Lecture Notes in Business Information Processing 584

LNBIP reports state-of-the-art results in areas related to business information systems and industrial application software development – timely, at a high level, and in both printed and electronic form.

The type of material published includes

- Proceedings (published in time for the respective event)
- Postproceedings (consisting of thoroughly revised and/or extended final papers)
- Other edited monographs (such as, for example, project reports or invited volumes)
- Tutorials (coherently integrated collections of lectures given at advanced courses, seminars, schools, etc.)
- Award-winning or exceptional theses

LNBIP is abstracted/indexed in DBLP, EI and Scopus. LNBIP volumes are also submitted for the inclusion in ISI Proceedings.

Krzysztof Węcel · Václav Řepa
Editors

Business Information Systems

26th International Conference, BIS 2026 Prague, Czech Republic, June 10–12, 2026 Proceedings

Springer

Editors
Krzysztof Węcel
Poznań Univ. of Economics and Business
Poznań, Poland

Václav Řepa
Prague Univ. of Economics and Business
Praha, Czech Republic

ISSN 1865-1348 ISSN 1865-1356 (electronic)
Lecture Notes in Business Information Processing
ISBN 978-3-032-26362-9 ISBN 978-3-032-26363-6 (eBook)
https://doi.org/10.1007/978-3-032-26363-6

This Springer imprint is published by the registered company Springer Nature Switzerland AG
The registered company address is: Gewerbestrasse 11, 6330 Cham, Switzerland

Preface

This volume contains the papers presented at BIS 2026: the 26th International Conference on Business Information Systems, held on June 10–12, 2026, in Prague. BIS is a conference with a long tradition, initiated in 1997. It brings together both scientists and practitioners interested in discussing up-to-date issues related to the development, implementation, and application of business information systems.

In recent years, artificial intelligence has evolved from a promising technological frontier into a central force shaping business strategy and innovation. Yet, as organizations have raced to adopt AI-driven tools and solutions, many have discovered that moving from experimentation to tangible results is far from straightforward. The 2026 theme, "From Hype to Impact: Turning AI into Real Business Value", reflected this critical shift in focus. Businesses are now challenged not by a lack of AI opportunities, but by the need to translate those opportunities into measurable outcomes that drive growth, efficiency, and competitiveness.

The Program Committee consisted of 67 members from 26 countries. All members were involved in a single-blind review process. There were 73 submissions. Each paper was reviewed by at least three Program Committee members, with additional reviews provided by subreviewers. Based on their feedback, 25 long and six short papers were accepted (acceptance rate 34% and 8% respectively). Similarly to the previous year, a significant number of contributions focused on the field of artificial intelligence. However, various application areas were studied where AI can provide real value.

The opening section of the proceedings is devoted to *Strategy, Architectures and Information Maturity*. The contributions examine the role of AI methods at a strategic level, as well as their support in architecture design. The second section reflects on *Information Safety*, understood not only as detecting fake news and disinformation, but also as securely sharing sensitive information in supply chains. The third section extends the discussion of trust issues towards systems. *Trustworthy AI* explores how to integrate AI into decision making and how to build trust in a chatbot used in management scenarios. The next section, *Process Management and Automation*, represents a well-established track at the conference This year, more emphasis is placed on the potential of employing LLMs and AI agents. *AI for Product Development*, the fifth section, investigates applications of AI in product development: from cost estimation, through description generation, to product experience management. The section *From Text to Knowledge* covers another popular topic at our conference. The contributions consider various techniques to better locate relevant pieces of information, using RAGs and AI agents. A specific subarea of NLP, *Speech Recognition*, is covered in the seventh section. The eighth section spans across AI development and presents several *Innovations in Machine Learning*, demonstrating that classical data analysis tools continue to be a strong pillar of research. In the ninth section, one can find a short paper elaborating on *Requirements for AI and BI Systems*, serving as a supplement to the first section. Lastly, the tenth section, *Various*

Applications, gathers papers that demonstrate unique research directions such as product passports, sustainability-aware accounting, and applications of machine learning in medicine.

We are confident that these proceedings offer valuable insights for both researchers and practitioners, and we hope they inspire further exploration, collaboration, and innovation at the intersection of business and information systems.

June 2026

Krzysztof Węcel
Václav Řepa

Organization

Program Committee Chairs

Krzysztof Węcel	Poznań University of Economics and Business, Poland
Václav Řepa	Prague University of Economics and Business, Czech Republic

Program Committee Members

Simone Agostinelli	Universitas Mercatorum, Italy
Rainer Alt	Leipzig University, Germany
André Pascal	University of Nantes, France
Dimitris Apostolou	University of Piraeus, Greece
Timothy Arndt	Cleveland State University, USA
Abdul Babar	Western Sydney University, Australia
Morad Benyoucef	University of Ottawa, Canada
Agnieszka Bitkowska	Warsaw University of Technology, Poland
Dominik Bork	TU Wien, Austria
Tomáš Bruckner	Prague University of Economics and Business, Czech Republic
François Charoy	Université de Lorraine, France
Rafael Corchuelo	University of Seville, Spain
Karl Cox	University of Brighton, UK
Jan Černý	Prague University of Economics and Business, Czech Republic
Sergiu Dascalu	University of Nevada, Reno, USA
Suzanne Embury	The University of Manchester, UK
Irene Bedilia Estrada Torres	University of Seville, Spain
Stefka Fidanova	Institute of Information and Communication Technologies, Bulgarian Academy of Sciences, Bulgaria
Agata Filipowska	Poznań University of Economics and Business, Poland
Adrian Florea	Lucian Blaga University of Sibiu, Romania
Naoki Fukuta	Shizuoka University, Japan
Jaap Gordijn	Vrije Universiteit Amsterdam, The Netherlands

Piotr Stolarski	Poznań University of Economics and Business, Poland
Milena Stróżyna	Poznań University of Economics and Business, Poland
Oleg Svatoš	Prague University of Economics and Business, Czech Republic
Hervé Verjus	Université Savoie Mont Blanc, France
Maxim Vidgof	Vienna University of Economics and Business, Austria
Daiva Vitkute-Adzgauskiene	Vytautas Magnus University, Lithuania
Hans Weigand	Tilburg University, The Netherlands
Krzysztof Węcel	Poznań University of Economics and Business, Poland
Zornitsa Yordanova	University of National and World Economy, Bulgaria

Additional Reviewers

Anschuetz, Christian
Czumałowska, Izabela
Gavric, Aleksandar
Huang, Rui
Jamali, Hossein
Kostrouchová, Veronika
Księżniak, Ewelina
Le, Vinh
Liu, Xiangrong
Michalski, Patrik
Otesbelgue, Alex
Plumhoff, Svenja
Ratermann, Jack
Riewe-Perła, Oskar
Rittelmeyer, Jack Daniel
Rossi, Jacopo
Saifee, Danish
Sawiński, Marcin
Tian, Yuxin
Triller, Marcus
Wei, Colin Ho
Yao, Ruiqi
Zhang, Rui
Zhang, Tuo

Organizing Committee

Jan Černý	Prague University of Economics and Business, Czech Republic
Pavel Kolesár	Prague University of Economics and Business, Czech Republic
Elżbieta Lewańska	Poznań University of Economics and Business, Poland

Contents

Strategy, Architectures and Information Maturity

Information Safety

Trustworthy AI

Process Management and Automation

AI for Product Development

From Text to Knowledge

Strategy, Architectures and Information Maturity

Analytics Maturity in Organizations: BI and AI Capability Development

Viktoriia Apalkova(✉) and Jürgen Fritz

School of Management Fribourg, University of Applied Sciences and Arts Western Switzerland, 1700 Fribourg, Switzerland
{viktoriia.apalkova,juergen.fritz}@hefr.ch

Abstract. Business Intelligence (BI) and Artificial Intelligence (AI) are central to organizational decision-making and digital transformation. Despite widespread adoption, organizations differ significantly in how effectively they develop and integrate these capabilities. These differences are often described as analytics maturity, yet the concept remains theoretically ambiguous and empirically underexplored, particularly in the context of BI–AI convergence.

This paper examines how analytics maturity is defined and developed in practice and which conditions shape its evolution. Based on a qualitative multiple-case study with interviews of internal analytics leaders, external consultants, and solution providers across energy, professional services, and software sectors, the study conceptualizes analytics maturity as a systemic organizational capability encompassing data foundations, governance, work practices, and decision-making processes.

The findings show that analytics maturity is not a linear progression toward advanced techniques, but a context-dependent and uneven capability shaped by data quality, leadership support, organizational learning, and trust in analytics outputs. Environmental factors such as regulation act primarily as boundary conditions. Drawing on the Technology–Organization–Environment framework and Dynamic Capabilities Theory, the study develops an integrated TOE $\times$ DCT framework that conceptualizes analytics maturity as the alignment between contextual conditions and dynamic capability processes. This framework advances theory beyond technology adoption and provides practical insights for building sustainable BI and AI capabilities.

Keywords: Analytics maturity · Data governance · Organizational capabilities

1 Introduction

Business Intelligence (BI) and Artificial Intelligence (AI) have become central to contemporary organizational decision-making and digital transformation. Organizations increasingly invest in analytics to improve efficiency, decision quality, and strategic adaptation, yet they differ markedly in how effectively they

K. Węcel and V. Řepa (Eds.): BIS 2026, LNBIP 584, pp. 3–16, 2026.
https://doi.org/10.1007/978-3-032-26363-6_1

develop and integrate BI and AI capabilities. While some embed analytics into core processes and decision routines, others remain limited to basic reporting or fragmented use cases. These differences are commonly described as variations in *analytics maturity*, but the concept remains theoretically ambiguous and empirically underexplored.

Prior research has proposed analytics maturity models that portray development as a staged progression from descriptive to predictive and prescriptive analytics [10,16,22]. Although useful as heuristics, these models are often technology-centric and implicitly normative. Empirical evidence suggests that analytics maturity depends on a broader set of conditions—including data architecture, leadership orientation, skills, governance, and trust in data and AI outputs—so that organizations with similar technological access may follow different development trajectories.

Recent studies therefore call for more context-sensitive and process-oriented perspectives that conceptualize analytics maturity as an evolving organizational capability shaped by learning and reconfiguration [19,28]. However, practitioner-based conceptualizations of analytics maturity and empirical accounts of how it develops in contexts of BI–AI convergence remain limited.

This paper addresses this gap through a qualitative interview study of organizations operating under diverse environmental and organizational conditions. Drawing on interviews with internal analytics leaders, external consultants, and solution providers across sectors including energy, professional services, software, and e-mobility, the study examines how analytics maturity is understood in practice and how it develops as a multidimensional capability spanning data foundations, governance, work practices, and decision-making.

The study is guided by two research questions: (1) *How is analytics maturity understood and manifested in organizational practice?* and (2) *Which environmental and organizational factors shape its development?* To address these questions, the analysis draws on the Technology–Organization–Environment (TOE) framework and Dynamic Capabilities Theory (DCT). TOE provides a structured lens for examining technological, organizational, and environmental conditions [3], while DCT explains how organizations develop and adapt capabilities through processes of sensing, seizing, and reconfiguration over time [30].

By combining these perspectives, the paper contributes to a more nuanced understanding of analytics maturity as a context-dependent and dynamically evolving organizational capability under conditions of BI–AI convergence.

The remainder of the paper is structured as follows. Section 2 reviews the literature and outlines the theoretical framing. Section 3 describes the methodology. Section 4 presents the findings, and Sect. 5 discusses implications for theory and practice.

2 Literature Overview

2.1 Analytics Maturity: Concepts and Limitations in Existing Research

The concept of analytics maturity has gained prominence as organizations increasingly rely on data-driven technologies for decision-making and performance improvement. Early research largely framed analytics maturity as a technological progression, often operationalized through staged maturity models describing a linear shift from descriptive to predictive and prescriptive analytics [1,13].

Despite their influence, these models have been widely criticized. They tend to prioritize technological sophistication over organizational context, implicitly presenting advanced analytics as a universal end state [8]. Moreover, maturity levels are often prescribed normatively without sufficient attention to strategic relevance, economic viability, or contextual feasibility [24,25]. Such models also understate the embeddedness of analytics in organizational processes, governance, and human judgment [26].

More recent studies reconceptualize analytics maturity as a composite construct encompassing data quality, governance, analytical skills, leadership orientation, and organizational culture [9,12]. While this broadens the concept beyond technical sophistication, empirical work still frequently relies on proxy measures such as tool adoption or self-assessed capabilities. Consequently, analytics maturity remains insufficiently theorized as an organizational capability rather than a purely technical state.

To reduce conceptual ambiguity, it is important to distinguish between BI, analytics, and AI. BI refers to the structured integration, processing, and visualization of data through dashboards, reporting systems, and predefined key performance indicators, primarily supporting descriptive and diagnostic analysis. Analytics represents the broader organizational capability to transform data into actionable insights, encompassing both BI and more advanced analytical approaches. AI constitutes an advanced layer of analytics that enables automation, prediction, and natural language interaction with data. In this sense, BI provides the foundational infrastructure for structured data use, while AI augments and extends analytics capabilities by accelerating insight generation and enabling new forms of interaction.

2.2 BI–AI Convergence and the Transformation of Analytics

The convergence of BI and AI technologies has complicated traditional views of analytics maturity. Conventional BI systems focused on structured data, standardized reporting, dashboards, and predefined KPIs, with maturity linked to reporting breadth and analytical sophistication [17].

AI-enabled analytics introduces machine learning, automation, natural-language interfaces, and the analysis of unstructured data, fundamentally changing how analytics is produced and used [23]. These systems support exploratory, conversational, and automated analysis, shifting analytical work closer to end users and reducing reliance on predefined logic. Rather than replacing BI, AI increasingly reshapes its role by lowering technical barriers, accelerating analysis, and broadening access to insights, while increasing dependence on data architecture, system integration, and governance [6,20].

In practice, BI and AI converge through the integration of dashboards, data pipelines, and AI-driven tools that enable automated reporting, natural language querying, and augmented decision support. This convergence shifts analytics from a tool-centric activity toward an embedded organizational capability integrated into workflows and decision processes. At the same time, issues of trust, explainability, accountability, and ethical use become more salient as AI-generated insights inform decisions [2].

Consequently, analytics maturity can no longer be defined by advanced techniques alone but by how organizations integrate BI infrastructure, AI capabilities, and human judgment. However, empirical research remains fragmented, often examining BI or AI in isolation. This gap highlights the need for qualitative, process-oriented studies that capture how analytics maturity is enacted in practice under increasing automation and AI-driven decision support.

2.3 Structural Conditions and Dynamic Processes of Analytics Maturity

The Technology–Organization–Environment (TOE) framework explains why analytics maturity differs across organizations by emphasizing the interaction of technological, organizational, and environmental conditions [3]. In the analytics context, technological factors include data availability, architecture, system integration, and tool usability [4]; organizational factors comprise leadership support, analytics-related skills, governance structures, and data-oriented culture [14,18]; and environmental factors include regulation, competitive intensity, market uncertainty, and vendor ecosystems [5,11].

While widely applied in BI and AI research, TOE-based studies often treat these factors as static and focus on initial adoption rather than post-adoption development, limiting their ability to explain divergent analytics maturity trajectories among organizations with similar conditions.

Dynamic Capabilities Theory (DCT) complements TOE by conceptualizing analytics maturity as an evolving organizational capability [27,28]. From this perspective, analytics maturity reflects an organization's ability to sense data-driven opportunities, seize them by embedding analytics into decision-making, and reconfigure structures, skills, and technologies over time. Recent studies emphasize learning, experimentation, and adaptation, showing that analytics maturity develops through iterative, non-linear processes rather than predefined stages [19,21].

Building on this perspective, analytics maturity can be conceptualized as a dynamic process involving several interrelated phases: (1) the establishment of data foundations through integration and quality improvement; (2) the generation of insights via BI-based reporting and analysis; (3) the embedding of analytics into decision-making processes; and (4) the transformation of organizational practices through automation and AI-enabled capabilities. This process varies across organizational units due to differences in legacy systems, skills, and strategic priorities.

Together, TOE and DCT suggest that analytics maturity is shaped by structural conditions but enacted through dynamic organizational processes. We therefore conceptualize analytics maturity as emerging from the interaction between contextual conditions (TOE) and capability development processes (DCT). While TOE explains the technological, organizational, and environmental conditions shaping feasibility, DCT explains how organizations develop, adapt, and sustain analytics capabilities over time.

2.4 Research Gap and Positioning of the Study

In summary, existing literature provides valuable but incomplete insights into analytics maturity. Maturity models offer descriptive structures but lack contextual sensitivity and theoretical depth. TOE-based studies identify key factors yet underexplore post-adoption dynamics, while DCT research emphasizes capability evolution but remains empirically limited in the analytics domain.

Moreover, prior research has insufficiently integrated BI and AI within a unified framework and has paid limited attention to their convergence in practice. The interplay between data foundations, analytical technologies, and human judgment remains underexplored, particularly regarding governance and decision-making.

This study addresses these gaps by conceptualizing analytics maturity as a context-dependent and dynamic organizational capability shaped by environmental conditions, organizational readiness, governance, and BI–AI convergence. Grounded in practitioners' experiences, it contributes to a more nuanced, theory-informed understanding of how analytics maturity is defined and developed in practice.

3 Methodology

3.1 Research Design

This study adopts a qualitative, exploratory multiple-case research design to investigate how organizations define and develop analytics maturity and which environmental and organizational conditions shape the evolution of BI and AI capabilities. Given the limited theoretical consensus on analytics maturity—particularly under conditions of BI–AI convergence—and the inherently processual nature of capability development, a qualitative approach is well suited to capturing managerial interpretations, organizational practices, and contextual contingencies [7].

The research is positioned within an interpretive paradigm, conceptualizing analytics maturity as a socially constructed and context-dependent phenomenon rather than as a purely technical attribute. This perspective enables theory elaboration and refinement by foregrounding how actors make sense of analytics, negotiate its role in organizational processes, and enact capability development over time. In doing so, the study provides an empirical basis for extending and contextualizing existing insights from the TOE-framework and DCT.

3.2 Cases and Data Collection

Four organizations were selected using theoretical sampling, guided by the objective of maximizing variation across key contextual dimensions relevant to analytics maturity, including sector, organizational size, regulatory exposure, and position within the analytics ecosystem. This sampling strategy supports theory-building by enabling comparison across contrasting organizational contexts and maturity trajectories [15].

The selected cases represent distinct positions along the analytics maturity spectrum and exhibit different relationships to BI and AI technologies, ranging from internal analytics users in highly regulated environments to external analytics providers operating across multiple industries. Table 1 provides an overview of the participating organizations in anonymized form.

Table 1. Overview of participating organizations (anonymized).

Case	Sector	Org. size	Interviewee role	Primary use of analytics
A	Energy	Large firm	HR, Project Manager	Internal transparency, HR analytics, process automation
B	e-Mobility	Startup	Founder	Benchmarking, trust-building, strategic sensemaking
C	Consulting	Large firm	Senior consultant	Analytics maturity assessment, governance
D	IT Software	SME	Founder, Director	Managerial self-service BI, ERP-centered analytics

This configuration enables cross-case comparison across (i) highly regulated vs. low-regulation environments, (ii) internal analytics users vs. external analytics providers, and (iii) large incumbent organizations vs. SMEs and startups. Such variation is essential for examining how analytics maturity is shaped by environmental constraints, organizational readiness, and strategic intent.

Primary data were collected through semi-structured interviews conducted between March and September 2025. Interviews lasted 45–60 min, were recorded, and transcribed verbatim. The interview protocol focused on analytics practices, BI and AI use, governance, and capability development; the full interview guide is provided in Appendix A. The semi-structured format ensured cross-case comparability while allowing respondents to elaborate on issues salient to their organizational context.

3.3 Data Analysis and Theoretical Integration

Data analysis followed a multi-stage coding process using MAXQDA. Transcripts were first open-coded to generate inductive first-order codes reflecting practices, perceptions, and contextual constraints. These codes were then aggregated into seven analytical dimensions: (1) Environmental and Market Influences; (2) Work Transformation and Role Reconfiguration; (3) BI–AI Convergence; (4) Process and Data Architecture; (5) Analytics Maturity and Organizational Readiness; (6) Trust, Governance, and Human Oversight; and (7) Sensemaking and Decision Support. Cross-case comparison was used to identify convergences, tensions, and boundary conditions. Analytical memos supported interpretation and theory integration.

Rather than imposing theory *a priori*, the TOE framework and Dynamic Capabilities Theory were applied as sensitizing lenses. TOE informed the categorization of contextual conditions, while DCT guided the interpretation of analytics maturity as an evolving capability involving sensing, seizing, and reconfiguring.

This analytical strategy followed an abductive logic, enabling iterative movement between empirical observations and theoretical concepts. Such an approach supports theory refinement and extension rather than hypothesis testing, allowing empirical insights to inform, challenge, and nuance existing theoretical explanations [29].

Several measures were taken to enhance research rigor. First, data triangulation was achieved through the inclusion of multiple organizational contexts and roles. Second, analytical transparency was ensured through systematic coding procedures, memo writing, and explicit documentation of analytical decisions. Third, anonymization of cases and interviewees was applied consistently to reduce social desirability bias and protect confidentiality. Finally, the study emphasizes theoretical rather than statistical generalization, contributing to conceptual understanding of analytics maturity under heterogeneous organizational and environmental conditions.

4 Results

The findings show that analytics maturity is understood not as a technological state, but as a multidimensional organizational capability shaped by data foundations, leadership, skills, governance, and environmental constraints. Across cases, BI and AI function as enablers rather than endpoints, and maturity is viewed as contextual, uneven, and evolving.

The results are presented in two parts. First, we synthesize practitioners' empirical definitions of analytics maturity. Second, we develop an integrative framework that explains how analytics maturity is shaped through the interaction of TOE dimensions and dynamic capability processes.

4.1 Defining Analytics Maturity: An Empirical Perspective

Across all four cases, analytics maturity is defined less by the sophistication of tools and more by the organization's ability to reliably generate, interpret, and act upon data. Interviewees consistently emphasized data quality, process integration, and decision relevance over advanced predictive techniques. Importantly, analytics maturity is described as non-linear and uneven—varying across functions, use cases, and organizational units. Even highly advanced organizations report pockets of low maturity, particularly in support functions or historically under-digitized domains (Table 2).

Table 2. Empirical Definition of *Analytics Maturity.*

Dimension	Empirical description	Illustrative anonymized quote
Data foundation	Clean, integrated data enabling reliable analysis	"If the data quality is not there, it doesn't matter which BI or AI tool you use—the answers will not be reliable." (Consult.–C)
Decision relevance	Analytics used to inform decisions, not only reporting	"The value is not the dashboard itself, but whether people actually use it to change how they work." (BI prov.–D)
Process embeddedness	Analytics embedded in daily processes	"Once data collection is part of the process, analytics becomes much more powerful." (HR–A)
Human interpretation	Continued reliance on managerial judgment	"People still rely on gut feeling for strategy, even if predictive analytics exists." (Consult.–C)
Organizational learning	Reflection, validation, and adaptation over time	"We are still on a learning curve—analytics helps us reflect and adjust our business model." (Founder–B)
Uneven maturity	Different maturity levels across functions	"In trading we are very advanced, but in HR or support functions the maturity is much lower." (HR–A)

Overall, analytics maturity emerges as a capability to make data actionable, rather than a function of adopting advanced BI or AI technologies per se.

Building on these findings, Fig. 1 presents an integrative framework that organizes analytics maturity as a matrix combining TOE dimensions (technological, organizational, environmental) and dynamic capability processes (sensing, seizing, transforming). The rows represent the contextual domains in which analytics maturity develops, while the columns capture the dynamic processes through which organizations identify, deploy, and continuously adapt analytics capabilities. The cells summarize empirically observed manifestations of analytics maturity across the four cases.

The framework shows that analytics maturity cannot be assessed solely by the presence of technologies or tools, but by how organizations mobilize these

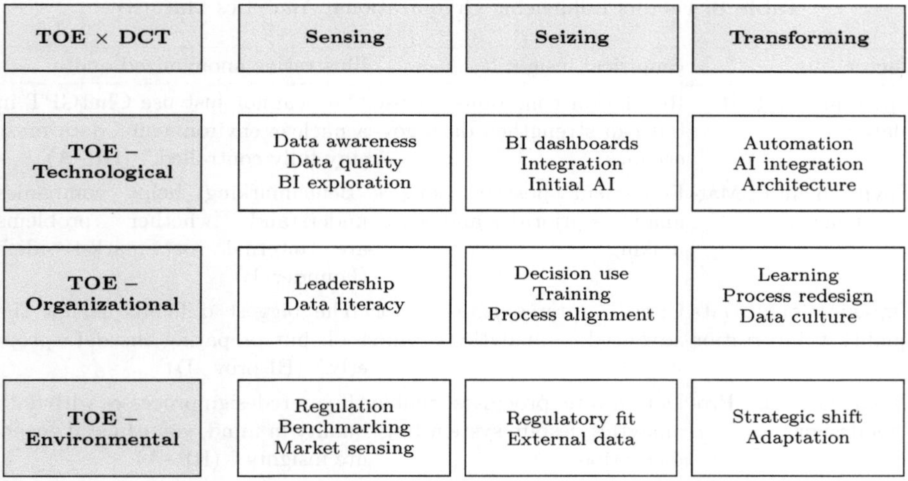

Fig. 1. Analytics maturity framework: TOE dimensions (rows) and DCT capability processes (columns)

resources dynamically. Lower levels of maturity are characterized by limited sensing capabilities, such as fragmented awareness of data sources, weak recognition of analytics value, and limited data literacy. More advanced organizations demonstrate seizing capabilities by embedding BI and AI into decision-making processes and aligning organizational practices with data use. High maturity emerges when organizations develop transforming capabilities, continuously adapting their data infrastructure, processes, and strategies based on analytics insights.

Importantly, maturity depends on the alignment of capabilities across TOE dimensions and dynamic capability processes. Organizations may exhibit advanced technological capabilities while lacking organizational readiness, or strong leadership support without sufficient data infrastructure.

4.2 Factors Shaping Organizational Analytics Maturity

The analysis identifies a set of interrelated factors that shape analytics maturity across organizations. These factors operate at technological, organizational, and environmental levels and interact with managerial practices. While all cases acknowledge the relevance of external conditions such as regulation and market structure, the findings show that organizational and managerial factors play a dominant role in determining maturity outcomes.

Leadership support, data literacy, and process design consistently emerge as central drivers of analytics maturity. At the same time, technological factors such as data quality and system integration remain foundational prerequisites, while environmental conditions primarily act as boundary constraints shaping the scope and direction of analytics use. Table 3 presents a classification of the main factors influencing analytics maturity, supported by representative quotes.

Table 3. Factors Influencing Organizational Analytics Maturity.

Factor	Empirical insight	Illustrative anonymized quote
Environmental: Regulation	Regulation constrains AI use but can strengthen data governance	"You cannot just use ChatGPT in a nuclear environment—data must stay fully controlled." (HR–A)
Environmental: Market structure	Ecosystem position shapes analytics priorities and sense-making	"Benchmarking helps companies understand whether problems are internal or market-wide." (Founder–B)
Organizational: Data quality & integration	Core prerequisite for advanced analytics and AI use	"The biggest difficulty is not the tool, but preparing the data properly." (BI prov.–D)
Organizational: Process design	Data-aware processes enable analytics despite system fragmentation	"If you redesign processes with data quality in mind, you can still generate insights." (HR–A)
Organizational: Size & complexity	Large firms require differentiated analytics; SMEs favor simplicity	"Small companies often need one dashboard; larger ones need many." (BI prov.–D)
Human/Managerial: Leadership support	Top management commitment drives prioritization and investment	"Since the new CEO arrived, data and AI became a strategic priority." (HR–A)
Human/Managerial: Skills & data literacy	Skills deficits limit adoption more than technology availability	"If companies knew how easy it is to work with data, things would look very different." (Founder–B)
Human/Managerial: Trust calibration	Under- or over-trust affects whether insights translate into action	"Some people don't trust the data at all, others trust it too much." (HR–A)

Taken together, these findings suggest that analytics maturity is shaped by configurations of conditions rather than single determinants. In particular, leadership orientation, data foundations, and organizational learning practices consistently emerge as central drivers, while environmental conditions primarily act as boundary constraints. The results further highlight that BI and AI capabilities alone are insufficient; their value depends on integration with organizational processes and human judgment.

5 Discussion

This study examines how organizations develop analytics maturity and the conditions shaping this process. Rather than reflecting a linear, technology-centric progression, analytics maturity emerges as a configurational organizational capability arising from the interaction between contextual conditions and dynamic capability processes. The TOE × DCT matrix (Fig. 1) captures this interplay by linking technological, organizational, and environmental factors with sensing, seizing, and transforming processes.

Contrary to maturity models that equate advancement with analytical sophistication, analytics maturity is defined in operational and organizational terms, emphasizing reliable data, process integration, and decision relevance. BI and AI tools function as enablers rather than defining features, and even technologically advanced organizations exhibit low maturity where these foundations are weak.

This perspective shifts the focus from analytics maturity as a technological endpoint to a capability-in-use. Within the TOE × DCT framework, maturity depends on how effectively organizations identify data-driven opportunities, embed analytics into decision-making, and continuously adapt their processes. Technology alone is therefore insufficient without corresponding organizational and managerial capability development.

5.1 BI–AI Convergence and Dynamic Capability Development

BI and AI are best understood as complementary elements within a broader capability development process rather than as sequential stages. BI primarily supports sensing and early seizing through structured reporting, while AI extends these capabilities through automation and advanced insight generation.

Rather than replacing BI, AI builds upon it—amplifying both the value and complexity of analytics use and reinforcing the importance of data quality, integration, and governance.

From a TOE × DCT perspective, analytics maturity depends on the alignment between contextual conditions and dynamic capability processes. Organizations may possess strong technological resources yet lack organizational readiness, or achieve relatively high maturity through leadership and clear use cases despite limited technological sophistication.

5.2 Human Judgment, Trust, and Governance

Human judgment and trust emerge as central to analytics maturity. While AI increases automation and analytical sophistication, it does not replace managerial interpretation; instead, effective use depends on combining human and machine intelligence. Trust calibration is critical: under-reliance limits the use of insights, while over-reliance may lead to uncritical acceptance, particularly in AI-driven contexts. Governance mechanisms—including data quality management, compliance, and human oversight—play a key role in balancing these risks.

Governance and trust thus act as cross-cutting elements that enable or constrain capability development. Analytics maturity depends not only on technological and organizational factors, but also on how organizations manage the interaction between human judgment and automated analytics.

5.3 Theoretical Contributions

This paper makes three contributions. First, it reconceptualizes analytics maturity as an organizational capability emerging from the alignment of TOE dimensions and dynamic capability processes, rather than as a linear or technology-driven progression. Second, it extends the TOE framework by showing that contextual factors shape the conditions for analytics maturity without determining outcomes directly. Third, it advances Dynamic Capabilities Theory by specifying how sensing, seizing, and transforming processes manifest in the context of BI–AI integration.

Integrating TOE and DCT provides a process-oriented and context-sensitive account of analytics maturity, addressing limitations of existing maturity models that overlook organizational dynamics and contextual variability.

5.4 Managerial Implications

For practitioners, achieving analytics maturity requires more than investments in BI and AI. Priority should be given to data quality, system integration, and process alignment, alongside leadership engagement and data literacy. The TOE × DCT matrix serves as a diagnostic tool to assess maturity across dimensions, identify gaps in sensing, seizing, and transforming capabilities, and align technological investments with organizational readiness and environmental constraints. Particular attention to governance and trust is essential, as these determine whether analytics insights translate into action.

5.5 Limitations and Future Research

The study is based on a limited number of qualitative interviews in the Swiss context, which may constrain generalizability. While the cases provide rich insights, future research could extend the analysis through larger samples, cross-country comparisons, and quantitative validation.

In addition, the qualitative design focuses on how analytics maturity is enacted rather than measured. Future studies may build on the TOE × DCT framework to develop quantitative instruments, examine links to organizational performance, and explore the evolution of analytics maturity over time under increasing BI–AI convergence.

Acknowledgments. This study was conducted as part of the BISWISS project, supported by the School of Management Fribourg (HES-SO).

Disclosure of Interests. The authors have no competing interests to declare that are relevant to the content of this article.

A Interview Protocol

Semi-structured interviews examined analytics maturity and BI–AI use. Key topics included **organizational context** (role, sector, size, regulation); **analytics**

maturity (definition, indicators, evolution); **analytics practices** (BI/AI solutions, data sources, decision use); **data and architecture** (data quality, integration); **work and skills** (role changes, skills, automation); **governance and trust** (data protection, trust in outputs, limits of automation); **environmental factors** (regulatory and market influences); and **sensemaking and outlook** (use of insights, future capability needs).

References

1. Ariyarathna, K., Peter, S.: Business analytics maturity models: a systematic review of literature. Focus **3**(10), 4 (2019)
2. Bahangulu, J.K., Owusu-Berko, L.: Algorithmic bias, data ethics, and governance: ensuring fairness, transparency and compliance in AI-powered business analytics applications. World J. Adv. Res. Rev. **25**(2), 1746–1763 (2025)
3. Baker, J.: The technology–organization–environment framework. In: Information Systems Theory: Explaining and Predicting Our Digital Society, vol. 1, pp. 231–245 (2011)
4. Chen, D.Q., Preston, D.S., Swink, M.: How the use of big data analytics affects value creation in supply chain management. J. Manag. Inf. Syst. **32**(4), 4–39 (2015)
5. Chong, J.L., Olesen, K.: A technology–organization–environment perspective on eco-effectiveness: a meta-analysis. Australas. J. Inf. Syst. **21** (2017)
6. Ebule, A.E.: Leveraging artificial intelligence in business intelligence systems for predictive analytics. Int. J. Sci. Res. Manage. (IJSRM) **13**(01), 1862–1879 (2025)
7. Gehman, J., Glaser, V.L., Eisenhardt, K.M., Gioia, D., Langley, A., Corley, K.G.: Finding theory-method fit: a comparison of three qualitative approaches to theory building. J. Manag. Inq. **27**(3), 284–300 (2018)
8. Grossman, R.L., Siegel, K.P.: Organizational models for big data and analytics. J. Organ. Des. **3**(1), 20–25 (2014)
9. Ioakeimidou, D., Chatzoudes, D., Chatzoglou, P.: Assessing data analytics maturity: proposing a new measurement scale. J. Bus. Anal. **8**(1), 55–69 (2025)
10. Król, K., Zdonek, D.: Analytics maturity models: an overview. Information **11**(3), 142 (2020)
11. Kumar, J., Rani, G., Rani, M., Rani, V.: Big data analytics adoption and its impact on SME market and financial performance: an analysis using the technology–organisation–environment (TOE) framework. Creat. Innov. Manag. (2025)
12. Langer, B.: Understanding data & analytics maturity: a systematic review of maturity model composition. Schmalenbach J. Bus. Res., 1–23 (2025)
13. Lemsa, S.: Challenges of advanced analytics maturity model development. In: ENVIRONMENT. TECHNOLOGY. RESOURCES. Proceedings of the International Scientific and Practical Conference, vol. 2, pp. 88–92 (2021)
14. Li, H., Dai, J., Gershberg, T., Vasarhelyi, M.A.: Understanding usage and value of audit analytics for internal auditors: an organizational approach. Int. J. Account. Inf. Syst. **28**, 59–76 (2018)
15. Ligita, T., Harvey, N., Wicking, K., Nurjannah, I., Francis, K.: A practical example of using theoretical sampling throughout a grounded theory study: a methodological paper. Qual. Res. J. **20**(1), 116–126 (2020)
16. Lismont, J., Vanthienen, J., Baesens, B., Lemahieu, W.: Defining analytics maturity indicators: a survey approach. Int. J. Inf. Manage. **37**(3), 114–124 (2017)

17. Majid, M.E., Marinova, D., Hossain, A., Chowdhury, M.E., Rummani, F.: Use of conventional business intelligence (BI) systems as the future of big data analysis. Am. J. Inf. Syst. **9**(1), 1–10 (2024)
18. Maroufkhani, P., Iranmanesh, M., Ghobakhloo, M.: Determinants of big data analytics adoption in small and medium-sized enterprises (SMEs). Ind. Manag. Data Syst. **123**(1), 278–301 (2023)
19. Mikalef, P., Krogstie, J.: Examining the interplay between big data analytics and contextual factors in driving process innovation capabilities. Eur. J. Inf. Syst. **29**(3), 260–287 (2020)
20. Pathak, A.: Leveraging AI for better data quality and insights. J. Comput. Sci. Technol. Stud. **7**(3), 291–300 (2025)
21. Pathak, S., Krishnaswamy, V., Sharma, M.: Unveiling the evolution of big data analytics capability: a comprehensive analysis. J. Scientometric Res. **13**(3), 791–805 (2024)
22. Rahman, M.M.: Data analytics for strategic business development: a systematic review analyzing its role in informing decisions, optimizing processes, and driving growth. J. Sustain. Dev. Policy **1**(01), 285–314 (2025)
23. Rane, N., Paramesha, M., Choudhary, S., Rane, J.: Business intelligence and business analytics with artificial intelligence and machine learning: trends, techniques, and opportunities (2024)
24. Röglinger, M., Pöppelbuß, J., Becker, J.: Maturity models in business process management. Bus. Process. Manag. J. **18**(2), 328–346 (2012)
25. Senna, P.P., Barros, A.C., Roca, J.B., Azevedo, A.: Development of a digital maturity model for Industry 4.0 based on the technology-organization-environment framework. Comput. Ind. Eng. **185**, 109645 (2023)
26. Shankararaman, V., Gottipati, S.: A framework for embedding analytics in a business process. In: 2015 IEEE 17th Conference on Business Informatics, vol. 2, pp. 49–54. IEEE (2015)
27. Sharma, R., Reynolds, P., Scheepers, R., Seddon, P.B., Shanks, G.: Business analytics and competitive advantage: a review and a research agenda. In: Bridging the Socio-technical Gap in Decision Support Systems, pp. 187–198 (2010)
28. Srinivasan, R., Swink, M.: An investigation of visibility and flexibility as complements to supply chain analytics: an organizational information processing theory perspective. Prod. Oper. Manag. **27**(10), 1849–1867 (2018)
29. Taylor, L.C.: Reassessing and refining theory in qualitative accounting research: an illustrative account of theorizing. Qual. Res. Account. Manag. **15**(4), 510–534 (2018)
30. Teece, D.J.: Explicating dynamic capabilities: the nature and microfoundations of (sustainable) enterprise performance. Strateg. Manag. J. **28**(13), 1319–1350 (2007)

Large Language Models for Generating ArchiMate Models

Benjamin Nast[1(✉)], Tim Arlt[1], Justus Dakowski[1], and Kurt Sandkuhl[1,2]

[1] University of Rostock, 18059 Rostock, Germany
{benjamin.nast,tim.arlt,justus.dakowski,kurt.sandkuhl}@uni-rostock.de
[2] Jönköping University, 55111 Jönköping, Sweden

Abstract. In many areas of conceptual modeling, large language models (LLMs) can be applied as assistive technology, for example, to gather domain knowledge to support model creation or to generate models from text. However, there is limited work on using LLMs to support enterprise architecture (EA) modeling. An LLM-based approach for generating EA models from text must consistently incorporate the different architectural layers of an EA. The aim of this paper is to contribute to this area by analyzing existing research, designing an approach to generating LLM-based models from text, and evaluating it experimentally. More concretely, an LLM-based approach designed for enterprise models is adapted for EA modeling with ArchiMate. The results of the experiments not only confirm feasibility but also a decent level of model quality. A set of recommendations for practical LLM use in EA modeling is abstracted, and implications for future research are derived.

Keywords: Large language models · Enterprise architecture · Enterprise modeling · Conceptual modeling · Modeling assistance

1 Introduction

Recent research on the application possibilities of large language models (LLMs) in conceptual modeling showed their potential as assistive technology for modelers, domain experts, and other participants in modeling projects. LLMs were successfully applied for various tasks, such as process execution [10], task extraction from textual descriptions [6,19], or gathering domain knowledge to support model creation [13]. There are also approaches that generate actual model files based on textual input. Sandkuhl et al. [17], for example, introduce a metamodel for prompt engineering that integrates the concepts of the modeling domain under consideration with the notation of the modeling language applied and the prompts (input and output).

However, existing work predominantly addresses business process models and does not cover enterprise architecture (EA) models (cf. Sect. 2.3), which are more complex due to multiple architectural layers (cf. Sect. 2.2). We argue that LLMs can also assist in EA modeling activities and focus our work on generating EA

K. Węcel and V. Řepa (Eds.): BIS 2026, LNBIP 584, pp. 17–31, 2026.
https://doi.org/10.1007/978-3-032-26363-6_2

models from text. Kolev et al. [7] developed a tool chain that combines the extraction of relevant elements of enterprise models from text with the creation of model files. We investigate whether and how this approach can be adjusted to support the creation of ArchiMate models. To this end, we selected a suitable scenario and examined the model generation for the relevant ArchiMate models and elements. We aim to answer the following research questions (RQs):

- *RQ1: What should the prompt for generating ArchiMate models look like?*
- *RQ2: Which criteria can be used to evaluate the LLM output?*

The paper is structured as follows: Sect. 2 gives an overview of LLMs, EA, and related work. Section 3 introduces the research method applied for this work. Section 4 describes the experiment conducted, and the results are discussed in Sect. 5. Section 6 summarizes the findings, abstracts recommendations for practical LLM use in EA modeling, and provides an outlook on future work.

2 Background and Related Work

2.1 Large Language Models

LLMs can translate, summarize, and generate text. They can be applied to question-answering, reasoning and search, transforming information into visual knowledge, and linguistics [1], and have been trained on large amounts of text data. For example, OpenAI's Generative Pretrained Transformer (GPT) series has been trained using books, web pages, and articles. Most LLMs are built on the Transformer architecture [23] and allow flexible customization through in-context learning during runtime in natural language, as pre-training was performed in a task-agnostic manner [3].

The input (prompts) is formulated to guide the LLM to perform a specific task, which is why prompt engineering is crucial [11]. Prompts can be optimized using prompt patterns [25], self-correction mechanisms to avoid undesired behavior [28], or by enhancing logical reasoning by introducing intermediate steps in natural language (Chain-of-Thoughts) [24]. The design of prompts often proceeds by trial and error because standardized engineering methods are rare [15].

2.2 Enterprise Architecture Management

An EA seeks to model, align, and understand the key interactions between business and IT, laying the foundation for an effective, strategic decision-making framework for digital business and technologies [14]. Enterprise architecture management (EAM) is thus an established discipline in many companies, aiming to coordinate the long-term development of the business and IT aspects [9]. It uses and maintains a coherent set of guidelines, principles, and governance rules to guide and support the design and development of an EA to achieve transformation goals. EAM uses a large set of different views for managing and documenting business-IT alignment [20], as defined by standards (e.g., ArchiMate and TOGAF). ArchiMate provides a visual modeling language covering the diverse elements of EAs [21].

2.3 Large Language Models in Enterprise Architecture Management

The state of research on LLM use in EAM was investigated through a systematic literature review (SLR) following the approach proposed by Kitchenham [5] in January 2026. The sub-research question to identify related work on LLM use in EAM is:

– *RQ-SLR: What previous scientific work is visible in publications about using LLMs in EAM?*

We used Scopus, IEEE Xplore, and AISeL as literature databases to provide broad coverage of computer science and information systems-related publications. The query was developed starting from the RQ-SLR and includes synonyms for its key terms. We searched the title, abstract, and keywords. The final query is:

((LLM OR "large language model" OR "foundation model" OR ChatGPT) AND ("enterprise architecture" OR EAM OR archimate))

Table 1 summarizes the number of hits for the query.

Table 1. Results of the systematic literature review.

	Number of Hits	Relevant
Scopus	30	5
AISeL	23	*1*
IEEE Xplore	0	0
Total	53	**5**

In Scopus, among the 30 hits for the query, 16 were conference proceedings or conference reviews. Three papers use the abbreviations EAM and LLM for terms not from the computer science domain; two are surveys of AI technologies for knowledge management in EAM and in sustainability management. Two papers focus on the use of LLMs in specific application fields (medicine, law) and also discuss potential impacts on EAs. These papers were not relevant. Furthermore, two papers focusing on integrating LLMs into EAs, from a security perspective and when transforming to the metaverse, were excluded. The 23 hits in AISeL were all applications of LLMs across different domains, addressing specific technical features of LLMs, their effects, or their integration. Only one relevant paper on LLMs and EA was identified, which was also found in Scopus.

The analysis of the five papers relevant for the RQ-SLR included, in the light of the RQs defined in the introduction, whether there is work directed to generating ArchiMate models: Zdravkovic et al. [29] propose using LLMs to support organizations in their work with business capabilities. LLMs are used to generate (textual) capability proposals or capability maps as part of the "capability broker". In the cybersecurity sector, when preparing the EA for new requirements,

Santos et al. [18] use an LLM as part of a behaviour-driven development strategy. The LLM automatically generates tests based on user stories and acceptance criteria. Quevedo et al. [16] apply ChatGPT to support understanding of microservice architectures in an enterprise by answering natural-language queries about them. The basis is the source code and an intermediate representation of the architecture, an enriched form of control call graphs. Kudryavtsev [8] proposes using LLMs as an assistive tool in digital business design. An app in the Miro collaboration platform allows for extracting information from company data or generating content recommendations for digital business activities. The paper summarizes a tool demo.

None of the above papers addresses the generation of actual EA models. Jung and Wienke [4] apply an LLM to generate a business capability map (BCM) from a textual description. The generated BCM is provided in CSV or JSON format and includes business capabilities with refinements and descriptions. This output could be used to add respective elements into EA models. So far, the work only addresses capabilities and does not generate models.

Related work on LLM use for model generation may also exist in other areas of conceptual modeling, such as process modeling or enterprise modeling. An SLR recently performed in this area [13] showed that, except for our own previous work, research focused on the generation of business process models, UML class models, or entity relationship models from textual descriptions. EA models differ from these types of models because they incorporate multiple perspectives within a single model. Only our work on generating enterprise models explicitly addresses multi-perspective models: we proposed a metamodel integrating prompt engineering, multi-perspective enterprise models, and LLM characteristics [17], along with a tool chain and a set of reusable prompts for generating multiple perspectives [7].

3 Research Method

The motivation of this work is to answer the RQs presented in the introduction and the decision to focus on supporting domain experts in creating models of the current EA. We employ a quasi-experimental approach. A quasi-experiment can be defined as "an experiment in which units are not assigned to conditions randomly" [2]. Our experiment protocol is oriented on the work of Wohlin et al. [27] and adapted as follows for our quasi-experimental setting.

Scoping: The study aims to conduct exploratory research to address the defined RQs. **Planning:** The *Treatment* is the specific combination of LLM and document set. The design results in four treatments: creating ArchiMate models with ChatGPT-5 and Claude Opus 4.1 based on two different document sets each. The *Independent Variables* are the two different LLMs and the two different document sets. The *Dependent Variables* are the defined evaluation criteria (see Sect. 4.5). *Controlled Variables* are the same prompt and uniform template for the output, identical textual description within each document set, and identical criteria for evaluation. **Execution:** The experiment starts with (1) the development of reference models. Based on this, (2) textual descriptions are created to be used as input for the LLMs. It continues with (3) engineering the prompts for the ArchiMate modeling language and the Archi tool file format. Then, (4) the models are generated and (5) evaluated based on defined criteria in the last step. **Analysis and Interpretation:** We map the outcomes of the evaluation to our RQs to discuss the results. **Presentation and Package:** The results are presented per RQ, and threats to validity are discussed. The prompts, outputs, and all other relevant material are made available in the paper or in our repository [12].

4 Experiment

4.1 Development of Reference Models

After reviewing the different case studies provided by The Open Group that apply ArchiMate in the context of TOGAF, we decided to use *ArchiSurance* (an insurance company) as the basis for our experiment. The *ArchiSurance* case study [22] is very complex and provides a lot of different models with varying complexities that build on each other. The baseline and goal architectures are provided in the respective ArchiMate/TOGAF perspectives. We made some changes to the models, added more, and changed the company's name to *Arche* to prevent the LLMs from immediately associating the models with the *ArchiSurance* case study. The models created, and their complexity, regarding the number of elements and relationships, are shown in Table 2; the model files can be found in our repository [12]. The models are present in three different layers to provide different perspectives, and one model combines these (*Layered*): *Business*, *Application*, and *Technology* layers.

Table 2. Number of elements and relationships in the reference models.

Layer	View	Elements	Rel.	Inter-persp. Rel.
Business	Organization Decomposition	10	12	0
	Functional Decomposition	30	68	0
	Business Process	28	39	0
Application	Application Usage	25	29	10
	Application Communication	31	45	0
Technology	Technology Usage CRM System	15	21	4
	Environments and Locations	46	60	0
	IoT Data Acquisition	19	27	0
Layered	Business Process Customer Data	49	72	16

"Rel." = Relationships, "Inter-persp. Rel." = Inter-perspective Relationships.

At the **Business Layer**, the following three models are selected for LLM-based generation. *Organization Decomposition* builds the internal structure of the *Arche* company and shows the most important departments and their locations. *Functional Decomposition* contains the most important business functions and represents the information flow between these functions and the business actors involved. *Business Process* represents the relationships between one or more business processes and/or their environment. It contains the two main processes *Issue New Policy* and *Handle Claim.*

The **Application Layer** contains application services that support the business and the applications that implement them. In *Application Usage*, it is shown how applications support the business processes. Our model is about the *Handle Claim* process and how it is supported by applications and systems. It also contains an abstraction of customer data and inter-perspective relationships that need to be modeled. *Application Communication* focuses on the cooperation of applications, whereby relationships between different application components with regard to information flows or their provided and used services.

The **Technology Layer** comprises the operations and information technology, representing the infrastructure of the company and supporting the business and application layers. *Technology Usage CRM* shows how hardware and software components support or realize the applications on the application layer. Our model shows how the Customer Relationship Management (CRM) system is realized by servers and system APIs. *Environments and Locations* includes the infrastructure and platforms that underlie the company's information systems, such as the CRM system, as well as physical devices, the network, and system software. The IoT gateway contained in this model is the content of the next model. The *IoT Data Acquisition* best fits the physical view, but the elements *Technology Function* and *Artifact* we modeled can not be represented in it. These two elements are required to represent the model without using derived relationship rules. The physical view comprises the physical environment and its connection with the IT infrastructure. This model was created to additionally cover elements of the physical layer, which is part of the technology layer. The model shows which different IoT devices of the company send data to the IoT gateway of the headquarter of *Arche* from an external location.

Layered comprises the three layers in one model. *Business Process Customer Data* represents the links across all layers and thus will be the largest model in terms of textual description. It is a good example of evaluating a complex, multi-layer model with many different ArchiMate elements and relationships.

4.2 Create Textual Descriptions for the Models

To create textual descriptions for the models to be generated by the LLMs to support domain experts, we defined two distinct document sets. In *Controlled*, care was taken to ensure that the exact names for the elements and relationships from the ArchiMate modeling language were used across all layers. No unnecessary information for modeling was used. This type of textual description is therefore very useful for an initial assessment of how well the prompts developed for our approach work. *Organized* is somewhat more realistic, and the elements and relationships of the ArchiMate were not described explicitly; synonyms were used. A comparison of the textual descriptions for *IoT Data Acquisition* is shown below (left: *Controlled*; right: *Organized*). *Organized* additionally contains information irrelevant for modeling (marked in blue):

The Location "External aggregates the Equipment "IoT Device", the Equipment "Car Black Box", the Equipment "Fitness Tracker", the Equipment "Home Security System", the Equipment "Weather Station", the Equipment "Smart Thermostat", the Facility "Smart Home" and the Distribution Network "Energy Network". The Facility "Smart Home" aggregates the Equipment "Home Security System", the Equipment "Weather Station" and the Equipment "Smart Thermostat". The Equipment "Smart Thermostat" is associated with the Distribution Network "Energy Network". The Equipment "Home Security System" is composed of the Equipment "Security Camera", the Equipment "Motion Sensor", the Equipment "Siren", the Equipment "Smoke Detector" and the Equipment "Water Leakage Detector". The Equipment "IoT Device" is specialized by the Equipment "Car Black Box", the Equipment "Fitness Tracker", the Equipment "Home Security System", the Equipment "Weather Station" and the Equipment "Smart Thermostat". The Equipment "IoT Device" is assigned to the Technology Function "Data Generation". The Location "Magdeburg Headquarters" aggregates the Node "IoT Gateway". The Node "IoT Gateway" is assigned to the Technology Function "Data Acquisition". The Technology Function "Data Generation" flows to the Technology Function "Data Acquisition". The Flow from the Technology Function "Data Generation" to the Technology Function "Data Acquisition" is associated with the Artifact "IoT_Data.json".	The tool "IoT Device", the tool "Car Black Box", the tool "Fitness Tracker", the tool "Home Security System", the tool "Weather Station", the tool "Smart Thermostat", the establishment "Smart Home" and the grid "Energy Network" refer to the site "External". The Home Security System, the Weather Station and the Smart Thermostat are part of the Smart Home. The Smart Thermostat is connected to the Energy Network, which is the biggest in this region. The Home Security System contains the tool "Security Camera", the tool "Motion Sensor", the tool "Siren", the tool "Smoke Detector" and the tool "Water Leakage Detector". The Home Security System is only available as a bundle for 299 USD. The Car Black Box, the Fitness Tracker, the Home Security System, the Weather Station and the Smart Thermostat are a variant of the tool "IoT Device". The "IoT Device" allocates the functionality "Data Generation". The battery of the Fitness Tracker lasts for eight days. The host "IoT Gateway" is part of the site "Magdeburg Headquarters". The IoT Gateway allocates the functionality "Data Acquisition". The functionality "Data Generation" streams to the functionality "Data Acquisition". The stream from the functionality "Data Generation" to the functionality "Data Acquisition" is connected with the file "IoT_Data.json".

4.3 Prompt Engineering

Sandkuhl et al. [17] (see Sect. 2.3) demonstrated, with simple examples, that their metamodel for reusable prompts could also be applicable to ArchiMate if the elements and relationships are defined in the prompts. Therefore, we first created a prompt chain from the existing prompt model concepts and added a part for ArchiMate: "*Export the model in the ArchiMate Model Exchange File Format.*" We tested this prompt chain for the simplest model, *Organization Decomposition* (*Controlled*), with no further information about the ArchiMate metamodel or required file format. Most of the results of GPT-5 and Opus 4.1 were not importable to Archi. A manual error analysis has revealed that the LLMs hallucinated regarding relationship types, and that the full syntax of the file format is not known to them. For this reason, we decided to create prompts for the ArchiMate modeling language and its file format (the complete prompt is available in [12]).

Prompt for Modeling Language: We defined the grammar of the modeling language based on the specification of ArchiMate 3.2 [21], which was given to the LLMs as PDF via the prompt chain. The language was renamed (*AUM8*) so that the LLMs do not associate it with the (partly incorrect) syntax of ArchiMate and so that it contains all elements and relationships relevant to our models.

Prompt for the File Format: The first part of this prompt is for mapping elements and relationships. We decided to explicitly define relationships rather than rules to avoid potential mapping errors (e.g., abstract elements being used incorrectly). The second part provides definitions of the necessary variables for creating views and instructions for adapting the provided XML template. The template is a minimal example that omits optional attributes (e.g., fonts or line colors) to avoid potential error sources and save tokens.

Final Prompt Chain: The final prompt chain is oriented on the structure of the tool chain of Kolev et al. [7] (see Sect. 2.3) and contains prompt model concepts defined by Sandkuhl et al. [17]. This is to explain the context, provide a response template and specification, and different prompt patterns:

> **Prompt 1:** I am trying to capture <purpose> of an insurance company using <model type> as described in the grammar of the AUM8 modeling language that is defined in the provided AUM8 Language Documentation.pdf. Please provide a less verbose and detailed outcome. Create a list of all non-abstract Elements, Relationship Connectors and Relationships for the following scenario: <scenario>.
> **Prompt 2:** Produce <model type(s)> for <purpose> by using the non-abstract Elements, Relationship Connectors and Relationships from your previously generated list in the AUM8 model exchange file format. For this customize the provided template AUM8 Model Exchange File Format.xml according to the instructions in the provided documentation AUM8 Model Exchange File Format Documentation.pdf.
> (Now the focus is to produce <model type> based on <earlier produced model type>.)

Two prompts and the template pattern (cf. [25]) were used to split the prompt into subtasks and to use the output of prompt 1 (a structured list of all elements and relationships) as input for the XML template in prompt 2. The placeholders (e.g., $< purpose >$, or $< modeltype(s) >$) are replaced for the respective models.

4.4 Generation of the Models

The models are generated using the prompts created (see Sect. 4.3) by inserting the scenario/textual descriptions (see Sect. 4.2). A new chat was started for each generation, as prior experiments with LLMs showed that the results otherwise suffered a significant loss in quality. The models for *Controlled* were generated first to test our prompt. To create the *Organized* models using the LLMs, another account was used to prevent the LLM from memorizing and reusing the sample solution provided by *Controlled*. However, we cannot rule out the possibility that the LLM has memorized our solution globally. In total, we had the two LLMs create 108 models, as we decided to generate each model three times because the outputs can vary significantly using the same input and LLM (see [7]). Each model was briefly evaluated, and the best of the three models generated for each textual description was selected and then evaluated in comparison to the previously developed reference models (see Sect. 4.1).

4.5 Evaluation Criteria

We use the evaluation criteria defined by Kolev et al. [7] for assessing multi-perspective enterprise models generated by LLMs. We have omitted *Component Identification* - because we consistently use the same designation for the individual components within the textual descriptions, and our different perspectives do not relate to each other - and *Relationship Precision* - since it is irrelevant for the evaluation of relationships within ArchiMate. In return, we have added and defined three further criteria that we consider particularly important for ArchiMate: *Clarity*, *Relevance of Information*, and *Completeness of Views*.

Importability assesses whether the LLM-generated output can be imported into Archi. The output is checked to ensure compliance with the required formats and standards, ensuring seamless integration with no errors. This criterion is essential as we aim to support non-expert modelers (domain experts). A model that cannot be imported is deemed unusable. We calculate the percentage of importability among all generated models. **Component Completeness** achieves 100% if all concepts from the textual description included as model components in the reference are also included in the LLM output. When components are missing, concepts are represented as the wrong component type, or the concept is represented as more than one component in the LLM output, the percentage can drop below 100%. **Correct Component Naming** evaluates the accuracy of the naming of the components. A component of the correct type in the LLM output that can be associated with a corresponding component in the reference still can have a label that is deviating from the reference. The percentage is measured again. **Relationship Completeness** achieves 100% if all relationships from the textual descriptions included as relationships in the reference are also included in the LLM output. In comparison to component completeness, a different relationship type between two components than in the reference does not necessarily indicate a mistake, as there may be different ways in the modeling language to express relationships. Therefore, 100% relationship completeness does not have to mean 100% identical relationships. **Completeness of Inter-perspective Relationships** measures if all relationships from the textual description between different perspectives included as relationships in the reference are also included in the LLM output. Again, we express this criterion in percentage. **Clarity** reflects how easily a human reader can understand the model. This includes layout aspects as well as semantic coherence and readability. It is thus a subjective assessment using a scale from *1 = unclear* to *4 = perfectly clear*. The layout aspects considered here are part of the ArchiMate 3.2 specification and originate from [26]; some examples include avoiding overlapping relationships, minimizing the number of intersecting lines, and using as few different element sizes as possible. Three of the authors (expert modelers) held several rounds of discussion to reach consensus on this criterion and thus address concerns about inter-rater reliability. **Relevance of Information** indicates if the information not relevant for modeling contained in *Organized* is included in the LLM output; therefore, it only applies to this document set. **Completeness of Views** was added because experiments with our prompts showed that some elements and relationships are present in the model but not in its view. It therefore represents the proportion of elements and relationships in the created views to the total number in the generated models.

5 Results and Discussion

Figure 1 presents the average values of the evaluation criteria for all models combined, and both document sets divided into GPT-5 and Opus 4.1. *Importability (I)* refers to all three generated models for each textual description; the other criteria were only applied to the most suitable (correct and complete) model selected by expert modelers. Overall, the *I* results for both LLMs are quite similar, ranging on average from 81.56% to 100% across layers and document sets. Both LLMs were mostly able to generate at least two of the three models that are importable, with Opus 4.1 achieving 100% for *Organized*.

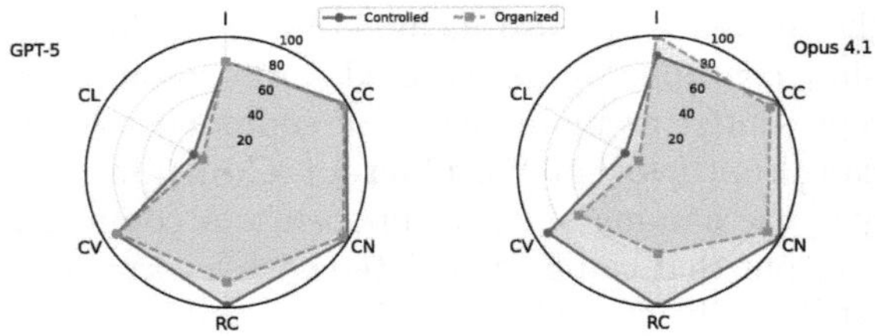

Fig. 1. Evaluation results for each LLM [left: GPT-5; right: Opus 4.1].

Component Completeness (CC) ranged between 92.78% and 100% between the different LLMs and document sets. The *Correct Component Naming (CN)* achieved the same percentage as *CC* for both LLMs for *Controlled* (GPT-5: 99.11%; Opus 4.1: 100%), and for *Organized*, only dropped slightly (GPT-5: from 97.44% to 95.78%; Opus 4.1: from 92.78% to 90.44%). This means that when the correct component is recognized, the correct name usually appears in the model. When it comes to *Relationship Completeness (RC)*, there are big differences between the two document sets. For *Controlled*, 98.67% with GPT-5 and 100% with Opus 4.1 were achieved, and for *Organized*, 81.33% (GPT-5) and 61% (Opus 4.1). When it comes to the *Completeness of the Views (CV)*, GPT-5 and Opus 4.1 achieved 90.78% for *Controlled*. Both LLMs achieved 100% for the models of the individual layers and only weakened in *Layered* (17% for both LLMs). Inter-perspective relationships are fully present in the models but are largely absent from the view (especially in *Layered*). For *Controlled*, *CV* achieved 89.78% with GPT-5 (only 31% with *Layered*) and 65% with Opus 4.1 (problems in almost all layers).

Upon closer inspection, recurring error patterns become apparent: inter-perspective relationships are often missing in the views, even though they exist in the model, suggesting inconsistencies between the model and the view generation process. Furthermore, relationships across layers are frequently incomplete, suggesting difficulties in maintaining consistency across abstraction levels.

At first glance, it seems that Opus 4.1 produces models with better *Clarity (CL)* in terms of the layout aspects mentioned in Sect. 4.5. However, this is not reflected in the evaluation, as many elements and relationships are missing from the model view and must be added. These missing elements and relationships are added as blocks, and are therefore not arranged by the LLM itself, which results in reduced *CL*. In general, it can be concluded that *CL* decreases for both LLMs with increasing complexity of the models and tends to be better for

Controlled. The average scores for clarity per LLM are *1.78* for GPT-5 and *1.67* for Opus 4.1 over both document sets. Regarding the *Relevance of Information*, both LLMs included the unnecessary information from *Organized* in the two models *Business Process* and *Functional Decomposition* (i.e., in two of the nine models). For example, a department responsible for a subprocess was added, which is not relevant to the model. As the *CL* scores were originally measured on an ordinal scale, we linearly transformed them to a percentage scale to ensure comparability with the other evaluation criteria. The transformation (from *1 = 0%* to *4 = 100%*) preserves the relative distances between this ordinal category while aligning the scale with the percentage-based evaluation metrics used for the other criteria.

Figure 2 shows the average values of the evaluation criteria per layer, broken down by combinations of LLMs and document sets. Across both LLMs and all layers, *Controlled* produced higher scores than *Organized*, resulting in near-perfect performance for *CC* and *CN* (ranging from 92.78% to 100%). *Organized* led to substantially higher variance across all criteria. For *Controlled*, GPT-5 and Opus 4.1 exhibited highly comparable performances, with the biggest differences in the *Application* and *Technology* layers. Both LLMs show the biggest weaknesses in *Layered.* For *Organized*, LLM-specific differences emerged. Opus 4.1 achieved higher scores in *I* across all layers, while GPT-5 had slightly lower *I* but higher scores in *RC*, particularly in the *Business* layer and in *Layered.* This indicates a trade-off between structural import readiness and relational coherence depending on the LLM. *Application* and *Technology* layers achieved the highest and most stable scores across all experimental conditions. These layers showed minimal sensitivity to the document sets or LLMs, suggesting that both LLMs handle models from these layers reliably. *Layered* was most challenging for both LLMs and document sets. This indicated a systematic difficulty in integrating multiple layers into a combined representation.

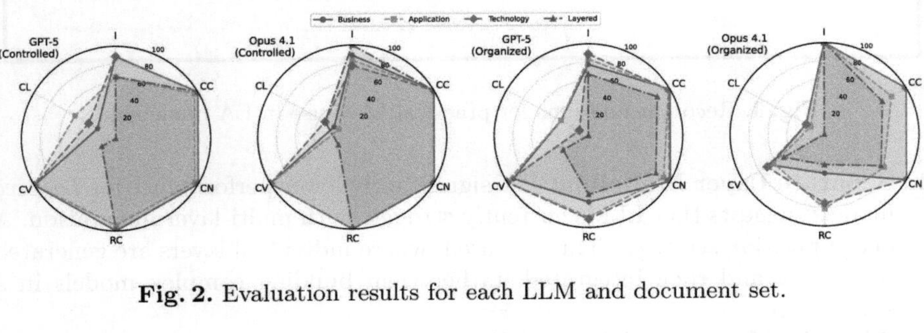

Fig. 2. Evaluation results for each LLM and document set.

6 Conclusion

6.1 Summary of Findings

This paper investigated the capability of LLMs to generate ArchiMate models from textual descriptions. In a quasi-experimental setting, we compared two state-of-the-art LLMs (GPT-5 and Opus 4.1) and used two distinct document sets (*Controlled* and *Organized*) that describe identical reference models. The results show that clearly defined prompts and output templates enable LLMs to generate largely complete and importable ArchiMate models, particularly when the input text is structured and modeling-oriented (RQ1).

The study provides a set of quantitative and qualitative evaluation criteria for systematically evaluating LLM-generated ArchiMate models (RQ2). Importability, completeness, and correctness capture syntactic and semantic accuracy, while qualitative criteria such as clarity and relevance of information address aspects of model usability that are essential in EA practice. Our study indicates that LLM-generated models can serve as initial artifacts that support the documentation of EAs in an early stage and facilitate collaboration between domain experts and enterprise architects.

6.2 Implications for EA Modeling Practice

The study on LLM use in EA modeling showed the feasibility of our proposed approach. Figure 3 presents the recommendations derived from the results, which are described below.

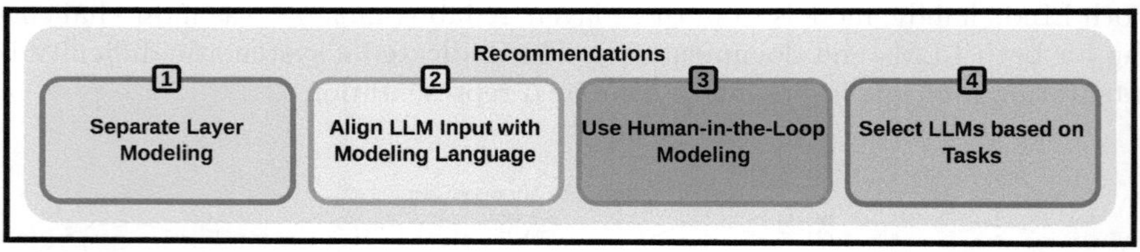

Fig. 3. Recommendations for practical LLM use in EA modeling.

1. **Separate Layer Modeling:** The significantly lower performance for *Layered* models suggests that LLMs currently struggle with multi-layer integration. A decomposition strategy should be used, where individual layers are generated separately and then integrated, rather than building complex models in a single step.
2. **Align LLM Input with Modeling Language:** Strong performance differences between the *Controlled* and *Organized* document sets indicate that LLM-based EA model generation requires structured, modeling-oriented input descriptions. Practitioners should therefore adopt lightweight preprocessing steps that align textual descriptions with modeling concepts and terminology.

3. **Use Human-in-the-Loop Modeling:** Limitations in *Clarity* and *Completeness of Views* highlight the necessity of human validation. EA models generated by LLMs should be treated as intermediate artifacts that require expert review and refinement, rather than as final modeling outcomes. We recommend a semi-automated modeling workflow in which LLMs are used for initial model generation, followed by iterative validation and refinement by human experts.
4. **Select LLMs based on Tasks:** The results indicate that different LLMs exhibit different strengths, for example, in terms of importability versus relational completeness. This suggests that LLMs should be dynamically selected or combined depending on the task.

6.3 Limitations and Future Work

While this study provides initial insights into the use of LLMs in EA modeling, several limitations arise from the experimental setup. The experiment is based on only two different LLMs and document sets, and is applied in only one domain. Future studies should include a broader range of LLMs (including open-source LLMs), domains, LLM configurations (e.g., different temperature values), and more diverse and realistic input data to expand generalizability. Due to the non-deterministic nature of LLMs, we decided to do three runs per model. Future experiments should investigate the robustness under single-run conditions.

Building on the recommendations derived in Sect. 6.2, future approaches should investigate incremental generation strategies, where individual layers are created and later integrated. To address the dependency on structured input, automatic preprocessing and alignment techniques for transforming unstructured text into modeling-ready input must be explored. Following the human-in-the-loop recommendation, interactive and semi-automatic workflows should be developed that combine LLM-based generation with expert validation and refinement. The observed differences between LLMs suggest the need for task-specific LLM selection or orchestration strategies, which should be systematically investigated in the future.

Disclosure of Interests. The authors have no competing interests to declare that are relevant to the content of this article.

References

1. Bommasani, R.: On the opportunities and risks of foundation models. arXiv preprint arXiv:2108.07258 (2021)
2. Cook, T.D., Campbell, D.T., Shadish, W.: Experimental and Quasi-experimental Designs for Generalized Causal Inference. Houghton Mifflin, Boston (2002)
3. Huang, W., Abbeel, P., Pathak, D., Mordatch, I.: Language models as zero-shot planners: extracting actionable knowledge for embodied agents. In: International Conference on Machine Learning, pp. 9118–9147. PMLR (2022)

4. Jung, J., Wienke, P.: Generating business capability maps using GenAI: a case study. In: Companion Proc. of The Practice of Enterprise Modeling (2024)
5. Kitchenham, B.: Procedures for performing systematic reviews. Keele, UK, Keele University **33**(2004), 1–26 (2004)
6. Klievtsova, et al.: Conversational process modelling: state of the art, applications, and implications in practice. In: Business Process Management Forum, pp. 319–336. Springer, Cham (2023)
7. Kolev, et al.: Grass-root enterprise modelling: how large language models can help. In: The Practice of Enterprise Modeling, pp. 123–139. Springer (2025)
8. Kudryavtsev, D.: AI-driven digital business design assistant: a prototype demo. In: ICSOB Companion (2023)
9. Lankhorst, M.: Enterprise Architecture at Work: Modelling, Communication, and Analysis. Springer, Heidelberg (2017)
10. Lins, L.F., Nascimento, N., Alencar, P., Oliveira, T., Cowan, D.: Comparing generative chatbots based on process requirements: a case study (2023)
11. Liu, et al.: Pre-train, prompt, and predict: a systematic survey of prompting methods in natural language processing. ACM Comput. Surv. **55**(9), 1–35 (2023)
12. Nast, B., Arlt, T., Dakowski, J., Sandkuhl, K.: Dataset for "Large Language Models for Generating ArchiMate Models" (2026). https://doi.org/10.5281/zenodo.18337615
13. Nast, B., Görgen, L., Müller, E., Triller, M., Sandkuhl, K.: Exploring large language models in enterprise modeling. Discov. Artif. Intell. **5**(1), 1–32 (2025)
14. Niemi, E., Pekkola, S.: Using enterprise architecture artefacts in an organisation. Enterp. Inf. Syst. **11**(3), 313–338 (2017)
15. Oppenlaender, J.: Prompt engineering for text-based generative art. arXiv preprint arXiv:2204.13988 **2** (2022)
16. Quevedo, E., Abdelfattah, A.S., Rodriguez, A., Yero, J., Cerny, T.: Evaluating ChatGPT's proficiency in understanding and answering microservice architecture queries using source code insights. SN Comput. Sci. **5**(4), 422 (2024)
17. Sandkuhl, K., Barn, B.S., Barat, S.: LLM support for enterprise modelling based on integrating prompt and enterprise modelling meta-models. Disco. Artif. Intell. (2026)
18. Santos, et al.: Increasing test coverage by automating BDD tests in proofs of concepts (POCs) using LLM. In: 23rd Brazilian Symp. on Software Quality, pp. 519–525 (2024)
19. Simon, C., Haag, S., Zakfeld, L.: Experiments on GPT-3 assisted process model development. In: 37th Int. Conf. on Modelling and Simulation, pp. 270–276 (2023)
20. Simon, D., Fischbach, K., Schoder, D.: Enterprise architecture management and its role in corporate strategic management. IseB **12**(1), 5–42 (2014)
21. The Open Group: ArchiMate®3.2 Specification. https://publications.opengroup.org/c226
22. The Open Group: ArchiSurance Case Study, Version3.2. https://publications.opengroup.org/y231
23. Vaswani, et al.: Attention is all you need. Adv. Neural Inf. Process. Syst. **30** (2017)
24. Wei, et al.: Chain-of-Thought prompting elicits reasoning in large language models. Adv. Neural. Inf. Process. Syst. **35**, 24824–24837 (2022)
25. White, J.: A prompt pattern catalog to enhance prompt engineering with ChatGPT. arXiv preprint arXiv:2302.11382 (2023)
26. Wierda, G.: Mastering ArchiMate Edition III: A Serious Introduction to the ArchiMate Enterprise Architecture Modeling Language. R&a (2017)

27. Wohlin, et al.: Experimentation in Software Engineering. Springer, Heidelberg (2024)
28. Wretblad, N., Gordh Riseby, F.: Bridging language & data: optimizing Text-to-SQL generation in large language models (2024)
29. Zdravkovic, J., Stirna, J., Tsai, C.H.: Pondering on capability brokering with LLM. In: International Conference on Advanced Information Systems Engineering, pp. 161–169. Springer (2025)

Strategic Choices for AI Transformation in Banking

Deepak Ravichandran[1(✉)] and Markus Bick[2]

[1] ESCP Business School, Paris, France
Deepak.ravichandran@edu.escp.eu
[2] ESCP Business School, Berlin, Germany
mbick@escp.eu

Abstract. Artificial Intelligence (AI) has demonstrably improved banking's financial performance, with Generative Artificial Intelligence (GenAI) predicted to add $200-340 billion through increased productivity. Despite growing organizational interest and investment in AI, GenAI implementation remains nascent, with no established frameworks and 95% of enterprise pilots failing to scale. The rise of GenAI has heightened strategic urgency for AI transformation. Value realization requires navigating complex strategic decisions. Digital transformation offers a useful analytical baseline for understanding AI strategy; however, AI exhibits distinctive characteristics including challenges to traditional resource classification, altered build vs. buy economics, and unprecedented development velocity that differentiate it from prior technology adoptions. This study examines how banking organizations and their leaders make strategic AI decisions through qualitative interviews of 10 leaders across diverse global institutions. We identify five strategic areas where banks face critical choices, shaped by five cross-cutting factors: leadership buy-in, regulatory context, organizational characteristics, legacy approaches, and perception of GenAI. Applying established strategic theories as interpretive lenses reveals that each offers partial insights, with AI's distinctive characteristics challenging direct theoretical application. We contribute a comprehensive framework mapping strategic choices available to banking leaders and demonstrate that understanding strategic AI decision-making requires drawing on multiple theoretical lenses, with careful contextualization.

Keywords: AI · Banking · Transformation · Value Creation

1 Introduction

Artificial Intelligence (AI) has demonstrably improved banking's financial performance, with research showing AI innovation positively influences return on assets [1]. This was based on data from 2010–2020, even before Generative Artificial Intelligence (GenAI) rose to prominence. McKinsey [2] predicts that GenAI could add value in the range of $200–340 billion in banking, largely through increased productivity. Furthermore, GenAI has the potential to shape future business models in Banking [3].

K. Węcel and V. Řepa (Eds.): BIS 2026, LNBIP 584, pp. 32–44, 2026.
https://doi.org/10.1007/978-3-032-26363-6_3

Banks are responding in terms of increased focus and investments in AI. A recent survey by Lloyds Bank [4] showed that over half of surveyed institutions plan to increase AI investment in the next 12 months. Furthermore, almost half of the institutions have established dedicated AI teams, with 20% partnering with external vendors to drive adoption [4].

Despite all the hype and potential, a recent MIT study [5] finds that Financial Services may be at the wrong side of transformation when it comes to GenAI. The study reports that 95% of enterprise pilots are failing. The recommendations, around buying vs. building, empowering line managers, and selecting tools that integrate seamlessly, all point to fundamental operating model decisions. Industry and academic research [3, 6] emphasize that realizing GenAI's potential requires rethinking operating models.

A number of theoretical frameworks have been employed to understand how organizations respond to technology-driven transformation, including dynamic capabilities [7]. There is also extensive literature on digital transformation [8], including research focused on banking [9, 10]. Banks have lived through digital transformation over the past decade, responding to fintech disruption by creating dedicated digital roles and restructuring operating models. This experience provides a natural reference point for understanding AI transformation. However, AI exhibits distinctive characteristics that may challenge existing frameworks: AI challenges traditional resource classification, low deployment costs alter build vs. buy economics, and development velocity is unprecedented. While banks have experience with traditional AI, the rise of GenAI has heightened both the stakes and the strategic urgency around AI transformation. We lack systematic understanding of how banks approach strategic decision-making for AI and to what extent they can draw upon digital transformation experience.

Accordingly, our research examines how banks are making strategic decisions around AI. Through qualitative interviews of banking leaders, we map the strategic choice landscape, identify factors shaping these choices, and interpret AI decision-making through established theoretical frameworks:

RQ1: What strategic decision areas and dimensions of choice do banks face when navigating AI?
RQ2: What contextual factors explain variation in choices across these decision areas?
RQ3: How does AI transformation compare to digital transformation?
RQ4: How do established strategic theories help interpret banks' strategic AI decisions?

This study offers both practical and theoretical contributions. For practitioners, it maps five strategic decision areas, the range of choices within each, and the contextual factors that shape them, helping leaders navigate AI decisions. For scholars, it demonstrates that AI's distinctive characteristics challenge established strategic frameworks, requiring multi-lens approaches and careful contextualization.

The paper is structured as follows. Section 2 establishes digital transformation as an analytical baseline, identifying relevant theoretical frameworks while qualifying the distinctive characteristics of AI transformation. Section 3 describes the research methodology used for the qualitative study. Section 4 synthesizes the findings, describing strategic choices and the factors that explain variation, comparing AI transformation with digital transformation, and interpreting the decisions through existing theoretical frameworks.

Finally, we present our conclusions in Sect. 5, including a future research agenda and highlighting some of the limitations of the study.

2 Literature Review

2.1 Digital Transformation as Analytical Baseline

Digital transformation offers a useful analytical baseline for this study. Vial [11] conceptualizes digital transformation as a process where digital technologies create disruptions triggering strategic responses from organizations that seek to alter their value creation paths while managing structural changes and organizational barriers. Research has shown that technology itself is only part of the puzzle: strategy [12], structure [13], processes [14], and culture [7] are all required to generate new paths for value creation [11, 15]. Recent studies have identified similar dynamics with GenAI, characterizing it as disruptive in nature [3, 16]. Banks have lived through digital transformation over the past decade, making it a natural comparison point for understanding their AI strategies. However, as Sect. 4 demonstrates, AI transformation exhibits characteristics that may differentiate it from prior technology adoptions.

2.2 Theoretical Lenses for Technology Transformation

Several theoretical frameworks have been applied to understand technology-driven transformation. We focus on three frameworks particularly relevant for strategic organizational decisions around technology adoption: the resource-based view (RBV), dynamic capabilities (DC), and transaction cost theory (TCT). RBV addresses resource questions, DC addresses organizational adaptation and transformation, and TCT addresses sourcing decisions.

RBV holds that competitive advantage derives from resources that are valuable, rare, inimitable, and non-substitutable [17]. Applied to digital transformation, RBV examines how IT capabilities serve as strategic resources that drive firm performance [18, 19]. For AI, RBV raises questions about which resources underpin capability and whether AI itself constitutes a strategic resource or is commoditized.

Dynamic capabilities address how organizations sense opportunities, seize them, and transform their resource base [20]. Karimi and Walter [7] demonstrate that dynamic capabilities enable strategic response to digital disruption. For AI, DC directs attention to how organizations identify opportunities, mobilize resources, and reconfigure structures to embed capabilities.

Transaction cost theory examines how organizations choose between buy and build based on asset specificity, uncertainty, and frequency [21]. TCT has been applied to IT transaction costs [22] and IT outsourcing partnerships [23]. For AI, TCT is relevant as GenAI potentially alters build economics while partnerships play increasing roles [3].

These theories, along with digital transformation literature [8, 12], informed our study design while remaining open to AI-specific considerations.

2.3 Characteristics of AI Transformation

AI, and particularly GenAI, exhibits characteristics that may limit direct applicability of existing frameworks. First, AI challenges traditional resource classification, paralleling human capital accumulation rather than functioning as conventional technology [24]. Second, GenAI enables rapid code generation and low-cost deployment, potentially altering traditional build vs. buy economics [3]. Third, AI exhibits unprecedented development velocity, with technology capabilities advancing at historically unprecedented speed. These characteristics naturally raise questions about how organizations navigate strategic AI decisions.

Beyond these characteristics, AI and particularly GenAI introduces distinct governance challenges that existing frameworks struggle to address. Unlike prior technologies, AI systems based on deep learning cannot be directly analyzed, specified, or audited against regulations in the conventional sense, as their behavior emerges unpredictably from training rather than intentional design. With GenAI specifically, this challenge becomes qualitatively different as large language models function as black boxes whose outputs cannot be reliably audited or demonstrated to comply with regulatory requirements, and whose safety guardrails cannot be guaranteed [25]. The academic literature reflects this nascent state of understanding, with a systematic review of AI governance frameworks finding that only a small minority of studies provide comprehensive answers to the fundamental questions of who is accountable, what requires governance, and how oversight should be implemented in practice [26]. The risks and complexity associated with AI adoption have prompted regulators across jurisdictions to develop AI-specific guidance, including the EU AI Act (2024), FCA and Bank of England guidance in the UK, and the Monetary Authority of Singapore's principles for fairness, ethics, accountability and transparency in financial AI [27]. The FSB has nonetheless noted that existing financial policy frameworks may not yet be sufficiently comprehensive given the pace and novelty of AI development in financial services [28]. For banking institutions navigating AI transformation, this rapidly evolving regulatory landscape adds a further layer of strategic complexity with no established precedent.

3 Research Methodology

3.1 Research Design

This study adopts an exploratory, qualitative approach grounded in interpretive methodology to understand how banking institutions and their leaders approach strategic decision-making regarding AI. Interpretive research recognizes that understanding organizational phenomena requires making sense of how participants interpret and give meaning to their experiences [29]. Given the nascent and rapidly evolving nature of AI in banking, this approach is particularly appropriate for developing grounded understanding of emerging practices. The interpretive lens allows us to capture the complexity of strategic considerations and the sense-making processes of leaders as they navigate AI decisions, considerations that quantitative methods might not adequately address at this early stage of theory development.

3.2 Data Collection and Analysis

We employed purposive heterogeneous sampling to capture diverse perspectives across geographies, bank types, and organizational sizes. Participants were identified through professional networks and referrals via informal networks, selected on the basis of their seniority and direct involvement in strategic AI decision-making, targeting individuals in analytics, data, and business leadership roles across diverse geographies and institution types.

The final sample of 10 participants represented diverse perspectives across the banking sector (Table 1). Nine participants held senior leadership positions (C-Level/Managing Director/Director level), with one Insights Lead included for their direct involvement in strategic AI decision-making.

Table 1. Participant Profile

Dimension	Distribution
Role	AI/Analytics Leadership: 6 (Chief Analytics Officer, Heads of Data/AI/Analytics) Business/Functional Heads (deep involvement in AI): 3 Insights Lead: 1
Geographic Coverage of Banks	North America: 3 (US) Europe: 4 (UK, Nordics, South Eastern Europe) Asia: 3
Banking Segments	Enterprise/Cross-functional (5), Retail banking (1), Investment banking (1), Private banking (2), Consumer finance (1)

Ten semi-structured interviews were conducted between October and December, 2025, lasting approximately 45 min on average (range: 35–65 min). Thematic saturation was largely reached after 8 interviews, with no substantively new decision areas or cross-cutting factors emerging in subsequent analysis; the remaining two interviews served as validation and confirmatory checks on identified patterns. Saturation appeared strongest for the scope and positioning, use case prioritization, and talent and capability development areas, where patterns converged consistently across participants, and thinner for build vs. buy strategy and governance, where greater contextual variation was observed. Given the contextual complexity of the phenomenon, we treat this as indicative rather than definitive saturation. The interview protocol explored five strategic decision areas: AI scope and positioning, governance models, use case prioritization, build vs. buy strategy, and talent development. Additional questions addressed enablers and barriers to AI adoption, with open-ended discussion allowing participants to raise topics beyond the structured protocol. All participants provided informed consent. Where participants consented to attribution, quotes are used throughout the findings to ground interpretations in the empirical material.

We employed a hybrid analytical approach. The five strategic decision areas (scope and positioning, governance, use case prioritization, build vs. buy, and talent development) served as our initial deductive framework, derived from digital transformation literature and strategic theories. Within this framework, we identified specific decision dimensions and choice patterns through iterative analysis of interview transcripts [30]. These dimensions emerged from patterns in how participants described their strategic choices, rather than from applying predefined theoretical categories.

Cross-cutting contextual factors (leadership buy-in, regulatory context, organizational characteristics, legacy approaches, and perception of GenAI) were identified through iterative analysis of interview transcripts. We analyzed patterns both within and across organizations to understand how these factors shaped strategic choices.

This approach draws on interpretive traditions in qualitative research [29], allowing us to both leverage existing theoretical frameworks and remain open to emergent insights specific to AI transformation in banking.

4 Findings

We structure our findings into four sub-sections: the five strategic decision areas, cross-cutting factors that shape choices, comparisons with digital transformation, and theoretical interpretations of AI decision-making.

4.1 The Five Strategic Decision Areas

Scope and Positioning of AI. AI scope and positioning varied widely across organizations along four dimensions:

Exclusivity of AI focus. Some organizations maintained dedicated "Pure AI" functions with clear separation from broader analytics activities (descriptive analytics, reporting), while others integrated AI within broader analytics remits. This correlated with organization size: larger organizations showed more separation. Even among large banks, however, the organizational level at which AI separated varied considerably. One organization had an AI head reporting directly to firmwide leadership. Approaches to GenAI also diverged, with some establishing dedicated GenAI functions while others integrated GenAI within existing AI teams.

Functional Positioning. AI functions reported into three organizational homes: most commonly to the Chief Operating Officer (COO), through the Chief Data Officer (CDO) or Chief Data and Analytics Officer (CDAO); alternatively to business leadership, with Business Intelligence (BI) reporting to the CDO; or within the technology organization. One participant emphasized benefits of reporting into business leadership, including tighter KPI alignment and appropriate decision authority: "you can't have someone in the tech world driving pricing decisions."

Analytics-Technology Ownership Boundary. Boundaries were clear for conventional AI but blurred for GenAI, creating friction as both analytics and technology implemented applications. Participants reflected on considerations such as whether domain expertise warranted keeping GenAI closer to AI teams, whether AI should own evaluations and governance while allowing development across the organization, or whether analytics should own use cases while partnering with technology for deployment.

Extent of Decentralization. Organizations adopted varying structural approaches. Some maintained fully centralized structures with a single center of excellence (COE) responsible for all AI applications. Others adopted federated models where COEs provided horizontal functions (e.g., governance, tools) while empowering business lines to build their own applications, sometimes alongside dedicated line of business AI teams. Some federated structures emerged unintentionally as GenAI democratized access to technology and simplified code generation, effectively bypassing centralized control.

Governance Models. Leaders universally acknowledged the need for strong governance capabilities, especially with generative AI use cases. Governance decisions centered on three key dimensions.

Organizational Positioning. Governance was either embedded within analytics (rolling up to CDO/CDAO) or separated completely (rolling up to central governance or risk functions). In separated models, AI teams partnered closely with governance while governance maintained independent reporting lines.

Frameworks for Generative AI. There were distinct governance approaches for GenAI, reflecting widespread risk aversion. One bank introduced additional GenAI-specific controls until reaching critical mass in use cases, while another adopted a risk-based framework prioritizing lower-risk applications initially. Heightened governance focused on reliability, explainability, and information security.

Vendor Governance. Although not a primary focus of discussion, governance for established vendor solutions appeared to follow different pathways, with contractual arrangements potentially enabling faster implementation than internal builds.

Use Case Prioritization. AI use case prioritization followed standard business case development in banking, with organizations applying variants of impact and feasibility assessments. Decisions centered on three dimensions.

Approach to Sourcing. Use cases were sourced through top-down strategic mandates, bottom-up innovation, and lateral inputs, with relative emphasis varying across organizations. Bottom-up surfacing was more common where talent came from Big Tech, while other leaders strongly emphasized top-down approaches, believing that top-down prioritization and business understanding of data value were key to impact: "most impactful projects are top down." One variant relied heavily on third-party vendors to bypass internal bureaucracies around budgeting and infrastructure.

Prioritization Frameworks. Organizations applied effort versus impact assessments with varying sophistication. One included innovation as a factor; another adopted a multi-tiered approach allocating different levels of central support based on strategic impact, from high-touch support for transformational initiatives to self-service tools for democratized use cases.

Executive Tracking. Executive-level scorecards for AI or other forms of tracking were reported by only a few participants. Notably, these organizations are recognized as technology and digital innovation leaders and have established track records of value creation through AI.

Build vs. Buy Strategy. The build vs. buy decision for AI capabilities varied across three dimensions.

Solution Sourcing Strategy. Organizations adopted markedly different baseline approaches. Some leaders maintained a strong build orientation, with one noting "90% of the systems were built." Others adopted buy-dominant strategies, heavily biased toward purchasing standard business applications rather than navigating internal approvals. A third pattern emerged around platform-centric sourcing, where organizations would buy if solutions were "packaged as part of an existing provider like Databricks or Snowflake," building on established platforms rather than best-of-breed point solutions.

Vendor Engagement Model. There were differences in vendor engagement approaches. Some participants emphasized full-service partnerships: "There is value in full service, integrating, testing, monitoring." Others preferred specialist or best-of-breed approaches, though one participant expressed frustration: "Too many suppliers with a sell anything to anyone mindset. Suppliers should differentiate, focusing on what they are specialized in." A third approach built capabilities on top of already-procured solutions like SAP or Oracle, leveraging existing vendor relationships rather than introducing new ones.

GenAI Integration Approach. There were varying perspectives on GenAI integration. Some participants viewed it as a build accelerator, using it to "accelerate legacy replacement" of mainframe applications. Others saw vendor rationalization opportunities, targeting "vendor solutions they paid for everything but used very little functionality."

Talent and Capability Development. Most participants referred to firmwide initiatives for upskilling in AI, with particular emphasis on generative AI literacy. Decisions centered on three dimensions.

Sourcing External Talent. Some leaders placed a strong emphasis on sourcing talent externally, especially from big tech. They thought it was an important channel to source ideas for AI use cases. However, another described unsuccessful attempts to hire from big tech: "People with big tech background struggle to function in a highly regulated industry. They often get frustrated with the processes and constraints."

Location Strategy. Most banks had presence across multiple locations with varying location strategies. Some participants described other locations as equal thought partners with no difference in work nature. Others differentiated technical versus business AI talent, sourcing technical skills from nearshore or offshore locations while keeping business talent in core markets for proximity to business and markets. Ability to source specialist data science skills also varied by local market.

Means of Upskilling. Upskilling approaches varied widely. Some leaders dismissed formal training programs, arguing AI adoption required fundamental mindset and cultural shifts rather than technical instruction. Others pursued firmwide AI literacy initiatives. US banks particularly emphasized hackathons for experiential learning, with one participant stressing the need to develop a probabilistic mindset. Several noted AI literacy becoming a baseline expectation in hiring and workforce development.

4.2 Cross-Cutting Factors: What Shapes These Choices

Five fundamental factors emerged as explaining variation in choices across the five strategic areas: Leadership buy-in, Regulatory context, Organizational characteristics, Legacy approaches, and Perception of GenAI. Table 2 illustrates how each cross-cutting factor shapes choices across the five strategic decision areas.

Table 2. Cross-Cutting Factors and Their Influence on Strategic Choices

	Leadership buy-in	Regulatory context	Org. Characteristics	Legacy approaches	Perception of GenAI
AI Positioning	Treating as business vs. tech mandate; Distinguishing AI vs. Data	*No link observed*	Size influences dedicated focus; Line of business influences strategic role	Legacy setup influences AI-Analytics organizational boundaries	Belief in GenAI potential influences GenAI organizational focus
Governance Models	Strategic emphasis influences governance frameworks	Regulatory jurisdiction influences risk frameworks	Size determines governance sophistication	Legacy governance models persist	Risk perception determines additional controls
Use Case Prioritisation	Leadership drives top-down prioritization and management scorecards	Regulatory constraints influence prioritization frameworks	Market context influences prioritization (retail vs. investment banking)	Historical frameworks continue	Bullish perception expands use cases; ROI expectations shape investments
Build vs. Buy Strategy	Strategic preference shapes default posture	Security concerns favour internal build; Data residency limits vendor options	Organization size determines internal build capacity	Existing data/tech infrastructure creates path dependency	Belief GenAI enables internal build vs. scepticism about quality and reliability
Talent and Capability Development	Leadership's background and tech proximity influence talent strategies	Data access restrictions limit offshore/nearshore talent deployment	Global footprint shapes location choices; Infra maturity determines skill needs	Existing outsourcing models continue	Technical vs. cultural framing influences talent strategy

4.3 Comparisons with Digital Transformation

Participants were asked to reflect on how AI transformation compared to their experience or understanding of digital transformation.

Continuities. Participants saw fundamental similarities: both require clean data foundations, organizational restructuring, leadership commitment, and change management. One noted: "See it similar in many ways. Both required you to clean up your data and get your data right."

Discontinuities. However, three critical differences emerged. First, AI demands a fundamental mindset shift from deterministic to probabilistic thinking, requiring the workforce to operate in a world where most outcomes are probabilistic. Second, AI's scope of disruption extends beyond channels and processes to challenge core work structures: "AI if correctly applied means business context knowledge becomes less relevant for humans. One person can serve multiple different contexts." With AI and agents, instead of writing requirements documents, "it's about prompting and iterating." Third, participants expected AI transformation to move faster, with generative AI "enabling teams of one" and reshaping roles at a pace digital transformation did not.

Participants differed on the relationship between digital and AI transformation. Some viewed digital transformation as a prerequisite: "You can't leapfrog to AI without having done a digital transformation." Others saw the relationship as more fluid, with AI potentially accelerating digital initiatives: "AI can probably help you move through a digital transformation faster."

4.4 Theoretical Interpretation

We examine how three established strategic frameworks illuminate AI decision-making patterns. Rather than testing theory applicability, we use Resource-Based View, Dynamic Capabilities, and Transaction Cost Theory as interpretive lenses.

Resource-Based View. Our RBV analysis identifies critical resources including data infrastructure, specialist talent, and computing infrastructure, though emphasis varied across participants. Resource quality matters: data quality constrains deployment, specialist talent remains scarce. However, as AI capabilities become broadly available, participants increasingly emphasized factors beyond traditional resources. Leadership commitment and organizational configuration emerged as more salient than resource possession, with one noting that advantage derives from "how organizations structure themselves around AI" rather than possessing AI technology. This suggests that as AI commoditizes, competitive advantage shifts from resource possession toward organizational ability to integrate and configure resources effectively, a finding more aligned with Dynamic Capabilities perspectives.

This suggests a proposition for future research: as AI capabilities commoditize, competitive advantage in banking may derive less from AI resource possession and more from organizational ability to integrate and configure those resources, an integration-based view of AI advantage that warrants empirical investigation.

Dynamic Capabilities. The DC framework offers insights into adaptation processes, with elements of sensing (opportunity identification), seizing (build vs. buy decisions), and transforming (org. reconfiguration) visible in our findings. However, a critical constraint emerged: one participant described technology moving at unprecedented speed, while another noted that organizations are not set up to harness efficiencies from GenAI.

The challenge is not absence of capabilities but transformation velocity: when technological change outpaces organizational adaptation, organizations struggle to execute. This reveals a boundary condition: DC assumes organizations can adapt if they possess dynamic capabilities, but unprecedented tech velocity can overwhelm adaptive capacity.

This reveals a boundary condition for dynamic capabilities theory in AI contexts: the framework's explanatory power may diminish when technological velocity systematically outpaces organizational adaptive capacity. Future research should examine how this velocity boundary condition operates across different institutional contexts and whether modified capability frameworks are needed for high-velocity technology environments.

Transaction Cost Theory. Standard TCT factors operate in our findings: high asset specificity and high frequency favor internal development. However, uncertainty perceptions varied considerably. Some viewed GenAI as a build accelerator. Others emphasized concerns: "GenAI hasn't changed the mindset" due to regulatory requirements, reliability monitoring, and integration complexity ("last mile integration has to be done by humans"). As one participant noted of the proof of concept (POC) stage: "POC is easy but going to production is hard." This variation in perceived uncertainty, shaped by risk tolerance and confidence in GenAI reliability, explains divergent build vs. buy strategies, demonstrating that with AI, uncertainty becomes subjectively perceived rather than objectively assessed.

Applying these frameworks reveals distinct yet complementary insights. RBV identifies critical resources but points toward integration ability as advantage commoditizes. DC explains adaptation processes but reveals velocity as a boundary condition. TCT clarifies sourcing choices but highlights how uncertainty is subjectively perceived. Together, these perspectives suggest that in AI contexts characterized by commoditization and perceived uncertainty, competitive advantage derives from how organizations integrate AI effectively, with uncertainty perceptions shaping sourcing decisions that enable this integration. Understanding strategic AI decision-making thus requires drawing on multiple theoretical lenses.

5 Conclusion

This study examined how banking organizations and their leaders make strategic decisions when navigating AI. Through interviews with ten leaders across diverse banking institutions, we identified five strategic decision areas, the contextual factors shaping choices, and how AI transformation diverges from digital transformation.

For practitioners, we provide a comprehensive framework mapping five strategic decision areas (scope and positioning, governance, use case prioritization, build vs. buy, and talent development) and five cross-cutting factors that shape choices across these areas. By identifying dimensions of choice and illustrating how contextual factors influence decisions, this framework enables leaders to better contextualize their own strategic choices, identify potential blind spots from implicit decisions, and understand the range of approaches available for AI decision-making. For scholars, we apply three established strategic theories as interpretive lenses to understand strategic AI decision-making.

Our analysis reveals that each framework illuminates different aspects of AI decision-making while AI's distinctive characteristics challenge direct application, suggesting that comprehensive understanding requires drawing on multiple theoretical perspectives.

Several limitations of this study warrant acknowledgment. A sample of ten leaders, while appropriate for exploratory research, limits the generalizability of findings. The study captures strategic choices at a single point in time during AI's rapid evolution. Additionally, findings rely primarily on self-reported perspectives; triangulation with internal documents, performance metrics, or vendor perspectives would strengthen robustness.

These limitations notwithstanding, the study points toward several directions for future research. Longitudinal studies could track how the five decision areas evolve as GenAI adoption matures. Quantitative research could test relationships between cross-cutting factors and strategic choices, or examine performance implications of different configurations. The two theoretical propositions proposed in this paper, that AI commoditization shifts competitive advantage toward integration ability and that technological velocity represents a boundary condition for dynamic capabilities theory, offer specific hypotheses for empirical investigation. Finally, while we apply established frameworks as interpretive lenses, future research could explore theoretical adaptations or integrations that more directly account for AI's distinctive characteristics, including its velocity, probabilistic nature, and challenge to traditional resource classification.

References

1. Gyau, E.B., Appiah, M., Gyamfi, B.A., Achie, T., Naeem, M.A.: Transforming banking: examining the role of AI technology innovation in boosting banks financial performance. Int. Rev. Financ. Anal. **96**, 103700 (2024)
2. McKinsey & Company: The Economic Potential of Generative AI: The Next Productivity Frontier. McKinsey & Company (2023)
3. Ravichandran, D., Bick, M.: Digital innovation with generative AI: business models for next-generation banking. In: Achilleos, A., Forti, S., Papadopoulos, G.A., Pappas, I. (eds.) I3E 2025. LNCS, vol. 16079, pp. 99–113. Springer, Cham (2026). https://doi.org/10.1007/978-3-032-06164-5_8
4. Lloyds Banking Group plc: UK Financial Institutions Double Down on AI as Productivity Surges. Lloyds Banking Group plc (2025)
5. MIT Sloan Management Review: The GenAI divide: state of AI in business 2025. MIT Sloan Manag. Rev. (2025)
6. McKinsey & Company: Scaling Gen AI in Banking: Choosing the Best Operating Model. McKinsey & Company (2024)
7. Karimi, J., Walter, Z.: The role of dynamic capabilities in responding to digital disruption: a factor-based study of the newspaper industry. J. Manag. Inf. Syst. **32**(1), 39–81 (2015)
8. Verhoef, P.C., et al.: Digital transformation: a multidisciplinary reflection and research agenda. J. Bus. Res. **122**, 889–901 (2021)
9. Vives, X.: Digital disruption in banking. Annu. Rev. Financ. Econ. **11**(1), 243–272 (2019)
10. Gomber, P., Koch, J.A., Siering, M.: Digital finance and FinTech: current research and future research directions. J. Bus. Econ. **87**(5), 537–580 (2017)
11. Vial, G.: Understanding digital transformation: a review and a research agenda. J. Strateg. Inf. Syst. **28**(2), 118–144 (2019)

12. Bharadwaj, A., El Sawy, O.A., Pavlou, P.A., Venkatraman, N.V.: Digital business strategy: toward a next generation of insights. MIS Q. **37**(2), 471–482 (2013)
13. Selander, L., Jarvenpaa, S.L.: Digital action repertoires and transforming a social movement organization. MIS Q. **40**(2), 331–352 (2016)
14. Carlo, J.L., Lyytinen, K., Boland, R.J., Jr.: Dialectics of collective minding: contradictory appropriations of information technology in a high-risk project. MIS Q. **36**(4), 1081–1108 (2012)
15. Svahn, F., Mathiassen, L., Lindgren, R.: Embracing digital innovation in incumbent firms. MIS Q. **41**(1), 239–254 (2017)
16. Kanbach, D.K., Heiduk, L., Blueher, G., Schreiter, M., Lahmann, A.: The GenAI is out of the bottle: generative artificial intelligence from a business model innovation perspective. Rev. Manag. Sci. **18**(4), 1189–1220 (2024)
17. Barney, J.: Firm resources and sustained competitive advantage. J. Manag. **17**(1), 99–120 (1991)
18. Nwankpa, J.K., Roumani, Y.: IT capability and digital transformation: a firm performance perspective. In: International Conference on Information Systems (ICIS) Proceedings (2016)
19. Bharadwaj, A.S.: A resource-based perspective on information technology capability and firm performance: an empirical investigation. MIS Q. **24**(1), 169–196 (2000)
20. Teece, D.J.: Explicating dynamic capabilities: the nature and microfoundations of (sustainable) enterprise performance. Strateg. Manag. J. **28**(13), 1319–1350 (2007)
21. Williamson, O.E.: The economic Institutions of Capitalism. Free Press, New York (1985)
22. Brynjolfsson, E.: Information assets, technology and organization. Manag. Sci. **40**(12), 1645–1662 (1994)
23. Lacity, M.C., Khan, S.A., Willcocks, L.P.: A review of the IT outsourcing literature: insights for practice. J. Strateg. Inf. Syst. **18**(3), 130–146 (2009)
24. Lu, C.H.: The impact of artificial intelligence on economic growth and welfare. J. Macroecon. **69**, 103342 (2021)
25. Judge, B., Nitzberg, M., Russell, S.: When code isn't law: rethinking regulation for artificial intelligence. Policy Soc. **44**(1), 85–97 (2025)
26. Batool, A., Zowghi, D., Bano, M.: AI governance: a systematic literature review. AI Ethics **5**, 3265–3279 (2025)
27. Monetary Authority of Singapore: Principles to Promote Fairness, Ethics, Accountability and Transparency in the Use of Artificial Intelligence and Data Analytics in Singapore's Financial Sector. MAS, Singapore (2019)
28. Financial Stability Board: The Financial Stability Implications of Artificial Intelligence. FSB, Basel (2024)
29. Myers, M.D.: Qualitative Research in Business and Management, 3rd edn. Sage Publications (2019)
30. Gioia, D.A., Corley, K.G., Hamilton, A.L.: Seeking qualitative rigor in inductive research: notes on the Gioia methodology. Organ. Res. Methods **16**(1), 15–31 (2013)

Information Safety

Towards a Generic Fake News Detection Method Independent of Linguistic Features

Satoru Onohara(✉) and Mamoru Mimura

National Defense Academy of Japan, Yokosuka, Kanagawa 239-8686, Japan
{em64006,mim}@nda.ac.jp

Abstract. The spread of fake news became a social issue following the 2016 U.S. presidential election, making the detection of fake news an urgent task. To address this, detection methods using machine learning models based on linguistic features have been proposed. However, these methods have been evaluated only on specific datasets, and their reliance on linguistic features poses challenges for generalizability. In this study, we propose a fake news detection model that does not rely on linguistic features. We use a large language model to select ten types of features—such as claim substantiation, source credibility, and sensational expressions—and to evaluate the degree of fake news associated with each feature. We compare the proposed model with a model that relies only on linguistic features. As a result, we demonstrate improved generalization performance on unseen datasets. On the other hand, an analysis of the features that contributed to fake news detection revealed variability across datasets, indicating that further investigation is needed to improve detection accuracy.

Keywords: fake news detection · large language model · features · generalization

1 Introduction

The term *fake news* attracted widespread interest following the 2016 United States presidential election. During this period, fake news spread widely on social media and gained more attention than articles from major media outlets. As a result, it became a serious social issue. The spread of fake news is a serious issue in modern society, and its detection has become an urgent challenge. Consequently, numerous studies have proposed various approaches to detect fake news and mitigate its social impact. In particular, fake news detection using machine learning models has emerged as a major research area, and many models based on natural language processing techniques and deep learning have been proposed [7,12].

Although many high-performance models have been proposed in previous studies [1,5], most of these studies evaluate detection performance using only a

K. Węcel and V. Řepa (Eds.): BIS 2026, LNBIP 584, pp. 47–59, 2026.
https://doi.org/10.1007/978-3-032-26363-6_4

single dataset. Some studies construct datasets that combine multiple domains to evaluate detection models [7]; however, few studies have explicitly examined the generalization ability of fake news detection models. As fake news evolves over time, detection models that lack generalization ability may fail to prevent the dissemination of misinformation, thereby increasing the risk of social disruption and undermining trust in information. Furthermore, while many approaches rely on linguistic features for fake news detection, it has been reported that fake news shares few common linguistic characteristics, leaving room for improvement in the generalization ability of detection models [5,9].

In this study, with the aim of addressing the limited generalization ability of existing fake news detection models, we select and evaluate ten types of features beyond linguistic characteristics using a large language model (LLM), including the basis of claims, source credibility, sensational expressions, and personal labeling, and develop a fake news detection model. We assess how well the proposed model can detect fake news in unknown datasets in order to evaluate its generalization ability. In addition, we investigate which features contribute to fake news detection.

The research questions (RQs) addressed in this study are as follows:

(RQ1) Does a fake news detection model that does not rely solely on linguistic features exhibit generalization ability?
(RQ2) Which features are effective for fake news detection?
(RQ3) Are the features effective for fake news detection consistent across different datasets?

To address these research questions, we evaluate the detection performance of the proposed model using four different datasets. The main contributions of this study are summarized as follows:

1. Compared with conventional models, the proposed model achieves higher detection performance on three of the four datasets, demonstrating strong generalization ability. However, the model shows limited performance on a specific dataset, indicating room for improvement.
2. Among the ten features, source credibility, claim substantiation, and sensational expressions exhibit high contributions across all datasets.
3. While certain features are effective for detection in all models, the features that contribute most to detection vary depending on the dataset, suggesting that further investigation is required to improve detection performance.

2 Related Work

With the widespread adoption of social media, a large amount of fake news has been disseminated, making it extremely difficult for individuals to verify its authenticity. Consequently, numerous methods for detecting fake news using machine learning techniques have been proposed.

Several studies have proposed fake news detection models based on linguistic and statistical features, such as TF-IDF, word embeddings, and handcrafted features, achieving high performance on individual datasets [1,4]. However, these approaches primarily focus on evaluation using a single dataset and do not sufficiently address cross-dataset generalization. Hakak et al. proposed a method that extracts 26 features from news articles, including statistical features like word count and sentence length, and named entities, and inputs them into machine learning models such as Random Forest [5]. Although this method showed high detection accuracy on a specific dataset, its accuracy decreased on a different one, leaving the issue of a lack of generalization ability. Recently, LLMs have been applied to fake news detection. Xu et al. utilized BERT-based models with additional formatting (length, capitalization frequency) and content features to improve detection performance [11,13,15]. However, the main weakness in their study is that they make no attempt to validate their approach on a different dataset, instead using the same dataset for both training and testing. Ishimaru et al. analyzed lexical features across multiple datasets and suggested that, because fake news shares few common linguistic characteristics, models tend to depend on features specific to the training data, resulting in limited generalization to unseen datasets [9]. In this study, we propose a fake news detection model that does not rely solely on linguistic features by having a LLM select and evaluate features. We evaluate the effectiveness of the proposed model on unseen datasets using multiple datasets to confirm its generalization ability. Furthermore, research is expanding toward evidence-based verification, as seen in various shared tasks such as FEVER or CLEF CheckThat!. Our approach aligns with this trend by focusing on evaluating the quality of information sources and the presence of supporting evidence, moving beyond simple linguistic patterns.

3 Related Techniques

In this study, we utilize Llama 3, one of the LLMs, as a tool for extracting feature quantities from news articles. The technical foundation of this approach is the Transformer model and its core self-attention mechanism. This section describes the technology used in this study.

3.1 Transformer Model

The Transformer is a neural network architecture for natural language processing developed by Google [14]. By employing self-attention and multi-head attention mechanisms, it can efficiently and in parallel learn long-range contextual dependencies in text. This enables the model to learn how strongly each word in a sentence is related to other words and to simultaneously analyze relationships between words from multiple perspectives, resulting in a richer contextual understanding.

3.2 Llama

Llama is an open-source LLM based on the Transformer architecture and developed by Meta. The Llama3-8B-Instruct model used in this study is freely available and achieves strong conversational and text generation performance with relatively modest computational resources. Leveraging these capabilities, the model is expected to evaluate not only superficial linguistic features but also abstract and complex concepts such as logical consistency, contradictions, and emotional exaggeration. In this study, we employ Llama3-8B-Instruct as a feature extractor to quantitatively assess features that conventional models fail to capture, with the aim of constructing a generic fake news detection model.

4 Proposal Method

An overview of the fake news detection method in this study is shown in Fig. 1. Conventional fake news detection methods have primarily relied on linguistic features such as the number of unique words and the frequency of specific named entities. However, linguistic characteristics commonly shared among fake news articles are limited. Therefore, constructing a general-purpose detection model based solely on such features has been challenging. To address this issue, we propose a method that leverages LLMs to identify features characteristic of fake news, with the aim of developing a general-purpose model that does not depend exclusively on linguistic features. Furthermore, we quantitatively evaluate the degree to which individual news articles constitute fake news using a LLM. We then examine the generalizability of the proposed approach through experiments on multiple heterogeneous datasets. This study uses four different datasets. Each dataset is preprocessed and then input into Llama 3 to extract features. Using the extracted features from one dataset, a Random Forest model is trained. After training, fake news detection is performed on the other datasets. This evaluation measures detection accuracy on unknown fake news and confirms the generalization ability of the proposed method. The details of each step are explained below.

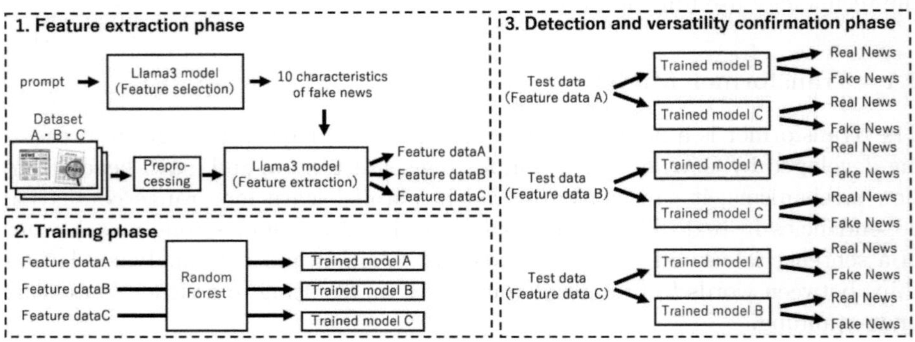

Fig. 1. Proposal method procedure

4.1 Preprocessing

In preprocessing, data cleansing was performed to allow Llama 3 to extract features from each news article. To ensure the integrity of each dataset, data cleansing involved deleting blank lines and replacement characters, as well as removing items other than the REAL or FAKE labels, article titles, and text.

4.2 Feature Extraction Phase

Conventional machine learning models have performed fake news detection using features like the number of unique words and word frequency. However, with the recent advent of LLMs, it has become possible to understand deeper meanings and perform detection by leveraging their advanced natural language understanding and reasoning capabilities. In this study, we extract features specific to fake news from news articles and detect fake news from multiple perspectives.

First, we input the prompt shown in Table 1 into Llama 3 and selected 10 types of fake news features, as shown in Table 2. Next, we provided Llama 3 with the news article's title and body text and instructed it, as in Table 1, to assign a score from 0 to 100 for each of the 10 fake news features for a quantitative evaluation. If Llama 3 was unable to quantitatively evaluate a feature, we imputed the score for that feature with the median of the entire dataset to prevent it from disproportionately affecting the model's training.

Table 1. Input Prompts

Purpose	Input prompts
Feature Selection	You are an expert in journalism research, specializing in identifying and analyzing fake news. What other types of information or characteristics are particularly useful in identifying fake news? Please provide specific examples and elaborate.
Quantitative Evaluation of Features	You are an AI assistant specialized in detecting fake news. Your task is to analyze the provided news article's title and text, and evaluate the degree of each of the 10 features defined below. For each feature, assign a **score ranging from 0 (indicating the characteristic is completely absent or strongly indicative of real news) to 100 (indicating the characteristic is extremely prominent and strongly indicative of fake news)**. A higher score means the article exhibits that specific fake news characteristic more strongly.

4.3 Training Phase

For each dataset, we input the feature data extracted by the Llama 3 model into a Random Forest classifier to create a trained model. Specifically, we convert the 10-dimensional scores extracted by the Llama 3 model into a feature vector and input it into the Random Forest model along with the true label of each news article (real news/fake news) to create a trained model for each respective dataset.

Table 2. Feature extraction

No.	10 types of fake news features
1	Linguistic Flaws (Grammar, Spelling, Awkward Phrasing)
2	Logical Inconsistency (Internal Contradictions, Illogical Flow)
3	Low Source Credibility (Unreliable or Vague Sources)
4	Lack of Supporting Evidence (Insufficient Justification)
5	Emotional/Sensational Language (Inflammatory Tone)
6	Lack of Specificity/Vagueness (Ambiguous Details)
7	Overuse of Rhetorical Questions (Leading Questions)
8	Extreme Language/Overuse of Emphatic Symbols (Exaggerated Phrasing)
9	Contextual Distortion/Misuse (Manipulated Context)
10	Labeling/Ad Hominem Attack (Personal Attacks)

4.4 Detection and Generalization Ability Confirmation Phase

For a single test dataset, we perform fake news detection using the trained model created in the training phase. We repeat this for all test datasets and evaluate the detection accuracy for each dataset. Furthermore, we confirm the generalization ability of the proposed model by comparing its detection accuracy with that of pre-trained models for fake news detection, specifically the BERT model [3,13] and RoBERTa model [6,11].

4.5 Importance of Each Feature

In this study, we extracted 10 types of fake news features, and we verify the extent to which each feature contributed to fake news detection.

Validation for this study uses Permutation Importance (PI). This method evaluates the contribution of each feature in a trained model by measuring how much the model's predictive performance (specifically, the F1-score in this study) decreases when a particular feature is randomly shuffled. This allows us to evaluate the general features needed for fake news detection. Specifically, the method calculates the amount of performance degradation when each feature is individually shuffled, using the original detection accuracy as a baseline, and evaluates this as the feature's importance.

5 Validation Experiments

5.1 Dataset

This study used four different datasets with varying genres. The breakdown of the datasets is shown in Table 3.

ISOT FAKENEWS is an English fake news dataset proposed by Ahmed et al., in which real news was collected from Reuters.com, and fake news was

Table 3. Dataset breakdown

Dataset name	Real News	Fake News
ISOT FAKENEWS	21417	23481
COVID-19	5600	5100
McIntire	3171	3164
MisInfoText	19203	18556

collected from unreliable websites flagged by Politifact and Wikipedia [1]. The dataset contains information such as article titles, text, and publication dates, with a large portion of the news being global and political in nature.

The COVID-19 dataset, proposed by Patwa et al., is a fake news dataset on the novel coronavirus disease. It was collected from 10,700 social media posts and articles from sources like Facebook, Twitter, and Instagram [10]. Real news in this dataset was gathered from official accounts of organizations like the World Health Organization (WHO) and medical institutions such as the Centers for Disease Control and Prevention (CDC). The fake news was collected from articles on social media related to COVID-19 that had been flagged as fake by well-known fact-checking websites like Politifact, Snopes, and Boomlive.

McIntire is known as a benchmark dataset for fake news detection, and it is constructed from articles primarily focused on politics and economics [8]. Real news was collected from sources like The New York Times, WSJ, Bloomberg, NPR, and The Guardian, while fake news was gathered from articles published on Kaggle.

MisInfoText is a dataset constructed by Torabi Asr et al. to analyze the impact of label reliability on fake news detection [2]. In this study, we used data collected from Politifact and, for binary classification, we labeled "true," "mostly true," and "half-true" as REAL, and "false," "mostly false," and "pants on fire!" as FAKE.

5.2 Experimental Environment

The experimental environment and the main libraries used in this study are summarized in Table 4.

5.3 Comparison of Detection Performance

For each dataset, we compare the fake news detection performance of BERT [3, 13] and RoBERTa [6,11], which are models pre-trained on more than 40,000 news articles for fake news detection, with that of the proposed method.

The detection performance for each dataset is shown in Fig. 2, Fig. 3, Fig. 4, and Fig. 5. In each graph, the vertical axis represents the classification models, and the horizontal axis represents the values of each evaluation metric. Since this

Table 4. Experimental Environment

CPU	Intel Core i9-14900KF 3.20 GHz
GPU	NVIDIA GeForce RTX 4090
Memory	128 GB
OS	Windows 11 Home
CUDA	11.8
Programming Language	Python 3.8.9
Transformers	4.46.3
Scikit-learn	1.3.2

study focuses on evaluating the performance of the detector, we pay particular attention to accuracy and F1-score.

Using ISOT FAKENEWS as the test dataset, the proposed model achieves an accuracy and F1-score of 0.91 with COVID-19 training and 0.87 with McIntire training. Although these results are inferior to those of the pre-trained models, they demonstrate that the proposed method can still achieve detection performance close to 90%. In contrast, when trained on MisInfoText, the proposed model shows significantly lower performance, with an accuracy of 0.81 and an F1-score of 0.79.

When COVID-19 is used as the test dataset, the proposed model achieves an accuracy of approximately 0.7, which is higher than that of the pre-trained models. With regard to the F1-score, except for the case where the model is trained on MisInfoText, we confirm that the proposed model shows higher generalization performance than the pre-trained models.

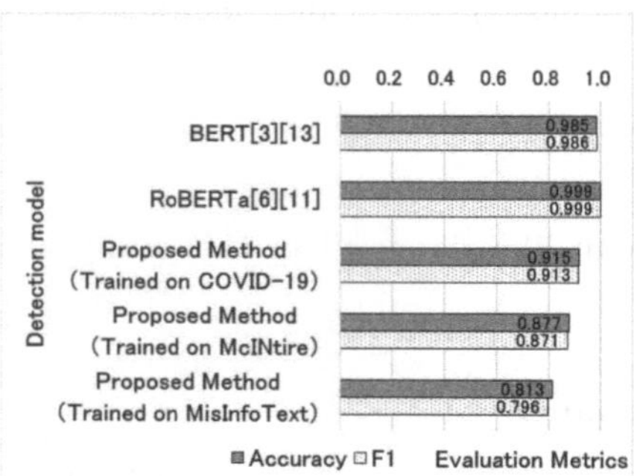

Fig. 2. Comparison of Detection Performance on ISOT FAKENEWS

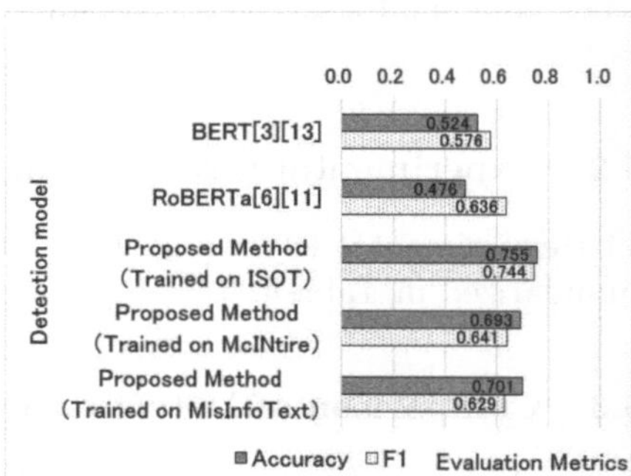

Fig. 3. Comparison of Detection Performance on COVID-19

When McIntire is used as the test dataset, the accuracy of the proposed model exceeds 0.7 in all cases, confirming that it exhibits higher generalization performance than the pre-trained models. However, focusing on the F1-score, we observe that when the model is trained on MisInfoText, its performance is inferior to that of the pre-trained models.

When MisInfoText is used as the test dataset, the proposed model achieves an accuracy of approximately 0.5 and an F1-score of approximately 0.3, indicating that the model exhibits very limited capability in detecting fake news.

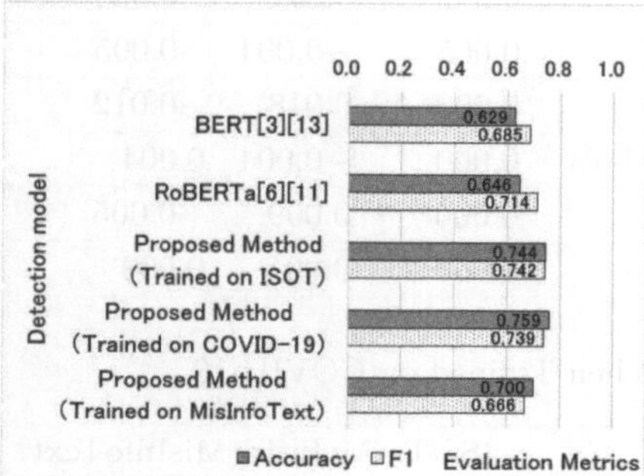

Fig. 4. Comparison of Detection Performance on McIntire

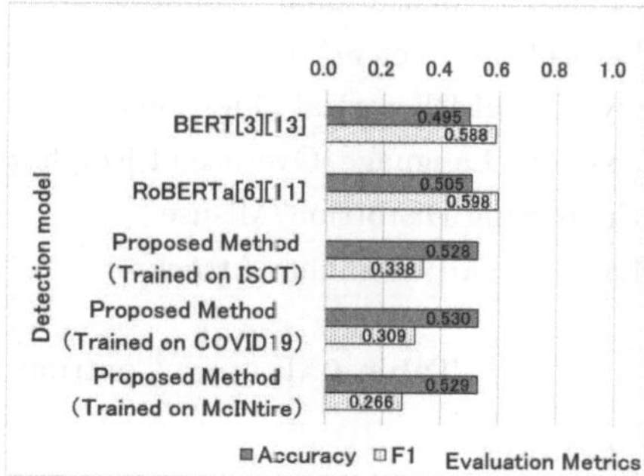

Fig. 5. Comparison of Detection Performance on MisInfoText

5.4 Important Features for Fake News Detection

We evaluated how much the ten types of fake news features assessed by Llama3 contribute to fake news detection. The evaluation results are shown in Tables 5, 6, 7 and 8.

The models trained on ISOT FAKENEWS and McIntire show high contributions from four features—Linguistic Flaws, Logical Inconsistency, Low Source Credibility, and Lack of Supporting Evidence—except when detecting MisInfoText. When MisInfoText is used for detection, we confirm that the contributions of all features are low.

The model trained on COVID-19 shows high contributions from four features—Low Source Credibility, Lack of Supporting Evidence, Emotional/Sensational Language, and Contextual Distortion/Misuse—except when detecting MisInfoText. The model trained on MisInfoText also shows high contributions from the same four features; however, we confirm that other features also contribute to the detection performance.

6 Discussion

6.1 Generalization Ability of the Proposed Method

Experimental results show that the proposed model achieves higher detection performance than pre-trained linguistic-feature-based models on most datasets,

Table 5. Feature Contributions When Trained on ISOT FAKENEWS

Features	COVID19	McIntire	MisInfoText
Linguistic Flaws	0.019	0.033	−0.044
Logical Inconsistency	0.005	0.013	−0.013
Low Source Credibility	0.050	0.019	−0.064
Lack of Supporting Evidence	0.082	0.037	−0.100
Emotional/Sensational Language	0.062	0.041	−0.043
Lack of Specificity/Vagueness	0.005	−0.004	−0.005
Overuse of Rhetorical Questions	0.002	0.018	−0.012
Extreme Language/Overuse of Emphatic Symbols	0.000	−0.004	0.004
Contextual Distortion/Misuse	0.000	0.009	−0.005
Labeling/Ad Hominem Attack	0.000	0.001	0.000

Table 6. Feature Contributions When Trained on COVID-19

Features	ISOT	McIntire	MisInfoText
Linguistic Flaws	0.000	0.002	−0.001
Logical Inconsistency	0.028	0.013	−0.021
Low Source Credibility	0.084	0.021	−0.081
Lack of Supporting Evidence	0.126	0.042	−0.111
Emotional/Sensational Language	0.246	0.108	−0.044
Lack of Specificity/Vagueness	0.069	0.022	−0.091
Overuse of Rhetorical Questions	0.012	0.004	−0.006
Extreme Language/Overuse of Emphatic Symbols	0.001	−0.001	−0.002
Contextual Distortion/Misuse	0.118	0.036	−0.064
Labeling/Ad Hominem Attack	−0.003	0.001	0.000

demonstrating its potential generalization ability. (RQ1) Although performance on the ISOT FAKENEWS dataset is slightly inferior, the proposed method still maintains high accuracy. In contrast, performance on the MisInfoText dataset remains limited, indicating that dataset characteristics strongly affect detection performance and that further improvement is required (Table 6).

The proposed method offers significant advantages for digital platforms and auditing organizations. By leveraging context-based features rather than database-specific patterns, the model enhances generalizability across news categories without extensive re-tuning. Automating feature extraction via LLMs reduces the human resources and costs typically required for manual fact-checking and complex feature engineering.

Table 7. Feature Contributions When Trained on McIntire

Features	ISOT	COVID19	MisInfoText
Linguistic Flaws	0.069	0.004	−0.039
Logical Inconsistency	0.005	−0.003	−0.010
Low Source Credibility	0.109	0.052	−0.083
Lack of Supporting Evidence	0.104	0.011	−0.147
Emotional/Sensational Language	0.120	0.026	−0.082
Lack of Specificity/Vagueness	−0.003	−0.061	−0.044
Overuse of Rhetorical Questions	−0.005	0.000	−0.002
Extreme Language/Overuse of Emphatic Symbols	−0.005	−0.010	0.002
Contextual Distortion/Misuse	−0.006	0.000	−0.001
Labeling/Ad Hominem Attack	−0.014	0.000	−0.004

Table 8. Feature Contributions When Trained on MisInfoText

Features	ISOT	COVID19	McIntire
Linguistic Flaws	−0.004	−0.001	−0.003
Logical Inconsistency	0.087	0.004	0.021
Low Source Credibility	0.083	0.047	0.025
Lack of Supporting Evidence	0.130	0.038	0.044
Emotional/Sensational Language	0.089	0.054	0.018
Lack of Specificity/Vagueness	−0.042	−0.026	−0.018
Overuse of Rhetorical Questions	0.040	0.001	0.007
Extreme Language/Overuse of Emphatic Symbols	0.067	−0.005	0.020
Contextual Distortion/Misuse	0.132	0.024	0.047
Labeling/Ad Hominem Attack	0.080	0.002	0.024

6.2 Limitations and Feature Variability

Analysis of feature importance reveals that source credibility, lack of supporting evidence, and emotional or sensational language consistently contribute to fake news detection across datasets. However, the importance of other features varies depending on the dataset, suggesting that a fixed feature set may not fully capture the diversity of fake news. In addition, Llama3 was unable to evaluate features for some articles due to input length limitations or insufficient information, which may affect detection performance (RQ2, RQ3) (Table 7).

6.3 Research Ethics

All datasets and libraries used in this study are publicly available, ensuring high reproducibility.

6.4 Limitations of the Study

In this study, experiments were conducted using four datasets. Although these datasets include labels assigned by fact-checking organizations, the definition of fake news is diverse. In addition, some datasets contain ambiguous labels, such as *half-true*, rather than a simple binary distinction between real and fake, leaving room for further validation of label reliability. To address these issues, future work should involve evaluations using multiple and diverse datasets.

The current prompts are designed to be generic to ensure task-independence. However, this abstractness may limit the transparency of how specific feature ratings are determined. Future work should focus on prompt optimization to improve the explanatory power of why certain datasets yield higher performance.

7 Conclusion

In this study, we proposed a fake news detection model leveraging abstract and contextual features extracted via an LLM. Experiments on multiple datasets demonstrated improved generalization over conventional models. Feature analysis revealed both common and dataset-dependent features, suggesting the effectiveness of multifaceted evaluation. While Llama-3-8B was utilized for efficiency, we recognize the potential of larger-scale models and are currently conducting experiments to evaluate how advanced reasoning further refines feature extraction and detection accuracy.

References

1. Ahmed, H., Traore, I., Saad, S.: Detection of online fake news using n-gram analysis and machine learning techniques. In: Traore, I., Woungang, I., Awad, A. (eds.) Intelligent, Secure, and Dependable Systems in Distributed and Cloud Environments, pp. 127–138. Springer, Cham (2017). https://doi.org/10.1007/978-3-319-69155-8
2. Asr, F.T., Taboada, M.: Big data and quality data for fake news and misinformation detection. Big Data Soc. **6**(1), 1–14 (2019)
3. Aymene: Fake-news-detection-BERT-based-uncased, hugging Face model
4. Garg, S., Sharma, D.K.: Linguistic features based framework for automatic fake news detection. Comput. Ind. Eng. **172**, 108432 (2022)
5. Hakak, S., Alazab, M., Khan, S., Gadekallu, T.R., Maddikunta, P.K.R., Khan, W.Z.: An ensemble machine learning approach through effective feature extraction to classify fake news. Futur. Gener. Comput. Syst. **117**, 47–58 (2021)
6. jy46604790: Fake-news-bert-detect, hugging Face model
7. Khan, J.Y., Khondaker, M.T.I., Afroz, S., Uddin, G., Iqbal, A.: A benchmark study of machine learning models for online fake news detection. Mach. Learn. Appl. **4**, 100032 (2021)
8. McIntire, G.: Fake and Real News Dataset. George McIntire's GitHub (2018)
9. Mimura, M., Ishimaru, T.: Analyzing common lexical features of fake news using multi-head attention weights. Internet Things **28**, 101409 (2024)

10. Patwa, P., et al.: Overview of CONSTRAINT 2021 shared tasks: detecting English COVID-19 fake news and Hindi hostile posts. In: Chakraborty, T., Shu, K., Bernard, H.R., Liu, H., Akhtar, M.S. (eds.) CONSTRAINT 2021. CCIS, vol. 1402, pp. 42–53. Springer, Cham (2021). https://doi.org/10.1007/978-3-030-73696-5_5
11. Poovozhi, T., Ahamed, S.A., Sankeerth, T., Reddy, S.S., Ganesh, T.: Fake news detection using BERT and ROBERTA. Int. J. Res. Appl. Sci. Eng. Technol. **13**, 2875–2880 (2025)
12. Rai, N., Kumar, D., Kaushik, N., Raj, C., Ali, A.: Fake news classification using transformer based enhanced LSTM and BERT. Int. J. Cognit. Comput. Eng. **3**, 98–105 (2022)
13. Rodríguez, Á.I., Lloret Iglesias, L.: Fake news detection using deep learning. arXiv preprint arXiv:1910.03496 (2019)
14. Vaswani, A., et al.: Attention is all you need. Adv. Neural Inf. Process. Syst. **30** (2017)
15. Xu, X., Xu, Z., Yu, P., Wang, J.: A hybrid attention framework for fake news detection with large language models. arXiv preprint arXiv:2501.11967 (2025)

Facilitating Disinformation Detection in Social Media with XScanner Approach

Dominik Szczepaniak and Adam Wójtowicz(✉)

Poznań University of Economics and Business, al. Niepodległości 10, 61-875 Poznań, Poland
adam.wojtowicz@ue.poznan.pl
https://www.ue.poznan.pl

Abstract. The social media adoption rate and business models make them an efficient environment for influencing users with disinformation content. In turn, the process of automated or semi-automated disinformation detection is challenging for many reasons. Numerous research methods and applications are published in this area, but they suffer from significant limitations related to their functionality or detection accuracy. These circumstances are the motivation for the presented work, which contributes with: a novel multi-criteria disinformation detection method implemented in the XScanner prototype application dedicated to the X service and a series of experiments designed to evaluate the properties of the XScanner method. XScanner application has the ability to operate on online data, to analyze the content, metadata, and interactions, and to produce fine-grained results for the analyst. XScanner LDA efficiency of 91% and F1-score of 0.87 show that the model maintains a balanced performance, effectively minimizing both false positives and false negatives. Through statistical analysis, the findings confirm that the identified criteria as well as XScanner application can be both effectively used to support a fact checker, community manager or security manager in the process of disinformation detection and labeling.

Keywords: disinformation detection · disinformation detection automation · disinformation detection tool · disinformation detection application

1 Introduction

The semantic distinction between disinformation, misinformation, and malinformation concepts is non-trivial and is a subject of scientific discourse [33]. In this work the focus is limited specifically to disinformation problem and European Commission's disinformation definition is assumed: verifiably false or misleading information that is created, presented and disseminated for economic gain or to intentionally deceive the public, and may cause public harm [9]. In practice disinformation production processes include publishing false information, content manipulation, creating false identities or documents, including multimedia

K. Węcel and V. Řepa (Eds.): BIS 2026, LNBIP 584, pp. 60–73, 2026.
https://doi.org/10.1007/978-3-032-26363-6_5

documents [10]. Mass dissemination of disinformation content is a significant challenge for modern societies as it is used in numerous fields: not only during armed conflicts but also beforehand as part of hybrid warfare [3] through spreading controversial and polarizing topics, or as part of a soft war: a long-term psychological, propaganda, media, information economic, or cultural operation that targets a society or a specific social group [17]. Another purpose of disinformation production is achieving political gains using crafted multimedia content or by providing false information or data [5,15]. Disinformation is used to create a certain view or mindset in society: infodemia conditions reliability and authenticity of information is difficult to verify, which leads to harmful social and economic decisions [21,27]. A significant portion of the disinformation content is produced to perform scam and theft in organized campaigns. They also slow down innovations as they can be aimed at raising mistrust towards innovative solutions, ideas, and technologies [4,13]. They can lead to a decrease in consumer and investor trust in specific companies or industries [8] and to additional costs spent by organizations for advertising actions against false information, content verification, or actions to maintain good relations with investors.

The high adoption rate of social media and the level of user engagement make social media an efficient tool for influencing its users with disinformation content. For example, disinformation content on X service spreads six times faster than genuine information [24]. Other factors that facilitate distribution of disinformation content in social media include information bubble phenomenon, also called filter bubble [19], and social media business models oriented on maximizing website traffic. They take advantage of social media users' psychological cognitive biases, which combined can even lead to accelerated spread of conspiracy theories [20]. Finally, in case of some social media, service provider's technical ability to manually adjust the content displayed to users can also play its role in disinformation spreading [2].

In turn, the process of automated or semi-automated disinformation detection in social media is challenging. There are numerous analytical methods [23,35,36,44] and tools [11,14,25,37,38,41,42] developed in this area, but they suffer from significant limitations related to their functionality or detection accuracy. Particularly analytical software tools are in this work's area of interest. Usually the given tool performs only on selected aspect of the analysis (such as analysis of account metadata, produced content or account interactions) and does not return fine-grained explainable results. These circumstances are the main motivation for the presented research which contributes with: a novel multicriteria disinformation detection method implemented in XScanner prototype application dedicated to X service, and series of research experiments designed and conducted to evaluate the properties of the XScanner method.

To deliver the stated contributions, a number of activities have been performed. XScanner prototype application to analyze users' accounts on X service has been developed: it uniquely combines metadata, content, interaction, and cross-platform analysis with fine-grained, explainable outputs. To validate the prepared application, and to support the application development process, X service accounts have been prepared forming test group. Their behavior is similar to accounts used to produce disinformation content. Also control groups consisting of actual user accounts on X have been formed. Finally, the experiments have been conducted using the proposed application on the previously prepared research groups, which has been followed by the statistical analysis of the obtained results. The findings confirm that a number of the proposed XScanner criteria can be effectively used to support a fact checker, community manager or security manager in the process of disinformation detection and labeling.

2 Related Works

2.1 Methods for Disinformation Creation

The production of fake news, which are spread mainly through social media and news sites, is one of the primary means in disinformation processes [12]. Nowadays, generative AI (genAI), particularly LLMs, are used for disinformation content production. LLM-based services are equipped with security features designed to prevent users from malicious content generation. Workarounds are practiced by passing appropriately crafted prompts that are not rejected by the filters [26]. The effectiveness of using LLMs in disinformation content production is demonstrated by experiments [40]. LLM technology development and availability allow disinformation actors to train custom models that do not impose any limitations on the content and are more specialized and effective. Disinformation content is created also through deepfake technology: genAI algorithms trained to generate realistic video of persons [39]. Currently, there are no publicly available tools to detect state-of-the-art deepfake content with 100% accuracy.

To increase an amount of published content and its impact, also the process of disinformation content publishing can be automated. Typically, bots are used to implement disinformation automation, which utilize social media accounts mimicking the activity of authentic users as well as software operating autonomously to communicate with end-users or publishing content according to a schedule. Mass interactions with selected content, by publishing, sharing or commenting particular posts, can build an impression of the popularity of a statement or a worldview. Bots also publish open-ended questions that encourage adding comments or filling surveys, interactions that increase the outreach of the content according to the nature of social media algorithms [18]. Accounts called cyborgs are used in the process of distributing disinformation and automate parts of their activities while still being actively managed by a real user [16]. They are used in Coordinated Inauthentic Behavior (CIB) [28] manipulative communication tactics that employ a number of authentic, fake, and duplicated social media accounts to operate as adversarial networks across various social media services.

There are ready-made applications that automate publishing of social media content, such as Buffer [6] or CoSchedule [7]. These applications allow for centralized account and content management: producing large amount of content in a short time and publishing it periodically in several services, adjusting publication time to the target time zone. Yet another solution is Zapier [43], which integrate not only with social media but also with email clients, workflow tools, sales systems, and CMSs. It also allows combining integrations into processes and designing event-driven processes to deploy complex disinformation scenarios. Some of the tools, such as AI-based Tweet Hunter [31], offer not only analytical and automation tools for publishing content, but also they assist operator in the creation of posts designed to attract reader interest and increase audience engagement. To eliminate risks related to above mentioned SaaS solutions, open source Huginn [22] and Automatisch.io [1] solutions are used, which provide an operator with full control over the users and the data.

2.2 Tools for Disinformation Detection on X Service

There are numerous research works on particular tools that are designed to analyze activity on X service for the spread of disinformation. One of them is Hoaxy [37], which provides its users with network visualizations that show how specific posts, topics, and trends are shared online, including who shares them and how the information propagates. The tool also allows checking the type of interactions: reposts, mentions, replies, and quotes. It requires passing the search phrase, and as a result, a number of dependency graphs are returned. Additionally, Hoaxy provides a chart with the cumulative post count on a timeline, which allows detecting popular topics and checking the identity of the involved parties. The main limitation of the application is that it only allows searching trends and identifying accounts involved in related discussions, as opposed to analyses for a specific account. Moreover, Hoaxy does not estimate the veracity of the given information, only its spread is tracked.

A tool that can facilitate detection of disinformation accounts is Botometer X. It is designed to analyze whether the behavioral patterns of X service account are similar to typical bot behavior. Botometer X analyzes an account's activity and assigns it a Bot Score, a metric of probability the account is to be automated. Bot Score is calculated based on the author's model [42]. Its first drawback is the data cut-off: Bot Score has been calculated on historical data collected before particular date in 2023. Thus the tool can be used mostly for analysis of historical trends, not as a full-fledged research tool. The second drawback is inability to detect bot accounts supported by AI tools, especially LLMs. Also it is unable to fully interpret aspects affecting the bot score value, therefore a researcher is not able to interpret the factors affecting the outcome.

Some tools focus on the worldview or political leanings of the accounts. TwitterTrails application estimates whether a given information is a fact or a rumor. The tool takes into account the visibility of information and the level of engagement was triggered by the information. The tool also analyzes the skepticism of posts related to the analyzed statement and it takes into account a partisan bias of the analyzed accounts. The proposed solution does not include any prevention steps related to the automation of content production and bot activities [38]. TwitterTrails applicability as a research tool is limited as it is no longer publicly available neither as an application nor in the form of a source code.

There are also software tools originating from IT industry that perform automatic analysis of selected aspects of accounts on X service. They allow partial automation of the analysis and their use does not require knowledge of advanced data analysis methods. The first is followerwonk [11]. The application provides the user with an analysis report containing the information regarding: account itself; the value of the Social Authority metric, which measures the strength of influence on other accounts; geolocation of related accounts presented in the form of a map; bar charts showing hourly percentage distribution of added entries for related accounts and for the analyzed account; keywords used by the analyzed account in the form of a word cloud; additional information such as language used, gender, or number of users observed. In addition to the analysis, the tool allows searching for accounts based on keywords in the account description, as well as comparing observer and observed lists between accounts.

The second tool that can be used to analyze X service accounts is Foller.me [14]. After the analysis, a report is displayed, which includes information about the analyzed account, and then, based on a sample of data from the list of posts, the tool returns statistics about the user's posts and a bar chart showing the user's activity by hour. In the report, there are also pointed out topics covered in the content, used hashtags, and tagged accounts.

The third tool is Simple Twitter Profile Analyzer (STPA) which generates a report that includes data such as average account activity by hour and day of the week, time zone, approximate user location, methods of interaction, e.g. mobile app or web app, most used hashtags and tagged users, and the analysis of the followed and followers based on the most common time zones and languages. The presented tool lacks UI adequate for requirements of typical users. Its use requires the ability to work with the Python environment and generate a custom authentication key for the X service API. Nevertheless, an important advantage of the discussed solution is its open-source nature, allowing free use, modification, and further distribution [41].

The application called onemilliontweetmap can be used to compare posted content between accounts [25]. The application displays posts from X service on a map and groups them by author location. It is possible to track down other users publishing content with the same subject as the analyzed account. For English language semantic analysis is supported. An alternative solution is Tweetmap allowing also for trend analysis for hashtags used within a given country.

3 Proposed XScanner Approach

The main purpose of the proposed XScanner application is to support and speed up the process of analyzing X service accounts in the context of disinformation labeling. The analysis of the preexisting solutions shows that there is a lack of solutions combining all key features, namely the ability: to operate on online data and to analyze the produced content, to analyze account metadata, to analyze account interactions, and to produce fine-grained results for the analyst. These shortcomings impact XScanner application design decisions. The application components shown in Fig. 1 analyze particular classes of information described in the following paragraphs.

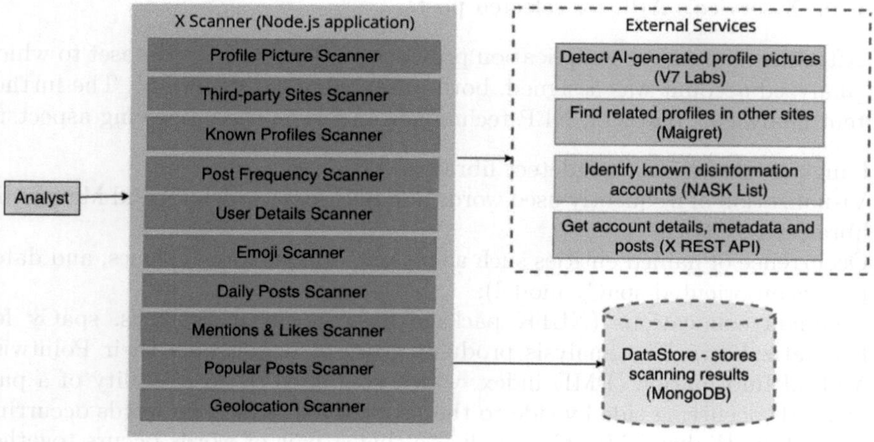

Fig. 1. XScanner application components

- Account metadata, which include: the full account name, description, creation date, its lifetime, the following and followers count, posts count, and information whether the account is marked as verified. Counted values are compared with the average values for previously conducted analyses.
- Posting temporal patterns, which include: last activity date; average number of posts on days when at least one entry was added; average number of total posts per day; sum of days in which no post was added; maximum number of posts in a day; estimated number of posts added via the scheduler tool; number of analyzed posts and the date of the oldest one; frequency of posting by hours in the form of a histogram; used language.
- Emoji and hashtags: emojis convey not only emotions but also their worldview [32], and they increase interaction and engagement of the content audience; hashtags can indicate the author's areas of interest; the application provides a list of the N most common emoji and hashtags.
- Profile image: to analyze profile images API by V7 Labs is used, which allows for detecting images generated with Generative Adversarial Network.
- Most tagged/liked accounts: analysis of the most frequently tagged accounts, the accounts most often liked by the analyzed account, and its watched and followed accounts reveals the network of relations between accounts.
- Presence on disinformation list, which has been prepared as part of the NASK Enable Verification campaign [29].
- Profiles with the same username on other services: Maigret tool was used to search for profiles on other social networks and websites (more than 2,500) related to the account under analysis.

- List of N most popular posts by the account, popularity is calculated as the sum of its public metrics: number of likes, shares, citations, and responses.
- Geolocation: for users who have provided their location data it is retrieved using X service's API, for selected posts.

After the analysis, the application provides a report and the dataset to which the analyzed account was assigned, both available in JSON format. The further content analysis is based on NLP techniques and covers the following aspects:

- Language detection (langdetect library);
- Visualization of frequently used words and phrases (wordcloud and Matplotlib libraries);
- Occurrence of named entities such as people, organizations, places, and dates (precision-oriented spaCy model);
- Common collocations (NLTK package for collocation analysis, spaCy for lemmatization). The analysis produces pairs of words with their Pointwise Mutual Information (PMI) index, which compares the probability of a pair of words occurring side by side to the probability of the two words occurring separately. Higher PMI values indicate that a pair of words occurs together more often than expected by chance.
- Vocabulary variety: the number of unique results from text lemmatization compared to the total number of analyzed words and posts, can be compared across accounts to detect anomalies.

The second XScanner module produces a graph showing relationships between the examined accounts. The graph is directed, with nodes representing accounts analyzed by the application. Each node is labeled with the account name, and edges indicate connections, with arrowheads showing which account follows the other. Node size increases with the number of outgoing edges, highlighting accounts with many connections.

4 Experiment Setup

To verify the usability of the proposed XScanner application, series of tests have been conducted. The goal of the tests is to response to the specific research questions regarding: effective identification an account's area of interest with the method; effective detection of anomalies in the activity of an account? determining whether the account is involved in distributing disinformation by distinguishing the test group accounts from the control group accounts?

Tests were conducted on real X service accounts. Two study groups were created: a control group and a test group, each with 100 accounts. Accounts qualified for testing had to publish content primarily in Polish. Initial accounts were selected from the most popular Polish-language accounts. Additional accounts were qualified using X service recommendation mechanisms as well as through mentions and interactions with already qualified accounts. The qualification process was conducted using the X service UI, and experimental data were collected via the X service API.

The criteria for qualifying accounts for the control group aim to maximize account authenticity. The following factors are considered for an account:

- belongs to a real person with a verified identity, or is an account representing an institution, company, or organization;
- is awarded a badge of authenticity by X service;
- belongs to at least one of the following groups: well-known people, publicists, OSINT and information analysis specialists, journalists, actors, reporters, politicians, athletes, and public officials;
- is linked with other accounts matched to the control group, while linking means interacting by replying to posts, sharing posts, or watching the account (auxiliary).

A test group consists of accounts that would be of interest to a researcher performing disinformation analysis. In addition to meeting the general criteria, an account that qualifies for a test group has to meet some of the specific criteria:

- publishes content of a provocative, offensive nature or that attacks social, ethnic, religious, professional, political groups and public figures;
- publishes content that contradicts the position represented by the widely recognized scientific community;
- it is not possible to determine account's owner, e.g., an account does not represent a true identity or does not identify the organization;
- impersonates another user, assuming that the victim owns an account on X service for which authenticity can be unambiguously verified;
- is on NASK list of accounts related to spread of disinformation;
- is linked to an account on the NASK list of accounts (auxiliary).

The following data have been collected for each of the accounts analyzed: username, account creation date and lifetime in years, hours of peak account activity, the result from the authenticity test of the profile image, the number of followed and followers, the total number of posts, average number of posts per active day and overall, the number of analyzed posts, maximum number of posts added in a day, and results of the semantic content analysis, detected lemmas count and unique words count. The result also includes the outcomes of semantic content analysis using interactive computational documents.

5 Results

Significant differences between the test group and the control group appear in publication frequency: the average number of posts in active days ($U = 1742$, $p < 0.001$, $r_{rb} = -0.6516$) (Fig. 2a) and the maximum posts in a single day ($U = 1776.5$, $p < 0.001$, $r_{rb} = -0.6447$) (Fig. 2b). Mann-Whitney U test with rank-biserial correlation has been performed to test the significance of differences for the indicated values. The test has been selected after conducting the Shapiro-Wilk normality test, which proved that the analyzed properties are not distributed normally. Performed tests have allowed rejecting the null hypothesis that the distributions for the analyzed datasets are similar. For both analyzed properties, values from the test group are stochastically larger than those of the control group. Similar procedure has been conducted for the following to followers ratio ($U = 281$, $p < 0.001$, $r_{rb} = 0.9438$) (Fig. 2c). However in this case, conducted tests have not allowed rejecting the hypothesis that the values in the control group is stochastically larger. The tests conducted on the lemmas to unique words ratio ($U = 2812$, $p < 0.001$, $r_{rb} = -0.4376$) (Fig. 2d) have allowed rejecting the null hypothesis that the analyzed groups are similar, and showed the ratio for the test group is stochastically larger than for the control group.

Another difference between the groups is related to availability of geolocation data. It has been available for 9% of control group accounts and only 1% of test group accounts. The proportion of accounts without clear periods of increased or decreased activity also differs: 2% in the control group versus 12% in the test group. Average activity hours are similar for both groups but standard deviations differ: control group activity is more uniform.

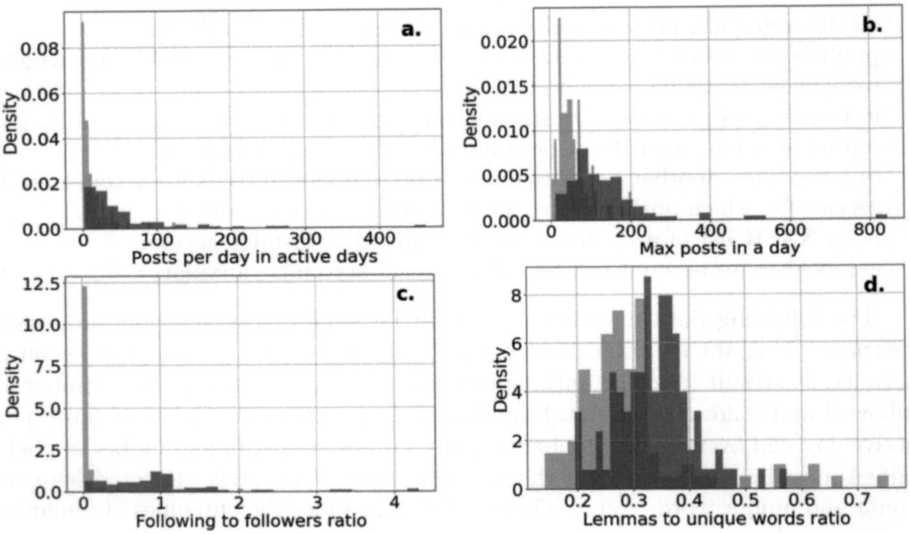

Fig. 2. Density of a. average number of posts in active days; b. max number of posts in a day; c. following to followers ratio; d. lemmas to unique words ratio. Red bars – control group; blue bars – test group. (Color figure online)

Conducting the direct analysis using the prepared tools does not allow to clearly distinguish the accounts belonging to each group. For this reason, a linear discriminant analysis (LDA) has been carried out based on the collected data. This analysis is aimed at preparing a model that would allow, based on the input provided, to assign an account to a group of accounts considered reliable, or to a group of accounts suspected of distributing disinformation.

For the analysis, data from 50 test accounts and 50 control accounts, are used, based on random selection. For each account, the following variables are used: account lifetime in years; average daily number of posts; average daily number of entries on active days during the study period; maximum number of posts added in a single day during the study period; followed to followers ratio; number of detected lemmas; detected lemmas to unique words ratio; initial hour of account activity; final hour of account activity; number of links to other accounts with accounts from the group to which the account belongs.

Each of the accounts in the training sample is pre-classified to the appropriate group. LDA model is prepared within Jupyter environment with Scikit-learn package providing machine learning, data processing, model selection and evaluation solutions [30]. Based on the cross-validation method, the efficiency of the obtained model is estimated at 91%. To test the model, a test group containing 15 accounts from both groups have been prepared. The accounts for the test group are selected randomly, and they exclude accounts used in the process of building the LDA model. The prepared model makes the correct classification for 26 cases, and misclassification occurs for one account from the control group and three accounts from the test group. The results obtained allow to conclude that account analysis using the prepared model can be a valuable component in the process of analyzing accounts on X service.

To evaluate the performance of the proposed model, precision, recall, and the F1-score effectiveness are calculated according to widely used formulas. The obtained results indicate that the model achieves a precision measure of 0.873, and the recall of 0.867. Obviously, the F1-score of 0.866 confirms that the model maintains a balanced performance, effectively minimizing both false positives and false negatives.

6 Discussion

The competing solutions described in Sect. 2.2 focus on particular data types such as account metadata, produced content data or account interaction data and do not provide the analyst with fine-grained, explainable outcomes. In turn, XScanner's main strength is related to its comprehensive approach to analysis the accounts. Not only the content of the posts is analyzed, but also the network of connections between the analyzed accounts, activity temporal patterns, image data, and a presence of similar accounts on other social networks. XScanner combines the analysis of profile metadata with published content and content metadata such as posting hours or geolocation data. The differences between XScanner and competing solutions have been shown in Table 1.

The comparison criteria shown in the header of Table 1 have been chosen because of their practical significance to the disinformation identification process. While the majority of the competing solutions have, similarly to XScanner, an ability to operate on online data and to analyze the produced content, only three of them have the ability to analyse account metadata, and only two competitors have the ability to analyze account interactions. Only one of the competing

Table 1. Feature comparison for the competing solutions and XScanner application

Solution	Operates on online data	Account metadata analysis	Content analysis	Interaction analysis	Is extensible	Fine-grained results
Hoaxy [37]	Yes	No	No	Yes	N/A	No
Botometer X [42]	No	No	Yes	Yes	N/A	No
TwitterTrails [38]	N/A	Yes	Yes	Yes	N/A	No
followerwonk [11]	Yes	Yes	Yes	No	N/A	No
Foller.me [14]	Yes	Yes	Yes	No	N/A	No
STPA [41]	Yes	No	Yes	No	Yes	No
onemillion-tweetmap [25]	Yes	No	Yes	No	N/A	Yes
XScanner	Yes	Yes	Yes	Yes	Yes	Yes

solutions produces fine-grained results for the analyst. None of the analyzed XScanner competitors has all these features.

A significant advantage of the application is that it provides the researcher with the detailed results and allows to interpret them. XScanner does not provide any fixed unified metric related to the analyzed profile or the published content. While it has been shown that with the proposed LDA model (cf. Sect. 5) it is feasible to classify accounts, an analyst still can interpret, based on their expert knowledge, particular factors separately. The other advantage is the ability to assign the particular accounts to different research groups, which allows for analyzing each group separately. It is also possible to study account activity over a defined period of time. XScanner allows exporting the analyzed dataset for further cross-analysis: performing Mann-Whitney U tests and constructing an LDA model based on data from XScanner are examples of such use case.

The application architecture allows for seamless extensions with additional features. It allows leveraging more capabilities offered by X service API or integrating it with other tools. XScanner can be used as a base for specific research and analytical extensions. The application allows multiple analyses to be performed simultaneously, making it possible to scale it by running multiple instances and routing the traffic to individual instances with load balancers.

The proposed XScanner approach has several limitations. The first one is the partial reliance on external services, such as an external API to analyze a user's profile image. There is a possibility that the service will be shut down at any time, or its business model will change, making its use unprofitable from the perspective of deriving financial benefits from the proposed application. There is a need to constantly monitor changes in the used APIs. The second limitation is missing a unified interface and the need to manually run the analysis of the content of entries and the network of links. It requires setting up the dedicated environment and installing required dependencies. This affects UX and the time needed to perform the analysis. The third limitation is related to possible biases in the study group construction process: despite the adopted strict criteria described in Sect. 4, the proposed approach has still imperfections in this area.

As for the sustainability of the disinformation detection solutions developed based on the XScanner approach, for economic scalability of high-volume deployments the X service Enterprise API version financed according to custom Enterprise plan is required.

7 Conclusions

Both declared contributions of the work have been delivered: a novel multicriteria disinformation detection method dedicated to X service, and series of research experiments designed and conducted to evaluate the properties of the XScanner approach. The competing solutions focus on selected aspects, whereas XScanner approach main strength is related to its comprehensive analysis of the accounts. Not only the content of the posts is analyzed, but also the network of connections between the accounts, activity temporal patterns, image data, and a presence of similar accounts on other social networks. An advantage of the application is that it provides the researcher with the detailed results and allows to interpret them. The other advantage is the ability to assign the analyzed accounts to different research groups, which allows for analyzing each group separately, also with a temporal separation of the groups. The application's architecture allows for easy and quick extensions with additional factors and for multiple analyses to be performed simultaneously. None of the analyzed XScanner competitors has all the analyzed features.

The second main contribution of this work is a series of research experiments designed to evaluate the properties of the approach. Lists of specific user accounts has been prepared and used to test the application. The process of preparing a list of accounts has allowed to find out the characteristics that can be used by a regular user to assess the credibility of other accounts. Quantitative evaluation of the prepared prototype makes verifying the assumptions from the prototype design phase stage possible. Several characteristics that distinguish accounts belonging to different groups can be identified: publishing time and frequency, number of interactions with other accounts, subject areas of published content, and vocabulary used. The proposed approach enables the collection of data, which have been used to conduct an analysis based on the LDA method. LDA efficiency of 91% and F1-score of 0.87 show that the model maintains a balanced performance, effectively minimizing both false positives and false negatives. The analysis confirms that the model could constitute a valuable component in the process of detecting accounts serving for disinformation purposes.

As for the future research works related to XScanner approach, they include works on increasing the automation of the account analysis process, applying more advanced ML methods, improving the usability of the proposed application, integrating XScanner application with other analytical applications, or integrating it into disinformation detection ecosystems such as OpenFact [34].

References

1. Automatisch: Create Flow | Automatisch Docs (2025). https://automatisch.io/docs/guide/create-flow
2. Baker-White, E.: Tiktok's secret 'heating' button can make anyone go viral. Forbes January **20** (2023)
3. Bilal, A.: Hybrid warfare–new threats, complexity, and 'trust' as the antidote. Nato Rev. **30**(11) (2021)
4. Blaskiewicz, R.: The Big Pharma conspiracy theory. Med. Writ. **22**(4), 259–261 (2013). https://doi.org/10.1179/2047480613Z.000000000142
5. Boatwright, B.C., Linvill, D.L., Warren, P.L.: Troll factories: the internet research agency and state-sponsored agenda building. Resource Centre Media Freedom Europe **29**, 192 (2018)
6. Buffer: Buffer (2026). https://buffer.com/publish
7. CoSchedule: Social Calendar (2026). https://coschedule.com/social-calendar
8. Dangwal, A.: 'No Weapon Sales To Israel': How A Lockheed Martin 'Tweet' Resulted In A Loss Of Billions Of Dollars To US Defense Giant (2022). https://eurasiantimes.com/no-weapons-sales-to-israel-how-a-lockheed-martin-tweet-resulted
9. European Commission: Om(2018) 236 final. tackling online disinformation: a European approach (2018). https://eur-lex.europa.eu/legal-content/EN/TXT/?uri=celex:52018DC0236
10. Fallis, D.: The varieties of disinformation. In: The Philosophy of Information Quality, pp. 135–161 (2014)
11. Fedica: Followerwonk: Tools for Twitter Analytics, Bio Search and More (2025). https://followerwonk.com/index.html
12. Figueira, Á., Oliveira, L.: The current state of fake news: challenges and opportunities (2017). https://doi.org/10.1016/j.procs.2017.11.106
13. Flaherty, E., Sturm, T., Farries, E.: The conspiracy of COVID-19 and 5g: spatial analysis fallacies in the age of data democratization. Soc. Sci. Med. **293**, 114546 (2022)
14. Foller.me: Foller.me Analytics for Twitter (2025). https://foller.me
15. Freelon, D., Wells, C.: Disinformation as political communication. Polit. Commun. **37**(2), 145–156 (2020)
16. García-Orosa, B.: Digital political communication: hybrid intelligence, algorithms. Autom. Disinform. Fourth Wave (2021). https://doi.org/10.1007/978-3-030-81568-4_1
17. Gross, M.L., Meisels, T.: Soft War: The Ethics of Unarmed Conflict. Cambridge University Press, Cambridge (2017)
18. Himelein-Wachowiak, M., et al.: Bots and Misinformation Spread on Social Media: Implications for COVID-19 (2021). https://doi.org/10.2196/26933. https://www.ncbi.nlm.nih.gov/pmc/articles/PMC8139392/
19. Holone, H.: The filter bubble and its effect on online personal health information. Croat. Med. J. **57**, 298 (2016). https://doi.org/10.3325/cmj.2016.57.298
20. Holoyda, B.J.: QAnon: a modern conspiracy theory and the assessment of its believers. J. Am. Acad. Psychiat. Law (2023). https://doi.org/10.29158/JAAPL.210053-21
21. Huang, B., Carley, K.M.: Disinformation and misinformation on twitter during the novel coronavirus outbreak. arXiv preprint arXiv:2006.04278 (2020)
22. Huginn: What is Huginn? (2023). https://github.com/huginn/huginn

23. Kaur, S., Kumar, P., Kumaraguru, P.: Automating fake news detection system using multi-level voting model. Soft. Comput. **24**(12), 9049–9069 (2020)
24. Langin, K.: Fake news spreads faster than true news on twitter–thanks to people, not bots. Science **8** (2018)
25. Maptimize: #onemilliontweetmap (2025). https://onemilliontweetmap.com
26. Metz, R.: 22-Year-Old's 'Jailbreak' Prompts "Unlock Next Level" in ChatGPT (2023). https://www.ndtv.com/world-news/chatgpt-22-year-olds-jailbreak-prompts-unlocks-next-level-in-chatgpt-3940173
27. Mu, Y., et al.: A large-scale comparative study of accurate COVID-19 information versus misinformation. arXiv preprint arXiv:2304.04811 (2023)
28. Murero, M.: Coordinated inauthentic behavior: an innovative manipulation tactic to amplify COVID-19 anti-vaccine communication outreach via social media. Front. Sociol. **8**, 1141416 (2023)
29. NASK: #włączweryfikację - nask (2023). https://nask.pl/weryfikuje
30. Pedregosa, F., et al.: Scikit-learn: machine learning in Python. J. Mach. Learn. Res. **12**, 2825–2830 (2011)
31. Pony Express Studio: Build & Monetize your Twitter Audience. Fast (2023). https://tweethunter.io
32. Bai, Q., Dan, Q., Mu, Z., Yang, M.: A systematic review of emoji: current research and future perspectives. Front. Psychol. **10**, 2221 (2019)
33. Santos-D'Amorim, K., de Oliveira Miranda, M.K.F.: Misinformation, disinformation, and malinformation: clarifying the definitions and examples in disinfodemic times. Encontros Bibli **26** (2021)
34. Sawiński, M., et al.: Openfact at checkthat! 2023: head-to-head GPT vs. BERT-a comparative study of transformers language models for the detection of check-worthy claims. In: CEUR Workshop Proceedings, vol. 3497 (2023)
35. Tacchini, E., Ballarin, G., Della Vedova, M.L., Moret, S., De Alfaro, L.: Some like it hoax: automated fake news detection in social networks. arXiv preprint arXiv:1704.07506 (2017)
36. Thota, A., Tilak, P., Ahluwalia, S., Lohia, N.: Fake news detection: a deep learning approach. SMU Data Sci. Rev. **1**(3), 10 (2018)
37. Trustees of Indiana University: Hoaxy (2025). https://hoaxy.osome.iu.edu
38. Westendorf, L., et al.: From personal genomics to twitter: visualizing the uncertainty of evidence. Nature **487**(7406), 190–195 (2017)
39. Westerlund, M.: The emergence of deepfake technology: a review. Technol. Innov. Manage. Rev. **9**(11), 39–52 (2019). https://doi.org/10.22215/timreview/1282
40. Williams, A.R., et al.: Large language models can consistently generate high-quality content for election disinformation operations. PLoS ONE **20**(3), e0317421 (2025)
41. x0rz: Simple Twitter Profile Analyzer (2025). https://github.com/x0rz/tweets_analyzer
42. Yang, K.C., Varol, O., Hui, P.M., Menczer, F.: Scalable and generalizable social bot detection through data selection. In: Proceedings of the AAAI Conference on Artificial Intelligence, vol. 34, pp. 1096–1103 (2020)
43. Zapier Inc.: Explore Ways to use Zapier by Industry, Role and Use Case (2023). https://zapier.com/explore
44. Zhou, Z., Guan, H., Bhat, M.M., Hsu, J.: Fake news detection via NLP is vulnerable to adversarial attacks. arXiv preprint arXiv:1901.09657 (2019)

Sensitive Information Sharing in Supply Chains to Overcome Shortages: Findings from a Design Study

Tom Meyer[1,2](✉), Frederik Möller[1,2], Thorsten Schoormann[1,3], and Ilka Jussen-Lengersdorf[1]

[1] Fraunhofer Institute for Software and Systems Engineering ISST, Speicherstraße 6, 44147 Dortmund, Germany
tom.meyer@isst.fraunhofer.de

[2] Data-Driven Enterprise, TU Braunschweig, Mühlenpfordtstraße 23, 38106 Braunschweig, Germany

[3] Department of People and Technology, Roskilde University, Universitetsvej 1, 4000 Roskilde, Denmark

Abstract. The awareness of potential supply chain shortages has been heightened by the news in recent years. If a shortage occurs, companies in a buyer-supplier relationship share sensitive information to mitigate and resolve the shortage. The information shared is often sensitive from a business perspective and companies must ensure not to reveal more information than needed. We employ a design science research study in a long-term and large-scale industrial initiative to address sensitivity concerns in information sharing during a shortage. We define and evaluate *sensitivity configurations for information sharing during shortages.* To do so, we draw on empirical data from an interview study and experiences of building digital artifacts within the automotive sector, allowing us to explore the correlations between sensitivity associated with sharing information in supply chain shortage situations.

Keywords: Information sharing · Sensitive information · Configuration · Design

1 Introduction

Globally occurring disruptions, such as the shortage of semiconductors [1], or natural disasters, shift supply chain resilience into the center of attention of companies. Sharing information efficiently between companies is essential during shortages to normalize operations [2], as the damage done can only be mitigated by reacting quickly [3], which means that there is an immediate need for information [1]. However, sharing operational supply chain (SC) information (e.g., production volumes) is non-trivial, as the information is highly sensitive and companies typically are hesitant to share [3, 4]. Going one step further (beyond aversion, solving, or ad hoc shortages), there is a growing perception of information sharing (IS) in SCs moving beyond a strictly "need-to-know" basis. Rather, this broader approach includes sharing information for value and optimization, which exceeds what is contractually and operationally necessary [3].

K. Węcel and V. Řepa (Eds.): BIS 2026, LNBIP 584, pp. 74–85, 2026.
https://doi.org/10.1007/978-3-032-26363-6_6

To overcome this challenge, we propose *sensitivity configurations for IS during shortages*. We do this by drawing from a design science research (DSR) project, in which multi-national companies from the automotive industry band together to jointly build and implement a type of data infrastructure in the form of a *data space*. Companies in a data space act as *data providers* (i.e., sending data) and *data consumers* (i.e., receiving data), and form relationships to exchange data, such as, about *production* or *stock volumes*, to optimize their SC efficiency or mitigate the consequences of shortages or delays [3, 5]. Our research is situated within a large-scale, multi-year industrial initiative that aims to design an Inter-Organizational Information System (IOIS) for IS in the European Automotive industry. The project started in August 2022 and includes contributions from more than 50 actors from eleven companies. It involves diverse stakeholders from business, management, and IT.

From a design perspective, this problem is exciting. On the one hand, the *scope* and *complexity* make it a highly interesting problem to explore, as it requires addressing the practical challenges of a complex IS process involving multiple stakeholders, each with their own motivations, by building a *digital artifact*. On the other hand, the DSR project applies to a fundamental problem prevailing in complex SCs and is transferable to types of SC. Consequently, this paper is guided by the following **research question**: *How to define IS configurations containing sensitive information?*

IS literature demonstrates how a SC's performance is influenced by IS overall [6] and by which concrete information, such as planning information [7]. While there are examples providing organizational and technical measures to bundle sensitive information for IS [3, 8], the willingness to share information differs between customer and supplier roles [9]. In pursuing the question, we focus on shortage management in which companies are forced to share sensitive information. We explore *sensitivity configurations for IS during shortages* to capture how information sensitivity in this complex relationship between data providers and data consumers can be codified and abstracted into reusable design knowledge, enabling "the selection of one from among a number of available alternatives" [10, p. 246]. We design configurations at different granularities to address sensitivity concerns, especially to lower the entry barrier for adopters and providing guidelines to researchers and practitioners [11].

In Sect. 2, we provide an overview of sensitivity IS in SCs. Section 3 explains the research design and steps performed. Section 4 elaborates on the problem space of sensitive IS during a shortage empirically and explains the sensitivity configurations as a solution. Section 5 discusses the contributions, and Sect. 6 concludes the paper.

2 Sharing Sensitive Information in Supply Chains

SCs are exposed to external disruption risks and operational SC risks [12]. If these risks occur, they constrain SC performance [13], which we refer to as a *shortage*. SC resilience the capability to respond to disruptions based on preparations and eventually grow the company's market share during disruption [2, 14]. One of its elements is SC visibility [14], which can be defined as "*the extent to which actors within a supply chain have access to or share information which they consider as key or useful to their operations and which they consider will be of mutual benefit*". [15, p. 1218] SC visibility is an essential component providing benefits ex-ante and ex-post disruption [14].

IS seeks to mitigate negative impacts on the SC, such as the *bullwhip effect* [16], and to enhance resilience [17]. The information flow in the SC is commonly covered via Electronic Data Interchange (EDI) [18], relying on UN/EDIFACT definitions covering data exchange for administration, commerce, and transport [19]. It has not been designed for the needs of granularity [20] and the sensitivity needed during shortage [8].

Despite the benefits, companies are reluctant to share sensitive information. Barriers arise from companies protecting their customer base [21], being afraid of antitrust violations [21], the loss of bargaining power [12], or information being used against them [22]. Research focused on factors influencing a company to share sensitive information [4, 8] that can be defined based on the fact that the "exchange is not desirable due to mistrust, unclear benefits, or other concerns." [8, p. 431] To address the concerns, technical approaches have been identified in the literature. Among others, multiparty privacy computing (MPC) [22] and usage control [8] support trust system-wise. Nevertheless, technical solutions must be complemented by organizational measures as e.g. the input information of MCP can be derived if the formula is known [22]. Further, implementation into legacy systems is needed to leverage their full potential.

3 A Design Science Research Study

3.1 The Research Project of PURIS

Our DSR project is embedded in a large-scale industry initiative aimed at solving multiple complex SC issues and the resulting *information needs* based on enhanced IS in an IOIS environment. PURIS is an interorganizational IS designed to solve information needs within SC execution. The initiative involves all roles relevant to car production, including automotive manufacturers, suppliers, IT service providers, standardization bodies, and applied research institutes. We are part of the initiative, particularly the first author is deeply engaged in the design process of PURIS. From a DSR perspective, our case is interesting, as the grand, industry-spanning scale (with all major companies), and unique access enables us to collect unique pieces of design knowledge.

PURIS provides different operational information exchanged between customers and suppliers. The information may be used to handle shortages and reduce their extent when applying monitoring logic. The information shared spans the demand and supply sides, with material-specific volumes available for up to 4 weeks at daily or higher granularity. Demand and production are both direct derivatives of a production plan. Customers share the requirements they consume (demand) while the suppliers share the planned production volumes (*production*). Both parties share stock levels (*stock*). Additionally, the latest information about deliveries (*delivery*) is shared by the partner responsible for transportation. Finally, for both inbound and outbound material, the *days of supply* per day are calculated and shared. PURIS harmonizes information that has been shared during shortages and makes it available for prevention.

3.2 Research Process and Methods

In the study, we employ BAUSTEIN [23] as our design method. The card deck approach to DSR us in representing the complexity of our real-world DSR project. The study consists of two design iterations. Our overall research objective is to lower the entry barrier of sensitive IS by providing configurations serving practitioners and researches as a guideline [11]. Thus, a *problem-centered design* has been used [23]. In the first design iteration, we derive configurations based on preferences communicated during an interview series. In the second design iteration, we incorporate logical and expert feedback. We finalize the configurations with a second logical evaluation from the supplier side and additional expert feedback (see Fig. 1).

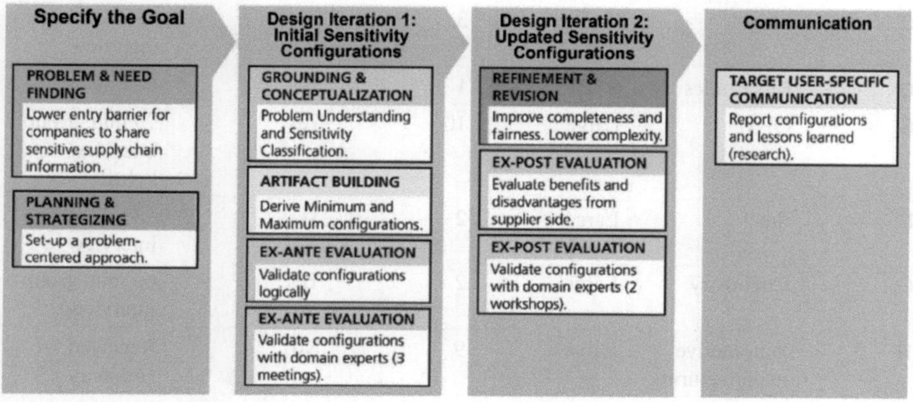

Fig. 1. Design science research process reported with BAUSTEIN [23].

Problem Understanding and Solution Objectives. PURIS emphasizes fairness in sensitive IS by following the quid pro quo principle [3]. It describes that information of equally perceived values must be shared incentivizing one's own sensitive information as a trading good [4]. The problem addressed by this study has been identified empirically. During rollout, partners, especially in their supplier role, were hesitant to adopt the system. We received feedback that the *information shared is very sensitive*, which often leads to higher complexity. Further, from a previous interview series, we knew that the sensitivity of the different information is perceived differently.

As a relatively low-effort solution, the team defined the objective *to create sensitivity configurations for IS,* lowering the entry barrier while improving visibility. To improve our understanding of the problem space, we re-assessed the protocols of a pre-existing interview series[1]. Section 4.1 reports how sensitivity correlates to complexity in sensitive IS. Next, we outline how the interview series has been conducted and analyzed.

Design Iteration 1 (Initial Sensitivity Configurations). An interview series with 36 participants in 10 companies[2] serves as the empirical *foundation* (see Table 1). The purpose of this study was to derive requirements for crafting configurations addressing

[1] How the interview series has been conducted is reported in design iteration 1 in Sect. 3.2.

[2] Given that this was the result of a large-scale research process, one of the authors of this paper was present at the interviews with eight of the eleven companies.

Table 1. Overview of interviews conducted.

Company Code	Domain	SME/Large[a]	Participants	Conducted by Author?	Note
A	Automotive manufacturing	SME	1	Yes	60 min
B	Automotive manufacturing	SME	1	Yes	60 min
C	Steel	Large	3	Yes	58 min. group interview
D	Electronics	SME	1	Yes	60 min
E	OEM	Large	10	Yes	90 min. group interview hybrid
F	Steel	Large	2	Yes	58 min. group interview
G	Chemistry	Large	2	Yes	60 min. group interview
H	Automotive manufacturing	Large	9	No	Received summary
I	OEM	Large	4	No	Received protocols
J	Automotive manufacturing	Large	3	No	Received summary

[a]Classification according to the company size in [24] based on headcount in 2025.

the hesitations of adopters. One interviewer and one protocol keeper conducted the interviews. The interviews were analysed based on the protocols and, when necessary, reaffirmed with the interviewees. Three companies conducted the interviews internally and provided the authors with their interview protocols or a summary. To harmonize across different interviewers, the authors iterated the protocols three times, applying one format and abstraction level. Statements have been paraphrased to preserve the semantics while fitting the abstraction level. The resulting protocols contain information about the usefulness of information, IS preferences, and notes on the benefits and disadvantages of sharing specific information.

To **ground our solution** we focused on the disadvantages and risks of sharing specific information noted in the protocols. Based on the paraphrased statements, we noticed that complexity in IS correlates with the information's sensitivity. In Sect. 4.1, we classify the sensitivity per information as a result.

After that, we **built an initial artifact** of IS configurations from the interview protocols. Based on the preferences, we derived a *minimum configuration* and a *maximum* *configuration* as a baseline. The maximum configuration represents the shared information as targeted at the beginning of this study. Three companies have favored the maximum configuration during the interviews. The *minimum configuration* creates an easy-to-implement starting point, allowing to assess the situation. Another three companies have favored it. It required demand, deliveries, and customer-stock information.

Within a **first ex-ante evaluation**, we evaluated the initial configurations regarding their consistency. To do so, we considered the benefits and risks mentioned in the protocols together with a heatmapping of the preferred information to share. Interestingly, the extracted minimum configuration deviated from previously considered quid-pro-quo IS [3]: Instead of the suppliers' production, the suppliers' committed deliveries have been considered as the counterpart of the customers' demand. Further, some companies preferred violating the quid-pro-quo IS by expecting the customer to only share *stock* levels. To allow the experts to select a favored minimum configuration, we added an alternative *minimum configuration* in which both sides share *stock* information.

The configurations have then been **evaluated** with five SC IS experts from three companies. The configurations, along with additional details, were shared with them before the meeting. In the meeting, author one explained the configurations and led the discussion, sharing his screen. The stakeholders discussed why companies don't want to share sensitive information, thinking from the customer and supplier perspectives. They suggested creating a fully permuted set of configurations. This helps standardize their IT and lets their business select how much information to share. Further, the participants regarded the *minimum configuration,* violating the quid pro quo principle [3], as unfair. Last, the participants acknowledged the abstraction provided by *days of supply.* It allows for assessing the situation without revealing *stock* and *production.*

Design Iteration 2 (Updated Sensitivity Configurations). We incorporated the feedback for **refinements and revisions**. To increase fairness, we excluded the single-sided *stock* from the *minimum configuration.* To create an exhaustive configuration set, we considered business-wise relevant combinations of *production, stock,* and *days of supply* based on the adapted *minimum configuration.* Further, we reduced the process complexity in the *maximum configuration.* To calculate the *days of supply*, one needs information from both parties. To reduce IS processes, we excluded the *days of supply.* Instead, it must be calculated after the necessary information has been shared. Finally, we visualized the delta to the *minimum configuration* to aid understanding during feedback. The resulting configurations are reported in Sect. 4.2.

To **logically evaluate** the new revision of configurations, we listed the benefits and disadvantages of each configuration. We emphasized the supplier's perspective on sensitivity and its associated complexity. The manufacturing strategy may need manual interventions to remain compliant (see Sect. 4.1). Thus, hiding *stock* or *production* information addresses complexity and sensitivity concerns.

The configurations have been **re-evaluated with the group of domain experts**. Feedback was collected from 10 participants across 8 companies. The first author protocoled feedback directly in the document he was screen sharing. Again, participants considered both perspectives. Suppliers preferred configurations with less sensitive information, because these are easier to adopt and help handle different contractual situations. From the customer's perspective, especially an OEM's, shortage configurations with less information are not favored because they already have worked with the maximum configuration. The experts note that the configurations can lower the integration cost, especially for companies on later tiers who work in many domains.

4 Results: Sensitivity Configurations

4.1 The Problem of Sensitivity in Supply Chain Information Sharing

Before diving into the configurations, we report on the sensitivity of operational information and the associated complexity of IS. We highlight and classify the relationship among complexity, sensitivity, and the nature of the configurations. This section draws from the grounding work conducted in design iteration 1 and has been enriched with knowledge gained during the evaluations. We start to elaborate on these factors based on a company's statement on sharing production information:

> *"In 1:n relationships it doesn't make sense to share the information due to political reasons. Company politics will define what will be shared in case of a disruption due to penalty fees, compliance and market conditions." – Company G*

Sharing *production information* in multi-customer (or multi-supplier) scenarios (1) risks compliance with anti-trust regulations. Anti-trust law prohibits companies to reveal business relationships to competitors and is sanctioned with hefty fines and prison sentences. Additionally, a company's manufacturing strategy influences complexity (2). If a company supplies multiple customers with the same material, the information must be assigned partner-wise. Lastly, sharing operational information partially allows the supplier to optimize their margin (3). During shortages, suppliers optimize their economic outcome, same as customers do [25]. The information is important for a partner's bargaining power and thus very sensitive (classification "*high*"). The complexity in IS comes from *hiding information* to address sensitivity.

For *stock information,* similar concerns arise. Stock levels are shared based on 1) the business relationship and eventually on their 2) contractual relationship. The latter may result in penalties, leading to suppliers tending to share less. Compliance-wise, 3) sharing information with multiple partners risks anti-trust violations and legal penalties. Summarized, the information may result in contractual or legal penalties. Thus, we consider it very sensitive (classification "*high*"). The complexity in IS stems from *hiding information* to comply with anti-trust regulations and avoid contractual fees.

The *days of supply* is a measure providing an abstract view of a partner's production and stock situation. It's an easy-to-understand measure indicating the criticality of the supply situation. Thus, we classify it as sensitive (classification "*medium*"). The complexity arises from the calculation needing deliveries and potential information hiding.

The *demand* reflects production (see Sect. 3.1) resulting in the same anti-trust requirements in multi-sourcing scenarios. Despite its sensitivity, we classify demand as not sensitive (classification "*low*") as it's mandatory to handle shortages. Still, complexity arises from information hiding to prevent violating anti-trust regulations.

The *deliveries* represent the committed and scheduled delivery volumes, that are essential during shortage. As it's the least sensitive information that could be shared to fulfil a demand, we classify the information as not sensitive (classification "*low*"). There is no additional complexity as a delivery is customer-specific.

4.2 Sensitivity Configurations for Information Sharing During Shortage

Below, we explain the configurations as our contribution. Each configuration represents a specific fit in shortage handling on different granularity levels. Each configuration is assigned a sensitivity classification (see Fig. 2) that has been defined based on the information shared in the configuration (see Sect. 4.1). A configuration covers a dyadic buyer-supplier IS relationship, sharing a view on the demand and supply situation. The five configurations are sorted based on the ascending class of sensitivity.

Sensitivity classification	Shortage configurations									
	Configuration		Customer				Supplier			
	ID	Name	Demand	Stock	Days of supply	Deliveries (arrival)	Deliveries	Days of supply	Stock	Production
Low	S01	Shortage minimum	✓			✓	✓			
Medium	S02	Shorage minimum + Days of supply	✓		✓	✓	✓	✓		
Medium	S03	Shortage minimum + Stock	✓	✓		✓	✓		✓	
High	S04	Shortage minimum + Stock + Days of supply	✓	✓	✓	✓	✓	✓	✓	
High	S05	Shortage maximum	✓	✓		✓	✓		✓	✓

Fig. 2. Sensitivity configurations for information sharing during shortage.

The first configuration, **Shortage Minimum (S01)**, is a minimalist configuration sharing as little information as possible. It allows to access the SC situation based on the customer's demand, the deliveries on route, and the committed deliveries. The information is more granular than EDI, reflecting requirements from the customers' production. The deliveries span a longer committed delivery schedule. The supplier provides volumes that can be committed for delivery during a shortage with estimated departure dates. In contrast, the actual arrival dates are confirmed or adjusted by the customer. As the data is purely logistical, the sensitivity classification is *low*. Given this configuration's position as *minimalist*, it is the foundation for configurations **S02**, **S03**, and **S04**. Each of them increases information granularity in SC visibility.

The second configuration, **Shortage Minimum + Days of Supply (S02)**, adds both parties' stock ranges and keeps the partners "*in charge*" (tier 1 feedback in design iteration 2) as production and stock are hidden. Thus, the sensitivity is classified *medium.*

The third configuration **Shortage Minimum + Stock (S03)** adds the stock information equally on both sides to **S01.** The sensitivity is slightly higher than for **S02** as stock levels are more precise than days of supply. The configuration received the review group's feedback of being suitable to build trust by raising granularity. As the production information remains unknown, the sensitivity is classified *medium.*

The fourth configuration **Shortage Minimum + Stock + Days of Supply (S04)** combines configurations **S02** and **S03** requiring more trust due to increased granularity and sensitivity. Despite the fact that the supplier hides production information, customers may abuse the information to infer production information based on the known formula for days of supply [22]. Thus, we raised this configuration's sensitivity to *high.*

The last configuration **Shortage Maximum (S05)** shares all information except for days of supply that are calculated based on the shared information. Due to sharing the production information, this configuration's sensitivity has been classified *high.*

5 Discussion

5.1 Contributions and Implications for Research and Practice

This study provides two contributions. The *first* contribution is the *classification of supply chain information sensitivity.* The interview data and the feedback sessions allowed us to provide deeper insights into the problem space of sensitivity, eventually classifying information into a *sensitivity class.* Further, we raised awareness of the complexity of IS. We showed that complexity correlates with the information's sensitivity. This sensitivity may be objectified based on the need for information hiding, depending on legal implications such as anti-trust and business implications such as bargaining power. Factors like the manufacturing strategy may amplify this need. We extend the understanding of sensitive IS as reported by, e.g., [4] who investigated the willingness to share sensitive information in customer-supplier relationships. During the study, we learned that the *quid-pro-quo principle* [3] is suitable to address fairness and the perceived value in IS. We extend it by implicitly accounting for the associated complexity in the *sensitivity classifications.* Sharing a measure abstracting the sensitive information but still serving the purpose of IS lowers the *sensitivity classification e.g.*, share *days of supply* instead of *production* and *stock* volumes. Similar approaches are recommended, like verifiable credentials proofing specific information abstractly [26].

Second, the *sensitivity configurations for IS during shortage* allow partners to align on appropriate levels of sensitivity before a shortage occurs. As outlined in Sect. 2, technical solutions need to be complemented by organizational measures. The latter can be an instrument to scale sensitive IS along SCs with legacy systems. The varying *levels of granularity can be applied based on perceived information sensitivity* and other factors. Partners may *switch between them* and align on protocols beforehand [14]. Further, lower sensitivity results in lower investment cost, eventually being a "signal of good faith" [27] towards adopters, especially suppliers. This provides several benefits. 1) Partners may collaborate earlier with less sensitive information to mitigate critical situations. 2) Lowering the entry barrier in terms of sensitivity lowers the complexity and adoption cost to fulfill the "tedious duty" of IS during shortages. This *money* incentive is perceived as more valuable than *coercion* [4]. On the contrary, configurations enable information hiding, creating a scalable approach. As today, partners must be enabled to practice fair-share allocation [13] even if it might negatively affect the overall SC.

The sensitivity configurations have been built based on the sensitivity classification. Both may be applied to the overall manufacturing domain due to similar regulations. When exploring further use cases and domains, the configurations might be applied in food and retail SCs to monitor and reduce food waste. In this scenario, days of supply may be used to identify waste based on the best-before date for e.g. short shelf-life products accounting for the biggest portion of waste and economic loss [28].

5.2 Limitations

First, the data is automotive-focused. While we provided ideas for the application in other domains, IS and shortages may be handled differently due to the sensitivity of operational information. For example, in pharmaceutical SCs regulations require stock visibility [27] changing the stock's sensitivity classification. Thus, the findings must be tested beyond a domain focus. *Second*, the configurations have been influenced by large companies, including major first-tier suppliers and OEMs in the automotive industry. While the SME perspective has been considered in the interview series, no representatives have been included in the evaluations. *Third*, the configurations have not been implemented and applied in a naturalistic setting. There is a lack of evidence of how companies apply them in their relationships, including coercion and resource dependency. During the evaluations, customers and suppliers had different perspectives on the configurations. OEMs tend to have a maximum configuration in place, while suppliers are interested in sharing less sensitive information. Nevertheless, it remains a business decision which configuration to use and how to collaborate.

6 Conclusion

Based on our DSR process, the question of how to define configurations containing sensitive information can be answered through a two-step approach: First, by defining a classification schema for information sensitivity, and second, by operationalizing sensitivity classifications into configurations through an iterative design and evaluation process, as described in our DSR cycles. The created sensitivity configurations for shortage handling, allow customers and suppliers to share information matching their business relationship and the criticality of a shortage. They allow companies to define protocols before the shortage persists. The configurations allow to limit the cost of information provisioning to an appropriate level. In particular, the suppliers' interests seem to be accommodated by the lower granularity configurations. They may balance information provisioning cost against, e.g., contractual penalties. Future research can implement the configurations and study their value during shortage for both parties. How and under which conditions they will be applied is a business decision worth to observe. The configurations likely won't change how coercion leads to sharing the maximum configurations but might facilitate IS if no coercion is applied. Limitations of this study arise from its automotive focus. Further, the interview series and evaluations are limited to a relatively small sample, may leading to bias in the contributions.

References

1. Brooks, K.J.: Semiconductor shortage puts brakes on Ford truck production (2021). https://www.cbsnews.com/news/ford-semiconductor-gm-toyota-microprocessor-chip-shortage/. Accessed 18 Jan 2026
2. Christopher, M., Peck, H.: Building the resilient supply chain. Int. J. Logist. Manag. **15**(2), 1–14 (2004)
3. Opriel, S., Möller, F., Strobel, G., Otto, B.: Data Sovereignty in inter-organizational information systems. Findings from demand and capacity management in the automotive industry. Bus. Inf. Syst. Eng. **67**, 833–853 (2024)
4. Burkhart, D., Bode, C.: Transparency in buyer-supplier relationships: the what and when of sensitive information exchanges. The what and when of sensitive information exchanges. In: Taneja, S. (ed.) Academy of Management Proceedings, vol. 2022, p. 10103 Academy of Management, Briarcliff Manor (2022)
5. Gieß, A., Schoormann, T., Möller, F., Gür, I.: Discovering data spaces: a classification of design options. Comput. Ind. **164**, 104212 (2025)
6. Dominguez, R., Cannella, S., Barbosa-Póvoa, A.P., Framinan, J.M.: Information sharing in supply chains with heterogeneous retailers. Omega **79**, 116–132 (2018)
7. Jonsson, P., Mattsson, S.-A.: The value of sharing planning information in supply chains. Int. J. Phys. Distrib. Logist. Manag. **43**(4), 282–299 (2013)
8. Opriel, S., Möller, F., Burkhardt, U., Otto, B.: Requirements for usage control based exchange of sensitive data in automotive supply chains. In: Bui, T. (ed.) Proceedings of the 54th Hawaii International Conference on System Sciences, pp. 431–440. University of Hawaii at Manoa, Hawaii (2021)
9. Peng, G., Trienekens, J., Omta, S., Wang, W.: Configuration of inter-organizational information exchange and the differences between buyers and sellers. Br. Food J. **116**(2), 292–316 (2014)
10. Simon, H.A.: Problem forming, problem finding and problem solving in design. Des. Syst. **3**, 245–257 (1995)
11. Offermann, P., Blom, S., Schönherr, M., Bub, U.: Artifact types in information systems design science – a literature review. In: Winter, R., Zhao, J.L., Aier, S. (eds.) DESRIST 2010. LNCS, vol. 6105, pp. 77–92. Springer, Heidelberg (2010). https://doi.org/10.1007/978-3-642-13335-0_6
12. Tang, C.S.: Perspectives in supply chain risk management. Int. J. Prod. Econ. **103**(2), 451–488 (2006)
13. Gatewood, A.K., Drake, M.J.: ASCM Supply Chain Dictionary (2024). https://www.ascm.org/learning-development/certifications-credentials/dictionary/. Accessed 06 Sept 2025
14. Hohenstein, N.-O., Feisel, E., Hartmann, E., Giunipero, L.: Research on the phenomenon of supply chain resilience. Int. J. Phys. Distrib. Logist. Manag. **45**(1/2), 90–117 (2015)
15. Barratt, M., Oke, A.: Antecedents of supply chain visibility in retail supply chains. A resource-based theory perspective. J. Oper. Manag. **25**(6), 1217–1233 (2007)
16. Lee, H.L., Padmanabhan, V., Whang, S.: The bullwhip effect in supply chains. MIT SMR **38**(3), 93–102 (1997)
17. Craighead, C.W., Blackhurst, J., Rungtusanatham, M.J., Handfield, R.B.: The severity of supply chain disruptions. Design characteristics and mitigation capabilities. Decis. Sci. **38**(1), 131–156 (2007)

18. OECD: OECD Data Explorer • ICT Access and Usage by Businesses (2015). https://data-explorer.oecd.org/vis?tm=edi%20usage&pg=0&hc[Measure]=&snb=1&vw=tb&df[ds]=dsDisseminateFinalDMZ&df[id]=DSD_ICT_B%40DF_BUSINESSES&df[ag]=OECD.STI.DEP&df[vs]=1.0&dq=EU27.A.C3A_B%2BC4_B%2BD1B_B%2BD2B_B%2BD2_B%2BD2A_B%2BD1A_B%2BD1_B%2BC3C_B._T.&pd=2023%2C2023&to[TIME_PERIOD]=false. Accessed 06 Sept 2025
19. United Nations Economic Commission for Europe: Part 1: Introduction | UNECE (2025). https://unece.org/trade/uncefact/unedifact-part-1-introduction. Accessed 12 Jan 2026
20. Meyer, T., Schoormann, T., Möller, F.: A reference architecture for digital twin-based supply chain information exchange. The PURIS case. In: Lucke, U., Stieglitz, S., Uebermickel, F., Lamprecht, A.-L., Klein, M. (eds.) The Wide Open. Offenheit von Source bis Science, p. 1593 Gesellschaft für Informatik e.V, Bonn (2025)
21. Clifton, C., Iyer, A., Cho, R., Jiang, W., Kantarcıoğlu, M., Vaidya, J.: An approach to securely identifying beneficial collaboration in decentralized logistics systems. Manuf. Serv. Oper. Manag. **10**(1), 108–125 (2008)
22. Atallah, M.J., Elmongui, H.G., Deshpande, V., Schwarz, L.B.: Secure supply-chain protocols. In: Chung, J.-Y., Zhang, L.-J. (eds.) CEC 2003. Proceedings IEEE International Conference on E-Commerce Technology. CEC 2003, pp. 293–302 IEEE Computer Society, Los Alamitos Calif. (2003)
23. Schoormann, T., Möller, F., Chandra Kruse, L., Otto, B.: BAUSTEIN. A design tool for configuring and representing design research. Inf. Syst. J. **34**(6), 1871–1901 (2024)
24. European Commission: SME definition (2023). https://single-market-economy.ec.europa.eu/smes/sme-definition_en. Accessed 20 June 2023
25. Tyborski, R.: Bezahlbare Autos werden zur Mangelware. Autobauer produzieren wegen der Chipengpässe vor allem teure, margenstarke Fahrzeuge. Der Nachfrageüberhang bei Elektroautos verknappt das Angebot für bezahlbare Modelle zusätzlich. Die Wartezeiten sind lang. Handelsblatt **1234**(ePaper), 5 (2022)
26. Sporny, M., Longley, D., Chadwick, D.: Verifiable Credentials Data Model (2022). https://www.w3.org/TR/2022/REC-vc-data-model-20220303/. Accessed 24 Jan 2026
27. Doney, P.M., Cannon, J.P.: An examination of the nature of trust in buyer-seller relationships. J. Mark. **61**(2), 35–51 (1997)
28. Mena, C., Adenso-Diaz, B., Yurt, O.: The causes of food waste in the supplier–retailer interface. Evidences from the UK and Spain. Resour. Conserv. Recycl. **55**(6), 648–658 (2011)

Trustworthy AI

An Evidence-First Reference Model for Trustworthy AI in Business Information Systems

Torsten Olivi Tiltack(✉), Yifei Dong, Kun Yu, and Fang Chen

University of Technology Sydney, Sydney, Australia
Torsten.Tiltack@student.uts.edu.au

Abstract. AI-supported decision support systems promise better organizational decisions, yet in many organizations trustworthiness is still handled through principles, documentation, or post hoc explanation rather than through the system design itself. The result is a persistent gap between responsible AI guidance and enforceable accountability in business information systems.

At its core, the paper presents AIJIM, an evidence-first reference model that treats trustworthiness as an architectural property. Using a design science perspective and a focused synthesis of recent literature, we derive five requirements: evidence binding, artifact-mandatory evaluation, audit-safe traceability, effective human oversight, and separation of governance from analytical execution. These requirements are consolidated into a domain-agnostic reference model and a conceptual implementation architecture that demonstrates constructability without prescribing a specific tool stack.

The result is a compact reference class for AI-supported decision support systems in which outputs remain reviewable, auditable, and governable across organizational contexts.

Keywords: Trustworthy AI · Decision Support · Business Information Systems

1 Introduction

Artificial intelligence (AI) now sits inside many organizational decision support systems, where it promises faster analysis and more consistent recommendations. Yet the same systems often struggle with a less glamorous question: whether an AI-supported decision can still be explained, reviewed, and defended once it enters routine organizational practice.

That tension has become increasingly visible in recent work on trustworthy and responsible AI. Across business information systems and adjacent fields, scholars repeatedly note that principles such as transparency, accountability, and human oversight rarely become reliable operational properties on their own [3,13]. In practice, organizations may endorse trustworthy AI while still running

K. Węcel and V. Řepa (Eds.): BIS 2026, LNBIP 584, pp. 89–101, 2026.
https://doi.org/10.1007/978-3-032-26363-6_7

systems in which outputs are weakly grounded, difficult to reconstruct, and hard to contest after the fact.

The problem is particularly acute in AI-supported decision support. Studies on implementation and evaluation show that deployments often stall when governance, review, and evidential grounding are treated as secondary concerns rather than as part of the information system itself [2,9]. Research on human–AI collaboration points in the same direction: oversight remains fragile when systems do not make reviewability and contestation structurally possible under real operating conditions [4,14].

This paper revisits the previously introduced AIJIM model [12] and reframes it as an evidence-first reference model for trustworthy AI in business information systems. The central claim is simple: trustworthiness should not be inferred from model behavior alone, nor delegated to policy documents after deployment. It needs architectural expression. AIJIM therefore treats evidence, analytical runs, evaluation artifacts, and governance constraints as first-class system elements through which trustworthiness becomes enforceable rather than merely desirable.

Relation to Prior Work. The original AIJIM contribution emerged from a domain-specific setting in environmental journalism [12]. Here, the model is generalized beyond that setting. The emphasis shifts away from newsroom-specific performance concerns and toward a cross-domain reference class for business information systems: systems in which evidence binding, audit-safe traceability, governance separation, and human authorization are built into the architecture itself.

The paper makes three contributions:

- It identifies a structural gap in BIS research: trustworthy AI is widely discussed, but rarely specified as an enforceable system design problem.
- It derives five design requirements for evidence-first, reviewable AI-supported decision support and consolidates them in the AIJIM reference model.
- It shows, through a reference implementation architecture, how these requirements can be instantiated without tying the model to a particular tool stack or domain.

The remainder of the paper proceeds as follows. Section 2 synthesizes related work and the gap it leaves open. Section 3 briefly explains the research method and derives the model requirements. Section 4 introduces the reference model, Sect. 5 details governance and audit mechanisms, and Sect. 6 outlines a reference implementation architecture and a minimal application scenario. Section 7 concludes the paper by discussing limitations and future work.

2 Background and Related Work

Research on AI-supported decision support systems (DSS) has long treated decision quality as a socio-technical matter rather than a purely computational one. As machine learning has become embedded in organizational decision processes, that perspective has broadened toward questions of governance, accountability, and oversight.

This section brings together four strands of prior work that jointly motivate the need for a system-level reference model: AI-supported DSS in information systems, trustworthy and responsible AI, governance and auditability, and human oversight in practice. Across these strands, the same limitation keeps resurfacing: much of the guidance remains principle-oriented, whereas the architectural conditions for enforceable trustworthiness stay underspecified.

2.1 AI-Supported Decision Support in Information Systems

Within BIS research, AI-supported DSS are commonly understood as socio-technical systems in which algorithmic components interact with human actors, organizational routines, and institutional constraints. This matters because the quality of AI-supported decisions cannot be judged by predictive performance alone. It also depends on whether outputs can be situated within the evidential and organizational context in which they are used.

A persistent concern is the opacity created when AI outputs travel further through an organization than their evidential basis does. Decision-makers may receive recommendations without a clear view of source data, uncertainty, or contextual limits, increasing the risk of over-reliance and diminished human agency [2]. Trust in such settings depends less on model accuracy in isolation than on whether the surrounding system preserves reviewability.

2.2 Trustworthy and Responsible AI in Organizational Contexts

The literature on trustworthy and responsible AI has responded by articulating principles such as transparency, fairness, accountability, and human control. These contributions are indispensable, but many stop at the level of normative guidance. Recent reviews and governance-oriented studies note that principle statements alone do not tell organizations how to build systems in which those principles are difficult to bypass [5,6,11,13].

For BIS research, the unresolved issue is therefore not whether trustworthy AI matters, but how it can be encoded in information system structures rather than left to discretionary compliance.

2.3 Governance, Auditability, and Accountability

Governance and accountability are especially salient where AI-supported decisions may have financial, legal, or societal consequences. Existing work stresses auditability, traceability, and clear responsibility allocation, yet the proposed remedies remain fragmented. Some focus on model explainability, others on organizational controls, internal accountability structures, or formal audit procedures [7,8,15].

What is still rare is an integrated design that binds evidence, analytical execution, evaluation outputs, and decision context into a reconstructable whole.

In many systems, auditability still amounts to logging events after the fact rather than preserving the conditions under which a decision can later be reconstructed and challenged.

2.4 Human Oversight and Socio-technical Perspectives

Human oversight is often invoked as a safeguard, but the literature makes clear that nominal human presence is not enough. Meaningful oversight requires systems that support review, contestation, and contextual interpretation of AI outputs [4,14]. Several studies warn that under time pressure or routine use, recommendations can harden into de facto decisions unless the system itself preserves decision points and responsibility boundaries [1,6,11].

2.5 Synthesis and Research Gap

Taken together, the literature points to a specific gap. Trustworthiness is usually discussed as principles, explainability as model-level technique, and governance as organizational procedure. Missing is a reference model for AI-supported decision support that makes these concerns mechanically enforceable through architecture. In particular, prior work does not provide an integrated model that consistently binds outputs to evidence, mandates evaluation artifacts, preserves audit-safe traceability, and separates analytical execution from governance. That gap motivates the evidence-first model developed next.

3 Research Method and Problem Setting

3.1 Research Method

This paper follows a design science research perspective in which the artifact is a prescriptive reference model for a recurrent class of BIS problems. The point of departure is the domain-specific AIJIM model introduced for AI-supported environmental journalism [12]. In the present study, that artifact is generalized into a domain-agnostic reference model through three closely connected steps: a focused synthesis of recent literature on trustworthy AI-supported DSS, a gap analysis of what that literature still leaves structurally underspecified, and an abstraction step that retains only those properties that must hold across domains.

Requirement derivation follows the same logic. The reviewed literature was used to identify recurring failure modes and governance needs, these observations were compared to the limitations of principle-oriented and model-centric approaches, and the resulting insights were abstracted into system requirements that can be expressed as enforceable architectural constraints. The aim is not to claim a universal ontology of trustworthy AI, but to define a small, reusable reference class for evidence-first decision support in business information systems.

3.2 Problem Setting

Artificial intelligence is increasingly embedded in decision support systems that inform high-stakes organizational decisions. The literature reviewed in Sect. 2.5 suggests a recurring pattern: many systems improve analytical capability while leaving open whether their outputs remain defensible once they are used in organizational practice.

The core problem is not simply opacity at the model level. It is the absence of system-level mechanisms that bind outputs to evidence, preserve execution context, require evaluative artifacts, and keep human authorization visible and effective over time. Where these mechanisms are weak, AI-supported outputs may be explainable in isolation yet still remain difficult to verify, reconstruct, or contest within the broader decision context.

This limitation is especially consequential in business information systems, where decisions often need to remain reviewable across organizational boundaries and time horizons. A trustworthy AI-supported DSS therefore cannot rely on abstract principles or procedural discipline alone; it needs architectural constraints that make reviewability and accountability durable properties of the system.

3.3 Derived System Requirements

Based on the synthesis of recent literature, we derive five core system requirements that an AI-supported decision support system must satisfy to be considered trustworthy in a business information systems context.

R1: Evidence Binding. AI-supported decisions must be explicitly bound to verifiable evidence. Multiple studies emphasize that trust in AI-assisted decision-making deteriorates when model outputs cannot be traced back to concrete data sources or evidential inputs. Without explicit evidence binding, AI outputs risk becoming detached recommendations that cannot be independently reviewed, contested, or validated. Every AI-derived claim or recommendation must therefore maintain a clear, persistent, and reviewable link to the evidence on which it is based. This requirement is necessary because the gap identified in Sect. 2.5 begins where outputs travel farther than their evidential basis, making later review and contestation unreliable.

R2: Artifact-Mandatory Evaluation. The literature frequently calls for transparency and explainability, yet often treats these aspects as optional or user-triggered features. To ensure auditability and accountability, evaluation artifacts—such as explanation representations, uncertainty cues, and provenance metadata—must be produced as mandatory outputs of every AI analysis. Artifact generation must not depend on downstream user actions or optional inspection, but be enforced at the system level as an integral part of the analytical process. This requirement is necessary because principle-oriented transparency does not resolve the Sect. 2.5 problem unless review context is generated automatically and preserved with each run.

R3: Audit Trail and Reproducibility. Numerous contributions highlight the importance of reproducibility and traceability in AI-supported decision support, particularly in regulated or high-risk environments. However, reproducibility is often addressed narrowly, for example through model retraining or dataset versioning. A trustworthy system must instead provide a complete audit trail that records when an analysis was performed, under which configuration, and within which decision context. This audit trail must enable independent reconstruction, review, and accountability assessment of past decisions. This requirement is necessary because the literature gap concerns not only knowing what the system did, but reconstructing why a decision state was admissible at a specific time.

R4: Human Oversight without Implicit Automation. While human-in-the-loop mechanisms are widely advocated, the literature also warns against forms of implicit automation in which human oversight becomes nominal rather than effective. Decision support systems must preserve human agency by ensuring that AI outputs inform decisions without autonomously triggering actions. Human oversight must be structurally enforced through system constraints that prevent AI components from bypassing review, authorization, or contestation processes. This requirement is necessary because, as discussed in Sect. 2.5, oversight fails in practice when review points exist only procedurally and can be eroded by routine use or time pressure.

R5: Separation of Governance, Evaluation, and Execution. A recurring limitation identified in existing systems is the conflation of analytical execution, evaluation, and governance logic. When these concerns are entangled, accountability becomes diffuse and policy enforcement inconsistent. A trustworthy decision support system must therefore enforce a strict separation between AI execution, evaluation of outputs, and governance or policy decisions. This separation enables independent control, clearer responsibility allocation, and systematic compliance with organizational and regulatory requirements. This requirement is necessary because the Sect. 2.5 gap is fundamentally architectural: without separated responsibilities, neither governance nor audit can remain stable when analytical components change.

3.4 Implications

Taken together, these requirements define the minimal conditions for an evidence-first reference model. They move the discussion from desirable principles to enforceable system properties and set up the model presented in the next section.

4 The Evidence-First Reference Model (AIJIM)

4.1 Model Overview

Building on the requirements in Sect. 3, this section introduces AIJIM as a domain-agnostic reference model for trustworthy AI-supported decision support in business information systems. Figure 1 provides a compact overview of the model entities, invariants, and the boundary between AI-supported analysis and human decision authority.

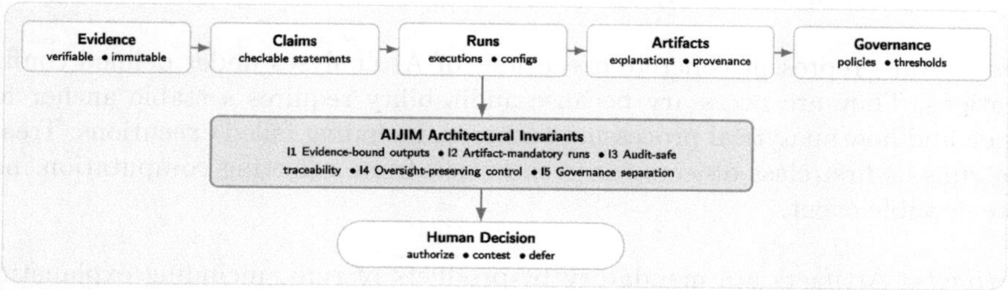

Fig. 1. AIJIM at a glance. Core entities, architectural invariants, and the explicit boundary between AI-supported analysis and human decision authority.

The model was originally proposed in a domain-specific context [12]; here it is reframed around enforceable trustworthiness at the information system level. The point is not to add another checklist of principles. It is to specify the structural conditions under which AI-supported outputs become reviewable, auditable, and governable in ordinary organizational use.

The subsections that follow unpack the model in four steps: core entities, invariants, the constraint view, and positioning within BIS. The sequence matters because the entities define what must be preserved, while the invariants explain why those elements cannot be treated as optional.

Reference Model Scope and Non-goals. AIJIM is a reference model, not a product architecture or implementation framework. It does not prescribe tools, algorithms, or platforms. Instead, it defines a reusable reference class of system relationships and invariants that can be instantiated across heterogeneous decision support settings where auditability, reviewability, and governance need to survive beyond a single model version or organizational procedure.

4.2 Core Entities and Relationships

The AIJIM reference model is structured around five core entities: *Evidence*, *Claims*, *Runs*, *Artifacts*, and *Governance Policies*. Each exists because one of the requirements in Sect. 3 would otherwise remain implicit and therefore easy to erode in practice.

Evidence. Evidence represents the verifiable basis on which AI analyses operate. It exists as a first-class entity because trustworthy review collapses when source material is treated as a transient input rather than as part of the decision record [2,9]. In AIJIM, evidence remains an immutable reference point that grounds later review.

Claims. Claims capture explicit, checkable analytical statements produced within the decision support process. They are modeled separately because organizational decisions are rarely made over raw model outputs alone; they are made over interpretable assertions that must be contestable and attributable to evidence and run context [4,14].

Runs. Runs represent concrete executions of AI analyses under defined configurations. They are necessary because auditability requires a stable anchor for when and how analytical processing occurred, including failed executions. Treating runs as first-class objects turns execution from a fleeting computation into a reviewable event.

Artifacts. Artifacts are mandatory by-products of runs, including explanation representations, uncertainty cues, provenance metadata, and diagnostic information. They exist because review cannot depend on optional inspection features or later reconstruction; the evaluative context must be produced together with the run [10].

Governance Policies. Governance policies define the constraints under which evaluated outputs may be used. They are represented separately because policy and authorization should shape admissibility without altering the analytical content itself. This keeps governance visible and independently auditable [3].

4.3 Model Invariants (Enforceable System Properties)

To ensure consistent enforcement across instantiations, AIJIM specifies five invariants:

- **I1 (Evidence-bound outputs):** No AI-supported claim or recommendation is reviewable unless it is explicitly bound to verifiable evidence.
- **I2 (Artifact-mandatory runs):** No analytical run is valid unless it produces the required evaluation artifacts.
- **I3 (Audit-safe traceability):** Every run is traceable to an execution and decision context sufficient for reconstruction and review.
- **I4 (Oversight-preserving control):** AI outputs cannot directly authorize actions; human authorization and contestation remain structurally supported.
- **I5 (Governance separation):** Governance decisions are evaluated independently of analytical execution logic.

These invariants are needed because the requirements in Sect. 3 are otherwise easy to dilute into aspirations or local best practices. In AIJIM, an invariant marks the boundary between an admissible and a non-admissible system state.

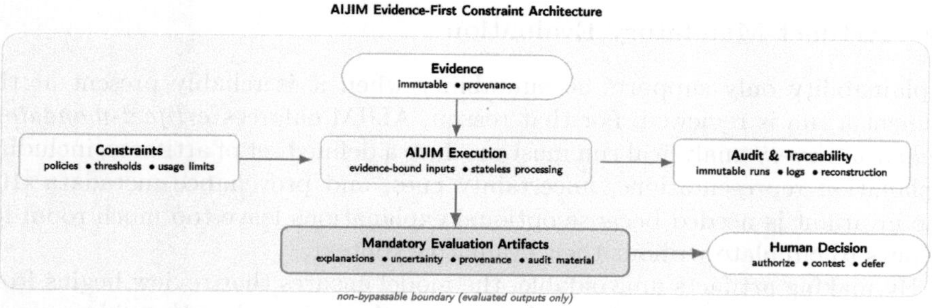

Fig. 2. AIJIM as an evidence-first constraint architecture. Trustworthiness is enforced through architectural boundaries rather than procedural steps or model-level assurances.

4.4 Constraint-Based System View

Figure 2 presents AIJIM as an evidence-first constraint architecture rather than a procedural lifecycle.

The constraint view is important because it shows why trustworthiness is not a matter of sequencing a few extra checks after inference. The architectural restrictions determine which outputs may continue through the system at all. Invariant-preserving constraints are therefore not decorative safeguards; they are the mechanism by which evidence binding, evaluation, and authorization remain coupled over time.

4.5 Positioning Within Business Information Systems

As a reference model, AIJIM remains deliberately domain-agnostic. The underlying need for evidence binding, auditability, and effective oversight recurs across business information systems even when domain workflows differ sharply [2,9]. The next section turns these invariants into governance and audit mechanisms; Sect. 6 then shows how they can be instantiated architecturally.

5 Governance and Audit Mechanisms

5.1 From Principles to Enforceable Mechanisms

A recurring lesson from recent literature is that trustworthy AI fails in practice when accountability and oversight remain external to the system [3,13]. In high-stakes decision support, manual review procedures and post hoc compliance checks are too easy to bypass, too uneven to scale, and too weak for retrospective reconstruction.

AIJIM therefore embeds governance and auditability as system responsibilities rather than downstream corrections. The following subsections explain why the model insists on artifact-mandatory evaluation, audit-safe traceability, explicit oversight, and a strict separation of execution, evaluation, and governance.

5.2 Artifact-Mandatory Evaluation

Explainability only supports accountability when it is reliably present at the moment a run is reviewed. For that reason, AIJIM enforces *artifact-mandatory evaluation*: every analytical run must produce a defined set of artifacts, including explanation representations, uncertainty cues, and provenance metadata [10]. The invariant is needed because optional explanations leave too much room for outputs to circulate without their evaluative context.

By making artifacts unavoidable, the model ensures that review begins from the same minimum evidential package every time. This directly addresses the practical concern that evaluation often remains too loosely coupled to deployment in organizational DSS [2,14].

5.3 Audit Trails and Reproducibility

Auditability requires more than logs. It requires preserving enough context to reconstruct what was run, on what basis, and under which conditions. AIJIM therefore treats runs and artifacts as immutable audit objects linked to evidence, configuration, and decision context. These bindings are necessary because otherwise traceability degrades into partial record-keeping that cannot support later accountability assessments [9].

Importantly, the model is failure-safe: denied or failed executions still produce reviewable records. That choice matters because the absence of an outcome can itself be organizationally consequential.

5.4 Human Oversight Without Implicit Automation

Human oversight is only meaningful if the system preserves a genuine authorization point. In AIJIM, AI outputs cannot directly trigger action; they must remain subject to review together with their evidence and artifacts. This constraint is necessary because nominal human-in-the-loop arrangements often collapse under routine use, time pressure, or automation bias [4,14].

Oversight is therefore not an informal override but an explicit, reviewable system function. That is what keeps human agency visible rather than symbolic.

5.5 Separation of Execution, Evaluation, and Governance

The model also insists on separating analytical execution, evaluation, and governance. This separation is needed because once these responsibilities are entangled, it becomes difficult to tell whether a downstream decision reflects analytical content, evaluative judgment, or policy logic [3]. In BIS settings, that ambiguity quickly undermines accountability.

By isolating these concerns, AIJIM allows analytical methods, review standards, and governance policies to evolve independently while preserving a coherent audit trail.

5.6 Summary

These mechanisms turn the model invariants into operational system constraints. Trustworthiness is not added after inference; it is preserved by the structure through which evidence, evaluation, and authorization remain tied together.

6 Reference Implementation Architecture

6.1 Purpose and Scope of the Reference Implementation

This section outlines a reference implementation architecture that demonstrates the constructability of AIJIM. It is a conceptual instantiation, not a production system or prescriptive software stack.

The architecture remains technology-agnostic and focuses on structural responsibilities. It is informed by a specification-driven design probe used in an applied organizational setting to test whether evidence binding, artifact-mandatory evaluation, audit-safe traceability, and governance separation can be enforced end-to-end through architecture rather than through documentation habits or discretionary controls.

6.2 Architectural Responsibilities and Separation of Concerns

The reference implementation organizes responsibilities according to the separation required by AIJIM.

Execution Responsibility. Stateless analytical components perform AI-based analysis on evidence-bound inputs under defined configurations. Execution may generate outputs, but it cannot authorize their use.

Evaluation and Artifact Responsibility. The evaluation responsibility generates and persists the mandatory artifacts for every run, including explanation representations, uncertainty cues, provenance metadata, and diagnostics. This responsibility exists because evaluative context must accompany outputs at generation time rather than depend on later user action [10].

Governance Responsibility. The governance responsibility evaluates already-evaluated outputs against organizational constraints such as escalation thresholds, oversight requirements, or usage restrictions. It remains separate so that policy decisions stay auditable without modifying analytical content [3].

6.3 Data Admissibility, Audit, and Oversight

Within this architecture, analytical execution produces outputs while governance determines admissibility and authorization. The arrangement prevents implicit automation and keeps human oversight structurally present as part of the decision path [4,14]. Each run preserves explicit bindings to inputs, configuration, outputs, and decision context, including failed runs, so that later reconstruction remains possible [9].

6.4 Minimal Application Scenario

A small newsroom instantiation illustrates the model's practical use without expanding scope. Source documents, transcripts, or sensor feeds serve as *Evidence.* A concrete extraction or scoring step is captured as a *Run.* The resulting summary, risk flag, or recommendation is accompanied by mandatory *Artifacts* such as provenance links and confidence cues. Editors or supervisors then apply *Governance Policies* before publication or escalation. Such a configuration has already been prototypically realized in an AI-assisted newsroom setting, which is precisely why the present paper treats the model as a generalizable BIS reference class rather than as a purely notional construct. The same mapping carries over to auditing or other DSS contexts: evidence remains the source basis, runs remain execution events, and artifacts remain the review package that makes outputs admissible.

6.5 Formative Design Evaluation

The model was also subjected to a compact formative expert review during its refinement. Across business information systems, governance, and applied AI practice, the feedback consistently supported the usefulness of evidence binding, mandatory artifacts, and separated governance responsibilities as means of making reviewable system states explicit. At the same time, the reviewers pointed to familiar trade-offs around operational overhead and implementation discipline. For the purposes of this paper, that evaluation does not serve as a standalone empirical result; it functions as a plausibility check that the proposed invariants remain intelligible and relevant outside the originating application setting.

7 Conclusion and Future Work

AIJIM reframes trustworthy AI in business information systems as an architectural problem. Instead of relying on principle statements or model-centric safeguards alone, the model specifies how evidence binding, mandatory evaluation artifacts, audit-safe traceability, human authorization, and governance separation can be treated as enforceable system properties [3,13].

This work has several limitations. First, the proposed reference model is conceptual and has not been evaluated through large-scale empirical deployment. Second, the formative evaluation focuses on plausibility and structural enforceability rather than measurable performance or organizational impact. Third, while the model is designed to be domain-agnostic, its illustration is grounded in a limited set of application contexts. These limitations point to the need for further empirical validation and domain-specific instantiations in future work.

Future work should examine AIJIM-based instantiations in varied BIS settings and study how these invariants affect reviewability, contestation, decision latency, and accountability under realistic operating conditions.

References

1. Alami, A., Jensen, V.V., Ernst, N.A.: Accountability in code review: the role of intrinsic drivers and the impact of LLMs. ACM Trans. Softw. Eng. Methodol. (2025). https://doi.org/10.1145/3721127
2. Cresswell, K., et al.: The need to strengthen the evaluation of the impact of artificial intelligence-based decision support systems on healthcare provision. Health Policy (2023). https://doi.org/10.1016/j.healthpol.2023.104889
3. Díaz Rodríguez, N., Ser, J., Coeckelbergh, M., López de Prado, M.: Connecting the dots in trustworthy artificial intelligence: from AI principles requirements to responsible AI systems and regulation. Inf. Fusion (2023). https://doi.org/10.1016/j.inffus.2023.101812
4. Gomez, C., Cho, S.M., Ke, S., Huang, C.M., Unberath, M.: Human-AI collaboration is not very collaborative yet: a taxonomy of interaction patterns in AI-assisted decision making from a systematic review. Front. Comput. Sci. (2023). https://doi.org/10.3389/fcomp.2023.1133555
5. Königstorfer, F.: A comprehensive review of techniques for documenting artificial intelligence. Digit. Policy Regul. Gov. (2024). https://doi.org/10.1108/dprg-01-2024-0008
6. Loufek, B., et al.: Embedding internal accountability into health care institutions for safe, effective, and ethical implementation of artificial intelligence into medical practice: a mayo clinic case study. Mayo Clin. Proc. Digit. Health (2024). https://doi.org/10.1016/j.mcpdig.2024.08.008
7. Murikah, W., Nthenge, J.K., Musyoka, F.: Bias and ethics of AI systems applied in auditing - a systematic review. Sci. Afr. (2024). https://doi.org/10.1016/j.sciaf.2024.e02281
8. Radanliev, P., Santos, O., Ani, U.: Generative AI cybersecurity and resilience. Front. Artif. Intell. (2025). https://doi.org/10.3389/frai.2025.1568360
9. Sáez, C., Ferri, P., García-Gómez, J.M.: Resilient artificial intelligence in health: synthesis and research agenda toward next-generation trustworthy clinical decision support. J. Med. Internet Res. (2024). https://doi.org/10.2196/51234
10. Sahoh, B., Choksuriwong, A.: The role of explainable artificial intelligence in high-stakes decision-making systems: a systematic review. J. Ambient. Intell. Humaniz. Comput. (2023). https://doi.org/10.1007/s12652-023-04789-3
11. Stetson, P.D., et al.: Responsible artificial intelligence governance in oncology. npj Digit. Med. (2025). https://doi.org/10.1038/s41746-025-01794-w
12. Tiltack, T.: AIJIM: a scalable model for real-time AI in environmental journalism. In: Proceedings of the International Conference on Sustainable Technology and Environmental Systems. LNNS. Springer (2024). https://doi.org/10.1007/978-3-032-07989-3_26
13. Wagner, B., Müller-Birn, C.: Responsible and accountable data science. Patterns (2022). https://doi.org/10.1016/j.patter.2022.100629
14. Wang, L., et al.: Human-centered design and evaluation of AI-empowered clinical decision support systems: a systematic review. Front. Comput. Sci. (2023). https://doi.org/10.3389/fcomp.2023.1122334
15. Weinberg, A.I., Faccia, A.: Machine learning for triple-entry accounting: enhancing transparency and oversight. J. Risk Financ. Manage. (2025). https://doi.org/10.3390/jrfm18090525

Anthropomorphic Cues in AI Chatbots: Boundary Conditions for Trust Formation

Tyge-F. Kummer[1], Markus Bick[2](✉), and Luca Laule[2]

[1] Queensland University of Technology, 2 George Street, Brisbane, QLD 4000, Australia
[2] ESCP Business School, Heubnerweg 8-10, 14059 Berlin, Germany
mbick@escp.eu

Abstract. AI-powered chatbots become increasingly embedded in everyday digital interactions. But the role of anthropomorphic design features in shaping user trust remains underexplored across contexts with differing stakes. This study investigates how anthropomorphic cues influence trust – measured through perceived benevolence, integrity, and ability – as well as the intention to follow AI-generated advice, in both high-stakes (healthcare) and low-stakes (retail) environments. Using a 2 × 2 between-subjects experimental design (N = 163), we find that anthropomorphism significantly increases all three trust dimensions and the intention to follow chatbot advice in low-stakes contexts, with trust levels increasing by over 30% compared to non-anthropomorphic versions. In contrast, in high-stakes settings, anthropomorphism improves perceived benevolence but has no significant effect on integrity, ability, or behavioural trust. These findings highlight the boundary conditions of anthropomorphic design: while beneficial in domains with comparatively limited consequences, such as retail, related cues do not increase professionalism or competence in more serious domains with a higher risk profile. Our findings offer actionable guidance for tailoring chatbot design to context, informing the deployment of trustworthy AI systems in both commercial and sensitive domains.

Keywords: Artificial Intelligence · experiment · anthropomorphism · trust

1 Introduction

AI-powered chatbots have become ubiquitous in modern digital ecosystems, playing a pivotal role in industries such as customer service, finance, and information technology. These conversational agents simulate human-like dialogue, offering automated assistance through natural language interfaces. While their technical capabilities continue to evolve rapidly, user adoption remains questionable due to concerns about trustworthiness and reliability [1]. Establishing trust is therefore critical to the sustained success of chatbot systems. Anthropomorphism is often considered as a potential solution as it describes adding human-like features such as sophisticated emotional expression to non-human entities such as a chatbot. It has been shown to foster emotional attachment, thereby enhancing trust and increasing user satisfaction in interactions with AI

K. Węcel and V. Řepa (Eds.): BIS 2026, LNBIP 584, pp. 102–113, 2026.
https://doi.org/10.1007/978-3-032-26363-6_8

[2, 3]. Moreover, interface design features, such as personalisation and conversational style, further contribute to emotional engagement and perceived warmth, highlighting the interplay between technical performance and social cues in shaping user trust [4].

Despite growing scholarly interest in trust in AI, research on anthropomorphism has predominantly examined specific industry contexts, such as information technology, hospitality and tourism, and financial services [5–7]. While these studies offer valuable insights, they often lack comparative perspectives that would enable a deeper understanding of how trust mechanisms operate across different domains. Limited attention has been paid to contextual comparisons, which are essential for assessing the generalisability of existing findings. For example, in high-stakes domains such as healthcare, trust may hinge on different factors than in low-stakes settings like retail, potentially altering the effectiveness of anthropomorphic cues. Building on Mayer et al.'s [8] trust framework and subsequent research in human-computer interaction (HCI), three key dimensions have emerged as central to trust formation: ability, benevolence, and integrity [9]. This study investigates the effect of anthropomorphic AI chatbots on these trust dimensions by addressing the following research questions:

RQ1: How does anthropomorphism displayed by AI chatbots affect trust across different contexts?
RQ2: How do trust drivers differ between contexts?

To address these questions, we conduct a 2 × 2 between-subjects experimental design, manipulating the level of anthropomorphic design (low vs. high) and industry context (high-stakes vs. low-stakes). Participants engage with simulated scenarios in either a high-stakes healthcare setting or a low-stakes retail setting.

The remainder of this paper presents the theoretical background and hypotheses (Sects. 2, 3), the methodology and results (Sects. 4, 5), followed by a discussion and conclusion (Sects. 6, 7).

2 Anthropomorphism in AI-Based Chatbots

Anthropomorphism describes the attribution of human characteristics to non-human agents. It has become a defining feature of AI-based chatbots. When these systems exhibit traits associated with emotion, cognition, or intention, users often perceive them as more human-like [10]. This perception is shaped by design elements such as fluent communication, natural language expression, and emotionally nuanced responses. As large language models continue to advance, the linguistic capabilities of chatbots have become increasingly sophisticated, making anthropomorphism not only more prevalent but also more influential in shaping user experience, while enhancing the interaction between user and chatbots [6].

A wide range of anthropomorphic features has been studied, including visual appearance [11, 12], language style [13], humour [7, 10], and competence [14]. While many studies report positive effects of anthropomorphism on trust and engagement, there is also growing concern about its implications. Some users express discomfort with chatbots that appear too human-like. This so-called uncanny valley effect is attributed to subtle inconsistencies that may trigger negative emotional responses as the AI lacks natural emotional behaviours, disrupting users' expectations and leading to a sense of unease while raising questions about authenticity, transparency, and ethical design [15, 16].

Trust is a central construct in understanding user interaction with AI chatbots. It is commonly defined as the willingness to accept vulnerability based on the expectation that another party will act in a beneficial or at least non-harmful manner. In the context of AI, trust influences whether users rely on chatbots for information, advice, or emotional support despite the inability to verify or control the system's actions. Mayer et al.'s [8] ABI model conceptualises trust through three dimensions: Ability, Benevolence, and Integrity. Although originally developed for interpersonal relationships, this framework has been widely applied to digital contexts, including e-commerce, healthcare, and AI system design [9].

In addition to the ABI model, we ground our analysis in the Task Technology Fit (TTF) model to explain context-related differences. TTF has been proposed for use in AI-human interaction, as it focuses on the fit between a task in a specific context, the available technology such as AI, and the personal characteristics of the user [17, 18]. However, TTF proposes that a good fit creates an ideal situation, yet it does not predict which specific constellations will arise. It is therefore necessary to investigate the conditions under which such ideal situations occur.

Despite the growing body of research on trust and anthropomorphism, much of the literature remains focused on specific contexts, such as marketing and commerce [11, 19]. While these studies offer valuable insights, they often lack comparative perspectives that would enable a deeper understanding of how trust mechanisms operate across different domains. Much of this research also relies on exploratory or correlational designs, limiting causal inference. Experimental approaches are needed to isolate the effects of anthropomorphic design and contextual factors on trust formation.

3 Hypotheses Development

To explore how anthropomorphism displayed by AI chatbots affects trust across different contexts (RQ1), we argue that anthropomorphic features are likely to influence the trust dimension as defined by the ABI model [6] to varying degrees. For example, a chatbot that communicates with empathy and warmth may be perceived as more benevolent but could be perceived as less competent if it does not use the expected professional language. These perceptions are shaped not only by the chatbot's design but also by the context in which it is deployed.

According to the Task Technology Fit (TTF) model [17, 18], tasks are driven by context, and technology is more likely to be used effectively when its capabilities align with the requirements of the task. In low-stakes settings such as retail, tasks typically involve browsing, selecting, or purchasing items, such activities that benefit from conversational, engaging, and emotionally resonant interactions. Anthropomorphic features, such as friendliness and humour, enhance the fit by making the chatbot more persuasive and enjoyable. In contrast, high-stakes settings such as healthcare demand precision and clinical accuracy. In these contexts, anthropomorphic traits may reduce perceived fit if they introduce ambiguity or emotional cues that conflict with the seriousness of the task. Furthermore, the uncanny valley effect may arise when anthropomorphic traits are perceived as inauthentic, potentially undermining trust. We postulate that this influences the trust perception as well as behavioural trust defined as observable actions that demonstrate trust, such as the intention to follow AI-generated advice [20].

Based on these considerations, we propose the following interaction effects between anthropomorphism and context:

H1a: In high-stakes contexts, chatbots with low anthropomorphism will be rated as more trustworthy than chatbots with high anthropomorphism.
H1b: In high-stakes contexts, the intention to follow the advice of AI chatbots with low anthropomorphism will be greater than the intention to follow the advice of chatbots with high anthropomorphism.
H2a: In low-stakes contexts, chatbots with high anthropomorphism will be rated as more trustworthy than chatbots with low anthropomorphism.
H2b: In low-stakes contexts, the intention to follow the advice of AI chatbots with high anthropomorphism will be greater than the intention to follow the advice of chatbots with low anthropomorphism.

To address the second research question, we focus on the three trust components identified by Mayer et al. [6]. We posit that the composition of trust varies across contexts because the relative importance of ability, integrity and benevolence differs depending on situational demands. As outlined above, in high-stakes settings the expectations for professionalism and accuracy are elevated. In such environments, anthropomorphic cues that introduce emotionality or informality may appear inappropriate, which can undermine the perception that the system adheres to relevant norms and standards. This can reduce perceived integrity.

A similar mechanism applies to perceived ability. In high-stakes tasks, users rely on signals of technical expertise and domain competence. Anthropomorphic features may shift attention away from analytical capability and towards social presence. Users may therefore infer that a highly anthropomorphic chatbot prioritises interpersonal engagement over task expertise, which reduces perceived competence.

Benevolence, however, is shaped by a different psychological process. Benevolence reflects perceptions of goodwill and positive intent rather than professional adequacy. Anthropomorphic cues that convey warmth or emotional expressiveness can enhance the sense that the chatbot cares about the user, even when the context is serious. Thus, anthropomorphism may decrease integrity and competence in high-stakes settings, while simultaneously increasing benevolence. We state:

H3a: In high-stake contexts, chatbots with high anthropomorphism will be rated as having less integrity than chatbots with low anthropomorphism.
H3b: In high-stake contexts, chatbots with high anthropomorphism will be rated as having less ability (competence) than chatbots with low anthropomorphism.
H3c: In high-stake context, chatbots with high anthropomorphism will be rated as having more benevolence than chatbots with low anthropomorphism.

In low-stakes contexts, we expect these effects to be more consistent and uniformly positive. Because the task is less consequential, users face fewer expectations regarding professionalism, expertise or adherence to formal standards. Assessments of integrity and ability rely less on strict professional benchmarks and more on general impressions formed during the interaction. As a result, individuals are more receptive to anthropomorphic cues in tasks that require minimal specialised knowledge or involve subjective judgement, such as fashion advice. In such situations, anthropomorphic features can enhance perceptions of integrity, competence and benevolence simultaneously. Therefore, we postulate:

H4a: In low-stake contexts, chatbots with high anthropomorphism will be rated as having more integrity than chatbots with low anthropomorphism.
H4b: In low-stake contexts, chatbots with high anthropomorphism will be rated as having more ability (competence) than chatbots with low anthropomorphism.
H4c: In low-stake context, chatbots with high anthropomorphism will be rated as having more benevolence than chatbots with low anthropomorphism.

4 Methodology

We conduct a 2 $\times$ 2 between-groups experiment with two independent variables: anthropomorphic design (low vs. high) and industry context (low-stakes vs. high-stakes). Fashion retail has been selected as the low-stakes context, while healthcare represents the high-stakes context. Participants are randomly assigned to one of the four experimental conditions.

4.1 Research Design

Each participant read a brief vignette simulating an interaction with an AI chatbot in one of the two industry contexts, featuring either high or low anthropomorphism. Each vignette includes a brief chat transcript displayed within a mock mobile phone interface screenshot to enhance realism. The interaction is structured into three segments: (1.) In the first interaction the chatbot introduces itself and provides context-related information. In the healthcare setting, the chatbot provides the results of a recent blood test, while the chatbot in the fashion retail context explains a product return process. (2.) The second interaction is used to further establish the relationship with the bot. In the healthcare setting, the chatbot explains why the results of the blood test are problematic while the chatbot in the low-stakes chatbot provides general fashion advice. (3.) The final interaction is used for a behavioural prompt. In the healthcare setting, the chatbot prescribes a suitable drug and asks the participant to confirm the treatment. In the fashion setting, the chatbot prompts the user to view specific products. In order to make the scenario realistic, the health scenario is based on diabetes, and a common diabetes drug is prescribed (Metformin 500 mg) [21]. The disease was selected because diabetes can occur at all ages and is a common condition in the USA [22]. However, in order to exclude biases because participants may already suffer from diabetes, a corresponding control question was added.

The depiction of an avatar, expressions of feelings, emojis and casual language were present in the high anthropomorphism versions (see Fig. 1). However, to ensure consistency across conditions, the core message remains identical in both the low and high anthropomorphism versions for each context to maintain information equivalence.

For example, in the healthcare condition, both vignettes communicate the same blood test results and prescribe the same drug. Generative AI (ChatGPT-4) was used to create the vignettes to ensure linguistic authenticity and contextual relevance. Manipulation checks based on ratings of perceived human-likeness and topic seriousness confirmed successful manipulations (Context: Wilks' $\lambda = .641$, $F(2, 158) = 44.31$, $p < .001$; AF: Wilks' $\lambda = .897$, $F(2, 158) = 9.07$, $p < .001$). Figure 1 presents the final third message with the behavioural prompt across the 4 experimental groups.

4.2 Data Collection and Research Design

Data collection took place in November 2025 and was conducted online via Prolific. Participants were incentivised in accordance with the Prolific guidelines. In total data from 179 participants was collected. 10 participants were removed because they failed the attention check question while an additional 6 participants were removed because their completion time was less than half of the median completion time, suggesting that they rushed though the survey and did not have sufficient time to read the scenario in detail, resulting in a total sample size of N = 163. A power analysis in G*Power 3.1 indicated that the available sample provides high statistical power for a MANOVA with four groups and five dependent variables ($f^2(V) = 0.0625$, $\alpha = 0.05$, power = 0.96). As G*Power does not support MANCOVA, the MANOVA specification was used as a conservative approximation.

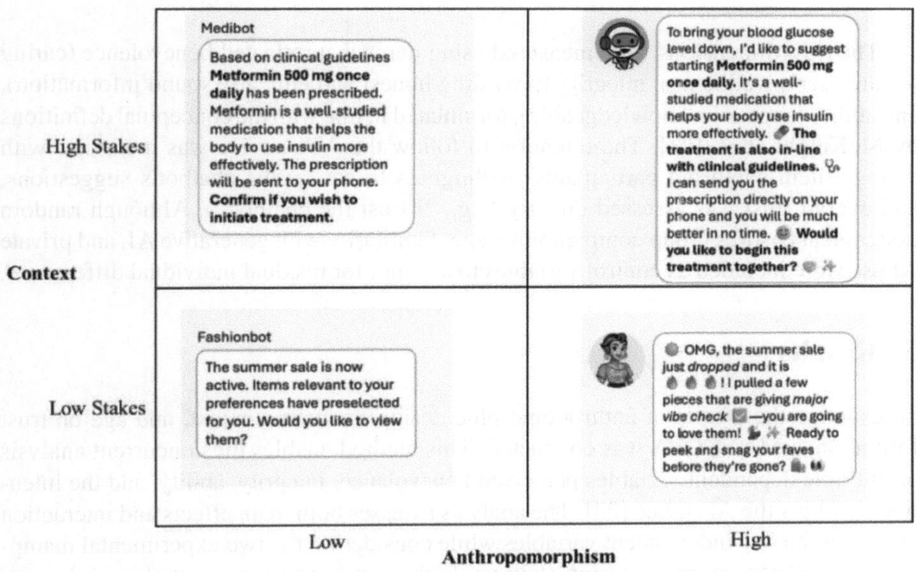

Fig. 1. Experimental Design: Behavioural Prompts Across Treatments

Participants were recruited from the USA to ensure a degree of homogeneity within the sample. Although the sample includes individuals of varying ages and levels of experience with AI to enhance generalisability, focusing on a single country helps maintain consistency in the availability of AI tools and the regulatory environment surrounding their use. Table 1 provides an overview of the sample's demographics.

Table 1. Overview of participant demographics

		Count (Percentage)	Mean
Gender	Female	80 (49.08%)	
	Male	82 (50.31%)	
	Non-Binary	1 (0.61%)	
Age (in years)			44.6
Education	No schooling completed	3 (1.84%	
	High school graduate, diploma or the equivalent	35 (21.47%)	
	Trade/technical/vocational training	18 (11.04%)	
	Bachelor's degree	70 (42.94%)	
	Master's degree	30 (18.40%)	
	Professional degree	1 (0.61%)	
	Doctorate degree	6 (3.68%)	

The trust dimensions were measured using items that reflected benevolence (caring for the user's wellbeing), integrity (providing honest and ethically sound information), and ability (appearing knowledgeable), formulated in line with the conceptual definitions by McKnight et al. [23]. The intention to follow the AI's advice was measured with a single item capturing participants' willingness to act on the chatbot's suggestions, and overall trust was assessed directly (e.g., "I trust the chatbot."). Although random assignment ensures group comparability, age, familiarity with generative AI, and private AI use were included as control variables to account for residual individual differences.

5 Results

To examine the effects of anthropomorphic design, industry context, and age on trust formation, a MANCOVA was conducted. This method enables the concurrent analysis of multiple dependent variables perceived benevolence, integrity, ability, and the intention to follow the AI advice [24]. The analysis assesses both main effects and interaction effects of the five independent variables while considering the two experimental manipulations anthropomorphic design (low vs. high) and industry context (low-stakes vs. high-stakes). Table 2 provides an overview of the descriptive statistics while Table 3 contains the MANCOVA results.

While the results depicted in Table 3 contain significant main effects, the presence of interaction effects suggests that these effects cannot be interpreted in isolation and must instead be examined in terms of how the variables jointly influence the outcome.

Table 2. Descriptive Statistics

Context	Anthro	Ability		Benevolence		Integrity		Trust		Intention	
		Mean	Std. D	Mean	Std. D	Mean	Std. D	Mean	Std. D	Mean	Std. D
Retail (low stakes)	Low (N = 40)	3.97	2.61	2.90	2.24	3.73	2.50	3.53	2.39	2.55	1.83
	High (N = 42)	5.38	1.08	4.33	1.90	5.17	1.32	4.55	1.60	3.36	1.08
	Total (N = 82)	4.70	2.09	3.63	2.18	4.46	2.10	4.05	2.07	2.96	1.54
Health (high stakes)	Low (N = 39)	5.44	1.10	4.15	1.53	4.95	1.32	4.51	1.50	2.92	1.22
	High (N = 42)	5.29	1.44	4.48	1.85	4.74	1.67	4.10	1.94	2.83	1.45
	Total (N = 81)	5.36	1.28	4.32	1.70	4.84	1.50	4.30	1.74	2.88	1.34

Table 3. MANCOVA results (* = p < 0.05, ** = p < 0.01, *** = p < 0.001)

Effect type	Factor	Statistic	Ability	Benevolence	Integrity	Trust	Intention
Covariates	Age	F(5,152)	**8.77****	0.06	**6.78***	**5.80***	3.38
		η^2_p	0.05	0.00	0.04	0.02	0.02
	Familiarity	F(5,152)	2.05	0.01	1.00	0.22	0.04
		η^2_p	0.01	0.00	0.01	0.00	0.00
	Private use	F(5,152)	0.39	1.20	0.18	0.62	2.62
		η^2_p	0.00	0.01	0.00	0.00	0.02
Main Effects	Context	F(5,152)	**7.25****	**5.47***	2.23	0.96	0.07
		η^2_p	0.04	0.03	0.01	0.01	0.00
	Anthro.	F(5,152)	**5.64***	**9.25****	**4.67***	1.04	2.71
		η^2_p	0.04	0.06	0.03	0.01	0.02
Interaction	Context × Anthro.	F(5,152)	**11.32*****	3.38	**10.76*****	**7.17****	**4.64***
		η^2_p	0.07	0.02	0.07	0.04	0.03

Table 4. Simple Effect Analysis (* = p < 0.05, ** = p < 0.01, *** = p < 0.001)

Variable	Context	Treatment	Mean difference (I-J)	St. Error
Trust	Retail	Low Anthro. (I), high Anthro. (J)	**−1.089****	0.416
	Health	Low Anthro. (I), high Anthro. (J)	0.488	0.416
Intention	Retail	Low Anthro. (I), high Anthro. (J)	**−0.843****	0.313
	Health	Low Anthro. (I), high Anthro. (J)	0.113	0.314
Ability	Retail	Low Anthro. (I), high Anthro. (J)	**−1.481*****	0.365
	Health	Low Anthro. (I), high Anthro. (J)	0.257	0.365
Integrity	Retail	Low Anthro. (I), high Anthro. (J)	**−1.498*****	0.389
	Health	Low Anthro. (I), high Anthro. (J)	0.310	0.390

Noteworthy, all interaction effects follow the same pattern, illustrated by the example of trust in Fig. 2. The simple effects analysis confirms that within the low stake retail environment, anthropomorphistic features improve the trust generation significantly (mean difference −1.089). However, in the high-stake health environment a descriptive trend in the opposite direction can be observed as the low anthropomorphistic scenario achieved a higher trust measure (mean difference 0.488). However, the corresponding simple effect analysis does not suggest that the differences within the health context are significant. H1 is therefore rejected while H2 is supported

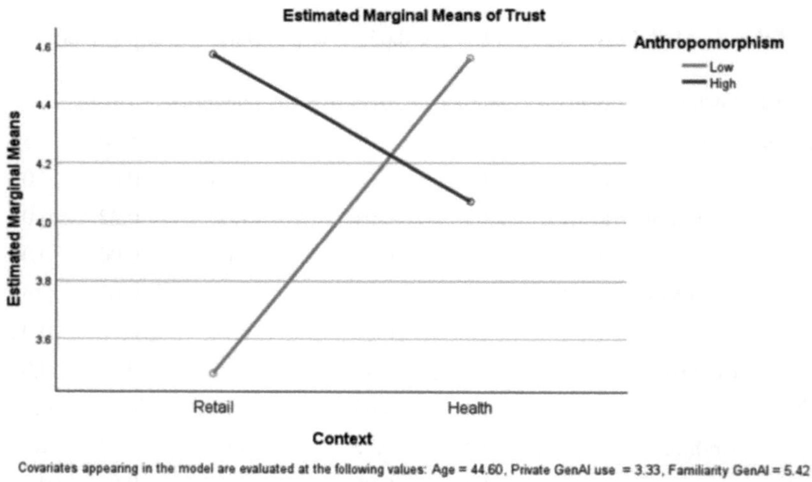

Fig. 2. Interaction effect between context and anthropomorphism on trust

The simple effect analysis in Table 4 further confirms the postulated relationships in relation to benevolence, integrity, and ability in the low-stakes retail context. Therefore, hypotheses 4a, 4b, and 4c are supported. As expected, benevolence does also not follow the interaction pattern and instead only a positive main effect emerges. The descriptive results suggest that the version with anthropomorphistic features has higher perceived benevolence. Hypotheses 3c is also supported. However, while integrity and ability are rated lower when anthropomorphistic features are present in a high-stakes scenario (see Table 2), the simple effects are not significant (Table 4). Hypotheses 3a and 3b are rejected.

6 Discussion

Consistent with prior research [2, 3, 5, 7, 13, 14], our results confirm that anthropomorphic features enhance trust in low-stakes environments, significantly increasing users' perceptions of benevolence, integrity, and ability, as well as their intention to follow AI advice. These findings reinforce the value of socially oriented chatbot design in settings where emotional engagement and user enjoyment are critical.

In contrast, the high-stakes healthcare context revealed a more nuanced pattern. While anthropomorphism significantly improved perceived benevolence, it did not produce meaningful gains in integrity, ability, or overall trust. These results suggest that the trust-enhancing potential of anthropomorphism may be contextually constrained, particularly when tasks demand accuracy, professionalism, and a clear communication of competence. Users may interpret emotional or casual cues in such contexts as inappropriate or misaligned with their expectations of technical rigor, potentially activating perceptions of risk rather than reassurance.

From a theoretical standpoint, the study contributes to the literature by integrating the ABI trust model [8] with the Task-Technology Fit framework [8] to interpret cross-contextual dynamics.

Moreover, the study offers meaningful practical implications. For designers of AI systems, especially in consumer-facing applications, these findings suggest that anthropomorphic elements such as emojis, emotional language, and avatar-based cues can be highly effective in informal or hedonic domains. In contrast, developers working in regulated, sensitive, or high-stakes environments should exercise greater caution. The design of AI interfaces in such settings may benefit more from cues of professionalism, competence, and transparency rather than social presence alone.

7 Conclusion and Future Research

Our study demonstrates that anthropomorphic cues in AI chatbots can differentially shape user trust depending on the application context. In low-stakes retail scenarios, such cues significantly enhance all three trust dimensions and the likelihood of following chatbot advice. In high-stakes healthcare settings, however, the effects are less consistent: benevolence increases, but perceived competence and integrity do not, leading to no significant overall trust gain.

Several limitations constrain the generalizability of our findings: First, the experimental design relied on a single use case per context (fashion retail and diabetes-related healthcare), which limits the ability to draw broader conclusions about trust formation across industries. Second, the trust outcomes were measured using a cross-sectional survey design, capturing user responses after a single, brief interaction. Future work should examine trust dynamics over time to assess whether initial impressions formed by anthropomorphic cues are reinforced, diminished, or reversed with repeated exposure. Moreover, future studies should explore which specific anthropomorphic features (e.g., visual elements, linguistic markers, or affective cues) contribute most to trust in different contexts. Disentangling these features could lead to a more granular design framework for context-sensitive chatbot development.

In sum, while this study reinforces established theoretical expectations, it provides clear, context-specific insights for the responsible design of AI chatbots. By identifying when anthropomorphism supports or undermines trust, this research contributes to a more nuanced understanding of human-AI interaction and offers a foundation for further inquiry into adaptive, user-sensitive chatbot design.

References

1. Zierau, N., Korbinian, F., Janson, A., Söllner, M., Leimeister, J.M.: The influence of AI-based chatbots and their design on users' trust and information sharing in online loan applications. In: Proceedings of the 54th Hawaii International Conference on System Sciences (HICSS) (2021)
2. Xie, Y., Zhu, K., Zhou, P., Liang, C.: How does anthropomorphism improve human-AI interaction satisfaction: a dual-path model. Comput. Hum. Behav. **148**, 107878 (2023). https://doi.org/10.1016/j.chb.2023.107878
3. Willems, J., Schmid, M.J., Vanderelst, D., Vogel, D., Ebinger, F.: AI-driven public services and the privacy paradox: do citizens really care about their privacy? Public Manag. Rev. **25**(11), 2116–2134 (2023). https://doi.org/10.1080/14719037.2022.2063934
4. Toader, D.-C., Boca, G., Toader, R., Măcelaru, M., Toader, C., Ighian, D., et al.: The effect of social presence and chatbot errors on trust. Sustainability **12**(1), 256 (2020). https://doi.org/10.3390/su12010256
5. Kumar, S., Jain, R., Sharma, A.: Anthropomorphic artificial intelligence drives consumer behavior: comprehensive literature review and research agenda. J. Internet Commer., 1–39 (2025). https://doi.org/10.1080/15332861.2025.2542138
6. Lee, S., Oh, H.: Anthropomorphism and its implications for advertising hotel brands. J. Bus. Res. **129**, 455–464 (2021). https://doi.org/10.1016/j.jbusres.2019.09.053
7. Schanke, S., Burtch, G., Ray, G.: Estimating the impact of "humanizing" customer service chatbots. Inf. Syst. Res. **32**(3), 736–751 (2021). https://doi.org/10.1287/isre.2021.1015
8. Mayer, R.C., Davis, J.H., Schoorman, F.D.: An integrative model of organizational trust. Acad. Manag. Rev. **20**(3), 709–734 (1995). https://doi.org/10.5465/amr.1995.9508080335
9. Lalot, F., Bertram, A.-M.: When the bot walks the talk: investigating the foundations of trust in an artificial intelligence (AI) chatbot. J. Exp. Psychol. Gen. **154**(2), 533–551 (2025). https://doi.org/10.1037/xge0001696
10. Moussawi, S., Koufaris, M., Benbunan-Fich, R.: How perceptions of intelligence and anthropomorphism affect adoption of personal intelligent agents. Electron. Mark. **31**(2), 343–364 (2021). https://doi.org/10.1007/s12525-020-00411-w
11. Pizzi, G., Vannucci, V., Mazzoli, V., Donvito, R.: I, chatbot! the impact of anthropomorphism and gaze direction on willingness to disclose personal information and behavioral intentions. Psychol. Mark. **40**(7), 1372–1387 (2023). https://doi.org/10.1002/mar.21813
12. Go, E., Sundar, S.S.: Humanizing chatbots: the effects of visual, identity and conversational cues on humanness perceptions. Comput. Hum. Behav. **97**, 304–316 (2019). https://doi.org/10.1016/j.chb.2019.01.020

13. Araujo, T.: Living up to the chatbot hype: the influence of anthropomorphic design cues and communicative agency framing on conversational agent and company perceptions. Comput. Hum. Behav. **85**, 183–189 (2018). https://doi.org/10.1016/j.chb.2018.03.051
14. Cheng, X., Zhang, X., Cohen, J., Mou, J.: Human vs. AI: understanding the impact of anthropomorphism on consumer response to chatbots from the perspective of trust and relationship norms. Inf. Process. Manag. **59**(3), 1 (2022). https://doi.org/10.1016/j.ipm.2022.102940
15. Mori, M., MacDorman, K.F., Kageki, N.: The uncanny valley [from the field]. IEEE Robot. Autom. Mag. **19**(2), 98–100 (2012). https://doi.org/10.1109/MRA.2012.2192811
16. Łukasik, A., Gut, A.: From robots to chatbots: unveiling the dynamics of human-AI interaction. Front. Psychol. **16**, 1569277 (2025). https://doi.org/10.3389/fpsyg.2025.1569277
17. Kummer, T.-F.: The balance enterprise. In: Rosemann, M. (ed.) The Future Enterprice (2025, forthcoming)
18. Goodhue, D.L., Thompson, R.L.: Task-technology fit and individual performance. MIS Q. **19**(2), 213–236 (1995). https://doi.org/10.2307/249689
19. Li, Y., Gan, Z., Zheng, B.: How do artificial intelligence chatbots affect customer purchase? uncovering the dual pathways of anthropomorphism on service evaluation. Inf. Syst. Front. **27**(1), 283–300 (2025). https://doi.org/10.1007/s10796-023-10438-x
20. Schmidt, P., Biessmann, F., Teubner, T.: Transparency and trust in artificial intelligence systems. J. Decis. Syst. **29**(4), 260–278 (2020). https://doi.org/10.1080/12460125.2020.1819094
21. Kalyani, R.R., Neumiller, J.J., Maruthur, N.M., Wexler, D.J.: Diagnosis and treatment of type 2 diabetes in adults: a review. JAMA J. Am. Med. Assoc. **334**(11), 984–1002 (2025). https://doi.org/10.1001/jama.2025.5956
22. Centers for Disease Control and Prevention. National Diabetes Statistics Report. https://www.cdc.gov/diabetes/php/data-research/
23. McKnight, D.H., Choudhury, V., Kacmar, C.: Developing and validating trust measures for e-commerce: an integrative typology. Inf. Syst. Res. **13**(3), 334–359 (2002). https://doi.org/10.1287/isre.13.3.334.81
24. Tabachnick, B.G., Fidell, L.S., Ullman, J.B.: Using Multivariate Statistics, 7 edn. Pearson, NY (2019)

Enhancing ChatGPT with a Decision Support Framework to Resolve Management Decision Scenarios

Tarmo Koppel(✉), Tarmo Kalvet, and Tanel Tammet

Tallinn University of Technology, Ehitajate tee 5, 19086 Tallinn, Estonia
correspondence@koppel.ee

Abstract. This study presents a novel approach to support management scenarios using a large language model (LLM) based decision support system (DSS) that integrates a Rational Decision-Making (RDM) framework with ChatGPT to evaluate alternative courses for action. The automated evaluation considers the problem, company context, confounding factors, and outcomes' ramifications. 72 business professionals tested the system's feasibility using their own management decision cases, assessing DSS output across six parameters: understanding, multi-faceted deliberation, output reliability, explainability, originality, and applicability. Results indicate ChatGPT's feasibility for the DSS task, with scores generally at or above 4 out of 5 across most parameters and domains. No significant differences were found across gender, business domains, or investment scenario types, suggesting consistent system performance. However, older and more experienced professionals assessed originality and applicability significantly more critically (Cohen's $d = 0.45$–0.61), indicating that domain expertise raises expectations for creative and practically grounded recommendations.

Keywords: LLM · ChatGPT · decision support · management

1 Introduction

Rapid advancements in artificial intelligence (AI) have led to the creation of numerous decision-making tools. However, businesses may be hesitant to incorporate these tools into critical processes such as decision-making, as it remains uncertain whether they truly deliver tangible value in managing decision-making within organizations. This study tests LLM-based decision support to resolve various management scenarios. The study aims to determine the feasibility of LLM based approach for analyzing these scenarios and producing an output for decision-makers. Most often, uncertainty is the source of difficulty in making decisions. Experienced managers have a large amount of knowledge in their memory gained from training and experience. Decision-making can also be done intuitively [1].

This study proposes an LLM-based decision support system that integrates a Rational Decision Making (RDM) framework with ChatGPT to analyze management investment decision scenarios. The approach advances the state of the art by combining structured

K. Węcel and V. Řepa (Eds.): BIS 2026, LNBIP 584, pp. 114–127, 2026.
https://doi.org/10.1007/978-3-032-26363-6_9

decision-making methodology with LLM capabilities, enabling systematic evaluation of decision alternatives while leveraging the natural language processing strengths of modern AI. Unlike traditional DSS that require extensive data engineering, the proposed system accepts natural language input describing business contexts and decision scenarios, making it more accessible to practitioners.

1.1 Decision Support Systems

Decision support systems (DSS) are computer-based tools and technologies designed to support an organization's decision-making activities. These systems use data, models, and analytical techniques to provide decision-makers with information and insights to help them make better, more informed decisions [2]. Benefits of using DSS include improved decision-making quality and speed, increased efficiency and productivity, and better resource allocation. However, the effectiveness of a DSS depends on the quality of its data and models, as well as the skills and experience of the users who interact with it [3–5]. Conceptual developments have been made to enhance the capabilities of decision support systems. Demirkan and Delen developed a conceptual framework for cloud DSS. DSS in the cloud offers benefits such as increased scale, scope, and speed [6]. The advancement of AI tools has reached a point where they can be integrated into decision-making support systems for practical applications, and their impact on decision-making is now significant [7].

AI-based DSS uses machine learning algorithms, natural language processing, and other AI techniques to analyze data, identify patterns, and make predictions or recommendations to inform decision-making. One of the critical benefits of AI-based DSS is its ability to handle large amounts of data and identify patterns and trends that may take time to become apparent to human decision-makers. AI-based DSS can also learn from past decisions and outcomes and use this knowledge to improve its accuracy and effectiveness over time. Different types of AI-based DSS exist, including rule-based systems, expert systems, neural networks, and decision trees. Rule-based systems use a set of predefined rules to make decisions based on the input data. Expert systems use knowledge and expertise from domain experts to provide recommendations or advice. Neural networks use algorithms that mimic the structure and function of the human brain to identify patterns and make predictions. Decision trees use a graphical representation of decisions and their possible outcomes to guide decision-making [8–11].

1.2 Large Language Model as a Decision Support System

One of the main advantages of using LLMs as DSS is their ability to process unstructured data. LLMs can also generate summaries of complex data, such as financial reports or medical records [12, 13]. At the strategic level, AI can aid in data collection and analysis, guiding evaluations, and improving decision-making processes.

Recent research has increasingly explored LLMs as foundations for decision support systems in business contexts. Alkayyal et al. introduced StrategicAI, a system that decomposes strategic decisions using logic trees combined with GPT-4o, demonstrating that human-AI collaboration significantly outperformed standalone ChatGPT in both problem identification and solution generation across business case studies [14]. Handler et al. framed this shift conceptually, arguing that LLMs' emergent capabilities and general-purpose nature introduce fundamentally new questions for DSS design across all phases of decision-making [15]. However, critical limitations persist: Khaldy highlighted risks including training data biases, interpretability challenges, and domain knowledge gaps, recommending human-in-the-loop oversight and explainable AI techniques [16]. Spatharioti et al. empirically demonstrated that while LLM-based tools dramatically accelerate decisions, they also increase overreliance on incorrect outputs, particularly for complex tasks [17]. Eigner and Händler further systematized these concerns through a dependency framework identifying technological, psychological, and decision-specific determinants that shape LLM-assisted decision quality [18]. Smirnov et al. proposed an integrated augmented intelligence approach combining conversational, generative, and evaluative AI with context-awareness, emphasizing that final decisions should remain with humans [19].

Multi-agent architectures and knowledge-augmented frameworks have further improved LLM reliability and explainability in complex decision environments [20–22]. In operational domains, LLM-driven DSS frameworks have demonstrated practical value for manufacturing, supply chain management, and energy optimization through natural language interfaces and structured reasoning [23–25]. Group and organizational decision support has also been explored, with LLMs analyzing meeting transcripts and supporting collaborative deliberation [26, 27]. However, these systems typically address domain-specific or operational decisions rather than strategic management scenarios requiring holistic evaluation of alternatives, contextual factors, and outcome ramifications - the gap our study addresses.

Few studies adopt a structured rational decision-making framework comparable to the approach presented in this paper. In healthcare, several studies have demonstrated LLMs' capacity for systematic evaluation of alternatives, with systems achieving moderate to high effectiveness in clinical decision-making tasks [28–30]. Structured frameworks integrating LLMs with optimization methods have shown promise for multi-criteria decision evaluation [23, 24]. Notably, Wang et al. (2025) proposed a Data Space and LLM-enabled system for drug development that employs the Best-Worst Method for weighting decision pipelines, representing a structured multi-criteria approach conceptually aligned with rational decision-making principles [31]. Similarly, multi-agent architectures have been developed to synthesize diverse analytical perspectives into coherent recommendations [27, 32]. However, these approaches typically embed domain-specific optimization algorithms rather than implementing a generalizable rational decision-making methodology accessible through natural language input, which distinguishes the present work.

1.3 Rational Decision Making (RDM) Models

The Rational Decision Making (RDM) models are recognized models for decision-making processes. RDM models focus on determining the most effective means of decision-making when presented with choices in well-structured situations. These provide a logical, systematic, and structured approach to decision-making. It is based on the assumption that individuals clearly understand their goals and objectives and can identify all available options and their potential outcomes. The model is widely used and effective for decision-making. It provides a clear and structured approach to decision-making that can be used in various contexts. However, it assumes that individuals have perfect information, which is often different in real-world decision-making situations. Therefore, the model should be used with other decision-making tools and techniques to ensure the best possible outcomes [7, 11].

RDM models utilize the rational, subjective utility model, which proposes that decision-makers strive to maximize the expected utility of available choices. This is achieved by developing utility functions that represent the decision maker's assessment of the relative weightings of each possible choice, thereby enabling the prediction and prescription of decisions [3].

The Rational Decision-Making models involve the following sequential steps [20, 21]: (1) **Identifying the problem**: This step involves identifying the problem or opportunity that requires a decision. It is essential to define the problem clearly and understand its root causes. (2) **Identifying the criteria or objectives of the decision**: In this step, the relevant information is gathered about the problem or opportunity. This includes quantitative and qualitative data and may involve conducting research, analyzing data, and seeking stakeholder input. (3) **Weighing or prioritizing the criteria**: Here, the criteria or objectives of the decision are weighed or prioritized. (4) **Identifying alternatives**: Based on the information gathered in step 2, a range of other options could solve the problem. It is essential to consider both obvious and less apparent alternatives and to evaluate their potential outcomes. (5) **Evaluating alternatives**: Each alternative is evaluated based on criteria or objectives, such as feasibility, cost, risk, and impact. This step involves weighing the pros and cons of each alternative and selecting the one that best meets the criteria. (6) **Computing and selecting the optimal alternative**: In this step, the alternative that is deemed to be the best is selected. This involves making a final decision and committing to a course of action.

2 Method

2.1 RDM as a Basis for LLM Driven DSS

In this work rational decision-making model is adapted to investment decision-making and tested as a LLM-based decision support system following these steps: Production or service deficiency → Investment decision criteria → Criteria prioritization → Course of action alternatives → Alternatives evaluation → Optimal solution for investment.

Our framework is based on a rational decision-making model for testing a large language model as a decision support system. In the first step, the researchers designed a prompt, which involves the first stages of RDM models: 1) Identifying the problem such as production or service deficiency; 2) Identifying the criteria or objectives of the investment decision 3) Weighing or prioritizing the criteria; and 4) Identifying alternative courses of action. The prompt instructs LLM to act as a decision support system by breaking down each step into a set of tasks that the model can perform. Test users adjusted input for their specific management decision scenario.

In the second step, the human test subjects interact with LLM, instructing it to complete the RDM stages: 5) Evaluating alternatives; and 6) Computing and selecting the optimal alternative for investment. Several sequential prompts instruct LLM to output relevant information for the given decision-making use case.

For example, in the case of production machinery investment alternatives, the model will include and analyze decision-relevant data, e.g., purchase price, maintenance costs, expected lifespan, and others. Also included is information about the company's financial condition and market outlook relevant to these products or services.

Based on this analysis, LLM could generate a report summarizing the risks and opportunities associated with investing in the production machinery. The report could include recommendations on which equipment to invest in.

The third step includes a human assessment of the LLM's decision support output. Test users analyze the output and determine its validity using personal expertise. An assessment framework developed by the lead author is used to provide a numerical evaluation of relevant decision support criteria.

2.2 System Design

This system is the combination of prompt engineering, LLM (ChatGPT), and RDM, which collectively act as a decision support system. The system includes the following components: (1) **Management decision scenario:** Provides context and sets the stage for the decision-making process. (2) **Business input:** The decision options (option 1, option 2, … option n) and the corresponding parameters for each option. These parameters include cost, risk, potential benefits, and other relevant factors. (3) **Decision criteria:** Serves as the basis for evaluating and comparing the decision options, e.g. financial viability, strategic alignment, feasibility. (4) **Resource availabilities**: Real-life restrictions related to resource availability, such as budget constraints, workforce limitations, time constraints, or the availability of raw materials. (5) **Prompt:** The prompt given to the virtual assistant providing the necessary information about the decision scenario, options, parameters, and criteria. (6) **Virtual Assistant:** Interface that interacts with the user, receives the prompt and manages the communication between the user and the system components. (7) **LLM (GPT-4o):** Processes the prompt provided by the virtual assistant and performs the following activities: Understanding options, Matching, Recommendation generation, Sensitivity analysis, Explanation. (8) **Rational decision-making model (RDM)**: Author's configured underlying decision-making framework a systematic to evaluate the decision options. It encompasses steps such as problem identification, gathering information, evaluating alternatives, making a decision, and implementing and monitoring the decision.

2.3 Prompt Design

Most businesses operate conservatively and are subject to well-established business theories and models. We used the rational decision maker (RDM) model to structure system inputs. In this study, the management decision scenarios were limited to investment decisions.

The prompts and dialogue were designed and planned, considering the context window of the LLM. The prompts were structured to include the following components of a management decision scenario: (1) **Task description**: process description and the protocol for the dialogue. (2) **Enterprise**: size, workers, types of facilities, activity history if relevant. (3) **Values**: guiding business values relevant to the decision-making. (4) **Product**: description of product or service that needs investment. (5) **Customers**: the main customer types and why they use the products/services. (6) **Decision**: requirements for the structure and the content of system output. (7) **Context**: business activity, the operating environment, internal and external. (8) **Confounding factors**: factors relevant to the scenario and investment. (9) **Situation**: the company's challenging situation, actors and challenges. (10) **Problem statement**: problem formulation and highlighting the critical process. (11) **Limitations**: all relevant limitations that may limit the available options, e.g., financial, human resource, market, etc. (12) **Case content**: narrowing down the decision to specific content, e.g., offers and product sheets from the suppliers of new machinery. (13) **Alternative actions**: options on management's table, including details, like initial cost, expected ROI per a given time, expected cost-benefit etc. (14) **Ramifications**: possible outcomes per each alternative action. This includes characterizing: the needed resources, e.g., a need to apply for a loan; the capabilities of the company to service the resources required over short and long periods; organizational, technological, and personnel changes, e.g., training, maintenance, etc.; the expected lifetime of the innovation; how the market and the competitors would react; and other relevant factors. (Link to prompt template)

2.4 Assessment Framework

Assessment of the LLM's output was carried out using a questionnaire. For each LLM, 19 questions formed six variables designed to characterize the decision support output concerning the given management scenario. Additional questions were asked to characterize the respondent's age and professional tenure. The variables were assessed on a 5-point Likert scale, where 1-"Do not agree"…5-"Totally agree"; points 2, 3, and 4 were left undefined for the continuous scale (Link to questionnaire). Next, an overview of variables is given with the number of questions in parenthesis (N). (1) **Understanding (N = 4):** Whether the assistant understood the company's context, problem, financial constraints, and available options. (2) **Multifaceted deliberation (N = 4):** Assistant's ability to provide well-considered answers on the basis of the company's values, context, and financial capabilities. (3) **Reliability of output (N = 3):** The degree to which the assistant's answers align with those of an experienced business consultant and the extent to which the assistant can make optimal decisions. (4) **Explainability (N = 3):** The logical coherence and transparency of the assistant's answers and the extent to which the assistant can provide additional explanations. (5) **Originality (N = 2):** Ability to provide innovative solutions and ideas that may not have been previously considered. (6) **Applicability (N = 3):** Are answers practical and relevant to real-life limitations?

2.5 Sample

The questionnaire was published electronically in Moodle's online learning platform, where the respondents were taking courses. Business professionals were instructed to use the assistant to output decision-support information. Based on median value, subsamples were formed on age and professional tenure. The sample consisted of 72 people, including 45 females and 27 males. Participants were from executive education and MBA-level courses at the university. They represented a variety of business domains, including production and manufacturing, services (retail, IT, healthcare, consulting), transportation and logistics, and public sector organizations.

Subgroups Categorized by Age: The median age was 42 years. The sample was divided into two subsamples based on age: "younger" (N = 31) and "older" (N = 41). The average age was also 42, whereas the minimum was 24 and the maximum was 62.

Subgroups Categorized by the Duration of Professional Experience: The median professional tenure was calculated at 20 years; likewise, two subsamples were formed: "novices" with less than 20 years of experience (N = 31) and "experienced" (N = 41). The average professional tenure was 18.7, with a minimum of 1 and a maximum of 45 years.

2.6 Test Procedure and Use Cases

Test users tested assistants and subjected each to a management scenario of their choosing. Prompts and dialogues were done in English. Prompts are entered sequentially to avoid text input limits. The user asks a series of control questions to ensure the LLM understands the task and the expected result. The assistant is then asked to suggest the best option for the given management scenario and provide argumentation, highlighting strengths and weaknesses. Next, the assistant is asked to argue why the other alternative options are less worthy and what their strengths and weaknesses are. For each alternative option, the assistant is asked how these match the company's values. Additionally, it is asked if other courses of action can be considered.

Test subjects referred to management decision use cases and all investment decision scenarios. The authors later analyzed these and divided them into three main investment scenarios, which served as subgroups for comparing the mean scores of decision support variables. The decision scenarios were the following (N shows how many test subjects used that scenario): (1) **Investing into hardware:** including machinery, equipment, facilities, and vehicles (N = 42). (2) **Investing into the main product or service development:** including R&D, IT enhancement, software, etc. (N = 13). (3) **Investing into support services:** including organization management, business model, HR, facilities maintenance, procurement, customer service, accounting, etc. (N = 17).

Additionally, the use cases were analyzed for sectorial features and were determined to take place in one of the following business domains: (1) **Production:** including hardware, mechanical parts, vehicles, food, textiles, ICT devices, utilities, etc. (N = 39). (2) **Service:** including retail, wholesale, ICT, healthcare, media, construction, cleaning, software development, consulting, travel, tourism, HR services, etc. (N = 28). (3) **Transportation:** including logistics, land, and sea transport (N = 3). (4) **Others:** including public sector (N = 2).

2.7 Statistical Analysis

The evaluation pursued three main goals: (1) to determine the overall quality of the LLM-based DSS output across six quality criteria (understanding, multifaceted deliberation, reliability, explainability, originality, and applicability); (2) to examine whether demographic factors (gender, age, professional experience) influence the assessment of DSS quality; and (3) to identify correlations between the quality criteria to understand interdependencies in DSS performance.

A structured questionnaire approach was followed to collect the questionnaire data. The results were collected in tabular format on a local machine. Descriptive statistics - scores as averages for each variable, together with standard deviations were calculated based on the structure introduced in Subsect. 2.4. A two-tailed Pearson product-moment correlation analysis was conducted to evaluate the relationship between the variables. While individual Likert-scale items are ordinal, each variable in this study is a composite average of 3–4 items, producing approximately continuous scores. Research has demonstrated that parametric statistics, including Pearson correlation, are robust when applied to such composite Likert-scale data [33] Significant correlations were flagged (* at .05 and ** at .01 level). To test the subgroup differences, an independent sample t-test was conducted. Additionally, the assumption of homogeneity of variances was checked using Levene's F test, where $p < .05$ was considered statistically significant. Assumption checks were conducted prior to analysis. When homogeneity of variance was violated (Levene's test, $p < .05$), Welch's t-test was applied instead of the standard independent samples t-test. Group differences among three or more groups were assessed using one-way ANOVA, with normality (Shapiro–Wilk test) and homogeneity (Levene's test) verified beforehand. Significant ANOVA results would be followed by Tukey's HSD post hoc test. Effect sizes were reported as Cohen's d for t-tests and eta-squared ($\eta 2$) for ANOVA. Statistical calculations were done with IBM SPSS Statistics 29.0.

3 Results

Descriptive statistics were performed to compare subsample means. Each variable's average score was calculated based on how the business professionals assessed the assistants' decision support output.

Gender-based subsamples were analyzed, and variables were compared pairwise. None of the variables returned statistical significance ($p > .05$), meaning men and women have assessed the variables highly similarly. Table 1 shows variables' mean scores (M) and standard deviations (SD) for gender-based subgroups.

Next, age-based subgroups' were analyzed to determine if they assessed variables differently. Indeed, a statistically significant difference was found in variable 5-originality $t(60) = 2.5$, $p = .013$, and variable 6-applicability $t(53) = 2.1$, $p = .040$. Older business professionals value ChatGPT's decision support output more critically, resulting in lower scores. The effect sizes for the significant age-based differences were medium to large (Cohen's d = .61 for originality, d = .50 for applicability).

Similarly, experience-based subgroups showed a statistically significant difference in variable 5-originality $t(66.9) = 2.6$, $p = .012$, and a marginally significant difference in variable 6-applicability $t(64.1) = 2.0$, $p = .052$, with novice professionals rating the DSS output more favorably than experienced professionals on both variables. Effect sizes were comparable (Cohen's d = .59 for originality, d = .45 for applicability), indicating medium practical differences between novice and experienced professionals.

Table 1. Average scores for ChatGPT's decision support by demographic subgroup, M(SD)

Variable	Males	Females	Younger	Older	Novices	Experienced
1. Understanding	4.5 (.5)	4.5 (.6)	4.6 (.6)	4.5 (.5)	4.5 (.6)	4.5 (.5)
2. Multifaceted deliberation	4.2 (.8)	4.2 (.8)	4.3 (.6)	4.0 (.9)	4.4 (.6)	4.1 (.9)
3. Reliability of output	3.8 (.9)	4.0 (1.0)	4.0 (.8)	3.9 (1.1)	4.0 (.7)	4.0 (1.1)
4. Explainability	4.3 (.8)	4.4 (.8)	4.5 (.5)	4.2 (1.0)	4.5 (.5)	4.2 (.9)
5. Originality	4.0 (1.0)	4.0 (1.3)	4.3 (.9)	3.6 (1.3)	4.4 (.9)	3.7 (1.3)
6. Applicability	4.0 (1.0)	4.0 (1.0)	4.2 (.7)	3.8 (1.2)	4.2 (.7)	3.8 (1.1)

A one-way analysis of variance (ANOVA) was conducted to determine if different management decision scenarios received different scores on decision support variables. ANOVA was performed separately on investment scenarios and business domains, as these categories had three or more subgroups. For both analyses, all variables returned statistically insignificant differences within subgroups ($p > .05$). Table 2 displays business domain-based subgroup scores, and Table 3 shows investment scenario-based subgroup scores. Effect sizes were small for both analyses (investment scenarios: $\eta 2$ ranging from .001 to .051; business domains: $\eta 2$ ranging from .011 to .077), confirming that the type of investment scenario or business domain explained very little variance in the assessment scores.

Pearson's correlation analysis showed notable correlations between the six measured variables (Table 4). Strong correlations ($r > .7$) were detected between 2-deliberation and 4-explainability; also between 2-deliberation and 6-applicability, additionally between 4-explainability and 6-applicability; and even between 5-originality and 6-applicability. All correlations were significant ($p < .01$).

Table 2. Average scores for ChatGPT's decision support output, business domain-based subgroups (Hardw.-investing into hardware, Prod. or serv.-investing into main product or service development, Sup. serv.-investing into support services).

Variable	Hardw.	Prod. or ser.	Sup. serv.
1. Understanding	4.6	4.5	4.3
2. Multifaceted deliberation	4.2	4.2	4.1
3. Reliability of output	4.1	3.8	3.9
4. Explainability	4.4	4.4	4.2
5. Originality	4.1	3.8	3.8
6. Applicability	4.0	4.1	3.8

Table 3. Average scores for ChatGPT's decision support output, investment scenario-based subgroups (Prod.-production, Serv.-service, Transp.-transportation, Oth-others).

Variable	Prod.	Serv.	Transp.	Oth.
1. Understanding	4.6	4.5	4.2	4.8
2. Multifaceted deliberation	4.2	4.3	3.5	4.5
3. Reliability of output	4.0	3.9	3.1	4.5
4. Explainability	4.4	4.4	3.4	5.0
5. Originality	4.1	3.9	3.8	3.5
6. Applicability	4.0	4.1	3.6	4.2

Table 4. Pearson's correlation coefficients between the main variables of ChatGPT-based decision support system output. ** Correlation is significant at the .01 level

Variable	1-und	2-delib	3-rel	4-exp	5-orig	6-app
1. Understanding (und)	1					
2. Multifaceted deliberation (delib)	58**	1				
3. Reliability of output (rel)	.35**	.65**	1			
4. Explainability (exp)	.57**	.74**	69**	1		
5. Originality (orig)	.32**	.58**	.54**	.51**	1	
6. Applicability (app)	.57**	.79**	.68**	.74**	.70**	1

4 Discussion

In healthcare, LLMs have been evaluated as decision support tools with moderate effectiveness, achieving scores around 3.7–4.5 out of 5 depending on specialization and system design, while highlighting the importance of structured prompting and domain-specific adaptation [28, 34, 35].

In this study, the strong positive correlations among key variables reveal interconnected capabilities essential for effective decision support. Assistants skilled at multifaceted deliberation-considering multiple facets of company values and financial capabilities-tend to excel at both explainability and applicability. This suggests that systematic, thorough thinking enables clearer communication of reasoning and more feasible recommendations that account for practical limitations. Similarly, the correlation between explainability and applicability indicates that assistants who communicate their reasoning effectively are more likely to consider real-world constraints when making recommendations. The link between originality and applicability further suggests that creative thinking may facilitate innovative solutions that nonetheless remain practically grounded. Demographic analysis revealed that older, more experienced professionals assess ChatGPT's output more critically, particularly regarding originality and applicability-possibly reflecting higher expectations for innovation or generational differences in AI acceptance. Notably, no significant gender-based differences emerged, indicating equitable system performance. The absence of significant variation across business domains and investment scenarios suggests uniform performance, though specialized systems might outperform generalized ones in specific contexts, warranting further research. These findings carry important implications for DSS development. User feedback mechanisms should be incorporated for continuous improvement, and training regimes must develop assistants' capabilities across multifaceted deliberation, explainability, originality, and applicability simultaneously. The major challenge in utilizing intelligent decision support systems for actual problems is building trust in them [7]. Transparency and explainability are qualities that could enhance user comprehension of decision-making processes within the system. It can aid in identifying potential biases or systematic errors, paving the way for rectification or mitigation strategies [36–38].

Despite the encouraging results, it is important to acknowledge the potential risks of overreliance on LLM-generated recommendations. LLMs may produce plausible-sounding but factually incorrect or contextually inappropriate advice, a phenomenon often referred to as "hallucination." Therefore, human oversight remains essential: the LLM-based DSS should be viewed as a decision support tool that augments, rather than replaces, human judgment.

Regarding domain-specific performance, the transportation domain (N = 3) and support services exhibited lower scores on several variables, including reliability of output (3.1 and 3.9, respectively) and applicability (3.6 and 3.8). While the ANOVA did not detect statistically significant differences, likely due to the small and unequal subgroup sizes, these lower scores may suggest that ChatGPT performs less effectively in specialized or operationally complex domains. These observations point to areas where domain-specific fine-tuning or supplementary data could improve performance.

5 Conclusions

The findings show that ChatGPT is a viable option for the DSS task, as it achieved high scores (generally 4 or above out of 5 for most domains) across all the measured decision support parameters. The highly rated parameter "Understanding" (4.5/5) indicates that the business professionals recognized ChatGPT's capability to understand the company's context, problems, financial constraints, and available options.

Older and more experienced professionals assessed the system's output significantly more critically on originality and applicability (Cohen's d ranging from .45 to .61), suggesting that greater domain expertise raises expectations for creative and practically grounded decision support. No significant differences were found across gender, business domains, or investment scenario types, indicating that the LLM-based DSS performs consistently regardless of context or user gender.

The results highlight the following criteria for designing effective DSS assistants that are more likely to provide effective solutions to companies' challenges: (1) Assistants must be skilled at considering multiple facets of the company's values and financial capabilities. (2) An assistant is to be able to provide logical and transparent explanations of their decisions. (3) An assistant is something that can think creatively and offer managers unique perspectives on a situation. (4) The assistant also needs to be able to provide practical and relevant recommendations considering company's real-life limitations. This study underscores the potential of LLM-based AI conversational assistants like ChatGPT in augmenting management decision-making, particularly in situations involving complex problems, and, with the help of business practitioners, provides evidence of their effectiveness in decision support roles.

Disclosure of Interests. The authors have no competing interests to declare that are relevant to the content of this article.

References

1. Simon, H.A.: Making management decisions: the role of intuition and emotion. Acad. Manag. Perspect. **1**, 57–64 (1987)
2. El-Najdawi, M.K., Stylianou, A.C.: Expert support systems: integrating AI technologies. Commun. ACM. **36**, 55-ff (1993)
3. Power, D.J.: Web-based and model-driven decision support systems: concepts and issues. In: AMCIS 2000 Proceedings, p. 387 (2000)
4. Power, D.J., Sharda, R.: Model-driven decision support systems: concepts and research directions. Decis. Support. Syst. **43**, 1044–1061 (2007). https://doi.org/10.1016/J.DSS.2005.05.030
5. Power, D.J.: Supporting decision-makers: an expanded framework. Inf. Sci. **1**, 1901–1915 (2001)
6. Demirkan, H., Delen, D.: Leveraging the capabilities of service-oriented decision support systems: putting analytics and big data in cloud. Decis. Support. Syst. **55**, 412–421 (2013)
7. Phillips-Wren, G.: AI tools in decision making support systems: a review. Int. J. Artif. Intell. Tools **21**, 1240005 (2012)
8. Quah, T.S., Tan, C.L., Raman, K.S., Srinivasan, B.: Towards integrating rule-based expert systems and neural networks. Decis. Support. Syst. **17**, 99–118 (1996). https://doi.org/10.1016/0167-9236(95)00016-X

9. Li, H., Love, P.E.D.: Combining rule-based expert systems and artificial neural networks for mark-up estimation. Constr. Manag. Econ. **17**, 169–176 (1999). https://doi.org/10.1080/014461999371664
10. Huysmans, J., Dejaeger, K., Mues, C., Vanthienen, J., Baesens, B.: An empirical evaluation of the comprehensibility of decision table, tree and rule based predictive models. Decis. Support. Syst. **51**, 141–154 (2011). https://doi.org/10.1016/J.DSS.2010.12.003
11. Aronson, J.E., Liang, T.-P., MacCarthy, R.V.: Decision Support Systems and Intelligent Systems. Pearson Prentice-Hall, Upper Saddle River (2005)
12. Bang, Y., et al.: A multitask, multilingual, multimodal evaluation of ChatGPT on reasoning, hallucination, and interactivity. In: Park, J.C., et al.: (eds.) Proceedings of the 13th International Joint Conference on Natural Language Processing and the 3rd Conference of the Asia-Pacific Chapter of the Association for Computational Linguistics (Volume 1: Long Papers), pp. 675–718. Association for Computational Linguistics, Nusa Dua, Bali (2023). https://doi.org/10.18653/v1/2023.ijcnlp-main.45
13. Liu, Y., et al.: Summary of ChatGPT-related research and perspective towards the future of large language models. Meta-Radiology **1**, 100017 (2023). https://doi.org/10.1016/J.METRAD.2023.100017
14. Alkayyal, M.: An LLM-based decision support system for strategic decision-making in business environments (2025)
15. Handler, A., Larsen, K.R., Hackathorn, R.: Large language models present new questions for decision support. Int. J. Inf. Manag. **79**, 102811 (2024). https://doi.org/10.1016/J.IJINFOMGT.2024.102811
16. Al Khaldy, M., Gheraibia, Y.: Evaluation and mitigation of the limitations of large language models in business decision-making. In: 2025 1st International Conference on Computational Intelligence Approaches and Applications (ICCIAA), pp. 1–6. IEEE (2025)
17. Spatharioti, S.E., Rothschild, D., Goldstein, D.G., Hofman, J.M.: Effects of LLM-based search on decision making: Speed, accuracy, and overreliance. In: Proceedings of the 2025 CHI Conference on Human Factors in Computing Systems, pp. 1–15 (2025)
18. Eigner, E., Händler, T.: Determinants of LLM-assisted Decision-Making. arXiv. abs/2402.17385 (2024)
19. Smirnov, A., Ponomarev, A., Shilov, N., Levashova, T.: LLM-assisted augmented intelligence for context-aware decision support: current trends and integrated approach. Proc. Copyr. **409**, 416 (2025)
20. Chen, M., Tao, Z., Tang, W., Qin, T., Yang, R., Zhu, C.: Enhancing emergency decision-making with knowledge graphs and large language models. Int. J. Disaster Risk Reduct. **113**, 104804 (2024). https://doi.org/10.1016/J.IJDRR.2024.104804
21. Öğdü, Ç.U., Arslanoğlu, K., Karaköse, M.: An adaptive multi-agent LLM-based clinical decision support system integrating biomedical rag and web intelligence. IEEE Access (2025)
22. Park, C., Lee, H., Lee, S., Jeong, O.: Synergistic joint model of knowledge graph and LLM for enhancing XAI-based clinical decision support systems. Mathematics **13** (2025). https://doi.org/10.3390/math13060949
23. Du, K., et al.: LLM-MANUF: an integrated framework of fine-tuning large language models for intelligent decision-making in manufacturing. Adv. Eng. Inform. **65**, 103263 (2025). https://doi.org/10.1016/J.AEI.2025.103263
24. Wong, K.K.L., Deng, L., Liu, Y., Li, A., Tu, J.: Design and implementation of a local LLM-driven decision support system for AI-enhanced supply chain management. J. Eng. Des., 1–27 (2026)
25. Li, H., Fu, X., Wang, K., Peng, J.: An LLM-assisted decision-making framework of rule-based control strategy for photovoltaic driven air conditioning systems. Energy **340**, 139328 (2025). https://doi.org/10.1016/J.ENERGY.2025.139328

26. Lubos, S., et al.: Towards group decision support with LLM-based meeting analysis. In: Adjunct Proceedings of the 33rd ACM Conference on User Modeling, Adaptation and Personalization, pp. 331–335. Association for Computing Machinery, New York (2025). https://doi.org/10.1145/3708319.3733646
27. Kalyuzhnaya, A., et al.: LLM agents for smart city management: enhancing decision support through multi-agent AI systems. Smart Cities **8**, 19 (2025)
28. Ammo, T., et al.: Evaluating ChatGPT-4o as a decision support tool in multidisciplinary sarcoma tumor boards: heterogeneous performance across various specialties. Front. Oncol. **14-2024** (2025). https://doi.org/10.3389/fonc.2024.1526288
29. Deng, R., et al.: CPGPrompt: translating clinical guidelines into LLM-executable decision support. arXiv preprint arXiv:2601.03475 (2026)
30. Hou, R., Xue, D., Sun, H., He, P., Zhang, W., Ruan, T.: CDAFlow: enhancing LLM clinical decision-making through agentic workflow. Expert Syst. Appl. **316**, 131806 (2026). https://doi.org/10.1016/J.ESWA.2026.131806
31. Wang, C., Ming, X., Zhang, X., Xu, J.: Data space and LLM enabled decision-making support system: an application in drug development. In: 2025 2nd International Conference on Electronic Engineering and Information Systems (EEISS), pp. 1–5. IEEE (2025)
32. Yu, Y., et al.: FINCON: a synthesized LLM multi-agent system with conceptual verbal reinforcement for enhanced financial decision making. Adv. Neural. Inf. Process. Syst. **37**, 137010–137045 (2024)
33. Norman, G.: Likert scales, levels of measurement and the "laws" of statistics. Adv. Health Sci. Educ. **15**, 625–632 (2010)
34. Jung, D., Butler, A., Park, J., Saperstein, Y.: Evaluating the impact of a specialized LLM on physician experience in clinical decision support: a comparison of ask Avo and ChatGPT-4. arXiv preprint arXiv:2409.15326 (2024)
35. Dymm, B., Goldenholz, D.M.: Prompting is all you need: how to make LLMs more helpful for clinical decision support. medRxiv. 2022–2026 (2026)
36. Dwivedi, R., et al.: Explainable AI (XAI): core ideas, techniques, and solutions. ACM Comput. Surv. **55**, 1–33 (2023)
37. Candelon, F., Evgeniou, T., Martens, D.: AI can be both accurate and transparent. https://hbr.org/ (2023)
38. Wirtz, B.W., Weyerer, J.C., Sturm, B.J.: The dark sides of artificial intelligence: an integrated AI governance framework for public administration. Int. J. Public Adm. **43**, 818–829 (2020)

Process Management and Automation

Unbottling the Bottlenecks: Analyzing the Consumer Process of Deposit Beverage Packaging Using a Human-Logged Process Mining Approach

Jeroen Baijens(✉), Paul Simonis, and Henri Duijsens

Knowledge Centre Data Intelligence, Zuyd University of Applied Sciences, Nieuw Eyckholt 300, 6419 DJ Heerlen, The Netherlands
jeroen.baijens@zuyd.nl

Abstract. Although recycling beverage packaging is increasingly important to reduce pollution and advance the circular economy, return rate targets are rarely achieved. In this exploratory research, which includes a case study guided by the PM^2 model, we investigate how process mining can be applied to identify constraints in the consumer process of deposit beverage packaging. To collect data, participants were asked to manually log their activities with deposit beverage packages. Our analysis, based on 74 collected cases, distinguished two cycles: short (process completion within 8 h) and long (process completion after 8 h). Within this distinction, descriptives show that the consumer-end process in short-cycles primarily leads to disposal, whereas in long-cycles it tends to result in the return of the packaging. These findings suggest that the short-cycle consumer process of deposit beverage packaging is an important constraint that limits the total return rate within our sample. Our case study gives rise to a novel approach to process mining that can help overcome some of the current pitfalls in process mining: Human-Logged Process Mining (HLPM). Our case study, together with our HLPM approach, show how process mining can contribute to the enhancement of a circular economy.

Keywords: Process Mining · Recycling Processes · Deposit Return Systems · Sustainability · Circular Economy

1 Introduction

Society is currently facing the urgent challenge of becoming more sustainable in order to meet environmental targets [8]. A critical aspect of this transition involves re-evaluating how waste streams are managed. In particular, end-of-use beverage packaging has come under increasing scrutiny due to the vast quantities of plastic packaging produced annually [23], underscoring the need to develop systems that promote reuse and recycling [40].

K. Węcel and V. Řepa (Eds.): BIS 2026, LNBIP 584, pp. 131–142, 2026.
https://doi.org/10.1007/978-3-032-26363-6_10

One effective strategy to extend the lifespan of packaging materials is the implementation of 'deposit return systems' (DRS). DRS incentivize consumers to return packaging by requiring an additional deposit at the point of purchase, which is refunded upon return of the packaging to designated collection points. DRS serve multiple purposes: they improve the quality and quantity of collected materials, reduce litter, and shift end-of-life responsibility to producers [38]. However, despite the introduction of DRS, not all packaging is successfully returned [40].

During the consumer process, which begins when the consumer takes possession of the deposit beverage packaging and ends when it is no longer in their possession, there is a risk that the packaging may be lost before it is returned, leading to several issues: it may end up as litter, or it may disrupt the efficiency of the reuse supply chain [15, 23, 29]. Therefore, developing effective DRS requires a deeper understanding of the consumer process with deposit beverage packaging. Such insights can help to optimize the return process and better support consumers in returning their packaging [23].

To gain this understanding, a data-driven analytical approach is needed to reconstruct and analyze real-world processes based on digital traces [23, 38, 40]. A promising method for this purpose is process mining, which is a technique that uses event data to describe and analyze processes, find bottlenecks, and identify opportunities for improvement [33]. Process mining for recycling, and particularly for DRS, represents a novel application area. Its novelty stems from different pitfalls when applying process mining, such as the availability of event logs from information systems, knowledge, and budget [13]. Nevertheless, process mining itself is a well-established and powerful analytical technique for advancing sustainability as it enables organizations to monitor processes, make processes more transparent, identify inefficiencies, and support improvements with empirical data [10].

Based on this, the objective of this study is to gain a deeper understanding of consumer processes surrounding DRS by employing process mining. The corresponding research question addressed in this study is:

How can process mining be applied to identify constraints in the consumer process of deposit beverage packaging?

To answer this question, deposit-related data was manually collected through a case study to generate an event log. This event log is then analyzed using process mining techniques to identify key constraints in the process. Based on this endeavor, we introduce Human-Logged Process Mining (HLPM), which is a process mining approach that uses manually recorded data by humans and can help overcome the current pitfalls when applying process mining to enhance sustainability.

We make three contributions with our work. Our first contribution is methodological. We employ HLPM in consumer processes to investigate constraints in DRS which is, to the best of our knowledge, unexplored in the current process mining and information systems literature. With this, we offer a novel approach to traditional process mining that helps overcome the current pitfalls when using process mining to enhance the circular economy. Also, we respond to recent academic calls to leverage process mining for enhancing circular processes, including reverse logistics and waste management [10].

Our second contribution is theoretical. Scholars have recently called that "building a suitable, efficient and convenient recycling system and improving the formal recycling rate of beverage packaging have become issues that need to be urgently resolved" [40, p. 2]. In our study, we address this call and investigate constraints in DRS with the aim of finding possibilities to increase return rates in DRS. More specifically, we add to the literature on DRS that, in our relatively homogeneous albeit small sample, the consumer process of deposit beverage packaging can be divided into two cycles: short (process completion within 8 h) and long (process completion after 8 h) and that the former one may yield the most potential to increase return rates.

Our third contribution lies in practice. Our case study and the introduction of HLPM together set the stage for scholars and practitioners in process mining. It enables them to collect data from processes that are not captured through automated systems. This approach makes it possible to identify constraints that limit progress toward a circular economy.

The remainder of this paper is structured as follows. First, we review the existing literature on DRS and process mining to establish the current state of research in the field. Next, we outline the research approach and present case study results. Finally, the discussion and conclusion are provided.

2 Research Background and Approach

This section introduces the theoretical background and outlines the research approach. It explains the role of DRS in the circular economy, the potential of process mining for analyzing consumer processes, and how these concepts are combined in our case study.

2.1 Deposit Return Systems

End-of-use beverage packaging causes major environmental pollution [11]. The recycling of beverage packaging is among the most powerful solutions to reduce this pollution [14], as the recycling of beverage packaging greatly contributes to reducing the emission of greenhouse gas [5]. To increase the recycling of beverage packaging, countries have implemented DRS in which "consumers pay deposits that are added to the price of products and receive refunds when they return the used products" [22, p. 303].

Originally, DRS were implemented since the 1970s in Sweden, Germany, Canada and some states in the US [40]. Currently, more than 40 countries worldwide employ DRS. While DRS initially was invented to save production costs [22], in the last decades DRS have been recognized as an efficient instrument to increase recycling [26]. Also, a well-functioning DRS is important to an effective circular economy [40] as it requires a closed-loop system [31]. Although it has been argued that a recycling rate of 95% can be achieved through the implementation of DRS [3], not all countries are able to reach this target. For instance, in Europe recycling rates range from 97% in Finland to 55% in Romania with only 2 out of 16 reporting countries achieving a return rate of 95% [25]. Consequently, there is a consensus that return rates should further be increased [16].

Although scholarship has acknowledged the importance of the efficient design of DRS to increase return rates [40], limited research has empirically investigated the potential of how improving DRS can enhance recycling rates [23]. In particular, much of the literature focuses on a theoretical analysis [1, 2] and the effectiveness of DRS in a specific country [19, 20]. Additionally, with the increase of the use of smart technology in waste management, new opportunities to monitor and improve recycling processes emerge under the label of 'intelligent recycling' [40]. A promising technique that may further enhance intelligent recycling is process mining, further explained in the following section.

2.2 Process Mining

Process mining is a data-driven approach that enables organizations to analyze their actual business processes based on event data [33]. This data is traditionally extracted from a firm's business information system and logged during daily process executions [24, 34, 37]. Instead of relying on predefined models or assumptions, process mining extracts insights directly from event data to reveal how processes are executed in practice [33]. The event data is often collected in event logs and must contain at least three key attributes: caseID, activity, and timestamp. The caseID uniquely identifies each process instance, the activity denotes the specific task that has been executed, and the timestamp records the moment at which the activity occurred.

Process mining comprises three primary analytical techniques: discovery, conformance, and enhancement. Discovery focuses on reconstructing a process model from event data. Conformance examines whether the observed process aligns with an existing model and vice versa. Enhancement aims to improve the process by identifying opportunities for optimization [33].

Process mining is gaining heightened attention from practitioners, with the increasing use of business information systems [32]. Its ability to provide insights into processes and optimize them based on event data and its application is well established in sectors such as manufacturing and healthcare. For example, it has been utilized to analyze and improve efficiency in production processes [27] and to improve patient care in hospitals [30].

Beyond efficiency improvements, process mining is increasingly recognized as a promising technique for enhancing sustainability in businesses. For instance, scholars have recently emphasized that there is a growing need for methods that integrate sustainability into process optimization and that process mining can play a key role in redesigning processes to reduce waste and use resources more efficiently [10]. This potential is illustrated by a case study, that applies process mining to reduce waste in food retail by analyzing stochastic processes [12]. Despite its promise for sustainability, process mining has seen limited application in recycling contexts, such as DRS.

Within DRS, understanding behavioral patterns are pivotal to achieving success, yet data collection on these patterns is inherently challenging, particularly when it comes to capturing event data from information systems. Nevertheless, process mining has previously been used to analyze behavioral patterns, as shown in a study that applied process mining to examine shopping behaviors in a mall setting [7]. This highlights process mining's versatility beyond operational processes, extending to behavioral studies.

One of the major challenges in process mining remains obtaining suitable data as many organizations lack event data that are directly usable [21]. While authors have acknowledged human's crucial role in the preparation of data for process mining [28], manual data collection by human activities has not been thoroughly investigated.

2.3 Research Approach

In response to a call to improve DRS, this study conducts an exploratory approach to investigate the consumer process of deposit beverage packaging using process mining techniques to gain data-driven insights. Therefore, we apply a case study based on student data to analyze a phenomenon in a natural setting [39]. The data for the case study was manually collected by students but set up in a structured manner to ensure a consistent and replicable data collection process, and a valid and reliable method, while still capturing naturalistic consumer behavior [17]. The methodology to guide the case study consisted of adapted steps from the PM^2 model [35], a well-known project methodology for process mining. The use of PM^2 ensures a systematic and transparent research process, from planning to process improvement.

3 Case Study: Consumer Process of Deposit Beverage Packaging

The steps conducted are based on the PM^2 model and include the following: (1) Planning, (2) Data Extraction and Processing, (3) Mining and analysis, (5) Evaluation, and (5) Process Improvement.

3.1 Planning

The main goal of this case study is to analyze the consumer process of deposit beverage packages, with the aim of identifying opportunities to improve return rates. By examining consumer process characteristics, such as return frequency, type of packaging, and potential barriers, this study seeks to uncover inefficiencies and patterns within DRS.

The process selected for analysis focuses specifically on the consumer process of students within DRS. This target group was chosen as young adults represent a meaningful and relevant demographic for studying return behavior [18]. As the most frequent consumers of single-use beverage packaging [6], they are well-positioned to provide insight into everyday deposit-return decisions. Insights drawn from this demographic can inform broader strategies aimed at improving return rates across diverse user groups. Also, younger people, on average, are more likely driven by self-interested behavior [36] which may result in a lower motivation to return beverage packages compared to other age groups [18]. Consequently, students likely demonstrate lower return rates in the consumer process and are therefore an important target group to increase return rates.

To prevent ambiguity between the research questions addressed in this paper and those pertaining to the case study, we designate the latter as 'Project Questions' (PQs) throughout this work. The PQs to the case study are:

- PQ1. What does the discovered process model reveal about the consumer process within DRS, and how is it performing?
- PQ2. Which process characteristics are associated with the return rate, based on the discovered process model?

3.2 Data Extraction and Processing

To extract data on the consumer process related to deposit beverage packaging, students collected data based on their personal interactions with deposit beverage packages in their daily life. The data was collected between February 11th and March 10th, 2025, involving 40 second-year Industrial Engineering & Management students from a large University of Applied Sciences in the Netherlands. As part of their coursework in the 'Data Modeling and Evaluation' course, each student was required to track their deposit beverage packages over the course of that period.

Students were instructed to behave as naturally as possible and not to alter their routines due to the data collection. To ensure consistency and data quality, students were provided with a detailed data dictionary (available in the online supplementary materials[1]), which specified the required structure and definitions for each data entry. This included fields such as *caseID*, *activity*, *timestamp*, and optional attributes. The data dictionary was refined based on a pilot study with a small group of students conducted during the previous teaching block, which helped identify feasible activities to track and provided the researcher with practical experience in data collection. Moreover, the participating students were assessed on the quality of their contributions, which formed an integral part of the overall course evaluation. This supported the adherence of the collected data to the necessary quality standards. Although the core activities were predefined, students were allowed to include additional events they considered relevant, such as *refilling* or *transporting* deposit beverage packages. While these were more difficult to standardize in the analysis, they offered valuable insights for future research.

To facilitate data collection, students were encouraged to use the smartphone app 'Anylog', which supports manual event tracking. This app enabled students to record events more easily, improving the accuracy and granularity of the data. The collected data was transformed into a structured event log suitable for process mining. Since each student collected their data individually, the datasets were subsequently consolidated into a single event log. The initial event log contained 86 cases. However, after inspection, several cases were removed due to incompleteness or incorrect usage of the data dictionary. These cases were deemed irrelevant for analysis. As a result, the final event log consisted of 74 usable cases, comprising a total of 380 events across 12 distinct activities.

3.3 Mining and Analysis

The mining and analysis is structured around two parts, each corresponding to a different PQ. To address PQ1, the event log used in the first analysis contains all defined activities and paths. Based on this event log, the first process model was mined, using all events (380) and cases (74). The model was generated in DISCO as a Directly-follows Graph (DFG) [9]. Due to the high number of process variants, the initial model resulted in a dense and unstructured DFG. Building on these insights, the complete event log was filtered using the path filter in DISCO. The filtering was configured with activities set to 100 percent and paths set to 0 percent. This resulted in a structured process with clearly

[1] https://doi.org/10.6084/m9.figshare.29598299.v1.

defined start and end points, as illustrated in Fig. 1. The refined model shows that each case starts with *obtain* or *buying*, passed through the activity *consume* and ends with one of the three activities: *dispose, deposit refunds* or *deposit collection bin.*

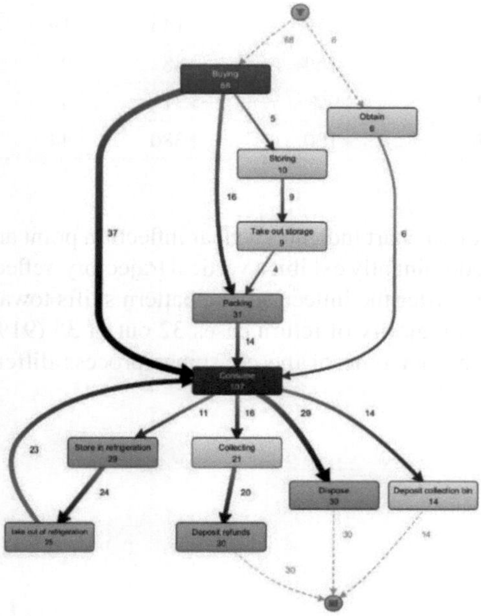

Fig. 1. DFG Refined Discovered Model on Consumer Process of Deposit Beverage Packaging.

With regard to the performance of the identified consumer process, the complete event logs revealed a return rate of 59,5%, as shown in Table 1. The packaging are perceived as *returned* if their trace ends with the activity *deposit refund* or *deposit collection bin* and perceived as *not return* if the trace ends with the activity *dispose.* The results indicate a slightly lower return rate compared to the national average in the Netherlands (68%) [25], which aligns with our expectation that younger people may exhibit lower return rates and indicates that our sample appears plausible.

Furthermore, additional attributes, such as the *type* of deposit beverage packaging, were collected during the data collection phase to identify patterns that might explain the consumer process. Although initial observations suggest that packaging *type* may influence return rates, the sample size was insufficient to support a more detailed analysis.

To address PQ2 and examine the process characteristics associated with return rates, several insightful analyses were performed. However, the most interesting finding emerged when the duration of each case was incorporated into the analysis. A dotted chart was created, in which cases were sorted by duration and plotted along the x-axis to highlight their respective time spans. Upon examining the chart, a clear pattern emerges: deposit beverage packages that are not returned (represented by red dots) tend to be associated with shorter case durations, whereas returned (green dots) are generally linked to longer durations, as illustrated in Fig. 2.

Table 1. Descriptive Statistics Type Frequency, Events and Return Rates.

Type	Frequency	Percentage	Events	Returned	Return Rate
Metal Can	28	38%	116	12	42,9%
Small PET Bottle	27	37%	145	19	70,4%
Big PET Bottle	12	16%	88	9	75%
Glass Bottle	7	9%	31	4	57,1%
Total	74	100	380	44	59,5%

For instance, the dotted chart indicates a clear inflection point around the 8 h. Before this point, the cases predominantly exhibit a vertical trajectory, reflecting no return 27 out of 39 (31% return rate). After the inflection, the pattern shifts toward a more horizontal orientation, indicating a majority of return cases 32 out of 35 (91% return rate). These findings suggest that the outcome of the consumer process differ notably if the case duration is longer than 8 h.

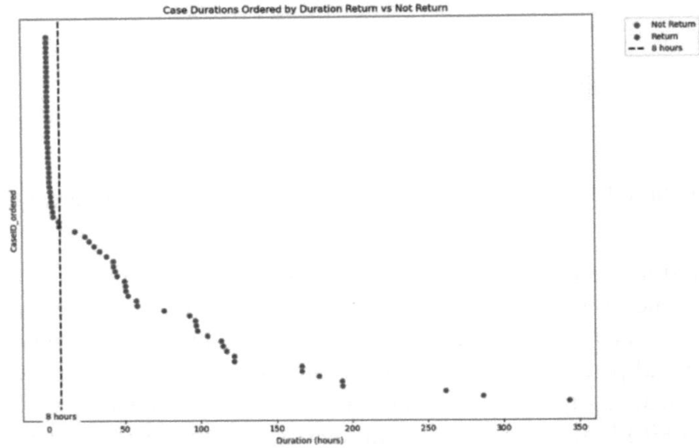

Fig. 2. Dotted Chart of Case Durations Highlighting Return vs. Not Return Process

3.4 Evaluation

In this section, we will evaluate the findings of different PQs in the Mining and Analysis section. In our analysis, we found lower return rates for participants that recorded relatively short times between the start (i.e., *buying* or *obtaining*) and end (i.e., *dispose*, *deposit refunds*, and *deposit collection bin*) of the process. On the other hand, we found higher return rates for participants that recorded relatively longer time between the start and end of the process. These results suggest the existence of two distinct patterns in consumer interaction with deposit beverage packaging. Based on the distribution of process durations in our dataset, we classified cases into short-cycle (process completion within 8 h) and long-cycle (process completion after 8 h). This observed pattern and the associated return rates indicate that the short-cycle process is a potential constraint in the effectiveness of DRS. Given the difference in return rates (i.e., 33% for short-cycle and 91% for long-cycle), targeting the short-cycle processes in the development of interventions to increase return rates may offer the greatest improvements in DRS.

3.5 Process Improvement

Based on the constraint that we identified in DRS, we can outline potential avenues for improvement to increase the return rates in the short-cycle consumer process.

It has been argued that the key to success of DRS is the design of the system, including the convenience of returning [4]. An increase in the amount of return locations specifically targeted at short-cycle processes would be potentially valuable as currently the majority of return locations concerns supermarkets while schools, event locations and train stations are also suitable as return locations. These locations are particularly relevant for short-cycle processes as findings show that people who are on the move, and are therefore likely to participate in the short-cycle process, tend to exhibit more disposal behavior compared to people who consume at home [6].

4 Discussion

This study conducts an exploratory approach by applying process mining techniques to collect student data, with the aim of uncovering constraints in the consumer process of deposit beverage packaging. By examining the consumer process within DRS and following the PM^2 method, the study demonstrates how process mining can be effectively applied to manually collected data and thereby answering the research question of this paper.

From a scientific view, this research advances two key domains: process mining and DRS scholarship. First, our study responds to recent academic calls to employ process mining for enhancing circular processes [10]. While process mining has been widely adopted in fields such as manufacturing and healthcare [26, 29], its application to consumer processes within circular systems remains underexplored due to several pitfalls, such as the availability of event logs and budget. To overcome these pitfalls, we introduce a novel approach to process mining: Human-Logged Process Mining (HLPM). Our case study demonstrates how HLPM has been used to analyze the consumer process of deposit beverage packages and to identify constraints. In doing so, the research contributes to the methodological development of process mining for sustainability applications. Second, our exploratory study contributes to research on DRS by carefully suggesting that to increase the return rates of beverage packaging, short-cycle consumer processes may be further investigated.

Several limitations of our study deserve mention. First, the data collection was conducted by a relatively small and homogeneous convenience-based sample of full-time bachelor students that collected 74 useful cases and is therefore prone to selection bias and lacks the possibility to generalize any findings. Importantly, as stated earlier, our current study is a purely pioneering and exploratory effort and does therefore not claim any generalizability. Future research needs to increase sample size and expand the participant pool towards other demographic groups to make findings more generalizable and to enhance the study's robustness. In addition, a larger sample size would also allow to conduct rigorous statistic testing to ensure that our exploratory findings, including the visually uncovered 8 h threshold, are not incidental. Second, the students followed a predefined data dictionary constructed based on a pilot study. While this suggests a careful and structured approach, it may not accurately reflect how such data would be collected at scale in real-world settings. Future research is needed to confirm the representativeness of the data dictionary used. Also, to assess and secure data quality, future research may include validation mechanisms such as cross-checking or triangulation with automated data. Third, the cases were analyzed on a per-case basis, without accounting for the possibility that a single event, such as purchasing a bottle crate, may relate to multiple individual cases. This simplification may have led to an overrepresentation of events. Future research could address this by incorporating more detailed data collection that captures multi-object relationships. Lastly, the scope of analysis is limited to general consumer process characteristics along the main paths, specifically focusing on return rates in relation to duration. Although additional information attributes, such as product type is available, these were not included in the current analysis. Future research could incorporate these attributes to enable a more comprehensive understanding of the consumer process.

5 Conclusion

Despite the fact that process mining is a well-established and powerful analytical technique for advancing sustainability in various industries, several pitfalls prevent the full potential of process mining from being realized in improving the circular economy. Our case study, which focuses on the manual creation of an event log of the consumer process within deposit return systems, gives rise to a Human-Logged Process Mining approach that can reveal constraints in processes that have remained hidden until now. The findings of our case study point towards potentially valuable areas within DRS where improvements may help unbottle the bottlenecks in DRS to further contribute to making the world more circular and sustainable.

References

1. Belzer, R.B.: Economic incentives for hazardous waste management: deposit-refund systems and used lubricating oil [Doctoral dissertation, Harvard University] (1989)
2. Bohm, P.: Deposit-Refund Systems: Theory and Applications to Environmental, Conservation, and Consumer Policy. Johns Hopkins University Press (1981)
3. Brisson, I.: Packaging waste and the environment: economics and policy. Resour. Conserv. Recycl. **8**, 183–292 (1993)
4. Campbell, B., Khachatryan, H., Behe, B., Hall, C., Dennis, J.: Crunch the can or throw the bottle? Effect of "bottle deposit laws" and municipal recycling programs. Resour. Conserv. Recycl. **106**, 98–109 (2016)

5. Choudhary, K., Sangwan, K.S., Goyal, D.: Environment and economic impacts assessment of PET waste recycling with conventional and renewable sources of energy. Procedia CIRP **80**, 422–427 (2019)
6. Conradie, M., Doms, B., Van de Koppel Maartje, Lenderink, T., Libbering, N.: Inlevergedrag kleine en grote statiegeldflessen (Nr. 2024/222). Ipsos I&O (2024)
7. Dogan, O., Bayo-Monton, J.-L., Fernandez-Llatas, C., Oztaysi, B.: Analyzing of gender behaviors from paths using process mining: a shopping mall application. Sensors **19**(3), 557 (2019)
8. European Commission: Klimaat- en energiedoelstellingen voor 2030 (2023). https://commission.europa.eu/energy-climate-change-environment/overall-targets-and-reporting_nl
9. Fluxicon: Disco (Version 4.1.9) [Computer software] (2025). https://fluxicon.com/disco
10. Graves, N., Koren, I., van der Aalst, W.M.: ReThink your processes! A review of process mining for sustainability. In: ICT4S Conference, Rennes, France (2023)
11. Gupt, Y., Sahay, S.: Review of extended producer responsibility: a case study approach. Waste Manag. Res. **33**(7), 595–611 (2015)
12. Kalenkova, A., Xia, L., Neumann, D.: Discovering and analyzing stochastic processes to reduce waste in food retail. arXiv preprint arXiv:2509.21322 (2025)
13. Kampik, T., Weske, M.: Event log generation: an industry perspective. In: Augusto, A., Gill, A., Bork, D., Nurcan, S., Reinhartz-Berger, I., Schmidt, R. (eds.) BPMDS EMMSAD 2022 2022. LNBIP, vol. 450, pp. 123–136. Springer, Cham (2022). https://doi.org/10.1007/978-3-031-07475-2_9
14. Kang, D., Auras, R., Singh, J.: Life cycle assessment of non-alcoholic single-serve polyethylene terephthalate beverage bottles in the state of California. Resour. Conserv. Recycl. **116**, 45–52 (2017)
15. Klein, C., Stikkelorum, M.: Niemand voorzag de zooi op straat door uitbreiding van statiegeld. NOS (2024). https://nos.nl/artikel/2527333-niemand-voorzag-de-zooi-op-straat-door-uitbreiding-van-statiegeld
16. Konstantoglou, A., Fotiadis, T., Folinas, D., Falaras, A., Rotsios, K.: Accessing consumer perceptions of the effectiveness of the deposit refund system. Sustainability **15**(12), 9429 (2023)
17. Kostewicz, D.E., King, S.A., Datchuk, S.M., Brennan, K.M., Casey, S.D.: Data collection and measurement assessment in behavioral research: 1958–2013. Behav. Anal. Res. Pract. **16**(1), 19–33 (2016)
18. Kremel, A.: Consumer behaviour in a circular system–how values promote and hinder the participation of young adults in the Swedish deposit-refund system for beverage packaging. Circ. Econ. Sustain. **4**(2), 1427–1446 (2024)
19. Lavee, D.: A cost-benefit analysis of a deposit–refund program for beverage containers in Israel. Waste Manag. **30**(2), 338–345 (2010)
20. Linderhof, V., Oosterhuis, F.H., Van Beukering, P.J., Bartelings, H.: Effectiveness of deposit-refund systems for household waste in the Netherlands: applying a partial equilibrium model. J. Environ. Manag. **232**, 842–850 (2019)
21. Martin, N., Fischer, D.A., Kerpedzhiev, G.D.: Opportunities and challenges for process mining in organizations: results of a Delphi study. Bus. Inf. Syst. Eng. **63**, 511–527 (2021)
22. Numata, D.: Optimal design of deposit–refund systems considering allocation of unredeemed deposits. Environ. Econ. Policy Stud. **13**, 303–321 (2011)
23. Picuno, C., Gerassimidou, S., You, W., Martin, O., Iacovidou, E.: The potential of deposit refund systems in closing the plastic beverage bottle loop: a review. Resour. Conserv. Recycl. **212**, 107962 (2025)
24. Racis, S., Spano, A.: Do not stay behind: embracing process mining in the italian public sector. In: Węcel, K. (ed.) BIS 2025. LNBIP, vol. 554, pp. 152–164. Springer, Cham (2025). https://doi.org/10.1007/978-3-031-94193-1_12

25. Reloop: Deposit return systems: How they perform (2025). https://www.reloopplatform.org/wp-content/u
26. Schneider, D.R., Tomić, T., Raal, R.: Economic viability of the DRS for beverage packaging waste—identification of economic drivers and system modelling. J. Sustain. Dev. Energy Water Environ. Syst. **9**, 1080386 (2021)
27. Stefanovic, D., Dakic, D., Stevanov, B., Lolic, T.: Process mining in manufacturing: goals, techniques and applications. In: Lalic, B., Majstorovic, V., Marjanovic, U., von Cieminski, G., Romero, D. (eds.) APMS 2020. IFIPAICT, vol. 591, pp. 54–62. Springer, Cham (2020). https://doi.org/10.1007/978-3-030-57993-7_7
28. Stein Dani, V., et al.: Towards understanding the role of the human in event log extraction. In: Marrella, A., Weber, B. (eds.) BPM 2021. LNBIP, vol. 436, pp. 86–98. Springer, Cham (2022). https://doi.org/10.1007/978-3-030-94343-1_7
29. Stikkelorum, M., Klein, C.: Statiegeldsysteem moet beter, inspectie dreigt met dwangsommen van ruim 300 miljoen. NOS (2024). https://nos.nl/artikel/2528562-statiegeldsysteem-moet-beter-inspectie-dreigt-met-dwangsommen-van-ruim-300-miljoen
30. Striani, F., Colucci, C., Corallo, A., Paiano, R., Pascarelli, C.: Process mining in healthcare: a systematic literature review and a case study. Adv. Sci. Technol. Eng. Syst. J. **7**(6), 151–160 (2022)
31. Svensson, N., Funck, E.K.: Management control in circular economy: exploring and theorizing the adaptation of management control to circular business models. J. Clean. Prod. **233**, 390–398 (2019)
32. Tentina, I., Mannhardt, F., Zerbato, F., van Dongen, B.: Can users trust process mining? In: Węcel, K. (ed.) BIS 2025. LNBIP, vol. 554, pp. 137–151. Springer, Cham (2025). https://doi.org/10.1007/978-3-031-94193-1_11
33. Van der Aalst, W.: Data Science in Action. Springer, Heidelberg (2016). https://doi.org/10.1007/978-3-662-49851-4
34. Van der Aalst, W.M., Schonenberg, M.H., Song, M.: Time prediction based on process mining. Inf. Syst. **36**(2), 450–475 (2011)
35. van Eck, M.L., Lu, X., Leemans, S.J.J., van der Aalst, W.M.P.: PM^2: a process mining project methodology. In: Zdravkovic, J., Kirikova, M., Johannesson, P. (eds.) CAiSE 2015. LNCS, vol. 9097, pp. 297–313. Springer, Cham (2015). https://doi.org/10.1007/978-3-319-19069-3_19
36. Van Lange, P.A., Otten, W., De Bruin, E.M., Joireman, J.A.: Development of prosocial, individualistic, and competitive orientations. J. Pers. Soc. Psychol. **73**(4), 733–746 (1997)
37. Vom Brocke, J., Jans, M., Mendling, J., Reijers, H.A.: A five-level framework for research on process mining. Bus. Inf. Syst. Eng. **63**(5), 483–490 (2021)
38. Walls, M.: Deposit-refund systems in practice and theory. SSRN (2011)
39. Yin, R.K.: Case Study Research and Applications: Design and Methods. SAGE Publications (2017)
40. Zhou, G., et al.: A systematic review of the deposit-refund system for beverage packaging: operating mode, key parameter and development trend. J. Clean. Prod. **251**, 119660 (2020)

AI-Driven Business Process Composition for Enterprise Information Exchange Within IE-BSE Framework: An Empirical Case Analysis on E-invoicing

Muhammad Raheel Raza[1(✉)], Fethi Rabhi[1(✉)], George Joukhadar[2], and Amitabh Kumar[1]

[1] School of Computer Science and Engineering, UNSW Sydney, Sydney, NSW 2052, Australia
{muhammad_raheel.raza,f.rabhi}@unsw.edu.au

[2] School of Information Systems, Technology and Management, UNSW Sydney, Sydney, NSW 2052, Australia

Abstract. Digitalization in supply chains has enabled the use of API-centric business services, enhancing workflow management as companies embrace digital transformation. However, API adoption is often hindered by internal organizational issues, complicating the identification and integration of suitable APIs. To tackle these challenges, the research article proposes the Information Exchange Business Service Ecosystem (IE-BSE) framework with an interactive method to understand user requirements accurately, which aids enterprises in leveraging publicly available APIs for document exchange. This framework includes a service discovery technique for identifying suitable APIs and a Business Process Builder tool for composing relevant business APIs, supported by a Knowledge Hub for E-invoicing APIs (KHEA), streamlining complex business processes. The BP-Builder uses pre-trained AI Agents and initiates an interactive method by enabling users to interact and ask questions to find the best suitable business APIs. Results ascertain potential accurate business processes, including several APIs, and allow the choice of a specific BP where Amazon Web Services (AWS) Step Functions creates automated business workflows.

Keywords: Information exchange · Business API · Technical API · API repository · API composition · API discovery · Business process · BP-Builder

1 Introduction

According to recent research [1], about 80% of businesses in the modern world are digitizing their supply chain operations and implementing cutting-edge technology at various levels of supply chain management (SCM). These contemporary digital technologies facilitate risk management, innovation, the creation of digital transformation strategies, and enhanced operational performance. Facilitating the inter-organizational interchange of business documents, including purchase orders and invoices, is a major

K. Węcel and V. Řepa (Eds.): BIS 2026, LNBIP 584, pp. 143–154, 2026.
https://doi.org/10.1007/978-3-032-26363-6_11

area that requires research emphasis. There are numerous potential approaches to using contemporary technologies and frameworks, such as Customer Relationship Management (CRM) systems, Enterprise Resource Planning (ERP), Cloud Computing, and Blockchain, to improve and streamline the implementation and maintenance of complex business processes that involve document exchanges and information sharing [2]. However, it can be challenging to use these technologies to transform business practices and maintain competitiveness, particularly when interacting with legacy systems [3].

According to a recent study [4], moving towards Application Programming Interface (API) ecosystems is one way to reduce both the challenges and complexity of developing business processes. One of the key elements of digital transformation that allows businesses to elevate customer value rapidly is API-centric business services. Evidence suggests that reputable businesses are employing APIs more frequently to execute their digital transformation initiatives [5]. Although there are numerous API marketplaces, their application has remained restricted to internal organization boundaries [6]. Businesses find contradicting information regarding APIs on API marketplaces. As a result, enterprises are challenged to identify suitable APIs for executing their different business processes [7]. While some recommendation algorithms offer recommendations on the technical attributes of APIs, they overlook their business aspects. Thus, an effective approach is crucial to evaluate the business traits that can help enterprises to select and provide pertinent services. To focus on the complexities of identifying suitable APIs and performing the integration of those APIs with the enterprise's internal BPs, the study addresses the following two fundamental research questions:

- RQ1: What sort of Business APIs should be provided by an ecosystem to support and enhance document exchanges in a supply chain?
- RQ2: How would enterprise systems be integrated with workflow technologies to assist business processes?

This research paper extends the IE-BSE framework, facilitating API sharing across enterprises for business document exchange. Via the BP-Builder tool, the framework allows businesses to identify potential business processes from a set of requirements and discover APIs based on their functionality in information exchange. The rest of the paper is structured as follows: Sect. 2 discusses the related work, with emphasis on the function of API ecosystems in information exchange. Section 3 outlines the research methodology used. Section 4 presents implementation techniques. The evaluation procedures are described in Sect. 5. Section 6 concludes the paper with future work.

2 Related Work

2.1 Technology-Based Information Exchange

Information Exchange (IE) is an essential aspect of supply chains, significantly affecting organizational relationships. Initially proposed in the 1970s, Electronic Data Interchange (EDI) [8] enables digital transactions of business documents, such as purchase orders and invoices, through standardized protocols like EDIFACT. Alongside EDI, technologies like Blockchain, Cloud Computing, and the Internet of Things have become increasingly important. However, Tilleli et al. [9] noted that high costs and limited experience hinder many firms from integrating these newer technologies into existing EDI systems. One viable solution is to employ APIs to help integrate legacy systems with persistent cloud technologies. According to Colanzi et al. [10], APIs enable communication between modern applications and legacy systems. Heshmatisafa et al. [11] highlight their accessibility in marketplaces, allowing for data transmission among systems and facilitating application features for stakeholders and developers. Maguire et al. [12] found that organizations favor external APIs for cost reduction, safer communication, and simpler long-term maintenance. Furthermore, an assessment by Bajaj et al. [13] suggested that APIs support microservices communication, improving internal business operations and expanding digital ecosystems by making services available to other companies.

According to the literature, the integration of APIs into enterprise business processes encounters several technical challenges. Key issues include difficulties in searching for and selecting suitable APIs for various supply chain business operations. According to Svensson [14], businesses seek the "best" solutions that meet their systematic requirements. Cremaschi et al. [15] indicated a common mismatch between business needs and available API information. Current API recommendation research focuses more on technical attributes than on business characteristics. Furthermore, some operations may require collaboration between multiple APIs, which can lead to resource inefficiencies. Moreover, considering the variety of workflow technologies utilized for support, König et al. [16] highlights the challenges of integrating external APIs into internal business processes due to the diversity of platforms and interoperability issues. Although there has been research [17] on API localization for various languages and cultures, there is a notable lack of studies focused on customizing APIs for specific application domains. Addressing these gaps is essential for developing effective integration solutions that are currently unaddressed in the literature.

2.2 Exploring Marketplaces and Ecosystems for Business APIs

To address challenges in business operations, the concept of a "Business API" is proposed, focusing on publicly available APIs that offer business services. Weir [18] identified key "business-oriented" API marketplaces as essential for businesses to find and use APIs effectively. Supported by examples like the agriculture-focused API marketplace utilizing 5G-IoT Big Data Infrastructure by Berto et al. [19] and Deng et al. [20] working on Transportation Cyber-physical Systems for cloud-connected transportation apps, these initiatives highlight the accessibility of business APIs. However, existing efforts do not cater to complex IE business processes. Moreover, enterprises face significant challenges in integrating external APIs into their operations, such as insufficient resources, difficulties in selecting suitable APIs, and restricted access. The complexity of merging external technical APIs with internal ones adds to the difficulty, requiring the creation of new business processes for extensive operations. In that context, Raza et al. [7] proposed an Information Exchange Business Service Ecosystem (IE-BSE) Framework where a BP-Builder tool allowed BPMN format inputs and generated API-based business processes using AWS Step Functions. However, understanding user requirements for identifying and selecting appropriate APIs remains a challenge. Additionally, limited research in the field hinders effective information exchange and slows down the adoption of API technologies.

3 Research Methodology

To evaluate these challenges, our study uses the Design Science Research Methodology (DSRM) [21]. DSRM is a problem-solving paradigm that seeks to increase human knowledge by generating new concepts and ideas. We chose the DSRM approach because of the depth of the procedures involved in generating artifacts, particularly in the context of Information Systems (IS). The DSRM process consists of the following four stages: (1) *Problem Identification:* involves identifying information exchange APIs and facilitating their integration into business processes; (2) *Defining Solution Objectives:* investigating open and business-like ecosystems allowing enterprises to employ and integrate accessible APIs into their IE processes; (3) *Design and Development:* addressing the research problems, we propose the Information Exchange Business Service Ecosystem (IE-BSE) as the main design artifact; (4) *Evaluation and Demonstration:* assess how well the framework works for IE situations in E-invoicing.

3.1 Proposed Framework

The IE-BSE framework [7] comprises the extended IE-BSE architecture in Fig. 1 and developer tools, which help enterprises to achieve their desired business goals.

The IE-BSE architecture is extended by increasing the number of possible ways the BP-Builder tool can accept desired business processes as input. In [7], the BP-Builder tool allows users to upload the desired BP in BPMN format and is analyzed by the BP Algorithm to generate target BPs. There is another interactive method that enables users to interact with the tool by asking questions in textual format. This uses Gemini AI Agents that analyze the texts and produce productive outputs. Both techniques are focused on facilitating users with feasible options and understanding the user requirements accurately. The three main services that comprise the IE-BSE architecture are as follows:

- **IE API Repository:** It is designed as an IE API catalogue that contains information about numerous external APIs, either from enterprise systems or from API marketplaces, classified into sub-categories, and stores all necessary information on the functions provided and how to access them.
- **API Publisher:** It assists enterprises in searching for and discovering suitable APIs for the IE API Repository for their utilization in different business processes. The discovery service can employ different search technologies, including Natural Language Processing (NLP) techniques, to help explore and recommend appropriate APIs for different businesses and business functions.
- **Business Process Builder (BP-Builder):** This service performs new API construction steps, such as combining multiple technical APIs to create new business APIs and combining multiple business APIs to create new business processes. This contributes to enriching the IE API Repository with new APIs and business processes that accomplish complex business processes. The composition is carried out via the BP-Builder tool, which is illustrated in Fig. 2.

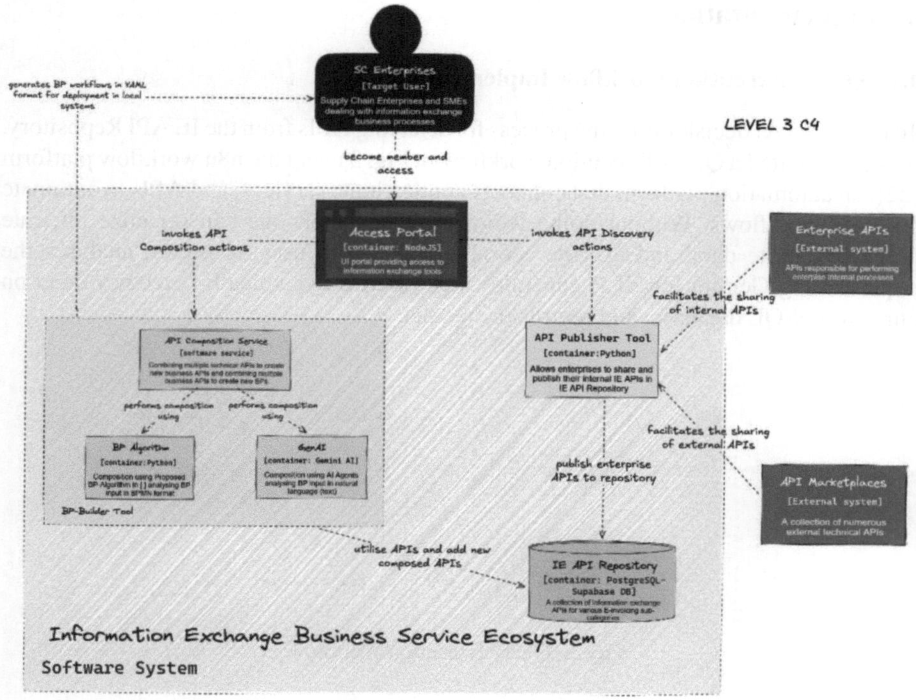

Fig. 1. Extended IE-BSE Architecture.

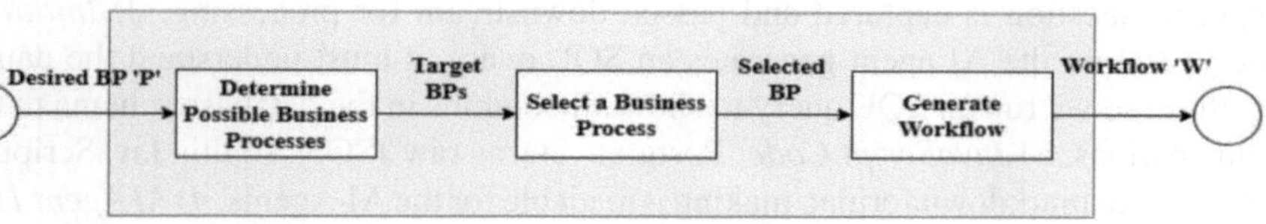

Fig. 2. Business Process of a BP-Builder [7]

The BP-builder tool enables users to input the Desired BP ‘P’ in BPMN format and determines possible business processes using Algorithm 1 [7]. This is one of the possible ways that BP-Builder operates by accepting inputs in BPMN format. Another way the BP-Builder can accept input is through a textual query format written in natural language. In this method, the user can express their requirements via questions/queries, which act as an input to the tool. The BP-Builder then initiates the Query Execution workflow (in Sect. 4.1) which generates a set of Target BPs. The user then selects the best possible option and generates a YAML format representation (in Sect. 5.1).

4 Implementation

4.1 Query Execution Workflow Implementation

To power the AI decision-making process for selecting APIs from the IE API Repository, we implemented a Query Execution workflow in Fig. 3 using the n8n workflow platform [22], an automation platform that connects applications, services, and APIs to automate business workflows. Without doing tedious human labor, one can organize intricate processes, route data, and execute actions. It listens to user messages, analyses the request using Gemini for NLP, generates SQL queries dynamically, executes them on our PostgreSQL database, and returns the results.

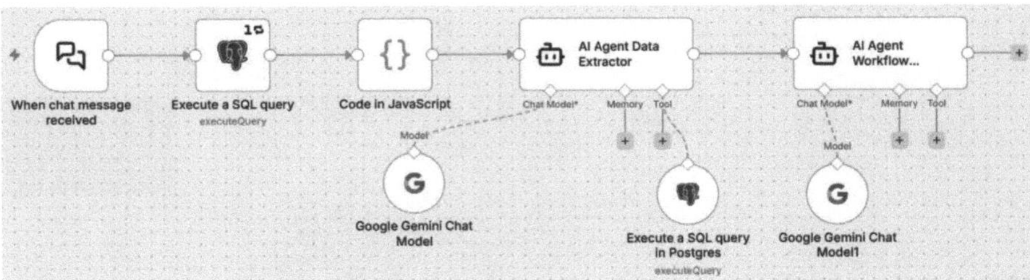

Fig. 3. Query Execution Workflow

Some of the basic components within the Query Execution Workflow above include: *1) Chat Trigger:* This is the entry point for the workflow, where the user's natural language question is captured and passed downstream for processing. *2) Initial SQL Query:* Before the AI agent generates an SQL query, it must understand the database structure, so we run an SQL query to show all columns in the database schema to avoid hallucinations. *3) JavaScript Code:* Postgres returns raw JSON, so this JavaScript code converts it to markdown format, making it readable for the AI Agents. *4) AI Agent 1:* This Gemini AI Agent for Data Extraction and Query Execution takes the user question + schema and produces a SQL query. It is connected to our IE API Repository in Supabase's PostgreSQL database. *5) AI Agent 2:* This AI Agent for Workflow Composition analyzes API query results and generates all possible valid workflow combinations based on input/output format compatibility. The algorithm that explains the mechanism behind the AI Agents employed is described in Sect. 4.2.

4.2 AI-Based Target BPs Generation Implementation

As described above, we have implemented AI Agents that allow users to write the desired business process in text and will execute a list of candidate business processes satisfying the user's query. If it could not find the exact BP, then the tool would suggest candidate BPs close to the desired BP. Algorithm 2 computes the possible Target BPs as provided below.

Algorithm 2: Algorithm for AI-based Target BPs Workflow Generation

```
Begin Algorithm
Input: UR: User Request in natural language
  DS: Database Schema
  CD: Column Descriptors
  SQLQuery: Predefined SQL queries at each stage
  CM: Compatibility matrix
  FR: Rules for format compatibility
  R: Result set
  APIrepository: PostgreSQL table containing API metadata
Output: TargetBPs: list of candidate BPs that satisfy the
textual query for the Desired BP
Function compatible (API_o1.Outformat,API_i1.Inpformat,F): finds the
compatible APIs by checking the output of API_oi and input of API_i1
/**** AI Agent 1: API Query Execution and Data Extraction ****/
/* Parsing the UR */
if UR contains "Extract from PDF" then add Extraction to steps
end if
if UR contains "Convert into UBL" then add Transformation to
steps end if
if UR contains "validate" then add Validation to steps
end if
if UR contains "send via Peppol or email" then Add Communication
to steps end if
for each step i in steps do
SELECT SQLQuery for step i
Ensure SQLQuery includes:
  - is_active = true
  - LOWER() for case-insensitive matching
  - Apply Filters only on category, input_formats,
    output_formats, network, business_rules
Execute SQLQuery against APIRepository and store results in R
for each steps i end for
/************* AI Agent 2: Workflow Composition ************/
API Grouping as per steps_i:
    Extraction, Transformation, Validation, Communication
for each step i from 1 to N-1 do
  | for each API_i1 in steps_i do
  |   | for each API_i2 in steps_i+1 do
  |   |   | if compatible (API_o1.Outformat,API_i1.Inpformat,F)
  |   |   |   then add API_i1 -> API_i2 to matrix CM
  |   |   | end if
  |   | end if
  | end if
end if {return TargetBPs in matrix CM}
/* generating valid TargetBPs using compatibility matrix CM */
for each TargetBP in TargetBPs do
  | Output: n "." API_i1 -> API_i2 . . . . -> API_iN
  | n++
end for {return numbered list of Target BPs}
/*********************** Main Program **********************/
Workflows = compatible (API_o1.Outformat,API_i1.Inpformat,F)
Output format:
    1. API_1 → API_2 → ... → API_n
    2. API_1 → API_2 → ... → API_n
    3. API_1 → API_2 → ... → API_k
  Return Workflows
End Algorithm
```

The main purpose of Algorithm 2 is to identify suitable APIs from the available *APIRepository* and to generate a list of *TargetBPs* satisfying the *UserRequest,* i.e., the

DesiredBP in natural language. The algorithm employs two Gemini AI Agents. AI Agent 1 is responsible for discovering appropriate APIs from the *APIRepository* that match the user requirements, i.e., comparing the inputs/outputs of each API. To do this, the *UserRequest* is parsed to identify several queries within a single query and to highlight which processing *steps* are required. After that, an SQL query looks for the inputs, outputs, and validation rules of each API within the *APIRepository* for each identified *steps.* This will give us the list of suitable APIs for the *UserRequest.* Here, the AI Agent 2 plays its role by checking the compatibility, i.e., the outputs of APIs for the first *step,* with the input of APIs for the next *step.* This gives us the compatibility graph for all the suitable API connections. Then, it computes all valid workflows going along all required *steps.* As a result, the algorithm outputs them as a list of *TargetBPs* as complete business processes for the DesiredBP.

5 Evaluation

The research work detailed in the article is still in its initial stages, and currently, our primary method of evaluation is testing a basic case study (E-invoicing) to verify that the system satisfies the functional requirements. We have used the same IE API Repository as mentioned in [7], consisting of a set of Transformation, Communication, and Validation APIs. To test the functionality of BP-Builder with another input alternative, Sect. 5.1 explains the testing scenario with the results achieved.

5.1 Testing Scenario

To test the BP-Builder tool, we designed the same testing scenario where a user wants to construct a simple "Send an Invoice" business process that fulfills the Australian e-invoicing requirements. We anticipate that all e-invoices are saved in PDF format and delivered via the PEPPOL network. The BP-Builder tool operates according to the given steps. **Step 1.** First, the BP-Builder tool allows users to write a textual query in natural language inside the chat section of our designed UI, as shown in Fig. 4. The query should be well-descriptive and, in a human-understandable and readable format.

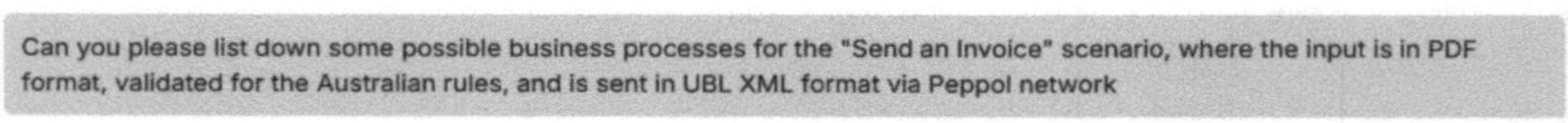

Fig. 4. Textual Query of the Desired Business Process

Step 2. After the Desired BP is expressed in textual format and uploaded, the algorithm mentioned in Sect. 4.2 executes the AI Agents to meet the criteria, employing accessible APIs from the Business API Repository. Thus, a list of Target BPs is displayed as shown in Table 1 which is a comprehensive list of business processes discovered by the algorithm for the given testing scenario. These business processes satisfy the Desired BP criteria by inspecting the input/output parameters of each underlying API.

Table 1. Possible Target BP Workflows for Desired BP

Business Process No.	Possible Business Processes
1*	UpBrainsXtract-> AmitTransform-> ESSValidator-> StorecoveSend
2	UpBrainsXtract-> AmitTransform -> ESSValidator-> AdemicoSend
3	UpBrainsXtract-> AmitTransform-> EcosioValidator-> StorecoveSend
4	UpBrainsXtract-> AmitTransform-> EcosioValidator-> AdemicoSend
5	UpBrainsXtract-> BabelwayTransform-> ESSValidator-> StorecoveSend
6	UpBrainsXtract-> BabelwayTransform-> ESSValidator-> AdemicoSend
7	UpBrainsXtract-> BabelwayTransform-> EcosioValidator-> StorecoveSend
8	UpBrainsXtract-> BabelwayTransform-> EcosioValidator-> AdemicoSend
9	EzzybillsExtract > AmitTransform-> ESSValidator-> StorecoveSend
10	EzzybillsExtract-> AmitTransform -> ESSValidator-> AdemicoSend
11	EzzybillsExtract > AmitTransform-> EcosioValidator-> StorecoveSend
12	EzzybillsExtract -> AmitTransform-> EcosioValidator-> AdemicoSend
13	EzzybillsExtract-> BabelwayTransform-> ESSValidator-> StorecoveSend
14	EzzybillsExtract -> BabelwayTransform-> ESSValidator-> AdemicoSend
15	EzzybillsExtract-> BabelwayTransform-> EcosioValidator-> StorecoveSend
16	EzzybillsExtract -> BabelwayTransform-> EcosioValidator-> AdemicoSend

Step 3. The user chooses the best business process that may guarantee a successful business function from the list of created business processes. The choices should correspond to the user's requirements, including business parameters. After that, the selection explains the underlying APIs that the Selected BP uses. The user has now chosen the UpbrainsXtract API to convert PDF to JSON, the AmitTransform API to convert JSON to UBL, a few validation rules in the ESSValidator API, and the StorecoveSend API to transmit invoices over PEPPOL. **Step 4.** After BP Selection, a workflow of the selected BP using AWS Step Functions is generated in a downloadable YAML format as in [7], which can be used by enterprises for customization and usage purposes.

5.2 Discussion

For the scenario mentioned in Sect. 5.1, we can assess the effectiveness, time efficiency, and user-friendliness of the BP Builder tool in comparison to other methods of API configuration for business processes. Table 2 presents a comparison of the time required by traditional approaches versus the BP Builder and provides an estimate of the time savings achieved using BP Builder in this context.

At this point, it is essential to highlight the effectiveness and reliability of the BP-Builder tool in terms of development time and complexity of business processes. Hypothetically, considering a single business process use case where PDF documents need

Table 2. Evaluation of Time taken by Traditional Methods and the BP-Builder tool

Traditional Approaches		BP-Builder	
Activities	Time required	Activities	Time Required
Set up a single API	3 h	Generate Lambda Functions for 1 API	1 h
Set up three APIs	9 h	Generate Lambda Functions for 3 API	3 h
Link APIs together	2 h	State Machine Set up	1 h
Integrate APIs	5 h	Release API Endpoint	1 h
UI Set up	2 h		
Total Time	**13–16 h**	**Total Time**	**5 h**
		Time Saved	***−11 h***

to be converted to UBL format, the BP-Builder may generate six possible business processes in approximately 3–5 s and complete the scenario mentioned in Sect. 5.1 in almost 5–10 s, providing twelve possible business process options. On the other hand, traditional approaches usually generate only one business process at a time. This indicates the substantial benefit of using the BP-Builder tool in terms of complexity, development time, and speed of development. Additionally, the BP-Builder also minimizes the cost of each business process by suggesting cost-effective options for the DesiredBP compared to traditional approaches, giving one solution at a time.

5.3 Limitations

Despite the cost savings offered by the BP-Builder tool, it has several limitations. There is often not a direct correlation between user requirements and available APIs, such as the lack of traditional methods to convert PDF invoices to UBL invoices. Users need to utilize multiple transformation APIs for these conversions. Furthermore, the tool relies on an exhaustive search for generating candidate business processes, which can be time-consuming. There is also the necessity for the API repository to contain rich metadata to facilitate effective searches. Additionally, while multiple APIs may appear to meet user requirements involving the PEPPOL communication protocol, various jurisdictional considerations complicate the selection process. Another limitation of the current version of BP-Builder is that each API is embedded in AWS Lambda functions, facilitating integration into the enterprise application. However, it does not support dynamic generation of Step Functions, necessitating the prior definition of AWS Lambda functions before invoking them through Step Functions. This design choice demands technical expertise and additional effort to ensure proper functionality. Moreover, maintaining the API Repository in this version requires manual intervention for upcoming new APIs.

6 Conclusion and Future Work

The research article presents an IE-BSE framework for integrating diverse information exchange APIs into business contexts. It includes extended architecture and developer tools to design, implement, and share APIs for information exchange workflows. The BP-Builder automates workflow generation from high-level business process requirements in natural language, evaluated via a "Send Invoice" scenario using e-invoicing APIs, producing workflows for integration as AWS Step Functions in YAML format.

The framework is currently in development with various potential future enhancements. Key focus areas include reducing the need for manual adjustments of generated workflows tailored for AWS and creating improved code generation templates for AWS Lambdas. Long-term initiatives aim to advance the Business API Repository by including features like advanced analytics, error diagnostics, and real-time monitoring, facilitating easier API usage for non-technical users. The integration of machine learning is also planned to offer AI-driven API recommendations, which would enhance API discovery and composition during the creation of business processes based on past experiences. Additionally, the framework aims to be validated through case studies across different domains, ensuring scalability, adaptability, and reliability in various business environments.

References

1. Susitha, E., Jayarathna, A., Herath, H.M.R.P.: Supply chain competitiveness through agility and digital technology: a bibliometric analysis. Supply Chain Anal. **7**, 100073 (2024). https://doi.org/10.1016/j.sca.2024.100073
2. van Engelenburg, S., Janssen, M., Klievink, B.: Design of a software architecture supporting business-to-government information sharing to improve public safety and security: combining business rules, events and blockchain technology. J. Intell. Inf. Syst. **52**, 595–618 (2019). https://doi.org/10.1007/s10844-017-0478-z
3. Chinazor, P.A., et al.: Transforming business scalability and operational flexibility with advanced cloud computing technologies. Comput. Sci. IT Res. J. **5**, 1469–1487 (2024). https://doi.org/10.51594/csitrj.v5i6.1248
4. Huhtamäki, J., et al.: Visualizing the geography of platform boundary resources: the case of the global API ecosystem. In: Annual Hawaii International Conference on System Sciences, pp. 5305–5314 (2017). https://doi.org/10.24251/hicss.2017.642
5. RAPID API: Best Practices for Implementing an Internal API Hub How a Phased Approach Delivers Successful Digital Transformation (2021)
6. Abbas, A.E., et al.: Business data sharing through data marketplaces: a systematic literature review. J. Theor. Appl. Electron. Commer. Res. **16**, 3321–3339 (2021). https://doi.org/10.3390/jtaer16070180
7. Raza, M.R., Rabhi, F., Joukhadar, G., Singh, R.: Enterprise information exchange via IE-BSE framework: a case study on e-invoicing. In: WorldCIST. Springer (2026)
8. Hasan, H., Ali, M.: A modern review of EDI: representation, protocols and security considerations. In: 2019 2nd IEEE MENACOMM. IEEE (2019)
9. Tilleli, F.: How Much Does EDI Cost. https://www.connectpointz.com/blog/how-much-does-edi-cost

10. Colanzi, T., et al.: Are we speaking the industry language? The practice and literature of modernizing legacy systems with microservices. In: ACM International Conference Proceeding Series, pp. 61–70 (2021). https://doi.org/10.1145/3483899.3483904
11. Heshmatisafa, S., et al.: Visualizing the maturing global API ecosystem. In: Proceedings of the 55th Hawaii International Conference on System Sciences (2022)
12. Maguire, T.K., Yoon, S., Chen, J.: Collaborating for COVID-19: hospital health information exchange and public health partnership. Telemed. e-Health (2023). https://doi.org/10.1089/tmj.2023.0056
13. Bajaj, D., Goel, A., Gupta, S.: A comprehensive microservice extraction approach integrating business functions and database entities. Int. Arab J. Inf. Technol. **21** (2024). https://doi.org/10.34028/iajit/21/1/3
14. Svensson, A.: What is the best API from a developer's perspective?: investigation of API development with fintech developers in the spotlight (2024)
15. Cremaschi, M., et al.: Toward automatic semantic API descriptions to support services composition (2017). https://doi.org/10.1007/978-3-319-67262-5_12
16. König, S., et al.: Executing automotive test workflows with BPMN and web service orchestration in software-defined car manufacturing. Prod. Eng. Res. Dev. (2024). https://doi.org/10.1007/s11740-024-01302-1
17. Malamas, N., et al.: A Multilayer architecture towards the development and distribution of multimodal interface applications on the edge. Sensors **24**, 5199 (2024). https://doi.org/10.3390/s24165199
18. Weir, L.: Enterprise API Management: Design and deliver valuable business APIs. Packt Publishing (2019)
19. Berto, F., et al.: A 5G-IoT enabled big data infrastructure for data-driven agronomy. In: 2022 IEEE GLOBECOM Workshops, GC Wkshps 2022 – Proceedings, pp. 588–594. Institute of Electrical and Electronics Engineers Inc. (2022). https://doi.org/10.1109/GCWkshps56602.2022.10008727
20. Deng, H.W., et al.: Commercial cloud computing for connected vehicle applications in transportation cyberphysical systems: a case study. IEEE Intell. Transp. Syst. Mag. **13**, 6–19 (2021). https://doi.org/10.1109/MITS.2020.3037314
21. Peffers, K., et al.: A design science research methodology for information systems research. J. Manag. Inf. Syst. **24**, 45–77 (2007). https://doi.org/10.2753/MIS0742-1222240302
22. n8n Workflow Automation. https://n8n.io/. Accessed 24 Jan 2026

VeriFlow: Multi-dimensional Verification of LLM-Generated Low-Code Workflows

Ahang Zuo(✉)

Univ. de Pau et des Pays de l'Adour, LIUPPA, 64000 Pau, France
ahang.zuo@univ-pau.fr

Abstract. Large language models (LLMs) are increasingly used to generate low-code workflows in platforms such as n8n, enabling rapid automation but also introducing structural flaws, unreachable paths, and mismatches between user intent and the produced workflow. We present *VeriFlow*, a multi-dimensional verification framework for LLM-generated workflows that combines three complementary analyses: (i) structural verification of workflow graphs, (ii) semantic verification that checks consistency between natural-language intent and workflow capabilities, ordering constraints, and parameter usage, and (iii) executable verification through a capability-aware sandbox that assesses reachability, parameter completeness, and execution readiness under a verification-oriented abstraction. VeriFlow produces interpretable diagnostic evidence, including missing capabilities, ordering inconsistencies, and parameter-level issues. Experiments on a benchmark of LLM-generated n8n workflows provide initial evidence that VeriFlow can reveal structural, semantic, and execution-related problems in an interpretable way, thereby supporting safer AI-assisted workflow engineering.

1 Introduction

Low-code/no-code (LCNC) workflow platforms such as n8n, Zapier, and Make are increasingly adopted to support rapid automation in modern business information systems. Their modular orchestration enables both developers and non-experts to assemble workflows with limited programming effort [3, 18,21]. With the emergence of large language models (LLMs), these platforms are now frequently augmented with natural-language-to-workflow generation: users describe an automation goal in plain language, and an LLM synthesizes a workflow specification (often JSON-based) that can be executed by the platform. Recent work on LLM-driven process modeling highlights both the potential and the reliability challenges of this paradigm, including structural omissions, malformed control-flow patterns, and incomplete configurations in generated artifacts [15,16].

Compared with workflows engineered manually, LLM-generated workflows may contain plausible but non-executable structures, incomplete parameterizations, disconnected fragments, unreachable paths, and incorrect uses of

K. Węcel and V. Řepa (Eds.): BIS 2026, LNBIP 584, pp. 155–168, 2026
https://doi.org/10.1007/978-3-032-26363-6_12

low-code components. They may also drift from the user's actual intent by selecting inappropriate triggers, actions, or conditions despite a superficially coherent workflow structure. Such failure modes are closely related to issues discussed in the literature on LLM hallucination, semantic instability, and unreliable tool use [11,13,27]. While many generated workflows appear reasonable on average, production use is risk-sensitive: even a small number of semantic or runtime mismatches may lead to costly silent failures. For this reason, verification should act as a *guardrail* for AI-assisted workflow engineering rather than as an argument that LLMs cannot generate useful workflows.

Existing workflow verification techniques, including structural analysis, soundness checking, and business process verification, typically assume carefully engineered models [1,6]. These assumptions do not always hold for LLM-generated LCNC artifacts, which may be underspecified, partially configured, and semantically unstable. This creates a need for verification methods that jointly reason about (i) workflow graph structure, (ii) consistency between the workflow and the natural-language request, and (iii) the ability of the workflow to execute under realistic configuration constraints.

In this paper, *verification* refers to automated checks over workflow structure, configuration, and intent-oriented consistency conditions, whereas *validation* refers to user-facing assessment of whether the generated workflow appears to satisfy the intended automation goal. VeriFlow primarily provides verification-oriented evidence, since semantic validation remains approximate when intent is expressed in natural language.

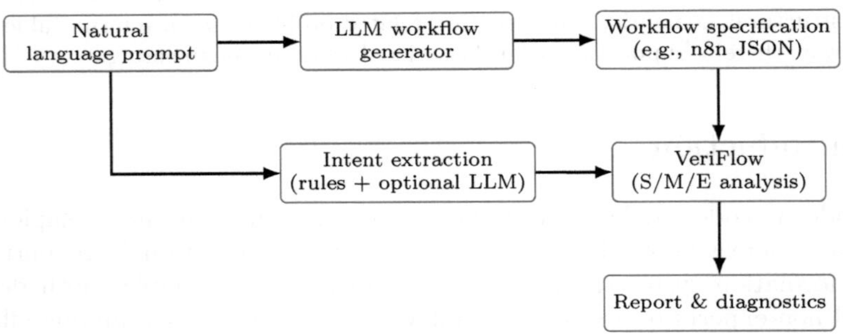

Fig. 1. VeriFlow pipeline from prompt and workflow to a verification report.

To address these challenges, we introduce *VeriFlow*, a multi-dimensional verification framework for LLM-generated low-code workflows. Figure 1 provides a high-level view of the pipeline. Given a natural-language prompt and an LLM-generated workflow specification, VeriFlow analyzes three complementary dimensions: (i) structural soundness of the workflow graph (node/edge consistency, reachability, suspicious cycles), (ii) semantic consistency between the workflow and the extracted intent (capability coverage, ordering constraints, trigger compatibility, and field/parameter alignment), and (iii) execution readiness assessed through a capability-aware sandbox that detects invalid parameters, runtime infeasibility, and other execution-related issues under a verification-oriented abstraction.

Running Example. Consider the prompt: *"When I receive a new Gmail invoice, extract the amount and append it to a Google Sheet, then notify me on Slack."* An LLM-generated workflow may appear structurally plausible while still containing (i) an unreachable branch, such as a disconnected filtering path, (ii) a semantic ordering mismatch, such as notifying before persisting the row, or (iii) an execution-related issue, such as an invalid Sheet ID. VeriFlow detects such issues and returns actionable diagnostics, including unreachable nodes, ordering conflicts, and parameter mismatches.

This paper makes the following contributions:

- A multi-dimensional verification framework for LLM-generated low-code workflows, combining structural, semantic, and execution-readiness analyses.
- A hybrid semantic consistency analysis method that combines rule-based reasoning with optional LLM-assisted intent extraction to detect intent–workflow mismatches.
- An open-source toolchain and a publicly released benchmark of LLM-generated n8n workflows (GenLLM), together with scripts to reproduce the reported results.

The remainder of the paper is organized as follows. Section 2 introduces the formal model. Section 3 presents the VeriFlow framework and its three modules. Section 4 describes the implementation and empirical evaluation. Section 5 discusses related work, and Sect. 6 concludes and outlines future directions.

2 Background

We model LLM-generated low-code workflows as graph-based artifacts equipped with platform-specific nodes, configuration parameters, and a natural-language intent description. The goal of this abstraction is not to preserve the full execution semantics of the underlying platform, but to provide a verification-oriented representation that supports three complementary analyses: structure, semantic consistency, and execution readiness.

2.1 Workflow Graph Model

A workflow is represented as a directed graph with node-local parameters:

$$W = (N, E, P),$$

where N is a finite set of nodes, $E \subseteq N \times N$ is the control-flow edge relation, and $P : N \to \mathcal{P}$ maps each node to a parameter dictionary. Intuitively, nodes represent workflow steps, edges represent control-flow connections, and parameter dictionaries capture the local configuration associated with each step.

Entry and exit nodes are defined as

$$\begin{aligned} Entry(W) &= \{n \in N \mid \nexists n' \in N.\,(n', n) \in E\}, \\ Exit(W) &= \{n \in N \mid \nexists n' \in N.\,(n, n') \in E\}. \end{aligned}$$

In VeriFlow, W is deterministically extracted from n8n JSON by mapping workflow nodes, connection objects, and parameter blocks to graph nodes, directed edges, and node-local configuration dictionaries, respectively. Runtime details that are not needed by the current analyses are intentionally abstracted away.

2.2 Capability and Intent Abstraction

To abstract over platform-specific node types, each node $n \in N$ is associated with a set of abstract capabilities:

$$cap(n) \subseteq \mathcal{C},$$

where $\mathcal{C}$ is a finite capability universe (e.g., *email*, *http*, *condition*, *transform*). In the current prototype, capabilities are assigned through a lightweight rule-based mapping over node types and related metadata.

Given a natural-language prompt, intent is extracted as

$$Intent = f_{\text{extract}}(Prompt) = (\mathcal{C}_{\text{req}}, \mathcal{O}, \mathcal{T}, \mathcal{F}),$$

where $\mathcal{C}_{\text{req}} \subseteq \mathcal{C}$ denotes the required capabilities, $\mathcal{O} \subseteq \mathcal{C}_{\text{req}} \times \mathcal{C}_{\text{req}}$ encodes precedence constraints, $\mathcal{T}$ denotes the expected trigger category, and $\mathcal{F}$ collects referenced fields or entities mentioned in the prompt. This intent representation is intentionally lightweight: it captures the aspects of the prompt needed for the current semantic checks rather than a fully formal specification of user requirements.

2.3 Executability Model

Many workflow failures stem from missing or inconsistent configuration. Let $\text{Req}(n)$ denote the required parameter keys for the type of node n. A node is parameter-complete if and only if

$$complete(n) = \mathbf{1}\big(\text{Req}(n) \subseteq \text{keys}(P(n))\big).$$

In addition to parameter completeness, execution readiness depends on whether the relevant nodes are reachable from entry nodes and whether the workflow can be checked in a bounded sandbox without immediate execution-related errors. This notion is approximate by design: VeriFlow assesses execution readiness under a verification-oriented abstraction rather than proving full correctness of platform execution semantics.

2.4 Three-Dimensional Verification View

VeriFlow characterizes each workflow along three complementary dimensions:

- **Structural correctness** $S(W) \in [0, 1]$, capturing graph-level properties such as connectivity, orphan nodes, suspicious cycles, and exit coverage;
- **Semantic consistency** $M(W, Intent) \in [0, 1]$, capturing capability coverage, ordering consistency, trigger compatibility, and field/parameter alignment;
- **Execution readiness** $E(W) \in [0, 1]$, capturing parameter completeness, reachability, and bounded sandbox success.

Thus,

$$\mathsf{VeriFlow}(W, Intent) = (S(W),\ M(W, Intent),\ E(W)).$$

The resulting three-dimensional profile is used together with diagnostic evidence. When needed, an aggregate score can be derived later for compact reporting, but the primary outcome remains the dimension-wise analysis.

3 The VeriFlow Framework

VeriFlow operationalizes the model of Sect. 2 through three complementary analyses: structural verification, semantic consistency analysis, and execution-readiness assessment, corresponding to $S(W)$, $M(W, Intent)$, and $E(W)$, respectively. Rather than attempting to prove full correctness of platform execution, VeriFlow provides a verification-oriented analysis profile together with concrete diagnostic evidence such as unreachable nodes, ordering violations, and missing parameters.

3.1 Architecture Overview

Figure 2 summarizes the pipeline. Given a workflow specification and its corresponding natural-language prompt, VeriFlow proceeds in three steps: (i) graph extraction with capability annotation, (ii) intent extraction using rules and, optionally, LLM refinement, and (iii) three verifiers producing (S, M, E) together with diagnostic evidence.

3.2 Graph Extraction and Capability Annotation

From an n8n JSON specification, we deterministically construct $W = (N, E, P)$ by parsing: (i) workflow nodes (N), (ii) connection objects (E), and (iii) parameter blocks (P). This transformation yields a verification-oriented abstraction rather than a complete encoding of all platform semantics.

Each node $n \in N$ is then associated with abstract capabilities through a lightweight rule-based mapping over node types and related metadata, for example `emailSend`$\mapsto \{email\}$, `httpRequest`$\mapsto \{http\}$, and `if`$\mapsto \{condition\}$. This capability layer supports platform-agnostic reasoning while preserving the distinctions needed for the current analyses.

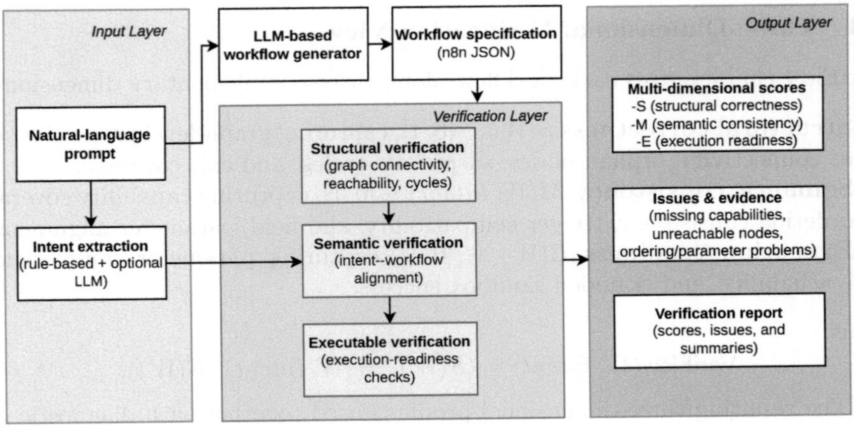

Fig. 2. VeriFlow architecture overview.

3.3 Intent Extraction

We extract *Intent* $= (\mathcal{C}_{\text{req}}, \mathcal{O}, \mathcal{T}, \mathcal{F})$ from the prompt using a hybrid pipeline. Here $\mathcal{T}$ denotes a possibly empty set of trigger constraints, including expected trigger categories and simple conjunction/disjunction patterns, rather than a single trigger label.

- **Rule-based extraction:** keyword patterns identify required capabilities and trigger cues, together with lightweight extraction of fields, entities, and simple values such as thresholds.
- **Optional LLM refinement:** when an API key is available, an LLM returns a strict JSON object validated against a schema; invalid or non-conformant outputs are discarded.

In the absence of external credentials, intent extraction remains fully deterministic. The resulting intent object is intentionally lightweight and captures only the aspects of the prompt needed by the current semantic checks.

3.4 Structural Verification

Structural verification evaluates graph integrity and basic control-flow consistency:

- **Reachability:** DFS/BFS from entry nodes identifies unreachable nodes and disconnected fragments [4].
- **Cycle analysis:** SCC-based analysis identifies suspicious cycles, i.e., cycles that may indicate unintended looping or malformed control flow under the current abstraction [23].
- **Exit coverage:** checking that at least one exit node is reachable from an entry node.

Sub-metrics are normalized and aggregated into $S(W)$, together with diagnostic evidence such as unreachable nodes, strongly connected components, and malformed connection keys.

3.5 Semantic Verification

Semantic verification checks whether the workflow is consistent with the extracted intent under the current abstraction:

- **Capability coverage:** $\mathcal{C}_{\text{req}} \subseteq \bigcup_{n \in N} \mathit{cap}(n)$.
- **Ordering consistency:** for each $(a \prec b) \in \mathcal{O}$, there exist $n_a, n_b \in N$ such that $a \in \mathit{cap}(n_a)$, $b \in \mathit{cap}(n_b)$, and $n_a \rightsquigarrow n_b$.
- **Trigger compatibility:** at least one trigger node satisfies $\mathcal{T}$.
- **Field/parameter alignment:** referenced fields or entities in $\mathcal{F}$ are matched against relevant node parameters and condition expressions using capability-specific heuristics.

These checks are aggregated into $M(W, \mathit{Intent})$ and accompanied by counterexamples indicating missing capabilities, violated ordering constraints, incompatible triggers, or unmatched fields.

3.6 Executable Verification

Executable verification assesses whether the workflow appears runnable under a bounded, side-effect-free sandbox with step budget $K_{\max}$. This assessment is approximate by design: it checks execution readiness under the current abstraction rather than proving full runtime correctness. We decompose $E(W)$ into three components.

Parameter Completeness.

$$E_{\text{param}}(W) = \frac{1}{|N|} \sum_{n \in N} \mathbf{1}\big(\text{Req}(n) \subseteq \text{keys}(P(n))\big).$$

Sandbox Reachability. Let $\mathit{Reach}_{\text{sb}}(W) = \{n \in N \mid \exists e \in \mathit{Entry}(W).\ e \rightsquigarrow_{\text{sb}} n\}$. Then

$$E_{\text{reach}}(W) = \frac{|\mathit{Reach}_{\text{sb}}(W)|}{|N|}.$$

Bounded Sandbox Success. Let $\mathsf{run}(W)$ denote attempted sandbox executions under admissible trigger events, and let $\mathsf{ok}(\rho)$ indicate termination within $K_{\max}$ without immediate execution-related errors:

$$E_{\text{run}}(W) = \frac{1}{|\mathsf{run}(W)|} \sum_{\rho \in \mathsf{run}(W)} \mathbf{1}\big(\mathsf{ok}(\rho)\big).$$

Finally, the execution-readiness score is

$$E(W) = \alpha E_{\text{param}}(W) + \beta E_{\text{reach}}(W) + \gamma E_{\text{run}}(W), \quad \alpha + \beta + \gamma = 1.$$

Authentication secrets, external service availability, and richer service-contract semantics are only partially modeled in the current sandbox and are therefore treated as out of scope for the present analysis.

3.7 Aggregation

We report the verification profile $(S(W), M(W, \mathit{Intent}), E(W))$ together with diagnostic evidence. When useful for compact reporting, an aggregate score may be derived from this three-dimensional profile, but the main outcome of VeriFlow remains the dimension-wise analysis rather than a single ranking value.

4 Tool Support and Evaluation

This section presents the VeriFlow toolchain, its software architecture, and the empirical evaluation of its effectiveness on LLM-generated low-code workflows. The goal is twofold: (i) demonstrate that the framework is implementable as a practical verification tool, and (ii) quantify its capability to detect structural, semantic, and execution-related defects in LLM-generated workflows. The design follows the formal foundations of Sect. 2 and instantiates the three verification dimensions $S(W)$, $M(W, \mathit{Intent})$, and $E(W)$.

4.1 Tool Architecture and Implementation

VeriFlow[1] is a modular Python 3.10 toolkit that implements the pipeline of Sect. 3. It comprises four components:

- **Graph extractor:** parses n8n workflow JSON into (N, E, P) with capability labels, and performs reachability, SCC-based cycle detection, exit coverage, and orphan detection.
- **Intent extractor:** derives intent from the prompt using rules, optionally refined by an LLM; outputs are validated against a strict JSON schema for reproducibility.
- **Semantic verifier:** checks capability coverage, ordering, trigger compatibility, and field/parameter alignment (Sect. 2), and produces counterexamples for debugging.
- **Executable sandbox:** simulates the behavior of common nodes (e.g., `HTTP Request`, `EmailSend`, `Set`, `IF`, `Schedule`) under side-effect–free sandbox semantics, checking parameter completeness, dead code, and bounded handling of cycles.

A command-line interface (CLI) with `typer` supports single-case analysis, DAG visualization, and batch benchmarking; each run outputs a structured JSON report with (S, M, E), issues, counterexamples, and a compact summary.

[1] https://github.com/ahzm/veriflow.

4.2 Benchmark Construction

We evaluate VeriFlow using the *GenLLM benchmark*, a systematically constructed collection of workflows generated from natural-language prompts. Each dataset W_k contains exactly k prompts (e.g., $W10$, $W20$, $W60$, $W100$), and one workflow is generated for each prompt using *GPT-4o-mini* under fixed decoding parameters. Thus, W_k denotes the *number of prompts*, not the structural size of the resulting workflows.

Prompts were constructed to cover common automation intents (email, HTTP, spreadsheet, messaging, conditional routing), and include both simple and multi-step instructions. For example: *"When a new invoice arrives in Gmail, extract the total and append it to Google Sheets, then notify Slack."* All prompts, generated workflows (n8n JSON), and evaluation scripts are released in the VeriFlow artifact repository.

To assess robustness under increased semantic difficulty, we additionally define constrained variants W_kC. These datasets contain the same number of prompts but with significantly more complex instructions involving nested conditions, multi-trigger dependencies, and parameter constraints, making them systematically harder to analyse.

Across the full set of W_k and W_kC families, the benchmark contains a total of *690 workflows*, covering a wide spectrum of structural patterns, semantic ambiguities, and execution-related conditions.

4.3 Research Questions

We evaluate VeriFlow on the GenLLM benchmark through two research questions:

RQ1. How consistent are the three verification dimensions (S, M, E) across benchmark families of increasing prompt-set size?

RQ2. What is the effect of hybrid intent extraction (rule vs. rule+LLM) on semantic consistency and on the aggregate outcome, for both unconstrained and constrained benchmark sets?

4.4 Experimental Setup

We process all 690 workflows with the same pipeline: (i) graph extraction from the n8n JSON specification; (ii) intent extraction using either rule-based heuristics or a rule+LLM hybrid refinement (*GPT-4o-mini*); (iii) computation of (S, M, E); and (iv) sandbox execution to detect missing parameters and execution-related failures. We additionally report an overall score $\mathit{Overall} = (S+M+E)/3$. For paired rule vs. rule+LLM comparisons, ΔM denotes the absolute difference in semantic consistency, while $\Delta M(\%)$ and $\Delta \mathit{Overall}(\%)$ denote the corresponding relative percentage changes.

Experiments were run on a MacOS workstation (M4 CPU, 32 GB RAM). The tool, prompts, workflows, and scripts are available in the VeriFlow artifact repository.

4.5 Results

Table 1 summarizes the verification results across all W_k and W_kC datasets. It reports the three verification dimensions: structural correctness S, semantic consistency M, and execution readiness E, all normalized to $[0,1]$, where higher values indicate better outcomes. For compact comparison, we also report *Overall* $= (S + M + E)/3$. Within each benchmark pair, the rule+LLM row is compared against the rule-only baseline through ΔM and the corresponding percentage deltas.

Table 1. GenLLM benchmark results (rule vs. hybrid extraction).

Benchmark	Extraction	S	M	E	Overall	ΔM	ΔM(%)	ΔOverall(%)
GenLLM_W10	rule	0.97	0.89	0.47	0.78	–	–	–
	rule+LLM	0.97	0.83	0.47	0.75	-0.07	-7.3%	-2.8%
GenLLM_W20	rule	0.99	0.90	0.93	0.94	–	–	–
	rule+LLM	0.99	0.90	0.93	0.94	-0.00	-0.1%	-0.1%
GenLLM_W30	rule	0.99	0.90	0.93	0.94	–	–	–
	rule+LLM	0.99	0.94	0.93	0.95	+0.04	+4.3%	+1.4%
GenLLM_W50	rule	0.98	0.92	0.94	0.95	–	–	–
	rule+LLM	0.98	0.96	0.94	0.96	+0.03	+3.4%	+1.1%
GenLLM_W60	rule	0.97	0.93	0.96	0.96	–	–	–
	rule+LLM	0.97	0.95	0.96	0.96	+0.02	+2.2%	+0.7%
GenLLM_W80	rule	0.97	0.97	0.97	0.97	–	–	–
	rule+LLM	0.97	0.97	0.97	0.97	+0.00	+0.5%	+0.2%
GenLLM_W100	rule	0.96	0.98	0.97	0.97	–	–	–
	rule+LLM	0.96	0.98	0.97	0.97	+0.00	+0.1%	+0.0%
GenLLM_W20C	rule	0.93	0.91	0.80	0.88	–	–	–
	rule+LLM	0.93	0.82	0.80	0.85	-0.09	-10.4%	-3.7%
GenLLM_W30C	rule	0.95	0.92	0.89	0.92	–	–	–
	rule+LLM	0.95	0.86	0.89	0.90	-0.05	-5.8%	-2.0%
GenLLM_W50C	rule	0.96	0.94	0.91	0.94	–	–	–
	rule+LLM	0.96	0.85	0.91	0.91	-0.09	-9.9%	-3.2%
GenLLM_W60C	rule	0.96	0.95	0.94	0.95	–	–	–
	rule+LLM	0.96	0.87	0.94	0.92	-0.08	-8.2%	-2.7%
GenLLM_W80C	rule	0.96	0.93	0.96	0.95	–	–	–
	rule+LLM	0.96	0.86	0.96	0.93	-0.07	-7.9%	-2.6%
GenLLM_W100C	rule	0.97	0.93	0.96	0.95	–	–	–
	rule+LLM	0.97	0.84	0.96	0.92	-0.09	-9.4%	-3.0%

RQ1 - Consistency Across Benchmark Families. Across unconstrained datasets with $k \geq 20$ (i.e., $W20$–$W100$), VeriFlow achieves consistently high scores: $S =$ 0.96–0.99, $E =$ 0.93–0.97, and *Overall* $=$ 0.94–0.97. The $W10$ set is an outlier with a markedly lower execution-readiness score ($E = 0.47$, $overall = 0.78$), indicating that execution readiness is sensitive to missing parameters and unreachable branches in small samples. This behavior is consistent with E being driven by parameter completeness and sandbox run success, which are strongly affected by a few non-executable workflows in small samples.

For constrained datasets (W_kC), scores decrease moderately compared to unconstrained sets, with semantic consistency emerging as the main source of degradation. While S remains high ($\approx$ 0.93–0.97) and E stays comparatively strong ($\approx$ 0.80–0.96), the semantic dimension is consistently more sensitive to increased prompt complexity and constraint density. Overall, the results remain consistent for $k \geq 20$, and the degradation observed on constrained sets is driven primarily by semantic difficulty rather than structural failure.

RQ2 - Effect of Hybrid Intent Extraction. Hybrid rule+LLM extraction has a mixed effect. It improves M on mid-sized unconstrained sets (e.g., $W30$–$W60$), is essentially neutral on larger unconstrained sets ($W80$–$W100$) and on $W20$, but consistently reduces M on all constrained sets (W_kC), with drops between −5.8% and −10.4%. This suggests that LLM refinement can introduce semantic noise under strict behavioral constraints, leading to lower semantic alignment. Overall, hybrid extraction is beneficial mainly for moderately ambiguous unconstrained prompts and should be applied cautiously when tight semantic conformance is required.

5 Related Work

Verification of LLM-generated low-code workflows sits at the intersection of (i) workflow/process model verification, (ii) requirement–behaviour alignment, (iii) quality and reliability of low-code/no-code (LCNC) platforms, and (iv) LLM-based workflow synthesis. We use *LCNC workflows* to denote executable automation artifacts in platforms such as n8n/Zapier/Make, as opposed to conceptual process models (e.g., BPMN or Petri nets).

5.1 Workflow Verification and Structural Soundness

Classical workflow verification builds on Petri-net and graph-based analysis to detect control-flow errors (e.g., deadlocks, improper completion, unreachable tasks) [1,6]. BPMN standards and tooling further support structural validity checks for manually designed models [19]. Recent studies show that LLMs can generate BPMN-like models, yet often introduce incomplete paths and inconsistent control-flow patterns [15,16], and vision papers anticipate broader AI-driven BPM scenarios [14]. These works motivate the structural dimension of VeriFlow, captured by $S(W)$, but do not address LCNC-specific failures stemming from partial configuration or runtime constraints. Beyond classical soundness analysis, recent work has studied formal and runtime verification of executable BPMN processes, including probabilistic model checking and runtime enforcement [7,9].

Related ideas also appear in software engineering research on static analysis, type checking, and service/interface compatibility. However, these approaches generally target engineered BPMN models, hand-written programs, or explicit formal specifications rather than LLM-generated LCNC workflows from natural-language prompts.

5.2 Semantic Alignment and Requirement–Behaviour Correspondence

A second stream assesses whether a process matches its intended behaviour. Conformance and alignment techniques compare observed behaviour with models and constraints, e.g., via replay-based alignment or mixed-paradigm checking [5,12]. Complementary NLP-based approaches map textual requirements to process structures or support semantic reasoning for compliance [2,24]. In our setting, the workflow is *generated* from a prompt and may exhibit semantic drift (missing/substituted actions, misinterpreted conditions/fields), consistent with documented hallucinations and behavioural instability in LLMs [13,27]. Uncertainty-based diagnostics can flag suspicious generations [11,28], but do not operationalize intent satisfaction for workflows. This motivates our semantic dimension $M(W, Intent)$, which checks capability coverage, ordering, and data/parameter usage against prompt-derived intent without assuming event logs or a ground-truth reference model.

5.3 LCNC Platforms and Executability-Oriented Quality

LCNC platforms have been analysed in terms of quality attributes and deployment risks [3,18,22], while process-aware information systems research studies robustness and runtime failures in executable process settings [20]. Verification work on low-code platforms often targets schema-level validation or model–data consistency [26]. For LLM-generated LCNC workflows, many critical defects arise at the *configuration/runtime* level (e.g., missing IDs/credentials, invalid parameter combinations, non-viable execution branches). Related runtime-oriented work has also explored predictive analytics and resource-aware decision support for executable BPMN processes, reinforcing the importance of execution-level reasoning in process-aware systems [8]. This motivates our execution-readiness dimension $E(W)$, implemented via a capability-aware sandbox that complements structural and semantic analyses with explicit execution-related checks.

5.4 LLM-Based Workflow Synthesis and Automation Pipelines

LLMs are increasingly used to generate structured workflows for automation and agentic systems [10,17,25]. While these systems demonstrate strong synthesis capability, they also report frequent failures such as missing parameters, incorrect ordering, and non-executable steps, underscoring the need for workflow-aware verification beyond generic uncertainty signals. Existing approaches generally do not provide workflow-specific verification support that jointly covers structure, intent satisfaction, and execution readiness for LCNC artifacts.

Overall, while workflow soundness/conformance, LCNC quality, and LLM failure modes are well studied, verification tailored to *LLM-generated LCNC workflows* remains limited. VeriFlow addresses this gap by combining structural, semantic, and execution-readiness analyses with actionable diagnostic evidence.

6 Conclusion and Future Work

This paper introduced *VeriFlow*, a multi-dimensional verification framework for LLM-generated low-code workflows, combining structural checks, semantic consistency analysis, and execution-readiness assessment. The toolchain provides end-to-end analysis, including DAG visualization, multi-dimensional scoring, and diagnostic reports. Our evaluation shows that, despite high aggregate scores on many benchmark sets, a non-negligible number of workflows still exhibit *long-tail* defects such as unreachable branches, intent–capability mismatches, and missing or invalid parameters. VeriFlow detects and localizes these issues through actionable diagnostic evidence, supporting verification as a practical *guardrail* for AI-assisted automation.

Future Work. Future work includes strengthening semantic consistency analysis, enriching the sandbox with richer behavioral modeling, broadening platform coverage beyond n8n, and integrating automated repair to connect verification more tightly with workflow synthesis.

References

1. van der Aalst, W.: Workflow verification: finding control-flow errors using petri-net-based techniques. Bus. Process Manag., 161–183 (2000)
2. Aysolmaz, B., Leopold, H., Reijers, H., Demirörs, O.: A semi-automated approach for generating natural language requirements documents based on business process models. Inf. Softw. Technol. **93**, 14–29 (2018)
3. Bock, A.C., Frank, U.: Low-code platform. Bus. Inform. Syst. Eng. **63**, 733–740 (2021). https://doi.org/10.1007/s12599-021-00726-8
4. Cormen, T.H., Leiserson, C.E., Rivest, R.L., Stein, C.: Introduction to Algorithms, 3rd edn. MIT Press (2009)
5. Dongen, B.V., Smedt, J., Ciccio, C.D., Mendling, J.: Conformance checking of mixed-paradigm process models. Inf. Syst. **102**, 101685 (2020)
6. Dumas, M., La Rosa, M., Mendling, J., Reijers, H.A.: Fundamentals of Business Process Management, 2nd edn. Springer (2018)
7. Falcone, Y., Salaün, G., Zuo, A.: Probabilistic model checking of bpmn processes at runtime. In: International Conference on Integrated Formal Methods, pp. 191–208. Springer (2022). https://doi.org/10.1007/978-3-031-07727-2_11
8. Falcone, Y., Salaün, G., Zuo, A.: Dynamic resource allocation for executable bpmn processes leveraging predictive analytics. In: IEEE 24th International Conference on Software Quality, Reliability and Security (QRS), pp. 689–700. IEEE (2024)
9. Falcone, Y., Salaün, G., Zuo, A.: Probabilistic runtime enforcement of executable bpmn processes. In: International Conference on Fundamental Approaches to Software Engineering. pp. 56–76. Springer (2024). https://doi.org/10.1007/978-3-031-57259-3_3

10. Fan, S., et al.: Workflowllm: enhancing workflow orchestration capability of large language models. ArXiv abs/ arXiv:2411.05451 (2024)
11. Farquhar, S., Kossen, J., Kuhn, L., Gal, Y.: Detecting hallucinations in large language models using semantic entropy. Nature **630**, 625–630 (2024)
12. García-Bañuelos, L., van Beest, N., Dumas, M., Rosa, M., Mertens, W.: Complete and interpretable conformance checking of business processes. IEEE Trans. Software Eng. **44**, 262–290 (2018)
13. Huang, L., Yu, W., Ma, W., et al.: A survey on hallucination in large language models: principles, taxonomy, challenges, and open questions. ACM Trans. Inform. Syst. **43**, 1–55 (2023)
14. Kampik, T., et al.: Large process models: a vision for business process management in the age of generative AI. KI - Künstliche Intelligenz (2023)
15. Kourani, H., Berti, A., Schuster, D., Aalst, W.M.: Evaluating large language models on business process modeling: Framework, benchmark, and self-improvement analysis. ArXiv abs/ arXiv:2412.00023 (2024)
16. Kourani, H., Berti, A., Schuster, D., Aalst, W.M.: Process modeling with large language models, pp. 229–244. CoRR abs/ arXiv: 2403.07541 (2024)
17. Li, Z., et al.: Autoflow: automated workflow generation for large language model agents. ArXiv abs/ arXiv: 2407.12821 (2024). https://doi.org/10.48550/arxiv.2407.12821
18. Naqvi, B., Kedziora, D., Zhang, L., Oyedeji, S.: Quality of low-code/no-code development platforms through the lens of iso 25010:2023. Computer **58**, 30–40 (2025)
19. Object Management Group: Business process model and notation (bpmn) version 2.0.2 (2013). https://www.omg.org/spec/BPMN/2.0.2/
20. Schwerz, A.L., Liberato, R., Pu, C., Ferreira, J.E.: Robust and reliable process-aware information systems. IEEE Trans. Serv. Comput. **14**, 820–833 (2021). https://doi.org/10.1109/tsc.2018.2824810
21. Silva, D.I.D., Shangavie, R., Ranathunga, R.: Role of quality assurance in low-code/no-code projects. In: 2024 International Conference on Information Networking (ICOIN), pp. 789–794 (2024). https://doi.org/10.1109/icoin59985.2024.10572203
22. Sufi, F.K.: Algorithms in low-code-no-code for research applications: a practical review. Algorithms **16**, 108 (2023). https://doi.org/10.3390/a16020108
23. Tarjan, R.: Depth-first search and linear graph algorithms. SIAM J. Comput. **1**(2), 146–160 (1972). https://doi.org/10.1137/0201010
24. Thayasivam, U., Verma, K., Kass, A., Vasquez, R.G.: Automatically mapping natural language requirements to domain-specific process models. In: Proceedings of the AAAI Conference on Artificial Intelligence (2011)
25. Xu, J., Du, W., Liu, X., Li, X.: LLM4Workflow: an LLM-based automated workflow model generation tool. In: 2024 39th IEEE/ACM International Conference on Automated Software Engineering (ASE), pp. 2394–2398 (2024)
26. Zaheri, M., Famelis, M., Syriani, E.: Catch me if you can: detecting model-data inconsistencies in low-code applications. J. Object Technol. (2024)
27. Zhang, Y., et al.: Siren's song in the ai ocean: a survey on hallucination in large language models. ArXiv abs/ arxiv:2309.01219 (2023)
28. Zhang, Y., Chen, J., Wang, J., et al.: Toolbehonest: a multi-level hallucination diagnostic benchmark for tool-augmented large language models (2024). https://doi.org/10.48550/arXiv.2406.20015

AI for Product Development

Toward a Method for Accurate and Explainable Cost Estimation Using Artificial Intelligence in Product Development

Claudia Michelberger[1(✉)], Kevin Klöpfer[2], and Marco F. Huber[1,2]

[1] Institute of Industrial Manufacturing and Management IFF, University of Stuttgart, 70569 Stuttgart, Germany
claudia.michelberger@iff.uni-stuttgart.de, marco.huber@ieee.org

[2] Fraunhofer Institute for Manufacturing Engineering and Automation IPA, 70569 Stuttgart, Germany
kevin.kloepfer@ipa.fraunhofer.de

Abstract. Cost estimation in the early phases of product development remains challenging due to high uncertainty, limited data, and a strong reliance on expert knowledge. To address these challenges, this paper presents and evaluates a proof-of-concept study for accurate and explainable cost estimation using artificial intelligence (AI) to support decision-making in product development. The proposed approach applies machine learning to generate cost estimates and employs methods from the field of explainable AI to identify cost drivers and quantify their influence on the estimated costs. In addition, a large language model is used to suggest product design improvements to reduce costs. The evaluation shows that the proposed approach can outperform both expert-based cost estimates and rule-based cost estimates generated by software tools in terms of accuracy and speed, while also improving explainability. Overall, the paper lays the groundwork for integrating accurate and explainable AI-assisted cost estimation into decision-making in product development.

Keywords: Cost estimation · Artificial intelligence · Machine learning · Explainable artificial intelligence · Large language models

1 Introduction

In enterprises, cost estimation is central to managing uncertainty and guiding decisions in the early phases of product development, particularly during the concept and design phases [8]. Cost estimates often determine whether a product is pursued, requires cost-driven improvements, or is abandoned, thereby shaping the economic viability of future products [2]. In the early phases, however, data are scarce and often incomplete, and cost estimates are largely based on expert knowledge [11]. As a result, cost estimation is not only prone to inaccuracy

K. Węcel and V. Řepa (Eds.): BIS 2026, LNBIP 584, pp. 171–182, 2026.
https://doi.org/10.1007/978-3-032-26363-6_13

but also time-consuming, creating delays in decision-making and increasing the risk of developing products that later prove economically unviable. Accordingly, design decisions made in the early phases can determine up to 80% of total costs [4], yet they are taken when knowledge about costs is at its lowest [18].

In this context, artificial intelligence (AI) offers opportunities to address these challenges. Several studies have shown that machine learning (ML) can deliver accurate cost estimates while reducing the time required for expert-based cost estimation and lowering reliance on expert knowledge [11,16]. However, most studies adopt a technical perspective and pay limited attention to how such methods can be applied within enterprises and integrated into existing product development processes, particularly in the early phases [19]. Moreover, many ML-based methods remain black boxes, making it difficult for experts to understand how cost estimates are generated and which product characteristics should be optimized to reduce costs [22]. This lack of transparency and interpretability limits trust and adoption [13]. Methods from the field of explainable AI (XAI) can address this limitation by identifying the cost drivers and quantifying their influence on estimated costs. Beyond explanation, early design decisions can benefit from actionable guidance on how to lower costs by making complex cost structures explicit and reducing reliance on expert knowledge. Large language models (LLMs) can complement XAI by transforming explanations into product design improvement suggestions. Together, these methods open a pathway toward accurate and explainable AI-assisted cost estimation and optimization.

The contribution of this paper is the proposal and evaluation of an approach for AI-assisted cost estimation in the early phases of product development. The approach combines ML for accurate cost estimation, XAI for identifying and quantifying cost drivers, and an LLM for translating these explanations into product design improvement suggestions. The approach is instantiated and evaluated in a proof-of-concept study using real-world data from sheet metal parts to assess its feasibility, accuracy, explainability, and practical usefulness compared to established expert-based and rule-based cost estimation methods.

This paper is structured as follows: Section 2 reviews related work. Section 3 introduces the approach. Section 4 presents the evaluation results. Section 5 discusses implications and limitations. Section 6 provides a summary.

2 Related Work

Cost estimation in the early phases mainly relies on parametric models, case-based reasoning, and rule-based methods [14]. While well established, these methods depend heavily on expert knowledge and struggle with uncertainty and incomplete data about product characteristics, particularly in the early phases [18]. In recent years, studies have explored the use of ML-based methods to address these limitations and report that they can deliver accurate cost estimates while reducing the manual effort required from experts [5,6]. For example, Manuguerra et al. [12] apply ML-based methods to estimate costs of sheet metal parts in the early phases and report low cost estimation errors. However, most studies focus on technical performance and provide limited insights into how such methods can be integrated into product development processes [20,21].

To improve the explainability of ML-based methods, XAI-based methods such as Local Interpretable Model-agnostic Explanations (LIME) [16] and SHapley Additive exPlanations (SHAP) [10] are used to explain how product characteristics influence costs. Only a few studies apply XAI-based methods specifically to cost estimation, for example in machining or vehicle component costing, where explanations help experts understand the cost drivers [13,22]. Nevertheless, existing work in AI-assisted cost estimation remains fragmented. ML-based methods focus on predictive performance, while XAI-based methods explain cost estimates, yet typically stop at explanation rather than supporting decision-making or assessing practical adoption. In the early phases, cost estimates raise the question of how costs can be reduced and which cost-driven design changes should be considered. Recent LLMs [1] offer a promising way to translate XAI-based explanations into actionable product design improvement suggestions. Consequently, there is still no integrated approach that combines ML-based cost estimation, XAI-based explanations, and LLM-based design guidance for decision-making. This gap motivates the approach proposed in this paper.

3 Approach

This section introduces an approach for accurate and explainable cost estimation in the early phases of product development. The approach focuses on using early available data to generate cost estimates, explain the underlying cost drivers, and suggest product design improvements to reduce costs. The approach follows a process consisting of five steps as illustrated in Figure 1.

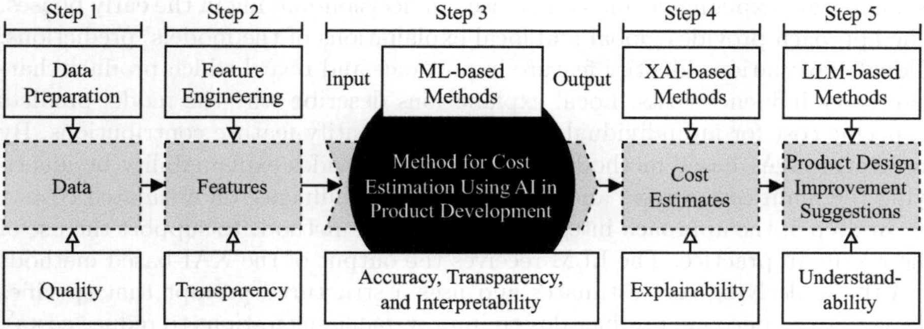

Fig. 1. Overall structure of the approach.

In Step 1, the approach begins with the available data, which come from concepts, preliminary specifications, or other early design documents [15]. These may include geometric dimensions such as length and width, weight, material type, and other characteristics relevant to the expected costs. As these data originate from early design documents, their quality may vary with regard to completeness, consistency, and granularity. The approach therefore includes a data preparation step to ensure that the data can be used consistently throughout the process. Data preparation covers handling missing values, plausibility checks, transformation of categorical attributes, normalization of attributes, and data harmonization and standardization, for example by mapping different material descriptions that refer to the same material to a single consistent description.

In Step 2, the approach integrates feature engineering to extract and derive features that improve the quality of the cost estimation. Relevant features can include geometric relationships such as surface area or volume estimates, indicators of product complexity, or ratios between dimensions. The goal is to create a set of features that capture both the physical characteristics of the product and the manufacturing effort, such as laser cutting and bending operations. This step is necessary because data in the early phases often lack detailed manufacturing attributes, and meaningful features must be derived from the available data.

In Step 3, the approach performs cost estimation using ML-based methods to generate cost estimates. The approach is largely model-agnostic and does not prescribe a single ML model. Instead, it can be instantiated with different model families, such as linear and regularized regression, tree-based models (e.g., random forests, gradient boosting, and extra trees), and neural networks. Using the features from Step 2 as input, the models capture complex relationships between product characteristics and costs and produce numerical cost estimates as output. The approach aims to obtain accurate cost estimates under the constraints of high-level early-phase data. In addition, the cost estimation step must meet basic requirements for transparency and interpretability to ensure that the resulting cost estimates can be understood and used reliably by experts.

In Step 4, the approach incorporates XAI-based methods to ensure that cost estimates are explainable and can be used in decision-making in the early phases. The approach provides global and local explanations of the models' predictions. Global explanations identify feature importance and reveal which product characteristics influence costs. Local explanations describe why the model predicts a specific cost for an individual product and quantify feature contributions. By integrating XAI-based methods, the approach provides explainability by identifying the main cost drivers and quantifying their influence on estimated costs.

In Step 5, the approach integrates LLM-based methods to support the use of the results in practice. The LLM receives the output of the XAI-based methods and the underlying cost estimates and uses a structured prompt that specifies the task (e.g., deriving product design improvement suggestions to reduce costs), the available inputs (e.g., estimated costs and identified cost drivers), and the decision context (e.g., early phases of product development) to generate product design improvement suggestions. For example, it can suggest alternative design options, such as adjustments in geometry or material choices, to reduce the expected costs. This step supports decision-making in the early phases, promotes acceptance of the approach, and can reduce manual analysis effort and enable a more efficient use of design engineering resources in product development.

In summary, the output of the approach consists of three results: the cost estimate, its explanation through XAI-based methods, and the product design improvement suggestions derived from LLM-based methods. Together, these results support decision-making in the early phases, even when limited data are available. The results allow design engineers to understand the cost implications of design choices, assess cost drivers, and identify cost-reduction opportunities.

4 Evaluation

The evaluation combines a quantitative benchmark comparing the approach in terms of accuracy and speed against expert-based and rule-based cost estimates with a qualitative expert study. The study assesses the explainability and usefulness of SHAP-based cost driver identification as well as the understandability and usefulness of LLM-based product design improvement suggestions.

4.1 Methodology

The evaluation follows Design Science Research (DSR), as the study focuses on the development and evaluation of an artifact [7]. DSR is well suited because it addresses the creation, instantiation, and evaluation of artifacts intended to solve practical problems. In this study, the artifact is realized as a proof-of-concept that integrates methods from ML, XAI, and LLMs to support cost estimation. The evaluation involves seven experts from the enterprise that provided the dataset. All experts have experience in part cost estimation and cost-related decision-making, with experience ranging from 1 to 17 years. They participated in both the quantitative and qualitative evaluation. The objective of the evaluation is not to demonstrate an optimized solution, but to assess whether the approach works under realistic conditions and provides value for decision-making. In particular, the evaluation examines whether the approach delivers accurate cost estimates, provides explainability, and supports decision-making by generating product design improvement suggestions. This perspective aligns with the understanding that evaluation should go beyond technical performance, as stated by Doshi-Velez and Kim [3]. Figure 2 shows the evaluation process.

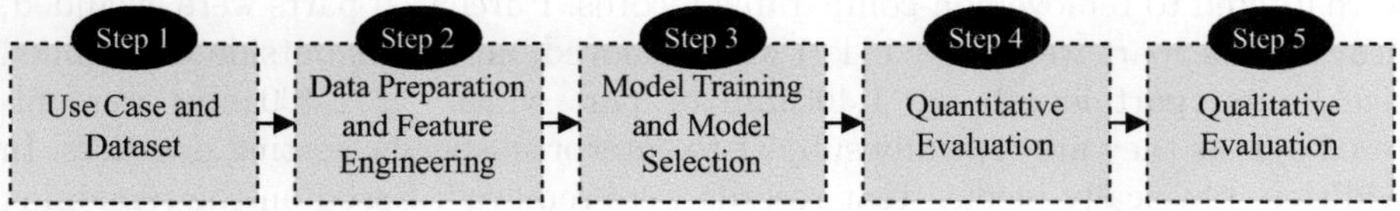

Fig. 2. Overall evaluation process of the methodology.

The evaluation process starts with defining the use case and dataset (Step 1). Then, data preparation and feature engineering are performed (Step 2), and a model is trained and selected using five-fold cross-validation (Step 3). Next, the quantitative evaluation benchmarks the selected model against expert-based and rule-based cost estimates using the ground-truth part costs as reference values (Step 4). Finally, the qualitative evaluation assesses the explainability and usefulness of cost drivers as well as the understandability and usefulness of product design improvement suggestions based on predefined evaluation criteria and expert ratings, with current expert practice serving as a baseline (Step 5).

4.2 Step 1: Use Case and Dataset

In Step 1, a real-world use case and the dataset were defined. The approach is domain-agnostic, and laser-cut and bent sheet metal parts were selected as a widely used and representative part type in mechanical engineering. The dataset was provided by a large German mechanical engineering enterprise and consists of 289 parts. Each record includes part-related attributes as shown in Table 1.

Table 1. Overview of part-related attributes available in the dataset.

#	Group	Attributes
1	Administrative	Part number, product area, description, source
2	Cost	Part cost (€)
3	Geometry	Part length (mm), part width (mm), part weight (kg)
4	Material	Material type, material thickness (mm)
5	Manufacturing	Number of piercings, cutout length (mm), number of bends

The dataset covers a wide range of part sizes, weights, materials, and geometric complexity, reflecting realistic variability. The objective of the use case is to estimate the manufacturing cost per part, including material and processing-related costs such as laser cutting and bending operations.

4.3 Step 2: Data Preparation and Feature Engineering

In Step 2, the data were prepared and features were engineered. The raw data were filtered to remove non-comparable records. Purchased parts were excluded, heavy parts (part weight $\geqq$ 15 kg) were removed, and parts outside the defined size limits (part length $\geqq$ 1,400 mm or part width $\geqq$ 1,400 mm) were filtered out, as they are typically subject to enterprise-specific costing practices. In addition, physically inconsistent records were removed. Based on the remaining 230 records, domain-informed features were constructed. Material types were mapped to reference material prices, and a material cost feature was derived by multiplying part weight with the corresponding material price. Administrative attributes were excluded from the feature set, for example, part descriptions, as they are non-standardized and would require manual normalization, while the approach focuses on structured early-phase product characteristics. Categorical features were one-hot encoded. The 230 records were then split into 196 records used for training and five-fold cross-validation in Step 3 and a separate hold-out set of 34 records reserved for the final evaluation in Step 4.

4.4 Step 3: Model Training and Model Selection

In Step 3, we selected model families commonly used for tabular data that perform robustly on small-to-medium datasets, including a linear baseline and established tree-based ensembles. Models were trained and compared in a unified machine learning (ML) pipeline using five-fold cross-validation with shuffled splits and a fixed random seed. Cross-validation was used for model selection and excluded the hold-out set for the final evaluation in Step 4. Performance was evaluated per fold using mean absolute error (MAE), mean absolute percentage error (MAPE), and a pseudo-R^2 metric. Table 2 shows the results.

Table 2. Cross-validation results used for model selection.

#	Model	MAE (€)	MAPE (%)	pseudo-R^2
1	XGBoost	0.622 ± 0.235	17.03 ± 6.92	0.936 ± 0.051
2	Gradient Boosting	0.705 ± 0.218	17.95 ± 6.43	0.928 ± 0.026
3	Extra Trees	0.718 ± 0.152	18.82 ± 5.03	0.902 ± 0.057
4	Random Forest	0.800 ± 0.159	21.76 ± 4.65	0.911 ± 0.029
5	CatBoost	0.815 ± 0.294	18.82 ± 4.30	0.859 ± 0.114
6	Linear Regression	1.158 ± 0.084	40.82 ± 8.50	0.850 ± 0.064

The results show that XGBoost achieves the lowest MAE and MAPE and the highest pseudo-R^2, indicating the best overall predictive performance. It was therefore selected for the subsequent benchmarking.

4.5 Step 4: Quantitative Evaluation

In Step 4, we evaluate the accuracy and speed of cost estimates under realistic early-phase conditions. All methods were evaluated on the same set of parts. The ML-based cost estimates were generated using XGBoost and evaluated on an unseen hold-out set of 34 records. The results were benchmarked against two practice-based methods. First, expert-based cost estimates, based on intuition and experience, were provided independently by seven experts from the enterprise that provided the dataset and aggregated using the mean across experts. Second, rule-based cost estimates were generated using WSi, a 3D software tool for cost estimation in sheet metal processing. The results are shown in Table 3.

Table 3. Comparison of cost estimation accuracy and speed.

#	Method	MAE (€)	MAPE (%)	RMSE (€)	Bias (€)	Time (s)
1	XGBoost	0.667	14.29	1.101	−0.056	< 1
2	Experts (mean)	0.950	31.96	1.440	0.006	16.5 ± 3.5
3	WSi	1.339	28.39	2.008	1.235	< 3

XGBoost outperforms experts' cost estimates and WSi across all accuracy metrics, with lower MAE and RMSE and roughly half the MAPE compared to WSi. While WSi shows a positive bias, indicating overestimation, the ML-based estimates exhibit a bias close to zero. Individual experts show systematic biases, whereas averaging their estimates cancels these biases, yielding an unbiased group estimate (bias = 0.006). Notably, the aggregated expert estimate achieves a lower error (MAE = 0.950) than the best individual expert (MAE = 0.974), meaning that no individual expert outperforms the group mean, a typical wisdom-of-the-crowds effect. Nevertheless, XGBoost outperforms both individual and aggregated expert estimates and requires negligible computation time, while expert estimates are more time-consuming, although fast due to experts being familiar with similar parts. This is relevant in the early phases, as high accuracy and low bias reduce the risk of economically unfavorable design decisions. However, predictive accuracy alone is not sufficient for practical adoption, as cost estimates must also be explainable to support decision-making.

4.6 Step 5: Qualitative Evaluation

In Step 5, a qualitative expert study was conducted to assess the explainability and usefulness of SHAP-based cost driver identification as well as the understandability and usefulness of LLM-generated product design improvement suggestions. Seven experts participated in individual semi-structured interviews following a predefined interview guide. Each interview lasted about 30 minutes.

First, SHAP-based explanations [10] for laser-cut and bent sheet metal parts were presented to the seven experts. SHAP was selected as an established method that provides global and local explanations and is well suited for the tree-based models used in this study, while alternative XAI-based methods could be applied analogously. Explanations were computed for the XGBoost model using TreeExplainer, a fast SHAP implementation specialized for tree-based models [9]. Experts were shown global and local explanations highlighting the main contributing features and their positive or negative contributions to the predicted cost. For example, a local explanation showed that part weight was the main cost driver, while cutout length and material thickness had smaller cost-increasing effects, and a low number of bends reduced the cost. The explanations were generally regarded as technically sound and suitable for identifying cost drivers. At the same time, all experts stated that interpreting them requires prior knowledge and contextual understanding, with four experts expressing this concern strongly and three to a lesser extent. As a result, translating the explanations into early-phase design decisions was perceived as cognitively demanding.

Second, the experts evaluated LLM-generated product design improvement suggestions produced by ChatGPT 5.2. The model was selected because it is widely used in practice. The suggestions were evaluated along two dimensions relevant in early-phase decision-making: understandability and usefulness. Understandability captures whether suggestions are clearly formulated and easy to understand, whereas usefulness reflects whether experts consider them relevant and applicable within realistic design constraints. For example, one suggestion proposed reducing material thickness from 8 mm to 7 mm to reduce costs, if technically feasible. For the boxplots, quartiles were computed using the inclusive median method. Figure 3 shows the understandability ratings.

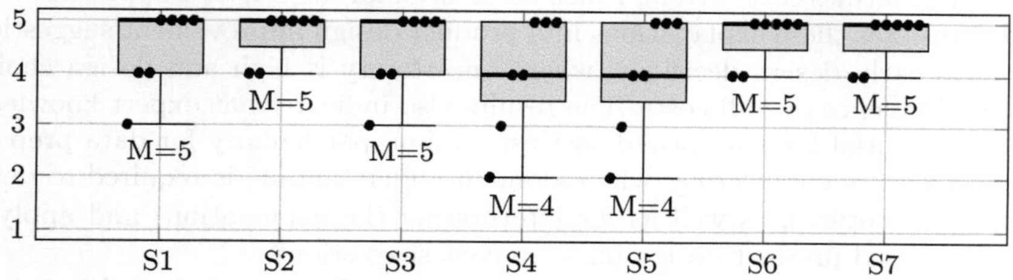

Fig. 3. Understandability (1=not understandable, ..., 5=very understandable) of LLM-based product design improvement suggestions (S1–S7), experts (n=7).

The high ratings indicate that the LLM-generated product design improvement suggestions translated complex inputs into accessible natural-language statements, reducing the cognitive effort required to engage with the results. However, high understandability alone does not ensure effective decision support. Figure 4 summarizes the usefulness ratings.

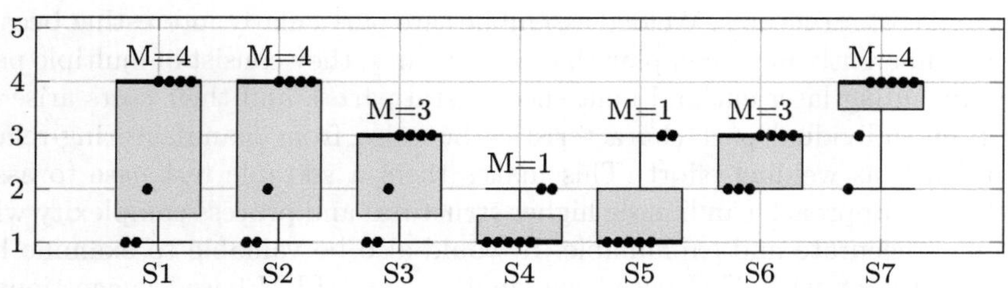

Fig. 4. Usefulness (1=not useful, ..., 5=very useful) of LLM-based product design improvement suggestions (S1–S7), experts (n=7).

In contrast, usefulness varies across the suggestions. While suggestions were rated as useful and relevant for early design decisions, others received low usefulness ratings because they were perceived as obvious (S4) or too generic (S5), e.g., stating that costs could be reduced by lowering part weight or suggesting optimization of the part design without specifying concrete changes. This indicates that decision support depends on both clarity and practical constraints.

In summary, the qualitative results show that SHAP-based identification of cost drivers increases transparency but does not automatically provide decision-relevant insights. The LLM-generated product design improvement suggestions were easy to understand, but their usefulness varied across suggestions.

5 Discussion

The evaluation indicates that the approach delivers accurate, fast, and explainable cost estimation even with limited data. By combining ML with XAI, the approach identifies cost drivers, which is essential for its practical application. An LLM translates these explanations into product design improvement suggestions to inform early design decisions, where uncertainty is high and design choices strongly influence overall costs. The results also indicate that expert knowledge remains essential for AI-assisted cost estimation, particularly for data preparation and feature engineering, where domain understanding is required to define meaningful features, as well as for interpreting the explanations and applying the LLM-based product design improvement suggestions.

An observation from the evaluation is that implicit knowledge, that is intuition and experience-based judgment that experts rely on when data are incomplete or inconsistent, currently does not flow into AI-assisted cost estimation in a systematic manner. While this proof-of-concept does not address this aspect, research on knowledge-based methods [11] and informed ML (IML) [17] shows that integrating knowledge into ML-based methods can improve robustness. This line of work highlights that capturing and formalizing implicit knowledge could become a next step for AI-assisted cost estimation, especially in the early phases of product development, where experience often compensates for missing data.

Future work should evaluate the approach on larger datasets across different part families, including welded assemblies, to assess scalability across product types and cost structures. Welded assemblies are particularly interesting because they are inherently more complex than single parts: they consist of multiple parts (often including laser-cut and bent sheet metal parts), and their costs arise not only from individual part characteristics but also from manufacturing-related factors such as welding effort. This makes them a suitable test case to assess whether the approach can handle higher structural and process complexity while remaining accurate and explainable. It would also be valuable to examine how experts interact with XAI-based explanations and LLM-based suggestions in real decision-making contexts and how well the approach adapts to different cost structures. Another research direction is the question of how implicit knowledge can be captured and incorporated meaningfully into AI-assisted cost estimation, for example through human-in-the-loop methods.

Overall, the findings show that accurate and explainable AI-assisted cost estimation is feasible and can support decision-making. However, accuracy alone is not sufficient. For practical adoption, an approach must provide explainability and actionable guidance while allowing experts to integrate their experience.

6 Summary

This paper presented a proof-of-concept study of an approach for accurate and explainable cost estimation in the early phases of product development by combining ML, XAI, and an LLM. The evaluation shows that the approach can outperform both expert-based cost estimates and rule-based cost estimates generated by software tools in terms of accuracy and speed while improving explainability, which is essential for practical adoption. By identifying cost drivers through XAI and translating these explanations into actionable product design improvement suggestions using an LLM, the approach supports decision-making. This is particularly relevant in early phases where data are limited, but design choices influence overall costs and the economic viability of future products.

Beyond technical performance, the study addresses a gap in research, which has largely focused on predictive accuracy rather than on applicability within product development processes. The integration of ML, XAI, and an LLM illustrates an end-to-end approach for embedding AI-assisted cost estimation into the early phases of product development and highlights how explainability can support transparency and interpretability. While the qualitative evaluation indicates that SHAP-based explanations alone provide limited decision support without additional interpretive context, the LLM-based design improvement suggestions were perceived as more actionable. Although the proof-of-concept is limited in scope to real-world data on laser-cut and bent sheet metal parts, it provides a foundation for future work that extends the approach to additional part families, including welded assemblies composed of multiple sheet metal parts.

Acknowledgment. ChatGPT 5.2 supported the generation of TikZ code for figures. All conceptual design and scientific content were verified by the authors.

Disclosure of Interests. The authors declare that they have no competing interests that could have influenced the work reported in this paper.

References

1. Baker, C., Rafferty, K., Price, M.: Large language models in mechanical engineering: a scoping review of applications, challenges, and future directions. Big Data Cognitive Comput. **9**(12), art. no. 305 (2025)
2. Björkdahl, J.: Strategies for digitalization in manufacturing firms. Calif. Manage. Rev. **62**(4), 17–36 (2020)
3. Doshi-Velez, F., Kim, B.: Towards a rigorous science of interpretable machine learning. Machine Learning (2017)
4. Ehrlenspiel, K., Kiewert, A., Lindemann, U., Mörtl, M.: Kostengünstig entwickeln und konstruieren (8th ed.). Springer (2020)

5. Hammann, D.: Big data and machine learning in cost estimation: an automotive case study. Inter. J. Product. Econ. **269**, art. no. 109137 (2024)
6. Hennebold, C., Klöpfer, K., Lettenbauer, P., Huber, M.: Machine learning based cost prediction for product development in mechanical engineering. Procedia CIRP **107**, 264–269 (2022)
7. Hevner, A.R., March, S.T., Park, J., Ram, S.: Design science in information systems research. Manag. Inf. Syst. Q. **28**, 75–105 (2004)
8. Hicks, B.J., Culley, S.J., Mullineux, G.: Cost estimation for standard components and systems in the early phases of the design process. J. Eng. Des. **13**(4), 271–292 (2002)
9. Lundberg, S.M., et al.: From local explanations to global understanding with explainable ai for trees. Nat. Mach. Intell. **2**(1), 56–67 (2020)
10. Lundberg, S.M., Lee, S.I.: A unified approach to interpreting model predictions. In: Proceedings of the 31st International Conference on Neural Information Processing Systems (NIPS 2017), Red Hook, United States, pp. 4768–4777 (2017)
11. Mandolini, M., Campi, F., Favi, C., Germani, M., Raffaeli, R.: A framework for analytical cost estimation of mechanical components based on manufacturing knowledge representation. Inter. J. Adv. Manufact. Technol. **107**(3), 1131–1151 (2020)
12. Manuguerra, L., Mandolini, M., Sartini, M., Germani, M.: Machine learning for costing sheet metals. In: Design Tools and Methods in Industrial Engineering IV, Palermo, Italy, pp. 133–141 (2025)
13. Moawad, A., Islam, E., Kim, N., Vijayagopal, R., Rousseau, A., Wu, W.B.: Explainable ai for a no-teardown vehicle component cost estimation: a top-down approach. IEEE Trans. Artifi. Intell. **2**(2), 185–199 (2021)
14. Niazi, A., Dai, J., Balabani, S., Seneviratne, L.: Product cost estimation: technique classification and methodology review. J. Manuf. Sci. Eng. **128**(2), 563–575 (2005)
15. Pahl, G., Beitz, W., Feldhusen, J., Grote, K.H.: Engineering Design: A Systematic Approach. Springer (2007)
16. Ribeiro, M.T., Singh, S., Guestrin, C.: Why should i trust you?: explaining the predictions of any classifier. In: Proceedings of the 22nd ACM SIGKDD International Conference on Knowledge Discovery and Data Mining, San Francisco, United States, pp. 1135–1144 (2016)
17. von Rueden, L., et al.: Informed machine learning – a taxonomy and survey of integrating prior knowledge into learning systems. IEEE Trans. Knowl. Data Eng. **35**(1), 614–633 (2023)
18. Röhrenbacher, S., Moerth-Teo, O., Schwarz, L., Schnöll, H., Ramsauer, C.: Product cost estimation in the early development phases - the case of powertrain systems and battery packs. In: Proceedings of the Conference on Resource Efficient Vehicles (REV 2021), Stockholm, Sweden, pp. 98–105 (2021)
19. Shamim, M.M.I., Hamid, A.B.A., Nyamasvisva, T.E., Rafi, N.S.B.: Advancement of artificial intelligence in cost estimation for project management success: a systematic review of machine learning, deep learning, regression, and hybrid models. Modelling **6**(2), art. no. 35 (2025)
20. Voltolini, R., Vasconcelos, K., Borsato, M., Peruzzini, M.: Product development cost estimation through ontological models – a literature review. J. Manag. Analytics **6**(2), 209–229 (2019)
21. Xie, J., Sun, L., Zhao, Y.F.: On the data quality and imbalance in machine learning-based design and manufacturing: a systematic review. J. Eng. **45**, 105–131 (2025)
22. Yoo, S., Kang, N.: Explainable artificial intelligence for manufacturing cost estimation and machining feature visualization. Expert Syst. Appli. **183**, art. no. 115430 (2021)

Optimizing AI-Generated Product Descriptions Through Behavioral Feedback: Evidence from a Production E-Commerce System

Marcin Koralewski(✉) and Filip Dratwiński

Zoovu, Rynek 39/40/423, 50-102 Wrocław, Poland
{m.koralewski,f.dratwinski}@zoovu.com
https://www.zoovu.com

Abstract. Large Language Models (LLMs) are increasingly deployed in electronic commerce to automate product description generation at scale. Despite their growing adoption in production systems, limited evidence exists on how variations in AI-generated descriptions influence consumer behavior in real-world commercial settings. The study contributes an approach for integrating behavioral analytics into AI-driven content generation systems and highlights adaptive prompt optimization as a practical decision-support mechanism in contemporary digital commerce.

This study proposes a behaviorally grounded, closed-loop framework for optimizing AI-generated product descriptions within a production e-commerce environment. Prompts are treated as configurable system-level controls whose effects are empirically evaluated using behavioral feedback. Latent content attributes are extracted from generated descriptions via topic modeling and linked to user clickout behavior using regression-based analysis with confidence intervals. The resulting estimates guide systematic prompt adaptations, which are validated through online A/B experimentation.

Keywords: Generative AI in E-commerce · Adaptive Prompt Optimization · Behavioral Feedback · A/B Testing · Topic Modeling

1 Introduction

The rapid adoption of generative artificial intelligence has transformed how content is produced and managed in electronic commerce. Large Language Models (LLMs) are now routinely used in e-commerce to automate tasks that traditionally required extensive manual work, such as generating product descriptions, personalizing customer communication, or creating marketing content [16]. As these technologies mature, a central challenge for digital commerce platforms is no longer whether content can be generated automatically, but how such systems

K. Węcel and V. Řepa (Eds.): BIS 2026, LNBIP 584, pp. 183–197, 2026.
https://doi.org/10.1007/978-3-032-26363-6_14

can be systematically optimized to align with consumer preferences and behavioral outcomes. While LLM-based descriptions often contain richer vocabulary, improved fluency, and more detailed information than human-written templates, their effectiveness largely depends on the prompts used to guide the model. Subtle variations in prompt wording can lead the LLM to emphasize different product features, present alternative narratives, or omit aspects relevant to consumer preferences [2]. This variability raises an important practical and scientific question: **which elements of product descriptions truly matter for user engagement, and can prompts be systematically optimized to include them?**

The relationship between the semantic structure of generated descriptions and user engagement remains underexplored. Existing approaches rarely link content-level features-such as topics, themes, or product attributes-to behavioral outcomes. Even fewer studies evaluate whether modifying the prompt to steer an LLM toward specific content can produce **causal improvements** in user engagement through controlled field experiments. To the best of our knowledge, **no prior research combines topic modeling, statistical modeling of click behavior, and prompt optimization validated through an A/B test in a live e-commerce environment**.

This study addresses this gap by proposing a closed-loop, behaviorally grounded framework for prompt optimization in electronic commerce. The proposed framework offers both empirical evidence and a generalizable methodological template for leveraging behavioral feedback to improve AI-generated content. The approach integrates large-scale generation of product descriptions with latent topic modeling and statistical analysis to identify which content attributes are associated with higher engagement. These insights are then used to adapt prompts, and their effectiveness is validated through online A/B testing. In doing so, the paper reframes prompt engineering as an adaptive optimization problem rather than a one-off design task.

From a theoretical perspective, this work is grounded in the Information Systems literature on adaptive decision support systems [3], in which computational tools iteratively refine their outputs based on observed outcomes. The proposed framework instantiates this principle in the context of AI-generated content: behavioral feedback from users drives systematic adaptation of the generation process, closing the loop between content production and consumption.

The findings suggest that even small, targeted modifications to prompts-derived from statistical analysis rather than intuition-can meaningfully improve user engagement. This work contributes to the growing literature on generative AI in e-commerce and provides actionable insights for retailers seeking to integrate LLMs into customer-facing systems.

2 Related Work

2.1 LLM-Based Product Description Generation in E-Commerce

Automated generation of product descriptions has long been explored in e-commerce [7,10], initially through template-based or rule-based systems and, more recently, through neural text generation models [11]. Transformer-based architectures enabled richer semantic representations and more fluent descriptions, with studies demonstrating improved product discoverability and perceived usefulness when descriptions are automatically enriched with additional attributes [14]. Research in this domain primarily assesses linguistic quality, factual correctness, and the alignment between generated content and product specifications.

Despite broad interest in potential of LLMs to follow flexible instructions, integrate product metadata, and generate coherent narratives [8], very few studies evaluate their real-world impact on customer behavior, leaving open the question of how specific elements of generated text (such as mention of particular attributes) shape consumer decision-making.

2.2 Topic Modeling and Content Feature Extraction for User Behavior Prediction

Topic modeling and other latent semantic analysis techniques are widely used to extract interpretable features from unstructured text [17]. In e-commerce, such methods help summarize product reviews, classify customer needs, and analyze product attributes mentioned by consumers. Prior research has shown that textual features can correlate with sales performance, conversion likelihood, or click behavior in advertising settings [9]. Logistic regression, generalized linear models, and related statistical techniques are often used to quantify associations between content-level variables and engagement metrics.

While topic modeling is commonly used to interpret large textual corpora, it is seldom connected to **automatically modifying the content generation process itself** (e.g., adjusting prompts) based on statistical findings. This creates a methodological gap that the present work aims to address.

2.3 Field Experiments and A/B Testing in E-Commerce

A/B testing is a standard methodology for evaluating changes in e-commerce interfaces [18], product recommendation algorithms [15], or marketing strategies. Best practices emphasize the importance of randomization, sufficient sample size, appropriate statistical tests, and transparent reporting of effect sizes and confidence intervals.

To date, no published work integrates **content feature extraction, significance testing, and prompt-controlled LLM generation** within a controlled field experiment.

2.4 Adaptive Systems and Behavioral Feedback in IS Research

Information Systems research has long examined how systems can adapt their behavior based on observed outcomes. Feedback-driven optimization is a core principle in decision support systems [4], [3], where system outputs are evaluated against measurable criteria and used to refine subsequent decisions. In digital commerce contexts, behavioral signals such as click-through rates, conversion, and dwell time have been used to optimize recommendation algorithms, interface design, and search ranking [15]. The present work extends this tradition to the domain of AI-generated content, treating prompt parameters as controllable system inputs and user engagement as the feedback signal driving iterative refinement.

2.5 Research Gap

Across these research streams, several gaps become evident:

- LLM-generated product descriptions have not been systematically linked to user engagement metrics such as clickout.
- No prior work combines topic modeling with statistical inference to identify which semantic features of generated descriptions influence user behavior.
- Prompt optimization driven by behavioral data, rather than heuristic or manual tuning, is largely unexplored.
- There is no published study validating prompt-engineered, content-optimized LLM descriptions through a real-world A/B field experiment.

This study addresses these gaps by introducing a framework that (1) extracts latent semantic topics from LLM-generated descriptions, (2) estimates their relationship with clickout using regression modeling, (3) incorporates statistically significant topics into optimized prompts, and (4) validates the resulting descriptions in a live A/B test with an online retailer.

3 Research Question

The goal of this study is to examine whether the semantic content of LLM-generated product descriptions can be systematically optimized using statistical analysis of latent topics to improve user engagement. Prior research has explored various aspects of automated text generation and prompt engineering, yet little is known about whether data-driven adjustments to prompts (grounded in the behavioral effects of specific content features) can produce measurable improvements in real e-commerce environments. To address this gap, we formulate the following research question:

Research Question
Can the semantic content of LLM-generated product descriptions be systematically optimized-using topic-level statistical analysis-to improve user clickout behavior in an e-commerce setting?

To empirically evaluate this question, we test whether prompts enriched with statistically identified positive content features lead to superior outcomes compared to a baseline prompt. This leads to the following hypothesis:

4 Materials and Methods

The methodology consists of five components: (1) data description, (2) baseline description generation, (3) topic modeling, (4) statistical modeling of topic effects, and (5) prompt optimization and experimental design.

4.1 Data Description

The study was conducted in collaboration with a major Canadian laptop retailer. The dataset includes user interactions collected through an online questionnaire, in which customers specified their preferences and were subsequently shown automatically generated product descriptions.

- Total questionnaire participants: 2258
- Users who completed the questionnaire and were shown a product: 1108
- Number of products shown in the study: 274
- Number of product descriptions generated: 20 thousand

Each record contains:

- Structured product metadata (e.g., processor, RAM, storage, display).
- The corresponding LLM-generated product description.
- A binary clickout indicator (1 = the user clicked the product; 0 = no click).
- User-provided need/preference information from the questionnaire.

Clickout is used as the primary behavioral performance metric.

4.2 Baseline Description Generation Pipeline

The baseline descriptions were generated using a single, fixed prompt containing three components:

- Template instructions guiding the model to write a product description.
- Product specification data extracted from the retailer's catalog.
- Customer need information, derived from questionnaire inputs and expressed as high-level requirements.

The prompt was executed on a commercial large language model (LLM). Because LLM outputs involve inherent randomness (stemming from sampling procedures), descriptions varied both across products and across repeated generations for same products.

Generation was conducted using OpenAI `gpt-4o-mini` with temperature=1. This setting reflects the production configuration of the content generation system, in which elevated temperature is used to ensure lexical diversity across descriptions generated for the same or similar products. While alternative temperature values were not systematically evaluated in this study, the choice is consistent with the goal of producing varied descriptions whose semantic content can be meaningfully analyzed via topic modeling. The effect of temperature on topic distribution and downstream engagement metrics remains an avenue for future investigation.

These baseline descriptions serve as the initial input for downstream topic extraction and statistical analysis.

4.3 Topic Modeling Procedure

To uncover latent semantic structure within the generated descriptions, topic modeling was applied using the Latent Dirichlet Allocation [LDA] algorithm [1].

Model Estimation. An LDA model (from `gensim` [13] Python library) with 18 topics was trained to represent recurring semantic patterns in generated descriptions. The number of topics was selected by evaluating UMass coherence scores across a range of candidate values. Table 1 reports the coherence scores for models trained with 14 to 30 topics. The model with 18 topics achieved the best coherence score of −5.24, and was therefore selected for subsequent analysis. Additionally, the model was estimated multiple times with different random seeds; the resulting topic structures were qualitatively consistent across runs, confirming the stability of the solution.

Table 1. UMass coherence scores for LDA models with varying number of topics.

Number of Topics	Coherence Score (UMass)
14	−5.436
18	−5.241
22	−6.109
26	−6.776
30	−8.037

For each description, every sentence was assigned to most relevant topic by `LDA.get_document_topics`. In result, union of sentence topics is assigned to description as description topics.

Topic Labeling
To improve interpretability and to ease interpretation for LLM, each topic's most representative sentences were extracted and passed to an LLM with the instruction to generate a concise, human-interpretable topic label (e.g., Camera and Microphone Quality, Battery Life, Performance).

This produced a set of semantically clear content categories used in the subsequent statistical modeling.

4.4 Statistical Modeling of Topic Effects on Clickout

To determine which topics influence user clickout behavior, a logistic regression model was fitted using topic indicators as explanatory variables.

Feature Construction
A feature matrix was constructed containing:

- One-hot encoded topic presence per description.
- One-hot encoded additional covariates: product brand, day of week, hour and similar metadata
- The binary clickout variable.

Regression Model
To estimate topic impact on clickout, Generalized Linear Model [GLM] [6] with a binomial family and logit link was estimated:

$$logit(p_i) = \beta_0 + \sum_{k=1}^{K} \beta_k Topic_{ik} \tag{1}$$

where main interest of this study is to use estimated coefficients β_k as measures of impact of presence of topic in description on clickout.

Statistical significance of coefficients was assessed using:

- p-values (< 0.05 threshold)
- 95% confidence intervals

Statistical significance of coefficients was calculated using Python `statsmodels` [12] library, with usage of `sm.GLM` with link `sm.genmod.families.links.logit`.

Only topics whose confidence intervals were strictly positive (entirely above zero) were classified as **positively associated** with clickout. Topics with strictly negative intervals were classified as **negatively associated**. These findings form the basis for prompt optimization.

To assess multicollinearity among topic indicators, Variance Inflation Factors (VIF) were computed for all predictors. All VIF values were below 3.0 (maximum: 2.80 for *Storage Capacity*), indicating no problematic collinearity among the topic features. The overall model fit was assessed using McFadden's pseudo $R^2 = 0.057$ and a likelihood ratio test ($p < 0.001$). The relatively modest pseudo R^2 is consistent with prior work on behavioral clickout modeling, where user engagement is influenced by numerous unobserved factors beyond description content [9]. The primary purpose of the model is not predictive accuracy but identification of statistically significant topic-level effects, for which coefficient estimates and confidence intervals are the appropriate evaluation criteria.

4.5 Prompt Optimization Procedure

Using the statistically identified topics, an enhanced prompt was constructed with explicit instructions:

- "Emphasize the following aspects: TOPIC_A, TOPIC_B, ..."
- "Refrain from describing: TOPIC_X, TOPIC_Y, ..."

The remainder of the prompt-including template, product data, and customer needs-was kept identical to the baseline version to ensure isolation of the effect. Identified instructions were included in the end of the prompt.

4.6 Experimental Design (A/B Test)

A field A/B test was conducted in the retailer's live environment, and lasted for a month.

Randomization and Traffic Split
Users completing the questionnaire were randomly assigned to:

- **Group A (baseline):** descriptions generated with the original prompt
- **Group B (optimized):** descriptions generated with the prompt enhanced with behaviorally-identified topics.

Traffic split was 50/50, blindly randomized. No statistically significant differences (as in device type, time of day, product mix) were observed.

Repeat exposure was controlled at the cookie level: once a user was assigned to a condition, all subsequent sessions from the same browser were served the same prompt variant, ensuring consistent treatment throughout the experiment. Users arriving organically from the web were assigned randomly upon first visit with no pre-stratification. The distributional balance between groups was verified post-hoc: device shares were nearly identical across conditions (Mobile: 61.2% vs. 60.1%, Desktop: 35.7% vs. 36.8%, Tablet: 3.0% vs. 3.1%), confirming that randomization produced comparable groups without requiring explicit stratification.

Product price distributions were not explicitly controlled during randomization. Post-hoc analysis indicated mean product prices of $1,254 in Group A and $1,170 in Group B. Notably, the baseline group (A) was exposed to higher-priced products on average, which would be expected to correlate with higher purchase intent and clickout likelihood. The fact that Group B nonetheless achieved a significantly higher clickout rate suggests that the observed uplift is not attributable to price differences, and may in fact represent a conservative estimate of the true prompt optimization effect.

Outcome Metric
The primary metric was **clickout rate**, defined as the fraction of users who clicked the recommended product after viewing its description.

Statistical Evaluation
Differences in clickout rates were evaluated using the **Boschloo exact test** [5] with expected p-value$<$ 0.05. Additionally, post-hoc power analysis was conducted to assess the robustness of the effect size.

5 Results

5.1 Topic Modeling Outcomes

Applying LDA with 18 latent topics to the corpus of generated product descriptions yielded a set of recurring semantic themes. After topic labeling via an LLM-based summarization step, 18 semantically distinct topics were identified. Table 1 confirms that this configuration yielded the best coherence score among evaluated alternatives.

The full set of identified topics is not disclosed, as the mapping between semantic content features and behavioral outcomes constitutes proprietary business knowledge of the participating retailer. The 15 topics available for disclosure are reported in Table 2, together with their regression coefficients. These topics correspond to common attribute categories in laptop purchasing decisions and provide meaningful content features for downstream behavioral analysis.

Logistic Regression Analysis of Topic Effects. To quantify the relationship between topic mentions and clickout behavior, a logistic regression model was fitted using binary topic indicators as predictors. Table 2 reports the estimated coefficients, p-values, and 95% confidence intervals for the six primary topics identified.

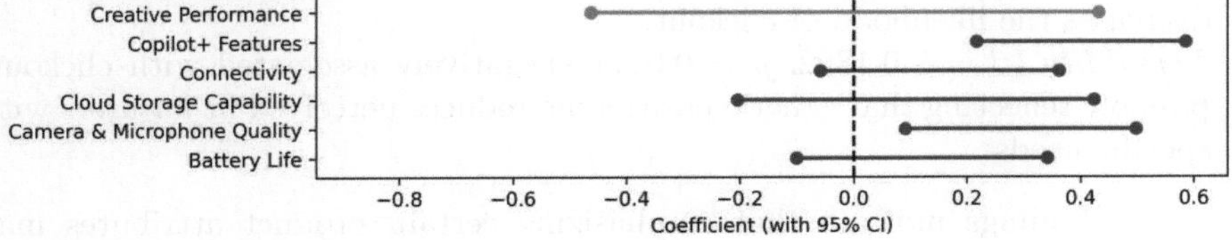

Fig. 1. Visualization of topic-level coefficients intervals from Table 2.

Only topics with confidence intervals strictly above or below zero were considered statistically meaningful predictors of clickout (as in Fig. 1). Five topics met this criterion:

Table 2. Logistic regression results for topic-level predictors of clickout.

Topic	Coefficient	95% CI	p-value
Battery Life	0.1213	[−0.100, 0.342]	0.283
Camera and Microphone Quality	**0.2947**	**[0.091, 0.498]**	**0.005**
Cloud Storage Capability	0.1095	[−0.204, 0.423]	0.494
Connectivity	0.1519	[−0.058, 0.362]	0.156
Copilot+ Features	**0.4012**	**[0.217, 0.586]**	**0.000**
Creative Performance	−0.0149	[−0.462, 0.432]	0.948
Display Quality	0.0825	[−0.098, 0.263]	0.370
Lightweight and Portable Design	**-0.2499**	**[-0.468, -0.032]**	**0.024**
Performance	0.1752	[−0.014, 0.365]	0.070
Processor Performance	0.0324	[−0.136, 0.201]	0.707
Productivity Features	−0.4237	[−0.874, 0.027]	0.065
Storage Capacity	**0.2010**	**[0.022, 0.380]**	**0.027**
Touchscreen Functionality	0.1258	[−0.026, 0.277]	0.104
Versatility	**-0.1802**	**[-0.318, -0.042]**	**0.011**

* Three topics omitted due to proprietary business constraints.

** Covariates (device type, day of week) included but not shown.

Positive Predictors

- *Camera and Microphone Quality* ($\beta = 0.2947$, $p = 0.005$)—significantly increases the likelihood of clickout.
- *Copilot+ Features* ($\beta = 0.4012$, $p < 0.001$)—the strongest positive predictor, suggesting that AI-related functionality is a salient driver of user engagement.
- *Storage Capacity* ($\beta = 0.2010$, $p = 0.027$)—positively associated with clickout, reflecting the practical importance of storage in purchase decisions.

Negative Predictors

- *Lightweight and Portable Design* ($\beta = -0.2499$, $p = 0.024$)—significantly decreases the likelihood of clickout.
- *Versatility* ($\beta = -0.1802$, $p = 0.011$)—negatively associated with clickout, possibly reflecting that generic positioning reduces perceived fit for users with specific needs.

These findings indicate that emphasizing certain product attributes may influence user engagement, whereas mentioning others may reduce interest.

5.2 Prompt Optimization Based on Significant Topics

Based on the regression results, the optimized prompt was constructed by inserting additional instructions with a goal to:

- **Emphasize:** Camera and Microphone Quality, Copilot+ Features, Storage Capacity
- **Avoid:** Lightweight and Portable Design, Versatility

All other components of the prompt-template, product data, and customer need information-remained unchanged relative to the baseline prompt to ensure a clean causal evaluation.

5.3 A/B Field Experiment Results

The A/B test was conducted over a one-month period on the live website of the participating retailer. Users who completed the preference questionnaire were randomly assigned to the baseline or optimized condition.

A total of **1108 users** were exposed to product descriptions after completing the questionnaire. The contingency table of clickout behavior is shown in Table 3.

Table 3. Clickout outcomes in the A/B field experiment.

Outcome	Baseline Prompt (A)	Optimized Prompt (B)	Total
Clickout	86	116	202
No Clickout	460	446	906
Total	**546**	**562**	**1108**

The clickout rate increased from 15.75% in the baseline condition to 20.64% in the optimized condition, representing:

- **Absolute uplift:** +4.89%
- **Relative uplift:** +31.04%

The Boschloo exact test yielded $p = 0.0188$, confirming statistical significance, with a post-hoc power of 0.664.

These results provide empirical evidence that prompt optimization based on statistically identified content features can meaningfully improve user engagement.

6 Discussion

The results demonstrate that variations in prompt-controlled content are associated with statistically significant differences in consumer clickout behavior. Rather than treating these differences as isolated performance gains, the findings suggest that prompts function as high-level control parameters that influence how product information is framed and prioritized by generative AI systems. The observed effects indicate that even modest shifts in the semantic emphasis of

AI-generated descriptions can alter user engagement in operational e-commerce settings.

In particular, three topics emerged as significant positive predictors of clickout: *Camera and Microphone Quality*, *Copilot+ Features*, and *Storage Capacity*. Two topics showed significant negative associations: *Lightweight and Portable Design* and *Versatility*. These results suggest that users interacting with a product recommendation interface pay closer attention to specific functional attributes while deprioritizing others, depending on their stated needs.

The negative effect of *Lightweight and Portable Design* warrants particular attention. The study was conducted in collaboration with a Canadian retailer during a period of widespread remote and hybrid work adoption. Under these conditions, a substantial share of the product catalog consisted of business-oriented laptops, for which portability is a secondary concern relative to performance, connectivity, and productivity features. Users shopping for such devices may perceive emphasis on lightweight design as misaligned with their primary use case, reducing perceived fit and consequently clickout likelihood. A similar interpretation applies to *Versatility*: generic positioning language may reduce perceived specificity for users with clearly defined professional needs. These interpretations remain context-dependent and should be validated in future work across different retail contexts and product mixes, for example by segmenting users by stated use case and analyzing topic-level engagement effects within each segment.

It should also be noted that LLMs are known to struggle with negative instructions—that is, being told what *not* to include [2]. To verify that the optimized prompt actually reduced the presence of *Lightweight and Portable Design* in generated descriptions, a post-hoc topic frequency analysis was conducted on Group B outputs. The topic appeared in 86% of baseline descriptions (Group A) compared to 19% in optimized descriptions (Group B), confirming that the negative instruction was partially effective. This caveat should be considered when interpreting the A/B test results.

The practical implication is that LLM-generated descriptions may follow similar professionalization as human-written ones: they can be strategically shaped to emphasize content that resonates with users. Importantly, the method proposed in this work does not rely on subjective judgments or domain intuition; instead, it identifies impactful content features empirically through topic-level statistical modeling. This creates a closed-loop system in which behavioral data informs prompt construction, and prompts in turn guide the LLM to produce more effective descriptions.

The field A/B test further demonstrates that these insights translate into measurable improvements in a real commercial environment. A relative uplift of over 30% in clickout rate suggests that targeted prompt optimization can provide tangible benefits to retailers using automated content generation. More broadly, the study contributes to literature on generative AI in e-commerce by showing that prompt design can function as a controllable lever for influencing downstream user behavior, rather than merely serving as an instruction interface for content creation.

7 Conclusions

This study demonstrates that the semantic content of LLM-generated product descriptions can be systematically optimized to improve user engagement in an e-commerce setting. By combining topic modeling with logistic regression, we identified specific content features that significantly influence clickout behavior. Incorporating these insights into an optimized prompt resulted in a measurable increase in clickout rates during a real-world A/B field experiment, providing empirical support for the hypothesis that data-driven prompt design can enhance the effectiveness of automated product descriptions.

The findings underscore the role of content-level features as actionable levers in generative AI systems. Rather than relying solely on intuition or manual prompt tuning, retailers can use behavioral data to guide LLMs toward producing descriptions that better align with user preferences. This contributes to a growing body of evidence that prompt engineering can serve as a practical, lightweight alternative to model fine-tuning for influencing downstream user behavior.

Despite these promising results, several limitations should be acknowledged. First, the study is constrained by its single-domain focus on laptop products within a single retail context, which limits the generalizability of the findings. Second, the experiment was conducted over a one-month period with a moderate sample size, and was not repeated across multiple time windows - a limitation that reduces the statistical power of the A/B test and leaves open the question of temporal stability of the identified effects. Third, the study relies on a single generative model (`gpt-4o-mini`), and prompt optimization effects may differ across LLM architectures or versions. Fourth, the topic modeling approach used (LDA) treats topics as independent and does not capture potential interactions or hierarchical relationships between semantic features. Richer representations, such as ontology-based models or contextual embeddings, may yield more nuanced content features and stronger behavioral predictions. Finally, several threats to validity should be noted:

- while randomization was applied and no significant differences between groups were observed on observable covariates, unobserved confounders cannot be fully ruled out,
- the one-month experiment window may not capture seasonal variation in user behavior,
- the modest statistical power of the test (0.66) suggests that smaller effects would not have been reliably detected.

Future research should validate the proposed framework across additional product categories, replicate the experiment over multiple time periods, explore richer semantic feature representations, and evaluate the stability of optimized prompts across different LLM architectures. Nonetheless, this work provides a clear demonstration that content-aware prompt optimization offers a viable path toward improving the real-world performance of LLM-driven e-commerce systems.

Acknowledgments. Authors thanks James Ansell for his continuous support and great collaboration during a study, what allowed for evaluation of approach.

Disclosure of Interests. Authors claim no competing interest.

References

1. Blei, D.M., Ng, A.Y., Jordan, M.I.: Latent Dirichlet allocation. J. Mach. Learn. Res. **3**, 993–1022 (2003)
2. Sahoo, P., Singh, A.K., Saha, S., Jain, V., Mondal, S., Chadha, A.: A systematic survey of prompt engineering in large language models. arXiv:2402.07927 (2025)
3. Power, D.J.: Decision support systems: a historical overview. In: Handbook on Decision Support Systems 1: Basic Themes, pp. 121–140. Springer, Heidelberg (2008). https://doi.org/10.1007/978-3-540-48713-5_7
4. Sprague, R.H.: A framework for the development of decision support systems. MIS Q. **4**(4), 1–26 (1980). https://doi.org/10.2307/248957
5. Boschloo, R.D.: Raised conditional level of significance for the 2 × 2-table when testing the equality of two probabilities. Stat. Neerl. **24**(1), 1–9 (1970). https://doi.org/10.1111/j.1467-9574.1970.tb00104.x
6. McCullagh, P.: Generalized linear models. Eur. J. Oper. Res. **16**(3), 285–292 (1984). https://doi.org/10.1016/0377-2217(84)90282-0
7. Wasilewski, A.: Harnessing generative AI for personalized e-commerce product descriptions: a framework and practical insights. Comput. Stand. Interfaces **94**, 104012 (2025). https://doi.org/10.1016/j.csi.2025.104012
8. Yu, T., Pan, Y., Jang, W.: Modeling consumer reactions to AI-generated content on e-commerce platforms. J. Theor. Appl. Electron. Commer. Res. **20**(4), 257 (2025). https://doi.org/10.3390/jtaer20040257
9. Li, X., Wu, C., Mai, F.: The effect of online reviews on product sales: a joint sentiment-topic analysis. Inf. Manag. **56**(2), 172–184 (2019). https://doi.org/10.1016/j.im.2018.04.007
10. Niemir, M., Mrugalska, B., Grajewska, D., Nitoń, B.: Leveraging generative artificial intelligence for enhancing the quality of product data. LogForum **21**(3), 317–326 (2025)
11. Krishnan, C., Mariappan, J.: The AI revolution in e-commerce: personalization and predictive analytics. In: Gaur, L., Abraham, A. (eds.) Role of Explainable Artificial Intelligence in E-Commerce. Studies in Computational Intelligence, vol. 1094, pp. 53–64. Springer, Cham (2024). https://doi.org/10.1007/978-3-031-55615-9_4
12. Seabold, S., Perktold, J.: Statsmodels: econometric and statistical modeling with Python. In: van der Walt, S., Millman, J. (eds.) Proceedings of the 9th Python in Science Conference, pp. 92–96 (2010). https://doi.org/10.25080/Majora-92bf1922-011
13. Řehůřek, R., Sojka, P.: Software framework for topic modelling with large corpora. In: Proceedings of the LREC 2010 Workshop on New Challenges for NLP Frameworks, pp. 45–50. ELRA, Valletta (2010)

14. Chen, Q., Lin, J., Zhang, Y., Yang, H., Zhou, J., Tang, J.: Towards knowledge-based personalized product description generation in e-commerce. In: Proceedings of the 25th ACM SIGKDD Conference on Knowledge Discovery and Data Mining, pp. 3040–3050. ACM, New York (2019). https://doi.org/10.1145/3292500.3330725
15. Gilotte, A., Calauzènes, C., Nedelec, T., Abraham, A., Dollé, S.: Offline A/B testing for recommender systems. In: Proceedings of the 11th ACM International Conference on Web Search and Data Mining, pp. 198–206. ACM, New York (2018). https://doi.org/10.1145/3159652.3159687
16. Ghaffari, S., Yousefimehr, B., Ghatee, M.: Generative-AI in e-commerce: use-cases and implementations. In: Proceedings of the 20th CSI International Symposium on Artificial Intelligence and Signal Processing, pp. 1–5 (2024). https://doi.org/10.1109/AISP61396.2024.10475266
17. Krishnan, A.: Exploring the power of topic modeling techniques in analyzing customer reviews. arXiv:2308.11520 (2023)
18. Quin, F., Weyns, D., Galster, M., Costa Silva, C.: A/B testing: a systematic literature review. arXiv:2308.04929 (2023)

Product Experience Management in E-Commerce -Potential of PXM Solutions in a Generational Comparison

Chiara Henßler, Lara Hönn, Hannah Lauber, Ralf-Christian Härting(✉), Patrick Ulrich, and Jo Scheppach

Aalen University of Applied Sciences, Beethovenstr. 1, 73430 Aalen, Germany
ralf.haerting@hs-aalen.de

Abstract. Rapid technological development and diverse product offerings in the fashion e-commerce sector have led to higher customer expectations regarding an optimal product experience. This study analyses the potential of product experience management (PXM) solutions to improve the product experience for both Generation X and Generation Z consumers in Germany. A quantitative research design was adopted, involving a survey of 481 participants from both generations. The data were analysed using partial least squares structural equation modeling (PLS-SEM) to identify which elements of product experience management influence the product experience across generational groups. The results reveal that the expectations of Generation X and Generation Z differ less than previously assumed, although specific areas exist where product experience management can improve the experience for each group. Based on these insights, recommendations are provided for tailoring product experience management strategies to the needs of both generations.

Keywords: Product Experience Management · PXM · Potential of PXM · E-Commerce · Generation X · Generation Z

1 Introduction

E-commerce, which represents a significant segment of Germany's retail landscape, primarily includes business-to-consumer (B2C) transactions. The number of e-commerce users in Germany has steadily increased, reaching approximately 47.68 million in 2025, reflecting ongoing growth trends [3]. Among these, the fashion sector is one of the most prominent, generating revenues of approximately €30.79 billion in 2025 [4].

In e-commerce, optimal product presentation is vital for generating revenue. Unlike physical retail, online fashion platforms must adhere to digital standards, such as consistently placing shopping carts and providing comprehensive, visually rich product information. This can include images, videos, augmented reality (AR), and virtual reality (VR) features, all of which enhance the consumer experience [5, 6]. Furthermore, the advancement of digitalisation is creating new possibilities for innovation in process and

K. Węcel and V. Řepa (Eds.): BIS 2026, LNBIP 584, pp. 198–209, 2026.
https://doi.org/10.1007/978-3-032-26363-6_15

data management. This approach enables more effective management of product data and the delivery of personalised customer experiences. These are crucial drivers of value creation in digital business models [2]. Moreover, social media platforms such as TikTok and Instagram have become essential channels that influence purchasing behaviour by providing consumers with easy access to products via embedded links and targeted advertising [7].

At the same time, continuous technological development and the increasing differentiation of product offerings are leading to constantly rising customer demands. In order to respond appropriately to changing requirements, the use of new technologies must be continuously optimised [1]. A fundamental issue is that, despite continuous technological advancement, companies encounter difficulties in rapidly and comprehensively adapting to the requirements of diverse consumers. As a consequence, the potential and opportunities that could be leveraged to improve communication with customers through the product experience are not being fully exploited [2]. The aim of this study is to examine the connection between PXM solutions and the needs of Generation X (Gen X) and Generation Z (Gen Z) in fashion e-commerce in Germany.

2 Related Research

PXM is an extension of Product Information Management (PIM) [8]. While PIM involves the central management and distribution of product data across various channels, PXM utilises this data in a targeted manner to create appealing, personalised product experiences. [9]. The main elements of the PXM process that provide an optimal product experience will be further delineated in the following paragraphs.

Product Data Management. Data management is the basis for data quality and consistency, from collection and management to provision. It facilitates the dissemination of reliable information across multiple channels and supports analysis, digital transformation and legal compliance. The maintenance of structured data has been demonstrated to optimise business-critical applications and automate processes [10].

Digital Shelf Analytics. The term 'digital shelf' describes the environment in which customers encounter products. Digital shelf analytics monitors these various shelves using AI-driven data collectors (crawlers) that collect, process and evaluate data from websites, marketplaces and competitors. This provides an overview of competitors and relevant key performance indicators (KPIs) [11].

Syndication: It describes the comprehensive process of distributing and synchronising product content across a network of channels, retailers and marketplaces. It forms the basis for scalable PXM and enables a company to deliver a compelling product experience at every touchpoint [12].

Contextualisation. In the process of contextualisation, it is imperative to adapt content to the customers' circumstances, such as location, language or age. The foundation for this approach is the aggregation of pertinent customer data in real time. This enables the targeted provision of information to the relevant customers at the optimal time [13].

Personalisation. The term can be defined as customisation based on personal data stored over a longer period of time. The collection of specific information about individual users is essential for the personalisation process. The available data represent information from past search interactions, which are analysed to determine the wishes and needs of the user in the current search process [14].

It is evident that PXM offers numerous benefits for both customers and companies. As a consequence, this leads to an improvement in customer loyalty and optimisation of the customer experience through the provision of consistent and relevant content across all touchpoints. PXM also exerts a favourable influence on the process of purchasing decisions, leading to a reduction in returns. Consequently, this contributes to higher conversion rates and increased sales. In essence, PXM assists companies in the creation of a product experience that is both appealing and seamless, thereby fostering robust customer relationships [15]. Furthermore, the most study ProDa4 (2025) shows that generative AI is increasingly being perceived as a fundamental tool for the optimisation of PXM [8]. In particular, it automates the creation, translation and personalisation of product information, thereby increasing efficiency and customer loyalty. However, it is important to note that this process simultaneously requires targeted training and technological development in order to address data protection and skills shortages [16].

Since the present study focuses on a generational comparison of Gen X and Gen Z, the main characteristics of the two generations will be discussed in the following.

Gen X (born 1965–1980) was shaped by an environment marked by economic instability, rising individualisation, and rapid digital transformation [23]. Gen X experienced an upbringing characterised by intensive support and an increasing presence of liberal elements [17]. Shifts in family structures led to an increase in non-traditional family configurations [18, 19]. Politically, Gen X was significantly influenced by key historical events, including the end of the Cold War [20]. Crises in the environment and public health, prompted a critical reassessment of the belief in unrestrained technological and societal progress [21, 22]. Technologically, Gen X witnessed the shift from analogue to digital technologies and displayed a strong capacity to adapt to innovation [23]. Their entry into the workforce was characterised by uncertainty and increasing demands for mobility and flexibility [24].

Gen Z (born 1996–2009) is considered the first generation to have grown up in a digitally connected environment from birth. Digital media and social networks have a significant impact on their socialisation and everyday lives [18, 28]. Despite the potential challenges posed by social instability, they place significant emphasis on maintaining strong social connections [29]. Politically and ecologically, Gen Z has been influenced by a series of pivotal events, including the coronavirus pandemic [30]. Their technological socialisation is characterised by permanent digital networking and media-based identity formation [31]. Regarding the employment sector, flexibility, continuous learning, and meaning-orientedness are at the forefront [32].

3 Hypotheses and Conceptual Model

Six hypotheses were derived from the literature review.

H1: Personalisation enhances the product experience in fashion e-commerce. Personalisation tailors digital touchpoints to individual customer needs, fostering stronger customer engagement and increasing purchase intention [33, 34, 45].

H2: High-quality product information improves the product experience in fashion e-commerce. Complete and accurate product data build customer trust and reduce returns, serving as a crucial basis for purchase decisions in online fashion retail [35].

H3: Interactive product presentation enhances the product experience in fashion e-commerce. Technologies such as AR and VR enable customers to engage more deeply with products, thereby improving satisfaction and purchase intention [36–39].

H4: Error-free translation of product information improves the product experience in fashion e-commerce. Providing product details in the customer's native language ensures clarity and smooth purchase processes, which is essential in globalised fashion e-commerce [40, 41].

H5: Consistent content across all channels enhances the product experience in fashion e-commerce. Omnichannel consistency builds trust and brand loyalty by preventing contradictory information, leading to more stable customer behaviour [42–44].

Based on the hypotheses a conceptual model that employs a structural equation model (SEM), which was simultaneously used for the data analysis, was developed (Fig. 1).

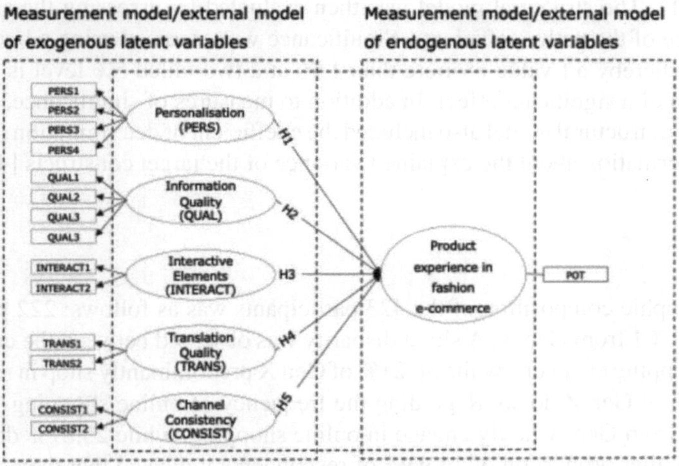

Fig. 1. Path model.

4 Methodology

The data were collected through an online-survey. Based on the theory-derived latent variables, specific items were developed, which enable the empirical measurement of the constructs and form the basis of the standardised questionnaire as manifest variables. A standardised formulation and structuring of the items ensure valid and reliable measurement of the underlying theoretical concepts [49]. Feedback on layout and phrasing obtained and incorporated through a pre-test with five participants. Responses were collected using a Likert scale, which allows for differentiated quantification of attitudes, opinions, or satisfaction, thereby facilitating the statistical analysis of latent variables [50]. The survey was conducted between 25 September and 10 October 2025. 481 participants completed the survey, of which 423 could be used for the evaluation.

The data were analysed using PLS-SEM in SmartPLS 4 to examine the hypothesised relationships between the latent variables. The measurement models were first evaluated using the PLS algorithm, which iteratively optimises the weighting of the indicators in order to maximise the explained variance of the endogenous constructs. Validation of the measurement model includes testing internal consistency using composite reliability (CR) and Cronbach's alpha (CA) [47, 51, 52]. The outer loadings of the indicators were examined to ensure item reliability. Convergent validity was assessed using the average variance extracted (AVE), which should be at least 0.5 to ensure that the latent construct explains at least 50% of the variance of its indicators. In addition, discriminant validity was assessed to ensure that the constructs in the model were sufficiently distinct from one another. This was confirmed, among other things, by the heterotrait-monotrait ratio (HTMT). The structural model was then evaluated by assessing the significance and relevance of the path coefficients. Significance was assessed using a bootstrapping procedure, whereby a t-value of more than 1.96 at a two-tailed 5% level is considered an indication of a significant effect. In addition to measures of significance, the quality criteria for the structural model also included the coefficient of determination (R^2), which provides information about the explained variance of the target constructs [47].

5 Results

The demographic composition of the 423 participants was as follows: 222 participants from Gen Z, 201 from Gen X. A slight disparity was observed between the cohorts with regard to shopping channels: while 58.21% of Gen X predominantly shop in retail stores, only 36.94% of Gen Z do so. Regarding the frequency of online shopping, 45.77% of participants from Gen X rarely engage in online shopping, while 25.87% do so once a month. A smaller proportion of 14.93% of respondents indicated that they shop online several times a month. In addition, 13.43% of respondents indicated that they never purchase fashion items online. 30.18% of the participants from Gen Z shop online once a month, 45.05% do so rarely, 23.87% several times a month, and only 0.9% have never purchased fashion items via online channels. Following, the SEM results for the two generations are presented, followed by the MGA results. Table 3 presents the measurement model results for Gen X. Constructs H1 and H3 meet the thresholds for CR ($CR > 0.70$), Cronbach's alpha (>0.70), and AVE (>0.50), indicating high internal consistency and convergent validity. Constructs H2, H4, and H5 fall below these recommended thresholds, suggesting limited reliability and convergent validity. All constructs exhibit HTMT ratios below 0.85, fulfilling discriminant validity requirements. The structural model explains 76% of the variance (R^2) in product experience (Table 1).

Table 1. Measurement model results Gen X

Hypothesis	CR (rho_c)	α	AVE	HTMT	f^2
H1	0,885	0,845	0,607	0,827	2,282
H2	0,569	0,529	0,276	0,252	0,026
H3	0,829	0,722	0,621	0,229	0,062
H4	0,572	−0,281	0,460	0,300	0,101
H5	0,591	0,469	0,414	0,211	0,004

For Gen Z (Table 2), all constructs show acceptable internal consistency, with CR values between 0.788 and 0.842. AVE values exceed 0.50 for all constructs except H2, where less than 50% of the indicator variance is explained by the latent construct. Cronbach's alpha ranges from 0.565 to 0.779; H1 and H2 meet the threshold, while the others fall slightly below but remain acceptable within an exploratory research context. HTMT values are all below 0.90, meeting discriminant validity criteria. R^2 is likewise 76%. One item was removed due to insufficient factor loading in order to improve model fit. Further adjustments, particularly for Gen X, were forgone to maintain measurement model comparability for MGA.

Table 2. Measurement model results Gen Z

Hypothesis	CR (rho_c)	α	AVE	HTMT	f^2
H1	0,842	0,779	0,519	0,859	2,329
H2	0,790	0,698	0,437	0,131	0,014
H3	0,794	0,701	0,570	0,260	0,031
H4	0,788	0,565	0,660	0,268	0,041
H5	0,825	0,685	0,611	0,323	0,000

The SEM results (Tables 3 and 4) indicate significant positive effects for H1 and H3 among Gen X, while H2, H4, and H5, are not significant. For Gen Z, H1, H3, and H4 show significant positive effects, while H2 and H5 do not.

Table 3. Structural model results Gen X

Hypothesis	β	SD	t	p	95% CI
H1	0,792	0,030	26,066	0,000	0,746 - 0,869
H2	0,091	0,058	1,575	0,115	(−0,078) - 0,173
H3	0,137	0,037	3,721	0,000	0,067 - 0,211
H4	−0,170	0,097	1,743	0,081	(−0,269) - 0,102
H5	0,033	0,054	0,620	0,535	(−0,098) - 0,102

Table 4. Structural model results Gen Z

Hypothesis	β	SD	t	p	95% CI
H1	0,813	0,022	36,315	0,000	0,769 - 0,857
H2	−0,066	0,047	1,412	0,158	(−0,150) - 0,039
H3	0,089	0,039	2,315	0,021	0,017 - 0,166
H4	0,120	0,047	2,579	0,010	0,026 - 0,207
H5	0,000	0,038	0,006	0,996	(−0,074) - 0,076

MGA reveals a marginally significant stronger effect of H2 on product experience for Gen X compared to Gen Z, and a significantly stronger negative effect of H4 for Gen Z versus Gen X. No significant group differences are found for H1, H3, and H5. Overall, personalisation and interactive elements have the greatest influence on product experience across both generations.

6 Discussion

The construct of *personalisation* (H1) is theoretically assumed to be a central determinant of product experience. The quantitative analyses validate this assumption, demonstrating that personalisation significantly impacts product experience across both generations. The MGA reveals no significant differences in this effect between Gen X and Gen Z, indicating that the influence can be considered equally strong across generations. This finding contradicts theoretical assumptions that Gen X is sceptical towards standardised advertising. The results suggest that the individual and personalised approach to Gen X reduces this scepticism by providing perceived benefits associated with personalisation. The findings underline the view that personalisation plays a crucial role in product experience across generations, with differences in emphasis and preferred elements between the cohorts. In order to optimise the product experience in the context of fashion e-commerce, it is essential to make use of personalisation, according to consumers from both Gen X and Gen Z.

The construct of *information quality* (H2) demonstrates a modest and statistically non-significant influence on the product experience for both generations. A direct influence of information quality cannot be confirmed. An influence might dependent on additional moderating factors, like disparate expectations and utilisation patterns across generations, as well as the fundamental prerequisite nature of information quality. With regard to the generations, the MGA indicates a significant difference. The findings show that the impact of information quality is more substantial for Gen X than for Gen Z, although marginal in both cases. The direction and strength of the relationship vary marginally between the cohorts. These statements are also consistent with the theoretical features and characteristics attributed to the cohort. The role of information quality must be viewed in a differentiated manner, and further research on moderating variables appears to be useful.

The findings indicate that *interactive elements* (H3) have a significant, but minor, influence on the product experience for both generations. While the influence has the second-highest path coefficient within Gen X model, it ranks third for Gen Z, suggesting a smaller but still relevant role. The MGA demonstrates no substantial disparities between the generations. The impact of interactive components can be regarded as analogous. Despite a tendency to exhibit lower levels of technological proficiency, Gen X demonstrates a pronounced interest in interactive components. Interactive elements such as product videos and 360° views in fashion e-commerce support product understanding and contribute to an increase in the perceived quality of the product experience.

The construct of *translation quality* (H4) shows significant generation-specific variations in terms of its impact on the product experience. For Gen Z, translation quality is the second most influential construct in the model, having a significant positive influence on the product experience. Gen X shows a negative, insignificant correlation, meaning that no cross-generational effect can be identified. The MGA confirms this divergence between generations and demonstrates a substantial impact of translation quality on product experience, which is more pronounced for Gen Z.

The results for *channel consistency* (H5) demonstrate that the correlation between channel consistency and product experience is negligible. The MGA confirms that there is no significant difference between generations in terms of the effect of channel consistency on the product experience.

As a critical reflection of the findings, it should be noted that the implementation and maintenance of PXM involve considerable costs. Innovative technologies in particular require high financial expenditure, which poses significant challenges for companies with limited financial resources. This can therefore have a considerable impact on the practical implementation of the measures developed in theory.

Although the key dimensions of the PXM were operationalized in a valid manner, the inclusion of additional items or exogenous latent variables would have allowed for an even more nuanced model examination. The number of items selected was determined by the need to limit the complexity and length of the questionnaire. Critical reflection reveals that a more comprehensive survey instrument could have provided potentially deeper insights into the relationships among the constructs under investigation. Future studies should consider expanding the model to strengthen its foundation.

Furthermore, the study is geographically limited to Germany. This restriction makes methodological sense, as generations are significantly shaped by national historical, cultural and social conditions and are therefore not transferable to other countries. For future research, it would be interesting to conduct comparative studies in other countries to analyse similarities and differences between Gen X and Gen Z in the context of PXM. In this study, it should also be noted that some of the companies examined operate not only in Germany but also across Europe and globally. Consequently, influencing factors cannot be entirely ruled out.

7 Conclusion

This study explores the potential of PXM to enhance the product experience in the context of fashion e-commerce by conducting a comparative analysis across different generations. The findings indicate that personalisation and interactive components emerge as the predominant factors influencing the product experience, with a substantial impact observed across both generations. The quality of translation is shown to be significant, albeit generation-specific, with members of Gen Z placing particular importance on it. Factors such as information quality and channel consistency were found to have a minimal or negligible impact. The findings emphasise the potential for technological and generation-specific optimisation of PXM-Strategies in order to address customer needs and realise competitive advantages in e-commerce. The determined requirements of the generations deviate from the theoretically postulated characteristics.

References

1. McKinsey & Company: State of fashion technology report 2022 (2022). https://www.mckinsey.com/industries/retail/our-insights/state-of-fashion-technology-report-2022/
2. Härting, R-C., Reichstein, C., Lämmle, P., Sprengel, A.: Potentials of digital business models in the retail industry – empirical results from European experts. In: Rudas I.J., Janos C., Toro C., Howlett R.J., Botzheim J., Jain, L.C. (eds.) Knowledge-Based and Intelligent Information & Engineering Systems: Proceedings of the 23rd International Conference, KES-2019, Budapest, Hungary, vol. 159, pp. 1053–1062. Elsevier (2019). https://doi.org/10.1016/j.procs.2019.09.274
3. Statista: Deutschland: Nutzeranzahl im Markt für E-Commerce 2029. Statista (2025). https://de.statista.com/prognosen/488012/prognose-der-e-commerce-nutzer-in-deutschland
4. Statista: Fashion - Germany. Statista (2025). https://www.statista.com/outlook/emo/fashion/germany?currency=EUR
5. Harwardt, M.: E-Commerce, Marktplätze und Online-Marketing: Eine praxisorientierte Einführung für Entscheider. Springer Fachmedien Wiesbaden (2025). https://doi.org/10.1007/978-3-658-46178-2
6. PwC: Retail & consumer goods on the way to the metaverse (2022). https://www.pwc.de/de/handel-und-konsumguter/pwc-retail-and-consumer-goods-on-the-way-to-the-metaverse.pdf
7. Zhao, W., Hu, F., Wang, J., Shu, T., Xu, Y.: A systematic literature review on social commerce: assessing the past and guiding the future. Electron. Commer. Res. Appl. **57**, 101219 (2023). https://doi.org/10.1016/j.elerap.2022.101219
8. Bösel, S., Härting, R.: ProData4 – Studie zu den Potentialen von generativer KI im Product Experience Management (PXM) (2024). https://sdzecom.de/proda-4-studie/
9. forbeyond consors GmbH: Transform product data & create experiences with PXM (2025). https://www.forbeyond.eu/en/competencies/pxm
10. forbeyond consors GmbH: Data management - strategies, systems and services (2025). https://www.forbeyond.eu/en/competencies/data-management

11. XPLN GmbH: Was ist Digital Shelf (Analytics)? Ziele, Erfolgsfaktoren, Lösungen (2025). https://xpln.com/de/insights/detail/was-ist-digital-shelf-analytics-ziele-erfolgsfaktoren-loesungen
12. Syndigo LLC: Product syndication. Syndigo (2025). https://syndigo.com/glossary/product-syndication/
13. ATAMYA: Was ist PXM? (n.d.) https://www.atamya.com/de/was-ist-pxm/
14. Lewandowski, D.: Personalisierung und Kontextualisierung: Konvergente Strategien, Methoden und Konzepte (2018). https://www.researchgate.net/publication/329214045_Personalisierung_und_Kontextualisierung_Konvergente_Strategien_Methoden_und_Konzepte
15. Schniedermann, R.: What is Product Experience Management (PXM) (2025). https://4allportal.com/blog/was-ist-pxm
16. SDZeCOM, & Hochschule Aalen: ProDa#4: Fokus: Potentiale von generativer KI im Product Experience Management (PXM) (2024). https://25358164.fs1.hubspotusercontent-eu1.net/hubfs/25358164/SDZeCOM_ProDa_4-Studie.pdf
17. Klaffke, M.: Generationen-Management: Konzepte, Instrumente, Good-Practice-Ansätze. Springer Fachmedien (2014). https://doi.org/10.1007/978-3-658-02325-6
18. IHK Niederbayern: Unterschiedliche Generationen und ihre Wertvorstellungen (2025). https://www.ihk-niederbayern.de/fokusthemen/fachkraefte/recruiting-generation-y-und-z/unterschiedliche-generationen-und-ihre-wertvorstellungen/
19. Mangelsdorf, M.: 30 Minuten Generation Y. GABAL-Verlag (2014). https://www.wiso-net.de/document/GABA__9783956230493 96
20. Zoch, G.: Thirty years after the fall of the Berlin wall—do east and west Germans still differ in their attitudes to women's employment? Eur. Sociol. Rev. **37**(5), 731–749 (2021)
21. Yap, C.K.: Chernobyl nuclear catastrophe: lessons for sustainability and human health. Front. Public Health **10**, Article no. 930208 (2025). https://doi.org/10.3389/fpubh.2022.930208
22. Uhrmacher, M., et al.: HIV pre-exposure prophylaxis during the SARS-CoV-2 pandemic: results from a prospective observational study in Germany. Front. Public Health **10**, 930208 (2022). https://doi.org/10.3389/fpubh.2022.930208
23. Pawlik, V.: Gen Z, Millennials und Generation X – Ein Überblick. Statista (2024). https://de.statista.com/statistik/studie/id/78414/dokument/gen-z-millennials-und-generation-x-ein-ueberblick/
24. Taylor Wessing: Generations at work: Different generations and their different priorities in the working world of the future (2020). https://www.taylorwessing.com/-/media/taylor-wessing/files/germany/2020/10/tw_2020_generations-at-work_eng.pdf
25. Munich Business School: Emotions on the Web (2017). https://www.munich-business-school.de/insights/en/2017/emotions-on-the-web/
26. Ward, S.: Generation X and generation golf: what advertisers need to know. J. Advert. Res. **45**(1), 19–34 (2005)
27. Nielsen Consumer LLC: The X factor: How Generation X is quietly driving trillions in consumer spend. NIQ (2025). https://nielseniq.com/global/en/insights/report/2025/the-x-factor/
28. Francis, T., Hoefel, F.: Generation Z characteristics and its implications for companies. McKinsey (n.d.). https://www.mckinsey.com/industries/consumer-packaged-goods/our-insights/true-gen-generation-z-and-its-implications-for-companies
29. Mützel, S., Mau, S.: Family diversity and social cohesion in Germany: patterns, challenges, and prospects. Zeitschrift für Soziologie **51**(3), 185–204 (2022)
30. Bertelsmann Stiftung: The Next Generation in Germany: Lebensrealitäten, Werte und Perspektiven (2023). https://www.bertelsmann-stiftung.de/fileadmin/files/BSt/Publikationen/GrauePublikationen/NextGermany_08lay.pdf
31. Tirocchi, S., Serpieri, R., Gentina, E.: Generation Z, values, and media: from influencers to BeReal. Front. Psychol. (2024). https://doi.org/10.3389/fpsyg.2024.10809394

32. Keller, A., Schmidt, B.: A comparative study of the expectations of Gen Z and the perception of their employers in Germany (IUBH Discussion Papers in Human Resources No. 1) (2020). https://www.econstor.eu/bitstream/10419/216780/1/iubh-dp-hr-1-2020.pdf
33. An, G.K., Ngo, T.T.A.: AI-powered personalized advertising and purchase intention in Vietnam's digital landscape: the role of trust, relevance, and usefulness. J. Open Innov. Technol. Mark. Complex. **11**(3), 100580 (2025). https://doi.org/10.1016/j.joitmc.2025.100580
34. McKinsey & Company: The value of getting personalization right - Or wrong - Is multiplying (2021). https://www.mckinsey.com/capabilities/growth-marketing-and-sales/our-insights/the-value-of-getting-personalization-right-or-wrong-is-multiplying
35. Taheri, B., Yousaf, A., Gannon, M., Mishra, A.: E-commerce website customer engagement: delineating the role of UTAUT, vividness, and compulsion. J. Retail. Consum. Serv. **79**, 103835 (2024). https://doi.org/.1016/j.jretconser.2024.103835
36. Schmidt, J., Reichstein, C., Härting, R.-C.: Influence of augmented reality on consumer behaviour in online retailing. In: Abramowicz, W., Auer, S., Stróżyna, M. (eds.) BIS 2021. LNBIP, vol. 444, pp. 131–143. Springer, Cham (2022). https://doi.org/10.1007/978-3-031-04216-4_14
37. Flavián, C., Ibáñez-Sánchez, S., Orús, C.: The impact of virtual, augmented and mixed reality technologies on the customer experience. J. Bus. Res. **100**, 547–560 (2019). https://doi.org/10.1016/j.jbusres.2018.10.050
38. Barta, S., Gurrea, R., Flavián, C.: Augmented reality experiences: consumer-centered augmented reality framework and research agenda. Psychol. Mark. **42**(2), 634–650 (2025). https://doi.org/10.1002/mar.22143
39. Uysal, E., et al.: Virtually mine: understanding consumer responses to virtual reality product presentations. J. Retail. (2025). https://doi.org/10.1016/j.jretai.2025.04.007
40. Araghi, S., Palangkaraya, A., Webster, E.: The impact of language translation quality on commerce: the example of patents. J. Int. Bus. Policy **7**(2), 224–246 (2024). https://doi.org/10.1057/s42214-023-00157-0
41. Fassott, G.: Internationaler E-Commerce: Chancen und Barrieren aus Konsumentensicht. DUV (2007). https://doi.org/10.1007/978-3-8350-9508-3
42. Verhoef, P.C., Kannan, P.K., Inman, J.J.: From multi-channel retailing to omni-channel retailing: introduction to the special issue on multi-channel retailing. J. Retail. **91**(2), 174–181 (2015). https://doi.org/10.1016/j.jretai.2015.02.005
43. Sharma, N., Fatima, J.K.: Influence of perceived value on omnichannel usage: mediating and moderating roles of the omnichannel shopping habit. J. Retail. Consum. Serv. **77**, 103627 (2024). https://doi.org/10.1016/j.jretconser.2023.103627
44. Chen, N., Yang, Y.: The impact of customer experience on consumer purchase intention in cross-border E-commerce - taking network structural embeddedness as mediator variable. J. Retail. Consum. Serv. **59**, 102344 (2021). https://doi.org/10.1016/j.jretconser.2020.102344
45. PwC: So tickt die Generation Z. PwC (2020). https://www.pwc.de/de/handel-und-konsumguter/so-tickt-die-generation-z.html
46. Chin, W., Cheah, J., Liu, Y., Ting, H., Lim, X., Cham, T.H.: Demystifying the role of causal-predictive modeling using partial least squares structural equation modeling in information systems research. Ind. Manag. Data Syst. **120**(12), 2161–2209 (2020)
47. Hair, J.F., Hult, G.T.M., Ringle, C.M., Sarstedt, M., Richter, N.F., Hauff, S.: Partial Least Squares Strukturgleichungsmodellierung (PLS-SEM): Eine anwendungsorientierte Einführung (2. Aufl.), Vahlen (2024)
48. Weiber, R., Sarstedt, M.: Strukturgleichungsmodellierung: Eine anwendungsorientierte Einführung in die Kausalanalyse mit Hilfe von AMOS, SmartPLS und SPSS. Springer Fachmedien (2021). https://doi.org/10.1007/978-3-658-32660-9
49. Döring, N.: Forschungsmethoden und Evaluation in den Sozial- und Humanwissenschaften. Springer, Heidelberg (2023). https://doi.org/10.1007/978-3-662-64762-2

50. Atteslander, P.: Methoden der empirischen Sozialforschung (14. Auflage). Erich Schmidt Verlag (2023)
51. Reichstein, C., Härting, R.-C., Häfner, F.: Challenges in the market launch of active assisted living solutions – empirical results from European experts. Procedia Comput. Sci. **176**, 2000–2009 (2020). https://doi.org/10.1016/j.procs.2020.09.247
52. Homburg, C., Baumgartner, H.: Beurteilung von Kausalmodellen. Bestandsaufnahme und Anwendungsempfehlungen. In: MAR, vol. 17, no. 3, pp. 162–176 (1995). https://doi.org/10.15358/0344-1369-1995-3-162

From Text to Knowledge

A Heterogeneous Agentic RAG Architecture for Administrative Knowledge Management

Adam Gałązkiewicz(✉)

Department of Information Technology Poznań University of Economics and Business
al, Niepodległości 10, 61-875 Poznań, Poland
adam.galazkiewicz@ue.poznan.pl

Abstract. The digital transformation of Higher Education Institutions (HEIs) has led to an influx of unstructured digital documents. Administrative repositories, containing orders, resolutions, and manuals, are difficult to navigate using keyword-based engines. This is problematic for the Polish language, where morphological complexity often renders simple BM25 algorithms ineffective. This paper presents the design and evaluation of an Agentic RAG system, deployed on-premise at the Poznań University of Economics and Business (PUEB). The proposed system employs an agentic workflow capable of multi-step reasoning. A comparative study of two locally hosted Small Language Models (SLMs) - the generalist open-weights OpenAI-OSS-20B and the native Polish SpeakLeash Bielik-11B-v3.0 - reveals trade-offs between reasoning capabilities and linguistic fluency. Based on these findings, a Heterogeneous Hybrid Architecture is proposed, where the generalist model handles logic, while the native model serves as a stylistic refinement layer.

Keywords: Agentic AI · Retrieval-Augmented Generation · Small Language Models · Data Sovereignty · Administrative Knowledge Management · Higher Education

1 Introduction

In the academic landscape, administrative efficiency correlates with the ability to access accurate information rapidly. Public institutions generate documents ranging from regulatory acts to financial directives. In the case of the Poznań University of Economics and Business (PUEB), such a repository comprises several thousand documents spanning nearly two decades. Manual retrieval is labor-intensive and error-prone, contributing to "administrative overhead".

While Large Language Models (LLMs) [1] have revolutionized information retrieval via Retrieval-Augmented Generation (RAG) [2–4], public institutions face hurdles. First, "Naive RAG" often fails when synthesizing information from multiple sources or performing deductions [5]. Second, strict privacy regulations (GDPR) prohibit processing sensitive data via public cloud APIs [6]. To address

K. Węcel and V. Řepa (Eds.): BIS 2026, LNBIP 584, pp. 213–224, 2026.
https://doi.org/10.1007/978-3-032-26363-6_16

these challenges, this paper proposes an Agentic RAG architecture deployed entirely on-premise. "Agentic" refers to the ability to act independently: breaking queries into sub-tasks, executing search tools iteratively, and verifying information [7]. This represents a leap from linear RAG pipelines.

A central research question of this study concerns the feasibility of Small Language Models (SLMs) - specifically in the 11B to 20B range - as cognitive engines. By 2026, the landscape has shifted towards efficient, local models. The performance of SpeakLeash Bielik-11B-v3.0, trained on Polish corpora, is compared against OpenAI-OSS-20B, a state-of-the-art open-weights Mixture-of-Experts (MoE) model. The contribution of this paper is threefold: (1) A reference architecture for secure, on-premise Agentic RAG; (2) A benchmark of Polish vs. Generalist SLMs in an administrative context; (3) A model for a hybrid pipeline decoupling reasoning from linguistic synthesis.

2 Related Works

Retrieving information from unstructured repositories is a core goal of Knowledge Management. Early sparse methods like BM25 suffer from the "vocabulary mismatch problem" [8]. This limitation is exacerbated in morphologically rich languages like Polish, where a noun can have dozens of forms that do not match the keyword without complex lemmatization [9].

Transformer-based models introduced Dense Retrieval, enabling semantic matching [10]. The Retrieval-Augmented Generation (RAG) framework [2] combined their retrieval capability with generative models [11]. However, early "Naive RAG" implementations faced the "Lost in the Middle" phenomenon [12], wherein models fail to use information placed in the middle of a long context window. Furthermore, Naive RAG is linear: if initial retrieval is poor, generation hallucinates. To overcome limitations of linear pipelines, research moved towards Agentic AI. ReAct [13] demonstrated that LLMs perform better when prompted to generate a reasoning trace. Toolformer [14] showed models can be fine-tuned to use external APIs. In the proposed system, the database is treated as a "tool" the agent can query iteratively. A critical aspect is "Data Sovereignty." Relying on US-based clouds raises GDPR concerns. Sovereign AI advocates for indigenous capabilities using local infrastructure [15]. The choice of SpeakLeash Bielik, trained on Polish infrastructure, aligns with this strategic direction.

By 2026, the focus of AI deployment has shifted from massive, cloud-hosted models to efficient, locally hostable Small Language Models (SLMs). Research by NVIDIA [16] and others indicates that for specific domain tasks, an SLM fine-tuned on high-quality data can match the performance of much larger generalist models. In the Polish ecosystem, the SpeakLeash project has been pivotal [17]. Their Bielik models are trained specifically to address the linguistic nuances of Polish [18,19]. Simultaneously, the release of OpenAI-OSS-20B as an open-weights model brought advanced "Reasoning" capabilities to the open-source community (e.g., Llama, Mistral) [20], challenging the dominance of closed-source models [21–23]. This study provides a timely comparison of these two approaches: native specialization versus generalist reasoning.

3 System Architecture

The system implements a containerized microservices architecture designed for high availability and strict data isolation. It is deployed entirely on-premise, ensuring that sensitive administrative data remains within the university's secure network perimeter.

Hardware Infrastructure. The deployment environment is built upon a high-performance workstation optimized for local LLM inference and vector search.

- **Compute Accelerator:** The system leverages an NVIDIA RTX 6000 Ada Generation GPU (48 GB GDDR6 ECC). The substantial VRAM capacity allows for hosting unquantized 20B+ parameter models alongside the embedding models without offloading to the CPU, ensuring low-latency responses essential for interactive chat.
- **Host System:** An Intel i9-13900KF processor paired with 64 GB of DDR5 RAM running Ubuntu Server 22.04 LTS.
- **Storage:** A 1TB NVMe SSD array provides high I/O throughput, critical for the vector database's read/write operations during indexing and retrieval.

Core Application. The core application logic relies on UEP AI Platform, based on the Onyx framework distributed under a "Free and Open Source Software" license [24,25]. The system is orchestrated via Docker Compose, managing a suite of interacting containers (Fig. 1):

- **Frontend and Backend Services**: The interface is served by a Next.js application, communicating with a FastAPI Python backend. The backend acts as the central orchestrator, managing user sessions, chat history in a relational database (PostgreSQL), and API calls to the inference engine. It implements a modular "Gen AI" abstraction layer that allows seamless switching between different LLM providers.
- **The Indexing Pipeline (Background Workers)**: A container handles the asynchronous data ingestion pipeline. This begins with Connector Polling, which monitors the mapped local directories for new PDF/DOCX files. Upon detection, the system initiates Document Processing to extract text and metadata. The data then undergoes Chunking, splitting documents into semantic segments (via Recursive Character Splitter, 512 tokens), before moving to the final Embedding stage, where text chunks are sent to the local embedding model server to generate vector representations.
- **Vector Database and Search Engine**: For retrieval, the standard UEP AI deployment utilizes Vespa (or PostgreSQL with pgvector in lighter configurations) as the vector store. This component indexes the dense vectors generated by `nomic-embed-text-v1` and executes hybrid search queries. The search mechanism combines Keyword Match (BM25) for the precise lookup of specific terms (e.g., "Regulation 33/2025") with Dense Vector Similarity (Dot Product) to handle the conceptual matching of user intent.

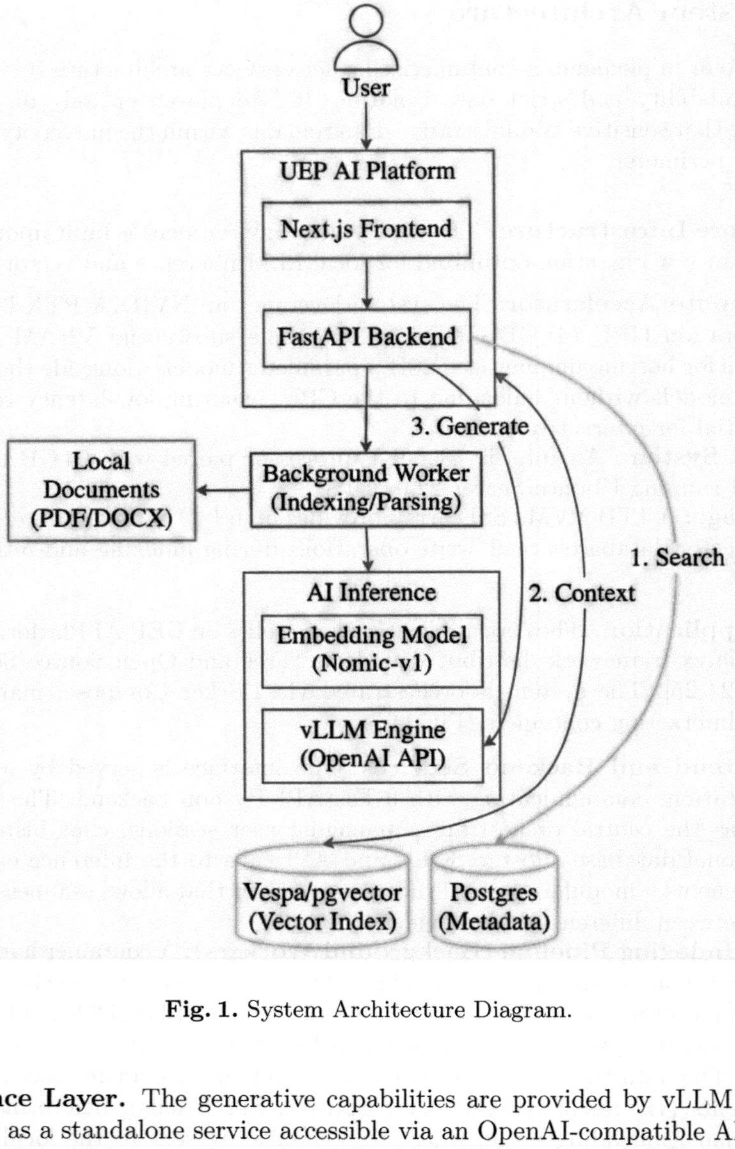

Fig. 1. System Architecture Diagram.

Inference Layer. The generative capabilities are provided by vLLM [26,27], running as a standalone service accessible via an OpenAI-compatible API. This decoupled architecture allows the UEP AI backend to treat the local model exactly as it would a remote cloud API. To support the complex agentic behaviors of the Bielik-11B [28] model, the vLLM service was deployed with specific flags enabling auto-tool-choice and the Hermes tool-call parser. This configuration is critical for translating the model's internal reasoning tokens into structured API calls that UEP AI can execute.

Data Ingestion. Proper data ingestion is the foundation of any RAG system. We utilized the `nomic-embed-text-v1` model (768 dimensions) for dense retrieval, hosted locally. This model was selected for its large context window, which is critical for long administrative documents, and robust multilingual support, while native Polish embedding models are considered for future iterations. To maximize retrieval precision, the model's specific protocol was adhered to by appending task-specific prefixes, where "search_query:" is prefixed to all user questions and "search_document:" is prefixed to all document chunks during indexing. This asymmetric instruction tuning aligns the vector space, ensuring that questions map closer to their relevant answers. Furthermore, to address the high morphological complexity of Polish legal texts, Multi-pass Indexing with Multilingual Expansion (Polish) was enabled. This mechanism augments the index with lemma variations, ensuring that a query for "Rektor" also retrieves documents containing "Rektora" or "Rektorowi," effectively bridging the lexical gap.

Prompt Engineering. One of the key findings of this study was the necessity of distinct prompting strategies for different models. While the generalist OpenAI-OSS-20B model followed simple instructions, the native Bielik-11B model required a more structured, "persona-based" system prompt to trigger agentic behavior reliably. Specifically, the system prompt for Bielik had to explicitly define the "Thought-Action-Observation" loop structure. It was observed that without rigid constraints (e.g., "Think step-by-step," "Do not answer until you have found the document"), the native model tended to hallucinate based on its pre-trained knowledge rather than using the search tool. This highlights a gap in current native model training: while they excel at language generation, they often lack the "Function Calling" fine-tuning present in global SOTA models.

4 Experimental Methodology

To rigorously assess the capabilities of the selected models in a domain-specific context, a multi-stage experimental protocol was designed. The methodology mirrors real-world usage scenarios, prioritizing practical utility over purely theoretical benchmarks.

Data Corpus. The knowledge base constitutes the foundational layer of the RAG system. For this study, a corpus of 4,342 documents sourced directly from the PUEB internal repository was ingested. This represents a curated subset of legally binding acts, specifically Rector's orders and Senate resolutions, with everyday administrative documents intentionally excluded to focus evaluation on the institution's complex regulatory core. The dataset spans a period of 17 years (2008–2025), reflecting the evolving legal and administrative framework of the institution. The corpus structure can be categorized as follows:

- **Primary Regulatory Acts (PDF)**: The vast majority of the dataset consists of Rector's orders and Senate resolutions in PDF format with accessible text layers. While text extraction was technically straightforward, the semantic segmentation proved complex due to the rigid administrative layout (headers, footers, side-notes, and multi-level listing styles like *§3, item 1, point a*).
- **Supplementary Attachments (DOCX)**: A smaller, yet semantically critical portion of the corpus comprises editable DOCX files. These serve predominantly as attachments to the main regulations (e.g., application forms, distinct tables of fees, or syllabus templates). The ingestion pipeline had to account for the fact that these documents often lack self-contained context and derive their meaning solely from the parent PDF regulation.

Queries Design. Standard academic benchmarks (like MMLU or HELM) are insufficient for evaluating specialized administrative tasks in the Polish language, particularly those requiring knowledge of internal university procedures. Consequently, a custom dataset consisting of 10 complex queries (Q1-Q10) was curated. The queries were developed to ensure they reflect genuine, high-frequency information needs. The dataset covers a spectrum of cognitive requirements:

- **Reasoning:** Questions requiring arithmetic operations or logical deduction based on retrieved premises (e.g., calculating the final fee for a document duplicate based on a base rate found in one paragraph and a multiplier found in another).
- **Synthesis:** Tasks requiring the aggregation of information scattered across multiple documents or separating a regulation from its specific attachments.
- **Fact Retrieval:** Direct questions about specific dates, names, or values.
- **Negative Constraints (Hallucination Traps):** Queries regarding non-existent procedures to test the model's adherence to truthfulness and its ability to admit ignorance.
- **Cross-Lingual Tasks:** Questions posed in English requiring answers derived from Polish source texts, testing the model's internal translation and alignment capabilities.

Execution Protocol. To evaluate the models in a setting that mimics a production environment, deterministic greedy decoding was replaced. Each query was executed 5 times for each model (Total $N = 100$ trials). Crucially, the sampling temperature was set to $\tau = 0.7$. While benchmarks typically use a temperature of 0.0 for reproducibility, a value of 0.7 was chosen to better reflect the configuration of live chat assistants, where a degree of generation diversity and linguistic fluency is desired. By averaging the results over 5 distinct runs, the randomness introduced by the higher temperature was mitigated while effectively capturing the models' stability and their tendency to hallucinate under non-deterministic conditions.

Evaluation Metrics. Given the nuanced nature of administrative language, automated metrics such as BLEU or ROUGE were deemed inadequate, as they focus on n-gram overlap rather than semantic correctness. A human-in-the-loop evaluation strategy using a 5-point Likert scale, assessed by domain experts, was employed:

- **5 (Excellent):** The answer is factually correct, logically sound, stylistically appropriate (formal Polish), and includes precise citations.
- **4 (Good):** The answer is factually correct but suffers from minor stylistic issues, unnecessary verbosity, or suboptimal formatting.
- **3 (Passable):** The model retrieved the correct document, but the synthesized answer is vague, incomplete, or requires user effort to interpret.
- **2 (Poor):** The model found the document but hallucinated the final answer or committed a significant logical error (e.g., wrong calculation).
- **1 (Failure):** Complete hallucination, failure to retrieve relevant documents, or a refusal to answer when information was available.

5 Results

The experimental results highlight a significant divergence in the capabilities of the two tested models. While both models successfully operated within the Agentic RAG framework, their behaviors differed fundamentally under the non-deterministic conditions ($\tau = 0.7$) typical of production environments. Results are summarized in Table 1. Figure 2 visualizes the average scores by question category while Table 2 presents a taxonomy of observed errors categorized into specific error types.

Table 1. Detailed Results (Average of 5 runs). Score (1–5), Time (s).

ID	Category	Description	OpenAI-OSS-20B		Bielik-11B	
			Score	Time	Score	Time
Q1	Reasoning	Duplicate ID Fee Calculation	5.0	12.5s	3.9	9.0 s
Q2	Fact	Committee Chairperson Name	4.8	8.4 s	4.6	7.2 s
Q3	Fact	Scholarship Deadline	4.8	9.1 s	4.5	6.5 s
Q4	Synthesis	List of Attachments	4.5	15.2 s	3.4	8.0 s
Q5	Conditional	Dean's Leave	4.9	11.0 s	4.3	8.5 s
Q6	Synthesis	Diploma Diff (FT vs PT)	4.7	14.5 s	4.0	9.2 s
Q7	Trap	Free Transport Tickets	5.0	6.0 s	4.3	4.5 s
Q8	Knowledge	Rector from 2005 Statute	4.6	8.0 s	4.4	7.0 s
Q9	Lang	English Query → Polish Ans	4.5	10.5 s	5.0	8.2 s
Q10	Metadata	Classification Symbol	4.2	13.0 s	2.9	6.0 s
AVG			**4.70**	**10.8s**	**4.13**	**7.4s**

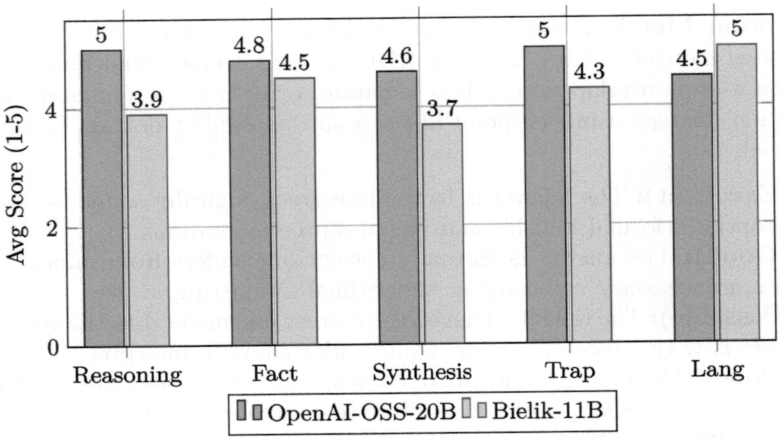

Fig. 2. Comparison of Average Scores by Question Category.

5.1 Detailed Analysis

Arithmetic and Logic. Query Q1 asked: *"What is the fee for issuing a duplicate electronic student ID?"*. This required retrieving a regulation stating the base fee (22 PLN) and a rule that duplicates cost 50% more.

- OpenAI-OSS-20B excelled here. It retrieved the document, identified the base fee, and explicitly performed the calculation ($22+11 = 33$). It effectively acted as a reasoning engine.
- Bielik-11B struggled with the final logic step. It consistently retrieved the correct document and identified the base fee, but usually failed to perform the calculation correctly, often answering with the base fee (22 PLN). This indicates that while its retrieval is strong, the model struggles with arithmetic without external tools.

Synthesis and Persistence. Queries requiring the synthesis of multiple documents (e.g., Q4 "List all attachments") exposed the "laziness" of the SLM.

- OpenAI-OSS-20B demonstrated robust agentic loops. In Q4, it performed an initial search, realized the list was incomplete, and executed two additional searches (Multi-hop).
- Bielik-11B showed improvement with careful prompt engineering. While prone to "premature convergence" in initial tests, a more structured prompt encouraged it to perform at least one additional verification step, leading to more complete, albeit not always perfect, answers.

Linguistic Fluency Query Q9 was posed in English: *"What is the deadline for submitting the thesis defense application?"*.

- Bielik-11B shone in this category. It correctly understood the English query, searched the Polish documents, and synthesized a grammatically perfect Polish response, as per system instructions.
- OpenAI-OSS-20B provided correct information but occasionally output "Anglicisms" (e.g., unnatural word order) or answered in English despite instructions to use Polish.

Table 2. Taxonomy of Observed Errors

Error Type	Definition	OSS-20B	Bielik-11B
Premature Stop	Agent stops searching before finding full info	2	7
Hallucination	Inventing facts not in documents	1	2
Logic Fail	Correct retrieval, wrong arithmetic/inference	0	4
Language Error	Grammatical errors or wrong language	5	0
Refusal	Refusing to answer when info is available	0	2

5.2 Discussion

Based on the error taxonomy analysis presented in Table 2, it is proposed as a theoretical framework that the optimal architecture for Public Administration AI is not a single model, but a Heterogeneous Pipeline. This proposal is not presented as an empirically tested system, but as a conceptual model grounded in the observed error distributions, intended to guide future benchmark studies. Currently, researchers often try to find one "Golden Model" that is both logically brilliant and linguistically native. The observed data suggests this is inefficient. Instead, future systems should decouple Reasoning from Articulation. A two-stage pipeline is envisaged:

- **Stage 1: The Orchestrator (Reasoning Engine)**. An optimized, high-logic model (like OpenAI-OSS-20B) receives the user query. Its role is to plan the search, execute API calls, filter results, and synthesize the factual core of the answer.
- **Stage 2: The Polisher (Linguistic Wrapper)**. The raw output from Stage 1 is fed into a Native SLM (like Bielik-11B), whose system prompt is restricted to reformulating the content in formal Polish administrative style without introducing new facts.

This approach leverages the "Reasoning" capabilities while maintaining the "Cultural Sovereignty" provided by local initiatives. Conceptual analysis of the error taxonomy (Table 2) suggests this architecture would mitigate the observed trade-offs. The proposed architecture can be directly adopted by public-sector information systems facing multilingual and legal-document constraints.

6 Future Works

The results of this study outline a clear roadmap for the further development of the proposed Agentic RAG architecture for administrative tasks. The limitations identified - specifically regarding arithmetic logic and search persistence in native models - will be addressed in the next phase of the project.

The current implementation relies on effective `nomic-embed-text-v1`. Future iterations will migrate to intfloat/multilingual-e5 [29]. Preliminary tests suggest this model offers superior semantic alignment for Polish legal phrasing, potentially improving the recall rate for the initial search step and reducing the need for multi-hop corrections. To solve the arithmetic failures, equipping the agent with a Code Interpreter tool is planned. By running a sandboxed Python environment (via Docker) alongside the LLM, the agent will be able to delegate calculation tasks to a deterministic engine. This hybrid approach combines the linguistic strength of the LLM with the mathematical precision of Python.

The system will be deployed to a pilot group of deanery staff. A feedback mechanism (Thumbs Up/Down) will be implemented to collect a dataset of real-world interactions. This data will be used to fine-tune the Bielik model specifically for the "Function Calling" task, aiming to cure the "laziness" observed in the current experiments. Finally, to improve accessibility, integration of OpenAI Whisper v3 for speech-to-text input is aimed for. This would allow administrative staff to query the database verbally during phone calls with students, significantly speeding up the resolution of routine inquiries.

7 Conclusions

This paper presented a comprehensive evaluation of an on-premise Agentic RAG system designed for university administration. By comparing a native Polish Small Language Model (SpeakLeash Bielik-11B) with a generalist open-weights model (OpenAI-OSS-20B), a fundamental trade-off in the current SLM landscape was highlighted.

Results show that generalist models like OpenAI-OSS-20B serve as superior "Agentic Engines." They possess the logical robustness required to plan multi-step searches, identify information gaps, and perform basic reasoning (e.g., arithmetic). However, they lack the cultural and stylistic polish required for official communication in Polish. Conversely, Bielik-11B generates text of high linguistic quality but struggles with complex, autonomous workflows, often giving up too early in the search process. The study confirms that deploying such advanced systems locally is technically feasible and cost-effective using consumer-grade hardware (like the RTX 6000 Ada). The combination of UEP AI and vLLM provides a robust, production-ready stack that rivals commercial cloud offerings while satisfying strict data sovereignty requirements (GDPR).

For institutions planning similar deployments, a hybrid approach is recommended. A viable strategy is to use a "Reasoning Model" (like OpenAI-OSS) for the internal thought process (planning, searching, filtering) and a "Native

Model" (like Bielik) for the final response generation. This ensures that the user receives an answer that is both logically accurate and stylistically impeccable. This architecture is highly transferable to other strict public-sector domains (e.g., healthcare, municipal offices). The transition to Agentic AI in public administration is inevitable. As open-weights models continue to improve, the gap between "Reasoning" and "Fluency" will close, enabling fully autonomous, secure, and linguistically proficient knowledge assistants for the public sector.

References

1. Zhao, W.X., et al.: A Survey of Large Language Models. arXiv:2303.18223 (2023)
2. Lewis, P., et al.: Retrieval-augmented generation for knowledge-intensive NLP tasks. In: Advances in Neural Information Processing Systems, vol. 33, pp. 9459–9474. Curran Associates, Inc. (2020)
3. Swacha, J., Gracel, M.: Retrieval-Augmented Generation (RAG) chatbots for education: a survey of applications. Appl. Sci. **15**(8), 4234 (2025). https://doi.org/10.3390/app15084234
4. Kuratomi, G., Pirozelli, P., Cozman, F.G., Peres, S.M.: A RAG-Based Institutional Assistant. arXiv:2501.13880 (2025)
5. Gao, Y., et al.: Retrieval-Augmented Generation for Large Language Models: A Survey. arXiv:2312.10997 (2023)
6. He, F., Zhu, T., Ye, D., Liu, B., Zhou, W., Yu, P.S.: The Emerged Security and Privacy of LLM Agent: A Survey with Case Studies. arXiv:2407.19354 (2024)
7. Wang, L., et al.: A survey on large language model based autonomous agents. Front. Comp. Sci. **18**(6), 186345 (2024). https://doi.org/10.1007/s11704-024-40231-1
8. Karpukhin, V., et al.: Dense passage retrieval for open-domain question answering. In: Proceedings of the 2020 Conference on Empirical Methods in Natural Language Processing, pp. 6769–6781. Association for Computational Linguistics (2020)
9. Rybak, P., Mroczkowski, R., Tracz, J., Gawlik, I.: KLEJ: comprehensive benchmark for Polish language understanding. In: Jurafsky, D., Chai, J., Schluter, N., Tetreault, J. (eds.) Proceedings of the 58th Annual Meeting of the Association for Computational Linguistics, pp. 1191–1201. Association for Computational Linguistics (2020). https://doi.org/10.18653/v1/2020.acl-main.111
10. Izacard, G., Grave, E.: Leveraging passage retrieval with generative models for open domain question answering. In: Proceedings of the 16th Conference of the European Chapter of the Association for Computational Linguistics: Main Volume, pp. 874–880. Association for Computational Linguistics (2021)
11. Lewis, M., et al.: BART: denoising sequence-to-sequence pre-training for natural language generation, translation, and comprehension. In: Proceedings of the 58th Annual Meeting of the Association for Computational Linguistics, pp. 7871–7880. Association for Computational Linguistics (2020)
12. Liu, N.F., et al.: Lost in the middle: how language models use long contexts. Trans. Assoc. Comput. Linguist. **12**, 157–173 (2024)
13. Yao, S., et al.: ReAct: synergizing reasoning and acting in language models. In: International Conference on Learning Representations. ICLR, Kigali (2023)
14. Schick, T., et al.: Toolformer: language models can teach themselves to use tools. In: Oh, A., Naumann, T., Globerson, A., Saenko, K., Hardt, M., Levine, S. (eds.) Advances in Neural Information Processing Systems, vol. 36, pp. 42385–42407. Curran Associates Inc., New Orleans (2023)

15. Jansen, B., Kadenko, N., Broeders, D., van Eeten, M., Borgolte, K., Fiebig, T.: Pushing boundaries: an empirical view on the digital sovereignty of six governments in the midst of geopolitical tensions. Gov. Inf. Q. **40**(4), 101862 (2023). https://doi.org/10.1016/j.giq.2023.101862
16. Belcak, P., et al.: Small Language Models are the Future of Agentic AI. arXiv:2506.02153 (2025)
17. SpeakLeash: Open PL LLM Leaderboard. https://huggingface.co/spaces/speakleash/open_pl_llm_leaderboard. Accessed 15 Jan 2026
18. Ociepa, K., Flis, Ł., Kinas, R., Wróbel, K., Gwoździej, A.: Bielik v3 Small: Technical report (2025). arXiv:2505.02550
19. Ociepa, K., Flis, Ł., Kinas, R., Wróbel, K., Gwoździej, A.: Bielik 11B v3: Multilingual Large Language Model for European Languages. arXiv:2601.11579 (2025)
20. Jiang, A.Q., et al.: Mistral 7B. arXiv:2310.06825 (2023)
21. OpenAI: Introducing gpt-oss models. https://openai.com/index/introducing-gpt-oss/. Accessed 15 Jan 2026
22. OpenAI: gpt-oss-20b Model Card. https://huggingface.co/openai/gpt-oss-20b. Accessed 15 Jan 2026
23. OpenAI API Documentation: gpt-oss-20b. https://platform.openai.com/docs/models/gpt-oss-20b. Accessed 15 Jan 2026
24. Onyx Documentation. https://docs.onyx.app/. Accessed 15 Jan 2026
25. Onyx AI Platform Repository. https://github.com/onyx-dot-app/onyx-foss. Accessed 15 Jan 2026
26. vLLM Documentation. https://docs.vllm.ai/en/. Accessed 15 Jan 2026
27. Kwon, W., et al.: Efficient memory management for large language model serving with pagedattention. In: Proceedings of the 29th Symposium on Operating Systems Principles, pp. 611–626. ACM, New York (2023). https://doi.org/10.1145/3600006.3613165
28. Ociepa, K., et al.: Bielik-11B-v3.0-Instruct model card. https://huggingface.co/speakleash/Bielik-11B-v3.0-Instruct. Accessed 15 Jan 2026
29. Wang, L., et al.: Text Embeddings by Weakly-Supervised Contrastive Pre-training. arXiv:2212.03528 (2022)

Agentic LLM Approach to Automated LOINC Code Assignment for Internal Laboratory Tests

Joël Fehr[1,2], Jing Fu[1], Luca Bernasconi[3], Cyril Fischer[1], and Felice Burn[1(✉)]

[1] Center of Excellence for AI & Data Science, Kantonsspital Aarau, 5000 Aarau, Switzerland
felice.burn@ksa.ch
[2] Department of Health Sciences and Technology (D-HEST), ETH Zurich, 8008 Zürich, Switzerland
[3] Institute of Laboratory Medicine, Kantonsspital Aarau, 5000 Aarau, Switzerland

Abstract. Standardized coding of laboratory data is essential for clinical interoperability, secondary data use, and multi-institutional research. Logical Observation Identifiers Names and Codes (LOINC®) provide a global standard for laboratory observations, but manual and automated mapping remain challenging due to heterogeneous local test descriptions, language differences, and evolving terminologies. We propose an agentic approach for automated LOINC coding that leverages a locally deployed large language model (LLM) interacting iteratively with the official LOINC Search API through a query-refinement loop. The method was evaluated on 151 frequently used laboratory tests extracted from German language routine clinical data. Performance was benchmarked against a retrieval augmented generation (RAG) baseline using multiple embedding models. The proposed approach consistently outperformed the RAG baseline, achieving a Top-1 accuracy of up to 85.4% and a Top-5 accuracy of up to 98.0%. The high Top-5 performance enables efficient expert-in-the-loop validation workflows. The agentic method demonstrated greater robustness to incomplete laboratory metadata and maintained competitive runtime while operating entirely locally. Agentic, API-driven LLM workflows offer a practical and transparent solution for automated LOINC coding in clinical settings. The approach supports interoperability, minimizes dependence on proprietary services, and is well suited for integration into routine hospital environments.

Keywords: Agentic AI · LLM · Automation · Data Mapping · LOINC · Laboratory Medicine

1 Introduction

Modern biomedicine increasingly depends on transforming large and heterogeneous clinical data streams into usable evidence to support research, quality

K. Węcel and V. Řepa (Eds.): BIS 2026, LNBIP 584, pp. 225–235, 2026.
https://doi.org/10.1007/978-3-032-26363-6_17

assessment, and clinical decision-making. The rapid expansion of digitized health data has enabled large-scale analyses but has also exposed persistent challenges in managing, linking, and integrating data across institutions and information systems [1,10]. In parallel, machine learning methods have matured into important tools for extracting value from these data, shifting the primary bottleneck from data availability to the representations and algorithms that render clinical data usable in practice [12]. A central and recurring limitation in this context is interoperability. When clinical data are encoded using incompatible formats and institution-specific conventions, downstream analysis, data reuse, and cross-site learning are substantially impaired, even when the underlying clinical measurements are conceptually equivalent [6,11].

Laboratory data represent a particularly high-value target for interoperability efforts. Laboratory tests are ubiquitous, high-volume, and essential for both direct patient care and secondary uses such as research and surveillance. However, equivalent tests are often represented using diverse local names and codes across laboratories and hospital information systems, complicating aggregation, benchmarking, and multi-institutional analyses [4]. Logical Observation Identifiers Names and Codes (LOINC®) [22], developed by the Regenstrief Institute,[1] provides a standardized terminology intended to assign laboratory observations universal identifiers with structured semantics. Despite this, achieving consistent LOINC coding remains operationally challenging. Mapping is time-consuming, and mismatches between institutions can undermine the benefits of standardization [4,17]. Incomplete local test descriptions and reliance on name-based mapping that omits key discriminating attributes increase the risk of systematic coding errors [17].

These challenges have motivated extensive research into automating the mapping of laboratory results to standardized LOINC codes. Early approaches focused on rule based and semi-automated methods, including parsing, synonym matching [5], and interactive tools such as RELMA®[2], which reduced mapping effort while maintaining high-quality results [26]. Subsequent work shifted toward data-driven machine learning approaches. Corpus-based supervised learning and information retrieval methods demonstrated that existing local-to-LOINC mappings can support mapping at new institutions [3], while traditional classifiers such as logistic regression and random forest proved effective for mapping raw laboratory data directly to LOINC codes [14]. Beyond text-based approaches, distributional methods leveraged similarities in observed result-value distributions to propose language-independent mappings [9], while linguistically informed methods addressed language-specific morphology and terminological variation [15]. More recently, neural and generative approaches have gained prominence. Pre-trained language models with contrastive fine-tuning improve generalization while reducing the need for manual feature engineering [20]. Retrieval-augmented generation (RAG)-based systems [7], combining text similarity, domain-specific embeddings, and generative AI, have further advanced

[1] https://www.regenstrief.org/.
[2] https://loinc.org/downloads/relma/.

automated laboratory test code mapping [8]. Nevertheless, important limitations remain. Local test names frequently omit critical information required for accurate LOINC selection, and name-based automation can propagate systematic mis-mappings [17]. Additional challenges include limited support for non-English languages [15], dependence on large institutional datasets [9], and the need to maintain mapping workflows as both LOINC and local databases evolve.

These challenges motivate new approaches based on large language models (LLMs), which can interact with external knowledge sources through iterative reasoning and action [18,24]. This capability enables the use of evolving data catalogs without explicit retraining or reliance on large task-specific datasets. In this study, we present an agentic approach to automated LOINC coding that employs an iterative queryrefinement loop, enabling an LLM to interact directly with the official LOINC Search API[3]. The model iteratively retrieves and ranks suitable LOINC candidates before final classification. We evaluate the approach on German-language clinical data, demonstrating its effectiveness beyond English centric scenarios while remaining transferable to other high-resource languages. The entire pipeline is executed locally to ensure that potentially sensitive data are not transmitted to proprietary LLM services, and we establish a RAG-based baseline for systematic comparison with the proposed agentic method.

2 Material and Methods

2.1 Data

The data used in this study were obtained from the clinical data platform of the Cantonal Hospital Aarau. All extracted data are in German. Laboratory information is sourced directly from the hospital's live laboratory information system. We initially retrieved the 200 most frequently performed laboratory tests. After review and consultation with laboratory staff, 151 laboratory codes were retained for further analysis. Codes that could not be uniquely mapped to a single LOINC code were excluded. For each of the 151 laboratory codes included, the following characteristics were extracted:

- **Laboratory test code** a short, unique internal identifier
- **Laboratory test name** the full, unique name of the test conveying test-specific attributes
- **Unit** the measurement unit used for reporting results
- **Reference range** the established reference interval

As a preprocessing step, we enriched the laboratory data using a manually curated dictionary of common abbreviations, prefixes, and suffixes. In addition, German-to-English translations of frequently occurring terms were added to better align internal laboratory descriptions with the English-language LOINC catalogue. After data extraction and preprocessing, each laboratory code was

[3] https://loinc.org/kb/api/search-api/.

annotated with a set of candidate LOINC codes. Laboratory professionals subsequently reviewed all candidates and performed a detailed refinement, comparing proposed mappings against the complete LOINC catalogue to assign one definitive LOINC code per laboratory test.

All experiments used the LOINC catalogue[4] [22], maintained by the Regenstrief Institute[5]. The catalogue is available as a collection of CSV files, enabling straightforward integration into downstream applications. In addition, we used the official LOINC Search API[6]. Table 1 provides an overview of the LOINC catalogue fields considered in this study.

2.2 Methodology

We propose an agentic framework that employs an iterative query refinement loop to align heterogeneous laboratory test descriptions with their corresponding LOINC codes. The effectiveness of this approach is evaluated by benchmarking it against a RAG baseline. The proposed query refinement strategy, illustrated in Fig. 1, tightly couples the retrieval and processing of LOINC candidates. The implementation is built directly on top of the official LOINC Search API. The pipeline maintains an iterative dialogue between the input laboratory test description, model-generated queries, and structured results returned by the API. Rather than performing a single-shot mapping, the task is decomposed into a sequence of steps, with each iteration informed by the outcomes of previous interactions.

Agentic Iterative Query-Refinement. Each session starts with a new laboratory test to be classified. The system is initialized with a fixed system prompt that defines expected behavior, output format, and relevant LOINC concepts, along with the extracted characteristics of the laboratory test. In each iteration, the language model proposes at most one search query, embedded in `<query>QUERY</query>` tags. This design enables automated extraction, logging, and routing of the query to the LOINC Search API. The API returns structured rows of candidate LOINC codes, which are summarized using a selected subset of columns (Table 1) and fed back into the model. When result sets are large, only a bounded preview of the highest-ranked candidates (based on `COMMON_TEST_RANK`) is provided. The model is explicitly instructed to refine its query if further exploration is required. This approach prevents excessive context growth while preserving exposure to relevant high-ranking codes and attributes such as specimen, property, method, or component. To ensure progress across iterations, all emitted queries are tracked, and repetitions are automatically blocked by re-prompting the model to generate a novel query. All screened LOINC candidates are accumulated to enable downstream analysis of search

[4] https://loinc.org.
[5] https://www.regenstrief.org/.
[6] https://loinc.org/kb/api/search-api/.

Table 1. Overview of the LOINC columns selected for this study. These columns were used in both the CSV-based experiments and the experiments that accessed LOINC via the API. A reference of the LOINC Database structure can be found here: https://loinc.org/kb/users-guide/loinc-database-structure/. Field names are reproduced from the LOINC® Table (v2.80); copyright © Regenstrief Institute, Inc. and the LOINC Committee. License: http://loinc.org/license.

Column Name	Description
LOINC_NUM	Unique LOINC code (identifier) for the term, represented as a code string with a check digit.
COMPONENT	First major axis of the fully specified name: the component or analyte being measured or observed.
PROPERTY	Second major axis: the type of property of the component that is being observed (e.g., mass, substance amount).
TIME_ASPCT	Third major axis: the temporal aspect of the measurement, such as a single point in time or an interval (e.g., 24 h).
SYSTEM	Fourth major axis: the specimen or system on which the observation is made (e.g., serum, urine, blood).
METHOD_TYP	Sixth major axis: the method or technique used to perform the measurement or observation.
CLASS	Classification used to group related terms for organizational and reporting purposes.
VersionLastChanged	LOINC version in which the record was most recently changed; if never updated after release, equals the value in VersionFirstReleased.
CHNG_TYPE	Coded indicator of the most recent type of change applied to the record (e.g., add, delete/deprecate, name change, major or minor change).
DefinitionDescription	Narrative definition or description of the term as a whole, including contextual information such as how and why it is used or its clinical utility.
STATUS	Lifecycle status of the concept (e.g., ACTIVE, TRIAL, DISCOURAGED, DEPRECATED) indicating whether and how it should be used.
EXAMPLE_UCUM_UNITS	UCUM (Unified Code for Units of Measure) is a standard covering all units used in international science, engineering, and business (www.unitsofmeasure.org). This field lists example UCUM units for this term.
LONG_COMMON_NAME	Human-readable LOINC name in a more natural format than the fully specified name, generally with abbreviations expanded.
COMMON_TEST_RANK	Numeric rank indicating how commonly this code is used as a test in U.S. laboratory data.
COMMON_ORDER_RANK	Numeric rank indicating how commonly this code is used as an orderable test in U.S. laboratories.

breadth. The refinement loop terminates when the model signals sufficient confidence. At termination, the model outputs a structured JSON object preceded by the <END_OF_SEARCH> keyword. A small number of corrective attempts are applied to ensure valid structured output, and a maximum iteration budget of 20 is enforced to prevent unbounded execution.

RAG Baseline. To benchmark the proposed agentic approach, we implemented a RAG-based baseline using a separate candidate retrieval step followed by

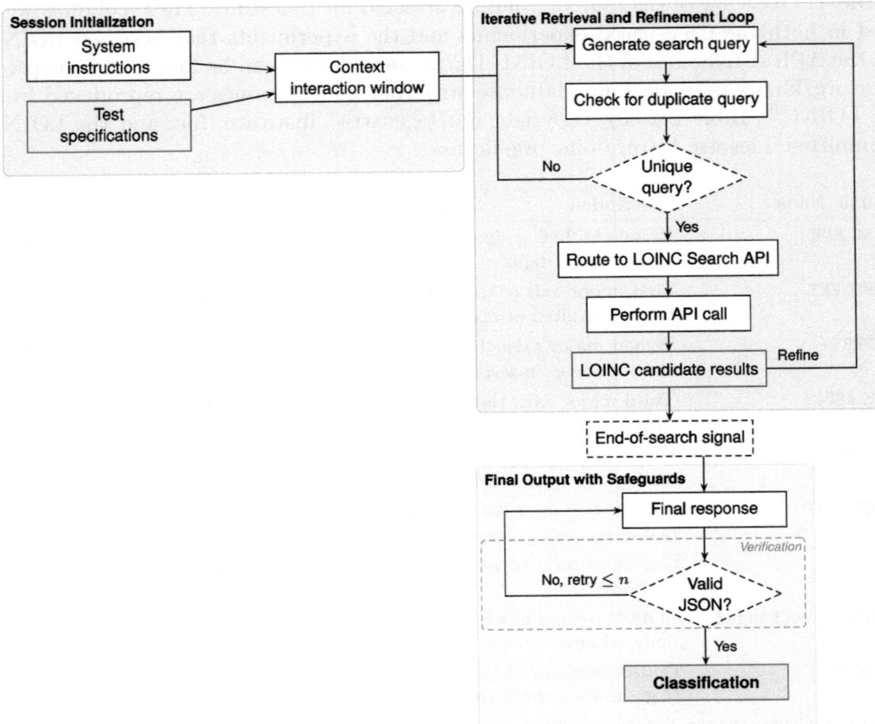

Fig. 1. Iterative retrieval: the system proposes queries, avoids duplicates, routes calls to the LOINC API, and iteratively refines until suitable candidates are found; output is validated via a JSON-format safeguard prior to final classification.

answer synthesis. The goal is to ground the language model's output in a curated set of semantically relevant LOINC codes retrieved from a vector index. The LOINC catalogue was downloaded as CSV files and transformed into concise textual representations using the fields listed in Table 1. These representations were indexed using the FAISS library [2], with structured metadata preserved to support ranking and sorting. The resulting vector store enables similarity-based retrieval of LOINC candidates. For each laboratory test, a new session is initialized using a system prompt similar to that of the query-refinement approach, but without instructions for iterative query generation. A similarity search retrieves the top-k most relevant LOINC candidates, which are then reordered using `COMMON_TEST_RANK`. The selected candidates, along with the laboratory test characteristics, are provided to the language model, which is instructed to select one code from the candidate set and emit the result in the same JSON format used by query-refinement method. As before, limited corrective attempts are applied to enforce valid structured output. Unlike the iterative approach, the RAG baseline performs a single-pass retrieval and classification step, grounding the model's output in a fixed, pre-indexed representation of active LOINC concepts.

2.3 Models and Embeddings

For all experiments, we used the same language model for both the agentic approach and the reader component of the RAG baseline: gpt-oss-120b[7] [13] with a context window of 50,000 and a temperature of 0.2. This open-source model demonstrated strong performance in preliminary experiments, reliably following system instructions, adhering to the prescribed workflows, and producing structured outputs. To assess the impact of embedding quality on RAG performance, we evaluated three embedding models spanning a range of computational cost and representational capacity:

- **multilingual-e5-large**[8] [23]
- **Qwen3-Embedding-4B**[9] [25]
- **embedding-gemma-300M**[10] [21]

Each embedding model was used to construct a separate FAISS index, enabling a systematic comparison of RAG performance against the proposed agentic approach.

3 Results

This section summarizes the outcomes of the experiments comparing the proposed agentic approach with the RAG baseline. We evaluate overall performance, runtime characteristics, robustness to missing laboratory attributes, and the effect of synonym-based input augmentation.

Across all experiments, the agentic approach with iterative query refinement consistently outperformed the RAG baseline in classification accuracy. Averaged over three runs, the agentic method achieved a Top-1 accuracy of 0.819 and a Top-5 accuracy of 0.954, while requiring an average of 19.11 seconds per laboratory test. In contrast, the strongest RAG configuration - using *Qwen3-Embedding-4B* as embedding model with a top-k setting of 50 - achieved a Top-1 accuracy of 0.684 and a Top-5 accuracy of 0.830, with a higher average runtime of 22.69 seconds per test. Although a RAG configuration using a smaller top-k value and lighter embeddings was the fastest overall, it also produced the weakest accuracy, indicating a clear trade-off between speed and performance in the RAG pipeline.

Increasing the top-k retrieval size consistently improved the performance of the RAG baseline across all embedding models. All RAG configurations performed better with top-k = 50 than with top-k = 30, but this improvement

[7] *unsloth/gpt-oss-120b-GGUF*: https://huggingface.co/unsloth/gpt-oss-120b-GGUF/tree/main.

[8] *intfloat/multilingual-e5-large:* https://huggingface.co/intfloat/multilingual-e5-large.

[9] *Qwen/Qwen3-Embedding-4B:* https://huggingface.co/Qwen/Qwen3-Embedding-4B.

[10] *google/embeddinggemma-300m:* https://huggingface.co/google/embeddinggemma-300m.

came at the cost of increased runtime. In contrast, the agentic approach did not rely on a fixed retrieval depth and maintained strong performance without requiring large candidate sets.

The best overall performance was achieved by the agentic approach augmented with synonyms and related terms generated by *MedGemma* [19]. This configuration reached a peak Top-1 accuracy of 0.854 and a peak Top-5 accuracy of 0.980. The strongest synonym-augmented RAG baseline also benefited from this enrichment but remained substantially behind, achieving a peak Top-1 accuracy of 0.735 and a peak Top-5 accuracy of 0.894.

Synonym augmentation had a markedly larger impact on the RAG baseline than on the agentic approach. For RAG, synonym enrichment substantially improved both Top-1 and Top-5 accuracy, reflecting its reliance on semantically rich input to compensate for single-pass retrieval. For the agentic approach, synonym augmentation led to a modest improvement in Top-1 accuracy but slightly reduced Top-5 accuracy, suggesting that the adaptive retrieval loop explores the relevant candidate space without extensive input expansion.

Ablation experiments further highlighted differences in robustness between the two methods. Removing key laboratory attributes negatively affected both approaches, but the performance degradation was more pronounced for the RAG baseline. In particular, omitting the measurement unit resulted in a larger accuracy drop than omitting the reference range for both methods, underscoring the importance of unit information for correct LOINC assignment. Overall, the agentic approach demonstrated greater resilience to missing or incomplete laboratory metadata.

In summary, the results demonstrate that the proposed agentic, iterative query refinement approach yields superior accuracy, competitive runtime, and improved robustness compared with a strong RAG baseline, particularly in scenarios with underspecified or non-English laboratory test descriptions.

4 Discussion

In this study, we introduced an agentic LLM-based approach that iteratively refines search queries through direct interaction with an external API, building on methods shown to be effective in prior work [18,24]. The proposed approach achieved strong performance, correctly assigning LOINC codes to 85.4% of laboratory tests and including the correct code within the top five candidates in 98.0% of cases. This high Top-5 accuracy highlights the suitability of the method for expert-in-the-loop workflows, where clinicians or laboratory specialists can efficiently validate a small set of ranked candidates rather than navigating the full LOINC catalogue.

Compared with prior approaches, the proposed method performs favorably across both semi-automated and fully automated settings. While its Top-1 accuracy is slightly below the semi-automated RELMA-based approach reported by Zunner et al. [26], it substantially reduces runtime and eliminates the need for manual expert interaction. Relative to fully automated methods, it outperforms Fidahussein and Vreeman's best model [3] as well as more recent neural approaches such as the contrastive T5-based model by Tu et al. [20], and achieves performance comparable to noisy-label methods reported by Parr et al. [14]. Direct comparison across studies remains challenging due to differences in datasets, languages, and annotation granularity, but the consistently strong Top-5 performance represents a notable advance over prior work.

In our experiments, the agentic approach consistently outperformed a strong RAG baseline, improving Top-1 and Top-5 accuracy while remaining competitive in terms of runtime. The analysis further showed that RAG-based methods are sensitive to retrieval depth and input quality, benefiting more strongly from synonym augmentation but also suffering larger performance drops when key attributes such as measurement units are omitted. These findings align with previous observations that RAG systems are highly sensitive to query formulation and input completeness [16]. In contrast, the iterative query refinement strategy demonstrated greater robustness to underspecified inputs, likely due to its ability to progressively explore and narrow the candidate space.

Beyond performance, the proposed approach offers conceptual advantages. By interacting directly with the official LOINC API, it enables automatic access to an up-to-date terminology without retraining. The explicit reasoning and query traces improve transparency and controllability, facilitating inspection, human supervision, and targeted error analysis. Moreover, the iterative workflow closely resembles how human experts approach LOINC mapping, supporting interpretability, maintainability, and adaptation to ongoing changes in the LOINC catalogue.

4.1 Limitations

Despite these promising results, several limitations should be acknowledged. First, the descriptive power of local laboratory test metadata is often limited. Incomplete or underspecified test descriptions make it difficult to capture all relevant attributes required for unambiguous LOINC assignment, which can constrain achievable performance regardless of the mapping strategy. Second, the runtime of the agentic approach remains relatively high, with an average classification time of approximately 19.11 seconds per laboratory test. This may become a bottleneck in large-scale or time-critical deployment scenarios where thousands of tests must be processed efficiently. This bottleneck could be mitigated through parallel processing of multiple queries including subagents such as "search agents", "verifiyers" and a general orchestrator supervising the whole process and delegating subtask to the corresponding agents. Parallel exploration could boost the processing speed while more specifically instructed subagents could increase the overall classification performance. Other strategies addressing these limitations could include richer input representations, caching strategies, or hybrid workflows.

5 Conclusion

We propose an agentic approach for automated LOINC coding that uses iterative query refinement with a locally deployed LLM and the official LOINC Search API. Evaluated on German-language routine laboratory data, the approach outperformed a RAG baseline in both Top-1 and Top-5 accuracy. Its high Top-5 performance supports efficient expert-in-the-loop validation, while local deployment and low maintenance requirements make it suitable for clinical environments, particularly in cases where sensitive data cannot leave the institution. Overall, the method offers a practical path toward improving laboratory data standardization and interoperability in routine care.

Acknowledgments. For this study no sensitive clinical patient data was involved. This material contains content from LOINC® (http://loinc.org), version 2.80 (released February 2025). LOINC is copyright © 1995–2025, Regenstrief Institute, Inc. and the Logical Observation Identifiers Names and Codes (LOINC) Committee and is available at no cost under the license at http://loinc.org/license. LOINC® is a registered United States trademark of Regenstrief Institute, Inc.

Disclosure of Interests. The authors declare no competing interests.

References

1. Austin, C., Kusumoto, F.: The application of big data in medicine: current implications and future directions. J. Interv. Card. Electrophysiol. **47**(1), 51–59 (2016)
2. Douze, M., et al.: The faiss library (2025). https://arxiv.org/abs/2401.08281
3. Fidahussein, M., Vreeman, D.J.: A corpus-based approach for automated loinc mapping. J. Am. Med. Inform. Assoc. **21**(1), 64–72 (2014). https://doi.org/10.1136/amiajnl-2012-001159
4. Frassica, J.J.: Frequency of laboratory test utilization in the intensive care unit and its implications for large scale data collection efforts. In: AMIA Annu. Symp. Proc, p. 844 (2003)
5. Lau, L.M., Johnson, K., Monson, K., Lam, S.H., Huff, S.M.: A method for the automated mapping of laboratory results to LOINC. In: Proc. AMIA Symp, pp. 472–476 (2000)
6. Lehne, M., Sass, J., Essenwanger, A., Schepers, J., Thun, S.: Why digital medicine depends on interoperability. NPJ Digital Med. **2**(1), 79 (2019)
7. Lewis, P., et al.: Retrieval-augmented generation for knowledge-intensive nlp tasks. In: Proceedings of the 34th International Conference on Neural Information Processing Systems, NIPS 2020. Curran Associates Inc., Red Hook, NY, USA (2020)
8. Liscio, A., Chiaravalloti, M.T., Dell'Isola, V.G., Moz, M.: Advancing LOINC mapping with AI: insights from LARA's RAG implementation and expert evaluation. In: Bellazzi, R., Juarez Herrero, J.M., Sacchi, L., Zupan, B. (eds.) AIME 2025. LNCS, vol. 15735. Springer, Cham (2025). https://doi.org/10.1007/978-3-031-95841-0_43
9. Liu, K., Witteveen-Lane, M., et al.: Bglm: big data-guided loinc mapping with multi-language support. JAMIA Open **5**(4) (2022). https://doi.org/10.1093/jamiaopen/ooac099

10. Martin-Sanchez, F., Verspoor, K.: Big data in medicine is driving big changes. Yearb. Med. Inform. **23**(01), 14–20 (2014)
11. de Mello, B.H., et al.: Semantic interoperability in health records standards: a systematic literature review. Heal. Technol. **12**(2), 255–272 (2022). https://doi.org/10.1007/s12553-022-00639-w
12. Obermeyer, Z., Emanuel, E.J.: Predicting the future—big data, machine learning, and clinical medicine. N. Engl. J. Med. **375**(13), 1216 (2016)
13. OpenAI, Agarwal, S., et al.: gpt-oss-120b & gpt-oss-20b model card (2025). https://arxiv.org/abs/2508.10925
14. Parr, S.K., Shotwell, M.S., Jeffery, A.D., Lasko, T.A., Matheny, M.E.: Automated mapping of laboratory tests to loinc codes using noisy labels in a national electronic health record system database. J. Am. Med. Inform. Assoc. **25**(10), 1292–1300 (2018). https://doi.org/10.1093/jamia/ocy110
15. Patel, N., Abel, Y., Brun, F., Mayoral, G.: Ensuring interoperability of laboratory tests and results: a linguistic approach for mapping french laboratory terminologies with loinc. In: International Conference on Computer Science Protecting Human Society Against Epidemics, pp. 14–22. Springer (2021)
16. Perçin, S., et al.: Investigating the robustness of retrieval-augmented generation at the query level. In: Arviv, O., et al (eds.) Proceedings of the Fourth Workshop on Generation, Evaluation and Metrics (GEM2), pp. 439–457. Association for Computational Linguistics, Vienna, Austria and virtual meeting (Jul 2025). https://aclanthology.org/2025.gem-1.38/
17. Rychert, J.: In support of interoperability: a laboratory perspective. Int. J. Lab. Hematol. **45**(4), 436–441 (2023). https://doi.org/10.1111/ijlh.14113
18. Schick, T., et al.: Toolformer: Language models can teach themselves to use tools (2023). https://arxiv.org/abs/2302.04761
19. Sellergren, A., et al.: Medgemma technical report (2025). https://arxiv.org/abs/2507.05201
20. Tu, T., et al.: Automated loinc standardization using pre-trained large language models. In: Parziale, A., Agrawal, M., Joshi, S., Chen, I.Y., Tang, S., Oala, L., Subbaswamy, A. (eds.) Proceedings of the 2nd Machine Learning for Health symposium. Proceedings of Machine Learning Research, 28 Nov, vol. 193, pp. 343–355. PMLR (2022). https://proceedings.mlr.press/v193/tu22a.html
21. Vera, H.S., et al.: Embeddinggemma: powerful and lightweight text representations (2025). https://arxiv.org/abs/2509.20354
22. Vreeman, D.J., McDonald, C.J., Huff, S.M.: LOINC® - a universal catalog of individual clinical observations and uniform representation of enumerated collections. Int. J. Funct. Inform. Personal. Med. **3**(4), 273–291 (2010)
23. Wang, L., Yang, N., Huang, X., Yang, L., Majumder, R., Wei, F.: Multilingual e5 text embeddings: A technical report (2024). https://arxiv.org/abs/2402.05672
24. Yao, S., et al.: React: Synergizing reasoning and acting in language models (2023). https://arxiv.org/abs/2210.03629
25. Zhang, Y., et al.: Qwen3 embedding: advancing text embedding and reranking through foundation models (2025). https://arxiv.org/abs/2506.05176
26. Zunner, C., Bürkle, T., Prokosch, H.U., Ganslandt, T.: Mapping local laboratory interface terms to loinc at a german university hospital using relma vol 5: a semi-automated approach. J. Am. Med. Inform. Assoc. **20**(2), 293–297 (2013). https://doi.org/10.1136/amiajnl-2012-001063

An AI-Enabled Method for Reconstructing Knowledge Maps of Transient Heterarchical Collaborations Using Large Language Models

Amanda McEachern Gaudet[1,2](✉), Amanda Peticca-Harris[2], and Carolyn McGregor[1,3]

[1] Faculty of Business and IT, Ontario Tech University, 2000 Simcoe St North, Oshawa, ON L1G 0C5, Canada
amanda.mceacherngaudet@ontariotechu.ca

[2] Grenoble Ecole de Management, 12 Rue Pierre Semard, 38000 Grenoble, France

[3] Faculty of Engineering and IT, University of Technology Sydney, 15 Broadway, Ultimo, NSW 2007, Australia

Abstract. Transdisciplinary innovation ecosystems are often organized through time-bound, multi-actor collaborations that operate without stable hierarchy structures commonly conceptualized as heterarchies. To date, efforts to recover relational knowledge in these transient heterarchies and to learn from the practices of historical projects remain limited. Existing tools for knowledge graphing and ecosystem mapping offer limited support for reconstructing relational data from these collaborations once actors disperse. Through our study, we demonstrate how a large language model (LLM) can assist in reconstructing the social network between actors by filling gaps left by actor mobility, organizational churn, and prior collaboration histories. We demonstrate this method through a single case study of Project Arrow, an all-Canadian electric vehicle concept project intended to mobilize national innovation capacity, and a transdisciplinary business heterarchical collaboration involving actors across industry, academia, and public-sector institutions. This paper contributes a methodological approach for retrospective relational knowledge reconstruction in transient innovation ecosystems and shows how LLM-supported prompt engineering can support the development of knowledge maps of heterarchical collaboration.

Keywords: Heterarchical collaboration · Knowledge map - Knowledge graphs · AI/Large language models · Business Innovation · Electric Vehicles

1 Introduction

Regional, national, and international innovation ecosystems bring together diverse actors to mobilize complementary resources for transdisciplinary solutions. These ecosystems are typically enacted through time-bound, project-based collaborations, where coordination relies on relational ties that cut across organizational boundaries. This study examines the challenge of retrospectively reconstructing relational knowledge in such collaborations, particularly when they are formed under time and resource constraints and when information is fragmented across actors, organizations, and sources.

K. Węcel and V. Řepa (Eds.): BIS 2026, LNBIP 584, pp. 236–248, 2026.
https://doi.org/10.1007/978-3-032-26363-6_18

While strategic collaborations can be formalized through bilateral, long-term agreements with hierarchical control, complex multilateral project-based collaborations often cannot. These arrangements frequently result in heterarchical collaboration, characterized by shifting relationships among actors and forms of coordination that cannot be fully captured by hierarchical or network models alone (Ling et al. 2026). Prior work identifies three features that make heterarchical collaborations difficult to reconstruct retrospectively: the coupling of micro- and macro-level dynamics, the role of actor agency within organizational structures, and discontinuous changes in the scope of the collaboration over time (Palmer & Cragin 2023). This inherent transience, where actors move roles, change organizations, or exit the collaboration, complicates efforts to recover relational knowledge once a project has concluded. As a result, reconstructing heterarchical collaborations has traditionally relied on labor-intensive historical methods, including interviews, archival documents, project artifacts, and manual internet searches.

Large language models (LLMs) are artificial intelligence systems capable of processing natural language to generate text, answer questions, and support human decision-making (Hogan 2021). Interaction with LLMs occurs through prompts, task-specific instructions that guide the model's output. The content and structure of these prompts are shaped through prompt engineering techniques, which have been shown to directly influence the relevance, quality, and traceability of LLM outputs. With their rapid expansion, LLMs present new opportunities to reconstruct missing relational information in retrospective innovation collaborations, particularly where public traces are dispersed and unevenly distributed across time and organizations (Ling et al. 2026). However, the use of LLM-constructed knowledge graphs to build retrospective knowledge maps for heterarchical collaborations remains underexplored. In particular, prompt engineering has not been examined as a mechanism for improving the quality, relevance, and traceability of LLM outputs in this context.

Project Arrow is a heterarchical collaboration established to support transdisciplinary innovation through the development of an all-Canadian electric vehicle concept. The project brought together actors from across the automotive sector, universities, and regional, provincial, and national government bodies, with the goal of showcasing Canada's innovation and supply-chain capacity and attracting an original equipment manufacturer (OEM) to locate in Canada. Heterarchical collaboration was particularly salient in this case because the project was executed under significant time and resource constraints, requiring the rapid assembly of actors with dispersed professional histories and prior affiliations that were not fully visible through formal project documentation. As a result, much of the relational knowledge underpinning collaboration was fragmented and difficult to reconstruct retrospectively. Accordingly, this study is guided by the research question: *How can missing, fragmented, and historically dispersed relational knowledge be reconstructed in transient heterarchical collaborations?* To address this question, we present constructive research demonstrating the use of LLMs in a human-in-the-loop approach to build retrospective knowledge maps, using Project Arrow as an illustrative case. In doing so, this paper contributes a methodological approach for reconstructing relational knowledge in transient innovation ecosystems by showing how iterative, prompt-based inquiry can support the incremental recovery of connections that are difficult to capture through interviews, documents, or keyword-based searches alone.

This approach is particularly useful when relational ties (e.g., trust, prior collaboration, informal reputation, career trajectories) must be inferred across dispersed organizational and project histories rather than retrieved as discrete facts.

2 Literature Review

2.1 Knowledge Graphs

Knowledge maps can be constructed using knowledge graphs, which represent real-world knowledge as nodes (entities of interest in a given context) and edges capturing relationships between those entities (Hogan et al. 2021). Although the term *knowledge graph* has appeared in the literature since the 1970s, their development accelerated following the launch of the Google Knowledge Graph in 2012 and the subsequent adoption of knowledge graph functionality by platforms such as Amazon, Facebook, and LinkedIn (Hogan et al. 2021). These implementations are typically described as *open knowledge graphs*. In contrast, *enterprise knowledge graphs* support knowledge representation and retrieval within a single organization (Galkin et al. 2017). In both cases, knowledge graph construction assumes relatively stable boundaries and ongoing curation over time. As a result, neither approach adequately supports retrospective relational reconstruction in business heterarchical collaborations.

Recent scholarship has increasingly focused on how knowledge graphs can be constructed automatically from heterogeneous and unstructured sources, including with large language models (LLMs). For example, Zhong et al. (2023) conducted a survey of automatic knowledge graph construction, reviewing 300 methods and outlining three steps: knowledge acquisition, knowledge refinement, and knowledge evolution. They note that extracting knowledge using LLMs represents a new direction for knowledge graph construction and see great potential to structure knowledge from the contextual information on which LLMs train (Zhong et al. 2023). Building on this, Ling et al. (2026) review LLM-enabled knowledge graph construction methodologies and categorize emerging approaches into prompt-based, fine-tuning, and agent-based pipelines. Specifically, they emphasize the challenge of harmonizing heterogeneous and often fragmented evidence into coherent graph structures, particularly where information is incomplete, unevenly distributed, or inconsistent across sources. Further, they highlight opportunities for LLMs to support knowledge graph construction by extracting and integrating relational information from distributed sources, while also identifying key constraints related to data quality and inconsistency, limitations in model reasoning and semantic control, and computational costs associated with iterative refinement and scaling (Ling et al. 2026).

Taken together, this scholarship positions LLMs as a promising mechanism for extracting and integrating relational information into knowledge graphs from heterogeneous, incomplete, and distributed sources. However, existing approaches remain largely general-purpose and offer limited guidance for (1) constraining LLM-generated knowledge graphs to user-defined boundaries, such as time-bound project collaborations, (2) producing traceable and auditable relational outputs that can be linked back to source evidence, and (3) supporting validation workflows when relational ties are implicit, uncertain, or inconsistently represented across sources.

Moreover, as illustrated in Palmer and Cragin's (2023) work on transdisciplinary innovation, knowledge graphs have primarily been mobilized to support data stewardship and sharing, rather than to reconstruct the relational structure of collaboration itself. Connecting this theoretical insight to practice, when attention does turn to mapping collaboration structure, existing tools are largely oriented toward visualization rather than discovery. For example, the tool Kumu.io supports the development of stakeholder maps and other visual representations of relationships. However, such tools are designed to represent relationships that are already known; they do not provide a way to infer or discover missing information needed to complete the mapping (Kumu.io 2026). This reinforces the need for approaches that support retrospective knowledge acquisition, rather than representation alone.

To enable retrospective knowledge acquisition, a human-in-the-loop approach may offer a practical solution for creating a knowledge map, enriched by AI tools such as LLMs. To interact with an LLM in a human-in-the-loop process, users must design and refine task-specific input queries, known as prompts (Marvin et al. 2024). This design and refinement, commonly referred to as prompt engineering, directly shapes LLM performance, including the risk of hallucinations and biased outputs, and is therefore central to this process.

Using LLMs to extract this kind of information can support a more comprehensive reconstruction, since LLMs draw on heterogeneous sources across industries and can surface interconnected perspectives that may be missed by conventional retrospective methods. For example, Ibrahim et al. (2024) identify several benefits of these techniques, including additional context and personalization, performance improvement, reliability, scalability, and transparency, and review application areas such as digital business recommendations in commerce, clinical decision-making, supply chain management, fraud detection, and customer relationship management (Ibrahim et al. 2024). However, translating these general capabilities into context-bounded, relational outputs for transient project collaborations remains methodologically underdeveloped. For example, Pather (2025) discusses how an interactive middle layer of human integration makes responses more reliable and correct. In other words, beyond the model itself, researchers still lack robust approaches for translating fragmented and heterogeneous source material into structured, context-bounded relational outputs through processes such as task decomposition, iterative prompting, validation, and traceability mechanisms. Thus, while LLMs show promise for extracting relational information, methodological guidance for doing so remains underdeveloped.

While these advances are significant, they each present limitations for retrospective relational reconstruction in transient heterarchical collaborations. Traditional retrospective methods provide depth but are often incomplete and time-intensive due to fragmented records and recall constraints. Knowledge graph and visualization tools support structured representation of known relationships but do not enable the discovery or inference of missing ties. Fully automated LLM approaches offer scalability but raise concerns regarding reliability, traceability, and the validation of inferred connections. In response to these limitations, this study develops a human-in-the-loop, LLM–GoT approach that combines structured prompt-based inquiry with iterative validation to support the reconstruction of relational knowledge from fragmented sources.

2.2 Prompt Engineering

In this section, we introduce the prompt engineering procedure that we later apply in our case study. Our approach is grounded in the Graph of Thoughts (GoT) framework (Besta et al. 2024), which we operationalize using the five-step prompt design logic articulated by Marvin et al. (2024). Together, these approaches enable structured, iterative prompt-based inquiry while supporting branching, evaluation, and recombination across alternative candidate outputs.

Marvin et al. (2024) propose a five-step foundational structure for prompt engineering that provides a useful baseline for organizing individual prompt cycles: (1) defining the goal, which establishes clear direction and purpose; (2) understanding the model's capabilities, such as whether it will generate text, images, or other outputs; (3) choosing an appropriate prompt format through clear, precise, and concise instructions; (4) providing relevant context, including background information about the topic, actors, or setting; and (5) testing and refining, where model outputs are evaluated and used to iteratively improve subsequent prompts. While this structure offers a strong sequential foundation for prompt design and refinement, it does not explicitly address how multiple prompt paths can be explored, compared, and selectively recombined in complex analytical tasks.

To address this limitation, we complement Marvin et al.'s (2024) structure with the Graph of Thoughts (GoT) framework. GoT formalizes prompt decomposition as a graph rather than a linear sequence, enabling prompts to branch into parallel subproblems, generate competing candidate outputs, and support systematic evaluation and recombination (Besta et al. 2024). This approach acknowledges that some analytical problems—particularly those involving historically dispersed, incomplete, or ambiguous information—do not have a straightforward step-by-step solution. We apply this combined approach to support the reconstruction of historically dispersed relational knowledge needed to build retrospective knowledge maps of transient collaborations. In practice, Marvin et al.'s (2024) five-step logic structures individual prompt cycles, while GoT oversees how those cycles branch, are evaluated, and recombined as the knowledge map is incrementally reconstructed.

GoT follows an iterative, staged procedure. *Stage 1 (goal prompting)* aligns with Marvin et al.'s (2024) first step, in which the system is prompted with an initial goal or main task. *Stage 2 (branching)* expands the task into sub-problems, producing multiple candidate paths. *Stage 3 (evaluation)* involves reviewing and critiquing each branch by verifying the outputs provided. *Stage 4 (control and refinement)* refines prompts to correct, redirect, or search further as needed, while selecting promising branches to carry forward and discarding less relevant paths. Stages 2–4 are repeated iteratively until the available information is exhausted or additional prompting no longer yields relevant outputs. Finally, *Stage 5 (solution or termination)* concludes the process once knowledge gaps are sufficiently addressed or a practical resource limit is reached (Hsu et al. 2024).

GoT prompting can be implemented in different ways depending on the level of automation and the degree of human oversight required. The first is informal, without automation, using tools such as whiteboards, sticky notes, and concept or argument maps (Pather et al. 2025). The second is fully automated, for example, in domains such as mathematical reasoning, planning, and code generation through software- and

LLM-based systems (Pather et al. 2025). The third approach, and the one adopted in this research, is human-in-the-loop (or human-guided) GoT, in which the definition of evaluation criteria, decisions about which branches matter, and the interpretation of ambiguous nodes are carried out by a human (Pather et al. 2025). This approach is particularly useful in settings where relational information is incomplete, uncertain, or context-dependent, and where the relevance and plausibility of information cannot be reliably assessed through automation alone. Prior work suggests that human-in-the-loop approaches can improve accuracy relative to fully automated prompting techniques (Pather et al. 2025) and enhance reasoning transparency by supporting a process that is more traceable and auditable, rather than functioning as a less transparent "black box" (Wei et al. 2022). In the application that follows, we use this human-in-the-loop GoT procedure to iteratively surface, assess, and refine relational ties and supporting leads needed to reconstruct a retrospective knowledge map.

3 Methodology

3.1 Case Context – Project Arrow

This study forms part of a broader research program examining regional electric vehicle (EV) innovation ecosystems in Canada[1]. Project Arrow was a time-bound, ad hoc project established to support transdisciplinary innovation through the creation of an all-Canadian-made electric vehicle concept for public launch at the 2023 Consumer Electronics Show (CES) in Las Vegas, Nevada, USA (Ontario Ministry of Economic Development, Job Creation and Trade 2023). The project addressed a socially relevant issue: demonstrating the capacity of a whole-vehicle electric supply chain in Canada. As such, it functioned as a targeted national economic development initiative aimed at showcasing national innovation capacity and supply chain capability.

Using a single-case study design (Yin 2018), the present study examines Project Arrow as a case of heterarchical collaboration in which heterogeneous, independent actors worked toward a shared sustainability-oriented innovation goal. Project Arrow involved a diverse set of organizations, mobilizing complementary resources and skillsets. This multi-actor configuration required rapid coordination across academic, industry, and government stakeholders. Several members of the Canadian supply chain were also engaged, alongside the sector's overarching association, the Automotive Parts Manufacturers' Association (APMA), and government stakeholders, including the Ontario Vehicle Innovation Network (OVIN), with the engineering and build lead happening at Automotive Centre for Excellence (ACE) at Ontario Tech University. The objective of this portion of the research was to construct an organizational network graph (i.e., the knowledge graph underlying the retrospective knowledge map), focusing on relational ties among these actors.

[1] This study received ethics approval from the Ontario Tech University Research Ethics Board 17743.

3.2 Data Collection and Analysis

Data collection combined primary and secondary sources. The first author collected primary data comprising eight semi-structured interviews with members of the Project Arrow collaboration who agreed to participate in the study (conducted between August 2024–April 2025), averaging approximately 45 min each). These interviews were triangulated with secondary data, including publicly available LinkedIn profiles and posts, as well as other accessible documents and news articles spanning the period of Project Arrow's development and public launch. In addition, internal memos (e.g., meeting notes, project updates, and coordination documents) accessible to the research team were utilized, providing private project materials not available through the internet. Throughout the paper, we use *knowledge graph* to refer to the underlying relational data structure, and *knowledge map* to denote its analytical or visual representation.

From the data collection process, the research team aimed to construct both (1) project timeline information and (2) a knowledge map of the heterarchical network for Project Arrow. The initial knowledge graph was constructed manually using event-based coding, with events coded by date, milestone, participating actors/organizations, and relational implications, and then linked to the Project Arrow timeline and associated ties (McEachern Gaudet & Peticca-Harris 2026). However, despite this triangulated approach, gaps remained in the relational knowledge required to fully reconstruct the collaboration network, particularly where ties were informal, historically dispersed, or not captured in project documentation. To address these limitations, we applied the prompt engineering procedure outlined above, using a human-in-the-loop GoT approach to iteratively develop, assess, and refine plausible relational connections and supporting leads from digital traces, rather than to replace primary or archival data. Accordingly, the knowledge map was further enriched through an interactive process with an LLM (ChatGPT 4.0), with outputs reviewed and retained only where they could be corroborated through available evidence.

Compared to the initial manually assembled relational data, the LLM-assisted process expanded and refined the information base by identifying additional relational ties particularly pre-existing actor-to-actor and actor-to-organization connections that were not visible in the primary data and by helping to explain why these relationships existed. In doing so, it improved the overall completeness and accuracy of the relational information used to construct the knowledge graph. However, while the LLM was effective in supporting relational inference and enrichment, it was not well suited to generating reliable visual representations, and external tools remained necessary for constructing a clear and usable knowledge map.

4 Results: Applying GoT Prompt Engineering to Project Arrow

After completing primary and secondary data collection, we applied the human-in-the-loop GoT prompt engineering procedure to the Project Arrow case to illustrate the empirical analytical work undertaken in reconstructing missing relational knowledge. Specifically, we engaged ChatGPT to address remaining gaps that persisted after manual knowledge-map construction. During this LLM prompt-based interaction process, GoT principles guided how prompts were structured, branched, evaluated, and refined, and we documented recurring prompting patterns as they were used to enrich the preliminary knowledge map developed during data collection. Following Besta et al. (2024), we operationalized the GoT procedure through five stages, as detailed below.

Step 1 – Defining the Goal. The initial goal of the GoT prompting process was to enrich the existing knowledge map of the heterarchical collaboration underlying Project Arrow. Specifically, we sought to: (a) explore whether an LLM (ChatGPT 4.0) could identify actor-to-actor connections that predated the formal commencement of Project Arrow and that helped draw actors into the collaboration from outside the focal collaborating organizations, and were therefore absent from the manually constructed knowledge map; and (b) examine whether such pre-existing connections could help explain participation decisions that could not be inferred from project documentation alone. At this stage, the goal was explicitly framed as knowledge enrichment rather than automated map generation or LLM-based visualization.

Step 2 – Branching Through Targeted Sub-Questions. To address these relational gaps, we generated a series of targeted sub-questions derived from the original prompting goal, consistent with the branching logic of the GoT framework (Besta et al. 2024). These sub-questions were designed to probe different relational dimensions, specifically actor-to-actor, actor-to-organization, and actor-to-geography connections, to surface links that were not captured through interviews or project documentation. For example, we began with a targeted *actor-to-actor* search, using the following prompt: *Can we find a connection between [actor] and anyone else that would suggest why he would decide to leave [previous employer] and join this project?*

The initial response contained only publicly available information regarding the actor's visit to Ontario Tech, which appeared to reinforce the project's legitimacy and credibility. However, this output did not address the underlying relational motivation implied by the prompt—namely, why the actor chose to join Project Arrow. Instead, the model reverted to readily available news coverage describing the actors' involvement in the project. This highlighted a clear gap between the question posed and the information retrieved. To address this limitation, we refined and redirected the prompts based on domain knowledge, explicitly testing alternative relational pathways that might explain participation decisions. These refinements included targeted *actor-to-geography queries, such as: Does [actor] have any connection to Canada?* As well as targeted *actor-to-organization* queries, such as: *Can we identify any specific suppliers in Canada that [actor] worked with prior to Project Arrow?*

These refined prompts initially yielded limited results and little additional clarity. However, the LLM offered an option to "dig deeper," which we selected. This deeper query moved beyond easily accessible, pre-populated summaries and prompted the model to search for less salient but potentially relevant relational traces. As a result, the LLM surfaced linkages to Canadian suppliers, which provided plausible relational leads for further verification. At each stage, we requested source links and reviewed the supporting evidence before proceeding to subsequent prompts, ensuring that candidate connections were treated as hypotheses rather than accepted facts.

Step 3 – Evaluation and Correction. With each prompt response, we evaluated the relevance and credibility of the information generated against existing interview data, project documents, and known elements of Project Arrow's history. This evaluation occurred iteratively after each branching cycle, before any new relational information was provisionally incorporated into the evolving knowledge map. Where outputs conflicted with established evidence or misrepresented relationships, we intervened through corrective follow-up prompts. These included prompts that explicitly challenged the inferred relationship (e.g., "*There is no evidence that [actor A] and [actor B] collaborated prior to Project Arrow—can you reassess this relationship and provide supporting sources?*") or narrowed the scope of inference (e.g., "*Limit your response to verifiable professional interactions prior to [YEAR], and cite specific sources.*"). In cases where the LLM continued to reproduce inaccurate or speculative relational representations despite repeated correction, the inferred ties were excluded from the knowledge map and documented as unresolved. These instances illustrate the limits of automated inference in reconstructing historically dispersed relational knowledge and reinforce the necessity of human judgment in validating LLM outputs within a human-in-the-loop process.

Step 4 – Selection and Recombination. Based on this evaluation, we selectively retained promising nodes and relationships, connecting them through vertices as candidate elements of the enriched knowledge map. Less relevant or weakly supported branches were discarded. Steps 2–4 were repeated iteratively as new gaps were identified, and additional relational hypotheses emerged.

Step 5 – Attempted Visualization and Termination. In the final stage, we requested that the LLM generates an enriched heterarchical collaboration knowledge map based on the combined manually coded and LLM-assisted information. While the LLM successfully synthesized relational content, the resulting visualizations were not reliable. For example, diagrams referenced legends that were missing or misaligned, and repeated correction requests did not resolve these issues across iterations. As a result, the primary contribution of the GoT-assisted process lay in content generation and relational inference rather than automated visualization. The LLM was effective in surfacing plausible relational leads and supporting incremental knowledge reconstruction, but visual representation required external tools and human curation.

5 Discussion

Using the case of Project Arrow, we demonstrate the potential for LLMs to enrich knowledge maps by enabling broader, more structured, and more systematic retrospective reviews of actor-to-actor, actor-to-geography, and actor-to-organization collaborations. In doing so, we directly address our research question, '*How can missing, fragmented, and historically dispersed relational knowledge be reconstructed in transient heterarchical collaborations?*' by showing how LLM-assisted, prompt-based inquiry can surface relational connections that are difficult to recover once projects conclude and actors disperse. This approach is particularly relevant for transdisciplinary projects organized through heterarchical collaboration, where coordination relies on dispersed experience, prior ties, and informal relationships rather than formal hierarchy.

The challenges encountered in reconstructing relational knowledge in Project Arrow are not unique to this case but reflect a broader structural feature of time-bound heterarchical collaboration. Once such projects conclude, actors return to their original organizations or move into new roles, and informal relational ties—such as prior collaboration, trust, or reputational familiarity are rarely captured in durable or centralized records. As a result, opportunities for retrospective learning are constrained less by a lack of collaborative activity than by the erosion and fragmentation of relational traces over time. This condition underscores the need for methodological approaches that can operate retrospectively across dispersed sources, rather than relying solely on contemporaneous documentation.

Our work responds to this need by moving beyond existing ecosystem mapping and visualization tools, such as Kumu.io, and shifting the analytic focus from representation to reconstruction. While visualization tools are effective for rendering known relationships, they do not support the discovery or inference of missing relational knowledge. In contrast, the LLM–GoT approach developed here combines human judgment with LLM-assisted inference to retrospectively reconstruct plausible relational connections that were not captured through interviews, documents, or keyword-based searches alone. In this sense, LLM-assisted reconstruction and visualization tools are best understood as complementary: reconstructed relational content can subsequently be rendered using visualization platforms.

Compared to existing approaches, the LLM–GoT method offers distinct advantages while addressing key limitations. Traditional retrospective methods, such as interviews and archival analysis, provide depth and contextual richness but are time-intensive and often incomplete due to recall limitations and missing records. Knowledge graph approaches and visualization tools, such as Kumu, enable structured representation of known relationships but do not support the discovery or inference of missing ties. Fully automated LLM-based extraction methods offer scalability but lack reliability and traceability, particularly in contexts of incomplete or ambiguous data. In contrast, the human-in-the-loop LLM–GoT approach combines the exploratory capacity of LLMs with human validation, enabling the systematic reconstruction of relational knowledge while maintaining interpretive control and evidentiary grounding. Despite the contributions, this study is not without limitations. Although the LLM supported the overarching goal of enriching the knowledge map, it also presented methodological challenges that required a human-in-the-loop approach. These included the need for highly explicit prompting across relational dimensions (actor-to-actor, actor-to-geography, actor-to-organization), the time required for deeper exploratory prompting, and the difficulty of determining when sufficient relational exploration had been achieved. While deeper queries required additional time (approximately 1 min and 23 s per query), this investment was not prohibitive given the richness of the insights generated. However, the process reinforced that relational inference cannot be fully automated. Human judgment remained essential for evaluating plausibility, correcting inaccuracies, and determining when inference should be constrained or terminated.

Recent research has also raised concerns about bias embedded in LLMs and their underlying knowledge graphs, including biases affecting minority populations Dehghani, F et al. 2025). In retrospective reconstruction, such biases risk amplifying this, particularly where actors already have uneven digital traces. In addition, prompt-based interactions may contribute new information to LLM training processes, depending on platform settings, with limited transparency regarding data retention. These issues further reinforce the importance of treating LLM outputs as provisional and subject to careful human evaluation.

Despite these limitations, the GoT-based, human-in-the-loop process enabled us to surface relational information that remained inaccessible through interviews, documents, and traditional search methods alone. As a pilot application, prompts were refined iteratively, allowing us to uncover connections, most notably a trust-based relationship between actors, that would not have emerged through standard keyword searches. While this process necessarily involved inference, it also supported ongoing validation and correction, consistent with Graph of Thoughts principles (Besta et al. 2024). The construction of the knowledge map visualization itself proved more challenging, as the LLM reverted to hierarchical or conventional network diagrams. As such, while LLMs were effective for relational inference, visualization required external tools and human curation. At a broader field level, this study contributes to research on innovation ecosystems, leadership-as-practice, and organizational behavior by offering a concrete methodological approach for examining coordination and influence in transient, multi-actor collaborations. By demonstrating how prompt engineering and GoT reasoning can support retrospective relational reconstruction, this study extends the methodological toolkit available for studying dispersed, informal, and historically contingent forms of organizing.

This method is most appropriate for time-bound, multi-actor heterarchical collaborations where participants—particularly senior individuals and organizations—have a visible digital, public presence. This enables relational traces to exist, even if they are dispersed across sources. In such contexts, LLM-assisted prompting can help surface and reconnect fragmented information. In settings where actors have a more limited digital presence, or where relational information is not externally observable, the approach may yield more limited or less reliable insights.

Building on this, we explicitly delineate the boundary conditions of the approach. First, the method is most effective in contexts where relational traces can be reconstructed from distributed public or semi-public sources. Second, it assumes that relational knowledge is at least partially observable and can be triangulated across heterogeneous data, rather than being fully tacit or private. Third, the approach is designed for retrospective reconstruction rather than real-time mapping and relies on human-in-the-loop validation to constrain LLM inference. In contexts where these conditions do not hold—such as low-visibility actors, highly confidential collaborations, or settings with limited digital traceability—the effectiveness of the method may be reduced.

Future research may extend this method by examining how different prompt engineering strategies shape the reconstruction of relational knowledge across contexts, by developing reusable prompt libraries for specific types of relational inference, or by comparing LLM-assisted reconstruction with participant-validated network accounts. Additional work could also explore hybrid approaches that integrate private organizational archives or participant-generated materials to mitigate visibility bias and further enrich retrospective knowledge maps of transient collaborations. Research using proprietary company data would be conducted with a private LLM to protect confidentiality.

6 Conclusion

This paper introduces a human-in-the-loop, LLM-enabled method for reconstructing relational knowledge in transient, heterarchical collaborations after project completion. Using Project Arrow as a case, we demonstrate how GoT–guided prompt engineering can support retrospective knowledge map reconstruction when actors have dispersed, and relational information is fragmented across organizations and digital traces. By combining manual, event-based coding with iterative, human-guided LLM inquiry, the approach surfaces relational connections, such as prior collaboration and trust, that are difficult to recover through interviews, documents, or keyword searches alone. While illustrated through a single case, the study establishes the feasibility of prompt-based LLM inquiry as a methodological contribution for research on heterarchical collaboration and innovation ecosystems.

Acknowledgments. The authors wish to thank those members of the Project Arrow team who participated in the interview process.

Disclosure of Interests. While McEachern-Gaudet and McGregor are at Ontario Tech University, neither was involved in Project Arrow. None of the authors have competing interests.

References

Besta, M., et al.: Graph of thoughts: solving elaborate problems with large language models. In: Proceedings of the AAAI Conference on Artificial Intelligence, vol. 38, no. 16, pp. 17682–17690 (2024). https://doi.org/10.1609/aaai.v38i16.29720

Dehghani, F., Dehghani, R., Naderzadeh Ardebili, Y., Rahnamayan, S.: Large language models in legal systems: a survey. Humanit. Soc. Sci. Commun. **12**(1), Article no. 1977 (2025). https://doi.org/10.1057/s41599-025-05924-3

Galkin, M., Auer, S., Vidal, M.-E., Scerri, S.: Enterprise knowledge graphs: a semantic approach for knowledge management in the next generation of enterprise information systems. In: International Conference on Enterprise Information Systems (2017)

Hogan, A., et al.: Knowledge graphs. ACM Comput. Surv. **54**(4), 1–37 (2021). https://doi.org/10.1145/3447772

Hsu, C.-Y., et al.: Thought graph: generating thought process for biological reasoning. In: Companion Proceedings of the ACM Web Conference 2024, 13 May 2024. https://doi.org/10.1145/3589335.3651572

Ibrahim, N., Aboulela, S., Ibrahim, A., Kashef, R.: A survey on augmenting knowledge graphs (KGs) with large language models (LLMs): models, evaluation metrics, benchmarks, and challenges. Discov. Artif. Intell. **4**(1), 76 (2024)

Kumu (2026). https://kumu.io

Ling, Y., Qin, Z., Ma, Z.: A review of knowledge graph construction using large language models in transportation: problems, methods, and challenges. Transp. Res. Part C Emerg. Technol. **183**, 105428 (2026). https://doi.org/10.1016/j.trc.2025.105428

McEachern Gaudet, A., Peticca-Harris, A.: Informal leadership practices in project ecosystems: the case of Project Arrow in redefining the automotive landscape in Canada [Paper submitted to the European Group for Organizational Studies (EGOS) Colloquium, Bergamo, Italy] (2026)

Marvin, G., Hellen, N., Jjingo, D., Nakatumba-Nabende, J.: Prompt engineering in large language models. In: Jacob, I.J., Piramuthu, S., Falkowski-Gilski, P. (eds.) ICDICI 2023. AIS, pp. 387–402. Springer, Singapore (2024). https://doi.org/10.1007/978-981-99-7962-2_30

Ontario Ministry of Economic Development, Job Creation and Trade: First all-Canadian, zero-emission concept vehicle designed in Ontario unveiled at Consumer Electronics Show. Ontario Newsroom, 5 January 2023. https://news.ontario.ca/en/release/1002625/first-all-canadian-zero-emission-concept-vehicle-designed-in-ontario-unveiled-at-consumer-electronics-show

Palmer, C.L., Cragin, M.H.: Curating for convergence: data stewardship for interdisciplinary inquiry. Libr. Trends **71**(1), 113–131 (2023). https://doi.org/10.1353/lib.2023.0007

Pather, K., et al.: Vis-CoT: a human-in-the-loop framework for interactive visualization and intervention in LLM chain-of-thought reasoning. arXiv preprint arXiv:2509.01412 (2025)

Wei, J., et al.: Chain-of-thought prompting elicits reasoning in large language models. In: Advances in Neural Information Processing Systems, vol. 35, pp. 24824–24837 (2022)

Yin, R.K.: Case study Research and Applications: Design and Methods, 6th edn. SAGE Publications (2018)

Zhong, L., Wu, J., Li, Q., Peng, H., Wu, X.: A comprehensive survey on automatic knowledge graph construction (2023)

Automatic knowledge graph construction. ACM Comput. Surv. **56**(4), 1–62. https://doi.org/10.1145/3618295

A Hybrid LLM-Based Architecture for Reliable Standardization of Heterogeneous Grant Information

Sergiusz Strykowski, Cyryl Leszczyński(✉), Stanisław Kumor, and Michał Śliwicki

Poznan University of Economics and Business, Niepodleglosci 10, Poznan, Poland
{sergiusz.strykowski,cyryl.leszczynski,stanislaw.kumor, michal.sliwicki}@ue.poznan.pl

Abstract. Public grants are an important instrument for financing socio-economic development, innovation, and public policy objectives. However, identifying and comparing key information on available grants remains difficult due to the fragmented, heterogeneous, and largely unstructured manner in which grant information is published by entities administrating grants.

Recent advances in LLMs enable new approaches to processing unstructured textual data and generating standardized representations that summarize and enhance key information and thus facilitate comparison. Nevertheless, their direct application in domains requiring high informational reliability is constrained by issues such as hallucination and limited reproducibility.

This paper examines the practical applicability and limitations of LLMs for standardizing grant information originating from heterogeneous, human-created sources. We propose a hybrid algorithmic architecture that bifurcates the standardization process into two complementary pathways. Descriptive textual fields are generated using a tightly controlled, parameter-constrained LLM pipeline, while hard factual data are extracted using predetermined, rule-based methods. This design restricts the scope of generative models to mitigate hallucination risks while preserving flexibility in processing unstructured content.

The proposed solution was implemented as a web-based system and successfully evaluated under real-world conditions. The results demonstrate that a constrained and selective application of LLMs can support effective standardization of heterogeneous information while mitigating the risks associated with hallucination and inconsistency. The proposed approach is not limited to the grant domain but is of a general nature and can be transferred to other business areas characterized by fragmented, unstructured, and inconsistently published information.

Keywords: Large Language Models · Information standardization · Public grants · Hybrid AI Architecture

1 Introduction

Public grants funded from national and European Union programs represent an important mechanism for financing socio-economic activities, innovation, and public policy objectives. For potential beneficiaries, effective access to information on available grants

K. Węcel and V. Řepa (Eds.): BIS 2026, LNBIP 584, pp. 249–259, 2026.
https://doi.org/10.1007/978-3-032-26363-6_19

is essential for informed planning and decision-making. In practice, however, the process of identifying, analyzing, and comparing grant opportunities remains complex and time-consuming.

This complexity arises primarily from the fragmented and heterogeneous manner in which grant information is published. Grant calls are disseminated by multiple intermediary bodies operating at different levels of public administration, each maintaining independent websites or information systems. The published content is typically unstructured or semi-structured and varies significantly in both scope and presentation. Key information—such as eligibility criteria, financial limits, deadlines, and objectives—is often embedded in narrative descriptions and expressed using inconsistent terminology. As a result, there is no single, consolidated source of grant information, and traditional keyword-based retrieval methods offer limited support for systematic analysis and comparison.

Recent advances in natural language processing, particularly the emergence of large language models (LLMs), have enabled new approaches to processing un-structured textual data. Owing to their capacity to model contextual dependencies and generate structured representations from free-form input, LLMs offer potential for standardizing grant descriptions originating from heterogeneous sources. In principle, such models can support the automated extraction and standardization of information without requiring task-specific supervised training for each new domain or source.

However, the direct application of LLMs to domains requiring high informational reliability introduces significant challenges. A well-documented limitation of these models is their tendency to generate content that is syntactically coherent but not fully grounded in the source material [5]. In the context of grant information, this behavior may result in the fabrication or incorrect inference of numerical values, dates, or eligibility conditions.

This paper investigates the practical applicability of large language models for the standardization of grant information published in heterogeneous, human-created sources. The central focus is not merely on automating data aggregation, but on identifying architectural constraints under which LLMs can be employed without compromising factual correctness. To this end, the paper proposes a hybrid algorithmic architecture that bifurcates the standardization process. It strategically combines a controlled, parameter-constrained LLM pathway for generating descriptive textual fields with predetermined, rule-based pathway for extracting hard factual data.

The proposed solution was implemented in the form of a web-based system. The system was evaluated under real-world conditions using data from multiple intermediary bodies administering grants and operating across various tiers of public administration or constituting specialized governmental agencies. The results demonstrate that a constrained and selective application of large language models can support effective standardization of heterogeneous information while mitigating the risks associated with hallucination and inconsistency. Accordingly, the proposed approach is not limited to the grant domain but is of a general nature and can be transferred to other business areas characterized by fragmented, unstructured, and inconsistently published information.

The reminder of this paper is structured as follows. Section 2 discusses related work on information extraction, and issues related to generating reliable highly structured summaries of unstructured text. Section 3 presents the characteristics of the public grant domain and the challenges associated with searching and selecting grant information. Section 4 outlines the proposed hybrid LLM-based architecture for standardized grant card generation and its evaluation under real-world conditions. Finally, Sect. 5 concludes the paper and discusses the directions for future work.

2 Related Work

The problem of automatically transforming unstructured natural language into structured formats (e.g., JSON or XML with predefined fields) has long been present in the literature on Natural Language Processing (NLP) and Information Extraction (IE). Traditional approaches, based on manually crafted rules, linguistic patterns, and statistical sequence models, were labor-intensive, brittle, and exhibited poor generalization to new domains [4]. Progress in this area was achieved with the adoption of deep neural networks, particularly recurrent architectures and sequence-to-sequence models with attention mechanisms, which enabled improved recognition of long-range informational dependencies in unstructured text [6]; this is especially relevant for working with generative models that produce target structures directly [19].

A major breakthrough came with the emergence of pretrained models based on the transformer architecture, called large language models (LLMs). Being trained in a self-supervised manner on massive text corpora, these model acquired rich, contextualized representations of language [3]. LLMs using zero-shot or few-shot settings, are capable not only of understanding complex natural language input but also of generating structured data from it [1, 21]. This approach, known as an in-context strategy (via prompt-engineering and answer-engineering), allows for efficient extraction of structured information by enabling to define an output schema only through a prompt, without the need for costly supervised training for each new task or domain [11]. However, according to [2], there are significant performance gaps between open-source and closed-source models in following specific constraints (lexical, structural, and relation-based) during text generation. Recent work has also emphasized that in practical applications, ensuring model outputs conform to the schema structure is challenging [20].

The most significant issue associated with the application of LLMs is hallucination. LLM hallucinations refer to the tendency of models to generate content that is coherent, grammatically correct, and seemingly plausible, yet factually incorrect, inconsistent with the provided context, or unsupported by external evidence [7]. The literature typically distinguishes two types of hallucinations in context-based tasks: (a) intrinsic hallucinations, which involve adding details, inferences, or statements not explicitly present in the source document, and (b) extrinsic hallucinations, which consist of incorporating information drawn from the model's own parametric knowledge that may be true in general but is not substantiated by the analyzed text [5, 13]. In the context of structured field extraction, hallucination may manifest as populating a required field with information that is merely inferred by the model or results from an incorrect interpretation of indirect cues.

Studies indicate that hallucinations often arise from a trade-off between faithfulness to the source and the fluency of the generated text. Models trained with the objective of next-token prediction are optimized to produce linguistically well-formed sequences, which may lead to the inclusion of tokens that statistically fit the context but lack factual grounding [5]. Additional risk factors include ambiguities in the source document, overgeneralization [14], pressure to satisfy all constraints of the output schema; e.g., the requirement to fill all fields even when information is missing which leads to fabricated or weakly supported content [12], and limitations of the attention window in the case of long summarization when hallucinations tend to occur more likely in the latter parts of the response [15].

Hallucination prevention strategies are an active area of research. These include advanced prompting techniques with explicit faithfulness constraints (e.g., "Answer only based on the provided text"), retrieval-augmented generation (RAG), which anchors generation to specific retrieved source passages [9], self-evaluation and multi-step verification methods (chain-of-verification). Nevertheless, the evaluation of faithfulness remains challenging and requires both automatic metrics (e.g., FactCC, QAFactEval) and expert human assessment [8].

3 Issues in Grant Search and Selection—Characteristics of the Domain

Public grants are a widely utilized instrument for financing the activities of socio-economic entities. In practice, however, the process of identifying, analyzing, and selecting suitable grants is complex and time-consuming, thereby hindering optimal management decision-making. The source of these difficulties lies not in isolated informational issues, but in the inherent characteristics of the domain in which grant information is published, processed, and utilized.

Information regarding available grants is published by their respective administering entities, commonly designated as intermediary bodies. These entities operate across various tiers of public administration—be it local or central—or constitute specialized governmental agencies. Grants themselves may originate from national or regional sources, funded either through national funds or European Union programs. Each administering institution typically maintains its own independent website or dedicated information system.

Consequently, a single, consolidated source of comprehensive grant information is absent. This fragmentation compels potential beneficiaries to proactively monitor a multitude of disparate portals. This not only imposes a significant temporal cost on the information-gathering process but also hinders the ability to form a complete and comparative overview of the funding landscape.

The institutional fragmentation is directly mirrored in the heterogeneity of publication formats. Grants are presented in diverse forms, ranging from static web pages and downloadable documents to extensive listings of announcements linked to local databases. Both the scope and the manner of presenting information vary considerably across sources, and critical terms—such as application deadlines, budgetary constraints, and eligibility criteria—are not consistently or clearly delineated. The absence of a standardized structure necessitates a manual, often context-dependent interpretation of content for the analysis and comparison of grants.

A defining characteristic of the grant domain is that information on grants is manually entered and updated by employees of intermediary institutions. This content is typically unstructured or semi-structured, encompassing both narrative descriptions and formal administrative requirements. Furthermore, grant descriptions are subject to frequent updates and amendments, which are not always clearly marked or systematically versioned.

In parallel, there exist aggregator portals that compile grant information within specific areas, such as European Union funding streams. These systems also rely on manual data entry, a practice which results in the duplication of identical information across multiple sources. This publication model fosters inconsistencies between descriptions of the same grant call and complicates the ongoing maintenance of data currency.

The described characteristics of the grant domain render traditional keyword-based information retrieval methods insufficient for the effective analysis and comparison of grants. The application of artificial intelligence techniques, particularly large language models (LLMs), creates the potential for processing unstructured content and standardizing information derived from multiple heterogeneous sources.

Concurrently, the practical deployment of these models reveals significant limitations, including a propensity for generating content inconsistent with the source material (hallucinations) and a lack of fully reproducible outputs. In the context of grant information—where reliability and fidelity to original documentation are paramount, this issue necessitates particular scrutiny.

Consequently, the core problem examined in this paper is not merely the aggregation of grant information using AI technology, but also the practical capabilities and constraints of employing this technology for the standardization of informational output. This challenge specifically concerns the boundaries within which large language models can be applied to standardize content from heterogeneous, manually created sources without compromising informational integrity.

4 Artificial Intelligence for Generating Standardized Grant Cards

To enable users to conduct an effective analysis and comparison of grants from diverse sources, a standardized grant card has been developed. The card comprises the following fields:

- Grant name – unique for each grant, serving as a human-readable identifier.
- Intermediary body – a name of the institution responsible for administering the grant, selected from a pre-defined list of verified institutions.
- Objectives – a list of objectives the grant is intended to support, set from a predefined range of topics; e.g., research, environmental protection, revitalization, energy transition.
- Applicable entities – size and type of entities eligible to apply for the grant, set from a predefined range of values.
- Range – geographical scope of the grant, set from a predefined range of region names.
- Financial information – a textual information relating to finances of the grant; e.g.; the maximum support amount the specific type of beneficiary may receive for specific types of activities.

- Goals – a textual description of goals the grant is intended to support; e.g., support for the development of critical technologies in the particular sector, support for activities aimed at particular social groups, etc.
- Qualified activities – a textual description of activities beneficiary may receive funding for.
- Beneficiaries – a textual description of entities that can apply for funding from the grant.
- Temporal facts – announcement, start and end dates for a grant call.
- Financial facts – grant total budget, minimum and maximum support amount for a single grant proposal, level of proposal funding in percentage.

The system was implemented in the form of a web platform. The overall conceptual architecture of the system is presented in Fig. 1.

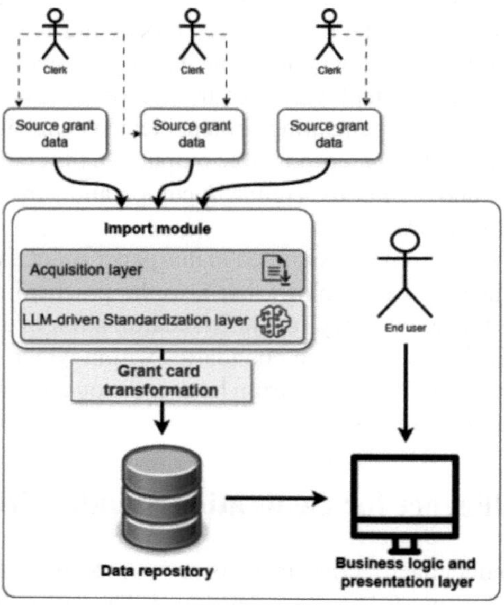

Fig. 1. The overall conceptual system architecture

The system architecture consists of the following components:

- Grant data importer module – consisting of 2 layers:
  - Acquisition layer: collects grant-related data from diverse Internet sources (web portals) run by intermediary institutions responsible for particular grants.
  - LLM-driven Standardization layer: transforms heterogeneous information content describing grant calls into standardized grant cards.
- Data repository – storage layer:
  - stores the standardized grant cards and other system data and data dictionaries.

- Business logic and presentation layer
  - provides search, filtering, comparing, and browsing on standardized grant cards

The data import module was implemented in the form of a proprietary algorithm utilizing artificial intelligence technology. The algorithm was developed using an iterative approach – the third version of the algorithm proved to be capable of generating a grant card containing a reliable set of information, consistent with the original data provided by the intermediary institutions at their websites or information systems.

Initially the algorithm iterated over a pre-defined list of pages while trying to detect certain key words and sections in a HTML document. This approach turned out to be insufficient due to the highly heterogenous nature of source webpages; e.g., one intermediary body listed the applicable entities as a list of image icons, while another described each one in a paragraph of text. As a result, the number of edge cases that would have to be accounted for resulted in an unsustainable system.

As an alternative solution, a generative web search approach has been implemented: for a specific grant, a chosen large language model would attempt to enrich the standardized grant card with as much information as it could gather from web-exploration; in this approach the data web retrieval has been relegated to AI as much as possible. This approach also turned out infeasible: by default, retrieval failures often lead to the LLM filling in the missing information with irrelevant or non-factual information [16], and even with proper data retrieval, the system can often conflict evidence, which lead to inconsistent standardized grant cards; e.g., the model confusing dates between similarly named grant calls. Additionally, due to the probabilistic nature of generative artificial intelligence, hallucinations occur after the retrieval process, even if the proper data has been obtained [17]: token prediction does not always align with real-world information, which results from the fact that LLMs training rewards fabricating information or guessing over acknowledging uncertainty or the lack of knowledge [18].

The final form of the algorithm, working correctly, is based on conclusions from the first two, not fully satisfactory approaches. The block diagram of the algorithm is shown in Fig. 2.

The algorithm for importing and standardizing grant data has been designed as a multi-stage process to transform unstructured, heterogeneous content from intermediary bodies into a coherent representation as a standardized grant card. A core principle of the algorithm is to restrict the use of large language models (LLMs), whose behavior is not fully deterministic, to generating only descriptive fields. In contrast, hard facts, such as numerical data and dates, are processed and generated using predetermined, rule-based methods.

The process begins with the initialization of data acquisition modules within the Acquisition layer. These modules interface with primary sources of grant data, such as websites or dedicated systems operated by intermediary bodies administering grant data. For each source, the Acquisition layer crawls a list of URLs, retrieves detailed grant descriptions, and extracts all available information as unstructured text. The collected data is stored in a cache, which retains an unmodified copy of the source material. At this stage, the algorithm performs no semantic interpretation, only ensuring the local availability of data for subsequent processing.

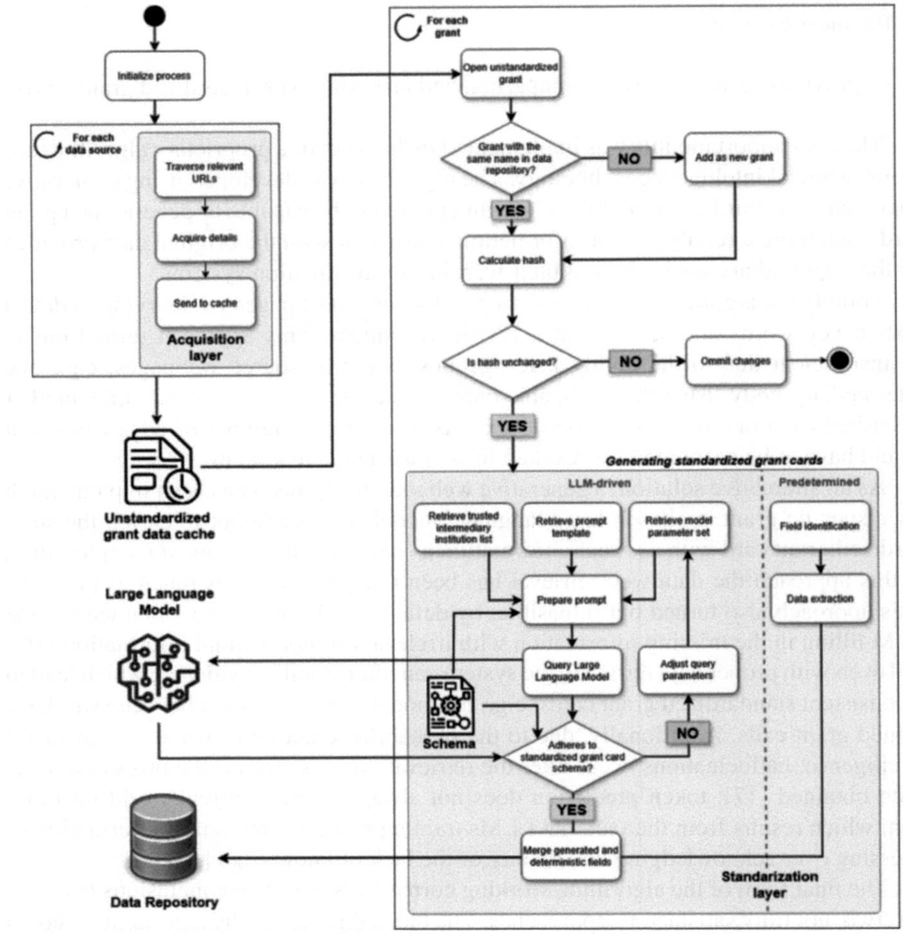

Fig. 2. Block diagram of the grant data standardization algorithm

Within the Standardization layer, each unstructured grant record is processed independently. The algorithm first queries the data repository to determine if a grant with the same name already exists. If not, the data is treated as a new grant entry. Next, an SHA-256 hash is computed from the entire unstructured data block. This hash is used to detect whether the source content has changed since the last retrieval. If the hash is unchanged, processing for that record is terminated to avoid unnecessary operations, re-generation of the grant card, and potential duplicates in the repository. If the hash differs, the unstructured data proceeds to the standardized grant card generation stage.

Grant card generation follows two parallel data processing pathways: an *LLM-driven path* and a *Predetermined path*. The former generates descriptive textual fields, while the latter extracts and populates hard factual fields containing numerical data and dates.

The LLM-driven path first assembles the input context for the model. This includes a list of verified intermediary bodies, a query template, a standardized grant card template, and a set of parameters to control the LLM's operation. Control parameters—such as temperature (regulating randomness), top-p, and top-k (limiting token selection to the most probable options)—are employed alongside maximum response length (max_tokens) and stop sequences. This combined parameter strategy reduces non-determinism and mitigates the risk of hallucination during grant card generation.

Using these components, a query is constructed and submitted to the LLM along with the unstructured source data, applying zero-shot and in-context learning strategies. The LLM's response is then validated for structural consistency against the predefined standardized grant card schema, which is formalized as a JSON schema. If the response does not conform, the algorithm adjusts the LLM control parameters and re-attempts generation. This iterative enforcement mechanism was developed and confirmed experimentally based on evaluations of LLM output quality.

Concurrently to the LLM-driven path, the Predetermined path operates. The Predetermined path ensures the accurate extraction of hard facts. It employs regular expressions and other deterministic parsing mechanisms to search the unstructured grant data for these facts. Identified values are directly mapped into the corresponding fields of the standardized grant card.

The dual-path architecture eliminates LLM hallucinations for fields requiring 100% correctness and alignment with the source information. The algorithm thus facilitates iterative and controlled processing of unstructured grant data, accommodating both the variability of content published by intermediary bodies and the inherent limitations of LLMs. The final output is a coherent repository of standardized grant cards, enabling systematic search, filtering, and comparison of grants sourcing across a broad range of intermediary institutions.

The algorithm was evaluated under real-world business conditions over a six-month period in the second half of 2025, with daily execution for importing grant data from intermediary bodies websites and systems. The evaluation involved 1,442 grants from 43 intermediary bodies representing various levels of public administration, from local government to central administration and specialized agencies. The grants covered 16 thematic areas, including research and development, entrepreneurship, energy transition, environmental protection, health, digitization, and education. Throughout the evaluation, domain experts analyzed the algorithmically generated grant cards, confirming the reliability and consistency of the output and attesting to its practical utility in operational business contexts.

5 Conclusion and Future Work

This paper analyzes the capacity and utility of artificial intelligence technology, specifically large language models (LLMs), for standardizing information being published in human-created, unstructured forms at various heterogeneous sources.

The proposed solution to this problem involves bifurcating the standardization process into two parallel data-processing pathways: an LLM-driven path and a Predetermined path. The former generates descriptive textual fields, while the latter extracts and populates hard factual fields containing numerical data and dates.

Implementation and evaluation of the developed solution within a real-world business context—namely, the sector dedicated to identifying and obtaining grants for co-financing socio-economic activities—confirm that direct, end-to-end generation of structured data using LLMs alone results in significant quality issues. These include information hallucination and data inconsistency, thereby limiting the models' direct applicability in domains requiring high informational reliability.

This work demonstrates that integrating predetermined data extraction mechanisms with the controlled application of large language models can substantially mitigate these problems while preserving the flexibility required to process un-structured content. The proposed standardized grant card framework facilitates effective searching, filtering, and comparison of grant data, irrespective of the original publication source. This, in turn, supports management decision-making based on the analysis of available grants.

Although the developed solution has been applied to the domain of publicly available grants, the results suggest that the identified challenges and the proposed architectural approach are generalizable and not domain specific. They are particularly relevant to a broad class of scenarios in which information is published in a fragmented, manual, and loosely structured or entirely unstructured, heterogeneous manner. Consequently, the proposed methodology can serve as a blueprint for designing standardization solutions in other business and administrative areas where both flexibility in processing descriptive content and the reliable preservation of hard facts are critical.

Future work may involve comparative performance analysis between the externally provided LLMs utilized in the current system and specialized models for information summarization, such as those based on the BART architecture [10]. Due to their smaller scale (comprising several billion parameters), such models can be deployed on local server infrastructure. This would enhance data privacy and significantly improve processing efficiency by eliminating the need to transmit queries to external LLM providers.

Disclosure of Interests. The authors declare no competing interests relevant to the content of this paper.

References

1. Brown, T.B., Mann, B., Ryder, N.: Language models are few-shot learners. In: Advances in Neural Information Processing Systems, vol. 33, pp. 1877–1901 (2020)
2. Chen, X., Wan, X.: Evaluating, understanding, and improving constrained text generation for large language models. https://arxiv.org/abs/2310.16343 (2024)
3. Devlin, J., Chang, M.W., Lee, K., Toutanova, K.: BERT: pre-training of deep bidirectional transformers for language understanding. In: Proceedings of NAACL-HLT (2019)
4. Grishman, R.: Information extraction: capabilities and challenges. Int. Winter Sch. Lang. Speech Technol. (2012)
5. Huang, L., et al.: A survey on hallucination in large language models: principles, taxonomy, challenges, and open questions. ACM Trans. Inf. Syst. **43**(2), 1–55 (2025)
6. Huang, L., Wu, L., Wang, L.: Knowledge graph-augmented abstractive summarization with semantic-driven cloze reward. In: Proceedings of ACL (2020)
7. Ji, Z., Lee, N., Frieske, R.: Survey of hallucination in natural language generation. ACM Comput. Surv. **55**(12), 1–38 (2023)

8. Kryscinski, W., McCann, B., Xiong, C., Socher, R.: Evaluating the factual consistency of abstractive text summarization. In: Proceedings of EMNLP (2020)
9. Lewis, P., Perez, E., Piktus, A.: Retrieval-Augmented generation for knowledge-intensive NLP tasks. In: Advances in Neural Information Processing Systems, vol. 34 (2020)
10. Lewis, M., et al.: BART: denoising sequence-to-sequence pre-training for natural language generation, translation, and comprehension. In: Proceedings of the 58th Annual Meeting of the Association for Computational Linguistics, pp. 7871–7880 (2020)
11. Liu, P., Yuan, W., Fu, J.: Pre-train, prompt, and predict: a systematic survey of prompting methods in natural language processing. ACM Comput. Surv. **55**(9), 1–35 (2023)
12. Lu, Y., et al.: Learning to generate structured output with schema reinforcement learning. In: Proceedings of the 63rd Annual Meeting of the Association for Computational Linguistics, vol. 1, pp. 4905–4918 (2025)
13. Maynez, J., Narayan, S., Bohnet, B., McDonald, R.: On faithfulness and factuality in abstractive summarization. In: Proceedings of ACL (2020)
14. Peters, U., Chin-Yee, B.: Generalization bias in large language model summarization of scientific research. R. Soc. Open Sci. **12**(4), 241776 (2025)
15. Yang, J., Yoon, S., Chang, H., Kim, B., Lee, H.: Hallucinate at the last in long response generation: a case study on long document summarization. https://arxiv.org/abs/2505.15291v3 (2026)
16. Yan, S.Q., Gu, J.C., Zhu, Y., Ling, Z.H.: Corrective retrieval augmented generation. https://arxiv.org/abs/2401.15884 (2024)
17. Wallat, J., Heuss, M., de Rijke, M., Anand, A.: Correctness is not faithfulness in retrieval augmented generation attributions. In: Proceedings of the 2025 International ACM SIGIR Conference on Innovative Concepts and Theories in Information Retrieval, pp. 22–32 (2025)
18. OpenAI: Why language models hallucinate (2025). https://openai.com/index/why-language-models-hallucinate
19. Zhang, Z.K., et al.: A survey of generative information extraction. In: Rambow, O., Wanner, L., Apidianaki, M., Al-Khalifa, H., Eugenio, B.D., Schockaert, S. (eds.) Proceedings of the 31st International Conference on Computational Linguistics. Association for Computational Linguistics (2025). https://aclanthology.org/2025.coling-main.324/
20. Shen, Z., Wang, D.Y.-B., Mishra, S.S., Xu, Z., Teng, Y., Ding, H.: SLOT: structuring the output of large language models. In: Potdar, S., Rojas-Barahona, L., Montella, S. (eds.) Proceedings of the 2025 Conference on Empirical Methods in Natural Language Processing: Industry Track, pp. 472–491. Association for Computational Linguistics (2025). https://doi.org/10.18653/v1/2025.emnlp-industry.32
21. Ke, W., et al.: Large language models in document intelligence: a comprehensive survey, recent advances, challenges, and future trends. ACM Trans. Inf. Syst. **44**(1), Article no. 18 (2025). https://doi.org/10.1145/3768156

Speech Recognition

Comparative Evaluation of Automatic Speech Recognition Models for Multi-accent University Admissions Interview Transcription

Diana Kalibatiene and Julius Jancevičius(✉)

Vilnius Gediminas Technical University, 10223 Vilnius, Lithuania
julius.jancevicius@vilniustech.lt

Abstract. University admissions increasingly rely on asynchronous video interviews, but manual review and transcription remain time-consuming and sensitive to transcription errors, particularly under accent variability. This paper presents a reproducible, privacy-oriented pipeline for processing authentic admissions interviews, including secure data preparation, automated personally identifiable information (PII) screening with human verification, dialect identification, and dialect-conditioned evaluation of automatic speech recognition (ASR) models. Dialect labels are inferred using a SpeechBrain ECAPA-TDNN accent identification model trained on CommonAccent. Transcription quality is assessed using word error rate (WER) for three transformer-based ASR systems: Whisper, HuBERT, and wav2vec2. Experiments are conducted on real applicant interviews and results are reported for dialect groups with more than 15 recordings. Across all evaluated dialects, Whisper yields the lowest WER (20–27%), while HuBERT and wav2vec2 exhibit higher error rates (31–46% and 44–64%, respectively). Dialect-aware ASR evaluation enhances transcription robustness across dialects, enabling fairer downstream decisions and more reliable early indicators for identifying students who may need support to mitigate attrition risk. The findings demonstrate that ASR accuracy is dialect-dependent in high-stakes educational settings and support dialect-conditioned model selection for more consistent transcription quality.

Keywords: Automatic Speech Recognition · Dialect Robustness · University Admissions Interviews · Privacy-Preserving Data Processing · Dialect Detection · Word Error Rate

1 Introduction

The evaluation of applicants to higher education institutions is a complex and time-consuming process due to its highly manual nature and multiple evaluation stages [1], such as evaluation of the applicant's documents, recommendation letters, video interviews, etc. The admissions process at universities typically involves multiple evaluation stages: the admissions department is responsible for the thorough review of all submitted documents, while university lecturers frequently utilise essay assessment, recommendation letter analysis, interviews as a means of evaluating applicants, with the objective of selecting the most suitable candidates [2].

K. Węcel and V. Řepa (Eds.): BIS 2026, LNBIP 584, pp. 263–276, 2026.
https://doi.org/10.1007/978-3-032-26363-6_20

Consequently, there is a need for a solution that improves accuracy while accelerating the overall processing pipeline, as video-based interviews have become an increasingly common component of university admissions processes [3]. To enable end-to-end automation of the evaluation workflow, the system must ensure reliable data preprocessing and accurate speech-to-text transcription. The broader multimodal preprocessing pipeline for applicant assessment is described in [4]. Transcription errors at this stage may propagate to downstream assessments and could disadvantage applicants by contributing to incorrect admission decisions [5].

Among these assessment steps, asynchronous video interview (AVI) assessment is quite complex and time-consuming [6]. AVI is a form of one-way, technology-mediated, selection interviewing [7]. Despite the fact that all applicants speak English, people's dialects around the world differ [8], that in addition to language irregularities, lead to errors in automatic speech recognition (ASR) systems [9, 10]. It has been noted that there is a paucity of research in this area, which means that it is not possible to determine which ASR system is most accurate for each language dialect [11].

Although determining dialect during asynchronous video interviews is not one of the main steps in assessing applicants, it is necessary to create a complete profile of the applicant and, in the event of admission, to monitor the applicant's progress in studies and take measures to reduce student dropout rates.

Consequently, the main aim of this research is to investigate which transcriber is most effective in processing audio interviews in various dialects in order to predict possible applicants progress in studies and take measures to reduce student dropout rates.

The main scientific contribution and novelty of this research are as follows. First, an automatic speech recognition (ASR) evaluation is conducted using speech from university admissions interviews; in contrast to most existing studies, which primarily rely on general-purpose corpora, the present work focuses on authentic, high-stakes interview data. Second, a multi-accent dataset is introduced and analysed, incorporating underrepresented varieties of English – namely Bermudian, Hong Kong, and Malaysian English – that remain rarely examined in prior ASR research. Third, an equity-oriented framework for educational assessment is developed, explicitly connecting ASR performance to fairness considerations and the potential implications for consistent and equitable evaluation of international applicants.

The paper is organized as follows. Section 2 reviews recent ASR evaluations for English speakers with diverse accents and dialects. Section 3 presents the transcription methodology, including data preparation, PII anonymization, and transcription. Section 4 reports experimental results on real applicant interviews, and Sect. 5 discusses their implications and limitations. Section 6 concludes the paper and outlines future work.

2 Related Works

Deep learning-based automatic speech recognition (ASR) is commonly evaluated using word error rate (WER) and is increasingly studied for robustness to accents and dialectal variation. Prior studies on accented and multilingual speech most frequently use OpenAI Whisper and FAIR self-supervised models (HuBERT and wav2vec2), reporting heterogeneous WER results across languages, datasets, and fine-tuning setups. In this section, these related works are compared in Table 1 to identify their performance ranges and limitations, and to motivate the need for this study's-controlled comparison and the proposed evaluation approach/model.

Table 1. Comparison of the related works on audio transcribers (Standard Deviations (SD))

Reference	Transcriber	Accuracy Metrics	Language
(1)	(2)	(3)	(4)
[25]	Whisper (large-v2)	WER = 0.866 (Words) and 0.767 (Sentences)	Kazakh
[12]	Whisper (base), HuBERT (large), wav2vec2 (large)	WER = 18.0 (MyST Dev), 26.28 (CSLU Read) WER = 19.8 (MyST Dev), 48.6 (CSLU Read) WER = 21.6 (MyST Dev), 54.0 (CSLU Read)	English
[26]	Whisper (large-v3)	WER = 4.1	Portuguese
[27]	HuBERT wav2vec2	WER%/SD = 23.4 (Moderate) WER%/SD = 36.3 (Moderate)	English
[28]	Whisper (base)	WER $\leq$ 0.3	English
[21]	Whisper (large), HuBERT (large), wav2vec2 (large)	WER = 12.5% WER = 10.7% WER = 9.8%	Telugu
[29]	HuBERT (large), wav2vec2 (large)	WER $\approx$ 22–30% WER $\approx$ 20%	English
[30]	wav2vec2 (fine-tuned)	XLSR-53: WER = 47.10% XLS-R-300M: WER = 48.94%	Kashmiri
[14]	Whisper (large-v2) Whisper (small) wav2vec2	WER = 28.86% WER = 32.17% WER = 14.42%	Bengali
[31]	HuBERT (large), wav2vec2 (large)	WER = 10.67% WER = 10.65%	English
[13]	Whisper (small) wav2vec2 (large)	WER = 45.33% WER = 34.31%	Badini

A close examination of the transcribers employed by other authors reveals three models that have gained particular popularity [12–14]. These studies employ the Whisper model, which was developed by OpenAI [15–18]. The HuBERT [19–21] and wav2vec2 [22, 23] models, developed by the Facebook AI Research (FAIR) team, have also gained significant popularity. The decision was taken to include the latter models in the comparison because, despite being from the same provider, the architecture of the aforementioned models (HuBERT and wav2vec2) is different [24].

In order to facilitate a more detailed examination of the extant literature, a set of relevant studies was analysed in order to develop a more comprehensive overview of prior work. The results of this analysis are summarised in Table 1.

Other practical ASR alternatives to the systems considered (see Table 1 column 2) include Vosk, DeepSpeech, ESPnet, NeMo (e.g., Conformer/RNN-T/CTC pipelines), and commercial cloud ASR APIs (e.g., Google, Azure, AWS) [25, 32]. However, these options are less suitable for this use case. Vosk and ESPnet typically require substantial ASR-specific engineering, such as decoding graphs, language models, and careful text normalization, and their off-the-shelf models may be constrained by language coverage and domain mismatch. DeepSpeech is largely deprecated and generally underperforms modern transformer-based approaches [33]. NeMo and related research toolkits introduce heavy GPU/software dependencies and can be challenging to deploy reproducibly across environments [34]. Finally, cloud ASR services raise privacy and compliance concerns, depend on network connectivity, and introduce recurring costs and vendor lock-in, which conflicts with the goal of local and reproducible evaluation [35].

Overall, the reviewed studies primarily rely on Whisper, HuBERT, and wav2vec2 and report WER values that vary widely by language, dataset, and fine-tuning strategy (see Table 1). Because these works use different evaluation conditions and often target different speech varieties, their results are not directly comparable and do not establish a consistent baseline for accented English. Alternative ASR solutions (e.g., Vosk, ESPnet, NeMo, and cloud APIs) introduce engineering overhead, deployment constraints, or privacy and cost risks, making them unsuitable for reproducible local evaluation. Therefore, a controlled comparison of the main transformer-based transcribers under a unified evaluation protocol is required, which motivates this study.

3 Materials and Methods

This section proposes a reproducible end-to-end pipeline for secure interview data handling that integrates automated PII screening with human verification, dialect labelling, and dialect-conditioned benchmarking of state-of-the-art ASR transcribers (Whisper, HuBERT, wav2vec2) using WER. The methodology (see Sect. 2) consists of three main stages – data preparation, PII check, transcription and evaluation.

3.1 Data Preparation

The data retrieval and preparation process is straightforward. Since authentic video recordings of applicants are used, the interviews are obtained securely using the available internal resources. The detailed data transfer process is presented in Fig. 1.

As shown in Fig. 1, the interviews are downloaded and immediately converted to an audio format. A preliminary transcription is generated at this stage to support the detection of personally identifiable information (PII) within the recordings. The subprocess covering basic transcription and the storage of the resulting files is indicated by the task marked with a "+" symbol and is detailed in Fig. 2.

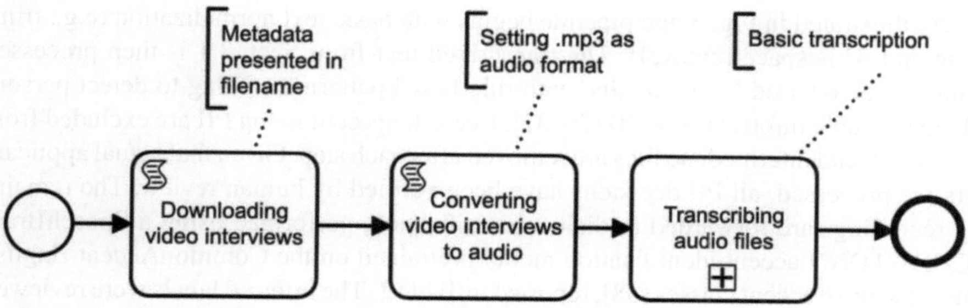

Fig. 1. Data preparation process.

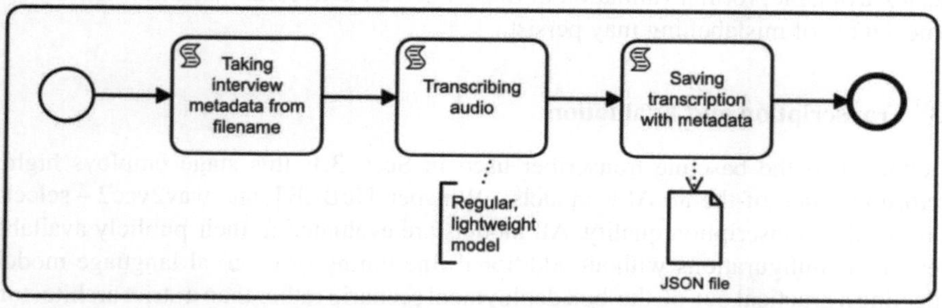

Fig. 2. Basic transcription subprocess for later PII verification.

3.2 Personally Identifiable Information Verification

As described in Sect. 3.1, at this stage the data have already been downloaded and prepared for use, including an initial transcription performed for PII verification. Only audio recordings that successfully pass the personally identifiable information (PII) screening are included in the final dataset. For these approved recordings, the dialect is then identified as the next step in the processing pipeline. A detailed overview of the PII verification pipeline is presented in Fig. 3.

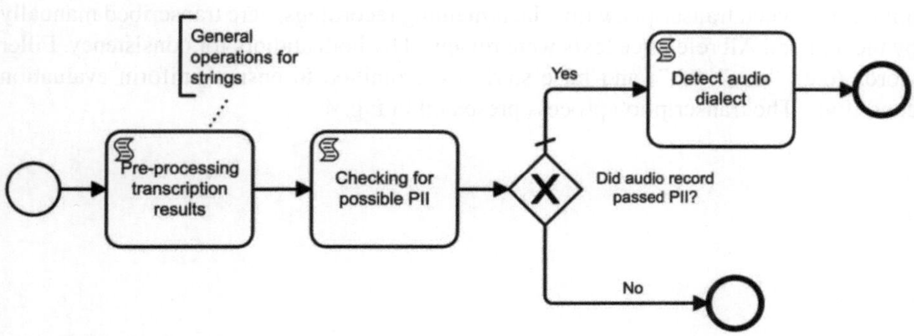

Fig. 3. Personally identifiable information (PII) verification and dialect detection process.

As illustrated in Fig. 3, the pipeline begins with basic text normalization (e.g., trimming and whitespace removal). The transcribed text from Sect. 3.1 is then processed using a spaCy-based NER pipeline with rule-based pattern matching to detect personally identifiable information (PII) [36, 37]. Recordings containing PII are excluded from the dataset, and intermediate files are removed after each step. Given that actual applicant data are processed, all PII decisions have been verified by human review. The remaining recordings are forwarded to dialect identification, performed using a SpeechBrain ECAPA-TDNN accent identification model pretrained on the CommonAccent English dataset with 16 accent classes [38], reported in Table 2. The inferred labels were reviewed by the authors, and in low-confidence cases the dialect was assigned manually based on the speaker's speech characteristics. Since self-reported nationality or dialect metadata was not available, formal validation of dialect detection accuracy was not feasible, and some degree of mislabelling may persist.

3.3 Transcription and Evaluation

In contrast to the baseline transcriber used in Sect. 3.1, this stage employs higher-performing state-of-the-art ASR models – Whisper, HuBERT, and wav2vec2 – selected to maximize transcription quality. All models are evaluated in their publicly available, pretrained configurations without additional fine-tuning or external language models, reflecting a practical out-of-the-box deployment scenario rather than a strict architectural comparison. Following a comprehensive review of the relevant literature (see Sect. 2), we selected the following models [12, 26, 31]:

1. Whisper (*large-v3*);
2. HuBERT (*hubert-large-ls960-ft*);
3. wav2vec2 (*wav2vec2-large-960h*).

To implement the method, each selected audio file is processed by all chosen transcriber models. This ensures a consistent basis for subsequent performance measurement and the systematic collection of experimental results. Word Error Rate (WER) is used as the primary evaluation metric for transcription verification. Reference transcriptions were obtained from two sources: a subset of recordings was accompanied by existing human-produced transcripts, while the remaining recordings were transcribed manually by the authors. All reference texts were reviewed by both authors for consistency. Filler words (e.g., "um," "uh") and false starts were omitted to ensure uniform evaluation conditions. The transcription process presented in Fig. 4.

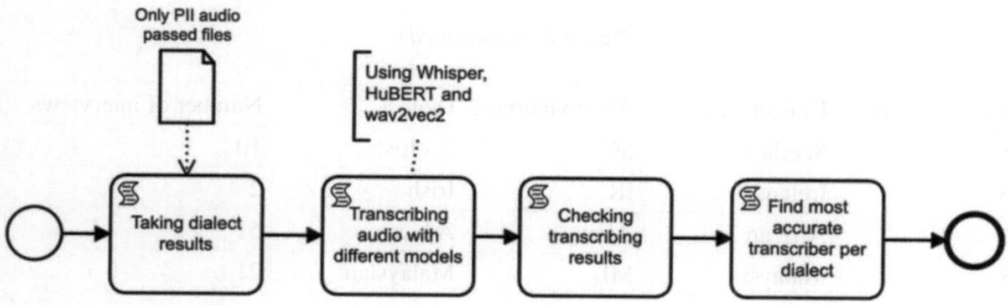

Fig. 4. Transcription process.

As shown in Fig. 4, the evaluation workflow operates exclusively on recordings that have passed PII verification. For each approved recording, the previously inferred dialect label is retrieved and attached as metadata. The audio is then transcribed independently using the selected ASR models (Whisper, HuBERT, and wav2vec2), ensuring identical inputs across systems. The resulting transcripts are assessed against the reference text to quantify transcription performance (e.g., using WER) under consistent evaluation criteria. Finally, performance scores are aggregated by dialect to identify the most accurate transcriber for each dialect group, enabling dialect-conditioned model selection.

4 Results

This section reports the outcomes of applying the methods described in Sect. 3. The results are organized into dialect identification and dialect-specific transcription performance of the selected ASR models for each identified dialect.

4.1 Dialect Detection

As described in Sect. 3, the dataset was compiled specifically for this study using authentic interview recordings from student applications. All necessary permissions for the use of these personal materials were obtained prior to analysis. Since applicants originate from diverse geographical regions, the number of recordings available per dialect varies according to the relative prevalence of that dialect in the applicant population. The distribution is reported in Table 2.

Table 2. Analysed dialect (accent) classes with number of interviews (Enumerator (enum)).

Class number	Dialect enum	Abbreviation	Dialect	Number of interviews
0	England	EN	English	132
1	United States	US	American	168
2	Canada	CA	Canadian	10
3	Australia	AU	Australian	48
4	Indian	IN	Indian	37

(*continued*)

Table 2. *(continued)*

Class number	Dialect enum	Abbreviation	Dialect	Number of interviews
5	Scotland	SC	Scottish	10
6	Ireland	IR	Irish	2
7	African	AF	African	51
8	Malaysia	ML	Malaysian	21
9	New Zealand	NZ	New Zealand	6
10	South Atlantic	SO	South Atlantic	0
11	Bermuda	BM	Bermudan	23
12	Philippines	PH	Philippine	17
13	Hong Kong	HK	Hong Kong	19
14	Wales	WL	Welsh	3
15	Singapore	SG	Singaporean	21

4.2 Transcription Results

Transcription performance is quantified using word error rate (WER) for each analysed dialect and for each evaluated model. To ensure a sufficient sample size for reliable comparison, results are reported only for dialect groups with more than 15 interviews (see Table 2). Lower WER values indicate higher transcription accuracy. For each dialect, the best-performing model (i.e., the model with the lowest WER) is highlighted. The transcription results are summarised in Table 3.

Table 3. Transcription results (Dialect (DI), Whisper (W), HuBERT (H), wav2vec2 (V), Number of Words (NoW)).

DI	WER %			Substitutions			Deletions			Insertions			NoW
	W	H	V	W	H	V	W	H	V	W	H	V	
AF	**27**	41	60	1065	1751	2821	529	328	458	193	645	671	6538
AU	**23**	39	55	844	1506	2350	397	251	293	153	653	782	6173
BM	**20**	31	44	442	717	1079	226	177	209	95	274	373	3761
EN	**25**	41	58	2460	4654	7337	1251	669	862	605	1941	2048	17551
HK	**27**	44	64	516	847	1364	199	175	204	77	282	318	2956
IN	**23**	42	64	641	1323	2286	333	230	257	138	492	573	4873
ML	**26**	46	62	468	875	1265	156	104	118	77	279	291	2707
PH	**22**	32	45	291	543	786	166	89	110	58	138	165	2374
SG	**23**	40	53	392	649	960	154	135	157	60	282	311	2685
US	**24**	40	58	2853	5246	8673	1444	819	924	660	2205	2578	20839

Whisper frequently achieves lower WER because it is an end-to-end encoder–decoder Transformer with a strong integrated language model. By contrast, HuBERT and wav2vec 2.0 are typically deployed as encoder – CTC systems and therefore exhibit weaker inherent language modelling unless supplemented with an external language model. In addition, Whisper was trained on approximately 680,000 h of diverse, weakly supervised multilingual audio, which contributes to improved robustness under accent variation, background noise, and other real-world recording conditions – factors that are widely recognised as drivers of elevated WER in applied settings [39].

To assess the statistical robustness of these results, per-recording WER distributions were computed for each dialect–model pair. Table 4 reports the mean WER, standard deviation (SD), and 95% confidence intervals (95CI) across individual recordings.

Table 4. Per-recording WER by dialect and model, reported as mean, standard deviation, and 95% confidence intervals (Dialect (DI), Mean WER (MW), Standard Deviation (SD), 95% Confidence Intervals (95CI)).

DI	Whisper			HuBERT			wav2vec2		
	MW	SD	95CI	MW	SD	95CI	MW	SD	95CI
AF	0.26	0.11	[0.23, 0.29]	0.43	0.19	[0.38, 0.48]	0.60	0.20	[0.54, 0.65]
AU	0.23	0.11	[0.20, 0.26]	0.44	0.23	[0.37, 0.50]	0.59	0.23	[0.53, 0.66]
BM	0.20	0.11	[0.15, 0.24]	0.34	0.18	[0.26, 0.41]	0.47	0.23	[0.38, 0.57]
CA	0.33	0.40	[0.08, 0.58]	0.39	0.19	[0.28, 0.51]	0.53	0.23	[0.39, 0.68]
EN	0.27	0.18	[0.24, 0.30]	0.48	0.29	[0.43, 0.52]	0.62	0.22	[0.58, 0.66]
HK	0.24	0.13	[0.18, 0.30]	0.45	0.15	[0.39, 0.52]	0.64	0.15	[0.57, 0.71]
IN	0.29	0.25	[0.22, 0.37]	0.50	0.24	[0.42, 0.58]	0.68	0.22	[0.61, 0.75]
IR	0.09	0.08	[-0.01, 0.20]	0.29	0.02	[0.27, 0.32]	0.35	0.03	[0.31, 0.39]
ML	0.24	0.12	[0.19, 0.29]	0.42	0.20	[0.33, 0.50]	0.57	0.20	[0.49, 0.66]
NZ	0.20	0.13	[0.10, 0.30]	0.46	0.26	[0.25, 0.67]	0.63	0.35	[0.35, 0.91]
PH	0.27	0.23	[0.16, 0.38]	0.38	0.22	[0.28, 0.49]	0.51	0.26	[0.39, 0.63]
SC	0.32	0.28	[0.15, 0.50]	0.53	0.29	[0.34, 0.71]	0.65	0.29	[0.47, 0.83]
SG	0.24	0.19	[0.16, 0.33]	0.47	0.27	[0.35, 0.58]	0.61	0.30	[0.48, 0.74]
US	0.30	0.32	[0.25, 0.35]	0.47	0.25	[0.43, 0.51]	0.65	0.26	[0.61, 0.68]
WL	0.20	0.14	[0.05, 0.36]	0.38	0.21	[0.14, 0.62]	0.48	0.20	[0.26, 0.71]

The wider confidence intervals observed for smaller dialect groups (e.g., Philippine with 17 recordings, Bermudan with 23) reflect greater uncertainty in the aggregate estimates for these categories, while larger groups such as American (n = 168) and English (n = 132) yield narrower intervals, indicating more stable performance estimates. High within-group variability is also notable for certain dialects, with standard deviations reaching 0.25–0.32 for Whisper on Indian, Scottish, and American English, suggesting that individual speaker characteristics beyond dialect also contribute to transcription difficulty.

To determine whether the observed differences between Whisper and the competing models are statistically significant, Wilcoxon signed-rank tests were conducted on paired per-recording WER values. This non-parametric test was chosen because per-recording WER distributions are not guaranteed to be normally distributed. Table 5 summarises the results.

Table 5. Wilcoxon signed-rank test results across dialect groups ($\alpha = 0.05$) with rank-biserial correlation as effect size (Number of Interviews (NI), P-value (PV), Significant (SG), Effect Size (ES)).

DI	NI	W vs H PV	W vs H SG	W vs H ES	W vs V PV	W vs V SG	W vs V ES
AF	51	2.51e−08	Yes	0.95	1.23e−09	Yes	0.99
AU	48	1.75e−10	Yes	0.96	1.97e−09	Yes	1.00
BM	23	5.45e−04	Yes	0.93	2.38e−07	Yes	1.00
CA	10	0.1289	No	0.84	0.0645	No	0.84
EN	132	9.84e−21	Yes	0.97	5.37e−23	Yes	1.00
HK	19	3.81e−05	Yes	0.97	3.81e−06	Yes	1.00
IN	37	7.56e−07	Yes	0.98	2.95e−07	Yes	1.00
IR	2	0.5000	No	1.00	0.5000	No	1.00
ML	21	2.41e−04	Yes	0.92	8.86e−05	Yes	1.00
NZ	6	0.0938	No	0.90	0.0312	Yes	1.00
PH	17	0.0032	Yes	0.93	6.55e−04	Yes	1.00
SC	10	0.0078	Yes	1.00	0.0039	Yes	1.00
SG	21	1.34e−05	Yes	0.97	9.54e−07	Yes	1.00
US	168	2.27e−21	Yes	0.94	8.77e−26	Yes	0.98
WL	3	0.2500	No	1.00	0.2500	No	1.00

Whisper significantly outperforms both HuBERT and wav2vec2 in 11 of the 15 evaluated dialect groups ($p < 0.05$). For the remaining four groups, i.e., Canadian ($n = 10$), Irish ($n = 2$), New Zealand ($n = 6$), and Welsh ($n = 3$), the differences were not statistically significant, likely due to insufficient sample sizes. The rank-biserial correlation effect sizes are consistently large across all significant comparisons, ranging from 0.92 to 1.00, indicating that Whisper produces lower per-recording WER than HuBERT and wav2vec2 in nearly all paired observations. These findings confirm that Whisper's advantage is statistically meaningful and practically relevant for the majority of dialect groups, while also highlighting the need for larger samples in underrepresented categories.

5 Discussion

The results show clear dialect-conditioned differences in ASR accuracy on authentic admissions interviews. For all dialect groups with sufficient data ($n > 15$), Whisper achieves the lowest WER (20–27%), while HuBERT and wav2vec2 produce markedly higher error rates (31–46% and 44–64%, respectively). This gap is consistent with Whisper's end-to-end encoder–decoder design and integrated language modelling, whereas HuBERT and wav2vec2 are evaluated as encoder–CTC systems without external language models, which likely increases substitution and insertion errors under spontaneous, accented interview speech. Wilcoxon signed-rank tests confirm that these differences are statistically significant for 11 of the 15 evaluated dialect groups ($p < 0.05$), with large effect sizes (rank-biserial correlation 0.92–1.00). The four non-significant groups (Canadian, Irish, New Zealand, and Welsh) have fewer than 10 recordings each, suggesting insufficient statistical power rather than comparable model performance. Per-recording confidence intervals further show that Whisper's advantage holds at the individual interview level, not only in aggregate.

These findings are relevant for equitable admissions assessment: systematic transcription errors for specific dialects can propagate to downstream text-based evaluation and disadvantage applicants. The high within-group variability observed for certain dialects (e.g., Indian and Scottish English exhibit standard deviations of 0.25–0.28 for Whisper) suggests that individual speaker characteristics beyond dialect also contribute to transcription difficulty. However, the analysis is constrained by strong class imbalance, automatically inferred dialect labels, and the absence of an external language model for the CTC-based systems, which may improve with optimized decoding and domain adaptation.

Future work should expand underrepresented dialect groups, validate dialect labels, and test enhanced decoding settings under the same privacy-preserving constraints.

6 Conclusions and Future Works

This study proposed a reproducible, privacy-oriented pipeline for processing authentic university admissions interviews, integrating secure data preparation, PII screening with human verification, dialect identification, and dialect-conditioned ASR evaluation. Using WER as the primary metric, supported by per-recording confidence intervals and Wilcoxon signed-rank tests with effect size analysis, the comparative results across dialect groups with sufficient data ($n > 15$) show that Whisper (large-v3) consistently and statistically significantly outperforms HuBERT and wav2vec2 on the collected interview recordings. The findings indicate that ASR performance is dialect-dependent and that model choice can materially affect transcription quality in high-stakes educational assessment settings.

Future work will expand the dataset to improve coverage of underrepresented dialect classes and enable more balanced comparisons, validate dialect labels and quantify dialect detection accuracy, and evaluate enhanced decoding for CTC-based systems under the same local, privacy-preserving constraints. In addition, downstream impact analyses will be conducted to measure how dialect-conditioned transcription errors affect subsequent interview scoring and fairness outcomes in admissions workflows.

Acknowledgments. These results are part of the project "Artificial intelligence and multimodal data fusion system for assessing and detecting fraud in applicants' videos" (FAIR-VID), which is funded by the Research Council of Lithuania (LMTLT), agreement No. S-ITP-25-14.

Disclosure of Interests. The authors declare no conflicts of interest.

References

1. Zhao, Y., Chen, X., Xue, H., Weiss, G.M.: A machine learning approach to graduate admissions and the role of letters of recommendation. PLoS ONE **18**, e0291107 (2023). https://doi.org/10.1371/journal.pone.0291107
2. Adwan, E.J., Al-Aradi, Y., Essa, M., Malabari, H.: A comprehensive study and development of unified mobile-based admission system for GCC universities. J. Comput. Theor. Appl. **1**, 212–230 (2023). https://doi.org/10.62411/jcta.9793
3. Roulin, N., Koutsoumpis, A., Abdulrazaq, S., Oostrom, J.K., Xie, Y., MacIntosh, A.: Assessing biasing factors in asynchronous video interviews: applicant completion decisions, video background, and evaluation format. Eur. J. Work Organ. Psychol. **35**, 129–146 (2026). https://doi.org/10.1080/1359432X.2025.2517592
4. Laukaitis, A., et al.: FAIR-VID: a multimodal pre-processing pipeline for student application analysis. Appl. Sci. **15**, 13127 (2025). https://doi.org/10.3390/app152413127
5. Gkrimpizi, T., Peristeras, V., Magnisalis, I.: Classification of barriers to digital transformation in higher education institutions: systematic literature review. Educ. Sci. **13**, 746 (2023). https://doi.org/10.3390/EDUCSCI13070746
6. Zhang, T., Koutsoumpis, A., Oostrom, J.K., Holtrop, D., Ghassemi, S., De Vries, R.E.: Can large language models assess personality from asynchronous video interviews? A comprehensive evaluation of validity, reliability, fairness, and rating patterns. IEEE Trans. Affect. Comput. **15**, 1769–1785 (2024). https://doi.org/10.1109/TAFFC.2024.3374875
7. Lukacik, E.-R., Bourdage, J.S., Roulin, N.: Into the void: a conceptual model and research agenda for the design and use of asynchronous video interviews. Hum. Resour. Manag. Rev. **32**, 100789 (2022). https://doi.org/10.1016/j.hrmr.2020.100789
8. Akram, W., Abdullah, N.B., Sartaj, R.: Linguistic diversity in English varieties: examining sociolects, dialects, and registers across continents **3**, 1071–1087 (2025)
9. Oye, E.: Accent and dialect adaptation in ASR: training custom Vosk models to improve recognition for non-native English speakers (2025)
10. Amartyaveer et al.: Improving dialect identification in Indian languages using multimodal features from dialect informed ASR. In: ICASSP, IEEE International Conference on Acoustics, Speech and Signal Processing - Proceedings (2025). https://doi.org/10.1109/ICASSP49660.2025.10889099
11. Das, A., Kumar, K., Wu, J.: Multi-dialect speech recognition in English using attention on ensemble of experts. In: ICASSP, IEEE International Conference on Acoustics, Speech and Signal Processing - Proceedings 2021, pp. 6244–6248, June 2021. https://doi.org/10.1109/ICASSP39728.2021.9413952
12. Singh, V.P., Sahidullah, M., Kinnunen, T.H.: Causal analysis of ASR errors for children: quantifying the impact of physiological, cognitive, and extrinsic factors. Comput. Speech Lang. **95** (2026). https://doi.org/10.1016/j.csl.2025.101859
13. Adnan, R., Hassani, H.: Which one performs better? Wav2Vec or whisper? Applying Both in Badini Kurdish speech to text (BKSTT) (2025)
14. Ridoy, M.S.I., Akter, S., Rahman, Md.A.: Adaptability of ASR models on low-resource language: a comparative study of whisper and Wav2Vec-BERT on Bangla (2025)
15. Jain, R., Barcovschi, A., Yiwere, M.Y., Corcoran, P., Cucu, H.: Exploring native and non-native English child speech recognition with whisper. IEEE Access **12**, 41601–41610 (2024). https://doi.org/10.1109/ACCESS.2024.3378738
16. Graham, C., Roll, N.: Evaluating OpenAI's whisper ASR: performance analysis across diverse accents and speaker traits. JASA Express Lett. **4** (2024). https://doi.org/10.1121/10.0024876
17. McGuire, M., Larson-Hall, J.: Assessing whisper automatic speech recognition and WER scoring for elicited imitation: steps toward automation. Res. Methods Appl. Linguist. **4** (2025). https://doi.org/10.1016/J.RMAL.2025.100197

18. Liu, Y., Yang, X., Qu, D.: Exploration of whisper fine-tuning strategies for low-resource ASR. EURASIP J. Audio Speech Music Process **2024** (2024). https://doi.org/10.1186/S13636-024-00349-3
19. Asaad, I., Jacquelin, M., Perrotin, O., Girin, L., Hueber, T.: Is self-supervised learning enough to fill in the gap? A study on speech inpainting. Comput. Speech Lang. **99** (2026). https://doi.org/10.1016/J.CSL.2025.101922
20. Picinini Méxas, R., Chu, Y., Park, U.: Multilingual speech-to-vocal tract visualization using deep learning for pronunciation training. EURASIP J. Audio Speech Music Process. **2026** (2026). https://doi.org/10.1186/S13636-025-00438-X
21. Satla, S., Shieh, C.-S.: Multi-model Telugu speech recognition: improving ASR with dialect classification and optimization techniques. Traitement du Signal **42**, 3159–3169 (2025). https://doi.org/10.18280/TS.420611
22. Ryumina, E., Axyonov, A., Abdulkadirov, T., Koryakovskaya, D., Ryumin, D.: Cross-lingual bimodal emotion recognition with LLM-based label smoothing. Big Data Cogn. Comput. **9** (2025). https://doi.org/10.3390/BDCC9110285
23. Oh, J., Lee, J.: Multilingual mobility: audio-based language id for automotive systems. Appl. Sci. **15** (2025). https://doi.org/10.3390/APP15169209
24. Huo, R., Dunbar, E.: Iterative refinement, not training objective, makes HuBERT Behave differently from Wav2vec 2.0. https://doi.org/10.21437/Interspeech.2025-514
25. Rakhimova, D., Duisenbekkyzy, Z., Adali, E.: Investigation of ASR models for low-resource Kazakh child speech: corpus development, model adaptation, and evaluation. Appl. Sci. **15** (2025). https://doi.org/10.3390/app15168989
26. da Silva, G.C., et al.: Assessing reading fluency in elementary grades: a machine learning approach. Comput. Educ. Artif. Intell. **8** (2025). https://doi.org/10.1016/j.caeai.2025.100411
27. Yu, C., Su, X., Qian, Z.: Multi-stage audio-visual fusion for dysarthric speech recognition with pre-trained models. IEEE Trans. Neural Syst. Rehabil. Eng. **31**, 1912–1921 (2023). https://doi.org/10.1109/TNSRE.2023.3262001
28. Pande, A., Mishra, D.: Assessment of pepper robot's speech recognition system through the lens of machine learning. Biomimetics **9** (2024). https://doi.org/10.3390/biomimetics9070391
29. Hu, S., et al.: Self-supervised ASR models and features for dysarthric and elderly speech recognition. IEEE/ACM Trans. Audio Speech Lang. Process. **32**, 3561–3575 (2024). https://doi.org/10.1109/TASLP.2024.3422839
30. Dar, M.A., Pushparaj, J.: A Wav2Vec2 model-based automatic speech recognition system for low-resource Kashmiri language. Int. J. Speech Technol. **29** (2026). https://doi.org/10.1007/s10772-025-10228-7
31. Sinha, A., Kathania, H.K., Kadiri, S.R., Narayanan, S.: Can layer-wise SSL features improve zero-shot ASR performance for children's speech? IEEE Signal Process. Lett. **32**, 3759–3763 (2025). https://doi.org/10.1109/LSP.2025.3602636
32. Fadel, W., Bouchentouf, T., Buvet, P.A., Bourja, O.: Adapting off-the-shelf speech recognition systems for novel words. Information **14**, 179 (2023). https://doi.org/10.3390/INFO14030179
33. Alshboul, M., Al Muaitah, A.R., Al-Issa, S., Al-Ayyoub, M.: Enhanced neural speech recognition of Quranic recitations via a large audio model. Appl. Sci. **15**, 9521 (2025). https://doi.org/10.3390/APP15179521
34. Medeiros, E., Corado, L., Rato, L., Quaresma, P., Salgueiro, P.: Domain adaptation speech-to-text for low-resource European Portuguese using deep learning. Future Internet **15**, 159 (2023). https://doi.org/10.3390/FI15050159
35. Chauhan, M., Shiaeles, S.: An analysis of cloud security frameworks, problems and proposed solutions. Network **3**, 422–450 (2023). https://doi.org/10.3390/NETWORK3030018

36. Kumar, M., Chaturvedi, K.K., Farooqi, M.S., Lal, S.B., Ranjan, R.: An algorithm for automatic text annotation for named entity recognition using SpaCy framework (2023). https://doi.org/10.21203/rs.3.rs-2930333/v1
37. Vedadri, Y.B., et al.: Transformative NLP in healthcare through clinical text analysis with spacy. In: 3rd International Conference on Multifunctional Materials: ICMM2024 2025, vol. 3361, p. 050031 (2025). https://doi.org/10.1063/5.0298371/3371998
38. Johnson, A., Shetty, V.M., Ostendorf, M., Alwan, A.: Leveraging multiple sources in automatic African American English dialect detection for adults and children. In: ICASSP, IEEE International Conference on Acoustics, Speech and Signal Processing - Proceedings 2023, June 2023. https://doi.org/10.1109/ICASSP49357.2023.10096614
39. Radford, A., Kim, J.W., Xu, T., Brockman, G., McLeavey, C., Sutskever, I.: Robust speech recognition via large-scale weak supervision. Proc. Mach. Learn. Res. **202**, 28492–28518 (2022)

Benchmarking ASR Models in German Medical Contexts: A Performance Analysis Using Anamnesis Conversations

Thomas Schuster[1(✉)], Julius Trögele[2], Nico Döring[2], Robin Krüger[2], Mathieu Hoffmann[2], and Holger Friedrich[2]

[1] Hochschule Pforzheim, Tiefenbronner Street 65, 75175 Pforzheim, Germany
thomas.schuster@hs-pforzheim.de
[2] XPACE GmbH, Blücherstraße 32, 75181 Pforzheim, Germany
{julius.troegele,nico.doering,robin.krueger,mathieu.hoffmann,
holger.friedrich}@xpace.de

Abstract. Automatic Speech Recognition (ASR) holds significant potential for reducing the workload of medical staff, primarily by automating documentation tasks. While numerous benchmarks exist for the English language, specific evaluations for the German-speaking medical context – particularly those considering dialects and accents – are still lacking. In this paper, we present a dataset of simulated doctor-patient conversations and evaluate a total of 29 different ASR models. Our test set encompasses open-weight models from the Whisper, Voxtral, and Wav2Vec2 families, as well as commercial state-of-the-art APIs (AssemblyAI, Deepgram). For evaluation, we employ three distinct metrics (WER, CER, BLEU) and provide an outlook on qualitative semantic analysis. The results reveal significant performance discrepancies among the models: while top-tier systems achieve very low Word Error Rates (WER), other models exhibit considerably higher error rates, especially when processing medical terminology or dialect-heavy speech.

Keywords: Automatic Speech Recognition · German Medical Context · Benchmarking · Data Sovereignty · Open-Weight Models

1 Introduction

Administrative and organizational duties, particularly clinical documentation, consume a substantial portion of the working hours of nursing staff and physicians. Voice technologies offer a promising solution by automatically transcribing and structuring doctor-patient interactions, such as anamnesis interviews. However, the requirements for such systems within the German-speaking medical landscape are exceptionally high and can be categorized into three main areas:

– **Medical Terminology:** A complex amalgamation of Latin, Greek, and German technical terms.

K. Węcel and V. Řepa (Eds.): BIS 2026, LNBIP 584, pp. 277–288, 2026.
https://doi.org/10.1007/978-3-032-26363-6_21

- **Speaker Diarization:** The precise attribution of utterances to either the physician or the patient.
- **Accents and Dialects:** In practice, patients rarely speak standard German (Hochdeutsch), and medical staff also exhibit diverse linguistic backgrounds.

The objective of this pilot study is to quantitatively benchmark the performance of modern ASR systems and assess their operational readiness for daily clinical application.

2 Related Work

The application of Automatic Speech Recognition (ASR) in healthcare has been a subject of extensive research, predominantly focusing on the English language. Studies have demonstrated that specialized models can significantly reduce documentation time [7,10]. However, the transferability of these findings to the German healthcare system is limited due to linguistic characteristics (e.g., compound words, case sensitivity) and strict privacy regulations (GDPR) [11].

Existing German ASR benchmarks focus largely on read speech or general conversation [3,13]. Unlike existing corpora, which predominantly feature controlled acoustic environments, there is a notable gap in evaluations dealing with the specific challenges of spontaneous medical dialogue. This includes the complex code-switching between regional dialects (patient) and highly specialized medical terminology (doctor). This study addresses these research gaps by providing a targeted benchmark for this domain.

3 Case Selection Strategy and Data Corpus

To conduct this investigation, we curated a dataset, which depicts four representative scenarios of a medical admission examination. Unlike traditional benchmarks that often rely on short sentence snippets, this study adopts a high-density approach: we selected four complete interview scenarios ranging from approximately 6.5 to 13.5 min in length. Collectively, the dataset encompasses 35 min of continuous audio and a transcription baseline of 4,872 words. Crucially, the scenarios exhibit a rich distribution of medical terminology distinguishing this corpus from generic dialogue benchmarks. The data was sourced from publicly available dialogue recordings on YouTube and subsequently manually transcribed. This manual transcription serves as the "ground truth" for evaluating the automatic transcriptions generated by the speech models.

3.1 Scenarios

Our dataset comprises the following four cases, covering various medical specialties and acoustic challenges:

1. **Back Pain (Standard):** A classic anamnesis interview (suspected prolapse) with clear articulation. This scenario serves as a baseline for general recognition performance.[1]

[1] Source: https://www.youtube.com/watch?v=Vv_eHFeKkBw.

2. **Lower Abdominal Pain (Diverticulitis):** A case involving more specific internal medicine terminology, testing the models' vocabulary.[2]
3. **Foreign Doctor:** A scenario (suspected deep vein thrombosis) in which the treating physician has a non-native accent. This tests the models' robustness regarding the diversity frequently found among medical personnel.[3]
4. **Strong Accent (Patient):** A complex scenario (Fabry disease) where the patient has a strong regional dialect and indistinct pronunciation. This poses the highest demands on acoustic modeling.[4]

3.2 Ground Truth Creation

Transcripts were created for each scenario. Two types of transcript data were generated as ground truth:

- **Full Text:** The raw spoken text, normalized (numbers written out, punctuation smoothed).
- **Speaker Recognition:** A segmented JSON file with attribution, recording every speaker change (Speaker A vs. Speaker B) along with the text content, to measure the models' ability to distinguish speakers (Diarization performance).

4 Methodology and Evaluation Setup

This section outlines our systematic approach to evaluating the ASR systems. We first detail the criteria for model selection, followed by the technical pipeline for inference and the metrics used for quality assessment.

4.1 Model Selection and Categorization

The selection of evaluated ASR (Automatic Speech Recognition) systems is based on current state-of-the-art architectures and their relevance for practical deployment in German-speaking regions. To create a comprehensive performance matrix, the models were divided into two primary categories (see Table 1):

1. **Multilingual and Domain-Specific Models:** This group includes architectures explicitly trained or fine-tuned on German speech data. It encompasses popular *Whisper* variants [14] as well as specialized models like *Wav2Vec2 XLS-R* [2,4] or *WhisperX* [6].
2. **Monolingual English Reference Models:** English-only checkpoints were intentionally included in the evaluation. As expected, these lead to significant degradation in recognition rates for German input. However, their inclusion serves to establish a *performance baseline* and to analyze the zero-shot behavior of generic speech architectures given phonetically similar but lexically foreign inputs [5,8].

[2] Source: https://www.youtube.com/watch?v=9mGj_ASu328.
[3] Source: https://www.youtube.com/watch?v=u3vLSuzMDvg.
[4] Source: https://www.youtube.com/watch?v=6NwEyPAvGIA.

4.2 Evaluation Pipeline

To ensure objective comparability, a generic inference pipeline was implemented. This guarantees that all models are evaluated under identical conditions:

- **Preprocessing:** Resampling of audio signals to 16 kHz and volume normalization (peak normalization) to ensure consistent input variance across all test samples.
- **Inference:** Use of standardized decoding logic based on *Greedy Decoding*. This isolates the acoustic performance of the model from algorithmic optimizations provided by search methods like Beam Search.
- **Postprocessing:** Text normalization via *lowercasing* and stripping of punctuation. This ensures that the calculation of *Word Error Rate* (WER) and *Character Error Rate* (CER) reflects purely lexical recognition performance.

As will be shown in the results, the monolingual English models (Wav2Vec2 EN, Whisper .en) predictably failed to provide usable transcriptions of the German anamnesis conversations. They primarily served as a negative control. The multimodal SeamlessM4T model also showed weaknesses in specific medical terminology compared to specialized ASR systems.

4.3 Evaluation Metrics

To quantitatively determine transcription quality and the structural correctness of speaker attribution, three complementary metrics are defined. The calculation is primarily based on the word or character level in comparison to a manually verified Ground Truth reference.

1. **Word Error Rate (WER):** Used as the primary measure of recognition performance, the WER defines the ratio of necessary edit operations (substitutions, deletions, insertions) to the total number of words in the reference. The calculation follows the Levenshtein distance: $WER = (S + D + I)/N$.
2. **Character Error Rate (CER):** Due to the morphological complexity of German (especially compound words), CER is used for fine-grained analysis. It is less sensitive to minor word formation variants and allows for a more precise assessment of phonetic recognition performance.
3. **Speaker-Attributed WER (SA-WER):** To evaluate the coupling of ASR and Diarization, SA-WER is employed. A word is only considered correctly recognized if both the lexical content and the assigned speaker label (Speaker ID) match the reference.
4. **BLEU Score:** As an additional metric, the BLEU Score is calculated to assess the semantic and syntactic integrity of the transcriptions. This metric evaluates the overlap of n-grams between the generated transcript and the reference, providing insight into the preservation of meaning beyond mere word accuracy.

Table 1. Overview of Evaluated ASR Models

Model	Checkpoint/Version	Type	Implementation	License
Multilingual & German Models				
Whisper (tiny)	openai/whisper-tiny	Local	Hugging Face	MIT
Whisper (base)	openai/whisper-base	Local	Hugging Face	MIT
Whisper (small)	openai/whisper-small	Local	Hugging Face	MIT
Whisper (medium)	openai/whisper-medium	Local	Hugging Face	MIT
Whisper (large)	openai/whisper-large	Local	Hugging Face	MIT
Whisper (v2)	openai/whisper-large-v3	Local	Hugging Face	MIT
Whisper (v3)	openai/whisper-large-v3	Local	Hugging Face	MIT
Faster-Whisper	large-v3 (CTranslate2)	Local	faster-whisper	MIT
WhisperX	whisperx-base	Local	whisperx	BSD-2
SeamlessM4T v2	facebook/seamless-m4t-v2-large	Local	Hugging Face	CC-BY-NC 4.0
Wav2Vec2 XLS-R (DE)	facebook/wav2vec2-large-xlsr-53-german	Local	Hugging Face	Apache 2.0
Wav2Vec2 XLS-R (DE)	maxidl/wav2vec2-large-xlsr-german	Local	Hugging Face	Apache 2.0
Wav2Vec2 XLS-R (DE)	jonatasgrosman/wav2vec2-xlsr-53-de	Local	Hugging Face	Apache 2.0
Voxtral (Mini)	voxtral-small-latest	API*	Mistral SDK	Apache 2.0
Voxtral (Small)	voxtral-mini-latest	API*	Mistral SDK	Apache 2.0
AssemblyAI	Universal-1	API	SDK	Proprietary
AssemblyAI (v2)	Universal-2	API	SDK	Proprietary
AssemblyAI (nano)	Universal-nano	API	SDK	Proprietary
Deepgram	Nova-2	API	SDK	Proprietary
English Models (Reference)				
Whisper (tiny)	openai/whisper-tiny.en	Local	Hugging Face	MIT
Whisper (base)	openai/whisper-base.en	Local	Hugging Face	MIT
Whisper (small)	openai/whisper-small.en	Local	Hugging Face	MIT
Whisper (medium)	openai/whisper-medium.en	Local	Hugging Face	MIT
Distil-Whisper (small)	distil-whisper/distil-small.en	Local	Hugging Face	MIT
Distil-Whisper (medium)	distil-whisper/distil-medium.en	Local	Hugging Face	MIT
Distil-Whisper (v2)	distil-large-v2	Local	Hugging Face	MIT
Distil-Whisper (v3)	distil-large-v3	Local	Hugging Face	MIT
Wav2Vec2 (base)	facebook/wav2vec2-base-960h	Local	Hugging Face	Apache 2.0
Wav2Vec2 (large)	facebook/wav2vec2-large-960h	Local	Hugging Face	Apache 2.0
Wav2Vec2 (large, libri)	facebook/wav2vec2-large-robust-ft-libri-960h	Local	Hugging Face	Apache 2.0
Wav2Vec2 (large,lv60)	facebook/wav2vec2-large-960h-lv60-self	Local	Hugging Face	Apache 2.0

*The Voxtral model from Mistral AI was tested via the API, but is also available for local operation (open weights) under the Apache 2.0 License.

5 Results

In the following sections, we present the quantitative and qualitative results of our study. We first analyze the raw transcription performance using Word Error Rate (WER) and Character Error Rate (CER), then examine the quality of speaker separation, and finally discuss the stability of the models across different acoustic scenarios.

5.1 Transcription Analysis Results

The evaluation shows a clear correlation between model architecture (parameter count, training data diversity) and the resulting Word Error Rate. Table 2 summarizes the aggregated results of the leading models.

- **High-Performance API Solutions:** The *AssemblyAI Universal* model demonstrates the lowest error rate in the test field with a WER of $\sim 3\,\%$. The low variance across all datasets indicates high robustness of the underlying *Conformer* architecture.
- **Efficiency Analysis (Mistral Voxtral):** The *Voxtral* series models show competitive performance. In particular, *Voxtral Small* achieves a WER of 7.1 %, signaling high efficiency per parameter relative to model size.
- **Open-Source Benchmarks:** *OpenAI Whisper Large-v3* achieves a WER of 12.6 %. Qualitatively, there is a tendency for errors in acoustically weak segments, underscoring the necessity for post-processing steps.
- **Degradation in Legacy Models:** Older architectures (e.g., *Wav2Vec2*) and compact Whisper variants show error rates of $> 20\,\%$, which can likely be classified as insufficient for automated medical documentation.

Table 2. Selective Comparison of ASR Performance

Model	WER (∅)	CER (∅)	BLEU
AssemblyAI Universal	0.0299	0.0194	0.942
Voxtral Small Latest	0.0711	0.0355	0.866
Voxtral Mini Latest	0.0846	0.0389	0.842
Whisper Large-v3 (Distilled)	0.1258	0.0809	0.817
Deepgram Nova-2	0.1433	0.0742	0.756
WhisperX-Base	0.2151	0.1033	0.663

5.2 Detailed Results and Model Comparison

The comparison of average Word Error Rates (WER) and Character Error Rates (CER) across the entire test corpus (see Fig. 1) reveals a clear stratification of the test field. While current SOTA (State-of-the-Art) models achieve error rates in the low single-digit percentage range, smaller and older open-source derivatives, in particular, show a significant gap to the required transcription quality.

Context-Dependent Robustness: Fig. 2 identifies acoustically challenging environments and domain-specific terminology as primary error drivers. While *AssemblyAI Universal* and *Mistral's Voxtral* remain highly robust, *Whisper Large-v3* degrades significantly with complex accents. Notably, severe hallucinations in older architectures and English-only baselines drive their WERs beyond 100 %, as insertions (I) surpass the ground truth word count (N) in the formula $WER = (S + D + I)/N$.

Statistical Stability and Reliability: Predictability of performance is essential for productive use in medical environments. The stability analysis reveals that models with high average WER also exhibit high variance and numerous outliers. As illustrated in the box-whisker plots in Fig. 3, models with larger interquartile ranges and long whiskers struggle with consistent acoustic modeling, being highly sensitive to speaker changes or noise. The top seven models demonstrate high precision and statistical stability, crucial for minimizing unpredictable hallucinations in medical documentation.

Semantic and Linguistic Integrity: The comparison of the top 7 models in Fig. 4 integrates the *BLEU Score* (Bilingual Evaluation Understudy) alongside WER and CER. A strong positive correlation is observed between low error rates and high BLEU values (best value > 0.94). This indicates that transcripts primarily from the leading models are not only lexically correct but also preserve the original semantic structure and syntax of the speakers almost without loss. This linguistic precision is a prerequisite for downstream automated analysis by LLM-based assistance systems.

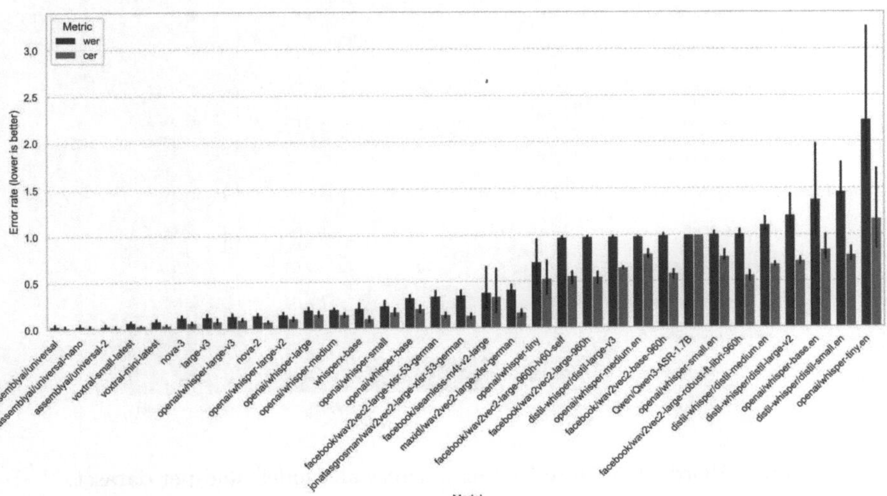

Fig. 1. Average WER and CER per Model (Full Text Evaluation).

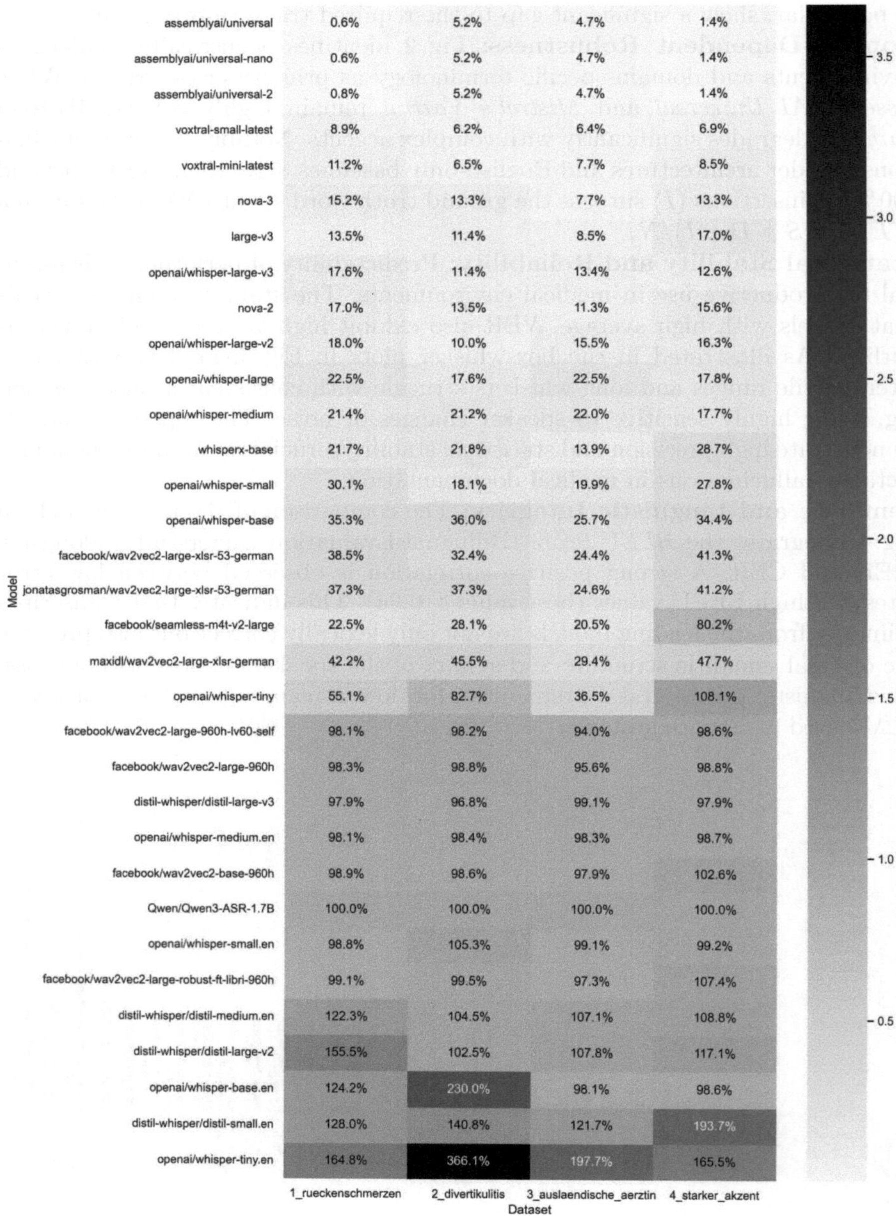

Fig. 2. Word Error Rate Heatmap across all models and per dataset.

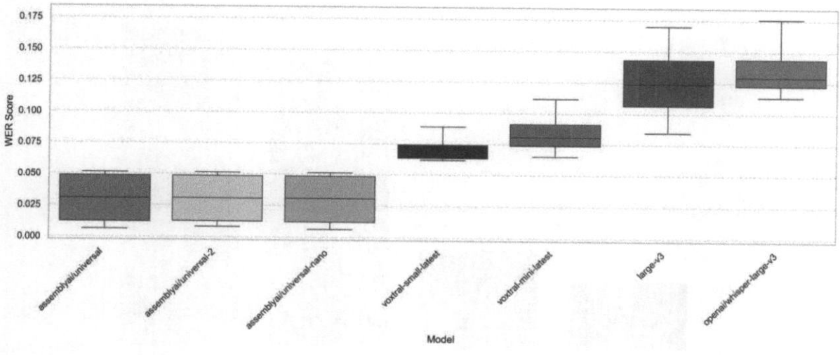

Fig. 3. Distribution of WER for the Top 7 Models (Stability Analysis).

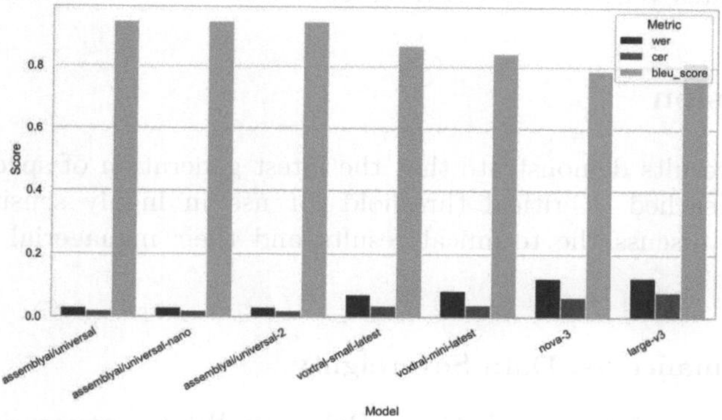

Fig. 4. Comparison of Top 7 Models by WER: WER, CER, and BLEU Score.

5.3 Speaker Recognition (Diarization)

The ability to distinguish between doctor and patient was evaluated separately.

- **Deepgram Nova-2:** Showed solid performance in speaker separation [9], but suffered from a somewhat higher base WER.
- **AssemblyAI:** Was able to score well in the attributed evaluation due to very high transcription accuracy, as fewer words were incorrectly assigned.
- **Open Source:** Many Open-Source wrappers (e.g., standard HuggingFace pipelines) do not offer integrated diarization, complicating deployment. Additional modules like Pyannote.audio [1,12] are necessary here.

Figure 5 shows that only commercial models provide attributed transcripts directly without extension. In our measurements, *Universal-2* from AssemblyAI demonstrated the most consistent results regarding speaker attribution.

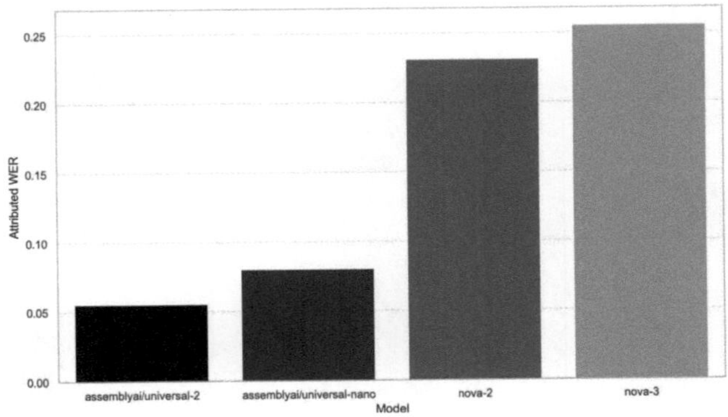

Fig. 5. Attributed WER (Speaker Attribution) for Models with Diarization Support.

6 Discussion

The present results demonstrate that the latest generation of specialized ASR models has reached a critical threshold for use in highly sensitive medical domains. We discuss the technical results and their managerial implications below.

6.1 Performance vs. Data Sovereignty

- **Model Sovereignty and Data Privacy:** While commercial APIs like *AssemblyAI* lead the quantitative benchmark, *Mistral Voxtral* (open-weights) in particular demonstrates that self-hosted solutions offer nearly equivalent performance. For deployment within the framework of GDPR-compliant processing, this represents a decisive advantage, as data sovereignty is maintained without accepting significant losses in transcription quality.
- **Semantic Fidelity:** Initial exploratory studies using an *LLM-as-a-Judge* evaluation show promising ratings for the top models, despite the metric's tendency to penalize structural rather than content-related divergences. These findings suggest high information preservation but require further validation through human evaluation.
- **Robustness to Technical Jargon:** The correlation between low WER values and high semantic ratings in *AssemblyAI* and *Voxtral* suggests that the models possess significant implicit knowledge of medical contexts.

6.2 Managerial Implications

For healthcare decision-makers, this study delineates a critical strategic trade-off between operational efficiency and institutional data governance. While proprietary Cloud APIs represent the current performance frontier ($\sim 3\%$ WER) and, they necessitate a reliance on external infrastructure, potentially complicating compliance with stringent data sovereignty mandates. Our findings demonstrate that high-performing open-weight models have reached a functional maturity ($\sim$ 7% WER) without compromising the integrity of clinical documentation. This positions them as a viable on-premise alternative.

From a process perspective, the marginal increase in error rates is mitigated by a human-in-the-loop (HITL) configuration. In this sociotechnical arrangement, the model serves as an automated drafting tool, while the physician maintains final accountability through expert verification. Consequently, the adoption of open-source architectures allows hospitals to internalize processing capabilities and minimize privacy-related externalities without compromising the overall utility of the clinical documentation workflow.

6.3 Limitations

A limitation of this pilot study is the number of distinct scenarios ($N = 4$). However, we argue that for an initial technology assessment, the depth of continuous dialogue (totaling roughly 35 min and nearly 5,000 words) outweighs purely quantitative sample sizes of short audio clips. The selected scenarios serve as "baseline acoustic archetypes" covering the most critical challenges (accent, dialect, terminology) found in German hospitals. Future large-scale studies should validate these findings across multi-center datasets.

7 Conclusion and Outlook

The evaluation confirms that automated assessment and logging are already feasible with current ASR models. *AssemblyAI Universal* (Cloud API) and *Mistral Voxtral* (open-weights) currently define the technological cutting edge. Due to data security requirements in the medical environment and already excellent out-of-the-box performance, *Voxtral* promises to be a very good basis for implementing concrete systems.

To overcome the limitations of a pilot study and strengthen generalizability, future iterations will expand the dataset to include further medical disciplines, diverse ambient noise conditions (e.g., emergency room environments), and additional regional dialects. Parallel to this, we will further deepen the semantic analysis level. Three focal points are planned:

1. **Hybrid Evaluation:** The combination of automated assessment methods (*LLM-as-a-Judge*) and systematic human evaluation to validate clinical relevance. The goal is to quantify the discrepancy between purely statistical error rates (WER) and actual information loss.
2. **Domain-Specific Error Metrics:** Usage of a *Keyword-specific Word Error Rate* (kWER) that explicitly relates the recognition rate to specialized medical vocabulary. Parallel to this, a *Human-centered Word Error Rate* (hWER) is intended to evaluate readability and post-processing effort for medical staff.

3. **Semantic Extraction:** The further development of agent systems that extract structured data formats (e.g., according to the FHIR standard) directly from stable transcripts to ensure interoperability with existing hospital systems.

References

1. Pyannote/pyannote-audio. https://github.com/pyannote/pyannote-audio, Accessed 12 Jan 2026
2. AI, M.: XLS-R: self-supervised speech processing for 128 languages. https://ai.meta.com/blog/xls-r-self-supervised-speech-processing-for-128-languages/, Accessed 12 Jan 2026
3. Ardila, R., e5t al.: Common voice: a massively-multilingual speech corpus. In: Calzolari, N., et al. (eds.) Proceedings of the Twelfth Language Resources and Evaluation Conference, pp. 4218–4222. European Language Resources Association. https://aclanthology.org/2020.lrec-1.520/
4. Babu, A., et al.: XLS-R: self-supervised cross-lingual speech representation learning at scale. In: Interspeech 2022, pp. 2278–2282 (2022). https://doi.org/10.21437/Interspeech.2022-143
5. Baevski, A., Zhou, Y., Mohamed, A., Auli, M.: wav2vec 2.0: a framework for self-supervised learning of speech representations. NeurIPS (2020)
6. Bain, M., Huh, J., Han, T., Zisserman, A.: Whisperx: time-accurate speech transcription of long-form audio. In: INTERSPEECH 2023 (2023)
7. Blackley, S.V., Schubert, V.D., Goss, F.R., Al Assad, W., Garabedian, P.M., Zhou, L.: Physician use of speech recognition versus typing in clinical documentation: a controlled observational study, vol. 141, 104178. https://doi.org/10.1016/j.ijmedinf.2020.104178
8. Conneau, A., Baevski, A., Collobert, R., Mohamed, A., Auli, M.: Unsupervised cross-lingual representation learning for speech recognition. In: Interspeech 2021, pp. 2426–2430 (2021). https://doi.org/10.21437/Interspeech.2021-329
9. Deepgram: Deepgram nova-2: The fastest and most accurate speech-to-text api (2024). https://deepgram.com/product/nova-2 Accessed 12 Jan 2026
10. Latif, S., Qadir, J., Qayyum, A., Usama, M., Younis, S.: Speech Technology for Healthcare: Opportunities, Challenges, and State of the Art, vol. 14, pp. 342–355 https://doi.org/10.1109/RBME.2020.3006860, https://ieeexplore.ieee.org/document/9133298
11. Nautsch, A., Jasserand, C., Kindt, E., Todisco, M., Trancoso, I., Evans, N.: The GDPR & Speech Data: Reflections of Legal and Technology Communities, First Steps Towards a Common Understanding, pp. 3695–369. https://doi.org/10.21437/Interspeech.2019-2647, https://www.isca-archive.org/interspeech_2019/nautsch19c_interspeech.html
12. Plaquet, A., Bredin, H.: Powerset multi-class cross entropy loss for neural speaker diarization. In: Proc. INTERSPEECH 2023 (2023)
13. Pratap, V., Xu, Q., Sriram, A., Synnaeve, G., Collobert, R.: MLS: A Large-Scale Multilingual Dataset for Speech Research, pp. 2757–2761.https://doi.org/10.21437/Interspeech.2020-2826, https://www.isca-archive.org/interspeech_2020/pratap20_interspeech.html
14. Radford, A., Kim, J.W., Xu, T., Brockman, G., McLeavey, C., Sutskever, I.: Robust speech recognition via large-scale weak supervision (2022)

Innovations in Machine Learning

Reliability Modelling of Economic Systems Using Decision Trees and Multi-valued Decision Diagrams

Elena Zaitseva[1(✉)], Vitaly Levashenko[1], and Egor Levashenko[2]

[1] Faculty of Management Science and Informatics, University of Zilina, Univerzitna 8215/1, 01026 Zilina, Slovakia
{elena.zaitseva,vitaly.levashenko}@fri.uniza.sk

[2] Prague University of Economics and Business, Nám. Winstona Churchilla 1938/4, 120 00 Prague 3-Žižkov, Czech Republic

Abstract. Contemporary economic systems, including global supply chains and corporate financial structures, are characterised by substantial uncertainty that complicates reliability modelling. Data on component reliability, interdependencies, and failure modes are often incomplete, vague, or derived from expert judgment, which challenges traditional probabilistic risk models. This paper introduces a novel methodology for data-driven construction of mathematical models of complex systems. We frame the problem as one of classifying a system's overall state (e.g., "Stable," "Vulnerable," "Distressed") based on the uncertain states of its constituent economic components. The core innovation lies in employing a decision-tree-based classifier capable of handling uncertain and categorical data, and algorithmically transforming it into a Multi-Valued Decision Diagram (MDD). The method remains compatible with fuzzy extensions, but the present implementation uses a crisp decision tree. The MDD serves as a formal, analyzable Multi-State System (MSS) model. The efficacy of the method is demonstrated through a case study on modelling the operational resilience of a multimodal logistics network, showcasing its utility for proactive economic risk management and decision support under uncertainty.

Keywords: Economic System · Reliability · Multi-Valued Decision Diagram (MDD) · Decision Tree · Importance Analysis · Business Process Resilience

1 Introduction

The stability and resilience of socio-economic systems are paramount concerns in an interconnected global landscape. Decision-makers in finance, logistics, and enterprise risk management require robust tools to model, analyse, and mitigate the risk of failures. Traditional reliability engineering techniques, such as Fault Tree Analysis (FTA) and Markov models, while powerful, are predicated on the availability of precise, statistically significant failure data—a condition rarely met in economic contexts [1, 2]. Data about economic systems is often uncertain and incompletely specified, due to knowledge gaps, subjective expert estimates, ambiguous performance thresholds, and inherently incomplete information about component interactions [3].

K. Węcel and V. Řepa (Eds.): BIS 2026, LNBIP 584, pp. 291–305, 2026.
https://doi.org/10.1007/978-3-032-26363-6_22

This epistemic gap necessitates a paradigm shift from purely probabilistic models to methodologies that can seamlessly integrate and reason with qualitative and incomplete data. Multi-State System (MSS) theory provides a suitable framework, as it allows components and the system itself to reside in multiple performance levels beyond simple binary "working/failed" states [4]. This aligns naturally with economic concepts such as "partial capacity," "degraded service," and "different credit rating tiers." The challenge, however, lies in constructing the MSS when the underlying data is not specified, since this model can be constructed from completely specified data.

Machine learning, specifically classification algorithms, offers a promising solution [1, 5–8]. Determining a system's state from its components' states is inherently a classification problem. Recent studies have begun exploring this link [5–8], but often remain confined to binary states [5] or rely on truth tables [6], which become computationally intractable for larger systems. In study [7], the use of a Multi-Valued Decision Diagram (MDD) has been explored for representing MSS based on uncertain data. However, this approach is oriented toward representing initial data using fuzzy values, which complicates the construction of the mathematical model. At the same time, the use of MDD for MSS representation is effective because it is a paradigm for representing and processing high-dimensional data [9]. In this paper, an integrated, end-to-end method for constructing MDD-based MSS as a mathematical model based on uncertain categorical data, along with its reliability analysis, is proposed. This method is considered for application in the economic domain. The advantages of this method are:

- Formalisation of the MSS model construction for economic systems as a classification task.
- Employment of a decision tree as the classifier, chosen for its transparency, ability to handle linguistic variables, and structural similarity to decision diagrams.
- Simply converting the induced decision tree into a canonical MDD is a compact, computationally efficient representation ideal for reliability analysis.
- Using well-known MDD-based algorithms to compute key reliability metrics: state probabilities, availability, and crucially, component Importance Measures for criticality analysis

In comparison with previously known methods for constructing a mathematical model of a system for reliability analysis based on incompletely defined data, this method allows for a significant reduction in the computational complexity of constructing such a model by eliminating the direct transition from the classification model of the system to the model used for reliability analysis (Fig. 1). The case study demonstrates that the proposed method identifies the most critical components of the logistics network and provides reliable estimates of system-level performance.

The remainder of the paper is structured as follows. Section 2 reviews the background on Multi-State Systems and Multi-Valued Decision Diagrams. Section 3 presents the proposed methodology. Section 4 describes the case study of a multimodal logistics network. Section 5 discusses implications and limitations. Section 6 concludes the paper.

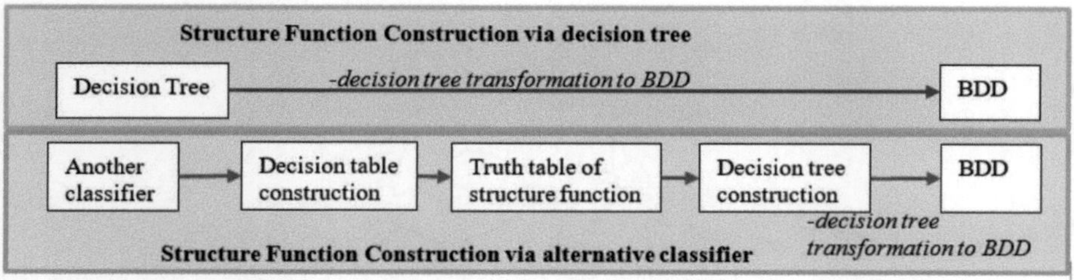

Fig. 1. The comparison of the proposed method and the method for a system reliability analysis based on another classifier

2 Background: MSS, MDDs, Reliability Measures and Classification

2.1 Multi-state Systems

An MSS is a mathematical model in reliability engineering that allows investigation of the subject from a perspective with several (not just one) working performance levels. For example, a system can be considered to have three performance levels: one represents failure, and the other two represent normal and stressed operation of a system. Different mathematical representations can be used for an MSS. One of them is a structure function, which unambiguously defines the correlation between the states of system components and system performance levels. The structure function of the MSS of n components is:

$$\phi(\boldsymbol{x}) : \{0,1, ..., m_1 - 1\} \times \cdots \times \{0,1, ..., m_n - 1\} \to \{0,1, ..., M - 1\} \quad (1)$$

where $\boldsymbol{x} = (x_1, x_2, ..., x_n)$ is the state vector of n components. Each component x_i can be in one of m_i states, e.g., $x_i \in \{0(\text{Failed}), 1(\text{Stressed}), 2(\text{Normal})\}$. The system output $\phi(\boldsymbol{x})$ takes values in M ordered levels, such as $\{0(\text{Collapse}), 1(\text{Distressed}), 2(\text{Stable}), 3(\text{Robust})\}$. This formalism perfectly captures graded economic conditions.

For example, in the study [10], a simple service system (Fig. 2) in a specific region was considered. This system has three components ($n = 3$) that are two service points and infrastructure. The service points 1 and 2 are interpreted as component 1 (x_1) and component 2 (x_2) of the system. The infrastructure is considered as component 3 (x_3) of this system. The service points can be operated or not, therefore $m_1 = m_2 = 2.$. The infrastructure can be modelled by 3 states ($m_3 = 3$): from failure when $x_3 = 0$ to a perfect state ($x_3 = 2$). According to [10], this system has three performance levels: non-operational (no customers are satisfied), partially operational (some customers are satisfied), and fully operational (all customers are satisfied). These performance levels of the system correspond to values 0, 1, and 2 of the structure function (1), respectively. The structure function of this system is defined in Table 1.

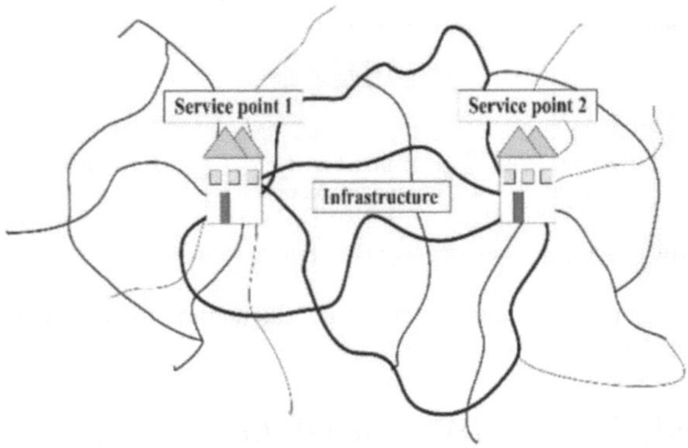

Fig. 2. A simple service system from [10] as an illustrative example of MSS

Table 1. The structure function of the simple service system.

Components states		x_3
x_1	x_2	0 1 2
0	0	0 0 0
0	1	0 1 1
1	0	0 1 1
1	1	0 2 2

Each system component should be associated with the probabilities of its states $p_{i,s}$:

$$p_{i,s} = Pr\{x_i = s_i\} \tag{2}$$

where $i = \{1, \ldots, n\}$ and $s_i \in \{0, \ldots, m_i - 1\}$.

For example, the probabilities of the service system (Fig. 2) are in Table 2.

Table 2. The probabilities of components of the simple service system

	Components and their states		
	x_1	x_2	x_3
	0 1	0 1	0 1 2
$p_{i,s}$	0.3 0.7	0.2 0.8	0.2 0.6 0.2

2.2 Multi-valued Decision Diagrams as Computational Models

An MDD is a directed acyclic graph providing a canonical and memory-efficient representation of the structure function $\phi(\boldsymbol{x})$ [9]. Non-terminal nodes represent component variables, edges represent component states (with associated probabilities $p_{i,s}$), and terminal nodes represent system states. MDDs enable efficient algorithms for calculating system reliability metrics [9, 11]. MDD construction for reliability analysis is well-studied and has been considered in many papers, particularly [9, 11, 12]. Using MDD as a computational model allows for:

- obtaining a compact and canonical representation of the structural function, avoiding exponential growth of truth tables or state lists;
- performing efficient and fast calculations of a range of reliability metrics (e.g., calculating the probability of system failure, finding minimum cuts);
- producing accurate results for system reliability metrics, unlike simulation-based methods;
- reflecting logical dependencies between components, enabling correct and simple analysis of the system topology without special processing of complex dependencies at the computational stage;

For example, the MDD for the simple service system in Fig. 2 is shown in Fig. 3. MDD is a tree-based structure that can be constructed from a decision tree by simple modification [7, 9].

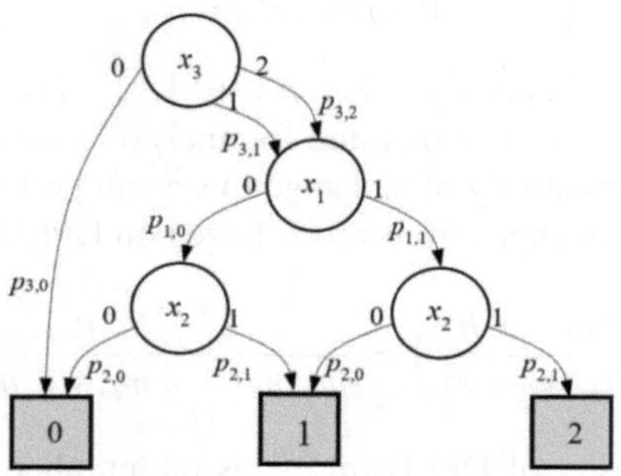

Fig. 3. MDD of the structure function of a simple service system

2.3 MDD-Based Analysis of MSS

The representation of MSS by the MDD enables calculations of various indices, measures, and metrics to evaluate system reliability. One of the basic metrics is the probability of an MSS performance level j ($j = 0, 1, \ldots, M$-1) [4]:

$$P_j = \Pr\{\phi(\boldsymbol{x}) = j\}. \tag{3}$$

Based on the probabilities of an MSS performance level (3) can be computed the availability and unavailability of MSS for performance level j ($j = 1, \ldots, M$-1) [4]:

$$A^{\geq j} = \sum\nolimits_{s=j}^{M-1} P_s, \tag{4}$$

$$U^{\geq j} = \sum_{s=0}^{j-1} P_s. \tag{5}$$

The calculation of the probability of an MSS performance level *j* based on the MDD is implemented by the sum of probabilities of all paths from the root node to the terminal node *j*. The probability of each path is calculated as the product of the probabilities of the component states $p_{i,s}$ involved in the path. A more detailed description of the probability calculation for an MSS performance level *j* can be found in [12].

For example, the performance levels probabilities of the simple service system based on its MDD (Fig. 3) are computed as: $P_0 = p_{3,0} + (p_{3,1} + p_{3,2}) \cdot p_{1,0} \cdot p_{2,0}$, $P_1 = (p_{3,1} + p_{3,2}) \cdot (p_{1,0} \cdot p_{2,1} + p_{1,1} \cdot p_{2,0})$, $P_2 = (p_{3,1} + p_{3,2}) \cdot p_{1,1} \cdot p_{2,1}$. For component probabilities in Table 2, for the simple service system $P_0 = 0.248$, $P_1 = 0.304$ and $P_2 = 0.448$.

Other metrics of reliability analysis for MSS are *Importance Measures* (IMs), which allow for quantifying the contribution of each system component to failure or operation. One possible method for calculating IMs based on MDD has been elaborated using *Direct Partial Logical Derivative* (DPLD). DPLD $\partial\phi(j \to h)/\partial x_i(s \to r)$ of the structure function $\phi(\boldsymbol{x})$ with respect to variable *i* allows indicating state vectors of the structure function for which the change of the variable x_i from the value *s* to the value *r* causes the change of the structure function value from *j* to *h*:

$$\partial\phi(j \to h)/\partial x_i(s \to r) = \begin{cases} 1, \, if\, \phi(s_i, \boldsymbol{x}) = j and \phi(r_i, \boldsymbol{x}) = h \\ 0, \, in\ the\ other\ case \end{cases}, \tag{6}$$

where $s, r \in \{0,1, \ldots, m_i - 1\}$ and $s \neq r$; $j, h \in \{0,1, \ldots, M_i - 1\}$ and $j \neq h$.

Structural Importance (SI) is a measure for analysing the topological properties of MSS, representing the probability of a change in system performance level from j to h when the i-th component changes from *s* to *r*. Based on DPLD (6) SI is defined as [7]:

$$SI_{i,s\to r}^{j\to h} = TD\left(\frac{\partial\phi(j \to h)}{\partial x_i(s \to r)}\right) = \frac{p_{i,s\to r}^{j\to h}}{m_1 \times \cdots \times m_{i-1} \times m_{i+1} \times \cdots \times m_n} \tag{7}$$

where TD(.) is truth density of DPLD; $p_{i,s\to r}^{j\to h}$ is the number of system states when a change of the *i*-th component state from *s* to *r* according to DPLD causes a change in the performance level of the system from *j* to *h*.

DPLD (7) based on MDD is computed based on the comparison of two sub-diagrams: from the root node to the terminal node *j*, with the condition of $x_i = s$ and from rote node to the terminal node *h* with the condition of $x_i = r$. The intersection of these sub-diagrams is the diagram of DPLD.

For example, in Fig. 4, the calculation of $\partial\phi(1 \to 0)/\partial x_1(1 \to 0)$ is shown. The result sub-diagram enables the determination of non-zero values of the derivatives, and the considered derivative has non-zero values for the state vectors (1 → 0 0 1) and (1 → 0 0 2). These state vectors indicate the critical states of a simple service system (Fig. 2): the failure of the first service point results in the system's non-operational state, provided that the second service point has failed and the infrastructure is either partially or fully operational.

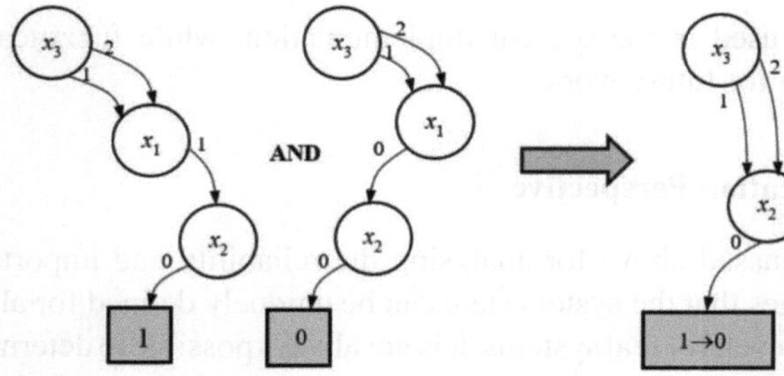

Fig. 4. DPLD $\partial\phi(1 \to 0)/\partial x_1(1 \to 0)$ calculation based on MDD

Birnbaum Importance (BI) is the probability of system performance level j if the system performance level changes from j to h depending on the change of the i-th component state from s to r and this measure is computed as [7]:

$$BI_{i,s\to r}^{j\to h} = \Pr\{\partial\phi(j \to h)/\partial x_i(s \to r) \neq 0\} \tag{8}$$

For example, SI and BI for all failures and degradation of the simple service system, depending on service points failure or infrastructure failure and degradation, are shown in Table 3. The degradation of the system's infrastructure has no impact on its operation. At the same time, the failure of the infrastructure leads to the system failing. Considering the topological properties of the system, it is more likely for the system to fail in a partial operational state ($SI_{3,1\to 0}^{1\to 0} = SI_{3,2\to 0}^{1\to 0} = 0.50$). But the probabilistic characteristics of the system ($BI_{3,s\to 0}^{j\to 0}$) show the large impact of the infrastructure failure on the breakdown of the system from a state of perfect functioning ($BI_{3,1\to 0}^{2\to 0} = BI_{3,2\to 0}^{2\to 0} = 0.56$). The failure of service points, based on the topological properties of the system, has a similar impact on the degradation or fault of this service system in a partly operational state. According to BI, this impact is more likely for the system degradation ($BI_{1,1\to 0}^{2\to 1} = 0.64$ and $BI_{2,1\to 0}^{2\to 1} = 0.56$) (Table 3).

Table 3. For the simple service system (Fig. 2, Table 1).

		Structural Importance					Birnbaum Importance				
		Components state changes					Components state changes				
		x_1	x_2	x_3			x_1	x_2	x_3		
		$1\to 0$	$1\to 0$	$2\to 1$	$2\to 0$	$1\to 0$	$1\to 0$	$1\to 0$	$2\to 1$	$2\to 0$	$1\to 0$
System performance level changes	$2\to 1$	0.33	0.33	0	0	0	0.64	0.56	0	0	0
	$2\to 0$	0	0	0	0.25	0.25	0	0	0	0.56	0.56
	$1\to 0$	0.33	0.33	0	0.50	0.50	0.16	0.24	0	0.38	0.38

The analysis of SI and BI enables us to consider the influence of a system's components on its operation or failure, as well as scenarios of the system's behaviour.

Although fuzzy decision trees may be used in cases of linguistic or interval uncertainty, the case study in this paper relies on crisp categorical data. Therefore, a standard decision tree was used in the present implementation, while fuzzification remains a potential extension for future work.

2.4 The Classification Perspective

The approach discussed above for analysing the reliability and importance of system components assumes that the system state can be uniquely defined for all possible component states. However, for real systems, it is not always possible to determine all possible correspondences between component states and system performance levels. Such data are incompletely specified, and a structure function cannot be constructed.

As was shown in the study [6], constructing $\phi(\boldsymbol{x})$ from incompletely specified data can be implemented as learning a classifier. This is possible because the structural function can be interpreted as a classifier that divides the states of the system components (input attributes) into M classes, which are labelled from 0 to M-1 (where M corresponds to the number of performance levels of the system). The training dataset comprises historical or simulated observations, where each sample is a pair ($\boldsymbol{x}$, $\phi(\boldsymbol{x})$). The features are the component states, and the label represents the system's performance levels. To achieve maximum consistency with the MDD representation of the MSS, it makes sense to use a decision tree as a classifier. Thus, the induced decision tree can be easily transformed into an MDD, a tree-based structure. The constructed MDD can be used for the reliability analysis considered above.

3 Proposed Methodology for Data-Driven MSS Analysis

The proposed method for the reliability analysis of MSS based on incompletely specified data includes two phases. The first of them is the MDD of the MSS construction. The MDD construction based on incompletely specified data requires two procedures: classifier induction using a decision tree and transformation of the decision tree into an MDD. The second is reliability analysis (the calculation of reliability indices, metrics, and measures). The observations for this method should be presented as categorical data.
Phase 1: MDD construction consists of two procedures: decision tree induction and its transformation into MDD:

- For the subsequent construction of MDD, the most suitable are ordered decision trees, in which the same attribute is present at each level. The algorithm recursively selects the component x_i that provides the greatest information gain regarding the system state $\phi(\boldsymbol{x})$. Splitting continues until a stopping criterion is met. Each leaf node L contains an instance that agrees with the system's performance level. A decision tree can be induced using algorithms such as C4.5, CART, or their variants. In the case study, a C4.5-type algorithm was used due to its suitability for categorical attributes and its tendency to produce compact, interpretable trees.
- There is a possibility to induct a decision tree with predefined properties, for example, an ordered decision tree that has equal attributes at each level [6].
- The decision tree is converted into an MDD using a three-step transformation [9]:

- *Merge Equivalent Leaves:* All leaves labelled with the same system state j are merged into a single terminal node j.
- *Merge Isomorphic Subtrees:* If two non-terminal nodes for the same variable x_i have identical child subgraphs, they are merged.
- *Eliminate Redundant Nodes:* Nodes where all edges point to the same child are removed.

Phase 2: Reliability Analysis based on the MDD and component state probabilities $p_{i,s}$(which can also be derived from data) allows computing:

- System State Probabilities according to (3).
- Component Importance Measures SI (6) and BI (7).

And implement analysis based on computed reliability metrics of system behaviour.

4 Case Study: Resilience of a Multi-modal Logistics Network

We model a *Multi-Modal Logistic Network* (MMLN) as an MSS with five critical nodes (components): two major ports (P1, P2), a key rail hub (RH), a customs clearance cluster (CC), and a regional trucking fleet (TF). Based on operational data and expert assessment, each component is assigned one of three states: 0 (Severe Disruption), 1 (Congested/Delayed), or 2 (Normal Flow). The network's overall service level (system state) is classified into four levels: 0 (Network Failure), 1 (Severely Degraded), 2 (Moderately Degraded), 3 (Normal Service). A dataset of 180 historical and simulated scenarios was created. The data is incompletely specified because there are 243 possible scenarios for this network. The probabilities of the network components' states are shown in Table 4.

Table 4. The probabilities of the Multi-Modal Logistic Network components' states

	Components				
	P1	P2	RH	CC	TF
$p_{i,0}$	0.05	0.03	0.07	0.05	0.10
$p_{i,1}$	0.20	0.27	0.25	0.40	0.30
$p_{i,2}$	0.75	0.70	0.68	0.55	0.60

Using the proposed method, the MDD of the considered MMLN is constructed and illustrated in Fig. 5. The steady-state probabilities of network performance levels are $P_3 = 0.3460$, $P_2 = 0.3217$, $P_1 = 0.1609$, $P_0 = 0.1714$. This quantitatively shows that approximately 82% of the network is operating ($A^{\geq 1} = 0.8286$), and among them, approximately 48% are at a degraded level or worse ($P_2 + P_1 = 0.4826$).

The criticality of the MMLN is determined by calculating the SI (Table 5) and BI (Table 6) measures.

According to the SI's measures in Table 5, RH and CC components have the greatest impact on this network operation, particularly on the potential for its complete failure when these components fail ($SI^{3\to0}_{RH,2\to0}$=0.1852, $SI^{3\to0}_{CC,2\to0} = 0.1852$, $SI^{2\to0}_{RH,2\to0} = 0.1358$, $SI^{2\to0}_{CC,2\to0} = 0.1358$, $SI^{1\to0}_{RH,2\to0} = 0.1358$, $SI^{1\to0}_{CC,2\to0} = 0.1358$, $SI^{2\to0}_{RH,1\to0} = 0.1975$, $SI^{2\to0}_{CC,1\to0} = 0.1975$, $SI^{1\to0}_{RH,1\to0} = 0.1975$, $SI^{1\to0}_{CC,1\to0} = 0.1975$). Also noteworthy is the TF component, which is the only one that affects system degradation from performance level 2 (Moderately Degraded) to performance level 1 (Severely Degraded) ($SI^{2\to1}_{TF,2\to1} = 0.3333$). This component, if it fails, has a similar impact on the overall network failure ($SI^{2\to0}_{TF,2\to0} = 0.3333$ and $SI^{1\to0}_{TF,1\to0} = 0.3333$). There are no other changes to the network operation affected by the TF component.

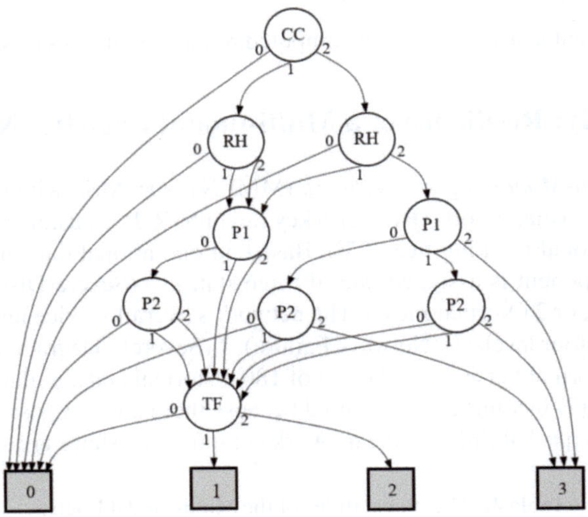

Fig. 5. MDD of Multi-Modal Logistic Network

Table 5. SI of Multi-Modal Logistic Network

			MMLN performance levels change					
			3 → 2	3 → 1	3 → 0	2 → 1	2 → 0	1 → 0
Components state change	P1	2 → 1	0.0247	0.0244	0.0244	0	0	0
		2 → 0	0.0123	0.0123	0.0494	0	0.0370	0.0370
		1 → 0	0	0	0	0	0.0494	0.0494
	P2	2 → 1	0.0247	0.1111	0.0247	0	0	0
		2 → 0	0.0123	0.1111	0.0494	0	0.0370	0.0370
		1 → 0	0	0.0370	0	0	0.0494	0.0494
	RH	2 → 1	0.0617	0.0617	0.0617	0	0	0

(continued)

Table 5. (*continued*)

			MMLN performance levels change					
			$3 \to 2$	$3 \to 1$	$3 \to 0$	$2 \to 1$	$2 \to 0$	$1 \to 0$
		$2 \to 0$	0	0	0.1851	0	0.1358	0.1358
		$1 \to 0$	0	0	0	0	0.1975	0.1975
	CC	$2 \to 1$	0.0617	0.0617	0.0617	0	0	0
		$2 \to 0$	0	0	0.1852	0	0.1358	0.1358
		$1 \to 0$	0	0	0	0	0.1975	0.1975
	TF	$2 \to 1$	0	0	0	0.3333	0	0
		$2 \to 0$	0	0	0	0	0.3333	0
		$1 \to 0$	0	0	0	0	0	0.3333

Criticality analysis based on BI measures is summarised in Table 6 and reveals critical insights. The obtained indices confirm and clarify the topological (structural) properties of the MMLN under consideration. The component CC has the greatest impact on MMLN's performance level from 3 "Normal Service" to "Network Failure" ($BI^{3\to0}_{CC,2\to0}$ = 0.6290), identifying it as the most significant single point of failure for maintaining peak performance. This component, although having a low probability of complete failure ($p_{CC,0} = 0.05$), exhibits a high BI for the transition network from performance level 2 to 0 depending on the failure of this component ($BI^{2\to0}_{CC,1\to0} = 0.5572$). These two BIs' measures indicate that if it becomes congested, it is extremely likely to cause a major network failure. This highlights a high-risk, high-impact vulnerability. The criticality of the component RH is similar ($BI^{3\to0}_{RH,2\to0} = 0.5088$, $BI^{2\to0}_{RH,2\to0} = 0.2639$, $BI^{2\to0}_{RH,1\to0} = 0.5691$, $BI^{1\to0}_{RH,1\to0} = 0.2846$). These BI measures indicate a high-risk vulnerability for this component that, if overloaded, has a high probability of causing a major MMLN outage with significant consequences.

Table 6. BI of Multi-Modal Logistic Network

			MMLN performance levels change					
			$3 \to 2$	$3 \to 1$	$3 \to 0$	$2 \to 1$	$2 \to 0$	$1 \to 0$
Components state change	P1	$2 \to 1$	0.0673	0.0337	0.0112	0	0	0
		$2 \to 0$	0.0606	0.0303	0.0213	0	0.0092	0.0046
		$1 \to 0$	0	0	0	0	0.0159	0.0080
	P2	$2 \to 1$	0.0561	0.3740	0.0094	0	0	0
		$2 \to 0$	0.0449	0.3740	0.0262	0	0.0153	0.0076
		$1 \to 0$	0	0.2805	0	0	0.0265	0.0133
	RH	$2 \to 1$	0.3052	0.1526	0.0509	0	0	0
		$2 \to 0$	0	0	0.5088	0	0.2639	0.1319

(*continued*)

Table 6. *(continued)*

			MMLN performance levels change					
			$3 \to 2$	$3 \to 1$	$3 \to 0$	$2 \to 1$	$2 \to 0$	$1 \to 0$
		$1 \to 0$	0	0	0	0	0.5691	0.2846
	CC	$2 \to 1$	0.3774	0.1887	0.0629	0	0	0
		$2 \to 0$	0	0	0.6290	0	0.1798	0.0899
		$1 \to 0$	0	0	0	0	0.5572	0.2786
	TF	$2 \to 1$	0	0	0	0.5362	0	0
		$2 \to 0$	0	0	0	0	0.5362	0
		$1 \to 0$	0	0	0	0	0	0.5362

From an economic perspective, the RH and CC components represent major logistical bottlenecks whose degradation disproportionately reduces overall throughput. Their high structural and Birnbaum importance indicates that even moderate congestion in these nodes can cause significant service-level losses, making them priority targets for investment and risk mitigation.

Above, we've outlined only a few possible conclusions about MMLN behaviour in scenarios where one of its components fails. The most vulnerable components in this network are the rail hub (RH) and the customs clearance cluster (CC). Investigating more detailed scenarios for this network required calculating other reliability metrics, such as minimum cuts. However, calculating just two IMs (SI and BI) provides a fairly comprehensive understanding of the system's most critical components.

5 Discussion and Implications

The main advantage of the proposed method for reliability analysis is that it relies on well-known, well-tested algorithms. The proposed method enables the creation of a mathematical model of a system for reliability analysis based on incompletely defined data using a classifier. Thus, a classification model of the system is initially created, which is then transformed into a mathematical model for reliability analysis (Fig. 1). As can be seen from Fig. 1, the computational efficiency of the proposed method is due to the elimination of additional transformations between these two models, which is typical of previously developed methods. This is made possible by using a decision tree as a classification model. Furthermore, the decision tree can be easily transformed into an MDD, a mathematical model that enables more efficient calculation of reliability indices and metrics [9].

The core of the proposed method is a decision tree classifier. Its effectiveness (classification accuracy) was evaluated as a function of the initial data's certainty. For this purpose, 15 datasets were generated, with the number of input attributes varying from 5 to 20. The values of the input and output attributes ranged from 2 to 7. MDD was constructed for each dataset. Datasets were then randomly split into training and test sets. The proportion of removed data varied from 5% to 85%. For each modified dataset, an MDD was created using the proposed method and compared with one constructed using fully specified data. The accuracy changes according to this evaluation are shown in Fig. 6.

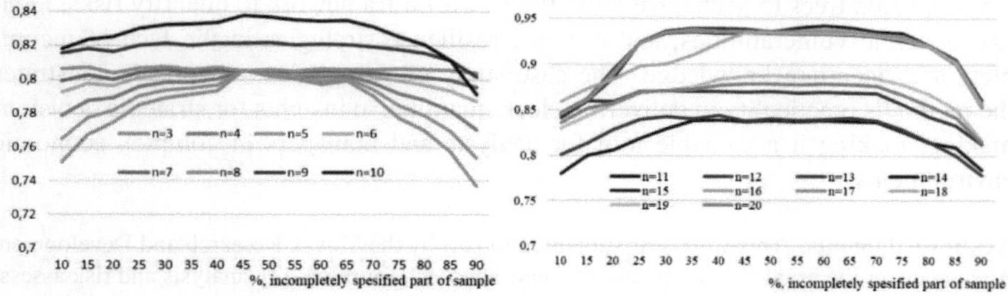

(a) (b)

Fig. 6. The evaluation of method sensitivity depending on the incompleteness of initial data

The proposed methodology presents a rigorous, data-driven pipeline for modelling economic risk and reliability with incomplete data. Key advantages include:

- Automates Model Building: The complex task of defining system logic (the structure function) is learned from data, reducing expert burden and potential bias.
- Enables Criticality Analysis: The seamless calculation of Birnbaum and Structural Importance from the MDD provides actionable intelligence for resource allocation, focusing investment on components whose improvement yields the greatest systemic resilience gain.
- Computational Efficiency: The MDD representation allows for the analysis of systems with dozens of components, a scale where truth-table-based approaches fail.
- Simple implementation: The proposed method is based on the use of well-known procedures and does not require the development of new and special algorithms.

The proposed approach moves beyond mere failure prediction to enable diagnostic and prescriptive analytics, answering questions like: "Which component's improvement would most increase system resilience?" or "Where is our risk exposure concentrated?".

The importance measures derived from the MDD enable decision-makers to prioritise investments in infrastructure components that most strongly influence network resilience [13, 14]. This supports evidence-based planning under uncertainty. The proposed data-driven MSS framework naturally supports resampling-based techniques such as bootstrap or leave-k-out validation. Evaluating the robustness of the results to variations in the training dataset is planned as part of future work.

Future work will explore sensitivity analysis, dynamic MDDs for time-dependent risks, and integration with prognostic models for predictive reliability and risk assessment.

6 Conclusion

This paper presents a novel synthesis of machine learning and multi-state system reliability theory, tailored for economic and risk analysis applications. By reframing system model construction as a classification problem and leveraging the transformation from decision trees to MDD, we provide a powerful framework to quantify risks, identify systemic vulnerabilities, and evaluate resilience strategies in the face of incomplete and uncertain knowledge. The case study on a logistics network demonstrates the method's practicality in delivering clear, quantitative insights for strategic decision-making, making it a valuable tool for analysts and managers in complex economic environments.

Acknowledgments. This work was supported in part by the Slovak Research and Development Agency under the grant "Development of a new approach for reliability analysis and risk assessment based on artificial intelligence" (reg.no. APVV-23-0033); and in part by the Ministry of Education, Science, Research, and Sport of the Slovak Republic under the grant "Reliability Analysis based on Machine Learning Methods" (VEGA 1/0331/25) and under the grant "Creation of new methods and algorithms of eXplainable Artificial Intelligence based on Importance Analysis" (VEGA 1/0090/25).

Disclosure of Interests. The authors have no competing interests to declare that are relevant to the content of this article.

References

1. Zio, E.: The future of risk assessment. Reliab. Eng. Syst. Saf. **177**, 176–190 (2018)
2. Park, S., Yang, J.-S.: Machine learning modeling to forecast uncertainty between capital sudden stop and boom. Expert Syst. Appl. **237**, 121662 (2024)
3. Sarazin, G., Mario, J., et al.: Reliability-oriented sensitivity analysis in presence of data-driven epistemic uncertainty. Reliab. Eng. Syst. Saf. **215**, 107733 (2021)
4. Lisnianski, A., Levitin, G.: Multi-state System Reliability: Assessment, Optimization and Applications. World Scientific (2003)
5. Zaitseva, E., Levashenko, V.: Reliability analysis based on aleatory and epistemic uncertainty using binary decision diagrams. Int. J. Intell. Syst. **2025**, 6471577 (2025)
6. Zaitseva, E., Levashenko, V.: Construction of a reliability structure function based on uncertain data. IEEE Trans. Reliab. **65**(4), 1710–1723 (2016)
7. Zaitseva, E., Levashenko, V., Rabcan, J.: A new method for analysis of multi-state systems based on multi-valued decision diagram under epistemic uncertainty. Reliab. Eng. Syst. Saf. **229**, 108868 (2023)
8. Wang, X., Huang, K., et al.: Reliability evaluation for a multi-state balanced system with a performance sharing mechanism in a multi-source shock environment. Proc. Inst. Mech. Eng. Part O: J. Risk Reliabil. **239**, 130171 (2025)
9. Xing, L.: A review of decision diagrams in system reliability modeling and analysis. Appl. Math. Model. **143**, 116039 (2025)
10. Kvassay, M., Rabcan, J., Rusnak P.: Multiple-valued logic in analysis of critical states of multi-state system. In: 2017 International Conference on Information and Digital Technologies, Zilina, Slovakia, pp. 212–217. IEEE (2017)

11. Zhang, T., Xing, L., et al.: MDD-based reliability analysis of multi-state system with common bus performance sharing. Proc. Inst. Mech. Eng. Part O: J. Risk Reliabil. **239**(5), 1134–1152 (2024)
12. Zaitseva, E., Levashenko, V., Kostolny, J.: Importance analysis based on logical differential calculus and binary decision diagram. Reliab. Eng. Syst. Saf. **138**, 135–144 (2015)
13. Hongjin, S., Ramachandran, V.: Analysis of risk factors in financial supply chain based on machine learning and IoT technology. J. Intell. Fuzzy Syst. Appl. Eng. Technol. **40**(4), 6421–6431 (2021)
14. Zhao, J., Zhou, N., Wan, Z.: Interpretable machine learning for default risk prediction in stress testing. J. Risk Model Validation **20**, 1–9 (2026)

Semi-supervised Streaming Anomaly Detection Using Next Activity Prediction: STAMP

Suhwan Lee(✉), Xixi Lu, and Hajo A. Reijers

Utrecht University, Utrecht, The Netherlands
{s.lee,x.lu,h.a.reijers}@uu.nl

Abstract. Business process execution can deviate from expected behavior, resulting in anomalous events or cases. Detecting such anomalies is important for ensuring compliance, reducing risks, and improving process reliability. Existing research has mainly addressed this problem in *offline* settings using *unsupervised* learning approaches. However, such approaches detect anomalies retrospectively on complete logs and do not leverage the anomaly labels provided by domain experts. In this paper, we propose **STAMP**, an approach for Semi-supervised sTreaming AnoMaly detection using next activity Prediction. STAMP integrates a next-activity prediction model with an anomaly classification model trained on a limited number of anomaly labels from domain experts. Both models are continuously updated in a streaming setting to capture recent process executions. We evaluate STAMP on benchmark event logs generated with three different noise levels. Our findings demonstrate that STAMP can improve recall in early anomaly detection compared with a fixed-threshold baseline while requiring only a modest number of labeled anomalies. These findings show how semi-supervised learning can leverage scarce expert feedback for anomaly detection in streaming process monitoring.

Keywords: Process Mining · Anomaly detection · Event streams · Predictive process monitoring

1 Introduction

Business processes are executed with the support of information systems, which record event data during execution [1]. These event logs provide the basis for analyzing and improving processes, as they capture the sequence of activities performed in real life. However, event logs may also contain irregular behavior that deviates from normal execution. Such deviations can indicate errors, compliance issues, or fraudulent activities [15]. Anomaly detection aims to identify these irregular behavior, enabling timely interventions that improve reliability and reduce risks in business operations.

Most existing research on anomaly detection assumes offline training, where models are trained once on complete event logs [12,13]. Such approaches are

K. Węcel and V. Řepa (Eds.): BIS 2026, LNBIP 584, pp. 306–318, 2026.
https://doi.org/10.1007/978-3-032-26363-6_23

limited in dynamic environments, as processes evolve and anomalies need to be detected during execution. Some studies address this limitation by analyzing events as they arrive [8]. However, these methods typically rely on unsupervised learning and have difficulties incorporating feedback from domain experts. Unsupervised detection is limited in getting the information that domain experts may provide when confirming anomalous processes.

Recently, semi-supervised learning has been explored for process anomaly detection to address this limitation [3,4]. These studies demonstrate the potential of using limited label information in anomaly detection. However, to the best of our knowledge, no study has investigated how expert-confirmed anomalies can be integrated into models in online settings. This gap highlights the need for approaches that combine online detection with semi-supervised learning to better support anomaly detection in real-world processes.

Building on this motivation, we propose **STAMP**, a semi-supervised approach for anomaly detection in event streams. Our method combines next activity prediction with an anomaly classifier and leverages limited anomaly labels confirmed by domain experts. These labels are used to update the models over time, allowing the models to adapt to potential process changes in online settings.

To evaluate the proposed approach, we conducted experiments on benchmark event logs with three varying noise levels. We analyze detection performance with respect to prefix length, number of anomaly labels, and classifier choice. The results show that STAMP can improve recall in early anomaly detection compared with a fixed-threshold baseline, while requiring only a modest number of anomaly labels. These findings suggest the potential of combining semi-supervised learning with online anomaly detection for streaming process monitoring, where expert feedback is limited.

The paper is organized as follows. Section 2 reviews related work on anomaly detection in event logs. Section 3 provides preliminaries, while the proposed approach is described in Sect. 4. The empirical evaluation is reported in Sect. 5. Section 6 summarizes the results. Finally, conclusions are presented in Sect. 7.

2 Related Work

Anomaly detection in event logs has been actively studied for more than a decade. Most studies focus either on offline settings with complete logs or on online settings where anomalies are detected as events arrive. In terms of learning type, the majority of approaches rely on unsupervised learning and do not utilize anomaly labels during the model training stage [7]. Only a few approaches explore semi-supervised learning to adapt potential expert feedback. In this section, we discuss existing anomaly detection approaches along two dimensions: (1) event log environment (offline vs. online) and (2) learning type (unsupervised vs. semi-supervised).

Many studies adopt *unsupervised* anomaly detection in *offline* settings, where models are trained on complete event logs without using anomaly labels. Pauwels and Calders [13] proposed a probabilistic approach based on Dynamic Bayesian

Networks to capture control-flow and attribute dependencies. Their method derives the anomaly scores from event likelihoods. Nolle et al. [12] introduced BINet, which detects anomalous events by assigning low predictive probabilities to unexpected attributes using gated recurrent units. Guan et al. [5] proposed GAMA, a graph-based neural approach that identifies anomalies based on the reconstruction error of event sequences. While these studies achieve strong detection performance, they are limited to offline settings and can not incorporate expert feedback or update models during execution.

To address the need for real-time anomaly detection, several studies propose methods for *online* event streams without using anomaly labels. Van Zelst et al. [17] introduced an online method that detects and filters infrequent behavior in event streams using probabilistic automata. Ko and Comuzzi [6] developed a statistical method that identifies anomalous traces based on leverage scores. The score is derived from the deviated traces to the overall distribution. Lee et al. [8] designed a framework that identifies anomalous events through deviations in next activity prediction. Musaj and Hassani [11] proposed an online autoencoder that detects anomalies at the prefix level based on reconstruction errors. While these studies demonstrate the potential of online anomaly detection, they operate in *unsupervised* settings and do not leverage anomaly labels to refine detection during the stream.

In addition to unsupervised methods, a few studies explore *semi-supervised* anomaly detection in *offline* settings. Elaziz et al. [3] introduced a deep reinforcement learning approach that combines a small number of labeled anomalies with a large pool of unlabeled traces. The labeled anomalies are used to reward correct classification decisions. Gong et al. [4] proposed a Transformer Autoencoder that leverages synthetically injected anomalies to detect trace-level anomalies. These studies demonstrate that a limited number of anomaly labels can improve detection accuracy. However, they remain on offline logs, where complete training data is available in advance.

In summary, although anomaly detection in event logs has been widely studied, the use of anomaly labels in real-time settings remains unexplored. Offline unsupervised methods learn from complete logs, while existing online unsupervised approaches do not incorporate feedback from domain experts. Offline semi-supervised methods leverage limited anomaly labels, yet they assume access to the complete logs. To bridge this gap, we propose an online semi-supervised approach for event-level anomaly detection. Our approach uses limited anomaly labels from domain experts for the training process and continuously updates the models as events arrive.

3 Preliminaries

In this section, we introduce the basic notations and definitions used throughout the paper. This includes notations for event logs, variants, anomaly labels, and the online evaluation setting with sliding windows.

Basic Notations. Let A denote the set of activity labels and $\mathbb{N}^+$ the domain of timestamps. An event is a tuple $e = (a, t, d_1, \ldots, d_l)$, where $a \in A$ is the executed activity, $t \in \mathbb{N}^+$ is the timestamp. d_i are additional attributes from domains D_i.

Each case j has a finite sequence $\sigma_j = \langle e_{i,j}, \ldots, e_{N_j,j} \rangle$ of events that belongs to case j, also referred to as the trace σ_j of case j. The prefix function $pref(\sigma_j, p)$ returns the first p events of σ_j, with $p \leq N_j$.

The event $\mathcal{E}$ contains all possible events, and $\mathcal{E}^*$ all finite event sequences. An event stream is then defined as an infinite sequence $\Psi : \mathbb{N}^+ \rightarrow \mathcal{E}$ representing events arriving over time. If multiple events share the same timestamp, we assume the order in the log reflects the execution order.

Given an event log L, the set of variants $Var(L) = v_1, \ldots, v_m$ contains all unique activity sequences in L. Each variant $v_i = \langle a_1, \ldots, a_n \rangle$ captures only the control-flow perspective of a case, without considering identifiers or additional attributes.

Anomalous Labels. In anomaly detection, labels can be defined either at the trace level or the event level. At the trace level, each trace σ can be associated with a binary label $y \in \{0, 1\}$, where $y = 1$ indicates that the trace is anomalous and $y = 0$ that is normal. At the event level, each event $e \in \sigma$ can be labeled as normal or anomalous, i.e., $y(e) \in \{0, 1\}$. Event-level labeling enables the detection of anomalies at the individual events, where a trace as a whole may still appear normal. In practice, such labels become available only upon case completion, i.e., after the last event $e_{N,j}$ of trace σ_j.

In this paper, we focus on event-level anomaly detection and investigate how limited expert feedback can be used to refine detection in streaming event logs.

Sliding Window. In streaming settings, models are trained and evaluated on the most recent data. We adopt a sliding window of size k that stores the last k events at time t, denoted W_t. As new events arrive, the window advances by discarding the oldest event and including the newest one. This ensures that the models adapt to recent processes and that evaluation reflects continuous performance in the online environment.

4 Method

We propose STAMP, a semi-supervised anomaly detection approach for streaming event data based on next activity prediction (NAP). The approach integrates predictive probabilities with a limited number of anomaly labels provided by domain experts and continuously updates the model during execution.

In the following, we explain the proposed STAMP approach step by step. Section 4.1 describes how a next activity prediction model is trained in online settings and used to obtain the probability distribution of possible activities. Afterwards, we explain how the anomaly detection classifier is trained on feature vectors from the NAP model in Sect. 4.2. Then, we discuss how both models are periodically updated in Sect. 4.3. We also describe how anomaly labels are acquired and used for retraining.

4.1 Next Activity Prediction Model

STAMP builds on a next activity prediction (NAP) model to estimate the likelihood of future process behavior. The framework is not tied to a specific NAP backbone, as long as the model outputs a probability distribution over next activities for a given prefix. In our implementation, the stream is processed online using a sliding window W_t of size k, which stores the k most recent events observed up to time t. From these events, prefix-based training instances are constructed for next activity prediction. In this work, we adopt prefix bucketing and index-based encoding, which are commonly used in the literature [9].

Each prefix $pref(\sigma_j, p)$ of a trace σ_j becomes one training instance, where the input is the activity sequence of length p observed so far and the target is the next activity a_{p+1} in the case. The predictive model is trained separately for each prefix length p. This allows the model to learn the likelihood of the next activity for prefixes of that length.

As the event stream progresses, the sliding window is continuously refreshed with newly arrived events. The NAP models are initialized as soon as training samples become available for the corresponding prefix length. The models are subsequently retrained using prefix-based training instances from the current window. We denote the NAP model at time t as M^t_{NAP}, which outputs a probability distribution over next activities:

$$M^t_{\text{NAP}}\big(pref(\sigma_j, p)\big) = P(a \mid pref(\sigma_j, p)), \quad a \in A$$

In our approach, the predictive probability distributions produced by the NAP model are used as input features for the anomaly classifier. This design enables a hybrid model that combines next-activity prediction signals with limited expert feedback for online semi-supervised anomaly detection.

4.2 Anomaly Detection Classifier

The anomaly classifier operates alongside the NAP model and predicts whether the arriving event e is anomalous. The goal of the classifier is to decide whether it is anomalous ($y(e) = 1$) or normal ($y(e) = 0$). Each event is represented by feature vectors x_e, constructed from three feature groups: (i) control-flow context encoded from the observed prefix, (ii) the activity label of the arriving event, and (iii) features derived from the NAP probability distribution. These features include the probability for the observed activity and the corresponding cross-entropy loss.

The anomaly classifier, denoted as M^t_{AD}, is trained on labeled instances $\{(x_e, y(e))\}$ obtained from expert feedback. Once trained, the classifier predicts for a new event, where $\hat{y}(e)$ denotes the predicted label:

$$M^t_{AD}(x_e) = \hat{y}(e), \quad \hat{y}(e) \in \{0, 1\}$$

To demonstrate how the three feature groups are combined, let us explain the anomaly detection process using Fig. 1. The sliding window in Fig. 1 contains three cases with Case IDs from 091 to 093. Suppose a new event with activity label D arrives for Case 091, whose preceding sequence is $\langle A, B, C \rangle$. The feature vector is constructed as follows. First, the context features are derived from the prefix $\langle A, B, C \rangle$ using index-based encoding with zero-padding. Second, the activity of the arrived event is encoded using the observed label D. Third, the NAP model produces a probability distribution over possible next activities, e.g., $[0.55, 0.25, 0.15, 0.05]$ for labels $[D, E, F, G]$. From this distribution, we compute the cross-entropy loss value (0.27) to quantify the mismatch between the predicted probabilities and the actual activity. Together, these components form a single feature vector that is used to train the anomaly detection classifier.

A single classifier is trained across all prefix lengths using one prefix bucket with zero-padding, which allows the classifier to share parameters across prefixes while ensuring sufficient training data.

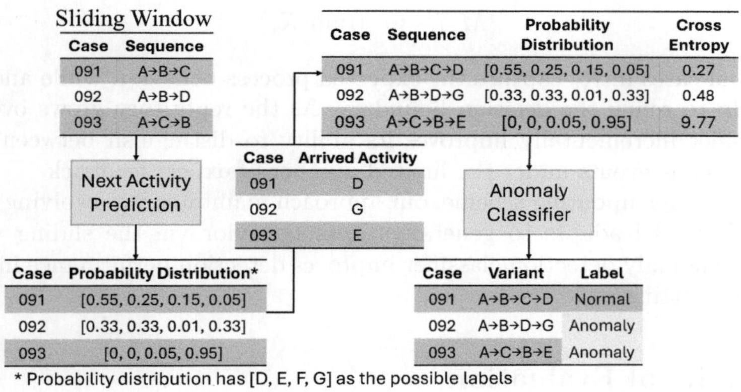

Fig. 1. Example of STAMP approach from Next activity prediction to Anomaly classification

4.3 Online Model Updating

In online environments, predictive models need to be updated as new events arrive in the stream [10]. In our approach, both the next activity prediction model and the anomaly detection classifier are updated at regular intervals.

Updates for the Next Activity Prediction Model. Updates are triggered after every i newly arrived events, where i is a fixed interval defined at the start of the experiment. At each update point, the NAP model is retrained using the data stored in the sliding window W_{t+1} of size k:

$$M_{\text{NAP}}^{t+1} \leftarrow \text{train}(W_t).$$

This updating strategy allows the model to adapt to recent process behavior, while the window size k controls how much past information is retained.

Label Acquisition. In practice, anomaly labels are scarce because their acquisition relies on the domain experts. Expert feedback is time-consuming and difficult to scale, only a limited number of labels can be obtained. To systematically evaluate how limited expert feedback can be incorporated, we simulate expert feedback at each update point. A subset of events $\mathcal{L}_t \subseteq W_t$ is randomly sampled, where $\mathcal{L}_t$ denotes the set of labeled events at time t. The sample size is set to N events per update, i.e., $|\mathcal{L}_t| = N$. To construct a controlled training set for the anomaly classifier, we enforce a 50% normal and 50% anomalous split. This balanced sampling is used to evaluate whether the classifier can learn from limited expert-labeled anomalies, rather than to reflect the class distribution of real-world event streams. The labeled set is stored in an anomaly repository $\mathcal{R}_t$, where it accumulates all labeled samples obtained up to time t.
Updating the Anomaly Detection Classifier. After label acquisition, the anomaly detection classifier is retrained using the repository.

$$M_{\mathrm{AD}}^{t+1} \leftarrow \mathrm{train}(\mathcal{R}_t)$$

Normal cases in $\mathcal{R}_t$ capture the expected process behavior, while anomalous cases help to refine the decision boundary. As the repository grows over time, the classifier incrementally improves its ability to distinguish between normal and anomalous events under the limited number of expert feedback.

Through this updating scheme, our approach maintains two evolving models. The NAP model adapts to general process behavior via the sliding window, while the anomaly detection classifier improves detection performance in a semi-supervised setting.

5 Empirical Evaluation

In our empirical evaluation, we assess the performance of the proposed semi-supervised anomaly detection approach in streaming settings. We compare STAMP against a baseline method and analyze the effects of prefix length, the number of revealed labels, and the classifier choice. The code and data to reproduce these experiments are available via https://github.com/ghksdl6025/online_semi_supervised_anomaly
Datasets. We have used three benchmark event logs with injected anomalous events originally introduced in [16]. The logs are generated from an event stream of a loan application process [2]. Anomalies are created by randomly injecting infrequent events at different probabilities, referred to as the *noise level*.

Each event log contains 5,000 cases with varying numbers of events, activity labels, and variants, as summarized in Table 1. We consider three noise levels: 5%, 10%, and 12.5%. These variations allow us to assess the method under different levels of anomalous events in the log.
Setup. In our proposed approach, we have two predictive models: the next activity prediction (NAP) model and the anomaly detection classifier. For the NAP model, we use a Random Forest (RF) classifier, which has been shown strong

Table 1. Descriptive statistics of event logs used in the evaluation

Noise level	Cases	Events	Activity labels	# Variants	Avg events/case	Median events/case
5%	5,000	78,504	21	2,422	16	15
10%	5,000	79,441	20	3,478	16	15
12.5%	5,000	83,183	21	3,800	17	16

performance in next-activity prediction [8]. For the anomaly detection classifier, we evaluate four classifiers: Random Forest (RF), Logistic Regression (LR), eXtreme Gradient Boosting (XGB), and Long Short-Term Memory (LSTM). We selected the classifiers to cover different prediction algorithms relevant to predictive monitoring and anomaly detection. LR serves as a simple linear baseline, RF and XGB represent tree-based ensemble methods suited to tabular feature representations and limited labeled data, and LSTM is included as a neural sequence-based alternative.

The NAP model is trained using prefix lengths ranging from 2 to 35, allowing the model to learn the process across short, medium, and long case prefixes. We use the first 2,500 events to initialize the first NAP model. This corresponds to approximately 3% of the full event stream and was used as a fixed design choice to provide sufficient event data for initial model training while preserving the online nature of the setting. Our approach maintains a sliding window of the most recent 2,500 events. Updates are triggered after every 1,250 newly arrived events. With this setting, the models are updated after approximately half of the window has been refreshed, balancing adaptation to recent behavior with stability in retraining. At each update point, a subset of events is randomly sampled from the sliding window, and their labels are revealed to simulate domain expert feedback. We consider four settings for the number of revealed labels: 20, 50, 100, and 200. Within each selected subset, labels are balanced between normal and anomalous events (50% each). This balanced sampling is used as a controlled evaluation setting for training and assessing the anomaly detection classifier under limited expert feedback.

To evaluate anomaly detection performance, we compute the precision, recall, and macro F1-score, which is commonly used in anomaly detection stud-

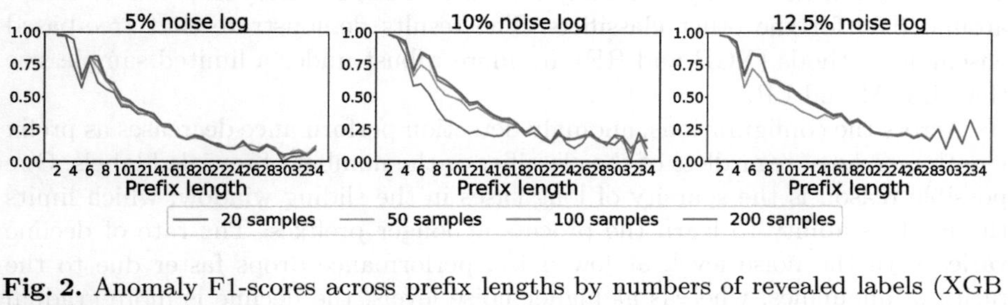

Fig. 2. Anomaly F1-scores across prefix lengths by numbers of revealed labels (XGB Classifier)

ies [12,14]. The macro F1-score gives equal weight to both normal and anomalous events, mitigating the bias that anomalies are much rarer than normal events. As a baseline, we implement the threshold-based anomaly detection approach proposed in [8]. This method directly uses the probability distribution from the NAP model and classifies events as anomalous when their probability falls below a fixed threshold. Following [8], we used 0.01 as a fixed threshold with the best anomaly F1-score performance.

6 Results and Discussion

We evaluate STAMP by examining the effects of revealed labels, classifier choice, and prefix length, and by comparing it against a fixed-threshold baseline.

6.1 Performance Comparison Across Revealed Labels and Classifiers

We analyze the anomaly detection performance of the proposed approach by varying (i) the number of revealed labels and (ii) the anomaly detection classifiers across different prefix lengths and noise levels.

Figure 2 shows anomaly F1-scores across prefix lengths using XGB as the anomaly detection classifier. The results are shown for four different numbers of revealed labels: 20, 50, 100, and 200. Overall, increasing the number of revealed labels improves detection performance, although the effect depends on the noise level. At low noise log (5%), the average anomaly F1-score across prefix lengths increases slightly from 0.30 with 20 revealed labels to 0.33 with 200 labels. At a 10% noise level, additional labels provide a clearer benefit with the average F1-score increasing from 0.30 to 0.39. In contrast, at a higher noise level (12.5%), the best performance is already achieved with the smallest amount of samples (0.42 with 20 labels). The results indicate that limited expert feedback is sufficient once anomalies become frequent, while additional labels could improve the detection performance at lower or moderate noise levels.

Next, Fig. 3 compares anomaly F1-scores across prefix lengths for four classifiers (RF, XGB, LR, and LSTM). XGB consistently achieves the highest performance, with RF showing comparable results across all noise levels. LSTM performs close to the tree-based ensembles but remains slightly behind both RF and XGB. However, LR shows the lowest performance. For example, at the 5% noise level, the average anomaly F1-score of LR is 0.22, compared to values around 0.30 for the other classifiers. The results demonstrate that tree-based ensemble methods (XGB and RF) are more robust under a limited sample size than LSTM and LR.

Across the configurations, anomaly detection performance decreases as prefix length increases, regardless of the classifier or the number of revealed labels. One possible reason is the sparsity of long cases in the sliding window, which limits the model's ability to learn the process at longer prefixes. The rate of decline varies with the noise level: at low noise, performance drops faster due to the rarity of anomalies, whereas at higher noise levels, the decline is more gradual because anomalous behavior remains represented at longer prefixes.

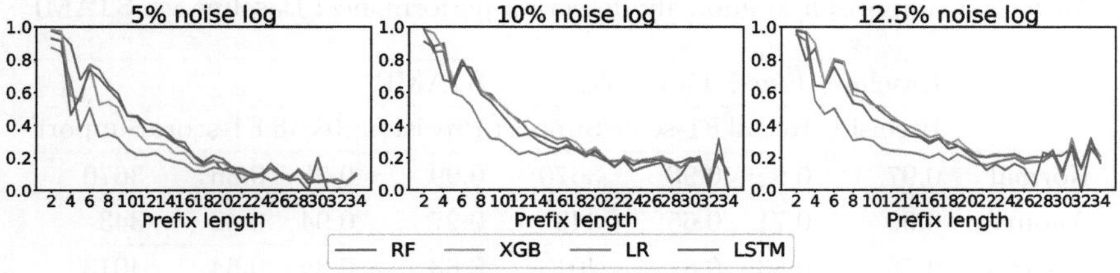

Fig. 3. Anomaly F1-scores across prefix lengths by classifiers

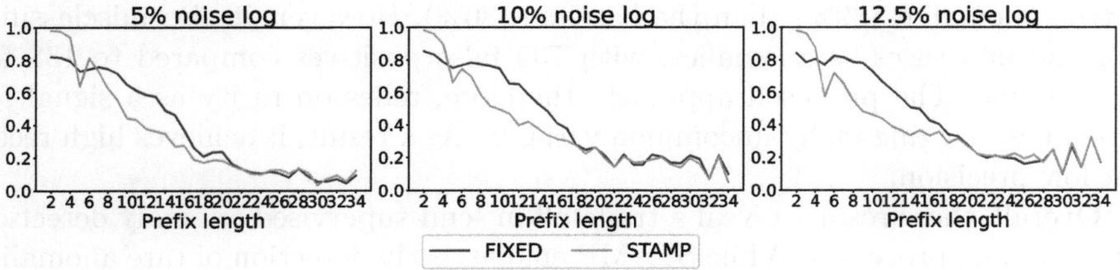

Fig. 4. Performance comparison: Baseline & STAMP Approach

6.2 Comparison with the Baseline Method

We now compare STAMP with the fixed-threshold baseline using the XGB classifier with 50 revealed labels.

Figure 4 compares anomaly F1-scores across prefix lengths at three noise levels (5%, 10%, and 12.5%). On average, the baseline achieves higher overall performance. However, the relative performance depends on the stage of the process. At early prefixes (lengths 2–6), STAMP consistently outperforms the baseline, achieving 0.87 and 0.85 at 5% and 10% noise, respectively. At medium prefixes (lengths 7–15), the baseline achieves higher results, with an F1-score greater than 0.1 in most noise levels. At the late prefixes (lengths 16–35), both methods converge to comparably low performance levels below 0.21. This can be due to the decreasing number of cases at longer prefixes. In addition, rare variants become more frequent at longer prefixes, which makes it difficult for both methods to detect anomalies.

To better understand the performance drop at medium prefixes, we examine a representative case at prefix length 12 in the 10% noise log. Table 2 reports the classification results for both methods. The baseline achieves an anomaly F1-score of 0.65, whereas STAMP reaches 0.42. STAMP detects most anomalies, achieving a recall of 0.94, but its anomaly precision is low at 0.27, resulting in many false positives. In contrast, the baseline achieves higher anomaly precision (0.60) at the cost of lower recall (0.71). This highlights a precision-recall trade-off between the two approaches.

An analysis of process variant distributions (Table 3) further explains the trade-off. Both methods primarily classify rare variants as anomalous, particularly variants that occur only once. STAMP identifies a slightly higher proportion

Table 2. Comparison of anomaly detection performance: Baseline vs. STAMP

	Baseline (Fixed Threshold)				STAMP			
	Precision	Recall	F1-score	Support	Precision	Recall	F1-score	Support
Normal	0.97	0.95	0.96	3670	0.99	0.76	0.86	3670
Anomaly	0.60	0.71	0.65	343	0.27	0.94	0.42	343
Macro avg	0.78	0.83	0.81	4013	0.63	0.85	0.64	4013

of true anomalies (89%) than the baseline (86%). However, it also misclassifies more normal cases as anomalies, with 735 false positives compared to 138 for the baseline. The proposed approach, therefore, relies on rarity as a signal for anomalies, flagging many uncommon variants. As a result, it achieves high recall but low precision.

Overall, these results reveal a trade-off in semi-supervised anomaly detection for streaming processes. While STAMP enables early detection of rare anomalies through higher recall, this improvement comes at the cost of increased false positives at later prefixes. This trade-off reflects the effect of limited expert feedback and variant rarity, underscoring the need for careful integration of supervision in streaming settings.

Table 3. Comparison of variant distribution for cases classified as anomalies: Baseline vs. STAMP

Cases in each variant	Baseline (Fixed Threshold)				STAMP			
	Actual Normal		Actual Anomaly		Actual Normal		Actual Anomaly	
	#variants	#cases	#variants	#cases	#variants	#cases	#variants	#cases
1	138	138	211	211	735	735	288	288
2	4	8	12	24	25	34	11	22
3	1	3	2	6	6	18	3	9
4	1	4	1	4	2	8	1	4
≥5	2	12	0	0	9	74	0	0
Total	146	165	226	245	777	869	303	323

7 Conclusion

In this paper, we proposed an online anomaly detection approach under the scenario where limited anomaly labels are obtained from domain experts. Our method combines next activity prediction with an anomaly classifier and leverages limited anomaly label information in a semi-supervised setting. This method addresses the practical challenge of expert involvement in real-world applications, where obtaining anomaly labels is costly and difficult to scale.

Our experimental evaluation shows that STAMP improves recall in early anomaly detection compared with a fixed-threshold baseline. Even a modest number of revealed labels can enhance detection performance, especially in early prefixes. Moreover, our results highlight the influence of the number of revealed labels, the choice of classifier, and the prefix length on detection performance.

The results suggest that STAMP is relevant for streaming business processes in which early anomaly recall is prioritized and flagged cases can be reviewed by analysts. Examples include operational monitoring settings such as order handling, claims processing, and service workflows. At the same time, the current study has several limitations. The evaluation is conducted under controlled settings using benchmark event logs with synthetic noise injection.

These findings contribute to the use of semi-supervised learning for process anomaly detection in online settings and provide a step toward more adaptive detection methods in practice. Future work includes exploring active label acquisition strategies, such as information gain-based sampling, to reduce reliance on domain experts further. In addition, integrating real-time explainability could help decision makers better understand why specific cases or events are flagged as anomalies.

References

1. van der Aalst, W.M.P.: Data science in action. In: Process mining. Springer (2016)
2. Dumas, M., La Rosa, M., Mendling, J., Reijers, H.A., et al.: Fundamentals of business process management. Springer (2013). https://doi.org/10.1007/978-3-662-56509-4
3. Elaziz, E.A., Fathalla, R., Shaheen, M.: Deep reinforcement learning for data-efficient weakly supervised business process anomaly detection. J. Big Data **10**(1) (2023)
4. Gong, Z., Fang, X., Wu, P.: Anomaly correction of business processes using transformer autoencoder. arXiv preprint arXiv:2404.10211 (2024)
5. Guan, W., Cao, J., Gu, Y., Qian, S.: Gama: a multi-graph-based anomaly detection framework for business processes via graph neural networks. Inform. Syst. **124** (2024)
6. Ko, J., Comuzzi, M.: Keeping our rivers clean: information-theoretic online anomaly detection for streaming business process events. Inform. Syst. **104** (2022)
7. Ko, J., Comuzzi, M.: A systematic review of anomaly detection for business process event logs. Bus. Inform. Syst. Eng. **65**(4) (2023)
8. Lee, S., Lu, X., Reijers, H.A.: The analysis of online event streams: predicting the next activity for anomaly detection. In: International Conference on Research Challenges in Information Science. Springer (2022). https://doi.org/10.1007/978-3-031-05760-1_15
9. Leontjeva, A., Conforti, R., Di Francescomarino, C., Dumas, M., Maggi, F.M.: complex symbolic sequence encodings for predictive monitoring of business processes. In: Motahari-Nezhad, H.R., Recker, J., Weidlich, M. (eds.) BPM 2015. LNCS, vol. 9253, pp. 297–313. Springer, Cham (2015). https://doi.org/10.1007/978-3-319-23063-4_21

10. Márquez-Chamorro, A.E., Nepomuceno-Chamorro, I.A., Resinas, M., Ruiz-Cortés, A.: Updating prediction models for predictive process monitoring. In: International Conference on Advanced Information Systems Engineering. Springer (2022). https://doi.org/10.1007/978-3-031-07472-1_18
11. Musaj, Z., Hassani, M.: Unsupervised anomaly detection of prefixes in event streams using online autoencoders. In: International Conference on Cooperative Information Systems. Springer (2024). https://doi.org/10.1007/978-3-031-81375-7_6
12. Nolle, T., Luettgen, S., Seeliger, A., Mühlhäuser, M.: Binet: multi-perspective business process anomaly classification. Inform. Syst. **103** (2022)
13. Pauwels, S., Calders, T.: An anomaly detection technique for business processes based on extended dynamic bayesian networks. In: Proceedings of the 34th ACM/SIGAPP Symposium on Applied Computing (2019)
14. Vitale, F., Pegoraro, M., van der Aalst, W.M., Mazzocca, N.: Control-flow anomaly detection by process mining-based feature extraction and dimensionality reduction. Knowl.-Based Syst. **310** (2025)
15. Woo, S.S., Yoon, D., Gim, Y., Park, E.: Raad: reinforced adversarial anomaly detector. In: Proceedings of the 39th ACM/SIGAPP Symposium on Applied Computing (2024)
16. van Zelst, S.J., Fani Sani, M., Ostovar, A., Conforti, R., La Rosa, M.: Filtering spurious events from event streams of business processes. In: Krogstie, J., Reijers, H.A. (eds.) CAiSE 2018. LNCS, vol. 10816, pp. 35–52. Springer, Cham (2018). https://doi.org/10.1007/978-3-319-91563-0_3
17. van Zelst, S.J., Sani, M.F., Ostovar, A., Conforti, R., La Rosa, M.: Detection and removal of infrequent behavior from event streams of business processes. Inform. Syst. **90** (2020)

Understanding Parking Behaviour and Traffic Perceptions in Tourism Regions: Results from a Large-Scale Survey on Sylt

Lars Emmerich and Matthias Wißotzki(✉)

Wismar University, Philipp-Müller-Street 14, 23966 Wismar, Germany
{lars.emmerich,matthias.wissotzki}@hs-wismar.de

Abstract. Innovative solutions are needed to meet the challenges of rapidly growing cities. In the resulting Smart Cities, the optimization of traffic flow impaired by parking search traffic is a central area of research. Like cities, regions with a strong focus on tourism also face such challenges. This study analyses parking behaviour and traffic perceptions on the German island of Sylt, a remarkably dense tourism hotspot. The analysis draws on a large-scale online survey encompassing residents and tourists alike. The final dataset enabled a differentiated analysis of seasonal perceptions, parking difficulties, and information needs. Results show substantial differences between residents and tourists regarding perceived congestion, parking-related stress, and typical search durations. Across groups, respondents expressed strong interest in digital parking information systems, especially real-time availability and location guidance. Significant relationships between local knowledge, visit frequency, age, and the willingness to adopt such systems are revealed. The findings provide empirically grounded implications for smart parking strategies and mobility planning in tourism regions, highlighting the potential of digital parking guidance and information systems to mitigate congestion and improve user experience.

Keywords: Smart City · Smart Parking · Parking Behaviour · Parking Guidance and Information System · Smart Infrastructures · Digital Administration · Tourism

1 Introduction

The global trend toward urbanization, with the proportion of the world's population living in cities expected to rise from around 57% in 2022 to 70% by 2050 [1], is accompanied by a significant increase in traffic volume [2]. Congested roads, traffic jams, emissions, noise pollution, and higher accident risks have become defining characteristics of modern urban mobility [3]. Parking and search traffic are significant drivers of these challenges: German drivers spend an average of 41 h per year searching for parking spaces, and in major cities like Berlin this figure exceeds 60 h [4]. In Rome, searching for on-street parking accounts for 11% of total travel time for trips to the city center [5]. Consequently, smart mobility concepts, especially smart parking systems, are of great interest to reduce

K. Węcel and V. Řepa (Eds.): BIS 2026, LNBIP 584, pp. 319–330, 2026.
https://doi.org/10.1007/978-3-032-26363-6_24

traffic searching for parking spaces and thus reduce overall traffic congestion, saving time, fuel, and emissions [6, 7].

However, these challenges are not limited to large metropolitan areas. Tourism-intensive regions experience similar mobility problems. A prominent example is the German island of Sylt, which, despite having only around 20,000 permanent residents [8], recorded 918,668 guests in 2024 [9].

Despite the increasing relevance of these issues, there is still a lack of quantitative empirical research on parking behaviour and perceptions of mobility in such tourist regions. This study aims to analyse perceptions of parking and traffic conditions in tourist regions using the practical example of the island of Sylt and to examine the relevance and acceptance of potential parking guidance and information systems (PGIS). By providing a comprehensive empirical data set on parking behaviour and mobility perceptions, this study therefore contributes to the discussion on smart mobility and offers practical insights for the development of PGIS in touristic regions.

2 Fundamental Concepts and Related Work

A systematic literature review was conducted following Kitchenham & Charters [10] to examine Smart Parking and PGIS. The review comprised a structured database search using a predefined search string, a complementary free-text search on Google Scholar, as well as forward and backward citation tracking. In total, 143 publications were identified. After applying predefined inclusion and exclusion criteria, 73 studies were deemed relevant for this paper. Among the selected studies, three works were identified that conducted surveys comparable to ours; however, none of them focused specifically on tourism [11–13].

The selected publications form the basis for the following section, which provides a high-level conceptual overview of the key concepts for this study, beginning with the smart city paradigm, rather than offering a detailed or exhaustive review of prior work.

The integration of digital network and communication technologies into existing urban infrastructure is commonly referred to as the smart city concept. Within smart cities, digital systems are employed to enhance quality of life and improve the efficiency of urban environments [6]. Smart mobility represents a core component of the smart city concept and encompasses the use of digital technologies in transportation and mobility systems to promote sustainable, safe, and efficient movement within cities and regions, while addressing the needs of users [14]. Smart parking constitutes a specific application area within smart mobility. It focuses on providing real-time information on parking availability for motorized individual transport, thereby reducing search time, fuel consumption, and unnecessary traffic. As a result, smart parking solutions can contribute to lower congestion levels and a more efficient overall transport system [6]. In contrast to systems that merely monitor parking availability, PGIS additionally provide navigation support to empty parking spaces, thereby actively assisting users in the parking search process [3, 15–17]. Modern PGIS represent a significant advancement over the early installations, which were primarily based on variable message signs [18]. Today, these systems include web-based platforms and, in most cases, smartphone applications [18, 19], enabling real-time access to availability data for multiple parking facilities and providing navigation to the selected locations [12]. However, system design and deployment are still largely driven by the need to address local mobility challenges, which often results in solutions tailored to specific contexts rather than universally transferable systems [20, 21].

Smart tourism refers to the use of advanced technologies to enhance the tourist experience through the integration of real-time data, intelligent infrastructure, and personalized services. A key component of this concept is a centralized smart tourism service platform, which integrates various tourism-related services and management solutions into a single digital ecosystem [22].

3 Context of Empirical Study

Sylt, Germany's largest North Sea Island, covers an area of approximately 99 km^2 and consists of twelve villages, with a permanent population of around 20,000 inhabitants [8]. In 2024, the island recorded 981,668 guests [9], underlining its strong dependence on tourism. With 237,642 arrivals in July and August alone Sylt is clearly subject to seasonal influxes of visitors, resulting in a particularly high tourist load in the summer. Most tourists arrive by car (63%), followed by train (32%), while air travel and other modes play only a minor role [23]. Guests traveling by car can use a car train or the ferry for their arrival and departure.

The parking situation on Sylt is characterized by limited and fragmented information. While an official website [24] provides an overview of off-street parking facilities, including two parking garages and approximately 60 designated parking areas, information is largely static and incomplete. Despite having the greatest impact on traffic flow due to its roadside location [25], on-street parking is neither systematically documented nor included in any comprehensive real-time availability overview. As a result, both residents and tourists face challenges in efficiently locating parking spaces.

Given this structure, a PGIS on the island of Sylt requires multi-source data collection. Sensors are suitable for parking lots with defined entrances and exits where they enable precise data under all weather conditions, while cameras are effective for monitoring larger areas when reliable data is only required in good weather, such as beach parking areas. Crowdsourcing offers a cost-effective solution for smaller roadside parking areas but depends on a large user base and strong incentives; given the average tourist stay of only seven days [9], it may be of limited relevance in the given setting.

4 Methodology

This study applies a quantitative survey-based research design to gain insights into perceived traffic and parking conditions, parking behaviour, and the relevance and optimal design of potential PGIS, in both relevant groups, residents and tourists in tourism-intensive regions, using the practical example of Sylt.

The overall survey research and questionnaire design was guided by established methodological recommendations for survey research [26], emphasizing clarity, reliability, and respondent motivation. An online format was selected to enable efficient data collection and broad reach, given the geographically dispersed target population.

4.1 Questionnaire Development

The questionnaire was developed in iterative steps, as recommended by Roopa and Rani [26]. First, the overarching objectives and information requirements were defined, then possible survey questions were formulated. Existing approaches from related studies were reviewed, incorporated and adapted to the specific context [11–13].

The final questionnaire consisted mainly of closed questions, multiple-choice questions, and questions with a 5-point Likert scale. The questionnaire also incorporated clear and concise wording, mutually exclusive response options, and logically ordered sections to minimize respondent burden and potential bias.

A pretest was conducted with 11 participants from the target group. Based on the pretest results, several adjustments were made. Questions on parking behaviour were displayed only to respondents who indicated car use, the number of visits to the island was converted from an open-ended to a categorical variable, and the classification of peak and off-seasons was refined to better reflect tourism dynamics.

4.2 Data Collection, Cleaning and Preparation

The online survey was conducted between September 16 and 29, 2024. Participation was voluntary. Recruitment of participants took place via online networks.

Prior to analysis, the dataset underwent a cleaning and validation process. The responses of participants classified as "other" were reviewed individually based on their text input. Records that could not be reliably assigned to either residents or tourists were removed to ensure analytical clarity. Entries containing implausible or incorrect values were excluded or corrected where appropriate. The literal responses on the Likert scales were converted into ordinal numerical scales from 1 to 5. In addition, a small number of free-text responses were recoded into predefined categories. Responses from individuals whose last visit to the island was more than ten years ago were excluded due to their limited relevance to the current traffic situation.

5 Results

This section presents the findings of the survey. First, the representativeness of the sample is determined. Subsequently, the descriptive results are presented and discussed. Finally, a set of exploratory hypotheses is examined, primarily through correlation analyses, to identify potential relationships between key variables.

5.1 Sample Description

After data cleaning, a total of 876 fully completed questionnaires were available for analysis. Of these, 256 respondents (29%) identified as residents of Sylt, while 620 respondents (71%) were classified as tourists. Both categorical and continuous variables were collected, with the latter primarily measured using 5-point Likert scales. Based on the defined thresholds by Bartlett et al. [27] the dataset presented in the Sylt case study can be considered representative at a 90% confidence level for both individual groups (residents and tourists) and at a 95% confidence level for analyses based on the full sample or only the tourist subgroup.

Regarding participant characteristics, 26% of respondents identified as male, 73% as female, and 1% preferred not to comment. The age distribution indicates that more than 99% of respondents belong to age groups legally permitted to drive a motor vehicle in Germany. The median age was 44. Participants were asked to assess their familiarity with the island of Sylt. On average, respondents agreed or strongly agreed with the statement that they were well acquainted with the island. Among tourists, 13% reported having visited Sylt one to three times, 12% four to six times, and 75% more than six times. The median value of the last visit was 2024, which led to time-relevant findings. The high share of repeated visitors and the before mentioned age distribution is typical for the island of Sylt [9, 23]. All participants were required to indicate which modes of transport they use on the island (Fig. 1). Overall, 87% reported using a car. Walking was the second most common mode, followed by cycling. Notable differences emerged between residents and tourists: 63% of tourists reported walking as a means of transport, compared to 45% of residents. Conversely, cycling was more prevalent among residents than among tourists. Public transport was only used by 17% of respondents overall, with a higher share among tourists than among residents.

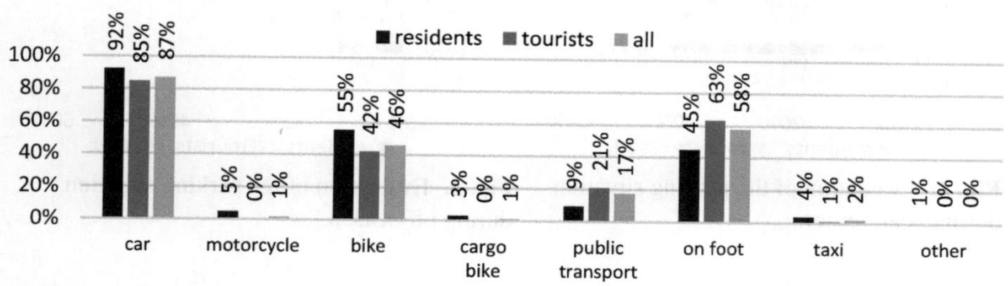

Fig. 1. Means of transport used by residents and tourists to get around the island of Sylt.

Among the 761 respondents who reported using a car it is shown, that when not using a car, participants most commonly rely on walking (57%) or cycling (43%). In contrast, public transport plays a secondary role (12%). Within the 115 respondents who stated that they do not use a car on Sylt at all (20 residents and 95 tourists), cycling is particularly prevalent among residents (80%, compared to 64% among tourists), whereas tourists more frequently rely on public transport (58%, compared to 37% among residents) and walking (72%, compared to 45% among residents). Overall, only 18% of car users also reported using public transport, whereas more than half (53%) of non-car users relied on public transport for mobility on the island. Among respondents using a car, 28% of residents and 23% of tourists relied exclusively on this mode of transport.

The sample was further complemented by information on respondents' car use behaviour. The frequency of car use is distributed relatively similarly between residents and tourists, where 51% use the car daily and 28% almost daily. In contrast, clear differences emerge regarding annual driving distance. While 64% of tourists reported driving 10,000 kms or more per year, this applied to only 38% of residents. This discrepancy can likely be attributed to the shorter travel distances typically covered on the island of Sylt.

5.2 Perceptions of Parking and Traffic

Participants were asked to assess the traffic and parking situation on Sylt separately for the peak and off-season. The peak season included the summer months (June–September) as well as major holiday periods such as Easter and New Year, which are typically associated with high tourist numbers. The answers were given on a five-point Likert scale and only by respondents who had experience with the respective season.

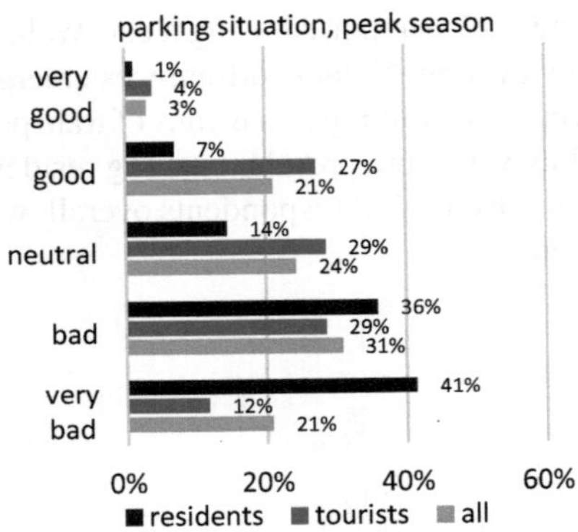

Fig. 2. Evaluation of the parking situation during peak season.

Fig. 3. Evaluation of the parking situation during off-season.

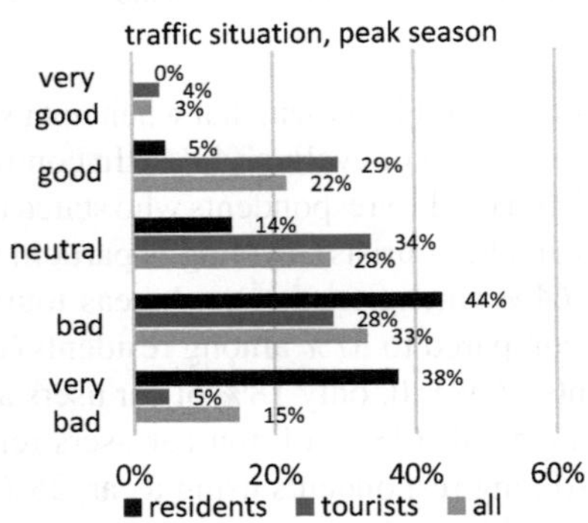

Fig. 4. Evaluation of the traffic situation during peak season.

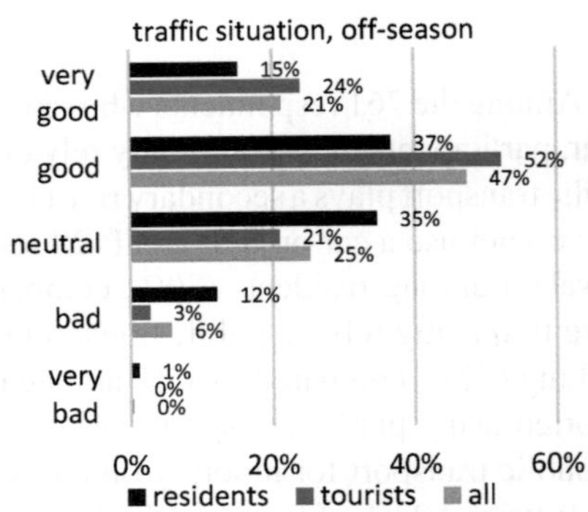

Fig. 5. Evaluation of the traffic situation during off-season.

The results show a clear seasonal contrast. During peak season (Fig. 2), the parking situation was rated negatively by both residents and tourists. Tourists evaluated the situation somewhat less critically. In contrast, assessments for the off-season (Fig. 3) were considerably more positive and more equally distributed in both groups.

A similar pattern emerged for perceptions of traffic conditions (Figs. 4 and 5). Overall, residents consistently rated both traffic and parking conditions more negatively than tourists, while both groups perceived a clear seasonal contrast. To further understand parking-related challenges, participants were asked to estimate how long they typically search for a parking space. As shown in Fig. 6, during the peak season, the median search time was 8 min for tourists and 10 min for residents.

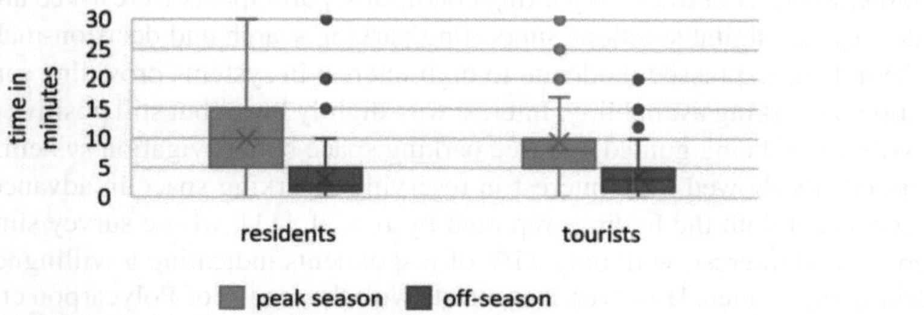

Fig. 6. Information on the time required to find a parking space on Sylt.

In the off-season, average search times dropped considerably to around 3 min. Participants were also asked to indicate where they experience the greatest difficulties when searching for parking spaces. More than 87% reported problems in town centres. Difficulties were reported less frequently at beaches (24%) and tourist attractions (18%). A smaller number of respondents indicated challenges in specific residential areas or locations (6%). When asked about the reasons for not being able to use a preferred parking space, the most frequently cited cause was that the parking facility was already occupied (89%). Some other individual relevant factors included high parking fees (25 respondents) and, less frequently, blocked or improperly used spaces.

When faced with a fully occupied parking facility, behavioural differences between residents and tourists became apparent. Residents were more likely to consider parking illegally, whereas tourists more often chose to wait for a space to become available or to continue searching in nearby areas (Fig. 7).

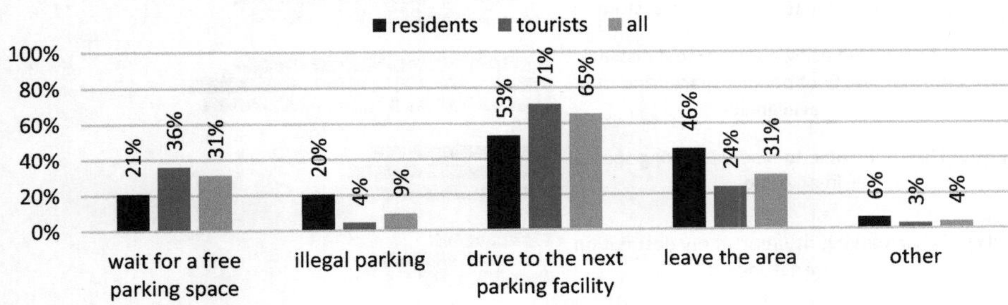

Fig. 7. Behaviour of residents and tourists when the desired parking spot on Sylt is occupied.

Overall, the findings demonstrate that parking pressure on Sylt is perceived as a significant issue, particularly during the peak season. Both residents and tourists experience difficulties, although their coping strategies and evaluations differ. The results underscore the relevance of improved parking management and information provision as potential measures to mitigate perceived congestion and inefficiencies.

5.3 Interest in Digital Parking Guidance and Information Systems

Following the assessment of parking conditions, participants were asked about their attitudes toward digital solutions supporting parking search and decision-making (Fig. 8). Respondents expressed moderate to high interest in systems providing real-time information on parking availability. Interest was slightly lower but still positive regarding the possibility of being guided to a free parking space by a navigation system. By contrast, respondents showed little interest in reserving a parking space in advance. This result is consistent with the findings reported by Ji et al. [11], whose survey similarly identified limited interest, with only 21% of respondents indicating a willingness to reserve parking in advance. However, it contrasts with the results of Polycarpou et al. [12], who reported a substantially higher level of interest (43%) in a fee-based parking reservation system. In addition, while Ji et al. [11] found that individuals planning a trip typically seek information about parking availability prior to departure, this behaviour could not be confirmed by the results of the present study. Real-time parking information in this context refers to continuously updated parking occupancy data collected through sensing infrastructure and disseminated to users with minimal latency, ensuring that current and reliable parking availability information is available at the start of the trip and at the latest upon arrival at the destination.

Differences between residents and tourists further contextualise these findings. Tourists generally expressed a slightly higher willingness to use digital parking assistance than residents. This aligns with earlier research [11] showing that residents tend to rely more on personal familiarity with the local environment, whereas non-residents benefit more strongly from external guidance.

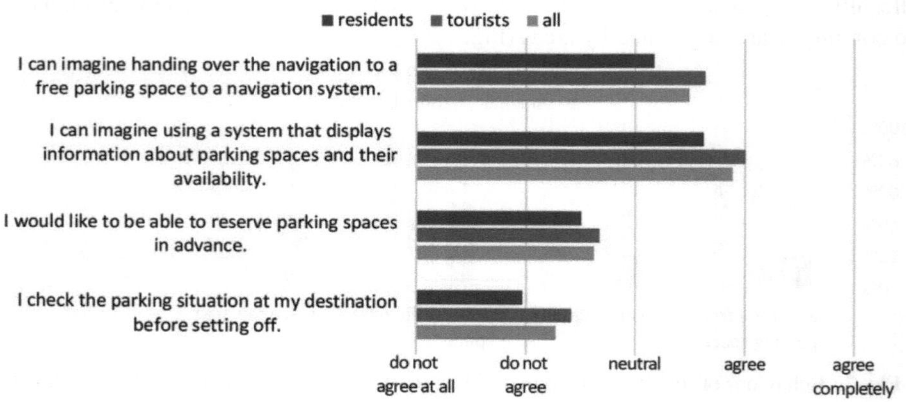

Fig. 8. Average rating of various statements on parking behaviour.

When asked which types of information would be most useful for parking, respondents emphasized the importance of the parking location, followed by cost information and real-time availability, as shown in Table 1. Importance was assessed using a five-point Likert scale, ranging from 1 (not important at all) to 5 (very important).

Table 1. Average importance of information about parking spaces.

	Parking fees	Accurate and up-to-date parking space availability	The location of the parking lot
residents	3.95	3.63	4.03
tourists	3.77	3.78	3.98
all	3.83	3.73	4.00

In terms of preferred information channels, smartphone applications were by far the most favoured option, selected by more than 80% of participants. This finding is consistent with the results reported by Polycarpou et al. [12] as well as by Ying & Sun [13]. Roadside signs (64%) were also considered useful, while websites (37%) and in-vehicle systems (36%) were mentioned less frequently. Radio-based information (5%) played only a marginal role. For the category "website" a clear difference appears, where tourists (41%), which favour them significantly more than residents (29%).

Overall, the findings indicate substantial potential for digital PGIS on Sylt, particularly those providing real-time availability information and location-based guidance via mobile applications. At the same time, the results highlight the importance of tailoring such systems to different user groups, as residents and tourists differ in both their needs and their willingness to adopt digital solutions.

5.4 Underlying Patterns

Relationships between selected variables were examined to identify patterns. Several hypotheses were formulated exploratively and tested using correlation analyses.

The first hypothesis proposed that local knowledge increases with the number of previous visits by tourists or with years of residence. The results (see Table 2) show a clear positive correlation at the confidence level of 99%. The second hypothesis assumed that increasing local knowledge is associated with a decreasing interest in using digital parking solutions (see Table 2). A significant negative correlation was found between local knowledge and the willingness to use a navigation system to locate available parking spaces. A similar, though slightly weaker, relationship was observed for interest in systems providing parking availability information. Therefore, and in line with previous research [11, 28] the results indicate that greater familiarity with the local environment reduces reliance on digital parking assistance.

The third hypothesis extended this relationship by proposing that increasing numbers of visits or years of residence are associated with decreasing interest in PGIS. This was confirmed, as both visiting frequency and length of residence showed significant negative correlations with interest in such systems at the 95% confidence level.

Table 2. Correlation matrix (r) of the effects of local knowledge, measured on a 5-point Likert scale, with significance levels indicated by * ($p < .1$), ** ($p < .05$), and *** ($p < .01$).

	n	1	2	3
(1) Local knowledge	755	–	–	–
(2) Number of visits	610	0.457***	–	–
(3) Years of residence	241	0.250***	–	–
(4) Interest in navigation	756	−0.104***	−0.1**	−0.153**
(5) Interest in PGIS	755	−0.067*	−0.113**	−0.201**

Based on the findings of Ji et al. [11] the fourth hypothesis assumed that the interest in using digital PGIS decreases with increasing driving frequency and annual mileage. Within the collected data no significant relationships were found.

Finally, the fifth hypothesis focused on age-related differences and assumed that younger persons have a higher interest in digital parking solutions. Using year of birth as an indicator, the analysis revealed a significant positive relationship between younger age and interest in digital parking solutions at the 99% confidence level. Younger participants were more inclined to use systems providing information on parking availability, to reserve parking spaces in advance, and to rely on navigation assistance, although the latter was slightly lower, shown at the 90% confidence level. Overall, the results indicate that younger users exhibit a greater openness toward digital and technology-based parking support systems.

6 Conclusion

This study examined perceived traffic and parking conditions, parking behaviour, and the relevance and optimal design of PGIS in a tourism-intensive context. Using Sylt as a case study, the analysis illustrates how high tourist volumes, limited spatial capacity, and fragmented parking information contribute to both perceived and actual mobility challenges. Overall, the findings underscore the urgent need to implement comprehensive PGIS solutions in practice to generate robust, real-world evidence on their effectiveness for sustainable traffic management. This need is particularly pronounced in tourism dominated regions, where efficient and environmentally friendly mobility is essential to maintaining accessibility, quality of life, and destination attractiveness. The survey results suggest that an effective PGIS should primarily provide real-time, location-specific information on parking availability, with a strong focus on peak-season conditions. Navigation support to available parking spaces is especially relevant for tourists, while residents, most likely due to greater local familiarity show lower interest. Features such as parking reservations and pre-trip information received limited acceptance. Users attach greatest importance to parking location, followed by parking costs and current availability, with smartphone-based access clearly preferred over other channels. A responsive web app is recommended to enable access via smartphones, browsers, and in-vehicle systems. Integration into a smart tourism service platform can enhance user appeal and revenue potential. Implementation should take place only after all parking areas are fully documented. At present, PGIS implementations are often fragmented and spatially limited. Advancing integrated, practice-oriented solutions therefore represents a significant opportunity to reduce parking search traffic, lower emissions, and contribute to more sustainable mobility patterns in tourism-dependent regions. From an academic perspective, the findings support and extend existing research by contributing to a deeper understanding of the interdependencies between smart parking and smart tourism. The collected data reliably highlights the changing demands placed on such a system by tourist traffic flows, thereby enabling the development of targeted systems. The transferability of the findings is limited by the strong tourism orientation of the study area and the high share of repeat visitors, which reduces insights into the behaviour of first-time visitors. In addition, the gender imbalance in the sample and the use of online survey recruitment may introduce self-selection bias and limit representativeness. As the study relies on self-reported data, responses may also be subject to recall and perception biases. Future research should therefore investigate comparable tourism-intensive regions, as mobility patterns and visitor structures will differ across destinations, and empirically test PGIS implementations or simulations to further validate and refine user-oriented mobility strategies.

References

1. BMZ Homepage. https://www.bmz.de/de/themen/stadtentwicklung. Accessed 02 Jan 2026
2. Das, P.: A methodology of evaluating urban parking system: case study of Delhi. Eur. Transp. **81**, 1–16 (2021)
3. Barone, R.E., Giuffrè, T., Siniscalchi, S.M., Morgano, M.A., Tesoriere, G.: Architecture for parking management in smart cities. IET Intel. Transp. Syst. **8**(5), 445–452 (2014)
4. Statista Homepage. https://de.statista.com/infografik/10532/so-lange-sind-die-deutschen-auf-parkplatzsuche. Accessed 10 Mar 2024
5. Mannini, L., Cipriani, E., Crisalli, U., Gemma, A., Vaccaro, G.: On-street parking search time estimation using FCD data. Transp. Res. Procedia **27**, 929–936 (2017)
6. Wilde, M.: Vernetzte Mobilität: Grundlagen, Konzepte und Geschäftsmodelle. Springer, Heidelberg (2023)
7. Winter, S., Goel, S.: Smart Parking in Fast-Growing Cities. Challenges and Solutions. TU Wien Academic Press (2021)
8. Sylt Marketing GmbH Homepage. https://www.sylt.de/fileadmin/Mediendatenbank_Sylt/05_Presse/smg-presse-basisinfo-facts-and-figures-sylt-2023.pdf. Accessed 25 Sep 2024
9. Sylt Marketing GmbH Homepage. https://www.sylt.de/fileadmin/Mediendatenbank/10_SMG/Presse/Sylt_Statistik_2024.pdf. Accessed 09 Jan 2026
10. Kitchenham, B., Charters, S.M.: Guidelines for performing Systematic Literature Reviews in Software Engineering, Technical Report EBSE 2007–001, Keele University and Durham University Joint Report (2007)
11. Ji, Y., Guo, W., Blythe, P., Tang, D., Wang, W.: Understanding drivers' perspective on parking guidance information. IET Intel. Transp. Syst. **8**(4), 398–406 (2014)
12. Polycarpou, E., Lambrinos, L., Protopapadakis, E.: Smart parking solutions for urban areas. In: 2013 IEEE 14th International Symposium on "A World of Wireless, Mobile and Multimedia Networks" (WoWMoM), pp. 1–6 (2013)

13. Ying, M., Sun, Y.: Discussion on parking management system based on parking behavior. In: 2020 International Conference on Urban Engineering and Management Science, pp. 513–516 (2020)
14. Muñoz-Villamizar, A., Solano-Charris, E.L., AzadDisfany, M., Reyes-Rubiano, L.: Study of urban-traffic congestion based on Google Maps API: the case of Boston. IFAC-PapersOnLine **54**(1), 211–216 (2021)
15. Bock, F., Di Martino, S., Sester, M.: What is the impact of on-street parking information for drivers? In: Web and Wireless Geographical Information Systems, vol. 11474, pp. 75–84 (2019)
16. Diaz Ogás, M.G., Fabregat, R., Aciar, S.: Survey of smart parking systems. Appl. Sci. **10**(11), 3872 (2020)
17. Song, J., Wen, Z.: Study on urban parking guidance information system design. In: Fourth International Conference on Machine Vision, vol. 83502G-2 (2011)
18. Verma P., Verma M.: Techniques for smart & innovative parking, critical observations and future directions: a review. In: 2015 International Conference on Control, Instrumentation, Communication and Computational Technologies (ICCICCT), pp. 431–437 (2015)
19. Derkach, M., Lysak, V., Skarga-Bandurova, I., Kotsiuba, I.: Parking guide service for large urban areas. In: 2019 10th IEEE International Conference on Intelligent Data Acquisition and Advanced Computing Systems: Technology and Applications (IDAACS), pp. 567–571 (2019)
20. Moini, N., Hill, D., Gruteser, M.: Impact analyses of curb-street parking guidance system on mobility and environment. In: TRID (2012)
21. Zhang, N., Lu, X., Tian, C., Duan, Z., Sun, Z., Zhang, T.: P2P network based smart parking system using edge computing. Mob. Netw. Appl. **25**(6), 2226–2239 (2020)
22. Li, Y., Yin, C., Xiong, Z., David, B., Chalon, R., Sheng, H.: Assistive systems for mobility in smart city: humans and goods. In: Krömker, H. (ed.), HCI in Mobility, Transport, and Automotive Systems, vol. 12791, pp. 89–104. Springer (2021)
23. Island Sylt Tourism Service Homepage. https://images.insel-sylt.de/content/uploads/2024/07/Auswertung-umfrage-nachhaltigkeit-2023.pdf. Accessed 11 Aug 2024
24. Sylt Marketing GmbH Homepage. https://www.sylt.de/anreise-mobilitaet/mobil-auf-der-insel/parkplaetze. Accessed 22 Aug 2024
25. Parmar, J., Das, P., Dave, S.M.: Study on demand and characteristics of parking system in urban areas: a review. J. Traffic Transp. Eng. (English Edition) **7**(1), 111–124 (2020)
26. Roopa, S., Rani, M.: Questionnaire designing for a survey. J. Indian Orthod. Soc. **46**, 273–277 (2012)
27. Bartlett, J.E., Kotrlik, J.W., Higgins, C.C.: Organizational research: determining appropriate sample size in survey research. Inf. Technol. Learn. Perform. J. **19**(1), 43–50 (2001)
28. Axhausen, K.W., Polak, J.W., Boltze, M., Puzicha, J.: Effectiveness of the parking guidance information system in Frankfurt am Main. Traffic Eng. Control 99–110 (1994)

Early Warning Detection of Honey Robbing from IoT Apiary Time Series in Precision Beekeeping

Igor Kurdin[1] (✉) and Aleksandra Kurdina[2]

[1] Department of Artificial Intelligence, Institute of Information Technology, Warsaw University of Life Sciences - SGGW, 02-787 Warsaw, Poland
igor_kurdin@sggw.edu.pl
[2] AmoHive, 02-627 Warsaw, Poland

Abstract. Honey robbing in honey bees is a fast, destructive event between colonies that can rapidly deplete food reserves, cause colony loss, and facilitate the spread of parasites and pathogens within an apiary. Early detection remains challenging because visual signs at early stages are often indistinguishable from normal foraging activity. This paper proposes a data-driven early warning approach for honey robbing based on online IoT monitoring of smart hives, with a focus on data quality, reproducibility, and readiness for integration into beehive monitoring systems. The study is based on a homogeneous network of ten AmoHive smart hives observed during a single nectar season, including one confirmed robbing case and nine reference hives. The paper contributes: (i) an open dataset combining raw IoT logs with standardized, cleaned, and quality-controlled time series together with a documented preprocessing workflow and provenance information; (ii) a formalization of a hidden early warning window from 10 to 1 days before the overt event, during which destructive weight loss accumulates without obvious external symptoms; and (iii) a lightweight and interpretable cumulative detector based on standard deviation, inter-hive normalization, and cumulative negative deviation, conceptually linked to approaches from statistical process control and negative cumulative summation. In the documented case, the system generated stable warnings several days before the overt robbing phase without false alarms in the studied network, demonstrating practical feasibility for precision beekeeping.

Keywords: Internet of Things · Precision Beekeeping · Honey robbing

1 Introduction

Honey robbing in the western honey bee (*Apis mellifera*) is a destructive inter-colony behavior in which workers invade neighboring colonies to steal stored food resources, typically during periods of nectar scarcity [1]. In biological terms, robbing is an extreme form of inter-colony competition [2]. In practical beekeeping, it is among the most dangerous apiary events because it can rapidly weaken or even collapse a colony and may facilitate the spread of pathogens and parasites between colonies [3]. From an

K. Węcel and V. Řepa (Eds.): BIS 2026, LNBIP 584, pp. 331–340, 2026.
https://doi.org/10.1007/978-3-032-26363-6_25

operational perspective, even a single robbing episode may therefore have consequences extending beyond one affected hive, making timely recognition important for both colony protection and apiary management.

Early detection of honey robbing remains difficult. Overt symptoms such as intense fighting at the hive entrance, dead bees, and damaged combs are usually visible only after the process has already escalated [4]. In its earlier phase, robbing may remain partly hidden and can be difficult to distinguish from intensified normal foraging or other short-term colony disturbances using routine visual inspection alone. As a result, practical intervention often relies on beekeeper experience and reactive action rather than on formal quantitative warning criteria.

Recent developments in the Internet of Things (IoT) and precision beekeeping have enabled continuous multi-sensor monitoring of honey bee colonies [5, 6]. Long-term recordings of hive weight, internal and external temperature, humidity, and related signals provide access to temporal patterns and anomalies that are not observable during periodic manual inspections [7]. In the present study, the apiary is treated as a controlled network of homogeneous smart hives, in which each hive is interpreted relative to the collective behavior of comparable neighboring hives [8]. Within this setting, hive weight is used as the primary signal because robbing is fundamentally associated with abnormal loss of stored resources, whereas temperature and humidity remain available as contextual variables for microclimatic interpretation.

Existing literature has established the value of IoT infrastructures for colony monitoring and has provided a growing number of datasets and analytical approaches for problems such as swarming, queen loss, overwintering, and general colony health assessment [5, 9]. Weight time series are particularly informative because they capture daily foraging dynamics, nectar inflow, internal consumption, and abrupt colony-level mass changes [7]. However, clearly documented robbing episodes remain rare in open datasets, and reproducible early-warning approaches specifically targeting robbing are still largely underdeveloped [9]. Prior technical work has shown that automated robbing recognition is feasible, including entrance-level audio/video approaches [10], yet lightweight and interpretable frameworks suitable for integration into online multi-hive monitoring systems remain scarce [6].

This gap is methodologically important because robbing differs from many broader colony-state classification tasks: it is a fast and destructive event that may unfold over hours to days and therefore requires early warning rather than post hoc detection [1, 4]. The present study focuses on a documented robbing case and asks whether a hidden robbing phase can be formalized and detected reproducibly in multi-hive IoT time series before overt robbing becomes visually obvious.

The objective of this study is to move from descriptive observation toward a formalized, reproducible, and data-driven framework for early robbing warning. Specifically, the paper: (i) presents an open IoT dataset from ten smart hives containing a documented honey robbing event together with its preceding hidden phase [11]; (ii) describes a deterministic workflow for transforming raw IoT logs into quality-controlled time series; (iii) formalizes a hidden early warning window preceding overt robbing; and (iv) proposes a lightweight, interpretable cumulative deviation detector conceptually linked to statistical process control and cumulative sum methods, demonstrated on a real robbing case in a homogeneous smart apiary. More broadly, the study treats honey robbing as a detectable collective anomaly in a controlled network of comparable hives.

2 Materials and Methods

2.1 Smart Hive Platform and Case Design

Data used in this study were collected using the AmoHive smart hive platform, an autonomous Internet of Things (IoT) monitoring system in which each hive is equipped with load cells for hive weight measurement, as well as internal and external temperature and humidity sensors, and a solar-powered energy supply, enabling continuous monitoring [8, 12]. The study analyzes one nectar season in a homogeneous smart apiary (see Fig. 1) of ten instrumented hives with comparable hardware configuration, sensor placement, measurement frequency, and logging structure, providing a controlled basis for inter-hive comparison.

Fig. 1. AmoHive smart apiary consisting of homogeneous solar-powered instrumented beehives used in this study.

During this period, one colony (Hive 883) experienced a clearly documented honey robbing event confirmed by field observations and an event log, while the remaining nine hives showed no robbing indications and served as reference controls. The curated dataset (raw logs, cleaned time series, preprocessing code, and quality-control summaries) is deposited on Zenodo [11].

2.2 Data Description and Preprocessing

For each of the ten hives, a separate raw data file was available. The recorded channels included hive weight, internal and external temperature, internal and external humidity, microcontroller temperature, solar power indicators, and timestamps. Data were logged in local time with a nominal sampling interval of approximately 60 min, with occasional longer gaps due to autonomous field operation.

Because the objective of this study is early warning of robbing-related abnormal resource loss, hive weight is treated as the primary detection channel, while temperature and humidity are retained as contextual variables for biological and microclimatic interpretation. Preprocessing included synchronization of raw IoT logs across hives, timestamp normalization, resampling to a common hourly grid, and rule-based interpolation and artifact removal. Each value in the cleaned dataset is accompanied by a provenance flag indicating whether it is directly observed, interpolated, or reconstructed, consistent with previous time-series datasets generated on the same smart hive platform [12]. The resulting daily series formed the basis for reproducible comparative analysis across the ten hives.

2.3 Operational Definition and Hidden Robbing Window

In this study, honey robbing is operationally defined as an inter-colony event characterized by intensive removal of stored food resources by workers from neighboring colonies, resulting in rapid loss of hive mass (weight). Based on field observations and event logs, the robbing incident at Hive 883 on 25–26 September 2023 is treated as a confirmed reference event. Analysis of inter-hive weight dynamics reveals that several days prior to the overt robbing phase, Hive 883 exhibits persistent negative deviations relative to the collective behavior of the apiary. Figure 2 (top panel) shows that these deviations accumulate gradually rather than manifesting as abrupt collapses, while the weight trajectories of the reference hives remain stable.

Importantly, during this period the internal temperature of Hive 883 remains within the inter-hive envelope observed across the apiary (Fig. 2, middle panel), indicating preserved thermoregulation and colony strength. To quantify these early deviations, we define a hidden robbing early warning window as the interval from 10 to 1 days preceding the overt event. For the present case, this window spans 15–24 September 2023, with a clear intensification of divergence beginning after 18–19 September.

2.4 Formal Problem Statement

Let

- $w_i(d)$ denotes the nocturnal reference weight of hive i on day d,
- $\Delta w_i(d) = w_i(d) - w_i(d_0)$ denotes the cumulative weight deviation relative to the start of the analysis window d_0,
- i^* denote the candidate hive affected by robbing (Hive 883),
- $H = [T_{\text{event}} - 10,\ T_{\text{event}} - 1]$ denotes the hidden robbing window (in days).

Given a multi-hive system of daily cumulative weight deviations $\{\Delta w_i(d)\}$, the task is to identify, within window H, statistically stable and accumulating negative deviations of $\Delta w_{i^*}(d)$ relative to the collective behavior of the remaining hives. Such deviations are interpreted as abnormal destructive weight loss associated with honey robbing, and the task is formulated as anomaly detection in a multi-hive monitoring system.

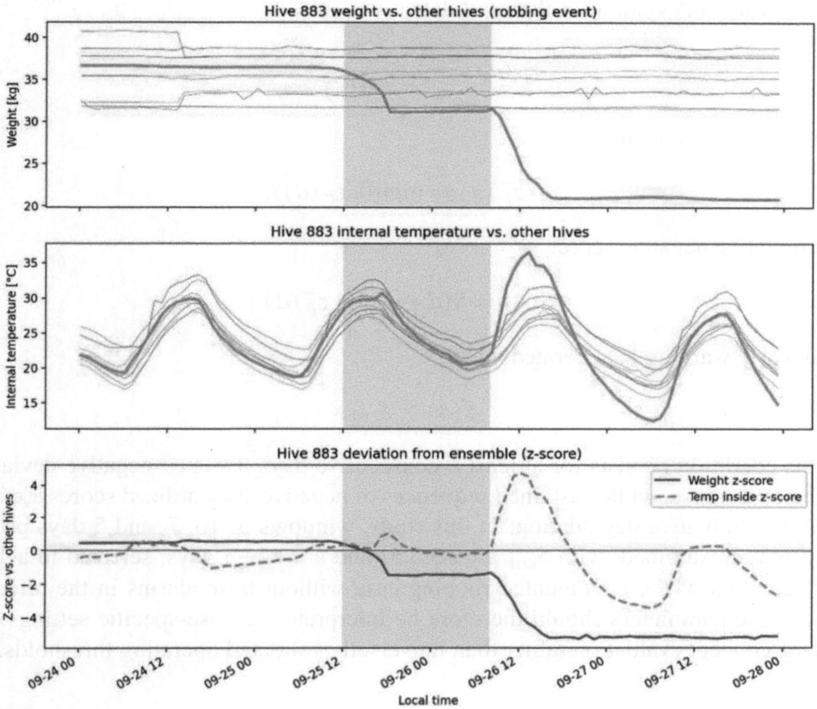

Fig. 2. Dynamics of Hive 883 relative to the apiary during a documented honey robbing event. Top: hive weight of Hive 883 compared with reference hives. Middle: internal temperature of Hive 883 compared with reference hives. Bottom: standardized deviation (z-score) of Hive 883 from the inter-hive ensemble for weight (solid line) and internal temperature (dashed line). The shaded area indicates the hidden robbing early warning window ($t = -10$ to -1 days before the overt event).

2.5 STD-Based CUSUM Detector

The apiary is modeled as a system of parallel processes, where each hive represents an individual process and normal behavior is defined by inter-hive dynamics. Honey robbing is interpreted as a persistent negative drift in the target process. This formulation naturally aligns with concepts from Statistical Process Control (SPC) and Cumulative Sum (CUSUM) monitoring [13].

For each day $d \in H$, we compute:

- Inter-hive baseline (excluding Hive 883):

$$\mu(d) = \frac{1}{N} \sum_{i \neq i^*} \Delta w_i(d), \sigma(d) = \text{std}(\Delta w_i(d)),$$

where N is the number of reference hives, and σ is estimated from the reference hives over the analysis window.

- Standardized deviation for the candidate hive:

$$z_{i^*}(d) = \frac{\Delta w_{i^*}(d) - \mu(d)}{\sigma(d)}.$$

- Negative component:

$$z_{i^*}^{-}(d) = \min(0, z_{i^*}(d)).$$

- Cumulative negative score:

$$S(d) = S(d-1) + \mid z_{i^*}^{-}(d) \mid .$$

An early warning is generated when:

$$S(d) \geq S_{\text{crit}},$$

and this condition persists for at least k consecutive days. Isolated negative deviations are treated as noise, while sustained sequences of negative standardized scores are interpreted as cumulative degradation. In this study, windows of 10, 7, and 5 days prior to the event are examined, with $S_{\text{crit}} \in [2.5,3.5]$ and $k = 2{-}3$ days, selected to achieve early detection of the documented robbing case without false alarms in the reference hives. These parameters should therefore be interpreted as case-specific settings for a proof-of-concept evaluation rather than universally validated operating thresholds.

2.6 Temperature Context

Although hive weight constitutes the primary detection channel, internal temperature provides important biological context for interpreting detected anomalies. Strong colonies typically maintain a stable positive difference between internal and external temperature. In the case of Hive 883, both the internal temperature dynamics during the hidden robbing phase and the difference between internal and external temperature remained similar to those of the other colonies, indicating that the colony remained in satisfactory condition relative to the rest of the hives.

3 Results

3.1 Weight Dynamics and the Documented Robbing Event

The reconstructed weight time series of Hive 883 exhibits three clearly distinguishable phases consistent with the documented robbing event. Prior to 17 September 2023, Hive 883 follows a typical late-summer to early-autumn pattern characterized by moderate diurnal variability and a gradual seasonal decline, closely matching the behavior of the reference hives.

Between 18 and 24 September, Hive 883 enters a hidden robbing phase in which cumulative weight deviation becomes systematically more negative than that of the nine reference hives, despite the absence of visible field symptoms. This divergence develops into a steadily increasing cumulative loss relative to the inter-hive baseline.

On 25–26 September, a sharp collapse of hive mass is observed, coinciding with classical field symptoms of honey robbing, followed by effective colony loss by 27 September. In contrast, the reference hives display only stable behavior or smooth seasonal decline throughout the same period. Within the multi-hive context, Hive 883 is therefore the only persistent negative outlier.

3.2 Behavior of the STD-Based CUSUM Detector

The STD-based CUSUM detector was applied to cumulative weight deviations using three analysis windows of 10, 7, and 5 days prior to the overt robbing event. In the 10-day window (15–24 September), the cumulative risk index $S(d)$ for Hive 883 begins to increase around 16–17 September and shows near-monotonic growth, reaching the critical region between 19 and 21 September.

In the 7-day window (18–24 September), $S(d)$ forms a strictly increasing risk trajectory without returning toward baseline, corresponding to a stable hidden robbing phase. In the 5-day window (20–24 September), the cumulative index remains in the high-risk region throughout most of the window, reflecting an advanced pre-collapse state.

For the 7-day hidden robbing window, the alert threshold S_{crit} was crossed on 21 September, approximately 4–6 days before the overt robbing phase observed on 25–26 September. After entering the alert region, $S(d)$ did not return to baseline, indicating a persistent destructive process rather than a transient fluctuation. For all nine reference hives, the cumulative negative score remained near zero throughout the same window, and no threshold crossings satisfying the persistence condition k were observed. Consequently, in this case study the detector produced no false alarms in the reference hives while generating a stable early warning signal several days before the overt robbing phase.

3.3 Visualization of Cumulative Risk Dynamics

Figure 3 illustrates the evolution of the cumulative CUSUM-based risk indicator $S(d)$ for all hives in the apiary. Thin lines correspond to the nine reference hives, while the highlighted curve represents Hive 883. The dashed horizontal line indicates the alert threshold.

For Hive 883, $S(d)$ remains near zero until 18 September, increases thereafter, crosses the alert threshold on 21 September, and subsequently accelerates during the hidden and overt robbing phases. None of the reference hives exhibit comparable accumulation or threshold crossings, highlighting the contrast between Hive 883 and the reference hives within this case study.

3.4 Temperature as Contextual Support

Internal temperature does not act as an independent early detector but provides important biological context for interpreting the weight-based signal. The internal temperature dynamics of Hive 883 remain broadly consistent with those of the reference hives during the hidden phase, supporting the interpretation that colony thermoregulation is preserved.

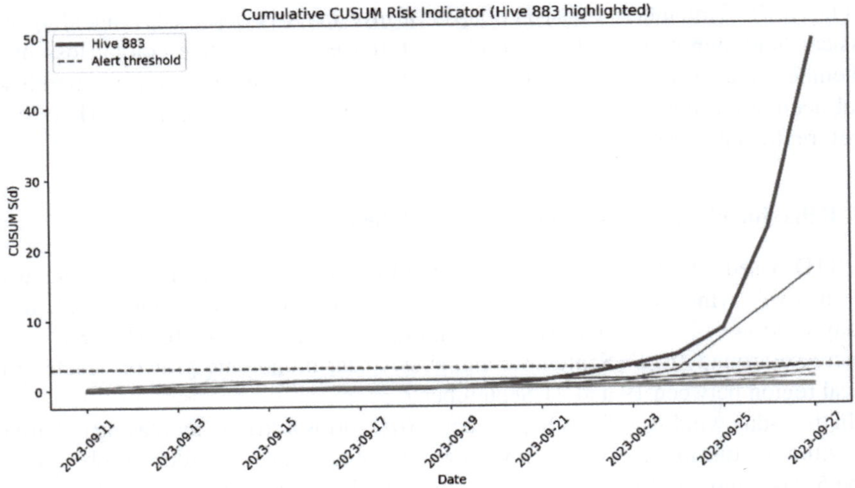

Fig. 3. Cumulative risk score $S(d)$ for all hives in the apiary. Thin lines show reference hives; the highlighted line shows Hive 883. The dashed horizontal line denotes the alert threshold S_{crit}.

In contrast, during the overt robbing phase, the internal temperature rises markedly above the level observed in the reference hives, consistent with intense activity of defending and robbing bees inside the hive (Fig. 2, middle panel). This pattern supports the biological plausibility of the detected robbing event.

4 Discussion and Conclusion

This study demonstrates that early warning of honey robbing based on smart hive data is technically feasible, statistically grounded, and biologically interpretable. A stable warning signal emerged approximately 4–6 days before the overt robbing phase, giving beekeepers time for preventive actions such as reducing the width of the hive entrance. Such actions may help protect an individual colony from collapse and reduce the risk of pathogen and disease transmission across the apiary, thus shifting apiary management toward a more predictive approach. The detector is suitable for integration into online IoT platforms. Its low computational complexity and reliance on online weight and temperature data make deployment feasible, while inter-hive normalization supports scalability, robustness, and early detection of a dangerous event in the apiary [3].

Several limitations should be acknowledged. The present study is based on a single, well-documented robbing case observed within one season and under specific climatic and management conditions. Broader validation across multiple locations, seasons, and apiary configurations is therefore required. The proposed detector and its parameter settings should be interpreted as proof-of-concept results from a single case rather than as generally validated operating rules. The current implementation focuses primarily on weight-based detection, with temperature used for biological context. The detector is designed to identify sustained cumulative negative divergence in hive weight from day to day rather than isolated abrupt losses of hive mass such as swarming.

Future work will focus on expanding the number of annotated robbing events across different hive types and climatic regions, including scenarios relevant to robbing warning in colonies outside an apiary setting. The open availability of data and processing pipelines supports reproducibility and facilitates independent validation. Overall, the results indicate that an online, data-driven early warning system for honey robbing is both conceptually sound and practically achievable in smart apiaries.

Acknowledgments. The authors thank professional beekeeper Serhiy Tonkovyd for support of the smart apiary and Rafał Dyba, Oleksiy Alekseev, and Oleg Klochko for technical support.

Disclosure of Interests. The authors declare no competing interests relevant to this article.

References

1. Wang, X., Huang, T., Ji, Q., Guo, J., Zhao, Y.: Honey robbing: causes, impacts and preventive measures. Insects **16**(1), 15 (2025). https://doi.org/10.3390/insects16010015
2. Rittschof, C.C., Nieh, J.C.: Honey robbing: could human changes to the environment transform a rare foraging tactic into a maladaptive behavior? Curr. Opin. Insect Sci. **45**, 84–90 (2021). https://doi.org/10.1016/j.cois.2021.02.005
3. Peck, D.T., Seeley, T.D.: Mite bombs or robber lures? The roles of drifting and robbing in transmission from collapsing honey bee colonies to their neighbors. PLoS ONE **14**(6), e0218392 (2019). https://doi.org/10.1371/journal.pone.0218392
4. Free, J.B.: The behaviour of robber honeybees. Behaviour **7**, 233–240 (1954). https://brill.com/view/journals/beh/7/1/article-p233_8.xml Accessed 04 Jan 2026
5. Danieli, P.P., Addeo, N.F., Lazzari, F., Manganello, F., Bovera, F.: Precision beekeeping systems: state of the art, pros and cons, and their application as tools for advancing the beekeeping sector. Animals **14**(1), 70 (2024). https://doi.org/10.3390/ani14010070
6. Hadjur, H., Ammar, D., Lefèvre, L.: Toward an intelligent and efficient beehive: a survey of precision beekeeping systems and services. Comput. Electron. Agric. **192**, 106604 (2022). https://doi.org/10.1016/j.compag.2021.106604
7. McMinn-Sauder, H.B.G., Colin, T., Gaines Day, H.R., Quinlan, G., Smart, A., Meikle, W.G., et al.: Next-generation colony weight monitoring: a review and prospectus. Apidologie **55**, Article 13 (2024). https://doi.org/10.1007/s13592-023-01050-8
8. Kurdin, I., Kurdina, A.: Internet of Things smart beehive network: homogeneous data, modeling, and forecasting the honey robbing phenomenon. Inventions **10**(2), 23 (2025). https://doi.org/10.3390/inventions10020023
9. Haddaoui, A., Khlifa, S., Chikhi, S., Varastehpour, S., Adjailia, A.: A comprehensive review of beekeeping datasets for precision apiculture research. In: Proceedings of the CoDIT 2024 (2024). https://doi.org/10.1109/CoDIT62066.2024.10708308
10. Tashakkori, R., Buchanan, G.B., Craig, L.M.: Analyses of audio and video recordings for detecting a honey bee hive robbery. In: Proceedings of the IEEE SoutheastCon 2020. Art. no. 9249684 (2020). https://doi.org/10.1109/SoutheastCon44009.2020.9249684
11. Kurdin, I., Kurdina, A.: Time-series dataset of non-invasive IoT measurements in Apis mellifera colonies: honey robbing phenomenon during autumn (2023; Ukraine). Zenodo (2025). https://doi.org/10.5281/zenodo.18078399
12. Kurdin, I., Kurdina, A.: Time-series dataset: fondant feeding in overwinteringApis mellifera colonies. BMC Res Notes (2026). https://doi.org/10.1186/s13104-026-07711-y

13. Cordier, Q., Prieur, H., Duclos, A.: Top surgeons study group: risk-adjusted observed minus expected cumulative sum (RA O-E CUSUM) chart for visualisation and monitoring of surgical outcomes. BMJ Qual. Saf. **34**(5), 330–338 (2025). https://doi.org/10.1136/bmjqs-2024-017935

Requirements for AI and BI Systems (short papers)

Human-AI Interaction Requirements in Public Sector Procurements

Mateen A. Abbasi[1], Tommi Mikkonen[1], Sinna Pirinen[1], and Aapo Koski[2,3](✉)

[1] University of Jyväskylä, Jyväskylä, Finland
{mateen.a.abbasi,tommi.j.mikkonen}@jyu.fi, sinna.e.pirinen@student.jyu.fi
[2] Tampere University, Tampere, Finland
[3] 61N Solutions Oy, Tampere, Finland
aapo.koski@tuni.fi, aapo.koski@61n.fi

Abstract. Public sector organizations increasingly procure AI-enabled ICT systems to support decision-making and service delivery. Although ethical AI frameworks emphasize transparency, accountability, and human oversight, these principles are rarely translated into explicit requirements in procurement processes. Consequently, humanAI interaction (HAI) is often left to vendor design choices. This paper conceptualizes HAI as a procurement-critical design dimension and proposes a taxonomy of interaction requirements tailored to public sector ICT procurement. The taxonomy enables contracting authorities to specify and govern interaction properties through procurement instruments, supporting both ethical compliance and sustainable value realization.

Keywords: humanAI interaction · public ICT procurement · responsible AI · accountability and transparency · AI value realization

1 Introduction

Public sector organizations are increasingly adopting AI-enabled ICT systems to support decision-making, service delivery, and operational efficiency. Such systems are used in a wide range of contexts, including administrative decision support, data-driven process automation, and predictive analytics in regulated and, in some cases, safety-critical environments [7]. Unlike in some other contexts, the procurement of ICT systems in the public sector takes place under strict legal and ethical requirements of transparency, lack of discrimination, and clear assignment of liability. All these aspects make AI system procurements a challenge for governance rather than a technical exercise.

In this study, AI refers broadly to computational techniques that generate predictions, classifications, or recommendations from data, including machine learning models and newer generative approaches such as large language models.

One of the most important issues is how human interaction with the AI system takes place. Ethical AI frameworks, regulatory guidance, and policy initiatives consistently emphasize human oversight, explainability, accountability, and

K. Węcel and V. Řepa (Eds.): BIS 2026, LNBIP 584, pp. 343–352, 2026.
https://doi.org/10.1007/978-3-032-26363-6_26

user trust [12]. However, these principles are typically articulated at a high level and implicitly assume that appropriate interaction mechanisms will be addressed during system design and implementation. In practice, public sector organizations rely primarily on procurement processes to define system requirements and govern supplier behavior [3]. If human-AI interaction (HAI) is specified in the procurement procedure at all, decisions regarding how the system should act are left in the hands of the suppliers. This significantly reduces the ability of the contracting authority to ensure that the principles are followed. In this regard, the issue of human interaction with AI-based systems in the public sector is viewed from the aspect of usability. This is inadequate since the behavior of the systems is based on probability. In public sector contexts, where AI-supported decisions may carry legal, societal, or safety-critical consequences, this gap poses significant governance risks. The emergence of regulatory initiatives such as the EU AI Act further highlights the need to operationalize oversight, transparency, and accountability as verifiable requirements rather than aspirational principles.

This paper argues that HAI must be considered a procurement-critical design dimension rather than an add-on in technical or ethical considerations. Based on previous research on ethical AI, humanAI interaction, and public sector ICT procurement, this paper proposes a structured taxonomy of HAI requirements tailored to public procurement contexts. The taxonomy identifies key interaction dimensions that can be explicitly specified, evaluated, and governed through procurement tools. By linking ethical AI principles with procurable and verifiable interaction requirements, the study contributes to responsible, value-oriented AI adoption in public sector information systems and offers practical guidance for contracting authorities to balance innovation, accountability, and sustainable value realization.

2 Background and Related Work

Research on AI in the public sector, humanAI interaction (HAI), and ethical AI provides important conceptual foundations, yet their integration into procurement practice remains limited. Existing HAI and ethical AI research focuses primarily on system design and development contexts, whereas public sector organizations typically influence system behavior through procurement requirements.

Public sector ICT procurement operates under strict legal and accountability constraints that shape verification, liability, and long-term operation [6]. The introduction of AI amplifies existing challenges such as requirement uncertainty and information asymmetry while introducing additional concerns related to opacity, probabilistic outputs, and loss of control [3,7].

HAI research examines how humans interpret, supervise, and collaborate with AI systems, emphasizing explainability, trust, and levels of automation [1,2]. Ethical and regulatory frameworks similarly stress principles such as transparency, human oversight, and accountability [4,9]. However, these principles are rarely translated into concrete requirements that can be specified in tender documents, evaluated during supplier selection, and verified during system deployment [11].

This paper addresses this gap by conceptualizing HAI as a procurement-critical design dimension and by proposing a taxonomy of interaction requirements that can be explicitly specified, evaluated, and governed through public sector ICT procurements.

3 Research Approach

This study adopts a conceptual design approach to develop a taxonomy of humanAI interaction (HAI) requirements for public sector ICT procurement. The taxonomy was derived through a literature synthesis across four domains: HAI research, ethical and responsible AI, requirements engineering, and public sector procurement.

Recurring themes across these domains—such as transparency, human oversight, accountability, user competence, and system adaptivity—were identified and consolidated into analytically distinct interaction requirement dimensions. Particular attention was paid to ensuring that the resulting dimensions correspond to properties that can be explicitly specified and evaluated within procurement processes.

To ensure practical relevance, the taxonomy was aligned with common public procurement lifecycle stages including needs assessment, tender specification, supplier evaluation, contracting, acceptance testing, and operational monitoring [14]. The contribution of the study is conceptual; empirical validation is left for future work.

4 Requirement Taxonomy for Public Sector Procurement

This section presents a taxonomy of HAI requirements that are explicitly formulated to be procurable in public sector ICT acquisitions. Existing ethical guidelines and regulatory frameworks emphasize human oversight, transparency, and accountability, but rarely translate into concrete requirements that can be specified, evaluated, and enforced through public procurement processes [8]. As a result, humanAI interaction is often ambiguous or left for AI vendors to implement.

The proposed taxonomy addresses the aforementioned gap by conceptualizing humanAI interaction not as a secondary usability or ethical concern but as a specific set of interaction characteristics that must be specified clearly in procurement documents. These characteristics define how AI systems are used and monitored and can be managed through the specifications and acceptance tests of the procurement. The taxonomy gives the procuring authority the capacity to influence the interaction design and accountability structures before systems are deployed.

The taxonomy comprises five dimensions: (1) transparency and explainability, (2) human oversight and control, (3) user competence and cognitive load, (4) accountability and traceability, and (5) adaptivity and behavioral predictability. Together, these dimensions capture the core ways in which humans and AI systems interact in public sector operational contexts.

Figure 1 presents an overview of this conceptual framework. It identifies the requirements of human–AI interaction as a separate governance layer that encircles and challenges the operations of AI-enabled systems. This structure not only specifies the requirements of human and AI interaction, but also emphasizes how interaction requirements mediate between ethical and legal expectations, organizational accountability, as well as the operations of AI systems.

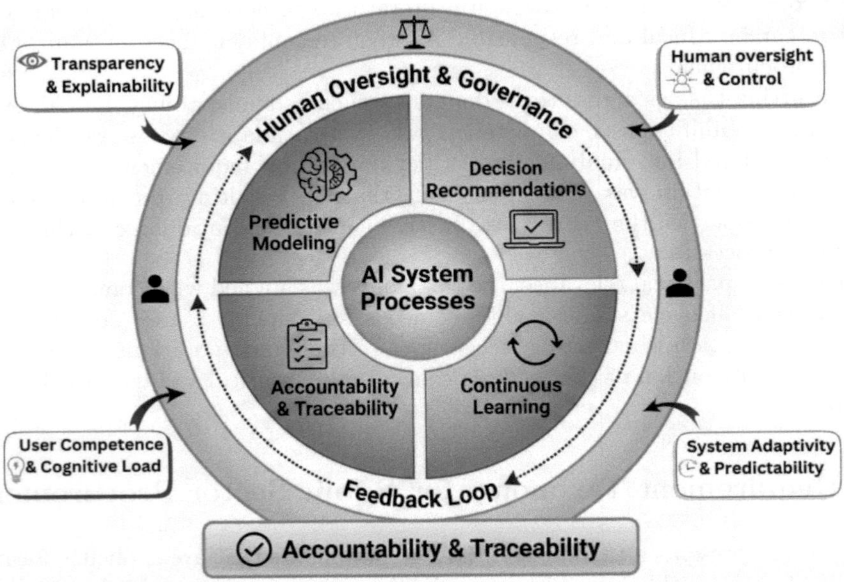

Fig. 1. HumanAI interaction requirements as a governance layer around AI system processes in public sector deployments

The remaining part of this section discusses each of the five dimensions, outlining their conceptual rationales, typical procurement-ready requirement formulations, and relevance for public-sector governance and accountability.

Transparency and Explainability. Transparency and explainability refer to the extent to which AI system outputs and reasoning processes are understandable to human users. In public sector contexts this is essential for legal accountability and the justification of decisions affecting citizens [15].

From a procurement perspective, transparency and explainability have to be formulated in concrete terms regarding interaction, rather than being considered as abstract system qualities. This involves specifying

- what aspects of system behavior must be explainable (e.g., individual decisions, model logic, data influences),
- to whom explanations must be available (e.g., end users, supervisors, auditors),
- at what stages explanations are required (e.g., in real time, post hoc, during audits).

Insufficiently specified transparency requirements risk leaving explainability as a best-effort feature rather than a guaranteed capability. Explicit procurement requirements can define minimum levels of explanation, acceptable forms of explanation, and verification methods during acceptance testing, thereby embedding transparency into contractual obligations.

Human Oversight and Control. Human oversight and control address how and under what conditions humans can supervise, intervene, or override AI-enabled processes. This dimension formalizes and operationalizes a well-established rule of keeping a human "in the loop" or "on the loop" [9,11]. In terms of procurement perspective, interaction mechanisms must be specified rather than assumed. The following requirements must be defined:

- decision points where human confirmation or authorization may be required,
- methods for overriding, suspending, or disabling automated recommendations,
- escalation paths for uncertainty, conflict, or unusual system behavior, and
- role-based control rights aligned with organizational responsibilities and obligations.

Without explicit procurement requirements, oversight mechanisms may be implemented in ways that are technically present but practically unusable, for example, due to poor interface design or excessive time pressure. Oversight as a key procurement requirement can ensure that control is not merely nominal but functional and aligned with the accountability structures within public sector organizations.

User Competence and Cognitive Load. This dimension concerns the relationship between AI system behaviors with human cognitive capabilities, with an emphasis on understanding, attention, and the effort required to effectively engage with an AI system. In the public sector, there is considerable variation in levels of competence and workload from experts to generalist civil servants. In procurement context, the issues of user competency and cognitive loads are dealt with through such explicit requirements as:

- user training, on-boarding, and certification,
- clarity of feedback, suggestions, warnings given through the system, and
- constraints on cognitive burden in time-critical situations.

From HAI perspective, poorly designed interaction can lead to automation bias, where users over-trust system outputs, or to underutilization, where users ignore AI support due to lack of understanding or confidence. By specifying competence and workload-related requirements, contracting authorities can shape systems that support calibrated trust and sustainable use.

Accountability andTraceability. Accountability and traceability refer to the ability to reconstruct, audit, and attribute AI-supported decisions and actions to human and system actors [13]. In the public sector, this dimension is essential for legal compliance, organizational governance, and public trust. Procurement-oriented requirements in this dimension may address:

- logging of inputs, outputs, and decision rationales,
- tracing system states, configurations, or model versions,
- attribution of actions to human roles and system components, and
- accessibility of records for audits and reviews.

By integrating traceability requirements into procurement contracts, contracting authorities can ensure that accountability depends on verifiable system capabilities throughout the system life cycle, not on vendor-allocated tools or discretion.

Adaptivity and Behavioral Predictability. AI systems may change their behavior over time due to learning, data drift, or model updates [4]. Although such adaptivity can offer performance improvements [2], for example, an increase in prediction accuracy, improved alignment with the operational context, or a decrease in error rates for specific sub-populations. Adaptivity introduces uncertainty about future system behavior, which is particularly problematic in regulated and accountability-driven public sector contexts [5].

In the context of the regulated public sector that emphasizes accountability, this level of uncertainty can pose a challenge to consistency, predictability, and equal treatment. The dynamic nature of system behaviors that are not governed in a straightforward manner might leave the users puzzled regarding the reasons behind the differential treatment of similar instances.
This dimension captures HAI requirements related to:

- constraints on autonomous learning and adaptation,
- mechanisms to notify users about changes in behavior,
- approval processes for model updates, and
- guarantees of behavioral stability for critical system functions.

From a procurement perspective, system adaptivity must be explicitly governed to balance innovation with predictability. It is crucial to define rules of change and how changes should be introduced and documented and accepted. Thus, a contracting authority is capable of gaining control over the adaptive AI.

Taxonomy as a Procurement-Oriented Design Construct. Although analytically distinct, the five dimensions are interdependent in practice: for example, human oversight presupposes transparency, and accountability requires traceability and control roles. The taxonomy is intended not as a checklist of features but as a procurement-oriented construct that enables interaction requirements to be specified, evaluated, and verified. Its value lies in supporting contracting authorities in identifying interaction-related risks and expectations and translating them into procurable requirement categories. This framing positions HAI as a locus of governance rather than solely a design concern.

5 Operationalizing HAI Requirements

While the taxonomy presented in Sect. 4 structures key dimensions of humanAI interaction, its practical value depends on whether these dimensions can be embedded into concrete public procurement practices. This section demonstrates how humanAI interaction requirements can be operationalized across the procurement life cycle and translated into instruments that contracting authorities already use in practice. The central argument is that humanAI interaction must be treated as an explicit object of procurement, subject to specification, evaluation, contracting, and verification. A set of interaction expectations should be formed through these processes to support governance, enforcement, and adaptation in time.

5.1 From Ethical Principles to Procurement Language

The principles that must be considered are transparency, accountability, and human agency. However, these principles are not directly actionable within procurement processes. To become operational, they must be translated into interaction-oriented requirements that can be expressed in tender documents, assessed during supplier selection, and verified before deployment. Across public procurement practice, this translation typically follows a recurring pattern:

$$\textit{Ethical principle} \rightarrow \textit{HAI requirement} \rightarrow \textit{Procurement clause} \qquad (1)$$

For example, the ethical principle of transparency may be translated into a requirement that the system provides user-friendly explanations regarding the recommendations supported by AI. Such a requirement will then be formulated as a mandatory functional requirement and will be tested for acceptance in scenario-based acceptance tests. In a similar way, there may emerge requirements regarding override and confirmation steps for the principle of human agency. Across the five taxonomy dimensions, such translations commonly result in three types of procurement clauses:

- **Mandatory requirements**, defining minimum acceptable interaction capabilities (e.g., availability of override functions, logging mechanisms, explanation interfaces).

- **Evaluation criteria**, differentiating competing solutions based on the quality of interaction design (e.g., usability of explanations, support for calibrated trust, clarity of system feedback).
- **Acceptance conditions**, specifying how interaction-related properties will be verified prior to deployment (e.g. scenario-based testing with end users).

By structuring ethical aspirations in this way, humanAI interaction concerns become part of the formal decision logic of procurement rather than remaining implicit expectations or post hoc evaluation criteria.

For example, a procurement clause in a public case-handling system might require that every AI-generated recommendation can be overridden by a human operator and that both the recommendation and the final decision are logged for audit purposes.

5.2 HAI Requirements Across the Procurement Life Cycle

Rules on HAI have to be understandable in any procurement process. Based on common public procurement process models, six key phases can be identified.

1. **Needs Assessment:** Identify where human oversight, explanation, and accountability must be preserved before automation decisions are made.
2. **Tender Specification:** Translate interaction expectations into requirement clauses defining explanation capabilities, override mechanisms, and traceability obligations.
3. **Supplier Evaluation:** Assess interaction design through demonstrations, prototypes, or interaction plans provided by suppliers.
4. **Contracting:** Define contractual obligations related to explanations, logging, and model updates affecting interaction behavior.
5. **Acceptance Testing:** Verify interaction requirements through scenario-based testing with representative users.
6. **Operational Monitoring:** Audit interaction behavior during system operation and manage updates affecting user interaction.

Addressing HAI across these phases reveals that interaction quality is not just an initial design problem, but a sustained governance concern.

5.3 Risks of Omission

If HAI is not addressed during procurement, several risks emerge. AI outputs may de facto determine decisions, reducing humans to passive verifiers. Human authority may erode if users cannot interpret or override system recommendations. Traceability and accountability suffer when explanation and role assignment are not contractually enforced, complicating audits and dispute resolution. Finally, adoption and value realization decline when users lack trust, understanding, or a sense of responsibility.

6 Discussion and Conclusions

This study positions humanAI interaction as a procurement-critical design dimension rather than solely a usability or ethical concern. Treating interaction requirements as procurable shifts part of the control over AI system behavior from vendors to contracting authorities and enables governance over transparency, oversight, and accountability throughout the system life-cycle.

The proposed taxonomy provides a structured way to translate ethical and regulatory principles into procurement instruments such as requirement clauses, evaluation criteria, and acceptance tests [10]. In this sense, procurement functions as an important governance mechanism for responsible AI deployment.

Acknowledgments. This work has been supported by Software Engineering Doctoral Pilot, funded by the Ministry of Education and Culture, Finland, and Business Finland (project ANSE, 1822/31/2025).

References

1. Abbasi, M.A., Ihantola, P., Mikkonen, T., Mäkitalo, N.: Towards human-AI synergy in requirements engineering: a framework and preliminary study. In: 2025 Sixth International Conference on Intelligent Data Science Technologies and Applications (IDSTA), pp. 81–88. IEEE (2025)
2. Amershi, S., et al.: Guidelines for human-AI interaction. In: Proceedings of the 2019 Chi Conference on Human Factors in Computing Systems, pp. 1–13 (2019)
3. Andersson, P.E., Arbin, K., Rosenqvist, C.: Assessing the value of artificial intelligence (AI) in governmental public procurement. J. Pub. Proc. **25**(1), 120–139 (2025)
4. Cavalcante Siebert, L., et al.: Meaningful human control: actionable properties for AI system development. AI Ethics **3**(1), 241–255 (2023)
5. Fischer-Abaigar, U., Kern, C., Barda, N., Kreuter, F.: Bridging the gap: towards an expanded toolkit for ai-driven decision-making in the public sector. Gov. Inf. Q. **41**(4), 101976 (2024)
6. Ghezzi, R., Mikkonen, T.: On public procurement of ICT systems: stakeholder views and emerging tensions. In: International Conference on Software Business, pp. 61–76. Springer (2023)
7. Hickok, M.: Public procurement of artificial intelligence systems: new risks and future proofing. AI Soc. **39**(3), 1213–1227 (2024)
8. Johnson, N., et al.: Legacy procurement practices shape how us cities govern AI: understanding government employees' practices, challenges, and needs. In: Proceedings of the 2025 ACM Conference on Fairness, Accountability, and Transparency, pp. 772–789 (2025)
9. Kazim, E., Koshiyama, A.S.: A high-level overview of AI ethics. Patterns **2**(9) (2021)
10. Koski, A., Pirinen, S., Mikkonen, T.: The ethical landscape in public procurement of ICT systems. In: International Conference on Software Business, pp. 35–43. Springer (2024)
11. Pérez y Madrid, A., Wright, C.: Trustworthy AI alone is not enough. Dykinson (2023)

12. Nagitta, P.O., Mugurusi, G., Obicci, P.A., Awuor, E.: Human-centered artificial intelligence for the public sector: the gate keeping role of the public procurement professional. Proc. Comput. Sci. **200**, 1084–1092 (2022)
13. Raji, I.D., et al.: Closing the AI accountability gap: defining an end-to-end framework for internal algorithmic auditing. In: Proceedings of the 2020 Conference on Fairness, Accountability, and Transparency, pp. 33–44 (2020)
14. Rolfstam, M.: Public Procurement and Innovation. Edward Elgar Publishing (2013)
15. Wachter, S., Mittelstadt, B., Floridi, L.: Why a right to explanation of automated decision-making does not exist in the general data protection regulation. Int. Data Privacy Law **7**(2), 76–99 (2017)

Adopting Generative AI – Preliminary Survey Results About Expectations About the Use and the Effects of Use from the Financial Industry

Katarina Cellarova[2], Joanna Kedziora[1], Mostafa Goudarzi[1], and Mikael Collan[1](✉)

[1] LUT Business School, Yliopistonkatu 34, 53851 Lappeenranta, Finland
{joanna.kedziora,mostafa.goudarzi,mikael.collan}@lut.fi
[2] Faculty of Law, Charles University, Prague, Czech Republic
katarina.cellarova@lut.fi

Abstract. This paper presents preliminary results from a survey study involving a financial organization that has started the adoption of the Generative Artificial Intelligence tool Microsoft CoPilot and the expectations their workforce has about the adoption of the tool. We concentrate on the task level and show results about the effort different types of tasks require and the expectations about the effort needed and the quality of the end-result when using CoPilot to do the same tasks. The results show that CoPilot users expect the tool to reduce the effort needed, while the quality is expected to remain at the same level or to be better. We identify many tasks for which CoPilot is perceived to be helpful. The results are new and relevant to knowledge-work focused organizations contemplating the adoption of Generative AI in finance and beyond.

Keywords: Generative AI · technology adoption · financial industry

1 Introduction

Adoption of generative AI is taking place right now in many "white collar" knowledge-work concentrated organizations [1–3]. In this paper the focus is on a Nordic financial institution operating in the retail finance market that is in the process of adopting generative artificial intelligence (GenAI) tools in the workplace, namely they are implementing Microsoft Copilot suite in everyday work. We have collected information through a survey administered in October - November 2025 and analyze the data collected.

In this research we look specifically at the work-related tasks (task-level) in the organization and how much effort the tasks require now (ex-ante) and how much effort the same tasks are expected to require with GenAI (ex-post). We are also interested in the user expectations regarding the quality of task outcomes with GenAI, also previously discussed in the literature [4, 5]. Our focus is on understanding the expectations that new GenAI users have on the ability of the tools to help them in frequently repeated

K. Węcel and V. Řepa (Eds.): BIS 2026, LNBIP 584, pp. 353–361, 2026.
https://doi.org/10.1007/978-3-032-26363-6_27

tasks by way of reducing the effort needed and to dig deeper into these expectations. We are interested in understanding what drives the adoption of GenAI and more generally, where GenAI is expected to work well and where it works well.

The work is related to the Lazy User Model [6, 7] that posits that the overall cost, including required effort, is an important factor in driving the adoption of solutions (and technology) and that the smaller the required effort is, the better the chances are that a solution is adopted. For frequently repeated tasks there are higher incentives to invest in learning as the effort spent on the investment is spread between the many instances a task is performed [8].

The adoption of GenAI in financial institutions has been looked at also in the past [3, 9, 10]. So far, generative AI adoption in financial services is often discussed at a high level, focusing on strategic benefits such as efficiency gains, innovation potential, and competitive advantage [1, 3]. However, new technologies affect daily work and concrete job tasks, which influence worker-level adoption decisions that ultimately translate to potential high-level gains. Existing studies show that financial institutions use GenAI across a wide range of activities, including customer service, advisory work, marketing, risk analysis, accounting, and document-intensive processes [3, 11, 12]. Research so far shows that in regulated banking environments successful adoption depends not only on technical performance, but also on organizational fit, system reliability, regulatory compliance, and operational readiness [4, 10]. These findings suggest that in order to understand what drives successful GenAI adoption close attention to how the technology is expected to change specific work tasks is required.

A task-level perspective is especially relevant in financial organizations, where many tasks are repetitive, standardized, and rich in textual content. Research in the context of accounting and finance shows that large language model-based tools can support drafting, summarization, report preparation, and explanatory documentation. These tools can reduce processing times and shift employee effort towards analytical, or decision-oriented work, even though human control is still necessary [11, 13]. In banking operations, GenAI systems have been studied for extracting information from financial documents and answering queries and combined with optical character recognition technologies, which show potential for partial automation of back-office workflows [14]. Studies on AI-based chatbots, also usable in the financial industry, show improvements in service efficiency, response times, and availability, when the tools are integrated into routine service processes [15, 16]. What we know so far is that GenAI is a relevant tool for performing recurring tasks that need retrieval of language, templates, and information, and that are common in knowledge-intensive office work, such as retail-banking.

Expected task-level benefits are also closely linked to task-level risks. Research on GenAI in financial services highlights concerns related to data privacy, governance, and responsible data practices, due to the sensitive nature of financial and personal information used [17]. A challenge is the risk of hallucinations and as result incorrect outputs, an especially problematic issue in banking, where accuracy, auditability, and compliance are critical [18]. Even though employees may expect GenAI to reduce effort and speed up task completion, additional (new) verification and control steps may be required, which may reduce potential overall efficiency gains. Concerns have been voiced about bias and lack of transparency in generative AI systems, which can reduce trust and increase decision-making risks, if the outputs are used without sufficient inspection [19].

This study focuses on employee expectations related to effort and quality at the task level during the early adoption of Microsoft Copilot in a Nordic financial institution. We focus on enhancing the micro-level understanding of where employees expect practical value from GenAI in their daily work [3, 4, 9]. This perspective aligns with the Lazy User Model, which emphasizes effort minimization as a key driver of adoption, particularly for frequently repeated tasks [6, 20]. It also supports the broader view that the business impact of GenAI depends less on algorithmic novelty and more on how effectively these technologies are adopted into everyday operational tasks [1, 2]. So far, to the best of our knowledge, there have not been many task-related / task-specific studies of GenAI in the financial industry space, nor have we found studies that link the adoption of GenAI with the Lazy User Model.

In the following section we present the method we have used to collect the data used and the data itself. Then we present some descriptive results and the results of a statistical analysis with analysis. Finally, we draw some conclusions and discuss avenues for further research.

2 Data Collection

We collected information through a survey administered with the Webropol on-line survey tool (www.webropol.co.uk) in October - November 2025. The population of respondents consists of 64 individuals working in expert and management roles in a Nordic financial institution engaging in retail finance. The population is 56% female / 44% male, and the 88% of the participants are between the ages of 25 and 55. Ninety-nine percent of the respondents have at least a bachelor level degree. The respondents predominantly (73%) work hybrid (part home part at the office), while 16% report working only at the office and 11% at home (distance).

The participants have all been given a Microsoft CoPilot license and 87% of them report that they have started using CoPilot for the first time, the rest report they are not yet using or have just tried the tool. The big picture is that we are looking at first-time users of CoPilot. Thirty-one percent of the respondents state that they use GenAI daily and 76% report that their use of GenAI is at least weekly. Fifty-nine percent of the population do not use digital assistants (such as Siri or Alexa), while 21% indicate at least weekly use. Ninety-one percent of the respondents have participated in CoPilot training (at work).

The respondents were asked to identify and specify three tasks they perform on a regular basis and to:

1. identify the process category to which each identified task belongs (“content creation”, “summarization”, “translation”, “data analysis”, “ideation and/or coding”, “other”)
2. estimate how difficult each task is for the respondent (scale of 1–5; “very easy”, “easy”, “neutral “hard”, “very hard”)
3. indicate how often they perform the task (“more seldom”, “weekly”, “several times per week”, “daily”, “several times per day”)

4. estimate how much effort the task requires without the CoPilot tool ("don´t know", "very low", "low", "medium", "high", "very high")
5. estimate / how much effort the task requires with the CoPilot tool ("don´t know", "very low", "low", "medium", "high", "very high")
6. how much they believe CoPilot affect the result of each task in terms of quality, time it takes to complete, and on how satisfied the respondent is with the process and the results – three questions ("much lower", "lower", "the same", "higher", "much higher")

They were also asked about the application (software) they use to perform the task. All in all, the maximum possible universe of task-specific answers was 192 (three tasks * 64 respondents) and the number tasks reported on was 186, but data is not fully complete for all asked for items (variables).

3 Results and Analysis

First, in Table 1 we report some descriptive results from the data. Most frequent task process category is content creation, followed by data analysis.

Table 1. Descriptive results from the data collection

	Content creation	Summari-zation	Translation	Data analysis	Ideation or coding	Other
Process category, n=186	57 (30.6%)	33 (17.7%)	16 (8.6%)	45 (24.2%)	18 (9.7%)	17 (9.1%)
	V. Easy	Easy	Neutral	Hard	V. Hard	
Difficulty, n=161	1 (0.6%)	41 (25.4%)	80 (49.7%)	33 (20.5%)	6 (3.7%)	
	M. Seldom	Weekly	Mult. Weekly	Daily	Mult. Daily	
Frequence, n=186	28 (15.1%)	24 (12.9%)	54 (29.0%)	59 (31.7%)	21 (11.3%)	
	Don't know	Very low	Low	Medium	High	Very High
Effort without CoPilot, n=186	0 (0%)	14 (7.5%)	58 (31.2%)	77 (41.4%)	37 (19.9%)	0 (0%)
Effort with CoPilot, n=185	11 (5.9%)	59 (31.9%)	84 (45.4%)	22 (11.9%)	4 (2.2%)	5 (2.7%)
	M. Lower	Lower	Same	Higher	M. Higher	
Diff. w. Copilot Quality, n=185	4 (2.2%)	10 (5.4%)	78 (42.2%)	74 (40%)	19 (10.3%)	
Diff. w. Copilot Time, n=186	37 (19.9%)	91 (48.9%)	31 (16.7%)	21 (11.3%)	6 (3.2%)	
Diff. w. Copilot Satisfaction, n=186	4 (2.2%)	10 (5.4%)	69 (37.1%)	82 (44.1%)	21 (11.3%)	

The difficulty of the tasks is estimated as mostly between easy and hard with only few tasks being estimated as very hard or very easy. More than 70% of the chosen tasks are performed at least multiple times weekly. The distributions of the estimated effort needed without copilot (ex-ante) and with copilot (expectation ex-post) are different and visible in Fig. 1.

The expectation is that on aggregate the effort with CoPilot is lower than without it (the distributions are different), while there are also tasks for which using CoPilot is estimated to mean having to spend more effort.

The difference in quality, time consumption, and satisfaction (or how content the respondent is with regards to the process) with and without CoPilot are interesting and show that the respondents expect the quality of the results of their chosen tasks to increase with Copilot (>50% expect higher or much higher quality), the time consumed by their chosen tasks to be lower (68,8% expect much lower or lower time consumption), and the task satisfaction to be higher (>55% expect higher or much higher satisfaction).

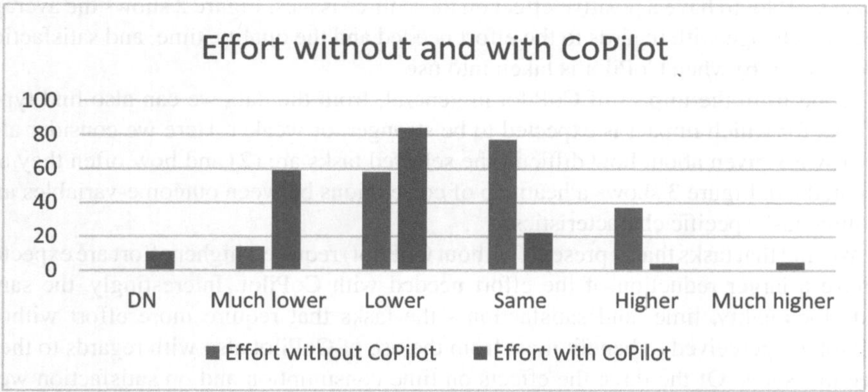

Fig. 1. Estimates of effort used without and with CoPilot (n = 186 /185)

When looking at the results with regards to the perceived changes in the effort needed with CoPilot, one can hypothesize based on the Lazy User Model that there are tasks for which CoPilot (GenAI) is a "winning solution" and for which the adoption of CoPilot is driven by the reduction in the effort needed.

Second, we go into deeper analysis and measure expectations of how CoPilot will affect work, with four outcome variables for each of three tasks reported. Firstly, we look at expectations about effort reduction for each task. This variable is derived from two questions–"estimate how much effort the task requires without the CoPilot tool" (4) and "estimate/how much effort the task requires with the CoPilot tool" (5). Both required responses are on a five-point Likert scale and "I don't know". On average, participants reported CoPilot will decrease effort for the task by 1 unit on the Likert scale. We find a statistically significant difference in the expected effort needed without and with CoPilot (Wilcoxon signed-rank test, paired data, $p < 0.001$).

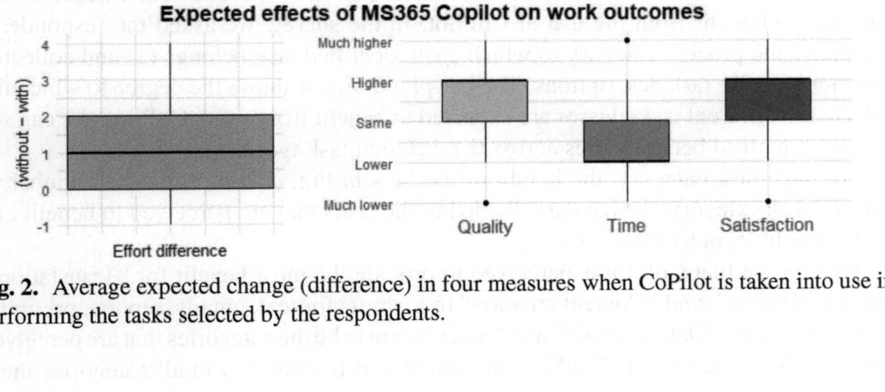

Fig. 2. Average expected change (difference) in four measures when CoPilot is taken into use in performing the tasks selected by the respondents.

Secondly, we measure the expected effect of CoPilot on three more measures about the expectations regarding the quality, time it takes to complete, and on how satisfied the respondent is with the process and the results (6). As seen in Table 1, the respondents expect CoPilot to have a positive effect on these three issues. Figure 2 shows the average expected change with regards to the effort needed and the quality, time, and satisfaction (questions 4–6) when CoPilot is taken into use.

Aside from the impact of CoPilot in general, from the data we can also find types of tasks for which impact is expected to be stronger, or weaker. Here we consider also the answers given about how difficult the selected tasks are (2) and how often they are executed (3). Figure 3 shows a heatmap of correlations between outcome-variables and the three task specific characteristics.

We find that tasks that at present (without CoPilot) require a higher effort are expected to have a larger reduction of the effort needed with CoPilot. Interestingly, the same holds for quality, time, and satisfaction - the tasks that require more effort without CoPilot are perceived to benefit most from the use of CoPilot also with regards to these three measures. Of the three the effects on time consumption and on satisfaction were statistically the most supported effects. Also, the frequency of performing a task seems to have positive effect on the expected time consumption of the task.

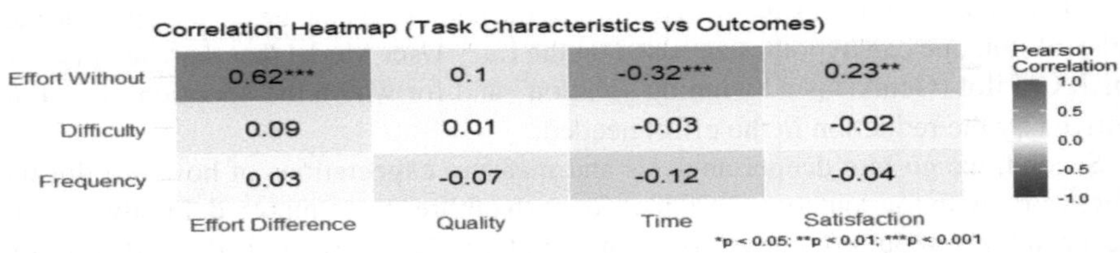

Fig. 3. Heatmap of correlations between task characteristics and outcome variables

The more often a task is performed the more on aggregate even a small reduction in time consumption affects the overall cost of performing the task. Based on the result, also time consumption (in addition to effort reduction) may be a driver of GenAI (CoPilot) adoption – and likely is for specific tasks particularly.

Lastly, we examine the categories of tasks and how the different categories are expected to benefit from the use of CoPilot. In the survey, we asked the respondents to identify the process category to which each identified task belongs (1) and collected also more precise task descriptions. The bar-plot in Fig. 4 shows the degree to which the tasks in the different task-classes are expected to benefit from using CoPilot. We can see that the perceived benefit varies across the different task types.

For each task category, the height of the bars in Fig. 4 shows the total number of tasks in each category, the bars are divided to the tasks that are perceived to benefit and not to benefit from CoPilot use.

We can see that CoPilot is perceived to provide the most benefit for "Translation", "Summarization", and "Content creation" (e.g. drafts for text, emails, reports, presentations) categories. "Data-analysis" and "other" seem to be the categories that are perceived from benefit the least from CoPilot. Importantly, it is clear that in all categories there

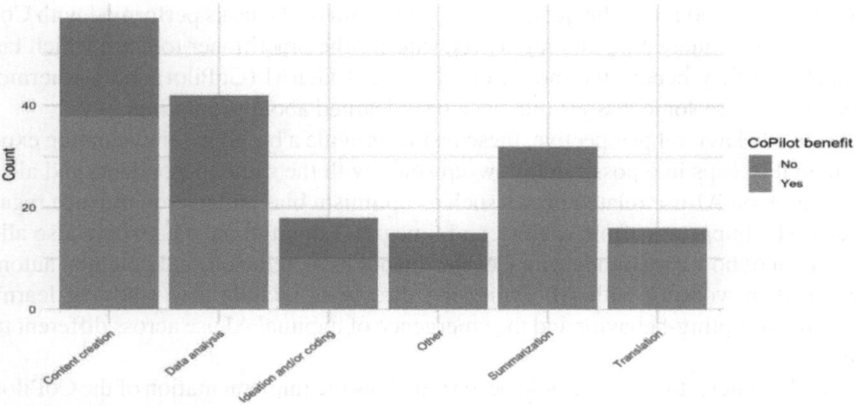

Fig. 4. Task categories and the proportion of tasks, where CoPilot is perceived to be beneficial to the task

are tasks that are perceived to benefit from CoPilot use, while there are differences with regards to the expectations.

4 Summary and Some Conclusions

This paper describes preliminary results from a survey studying the expectations about the use of GenAI tools (CoPilot) in a Nordic financial organization. The results are task-level and tell us about the expectations regarding how GenAI is expected to perform in specific tasks identified by the respondents. The main results show that the respondents seem to generally expect that they will benefit from using GenAI tools in the identified tasks and with regards to the quality of outcome, time consumption, and satisfaction (in completing the task). The respondents generally expect CoPilot to reduce their effort in completing tasks. The more effort tasks require without GenAI, the more GenAI is expected to contribute. CoPilot is expected to be most beneficial in tasks that involve translation, summarization, and content creation.

The results can be interpreted from the technology adoption point-of-view, and it can be hypothesized, based on the Lazy User Model that the overall "cost" reduction (in terms of effort and time use) are drivers of GenAI adoption among the respondents, and that the increased (job) satisfaction is positive for the adoption. One thing that comes to mind is that increased job satisfaction is a form of negative cost of performing a task.

As a caveat we point out that the results are preliminary and as the population is rather small (64), while the number of tasks identified is more numerous (186), the presented results cannot be generalized to represent a larger population of financial white-collar workers / task performed by them. However, the results are interesting and shed light on task-specific expectations of using GenAI in general.

There are several avenues for further research that have been opened by this research. One very promising one is to make a follow-up, longitudinal, survey to collect information about the actual effect the CoPilot tool has had on the effort required to perform the identified tasks and about the quality of the end-result of the tasks performed with CoPilot. It would be interesting and highly relevant for the practitioner to learn which tasks are such that they benefit the most from the use of GenAI (CoPilot) and furthermore, whether there are some lessons that have been learned about prompting.

From a behavioral perspective, these results provide a baseline for evaluating expectation–reality gaps in a possible follow-up study with the same respondents and allows for research on AI-use related biases such as optimism bias and overconfidence regarding GenAI's impact on effort, quality, and time use. Longitudinal data would also allow assessment of how experience with CoPilot shapes trust, reliance, and potential automation (bias) in working with AI. Promising directions include also studying learning effects in prompting-behavior and the emergence of habitual AI use across different task types.

Another interesting issue would be to study how the implementation of the CoPilot as a tool has taken place in the case-firm and to study how much benefit the users have been able to draw from GenAI training sessions they have participated in. Another interesting avenue is to do a comparative study with a survey that is similar (or same) and to compare results between organizations. All in all, there are many interesting avenues for further research.

Acknowledgments. This research was supported by the Czech Science Foundation (23-07419M). Thanks go to the respondents and the collaborating Nordic financial institution.

Disclosure of Interests. The authors have no competing interests to declare that are relevant to the content of this article.

References

1. Chen, B., Wu, Z., Zhao, R.: From fiction to fact: the growing role of generative AI in business and finance. J. Chin. Econ. Bus. Stud. **21**, 471–496 (2023)
2. Generative AI in banking and financial services | McKinsey. https://www.mckinsey.com/industries/financial-services/our-insights/capturing-the-full-value-of-generative-ai-in-banking
3. Lee, D.K.C., Guan, C., Yu, Y., Ding, Q.: A comprehensive review of generative AI in finance. FinTech **3**, 460–478 (2024)
4. Moharrak, M., Mogaji, E.: Generative AI in banking: empirical insights on integration, challenges and opportunities in a regulated industry. Int. J. Bank Market. (2024). https://doi.org/10.1108/IJBM-08-2024-0490
5. Khan, M.S., Umer, H.: ChatGPT in finance: applications, challenges, and solutions. Heliyon **10**, (2024)
6. Collan, M., Tétard, F.: Lazy user theory of solution selection. 273–278 (2007)
7. Tetard, F., Collan, M.: Lazy user theory: a dynamic model to understand user selection of products and services. In: 2009 42nd Hawaii International Conference on System Sciences, pp. 1–9 (2009). https://doi.org/10.1109/HICSS.2009.287
8. Loureiro, S.M.C., Guerreiro, J., Tussyadiah, I.: Artificial intelligence in business: state of the art and future research agenda. J. Bus. Res. **129**, 911–926 (2021)
9. Chen, Y., Yan, S., Jin, Y., Li, J., Jin, X.: Generative artificial intelligence in finance: a systematic literature review and a research agenda. Digit. Technol. Res. Appl. **4**, 14–32 (2025)

10. Vuković, D.B., Dekpo-Adza, S., Matović, S.: AI integration in financial services: a systematic review of trends and regulatory challenges. Humanit. Soc. Sci. Commun. **12**, 562 (2025)
11. Dong, M.M., Stratopoulos, T.C., Wang, V.X.: A scoping review of ChatGPT research in accounting and finance. Int. J. Account. Inf. Syst. **55**, 100715 (2024)
12. Sai, S., et al.: Generative AI for finance: applications, case studies and challenges. Expert. Syst. **42**, e70018 (2025)
13. Zhao, J., Wang, X.: Unleashing efficiency and insights: exploring the potential applications and challenges of ChatGPT in accounting. J. Corp. Account. Finan. (Wiley) **35**, 269–276 (2024)
14. Qiu, Y., Duvvuri, V.C., Yadavalli, P., Prasad, N.: Evaluation of generative AI Q&A Chatbot chained to optical character recognition models for financial documents. In: Proceedings of the 2024 8th International Conference on Machine Learning and Soft Computing, pp. 101–110. ACM, New York, NY, USA, (2024). https://doi.org/10.1145/3647750.3647766
15. Bavaresco, R., et al.: Conversational agents in business: a systematic literature review and future research directions. Comput. Sci. Rev. **36**, 100239 (2020)
16. Nguyen, T.H., Le, X.C.: Artificial intelligence-based chatbots – a motivation underlying sustainable development in banking: standpoint of customer experience and behavioral outcomes. Cogent Bus. Manage. **12**, 2443570 (2025)
17. Shalini, R., Bagrecha, C.: A study on generative AI and its impact on banking and financial services sector: data privacy & sustainable perspective. In: 2023 IEEE Technology & Engineering Management Conference - Asia Pacific (TEMSCON-ASPAC), pp. 1–5 (2023). https://doi.org/10.1109/TEMSCON-ASPAC59527.2023.10531592
18. Wach, K., et al.: The dark side of generative artificial intelligence: a critical analysis of controversies and risks of ChatGPT. Entrep. Bus. Econ. Rev. **11**, 7–30 (2023)
19. Mirestean, A., et al.: Powering the digital economy: opportunities and risks of artificial intelligence in finance. Dep. Papers **2021**, 1 (2021)
20. Collan, M., Tétard, F.: Lazy user model: solution selection and discussion about switching costs. In: Salmela, H., Sell, A. (eds.) Nordic Contributions in IS Research, pp. 56–68. Springer, Heidelberg (2011). https://doi.org/10.1007/978-3-642-22766-0_7

Analysis of the Relationship Between the Use of Cloud Business Intelligence Systems and Selected Aspects of Enterprise Functioning

Damian Dziembek[1](✉) and Paula Bajdor[2]

[1] Czestochowa University of Technology, Czestochowa, Poland
damian.dziembek@pcz.pl
[2] Warsaw University of Technology, Warsaw, Poland
paula.bajdor@pw.edu.pl

Abstract. This article examines how the use of Cloud Business Intelligence (Cloud BI) systems relates to selected areas of enterprise operations. The study was conducted through an online CAWI survey among 400 medium-sized and large companies in Poland that use Cloud BI. Using Spearman's rank correlation, the analysis shows that neither the overall impact of Cloud BI nor the length of its use produces consistently strong or positive effects across all operational areas. However, several significant relationships were found within specific aspects of Cloud BI use, indicating its multidimensional and systemic nature. These results provide a clearer understanding of the role of Cloud BI in enterprise management.

Keywords: Cloud Computing · Business Intelligence · Cloud Business Intelligence

1 Introduction

Modern enterprises are experiencing a dynamic increase in the amount of data generated and processed (e.g., in ERP systems, IoT, email, corporate portals, social media, and other digital sources), which requires the use of Business Intelligence (BI) systems. BI systems are designed not only to support decision-making but also to transform data into knowledge, as well as integrate, analyze, and visualize information from various sources. The development of cloud technologies has led to the emergence of a new generation of BI systems, known as Cloud Business Intelligence (CBI), which leverage external infrastructure for analytical processes without the need to invest in local IT resources, ensuring flexibility, scalability, and a pay-as-you-go model. CBI systems enable dynamic data analysis, support better decisions, increase operational efficiency and process transparency, and facilitate the forecasting of trends and threats.

Despite a wide range of research (e.g., [1, 2, 3, 4, 5]), there is still a gap in the empirical analysis of the relationship between Cloud BI use and specific aspects of enterprise operations. In particular, the relationships between the overall assessment of CBI impact, its duration of use, and the assessment of individual aspects of its use have

K. Węcel and V. Řepa (Eds.): BIS 2026, LNBIP 584, pp. 362–370, 2026.
https://doi.org/10.1007/978-3-032-26363-6_28

not been sufficiently investigated. There is also a lack of research on the strength and direction of these relationships. The aim of this article is to analyze the relationship between Cloud BI use and selected aspects of enterprise operations, with particular emphasis on the strength and direction of these relationships. The following research questions were formulated:

- RQ1: Is the overall impact of Cloud BI related to the assessment of its individual aspects? RQ2: Does the number of years of Cloud BI use influence the assessment of these aspects?
- RQ3: Are there any interdependencies between the individual aspects of Cloud BI?

Based on this, the following research hypotheses were formulated:

- H1: The overall impact of Cloud BI on enterprise operations positively influences the implementation of individual aspects of Cloud BI.
- H2: The number of years of Cloud BI use positively influences the implementation of individual aspects of Cloud BI.
- H3: There is a significant interdependency between individual aspects of Cloud BI.

The hypotheses are considered confirmed if the strength of the interdependency exceeds 0.5. Achieving this research objective will allow for a better understanding of the role of Cloud BI in enterprise management and provide practical guidance for managers responsible for the use and development of analytical systems.

2 Literature Review

In a dynamic market environment, rapid data processing, knowledge generation, and sound decision-making are crucial to maintaining a company's position. BI systems make it easier for managers at various levels to collect, integrate, analyze, and visualize data to support and streamline the organization's decision-making process [6]. The desire to reduce the costs of implementing and maintaining BI systems, increase access to internal and external data, reduce dependence on IT specialists, reduce reporting burdens, and leverage the benefits of cloud computing have led IT vendors to develop and implement Cloud Business Intelligence (CBI) systems.

CBI is a new way of implementing business intelligence: instead of deploying costly and complex software locally, BI software runs in the cloud, which ensures easier development, simpler installation, and use thanks to lower costs and easier implementation [7]. Cloud BI offers reporting, analysis, data mining, visualization, and forecasting in a cloud architecture. Integrating BI with the cloud increases scalability, data availability, and speed of response to market changes [8]. Compared to traditional BI systems, cloud solutions shorten analysis time, facilitate access to data from multiple sources, and improve management efficiency [9]. These systems also better cope with large data volumes and advanced analytics [10].

Cloud Business Intelligence can support both operational and strategic decisions, enabling trend analysis, anomaly identification, and scenario-based decision-making. Consequently, Cloud BI can be defined as the delivery of BI systems in a cloud environment in which analytical tools, data warehouses, and reporting mechanisms operate as a service accessible via the Internet, synergistically combining the cost-effectiveness, flexibility, availability, and scalability of the cloud with the potential of data analytics.

Cloud BI works by replicating data to a cloud platform, where it is updated and made available to users. It can operate in IaaS, PaaS, and SaaS models, as well as in public, private, and hybrid clouds. Examples include Amazon EC2, Amazon Redshift, Azure Synapse, Power BI, Tableau Cloud, and SAP Analytics Cloud.

The literature highlights the numerous benefits of Cloud BI: ease of use, accessibility across devices, rapid deployment, lower costs, flexibility, improved data integration, and high levels of security. Challenges include data protection, vendor lock-in, network outages, integration difficulties, and data access delays [11, 12, 13].

The pay-as-you-go model makes Cloud BI particularly attractive to small and medium-sized businesses, for whom traditional BI systems were prohibitively expensive. However, the value of a CBI system depends on its integration with business processes and the analytical skills of users. Nowadays, cloud-based analytical platforms are a key element of digital transformation, supporting the processing of large data sets and integration with technologies such as AI and LM.

3 The Research Methodology

3.1 The Characteristics of the Respondents

To achieve the adopted research objective and verify the research hypotheses, the authors conducted a survey. The research sample included 400 Polish enterprises (200 medium-sized and 200 large), primarily from the industrial and commercial sectors, all of which were using a CBI. A sample of 400 enterprises can be considered representative because it exceeds the minimum sample size of approximately 384, which ensures a 95% confidence level and a ± 5% estimation error for large populations. With appropriate sampling, it enables reliable generalization of results. The selection of 200 medium-sized and large enterprises stems from the need to ensure comparability of analyses between groups and to increase the reliability of inferences, as equal-sized samples enable more stable estimates and eliminate the risk of one category dominating the study results. The sample was selected randomly, which limits the risk of selection bias, with the exclusion criterion being the lack of use of CBI solutions in the enterprise, and the survey itself was conducted in the period from September to December 2024.

To conduct empirical research, a survey questionnaire was developed. The survey questionnaire developed to conduct the research consisted of the following parts: an introduction addressed to research respondents, which included the purpose of the research, the duration of the research, and assurance of confidentiality and anonymity, and relevant questions covering issues related to CBI in the enterprise. The survey was conducted using CAWI. The nature of the answers to individual questions was a 5-point Likert scale (5-definitely yes, 4-yes, 3-do not know, 2-no, 1-definitely no).

The sample was evenly distributed by company size, with 50% medium-sized and 50% large enterprises from various industries. Analysis of the collected data indicates that the majority of surveyed companies operated in the industrial sector (50%) and trade (20%). The largest respondent groups were IT department specialists (76%) and management representatives (19%), while managers of other departments and specialists comprised a small proportion (3%). Consequently, the research engaged personnel with a comprehensive understanding of IT solutions, decision-making authority regarding cloud IT system implementation, and knowledge of the effects of CBI system use within their organizations. On average, the surveyed enterprises in Poland have utilized CBI for over five years, suggesting that this duration is sufficient to accumulate knowledge and experience regarding the impact of such solutions on business activities.

4 Research Results

4.1 Variables List and Reliability Analysis

Table 1 presents the list of variables used for further analysis, their descriptions, symbols, and Cronbach's Alpha values.

Reliability analysis is most often associated with the development of complex scales, particularly summary scales composed of multiple individual items (questions). The reliability of a scale—understood as its internal consistency—provides information about how accurately the scale measures what it is intended to measure, that is, how well the individual items reflect the overall construct. In reliability analysis, the most commonly used indicator is Cronbach's Alpha coefficient, which measures the ratio of the variance of individual items to the variance of the entire scale (the sum of those items). Its value ranges from 0 to 1, with higher values indicating greater reliability. For all groups of variables examined, Cronbach's Alpha was above 0.6, indicating high reliability of the analyses. Moreover, the scale used is a reliable measurement tool characterized by high consistency.

4.2 Correlation Analysis

Spearman's rank correlation coefficient was used to assess the association among all variables. In the first step, it was examined whether there were any significant correlations between the number of years of using BA in Cloud and the assessment of individual aspects of BA in Cloud influencing its functioning (Table 2).

Positive values indicate a positive monotonic relationship – as the value of one variable increases, the value of the other also decreases. Negative values indicate a negative monotonic relationship – as the value of one variable increases, the value of the other usually decreases as well. As Table 2 shows, there are statistically significant correlations between the selected dependent and independent variables:

- analyzing the correlation between variable x_1 and the remaining dependent variables, it is clear that only in two cases were two negative, moderately strong relationships observed. When the value of one variable increases, the value of the other typically decreases, and the strength of this relationship is significant, although not perfect, indicating a moderate relationship. In the first case, a Spearman correlation of −0.58 between variables x_1 and y1 indicates a moderate, negative (inverse) monotonic relationship. Therefore, it can be concluded that the longer a company uses CBI, the less effective the decision-making process becomes. This may be due to the fact that while a clear, positive change in the effectiveness of the decision-making process occurred in the initial

Table 1. The variables' description and reliability analysis

Variable	Label	Cronbach's Alpha
Independent variables		
Years of using CBI	x_1	–
Overall impact of CBI on business operations	x_2	–
Dependent variables		
Decision-making process efficiency	y_1	0,63
Decision-making process effectiveness	y_2	0,67
Decision-making process speed	y_3	0,65
Business analysis quality	y_4	0,63
Ability to create and monitor enterprise strategies	y_5	0,60
Improve and optimize business processes	y_6	0,65
Accelerate forecasting analyses	y_7	0,66
Increase the efficiency of enterprise resource utilization	y_8	0,64
Streamline data management processes	y_9	0,67
Information support for current and new business processes	y_{10}	0,69
Improve work efficiency	y_{11}	0,66
Better control of production/service costs	y_{12}	0,69
Improve analysis of promotional and sales campaigns	y_{13}	0,63
Increase the effectiveness of business analyses	y_{14}	0,60
Improve data security	y_{15}	0,62
Improve fraud detection	y_{16}	0,62
More effective value chain analysis	y_{17}	0,61
More effective customer profiling	y_{18}	0,63
More effective inventory and distribution analysis	y_{19}	0,65
More effective monitoring of project outcomes	y_{20}	0,63
Real-time decision-making	y_{21}	0,67

years of CBI use, in subsequent years, this change simply ceased to be noticeable, thus losing its "novelty appeal". A similar situation occurs in the case of decision-making effectiveness, where a value of −0.62 in the Spearman correlation between variables x_1 and y_2 also indicates a moderate, negative (inverse) monotonic relationship, and the strength of this relationship is significant, although not perfect. This means that the longer a company uses CBI, the less effective the decision-making process becomes. The remaining relationships are also negative but characterized by very weak strength of relationship – in the case of the relationship between variable x_1 and variables y_{10} (−0.22), y_{11} (−0.19), and y_{12} (−0.32). Only in two cases was a positive monotonic relationship observed – for variables y_4 (0.21), y_6 (0.1), and y_{14} (0.09). However, these values are so low that they are interpreted as a nearly nonexistent relationship.

Table 2. The correlation analysis results between the x_1 and x_2 and y_1–y_{21}

	x_1	x_2
y_1	-0,588800	0,180775
y_2	-0,620164	0,233354
y_3	-0,005995	0,050738
y_4	0,217144	0,664211
y_5	0,035074	0,417692
y_6	0,099161	-0,038113
y_7	0,003428	0,020756
y_8	0,088312	-0,015566
y_9	0,012699	0,073005
y_{10}	-0,227814	0,117986
y_{11}	-0,198237	0,366691
y_{12}	-0,329069	-0,183346
y_{13}	-0,096241	0,733382
y_{14}	0,105659	0,382037
y_{15}	0,053702	-0,041979
y_{16}	0,030642	-0,052565
y_{17}	0,019067	-0,009979
y_{18}	0,005395	-0,059627
y_{19}	-0,010879	0,066110
y_{20}	0,001414	-0,098893
y_{21}	0,042080	-0,573922

- the situation is somewhat different in the case of correlations between variable x_2 and the remaining dependent variables. A fairly strong positive relationship exists. The strongest relationships are between x_2 and y_{13} (0.73), x_2 and y_4 (0.66), and x_2 and y_5 (0.41). Therefore, it can be concluded that the greater the impact of CBI on the company's operations, the better the analysis of promotional and sales campaigns, the improved the quality of business analyses, and the easier it is to develop and monitor the company's strategy. Weaker, but still positive, relationships exist between variable x_1 and the following variables: y_1 (0.18), y_2 (0.23), y_{11} (0.36), y_{14} (0.38). There are also three negative relationships: between variable x_2 and y_{12} (–0.18), y_{20} (–0.09), and y_{21} (–0.57). The latter indicates moderate dependence, so it can be stated that the greater the impact of CBI on the enterprise's functioning, the worse the ability to make real-time decisions.

Summarizing the above results, it can be concluded that although several relationships exist between variables x_1 and x_2 and the dependent variables, neither hypothesis H1 nor H2 was supported. This is because, under the first hypothesis, only 8 of 21 correlations were observed, and the two strongest were negative. In the second case, 11 of 21 correlations were observed, but only 8 indicated a moderately strong positive relationship. Therefore, it can be concluded that neither the duration of CBI use nor its overall impact on the company's operations improves the company's performance in the analyzed aspects.

In the next step, it was examined whether there were significant relationships among the individual aspects of CBI's impact on the enterprise's functioning (Fig. 1).

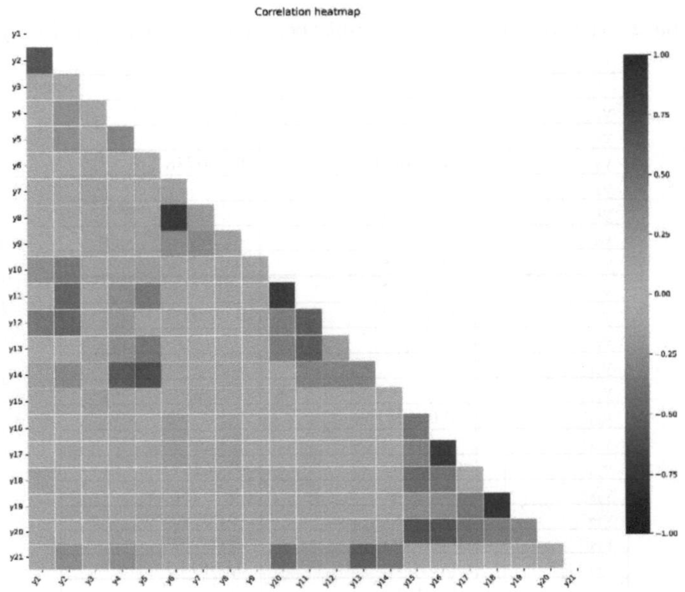

Fig. 1. The correlation analysis results between the y_1–y_{21}

Analyzing the obtained results, it is clearly visible that there are a number of relationships between the analyzed variables:

- a very strong positive relationship between y_6 and y_8 (0.81), y_{10} and y_{11} (0.80), and y_{16} and y_{17} (0.79). It follows that improving and optimizing business processes increases the efficiency of enterprise resource utilization, information support for current and new business processes increases work efficiency, and better fraud detection leads to more effective value chain analysis.
- a strong positive relationship between y_5 and y_{14} (0.66), y_{15} and y_{20} (0.63), y_{16} and y_{20} (0.62), and y_1 and y_2 (0.65). Therefore, it can be concluded that increasing the ability to create and monitor enterprise strategies positively influences the effectiveness of business analyses, improves data security and enables more effective fraud detection, enhances the monitoring of project outcomes, and increases decision-making efficiency.
- the moderate positive relationship between y_2 and y_{11} (0.52), y_{11} and y_{12}, y_{13} (0.59), y_2 and y_{12} (0.52), and y_4 and y_{14} (0.58) suggests that higher decision-making efficiency slightly influences increased work efficiency and better control of production/service costs. Increased work efficiency positively influences better control of production/service costs and improved analysis of promotional and sales campaigns. A higher level of business analysis quality increases the effectiveness of business analyses.

– there is one rather strong negative relationship between variables y_{18} and y19 (–0.75), indicating that more effective customer profiling negatively impacts inventory and distribution analyses. In summary, it can be concluded that hypothesis H3 was partially positively verified, as there were indeed a number of correlations between the analyzed variables, but only 13 of them were characterized by a strong relationship. The remaining ones indicated a moderately strong or weak relationship.

5 Conclusions

The research confirmed that Cloud Business Intelligence systems play a significant role in supporting the operations and development of modern enterprises and enabled the achievement of the article's main goal: to analyze the relationship between the use of Cloud Business Intelligence systems and selected aspects of enterprise operations. The results indicate that the impact of Cloud BI on enterprise operations is neither clearly linear nor universal. Neither the duration of Cloud BI use nor the overall assessment of its impact on enterprise operations automatically translates into improvements in all analyzed areas, such as efficiency, effectiveness, or speed of decision-making processes.

Correlation analysis revealed that hypotheses H1 and H2 were not positively verified, as the observed correlations were often weak or moderate, and some were negative. These results suggest that the benefits of implementing Cloud BI may be most noticeable in the initial period of use, but their impact may stabilize or weaken in the long term. This may be due, among other things, to the "novelty effect," insufficient development of users' analytical skills, or limited integration of Cloud BI systems with key business processes. At the same time, hypothesis H3 was partially confirmed, indicating significant relationships among individual aspects of enterprise operations supported by Cloud BI. Particularly strong correlations were observed between business process optimization and resource efficiency, information support and work efficiency, and fraud detection and value chain analysis. These results confirm that the value generated by Cloud BI is systemic, manifesting primarily in connections across various management areas rather than in isolated effects of individual functionalities.

The research findings have significant practical implications. They indicate that implementing Cloud Business Intelligence systems should be considered an element of a long-term strategy for developing analytical competencies and digital transformation within an enterprise, rather than solely as a technological investment. Integrating Cloud BI into decision-making processes and actively leveraging the generated analyses in operational and strategic management is crucial.

The conducted research has certain limitations, such as the limited number of companies surveyed and the diversity of industries, which may affect the generality of the conclusions. Furthermore, the rapid development of Cloud BI technology means that the results may require updating as new solutions and trends emerge. Therefore, further research should include a broader range of companies from various sectors and analyze the long-term effects of Cloud BI implementation. It is also important to explore the impact of organizational and cultural factors on the effectiveness of these systems. The obtained data provide an important contribution to understanding the mechanisms of Cloud BI and can serve practitioners and decision-makers as a basis for better planning digital transformation strategies for enterprises.

References

1. Sultan, H., Chan, L.K., Siew, P.H., Lee, C.K.: Factors influencing cloud business intelligence adoption and use at organisational level. In: ITM Web of Conferences, vol. 67, Article 01019 (2024)
2. Owusu, K.: Determinants of cloud business intelligence adoption among Ghanaian SMEs. Int. J. Cloud Appl. Comput. **10**(4), 1–20 (2020)
3. El Malah, K., Nasr, M.: Cloud business intelligence. Int. J. Adv. Netw. Appl. **10**(06), 4120–4124 (2019)
4. Moyo, M., Loock, M.: Conceptualising a cloud business intelligence security evaluation framework. Information **12**(3), 128 (2021)
5. Dziembek, D., Ziora, L.: Cloud-based business intelligence solutions in the management of polish companies. In: Silaghi, G.C., et al. Advances in Information Systems Development. ISD 2022. Lecture Notes in Information Systems and Organisation, vol. 63, Springer, Cham, pp. 35–52 (2023)
6. Fink, L., Yogev, N., Even, A.: Business intelligence and organizational learning: an empirical investigation of value creation processes. Inf. Manage. 54(1) (2017)
7. Ouf, S., Nasr, M.: Business intelligence in the cloud. In: 2011 IEEE 3rd International Conference on Communication Software and Networks, Xi'an, China, pp. 650–655 (2011)
8. Indriasari, E., Meyliana, Hidayanto, A.N., Prabowo, H.: Key benefits, challenges, and risk of cloud business intelligence: a systematic literature review. Int. J. Mech. Eng. Technol. **9**(9), 819–831 (2018)
9. El Ghalbzouri, H., El Bouhdidi, J.: Integrating Business Intelligence with Cloud Computing: State of the Art and Fundamental Concepts. In: M. Ben Ahmed, et al (Eds.), Networking, Intelligent Systems and Security, Springer, 197–213, (2022)
10. Dziembek, D. Ziora, L.: Cloud-based business intelligence solutions in the management of polish companies. In: Buchmann, R.A. et al. (eds.). Information Systems Development: Artificial Intelligence for Information Systems Development and Operations (ISD2022 Proceedings). Cluj-Napoca, Romania: Risoprint (2022)
11. Dashora, S., Gupta, N., Tanwar, M.P.S., Singh, A., Kaur, S.: Cloud-based data analytics for business intelligence. Int. J. Res. Appl. Sci. Eng. Technol. (IJRASET) **11**, Issue XI (2023)
12. Patel, D.B.: Building scalable business intelligence systems in the cloud: a technical approach. Int. J. Sci. Res. Arch. **2**(1), 212–215 (2021)
13. Olszak, C.M.: Business intelligence in cloud. Polish J. Manage. Stud. **10**(2), 115–125 (2014)

Various applications

Blockchain-Based Digital Product Passports and Their Feasibility in Steelmaking

Sadeer Beden(✉), Connor Blake Hurley, Cinzia Giannetti, and Arnold Beckmann

Swansea University, Swansea SA1 8EN, UK
sadeer.beden@swansea.ac.uk

Abstract. The transition toward a circular economy requires continuous tracking of material lifecycles through Digital Product Passports (DPP). Blockchain has been proposed for DPP implementations due to their immutable nature, but its application within the steelmaking sector remains largely unexplored. This paper investigates the technical feasibility of a permissioned blockchain framework to serve as a foundational infrastructure for steel DPPs. The proposed framework utilises Hyperledger Fabric with a hybrid storage strategy and cryptographic hash pointers to ensure data integrity and scalability. To validate the framework, we conducted a performance assessment simulating approximately 11.5 years of industrial activity across a 12-node distributed network. The simulation processed over 48 million transactions, displaying ledger stability and storage scalability under operational pressure. Our results display a consistent mean throughput of approx. 210 TPS and stable transaction latency even as the ledger grew linearly. The hybrid data strategy provided pruning that effectively managed storage overhead. These findings suggest that permissioned blockchains are technically feasible to serve as the foundational framework covering the requirements of DPP implementations within the steel supply chain.

Keywords: Blockchain · Digital Product Passport (DPP) · Steelmaking · Hyperledger Fabric

1 Introduction

As part of the circular economy movement, there is a regulatory push to record the full lifecycle of a product [5], leading to the introduction of Digital Product Passports (DPP) [8]. These passports serve as the digital backbone for this transition and are becoming a mandatory requirement to produce and sell products in the European market under the Ecodesign for Sustainable Products Regulation (ESPR). Under this framework, DPPs are designed to function as digital identity cards throughout a product's lifecycle, storing a variety of data such as material origins, environmental footprints, and recyclability [4].

K. Węcel and V. Řepa (Eds.): BIS 2026, LNBIP 584, pp. 373–384, 2026.
https://doi.org/10.1007/978-3-032-26363-6_29

However, current DPP implementations remain fragmented, often facing limitations with data integration, storage scalability, as well as privacy, transparency, and security [13]. Traditional centralised databases require stakeholders to trust a single managing entity, creating potential conflicts of interest.

Blockchain technology has emerged as a potential solution to address these challenges [3]. Blockchain is a distributed ledger technology that records information across multiple nodes, ensuring that no one single party can alter on-chain information without leaving evidence. This approach provides the transparency, security, and integrity required for multi-stakeholder supply chains. Blockchain also provides smart contracts to enable automation of tasks such as updating, collating and verifying information [10]. The use of cryptographic hashes and links to existing databases provides flexibility, allowing companies to integrate the framework with their established data infrastructures. These core characteristics justify the adoption of blockchain, making it suitable for supporting DPP implementations.

The steel industry is one domain that is transitioning towards the adoption of DPP. Steelmaking encompasses many complex processes, from raw material extraction to finishing processes, all of which generate disparate data points that must make their way into the DPP. Sharing this data across stakeholders without exposing proprietary information requires a decentralised approach. Despite the potential, there is limited literature investigating the adoption of blockchain-driven DPPs for the steelmaking industry.

This paper addresses this gap by evaluating the performance of a blockchain-based framework tailored for steel manufacturing. The scope is not to propose a comprehensive DPP with complex application-layer interactions e.g., audits or economic cost analyses. Instead, the focus is on the performance evaluation of this framework using a simulated system, specifically to establish a baseline for throughput, latency, and storage scalability in this domain.

To achieve this aim, our objectives are to identify a suitable architecture, design a scalable framework, and validate its performance under realistic industrial stress. Consequently, we investigate the following research questions:

- What are the available and most suitable blockchain technologies for this task?
- How can we assess and evaluate the impact and technical feasibility of using blockchain technologies for a steelmaking DPP?
- How can we validate this assessment with an experiment modelling a realistic segment of the UK's steel supply chain?

The contributions of this paper are twofold: (1) A comparative evaluation of blockchain technologies for industrial DPP feasibility, and (2) The deployment of a realistic demonstrator based on steel supply chain parameters to evaluate the performance of the proposed framework. The full results are available in the open-source repository.[1]

[1] https://github.com/bedening/steel-dpp-feasibility-experiment.

2 Literature Review

This section reviews blockchain-based DPP implementations with similar methodologies and application domains to provide a basis for our first research question.

Hulea et al. [6] implemented a DPP using Hyperledger Fabric for product lifecycle management. Particularly, their data model captured *Product, Manufacturer, Supplier* and *Material* information, using *cheqd.io* to create unique product identification for each category. The chaincodes were created using *Node.js* and executed CRUD operations. The authors stated that their evaluation focused on response time of CRUD operations, omitting other impacts such as high-volume throughput and storage bloat. Our methodology challenges this by stress-testing these parameters under steelmaking conditions.

Kim et al. [11] focused on solving supply chain privacy using a multi-channel Hyperledger Fabric architecture. The authors set up multiple channels to manage different product stages (material supply chain, product manufacturing, recycling) within the supply chain. The data was segmented into its corresponding channel based on the lifecycle stage of each product, and assigned decentralised identifiers for improved security. The authors stated that although this overall approach enhanced system security and privacy, challenges relating to data integration across various channels remained. In contrast, our focus is less on specific system architecture, and instead aims to understand the feasibility of DPP for steelmaking. We argue that a single-channel hybrid approach with off-chain storage provides a scalable solution as a baseline for the steel industry.

Paolucci et al. [15] investigated the use of the DPP for electronics manufacturing. The authors developed a DPP prototype using eXtended Markup Language (XML) for data digitalisation and blockchain technology for data communication and storage. They validated their model using Ganache, a local Ethereum testing environment, which demonstrated the advantages of adopting Ethereum to track ownership of a washing machine product over its lifecycle. However, the paper also highlighted the limitations in data privacy inherent in Ethereum. This presents a challenge for our use case, which requires the protection of proprietary manufacturing data. The authors further abstracted from details relating to network latency and consensus overhead of a distributed production system. We address these gaps by deploying a distributed permissioned network.

Kannappan et al. [9] proposed a system that combined blockchain and digital twin technologies to enable the creation and sharing of product lifecycle data for DPP. The authors utilised a multi-layer architecture where Ethereum was employed for automation, security, and improved traceability using smart contracts. The authors deployed their network in a development mode that forced instant transactions. This assumption masked the throughput bottlenecks inherent to permissionless networks. Our research addresses this gap by configuring consensus protocols to reflect representative industrial latency.

Xia et al. [18] focused on integrating blockchain technology with DPP in the Reverse Supply Chain (RSC). The authors presented a novel conceptual framework comprising four layers: user interface, application service, blockchain, and data. This structure managed user access, data standardisation, and the distributed ledger of the RSC. The authors stated that RSC often faces issues with uncertainty and low trust, which blockchain generally overcomes. Similarly, Stodt et al. [17] designed a blockchain-enabled DPP framework for healthcare devices such as pacemakers and surgical instruments. This approach established a primary security layer to defend against cyberattacks. They formulated a multi-stage framework covering the full lifecycle of devices, from manufacturing to recycling. Both studies rely on theoretical designs but leave implementation as future work. This highlights a recurring limitation in current literature where theoretical blockchain architectures are rarely validated against realistic industrial constraints. In contrast, this paper evaluates the feasibility of a blockchain-driven DPP for steelmaking based on a realistic use-case.

Furthermore, Canciani et al. [2] proposed a hybrid blockchain to address existing challenges of implementing blockchain-based DPP. Their design used a public blockchain to mirror the state of private data for end-user access. However, this hybrid approach introduced additional layers of complexity that might not be suitable for all industrial contexts. In contrast, our approach explores a different blockchain model tailored to the specific operational demands of the steel industry, prioritising feasibility over architectural complexity.

In summary, current literature lacks rigorous performance evaluations of blockchain-based DPPs within high-volume industrial settings. While conceptual frameworks have been proposed for other sectors, empirical data regarding throughput and storage scalability remain scarce, particularly for the unique demands of steel manufacturing. This paper addresses this research gap by characterising the technical resilience of a permissioned blockchain infrastructure under realistic industrial stress levels.

3 Research Methodology

This research follows a structured methodology to evaluate the technical viability of blockchain as a framework for DPPs in the steel supply chain. The process consists of three distinct phases. First, we evaluate the infrastructure of blockchains suitable for industrial data. Second, we design a hybrid on-chain and off-chain architecture tailored to manufacturing privacy and scalability requirements. Third, we simulate and stress-test the framework using real-world production parameters to establish a performance baseline for throughput and latency. Our use case focuses on system capabilities under intensive conditions rather than specific end-user features of DPP.

3.1 Assessing Blockchain Infrastructures

The steel industry presents unique challenges, recording high transaction volumes, sensitive propriety data, and the need for low-latency verification. As established in the literature, we evaluate three architectural types to address these needs:

- Permissioned Blockchains (e.g., Hyperledger Fabric): These are privatised frameworks that provide a controlled environment where participants on the blockchain are pre-authorised. Additionally, they offer modular consensus mechanisms and fine-grained access control, which are essential when handling sensitive data. Existing studies show private blockchains provide higher transaction *Throughput Per Second* (TPS) with lower latency compared to public blockchains [12].
- Permissionless Blockchains (e.g., Ethereum): These are public frameworks offering decentralisation and high transparency but often at the cost of a transaction fee [14]. They can handle multiple transactions but output a lower TPS and higher latency compared to permissioned blockchains. Additionally, all metadata is publicly visible, which conflicts with privacy requirements in steel manufacturing.
- Decentralised Off-chain Storage (e.g., IPFS, Arweave): These frameworks are effective for storing large documents and certificates [7]. They often focus on one-off payments but lack computational logic and real-time management.

Table 1 summarises the trade-offs between these architectures, demonstrating that permissioned models are best suited for industrial supply chains. We select Hyperledger Fabric for our framework for many reasons, including its channel-based architecture that ensures data privacy between specific consortium members, required for proprietary steel data. Furthermore, its modular consensus and lack of cryptocurrency satisfy the throughput demands of the steel sector more effectively compared to other permissioned blockchains.

Table 1. High level summary of blockchain architectures

	Permissioned	Permissionless	Off-chain
Throughput	Higher ($> 2,000$ TPS)	Lower ($\approx 15-30$ TPS)	N/A (Storage only)
Latency	Milliseconds to seconds	Seconds to minutes	Variable
Data Privacy	Higher (Channels)	Lower (Public Ledger)	Variable (Encrypted)
Costs	Internal costs	Per transaction	Storage-based fees
Governance	Centralised consensus	Decentralised	Decentralised

Beyond infrastructure, storing DPP data directly on the blockchain will eventually lead to ledger bloating and scalability issues [1]. To mitigate this, our study implements a hybrid data strategy that utilises hash pointers [16]. Hyperledger Fabric serves as the on-chain infrastructure to store unique product IDs and cryptographic hashes. Additionally, we use CouchDB as the world state database over alternatives like LevelDB, as CouchDB supports rich JSON querying needed for complex DPP metadata. The primary data payload remains in secure off-chain databases. This approach ensures data integrity, as any off-chain modifications will result in a hash mismatch. In the event of a mismatch, the smart contract flags the DPP as invalid and halts further state transitions until the authentic payload is restored from backups.

3.2 Framework Architecture and Lifecycle

Figure 1 represents the application of our proposed framework to a physical steel product. The product transforms with different properties and ownership throughout its lifecycle, which is recorded and tracked through a DPP.

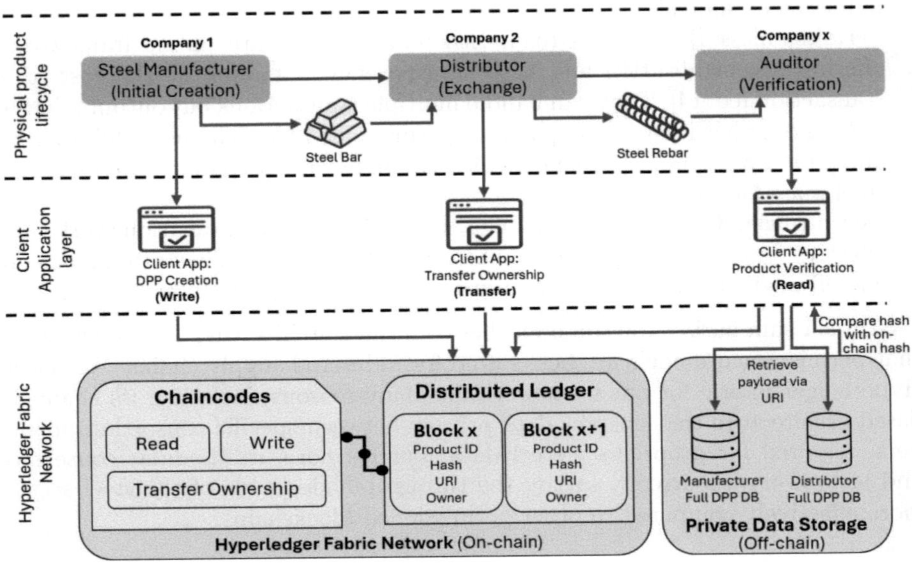

Fig. 1. Proposed Blockchain-based Digital Product Passport for Steelmaking.

The proposed framework reflects the multi-stage lifecycle of steel, tracking a product from its initial creation through various transformations. Typically, this lifecycle is dynamic and decentralised, involving multiple stakeholders, manufacturers, and distributors. We model these interactions as a series of digital state transitions within the blockchain environment. We create smart contracts (chaincodes) implemented via Hyperledger Fabric that execute the following fundamental operations:

- **Write**: Simulating the creation of a new DPP with batch-specific data (e.g., chemical composition and initial carbon footprint). This operation generates a unique product ID and a cryptographic hash of the initial production data.
- **Read**: Enable stakeholders to retrieve the current *State of Truth* for a specific product. This operation returns the on-chain hash, a pointer to the off-chain data, and a validation status, serving as a mechanism to verify the product's documentation matches the record on the ledger.
- **Transfer Ownership**: Simulating the exchange of the product (e.g., from steel bar to rebar). This process updates the *owner* attribute on-chain while maintaining a linked history of previous owners, ensuring transparency.

4 DPP Use Case and Implementation

The objective of this experiment is to evaluate the technical feasibility of a blockchain-driven DPP for the UK steel sector. We simulate the creation and management of DPPs for rebar and tin can production over an extended duration. In this scenario, all products originate as raw steel batches that undergo transformation into specific materials by downstream manufacturers.

To determine the suitability of the framework for this industrial context, we establish three evaluation criteria based on the primary barriers to high-volume blockchain deployment: *(1) Transaction throughput*: the capacity to process concurrent transactions per second, *(2) Latency*: the duration required for a transaction to be committed to the ledger, and *(3) Storage scalability*: the ledger's capacity to manage data growth over a simulated decade of production. We focus exclusively on these metrics because they represent the operational bottlenecks for enterprise ledgers in steel manufacturing.

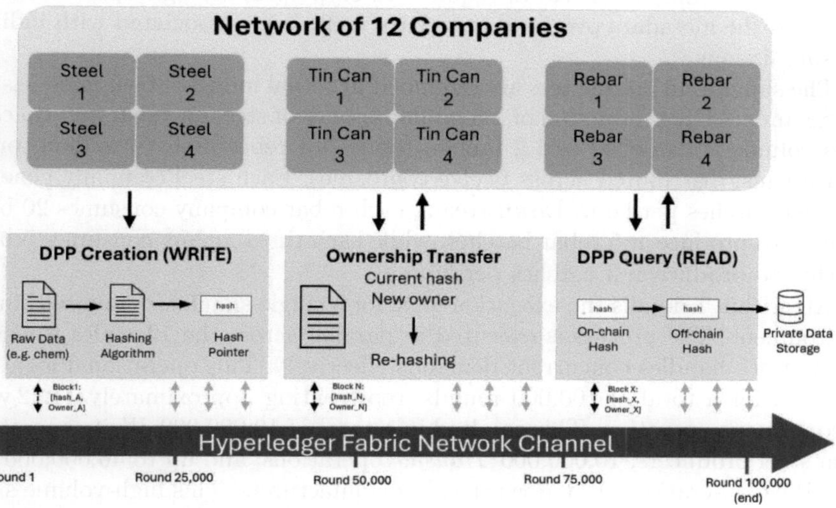

Fig. 2. Proposed Implementation use case network and channel.

The implemented system comprises 12 organisations, as illustrated in Fig. 2. Each organisation operates a dedicated Linux server running Ubuntu 24.04.2 LTS, equipped with 4 vCPUs and 8GB of RAM. To evaluate storage performance across varying capacities, nodes were configured with either 250GB or 500GB of SSD storage.

Each organisation maintains a peer node to host the ledger and execute smart contracts (chaincodes). Additionally, three companies also host an orderer, a specialised node responsible for gathering endorsed transactions, sequencing them into batches, and distributing blocks to the peers. These orderers utilise

Raft consensus protocol to ensure a decentralised and synchronised transaction order across the network.

These peers and orderers join one common channel that forms the private communication backbone of the network. Although Hyperledger Fabric allows for partitioning, we utilise a single channel architecture to establish a baseline for simplicity. This environment hosts the chaincode, which implements the smart contracts and logic required for our steelmaking use case. The ledger executes three primary operations: write, read, and change ownership. These functions simulate product creation, data retrieval, and material movement. This experiment focuses on the two fundamental operations: production creation *(Write)* and changing product ownership *(Transfer)*.

To simulate an industrial environment, the experiment is structured into hourly rounds using batched transactions. We define a transaction as a direct interaction between a company server and the blockchain network. We utilise batching instead of individual operations to align with standard industrial production cycles. This approach also enhances storage efficiency, as each transaction in the 12-company network requires 12 cryptographic signatures. Batching mitigates the metadata overhead and space inefficiency associated with individual submissions.

The simulation parameters are grounded in actual industrial volumes, assuming an annual UK production of 1.5 million tonnes of steel for rebar and tin cans. This volume is modelled as 1.2 million tonnes for rebar and 0.3 million tonnes for tin cans, distributed across twelve companies. Each steel company generate 25 billet batches per hour. Downstream, each rebar company consumes 20 billet batches to produce 1–5 rebar batches, while each tin company consumes 5 billet batches to produce 1–3 batches per hour.

Algorithm 1 details the execution logic for a single simulated hour within the environment. The process is executed in parallel across the 12 nodes to ensure the network handles concurrent demands effectively. This operational logic was executed for a total of 100,000 rounds, representing approximately 11.42 years of continuous operation. This resulted in a total of 10,000,000 *Write* operations from steel producers, 10,000,000 *Transfer* operations, and up to 46,000,000 further *Write* operations from downstream manufacturers. This high-volume simulation allows for a comprehensive assessment of the ledger's stability and storage requirements over an extended industrial lifecycle.

4.1 Results and Discussion

We distinguish between two types of transactions in our experiment. External transactions refer to the batched requests sent by company servers to the blockchain network. Internal transactions represent the individual DPPs processed within those batches. For the purpose of evaluating industrial feasibility instead of blockchain performance, we consider internal transactions as the basis for our evaluations.

Table 2 summarises overall measures. During the simulated period, the network successfully processed a total of 48,007,083 transactions in 143.37 h exe-

Algorithm 1. Simulation of a single round representing 1 hour.

```
parallel for each Company n ∈ {1...12} do          ▷ Executed in parallel threads
if n is Steel company i then
    Execute Batch_Write(25 units)                   ▷ Initialises 100 total DPPs
end if
if n is Tin company j then
    Execute Batch_Transfer(5 units) from Steel company
    x ← random(1, 3)
    Execute Batch_Write(x × 5 units)                ▷ Creates 20–60 Tin DPPs
end if
if n is Rebar company k then
    Execute Batch_Transfer(20 units) from Steel company
    y ← random(1, 5)
    Execute Batch_Write(y × 20 units)               ▷ Creates 80–400 Rebar DPPs
end if
end parallel for
```

Table 2. Experiment total transactions and time after 100,000 rounds.

Organisation	Total Transactions	Total Time
steelCompany1	2,500,000	26,897.58 s
steelCompany2	2,500,000	26,301.74 s
steelCompany3	2,500,000	25,089.03 s
steelCompany4	2,500,000	23,876.81 s
tinCompany1	1,499,559	43,271.35 s
tinCompany2	1,500,156	43,451.32 s
tinCompany3	1,500,380	41,974.19 s
tinCompany4	1,500,902	41,270.80 s
rebarCompany1	8,002,044	61,209.73 s
rebarCompany2	8,001,830	60,238.54 s
rebarCompany3	8,001,892	60,880.19 s
rebarCompany4	8,000,320	61,666.23 s
	48,007,083	**516,127.51 s**

cution effort. Specifically, the rebar companies handled the highest volume of the network load, accumulating over 32,000,000 transactions and maintaining consistent execution times. The processed volume demonstrates that the Hyperledger Fabric infrastructure can handle over a decade of simulated industrial data within a short execution window.

To analyse the performance of the simulated system, Fig. 3 displays throughput as internal transactions per second (TPS). The data is grouped into intervals, where each interval represents the average of 1,000 rounds. The system shows a stable mean TPS staying in the range 200 to 220 throughout the experiment,

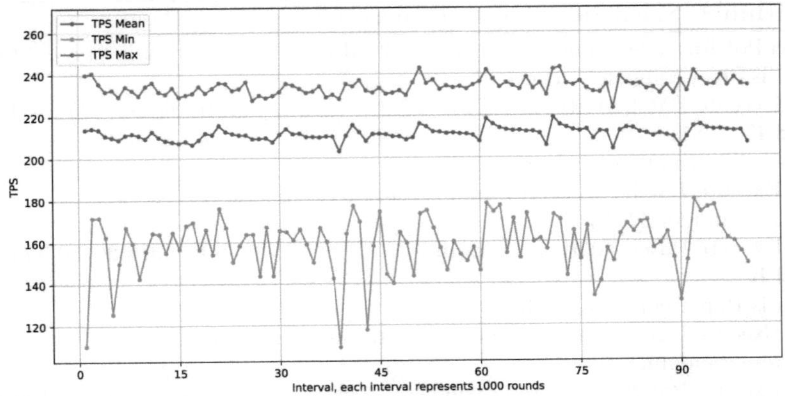

Fig. 3. Experiment results displaying internal transactions per second.

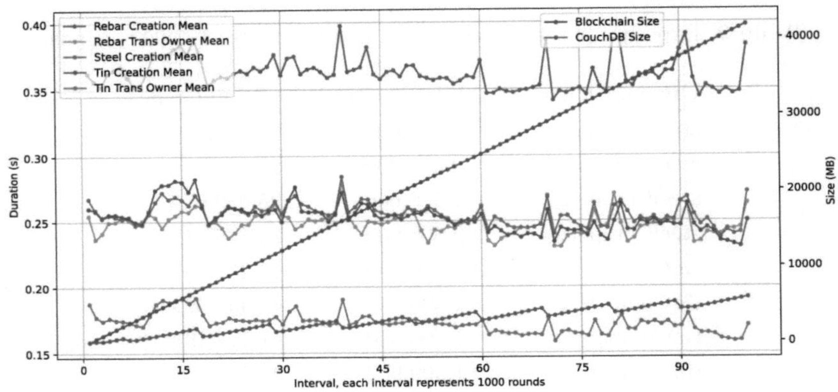

Fig. 4. Experiment results displaying throughput, latency, and size.

with regular min TPS troughs related to wider system updates like pruning of CouchDB. A stable mean TPS indicates that this permissioned architecture effectively accommodates the transaction volumes for the steel domain.

To further analyse the stability of the system, Fig. 4 displays the performance for the different batch transactions alongside the growth of the ledger, again with a grouping of data into intervals of 1,000 rounds. The primary Y-axis represents the transaction latency/duration in seconds, while the secondary Y-axis represents the storage size values for the blockchain and CouchDB databases. The findings indicate that the performance of each transaction type remains stable over the full duration of the experiment, with latency fluctuating between 0.15 s and 0.40 s. Despite this stability, specific points of correlation were observed where all transaction types experienced a simultaneous increase in latency (e.g., at interval 40). This suggests that external environmental factors temporarily impacted performance, rather than an inherent bottleneck within the chaincode logic.

As expected, the blockchain grew linearly to approximately 42GB to store transaction history and cryptographic hashes. The CouchDB world state database remained significantly smaller, peaking near 5GB. Notably, the size of CouchDB exhibits "jumps" at regular intervals. This is due to the internal database pruning process that occurs periodically to optimise storage.

5 Conclusion

This paper validates the feasibility of a permissioned blockchain as the foundational infrastructure for Digital Product Passports (DPP) in the steel industry. Addressing our first research question, we establish that permissioned ledgers, specifically Hyperledger Fabric, are the most suitable blockchain technologies due to their high throughput and privacy controls. This research addresses a literature gap by providing a rigorous evaluation of blockchain performance in an industrial domain requiring both high transaction volumes and long-term data integrity.

The experimental results demonstrate the framework's feasibility for industrial applications, effectively handling the steel industry's throughput demands with low latency. During stress testing, we recorded a mean throughput of approx. 210 TPS, which far exceeded the peak demand of our realistic experiment workload of 540 transactions per hour. Additionally, off-chain storage via hash pointers effectively mitigated the risk of ledger bloat, ensuring storage scalability over a product's lifecycle. The successful pruning of the CouchDB world state database, which remained significantly smaller than the total blockchain ledger, further demonstrated this scalability.

Future work focuses on evolving our implementation into a functional DPP ecosystem. This research abstracted the data model to focus on baseline infrastructure throughput. Future iterations need to incorporate specific DPP semantics, interoperability standards, and regulatory compliance data.

Acknowledgments. For the purpose of open access, the authors have applied a CC BY licence to any Author Accepted Manuscript version arising from this submission. This project was enabled through EPSRC-funded project SUSTAIN Future Manufacturing Research Hub (EP/S018107/1).

Disclosure of Interests. The authors declare no conflict of interest.

References

1. Alzoubi, Y.I., Mishra, A.: Techniques to alleviate blockchain bloat: potentials, challenges, and recommendations. Comput. Electr. Eng. **116**, 109216 (2024)
2. Canciani, A., Felicioli, C., Severino, F., Tortola, D.: Enhancing supply chain transparency through blockchain product passports. In: 2024 IEEE International Conference on Pervasive Computing and Communications Workshops and other Affiliated Events (PerCom Workshops), pp. 751–756 (2024)

3. Doguchaeva, S., Zubkova, S., Katrashova, Y.: Blockchain in public supply chain management: advantages and risks. Transp. Res. Proc **63**, 2172–2178 (2022)
4. European Union: Regulation (EU) 2024/1781 (Ecodesign for sustainable products). Official Journal of the European Union (2024). https://eur-lex.europa.eu/eli/reg/2024/1781/oj
5. Geissdoerfer, M., Savaget, P., Bocken, N.M., Hultink, E.J.: The circular economy – a new sustainability paradigm? J. Clean. Prod. **143**, 757–768 (2017)
6. Hulea, M., Miron, R., Muresan, V.: Digital product passport implementation based on multi-blockchain approach with decentralized identifier provider. Appl. Sci. **14**(11) (2024)
7. Ismail, A., Toohey, M., Lee, Y.C., Dong, Z., Zomaya, A.Y.: Cost and performance analysis on decentralized file systems for blockchain-based applications: State-of-the-art report. In: 2022 IEEE International Conference on Blockchain (Blockchain), pp. 230–237 (2022)
8. Jensen, S.F., Kristensen, J.H., Adamsen, S., Christensen, A., Waehrens, B.V.: Digital product passports for a circular economy: data needs for product life cycle decision-making. Sustainable Prod. Consumpt. **37**, 242–255 (2023)
9. Kannappan, R., Hatin, J., Bertin, E., Crespi, N.: Enhancing digital product passport through decentralized digital twins. In: 2025 12th IFIP International Conference on New Technologies, Mobility and Security (NTMS), pp. 300–308 (2025)
10. Khan, S.N., Loukil, F., Ghedira-Guegan, C., Benkhelifa, E., Bani-Hani, A.: Blockchain smart contracts: applications, challenges, and future trends. Peer-to-peer Netw. Appl. **14**(5), 2901–2925 (2021)
11. Kim, J., Lee, S., Kim, H.: Blockchain-based digital product passport for the circular economy. In: 2024 International Conference on Platform Technology and Service (PlatCon), pp. 188–191 (2024)
12. Kwadzode, D.: Performance comparison of blockchain platforms for modeling financial transactions: a case study of Ethereum and hyperledger fabric. Int. J. Fin. Econom. Bus. **4**, 50–58 (2025)
13. Lopes, C., Barata, J.: Digital product passport: a review and research agenda. Proc. Comput. Sci. **246**, 981–990 (2024)
14. Mohammed, A.H., Abdulateef, A.A., Abdulateef, I.A.: Hyperledger, Ethereum and blockchain technology: a short overview. In: 2021 3rd International Congress on Human-Computer Interaction, Optimization and Robotic Applications (HORA), pp. 1–6 (2021)
15. Paolucci, A., Gianvincenzi, M., Marconi, M., Favi, C., Pennino, D.: Development of a decentralized digital product passport for enhanced lifecycle management of electrical and electronic equipment. Proc. CIRP **135**, 356–361 (2025)
16. Sheth, H., Dattani, J.: Overview of blockchain technology. Asian J. Converg. Technol. (AJCT) (2019)
17. Stodt, F., Ruf, P., Reich, C.: Blockchain-enabled digital product passports for enhancing security and lifecycle management in healthcare devices. In: 2024 8th Cyber Security in Networking Conference (CSNet), pp. 44–51 (2024)
18. Xia, H., Li, J., Li, Q.J., Milisavljevic-Syed, J., Salonitis, K.: Integrating blockchain with digital product passports for managing reverse supply chain. Proc. CIRP **132**, 215–220 (2025), 12th CIRP Global Web Conference (2024)

Activity-Based Cost and GHG Accounting: Designing and Developing a Real-Time Add-On Application

Walter S. A. Schwaiger(✉), Josef Baumüller, and Lalla Hasnae Alaoui

Institute of Management Science, TU-Wien, Theresianumgasse 27, 1040 Vienna, Austria
{walter.schwaiger,josef.baumueller,lalla.alaoui}@tuwien.ac.at

Abstract. The problem of designing and developing information system applications is like sitting on the fence because the knowledge of two very different domains must be aligned, i.e. the business domain the application refers to and the information system engineering domain responsible for the application's design and development. In this article 'activity-based cost & GHG accounting' is selected due to its recent appearance for solving the design and development problem by establishing a 'real-time add-on' digital GHG accounting information system (GHG-AIS) application with the 'object-oriented' domain engineering methodology. The 'real-time' capability is the key feature of the digital AIS application that distinguishes it from a 'manual' – e.g. spreadsheet – application, and the 'add-on' feature assures compatibility to the production information systems incorporated in existing ERP systems.

Keywords: Activity-Based Cost & Greenhous Gas (GHG) accounting · GHG-Protocol initiative · ERP system · digital accounting information system

1 Introduction

Climate change and mitigating corresponding risks is one of today's main challenges to society. Managing GHG emissions, which are closely related to climate change, requires next to a planning and control systems also an adequate GHG accounting system for assessing these emissions. Concerning GHG accounting there exist two main streams, i.e. the Life cycle assessment (LCA) standards [1] of the International Organization for Standardization (ISO) and the GHG accounting and reporting standards related to the corporate level [2, 3] and the product level [4] of the GHG Protocol initiative. 'Life cycle inventory (LCI) is the crucial phase of Life cycle assessment (LCA) in which the system's input and output data are quantified and accumulated via an LCI method, i.e. process based modeling, Input output (IO) LCI and Hybrid method.' [5, p. 266]. In contrast to that, GHG Protocol's GHG accounting is an activity-based (AB) accounting what makes it compatible with activity-based management accounting systems which are already implemented in most ERP systems.

Activity-based (AB) cost & GHG accounting [6] deals with the assessment of production costs and GHG Protocol compliant cradle-to-gate product carbon footprints in

K. Węcel and V. Řepa (Eds.): BIS 2026, LNBIP 584, pp. 385–394, 2026.
https://doi.org/10.1007/978-3-032-26363-6_30

multi-level production systems characterized with multi-level product (bill-of-material) structures and production (routing) structures. But it does not address the design and development of digital GHG accounting information systems (GHG-AIS) that can be either fully integrated into existing ERP systems, or that can extend existing ERP systems as a real-time add-on application. A 'real-time add-on' digital GHG AIS application should be of special interest to companies that currently use manual – e.g. spreadsheet-based – applications to calculate the finished products carbon footprints.

For building the digital GHG-AIS application the GHG accounting knowledge must be extended by information system engineering (ISE) knowledge. The domain engineering methodology from Arango [7] specifies three stages, i.e. 1) the conceptualization of the domain, 2) the transformation of the conceptualization into a design for the application and 3) the development of the application from its design. This methodology is concretized to address the design and development problem as 'object-oriented' domain engineering methodology that follows Evans' [8] suggestion to apply the object-oriented paradigm to the modeling and to the programming language.

The article is organized as follows. In Sect. 2 the GHG accounting knowledge of AB-cost & GHG accounting is conceptualized by representing it in form of metrics and as UML class diagram. In Sect. 3 the production information system underlying ERP systems is conceptualized according to ISO/IEC's Enterprise Control System Integration (ECSI) standard [9], and the thereof resulting conceptual and operational designs of the AB-GHG-AIS are derived. In Sect. 4 the operational AB-GHG-AIS design is implemented by using the R-Tidyverse programming language in an object-oriented way to develop the add-on GHG application for the 'Molding Inc.' company, which serves as demonstration use case. In the final section the paper is concluded.

2 Activity-Based (AB)-GHG-Accounting: Knowledge Representation

AB-GHG accounting within AB-cost & GHG accounting distinguishes three categories of metrics to assess the GHG emission of a finished product (product carbon footprint), i.e. the 3-Levers-of-Emission-Control (3-LoEC)-metrics, the Emission Liability (EL)-metrics and aggregation metrics for summing the emissions of the activities.

Equation (1) shows the calculation of the activity's carbon footprint (ACF) by multiplying the consumed energy (EC) – this is the product of the resource input (rE) and the applied power level (powE) – with the energy's emission factor (emE). The sub-indices indicate the objects (entities) involved so explicate existing interdependencies.

Equations (2) and (3) show the calculation of the activity's emission liability for the consumed material resource (AMEL) and the used equipment resource (AEEL) by multiplying the corresponding resource inputs (rM and rE) with the emission liability per unit of material (uMEL) and per capacity unit of the equipment resource (cuEEL). Equation (4) shows the calculation of cuEEL by dividing the emission liability of the equipment (uEEL) with the equipment's life-time capacity (ltCapacity).

Equations (5), (6) and (7) show the calculation of the product activity carbon footprint (PACF), the product equipment carbon footprint (PECF) and the product material carbon footprint (PMCF) by summing the corresponding carbon footprints and emission liabilities over all activities and the therein used equipment and consumed materials. In Eq. (8) the partial carbon footprints are summed to the product carbon footprint (PCF) by grouping them into the product's internal and external carbon footprints (Fig. 1).

$$\underbrace{ACF_{acty,eqip(eny),fP}}_{[kgCO_2e]} = \underbrace{EC_{acty,eqip(eny),fP}}_{\left[\frac{kWh}{unit.fP}\right]} \cdot \underbrace{emE_{eny,scope}}_{\left[\frac{kgCO_2e}{kWh}\right]} = \underbrace{(rE_{acty,eqip(eny),fP}}_{\left[\frac{res.input}{unit.fP}\right]} \cdot \underbrace{powE_{acty,eqip(eny),fP})}_{\left[\frac{kW}{res.unit} or \frac{kWh}{res.unit}\right]} \cdot \underbrace{emE_{eny,scope}}_{\left[\frac{kgCO_2e}{kWh}\right]} \tag{1}$$

$$\underbrace{AMEL_{acty,mat,fP}}_{[kgCO_2e]} = \underbrace{rM_{acty,mat,fP}}_{\left[\frac{res.input}{unit.fP}\right]} \cdot \underbrace{uMEL_{mat,scope3}}_{\left[\frac{kgCO_2e}{res.input}\right]} \tag{2}$$

$$\underbrace{AEEL_{acty,eqip,fP}}_{[kgCO_2e]} = \underbrace{rE_{acty,eqip,fP}}_{\left[\frac{res.input}{unit.fP}\right]} \cdot \underbrace{cuEEL_{eqip,scope3}}_{\left[\frac{kgCO_2e}{res.input}\right]} \tag{3}$$

$$\underbrace{cuEEL_{eqip,scope3}}_{\left[\frac{kgCO_2e}{res.input}\right]} = \underbrace{uEEL_{eqip,scope3}}_{\left[\frac{kgCO_2e}{res.input}\right]} / \underbrace{ltCapacity_{eqip}}_{[time\ or\ quantity]} \tag{4}$$

$$PACF_{fP} = \Sigma_{acty}\Sigma_{eqip} ACF_{acty,eqip,fP} \tag{5}$$

$$PECF_{fP} = \Sigma_{acty}\Sigma_{eqip} AEEL_{acty,eqip,fP} \tag{6}$$

$$PMCF_{fP} = \Sigma_{acty}\Sigma_{mat} AMEL_{acty,mat,fP} \tag{7}$$

$$PCF_{fP} = \underbrace{PCF_{fP}^{int}}_{PACF_{fP}} + \underbrace{PCF_{fP}^{ext}}_{PMCF_{fP}+PECF_{fP}} \tag{8}$$

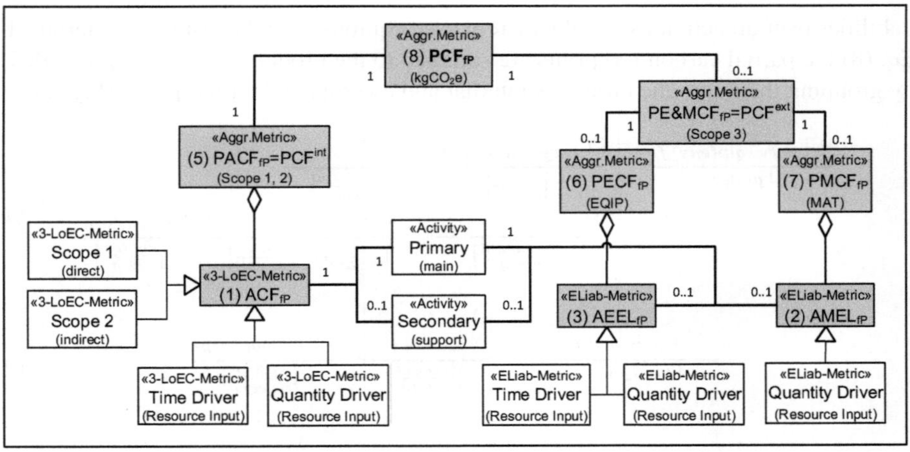

Fig. 1. AB-GHG-Accounting – Conceptualization in UML-CD language

3 Add-On AB-GHG-AIS: Conceptual and Operational Design

For building a generic AB-GHG-AIS that is compliant to ERP systems, ISO/IEC's Enterprise Control System Integration (ECSI) standard [9] is used. This standard specifies the production information system which connects the enterprise (ERP) system with the production control system, and it is at the core of the 'Industry 4.0' initiative.

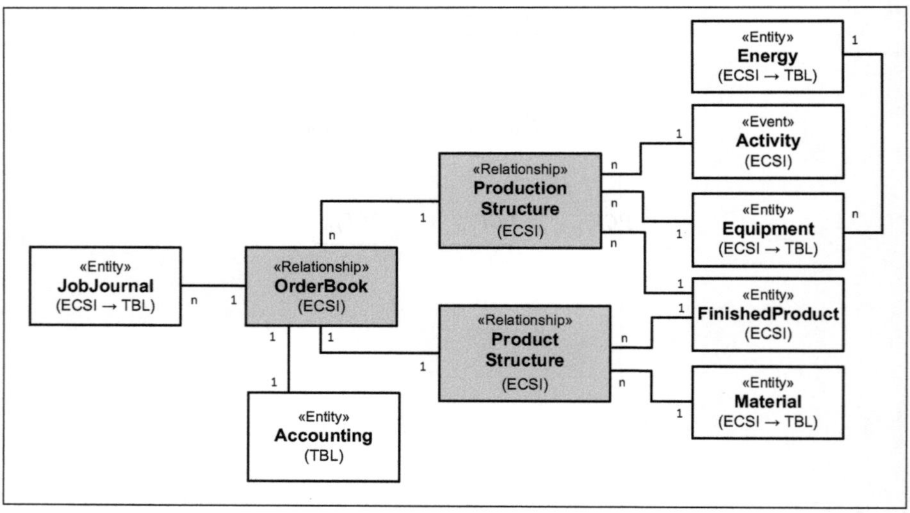

Fig. 2. AB-GHG-AIS: Conceptual design – Entity, event and relationship types

Figure 2 shows the standardized ECSI data for the production information system indicated with ECSI references in parentheses. It consists of the 'Activity' event type and the three input entity types, i.e. 'Material', 'Equipment' and 'Energy' as well as the output entity type 'Finished Product' at the figure's right side. The middle of the figure shows the relationship types in form of the 'Production Structure', i.e. which activities are needed for finishing the product (routing data) and the 'Product Structure', i.e. which materials are needed in production (bill-of-material data). These master ECSI data of the production information system are combined with the transactional ECSI data on its left side. The 'OrderBook' relationship type combines the production and product structures needed for manufacturing ordered products, and in the 'JobJournal' entity type the transactional data for manufacturing the products are collected.

The conceptualization of the ERP system's production information system in Fig. 2 applies McCarthy's [10] 'object-oriented design science paradigm' for conceptualizing AIS designs, and it uses Olivé's type-based modeling language [11] by distinguishing the three categories of types, i.e. entity type, event type and relationship type. For including AB-GHG accounting into the system additional GHG data is inserted into the Material, Equipment and Energy input resources what is indicated by the arrow from ECSI to TBL. For the design's operationalization the GHG accounting's metrics are inserted into the JobJournal and the Accounting entity type.

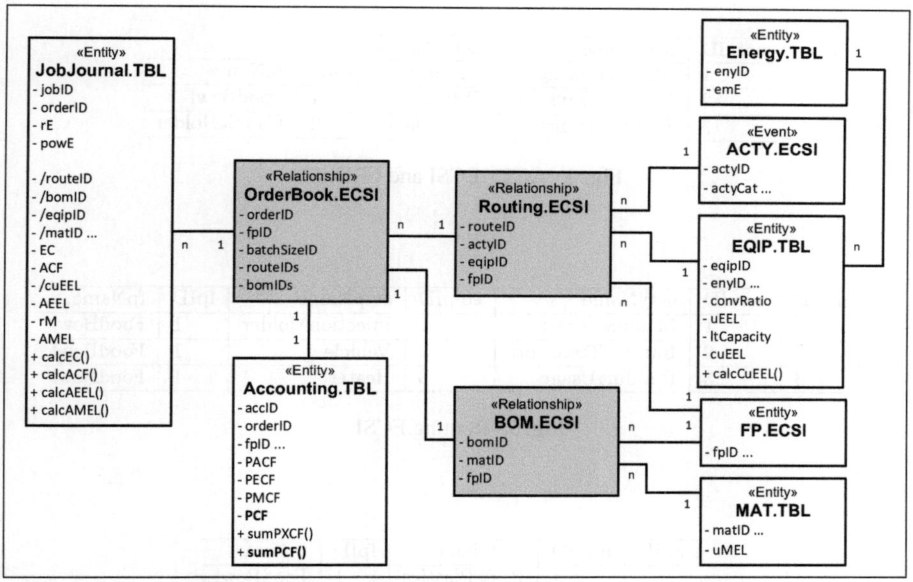

Fig. 3. AB-GHG-AIS: Operational design – Classes with attributes and methods

Figure 3 shows the operationalized design of the AB-GHG-AIS that now contains 'classes' for the entity, event and relationship types from the system's conceptual design. This change is indicated by the ECSI and TBL suffixes attached to the names of the corresponding classes. The classes for the input resources, i.e. MAT.TBL, EQIP.TBL and Energy.TBL have additional GHG attributes. The JobJournal.TBL class includes the 3-LoEC- and the EL-metrics shown in Eqs. (1) to (3), and the aggregation metrics in Eqs. (5) to (8) are located in the Accounting.TBL class.

4 Add-On AB-GHG-AIS: Development with R-Tidyverse

Following the object-oriented domain engineering methodology, the object-oriented operationalization of the AB-GHG-AIS in Fig. 3 is implemented with the R-Tidyverse programming language [12, p. 149] – in an object-oriented way – by transforming the entity, event and relationship classes into class-like tibble format 'tables' where the 'attributes' of the classes are 'variables', the 'methods' are 'table functions' and the 'instances' of the classes are 'observations'.

The 'Molding Inc.' company serves as use case for showing the development of an 'object-oriented' AB-GHG-AIS application with the R-Tidyverse programming language. In the example considered, Molding Inc. finishes food-bowls in a batch-production system with an injection molding equipment via three activities, i.e. the Manufacturing, the InternalTransport and BuildingUsage activity. The peculiarities of the developed application are its real-time and add-on features.

actyID	actyName	actyCat
1	Manufacturing	Primary
2	InternalTransport	Primary
3	BuildingUsage	Secondary

fpID	fpName
1	FoodBowl
2	CandleHolder

Fig. 4. ACTY.ECSI and FP.ECSI

routeID	actyID	actyName	eqipID	eqipName	fpID	fpName
1	1	Manufacturing	1	InjectionMolder	1	FoodBowl
2	2	InternalTransport	2	Vehicle	1	FoodBowl
3	3	BuildingUsage	3	Heater	1	FoodBowl

Fig. 5. Routing.ECSI

bomID	matID	matName	fpID	fpName
1	1	PLA Plastics	1	FoodBowl

Fig. 6. BOM.ECSI

Figures 4, 5 and 6 show the ECSI master tables that stay the same in the AB-GHG-AIS. The left panel of Fig. 4 shows the three activities in the ACTY.ECSI table that are needed to finish the FoodBowl as shown in the figure's right panel. The Routing.ECSI and the BOM.ECSI tables in Fig. 5 and Fig. 6 specify the production structure in form of the three activities and the product structure for the simple case where only PLC plastics is needed for the food-bowl production.

orderID	fpID	batchSizeAct	routeIDs	bomIDs
1	1	100	1, 2, 3	1, NA, NA
2	1	80	1, 2, 3	1, NA, NA

Fig. 7. OrderBook.ECSI

jobID	orderID	routeID	eqipID	rEact	eqipUOM	powEact	powUOM
1	1	1	1	1.111	h/Batch	7.684	kW/h
2	1	2	2	1.111	h/Batch	9.940	kWh/l
3	1	3	3	1.111	h/Batch	1.359	kW/h
4	2	1	1	0.933	h/Batch	7.290	kW/h
5	2	2	2	0.933	h/Batch	9.940	kWh/l
6	2	3	3	0.933	h/Batch	1.359	kW/h

Fig. 8. JobJournal.ECSI (1/2) with routeID related data

jobID	orderID	bomID	matID	rMact	matUOM
1	1	1	1	12.400	kg/Batch
2	1	NA	NA	NA	kg/Batch
3	1	NA	NA	NA	kg/Batch
4	2	1	1	10.416	kg/Batch
5	2	NA	NA	NA	kg/Batch
6	2	NA	NA	NA	kg/Batch

Fig. 9. JobJournal.ECSI (2/2) with bomID related data

Figures 7, 8 and 9 show the ECSI transaction tables as they are received from the ERP system and on which the real-time add-on features of AB-GHG-AIS are based.

In the OrderBook.ECSI table in Fig. 7 the production and the product structures for manufacturing the ordered food-bowls in the batch-production system are specified. The table shows exemplary two production orders which are produced in the same way and only the batch sizes differ, i.e. 100 units in the first and 80 units in the second order. The JobJournal.ECSI shown in two parts, i.e. in Fig. 8 and Fig. 9 contains the actual inputs in the activities of the equipment resource (rEact) and the material resource (rMact) as well as the actual power levels the equipment is applied (powEact).

eqipID	eqipName	enyID	nomPow	convRatio	ltCapacity	uEEL	ueelUOM
1	InjectionMolder	1	28	NA	20000	11900	kgCO2e/eqipID
2	Vehicle	2	NA	0.0058	NA	NA	kgCO2e/eqipID
3	Heater	3	NA	NA	NA	NA	kgCO2e/eqipID

Fig. 10. EQIP.TBL (with uEEL)

matID	matName	uMEL	umelUOM
1	PLA Plastics	0.5	kgCO2e/kg

enyID	enyName	emE
1	Electricity	0.127
2	Diesel	0.271
3	Gas	0.200

Fig. 11. MAT.TBL (with uMEL) and Energy.TBL (with emE)

Figure 10 and Fig. 11 show the three ECSI master tables, i.e. EQIP.TBL, MAT.TBL and Energy.TBL that are extended with additional GHG data as specified in the corresponding classes in Fig. 3. With the data in the master and transaction tables presented so far, all GHG information can be calculated via the metrics in Eqs. (1) to (8).

jobID	orderID	routeID	rEact	powEact	EC	emEact	ACF	UOM
1	1	1	1.111	7.684	8.5369	0.127	1.0842	kgCO2e
2	1	2	1.111	9.940	0.0641	0.271	0.0174	kgCO2e
3	1	3	1.111	1.359	1.5098	0.200	0.3020	kgCO2e
4	2	1	0.933	7.290	6.8016	0.114	0.7754	kgCO2e
5	2	2	0.933	9.940	0.0538	0.271	0.0146	kgCO2e
6	2	3	0.933	1.359	1.2679	0.200	0.2536	kgCO2e

Fig. 12. JobJournal.TBL (1/2) with ACF

jobID	orderID	routeID	EC	ACF	AEEL	bomID	AMEL	UOM
1	1	1	8.5369	1.0842	0.6610	1	6.200	kgCO2e
2	1	2	0.0641	0.0174	NA	NA	NA	kgCO2e
3	1	3	1.5098	0.3020	NA	NA	NA	kgCO2e
4	2	1	6.8016	0.7754	0.5551	1	5.208	kgCO2e
5	2	2	0.0538	0.0146	NA	NA	NA	kgCO2e
6	2	3	1.2679	0.2536	NA	NA	NA	kgCO2e

Fig. 13. JobJournal.TBL (2/2) with AEEL and AMEL

Figure 12 and Fig. 13 show the job-specific GHG information in JobJournal.TBL concerning the food-bowls activity-related partial carbon footprints, i.e. ACF, AECF and AMCF. They are calculated via the 3-LoEC- and EL-metrics in Eqs. (1) to (3) and implemented in R-Tidyverse as 'table functions'.

```
calcACF <- function(JobJournal.TBL) {
  JobJournal.TBL %>%
    mutate(ACF = EC * emEact,
           UOM = "kgCO2e")
}
```

Fig. 14. Calculating ACF with calcACF() function

Figure 14 shows exemplarily the 'calcACF' table function for calculating the activity carbon footprint (ACF) by multiplying the energy consumption (EC) with the emission factor (emEact) as defined in the 3-LoEC-metric in Eq. (1). It is called 'table function' as the function's input is the table that gets extended, in this case by the 'ACF' variable in the 'JobJournal.TBL' table.

accID	orderID	actyIDs	eqipIDs	enyIDs	matIDs	fpID	PACF	PECF	PMCF	PCF
1	1	1, 2, 3	1, 2, 3	1, 2, 3	1, NA, NA	1	1.4035	0.6610	6.200	8.2646
2	2	1, 2, 3	1, 2, 3	1, 2, 3	1, NA, NA	1	1.0435	0.5551	5.208	6.8067

Fig. 15. Acounting.TBL with PCF and PACF, PECF and PMCF

```
sumPXCF <- function(Accounting.TBL) {
  Accounting.TBL %>%
    left_join(JobJournal.TBL %>% group_by(orderID) %>%
      summarise(
        PACF = sum(ACF, na.rm = TRUE),
        PECF = sum(AEEL, na.rm = TRUE),
        PMCF = sum(AMEL, na.rm = TRUE),.groups = "drop"),
      join_by(orderID)) %>%
    add_column(UOM = "kgCO2e")
}
```

Fig. 16. Calculating PXCF with sumPXCF() function

Figure 15 shows the order-specific GHG information in Accounting.TBL concerning the food-bowls production-related partial carbon footprints, i.e. PACF, PECF and PMCF. Summing up, gives the PCF of 8.2646 and 6.8067 kgCO_2e for the production of 100 and 80 food-bowls in the first and second order. The three production-related partial carbon footprints are calculated via the aggregation-metrics in Eqs. (5) to (7) and implemented in the common 'sumPXCF' table functions shown in Fig. 16. As all calculations are executed online with respect to the data received from the ERP system's production information system, the 'digital AB-GHG-AIS application' developed with the R-Tidyverse programming language is a 'real-time add-on' application.

5 Conclusion

The paper's primary research objective relates to the building of a 'digital GHG-AIS application' that is compliant to the GHG Protocol's specification of GHG accounting, that can be integrated – as add-on – with production information systems of existing ERP systems and that allows real-time reporting of the finished products carbon footprints.

This objective was achieved by using the 'object-oriented' domain engineering methodology 1) for the conceptual modeling of the ECSI-production information system, 2) for the derivation of the digital GHG-AIS's design by operationalizing the production information system's conceptualization with the AB-GHG accounting knowledge and

3) for the development of the design compliant GHG-AIS application in the R-Tidyverse data science language applied in an object-oriented way.

The real-time and add-on features of the GHG-AIS application should be beneficial especially for enterprises that currently use manual – e.g. spreadsheet-based – GHG-AIS applications for assessing the carbon footprints of their finished products. The main limitation is the not yet clarified well-functioning of the ECSI interface connection and the reliable delivery of the master and actual transactional data. This has to be checked and validated next. Concerning the scope of the digital GHG AIS application, an extension to more advanced multi-level production information systems is needed for allowing further important application fields. Finally, the GHG accounting system only is the prerequisite and the starting point for the planning and control system needed for successfully mitigating climate change and corresponding risks.

References

1. ISO-LCA (14040): Environmental management - Life Cycle Assessment - Principles and framework, ISO 14040:2006. https://www.iso.org/standard/76121.html
2. GHG-Protocol's Corporate Standard: A Corporate Accounting and Reporting Standard (2004)
3. GHG-Protocol's Scope 3 Standard: Corporate Value Chain (Scope 3) Accounting and Reporting Standard (2011)
4. GHG-Protocol's Product Standard: Product Life Cycle Accounting and Reporting Standard (2011)
5. Islam, S., Ponnambalam, S.G., Lam, H.L.: Review on life cycle inventory: methods, examples and applications. J. Clean. Prod. **136**, 266–278 (2016)
6. Schwaiger, W.S.A., Baumüller, J., Alaoui, L.H.: Activity-based cost & GHG accounting: conceptualization, design and implementation. In: 25th International Conference on Business Information Systems (BIS 2025), Poznan, 25–27 June 2025, pp. 283–296 (2025)
7. Arango, G.: Domain analysis - from art form to engineering discipline, pp. 152–159 (1989)
8. Evans, E.: Domain-Driven Design - Tackling Complexity in the Heart of Software. Addison Wesley, Boston (2004)
9. ISO/IEC-ECSI: Enterprise-control system integration - Part 1: Models and terminology, IEC 62264-1:2013 (2013). https://www.iso.org/standard/57308.html
10. McCarthy, W.E.: Accounting information systems: research directions and perspectives. J. Inf. Syst. **2**, 29–32 (1987)
11. Olivé, A.: Conceptual Modeling of Information Systems. Springer, Heidelberg (2007). https://doi.org/10.1007/978-3-540-39390-0
12. Wickham, H., Grolemund, G.: R for Data Science - Import, Tidy, Transform, Visualize, and Model Data. O'Reilly, Beijing (2020)

Integrated Method for Exploring Causal Effects of Sensitivity to Post-stroke Treatment

Virgilijus Sakalauskas(✉) and Dalia Kriksciuniene

Kauno kolegija, Pramones Pr. 20, 50468 Kaunas, Lithuania
{virgilijus.sakalauskas,dalia.kriksciuniene}@go.kauko.lt

Abstract. Machine learning models are increasingly used to explore survival and treatment outcomes for stroke patients. This study addresses that gap by applying causal inference methods to estimate the survival impact of different stroke treatment strategies by using real-world clinical data. The investigation was conducted by analysing records from 944 stroke patients treated at the Clinical Centre of Montenegro. The data variables included demographic characteristics, clinical status, stroke type, and treatment information. The proposed method addressed the observed problem of high deviation and differences in sensitivity across medical treatment types within patient groups with the same stroke type diagnosis. Propensity Score Matching was used to construct comparable patient groups based on demographic and medical data and to reduce bias inherent in observational data. The causal forests machine learning method was applied to explore causal relationships and estimate individual patterns that affect survival and recovery across patient subgroups. The applied method revealed age, gender, and health status effects, highlighting differences in patient responses to treatment, as compared to the comparative evaluation without group matching and causal effect research.

Keywords: Propensity score matching · causal forests · stroke risk reduction · stroke causal effects

1 Introduction and Literature Review

Despite continuous advancements in stroke diagnostics and acute care, the variability in patient outcomes affected by stroke persists, particularly in terms of mortality. This inconsistency suggests that clinical outcomes are not solely dictated by biological factors or standard interventions, but also by nuanced, patient-specific variables and treatment decisions made in complex hospital environments. Understanding how different treatment strategies causally influence stroke-related mortality, rather than merely correlate with outcomes, is therefore critical to improving patient survival and personalising care. Global analyses in [1, 2] reveal persistent disparities in stroke mortality and risk factors across regions and socioeconomic groups.

While traditional machine learning models have shown promise in predicting stroke outcomes, their reliance on correlations limits their usefulness in clinical decision-making. As a result, these models may identify associations between treatment choices

K. Węcel and V. Řepa (Eds.): BIS 2026, LNBIP 584, pp. 395–403, 2026.
https://doi.org/10.1007/978-3-032-26363-6_31

and outcomes without identifying whether those treatments actually caused the observed differences. Consequently, there is growing interest in applying causal inference methods to healthcare data to estimate treatment effects with greater validity [3, 4].

Causal inference bridges the gap between prediction and explanation. Among these methods, Propensity Score Matching (PSM) has emerged as a foundational technique. Initially proposed by Rosenbaum and Rubin [5], PSM addresses selection bias in observational studies by creating quasi-randomised groups with similar distributions of covariates. When appropriately applied, PSM enables researchers to compare treatment effects as if they originated from a randomised controlled trial, thereby approximating experimental conditions using real-world data.

However, PSM by itself is limited to average treatment effects and does not accommodate the complexity of treatment effect heterogeneity. This is where more flexible machine learning-based approaches, like causal forests, offer added value. Introduced by Wager and Athey [6], causal forests extend the random forest algorithm to estimate Conditional Average Treatment Effects (CATEs) at the individual level. This not only quantifies the expected benefit of a treatment for a given patient profile but also helps to identify which subgroups benefit most.

Recent studies have begun to explore these tools in clinical settings. For example, the research in [7–9] demonstrated the value of machine learning methods, including causal forests, for estimating treatment effects with healthcare data. In stroke research, similar techniques have been used to assess the impact of rehabilitation timing, treatment outcomes, anticoagulation, and thrombolysis therapies (see [10, 11]).

Our work contributes to this emerging field by applying a combined PSM and causal forest approach to real-world stroke data from 944 patients at the Clinical Centre of Montenegro, with a specific focus on treatment-related differences in survival. This combination of balancing groups through PSM and capturing nuanced effects through causal forests provides a more refined and clinically relevant understanding of how different interventions influence stroke-related mortality. Unlike global models that output a single effect size, causal forests highlight variability in treatment responses across patients, offering clinicians not just a better average, but a roadmap for targeted decision-making.

The next section describes the data used for research. In Sect. 3, we shortly highlight the Propensity Score Matching and Causal Forest methods. The Results and Conclusions are presented in Sects. 4 and 5 respectively.

2 Clinical Data Description

The database applied for evaluating treatment effects on stroke-related survival consists of stroke patients records from neurology department of the Clinical Centre of Podgorica, Montenegro collected between February 25, 2017, and December 18, 2019. After cleansing and selecting adequate variables from the original database we selected structured 944 records of stroke patients and 8 variables. The data of stroke patients varies by age (13 to 96 years) and gender (485-male, 427-female). The short example of database structure and data records is presented in Table 1.

The variables and their codification are explained in Table 2.

A stroke occurs when the blood supply to part of the brain is disrupted, leading to potential brain damage. Broadly, strokes are categorized into two main types: ischemic

Table 1. Sample of data records and variables

Vital Status	Stroke Type	Treatment methods	Health Status	Age	Gender	Past Stroke	Smoke
1	3	0	1	17	2	0	2
1	3	0	2	16	1	0	2
0	2	0	0	13	2	1	3
0	1	0	0	96	1	0	2
0	1	0	9	94	2	0	3
0	4	0	0	93	2	0	3
0	1	2	0	94	1	0	2

Table 2. The definition of stroke clinical database variables

Variable name	Meaning and coding of data
Vital Status	- 0:Event (death), 1: Alive
Stroke Type	- 1: Ischemic, 2: Hemorag, 3: SAH, 4: Unspecified
Treatment methods	- 0:other treatments,1:Anticoagulation, 2:Antiplatelet Therapy
Health Status	- Health score before stroke from 0:best to 9:worst: 0: Without symptoms; 1: Without significant disability despite symptoms; 2: Minor disability; 3: Moderate disability, but able to walk independency; 4: Moderate disability, not able to walk independency; 5: Major disability; 9: Unknown
Age	- Patient age, years
Gender	- 1:Male, 2:Female, 9:Unspecified
Past Stroke	- Stroke in the past. 1:Yes, registered in the patient health record, 0:No
Smoke Status	1-Smokes, 2-No, 3-Smoked before

and hemorrhagic. Ischemic strokes, which account for approximately 87% of all cases, result from a blockage in the blood vessels supplying the brain. Hemorrhagic strokes involve bleeding in or around the brain and are divided into two categories based on the location and source of bleeding:

- *Intracerebral hemorrhage* occurs when a blood vessel ruptures within the brain tissue itself.
- *Subarachnoid hemorrhage* (SAH) involves bleeding in the space between the brain and the surrounding membranes, typically caused by a ruptured aneurysm.

SAH represents about 5–6% of all stroke cases and is classified separately due to its distinct origin and clinical features. Other stroke types include cryptogenic stroke, brain stem stroke, and various less frequent forms.

In this study, we compare the effectiveness of two stroke treatment strategies:

- ANTIKOAG (Anticoagulants): These drugs target clotting factors to prevent the formation of blood clots. Examples include warfarin, heparin, and DOACs. They are typically used for conditions such as atrial fibrillation or venous thromboembolism.
- ANTIAGREGAC (Antiplatelets): These agents, such as aspirin and clopidogrel, inhibit platelet aggregation and are commonly prescribed after ischemic strokes or myocardial infarction.

Both therapies aim to reduce the risk of stroke but operate at different stages of the clotting cascade and are used in distinct clinical contexts.

Our goal for this research is to compare these two treatment types-coded as 1 (anticoagulants) and 2 (antiplatelets) - against each other, as well as against other treatment methods not falling into either category, which are coded as 0.

3 Methods Description

This study employed two steps to evaluate the impact of different stroke treatments on survival: first, we applied Propensity Score Matching (PSM) to mitigate bias in our comparisons, and then utilised a machine learning approach called Causal Forests to estimate how treatment effects may vary across different patient types.

3.1 Propensity Score Matching (PSM)

Because patients in our dataset were not randomly assigned to treatment groups, direct comparisons could be misleading. For example, patients who received anticoagulants may be older or have different health risks than those who received antiplatelets. To make the groups more comparable, we used Propensity Score Matching.

A propensity score represents the probability that a patient would receive a specific treatment, based on characteristics such as age, gender, stroke type, past health conditions, and smoking status. We calculated these scores using logistic regression, then matched patients who received one treatment with similar patients who received another. Then we match each patient who received the treatment with another patient who didn't, but who has a very similar health profile. To make sure the matches were good, we set a limit (called a caliper) so that patients were only paired if their scores were close enough-this helps avoid pairing people who are too different.

After matching, the groups were more balanced. That means their baseline characteristics looked very similar, which helps us focus on the effect of the treatment itself - not the differences between patients.

3.2 Causal Forests

Once we had balanced treatment groups, we wanted to go further and understand how treatment effects might differ across individual patients. For this, we used a method called Causal Forests, which is based on decision trees.

Causal Forests work by splitting the data into many small groups where patients are similar, and then estimating the treatment effect within each group. These small trees are combined into a large "forest" that provides an estimate of how much a treatment helps or harms each patient- this is known as the Conditional Average Treatment Effect (CATE).

We trained the Causal Forest model using the matched data and the same patient characteristics used in the PSM step. This allowed us to estimate the average benefit of treatment and see how that benefit changes depending on factors like age, health status, or stroke history.

Together, these methods allowed us to compare treatments fairly and explore which types of patients benefit the most from each therapy.

4 Results

We evaluated the causal effect of three treatment strategies on stroke-related mortality using matched datasets and Causal Forest analysis. The treatments compared were:

- ***Treatment 2***: Antiplatelet therapy (ANTIAGREGAC)
- ***Treatment 1***: Anticoagulant therapy (ANTIKOAG)
- ***Treatment 0***: Other medications or no targeted treatment

Each comparison included a Propensity Score Matching (PSM) step to ensure balanced cohorts, followed by estimation of individual treatment effects using Causal Forests. All analyses from our data were conducted using Python libraries. For implementing Propensity Score Matching (PSM), we used pandas for data loading and manipulation, numpy for numerical operations, and scikit-learn (sklearn) to build the logistic regression model used to estimate propensity scores. Visualization of covariate balance before and after matching was performed using matplotlib and seaborn.

To estimate heterogeneous treatment effects, we applied the Causal Forest method using the CausalForestDML class from the econml library—one of the most established implementations of causal forests in Python. The scikit-learn library was also used within this framework for modeling and preprocessing. Matplotlib and seaborn were again employed to visualize CATE distributions, scatterplots, and feature importance rankings. Below we present the results of our calculations. The Table 3 shows number of patients after PSM, Average Treatment Effect (ATE) and Max ATE. The number of matched pairs used for each analysis means the patients with similar characteristics from both treatment groups, selected using Propensity Score Matching to reduce bias. ATE here stands for the average difference in survival probability caused by the treatment. A positive ATE means the treatment increased survival; a negative ATE suggests the opposite. Max ATE is the largest estimated individual-level benefit observed in the sample, showing how effective the treatment was for the best responders.

The Antiplatelet therapy (treatment 2) consistently showed the most positive and reliable impact on survival after stroke, both compared to anticoagulants and to no specific treatment. An approximately 8.6% survival chance is higher compared to Anticoagulant therapy (treatment 1), and 15% higher than no targeted treatment (treatment 0).

On the other hand, Anticoagulant therapy showed no consistent benefit, with ATE at -6.5%, possibly resulting in some harm, depending on the patient's profile.

The differences in maximum ATE across groups suggest that individual factors - such as age, stroke type, or baseline health play a significant role in treatment response.

Table 3. Treatment main parameters comparision

Comparison	Treatment Codes	Patients after PSM	ATE (Average Treatment Effect)	Max ATE
Antiplatelet vs Anticoagulant	2 vs 1	671	0.08597	0.37012
Antiplatelet vs No Targeted Treatment	2 vs 0	675	0.15038	0.37905
Anticoagulant vs No Targeted Treatment	1 vs 0	219	–0.06503	0.05137

These results support moving beyond average effects to more personalised treatment planning, guided by Causal Forest insights.

Next we compare balanced covariate of all treatments after PSM step (Fig. 1). Treatments 2 vs 1 and 2 vs 0 show excellent covariate balance, indicating that patients in each group had very similar starting characteristics, making it possible to focus on the treatment's effect without confounding differences between individuals. This helps the Causal Forest algorithm achieve high survival scores for antiplatelet therapy (treatment 2). On the contrary, the low covariate balance of treatment 1 vs 0 led to pure Average Treatment Effect results.

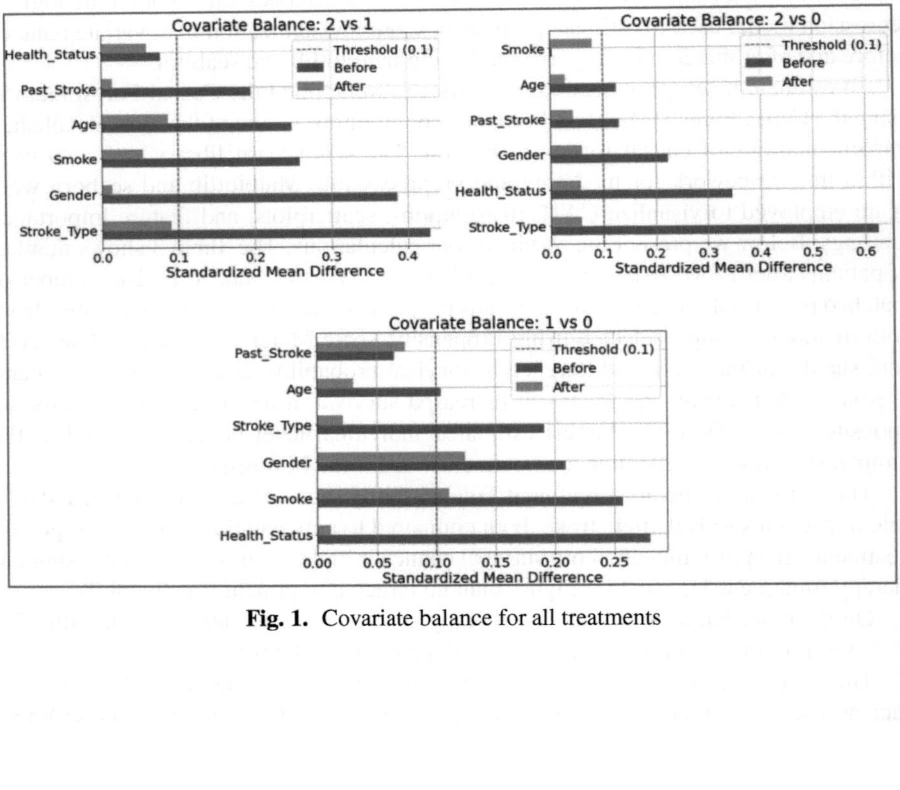

Fig. 1. Covariate balance for all treatments

In Causal Forests, feature importance doesn't show which variables predict outcomes (like in standard models) - it indicates which variables help explain differences in treatment effects between patients. Our model for all treatments ranked features in a very similar way (see Fig. 2).

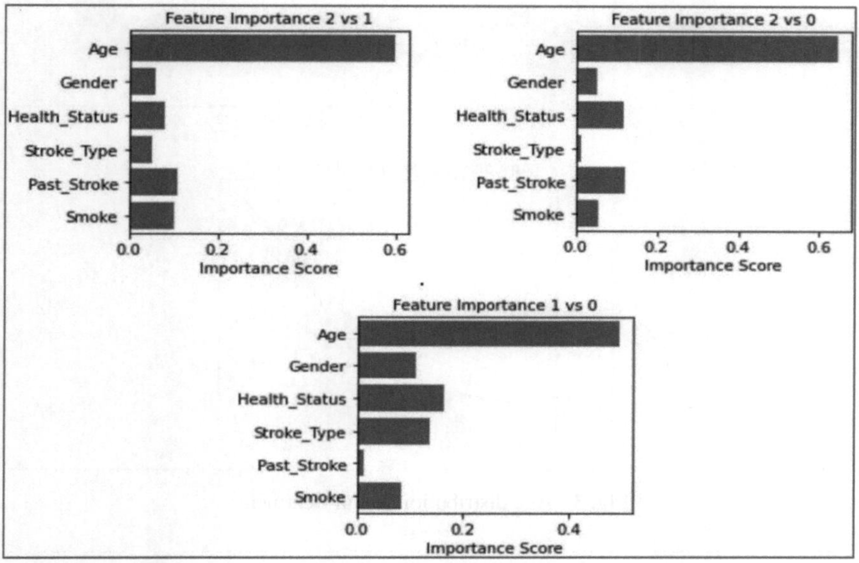

Fig. 2. Features importance

The most important are *Age, Health Status* and *Past Stroke. Factors less influencing the differences in treatment effects are Gender, Stroke Type and Smoking.* Worth mentioning that *Age* is more than 3 times more important than any other feature. Therefore, it would be very interesting to see how Age is distributed along the Estimated Treatment Effect (CATE) (see Fig. 3).

Each plot illustrates the relationship between age and the effectiveness of stroke treatments. The vertical axis shows the estimated benefit of treatment (CATE), and the horizontal axis is Age. Higher values mean more benefit.

The research shows that ***Age* is a strong modifier** of treatment response. Antiplatelets (Treatment 2 vs 0) tend to offer consistent and increasing benefit with age, especially notable after 70. In treatment 2 vs 1 we see the constant survival percent till 65 years, and we observe a sharp drop in survival in the range from 65 to 80. The Age distribution for Anticoagulants versus No treatments looks very strange. In this case, Anticoagulants should not be used for patients younger than 80 years of age, as they reduce the likelihood of survival.

These patterns underscore the need for **age-sensitive treatment strategies** in stroke care. **Older patients** generally benefit more from treatment, especially **Antiplatelets. Anticoagulants** may not help younger people and should be used more carefully. Age really matters when choosing the right treatment.

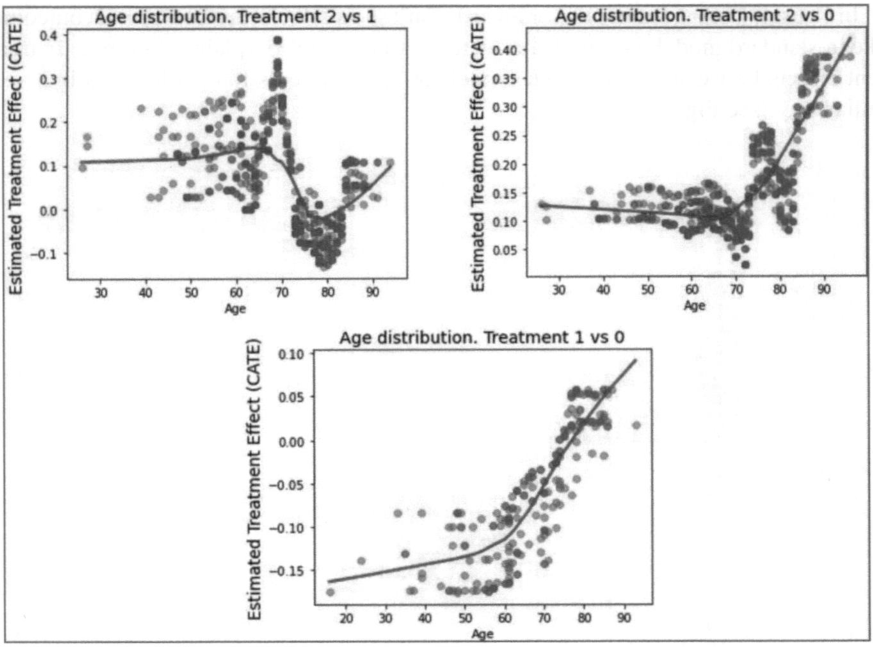

Fig. 3. Age distribution for all treatment

5 Conclusion Remarks

This study demonstrates the practical value of causal inference methods for evaluating treatment effectiveness in stroke care using real observational clinical data. By using Propensity Score Matching with Causal Forest models, we moved beyond traditional risk prediction and association-based analyses to estimate both average and individual-level treatment effects on stroke-related survival.

The empirical findings showed that ***antiplatelet therapy*** consistently provides the greatest survival benefit among the treatment strategies. In contrast, ***anticoagulant therapy*** was limited and, in some patient subgroups, has negative effects on survival. The research highlights that treatment effectiveness is not the same across the patient population and strongly depends on individual characteristics. In particular, age and health status emerged as the dominant factors shaping treatment response. The observed heterogeneity in treatment effects underscores the importance of personalised treatment strategies.

From a methodological point, the study illustrates how causal machine learning techniques can enhance clinical decision support. *Propensity Score Matching* helped mitigate confounding and selection bias, approximating the conditions of a randomised experiment, while *Causal Forests* captured complex, non-linear interactions and revealed subgroup-specific treatment effects. Together, these methods provide clinicians and healthcare decision-makers with interpretable and actionable insights that are not accessible through standard predictive models or descriptive statistics.

The analysis relies on retrospective data from a single clinical centre, which may limit the generalisability of the results. Although the applied causal methods reduce bias, unobserved patients cannot be fully excluded. Additionally, treatment classification was restricted to broad therapeutic categories and did not account for dosage, timing, or adherence, which may further influence outcomes.

Future research should further validate on diverse clinical datasets and real-world settings to confirm its robustness and generalisability. Extending the causal framework to dynamic or longitudinal models could further improve the understanding of how treatment effects evolve over time. Despite these limitations, the present study provides strong evidence that causal inference combined with machine learning offers a powerful and clinically meaningful framework for evaluating stroke therapies and supporting more targeted, data-driven treatment decisions.

These findings highlight the importance of **personalised treatment decisions,** as patient characteristics - especially Age - strongly influence treatment response. Causal forest analysis proved valuable in uncovering these individual-level differences, supporting more targeted and effective stroke care strategies.

References

1. Pantoja-Ruiz, C., et al.: Socioeconomic status and stroke: a review of the latest evidence on inequalities and their drivers. Stroke **56**(3), 794–805 (2025)
2. Yadav, R.S., et al.: Social determinants of stroke hospitalization and mortality in United States' counties. J. Clin. Med. **11**(14), 4101 (2022). https://doi.org/10.3390/jcm11144101
3. Jawadekar, N., et al.: Practical guide to honest causal forests for identifying heterogeneous treatment effects. Am. J. Epidemiol. **192**(7), 1155–1165 (2023)
4. Wu, X., Peng, S., Li, J.: Causal inference in the medical domain: a survey. Appl. Intell. **54**, 4911–4934 (2024)
5. Rosenbaum, P.R., Rubin, D.B.: The central role of the propensity score in observational studies for causal effects. Biometrika **70**(1), 41–55 (1983)
6. Wager, S., Athey, S.: Estimation and inference of heterogeneous treatment effects using random forests. J. Am. Stat. Assoc. **113**(523), 1228–1242 (2018)
7. Athey, S., Tibshirani, J., Wager, S.: Generalized random forests. Ann. Stat. **47**(2), 1148–1178 (2019)
8. Künzel, S.R., Sekhon, J.S., Bickel, P.J., Yu, B.: Metalearners for estimating heterogeneous treatment effects using machine learning. Proc. Natl. Acad. Sci. U.S.A. **116**(10), 4156–4165 (2019)
9. Nie, X., Wager, S.: Quasi-oracle estimation of heterogeneous treatment effects. Biometrika **108**(2), 299–319 (2021)
10. Feuerriegel, S., Frauen, D., Melnychuk, V., et al.: Causal machine learning for predicting treatment outcomes. Nat. Med. **30**, 958–968 (2024). https://doi.org/10.1038/s41591-024-02902-1
11. Zhang, B., Silverman, S., Schwammn, L.H., Ji, X., Singhal, A.B.: Effectiveness of metformin pretreatment for stroke severity: a propensity score matching study. CNS Neurosci. Ther. **30**, e70004 (2024). https://doi.org/10.1111/cns.70004

Author Index

K. Węcel and V. Řepa (Eds.): BIS 2026, LNBIP 584, pp. 405–406, 2026.
https://doi.org/10.1007/978-3-032-26363-6

MIX
Papier aus verantwortungsvollen Quellen
Paper from responsible sources
FSC® C105338

If you have any concerns about our products,
you can contact us on
ProductSafety@springernature.com

In case Publisher is established outside the EU,
the EU authorized representative is:
Springer Nature Customer Service Center GmbH
Europaplatz 3, 69115 Heidelberg, Germany

Printed by Libri Plureos GmbH
in Hamburg, Germany